PEARS WORD-PUZZLER'S DICTIONARY

PEARS
WORD-PUZZLER'S DICTIONARY

Compiled, Written and Edited by
PETER NEWBY

PELHAM BOOKS
London

First published in Great Britain by
Pelham Books Ltd
44 Bedford Square
London WC1B 3DU
1983

British Library Cataloguing in Publication Data
Newby, Peter
Pears word-puzzler's dictionary
1. Word games—Dictionaries
I. Title
793.73′03′21   GV1507.W8

ISBN 0 7207 1375 7 (hardback)
ISBN 0 7207 1462 1 (paperback)
Typeset by Rowland Phototypesetting Ltd
Bury St Edmunds, Suffolk.
Printed and bound in Great Britain by
Billing and Sons, Worcester.

To my parents,
Thomas and Mavis Louisa Newby

CONTENTS

HOW TO USE THIS BOOK

With *Pears Word-Puzzler's Dictionary* the object has been to produce a unique work of reference, different from any other crossword dictionary. In the pages that follow you will find listed 30,000 words, names, abbreviations, prefixes and suffixes, specially selected and arranged with the crossword-puzzle solver, the word-game enthusiast and the word-puzzle compiler in mind. The descriptive words have been given concise definitions expressly geared to solving word puzzles. Where the volume of examples justifies, entries are shown with their respective validity for various word games.

The main aim of this dictionary is to enable the user to find quickly the word he or she wants. For this reason the information is divided into main subject categories (The Arts, Geography, History, Languages, Religion and Mythology, Science and Technology, etc.) each of which is split into various sub-sections. In the sub-sections the relevant words are arranged alphabetically and according to the number of letters.

Much of the material has a general reference value – whether it is giving the meanings of personal names or listing popes and antipopes – but the idea behind the enterprise has been to provide a practical tool for crossword solvers and word-game players.

FOR CROSSWORD SOLVERS

It is impossible for any one book to list the sum of words available to the crossword compiler. However, what *is* possible is to help the crossword solver get to grips with the puzzle. Compilers vary, of course: some stick strictly to a named dictionary while others feel free to select words and phrases from any source. (One national woman's magazine even has a compiler who invents his (or her) own phrases when faced with an awkward gap to fill!) What this book sets out to do, therefore, is to give words for the subjects most commonly used by compilers. For reasons of space and to keep the dictionary of manageable proportions, the most obvious words are not included (e.g. under ANIMALS you will find no cow or cat or dog, but you will find dzo, pard and dhole). While avoiding 'everyday' words emphasis has been placed on the less predictable words which get into the crossword because 'nothing else will fit'.

However much the styles of different crosswords vary, the compilers themselves do share certain tendencies and it is an awareness of these that has governed the choice of words.

A LOVE OF AMBIGUITY

The use of ambiguity is a favourite ploy of compilers, especially those who work on the so-called 'easy' crosswords. A simple one-word clue such as *dish (5)* could mean a foodstuff, a drink, a vessel, a geographical or other concavity, distribution of print type or even an attractive female. This book covers most of the five-letter words which could answer that clue. Ambiguity is also used by the cryptic crossword-puzzle compiler who delights in choosing the obscure meaning of an everyday word and in the pages that follow you will find some *very* obscure meanings of some *very* usual words (e.g. you will not find 'quiz' under GAMES, but you will find it as a 'monocle' in CLOTHING, MATERIALS AND ORNAMENTATION and as 'an odd-looking person' under STRANGERS).

A LOVE OF COMPLEXITY

The more complex the clue the more likely is the word to be unusual. For example, if a clue is merely 'a European river' it will be one of the famous ones, but should the clue be more specific than that you can be assured that you will either need a good atlas or this book.

A LOVE OF ANAGRAMS

Anagrams are usually easy to spot because the clues more often than not take the form of awkward, strange or silly phrases. Of course, while recognizing that what you are looking for is an anagram, working out the anagram itself may not be so simple. However, you will know the number of letters required and the clue should give you some indication of the subject, so turning to the appropriate page in the dictionary should help solve your problem.

INTELLECTUAL ARROGANCE

Some compilers delight in choosing obscure quotations from little-known books leaving the solver to guess the missing word. Fortunately this usually prevents ambiguity, so that the subject can only be in one category and, if this book covers it, you should get your answer.

Equally helpful to crossword addicts will be the various symbols mainly intended for word-game players. Knowing that a particular proper noun has an alternative meaning could well be useful to a crossword solver and knowing that a word is *foreign* or *obsolete* will make sense of such clues as 'American' or 'old'.

FINDING THE WORD YOU NEED

Suppose, for example, you are seeking a 5-letter word which is the name of a bird.

(1) Turn to the CONTENTS on page 8 and this will show that the FAUNA–BIRDS section of NATURAL HISTORY begins on page 236.

(2) Ignoring the 2-letter, 3-letter and 4-letter birds, all of which are alphabetically listed according to the number of letters in each word, you come quickly to the 5-letter birds. Each of these 5-letter birds is listed with a short description to enable you to select the most appropriate.

Alternatively your crossword may give a 5-letter-word bird name in the clue but you do not appreciate its relevance. Follow the same pattern as above and read the given description.

FOR WORD-GAME PLAYERS

When you play Scrabble® at home you may choose any dictionary you like to verify the words played and challenged during a game. If you take part in the National Scrabble Championships or in competitions organized by one of the hundred and more Scrabble Clubs that exist in the United Kingdom then you will need to refer to the currently specified reference dictionary. Originally the *Shorter Oxford English Dictionary* was selected but, in 1980, *Chambers Twentieth Century Dictionary* replaced it as the UK Scrabble 'word bible' and *Chambers* is also used extensively throughout the Commonwealth for this purpose. In the United States and Canada the *Official Scrabble Players' Dictionary* (which is not valid in the UK nor has a British equivalent) is the standard reference for all the English-speaking Scrabble Clubs, tournaments and championships. The French Canadians not only use a totally different dictionary (*Larousse*) but play a completely different version of Scrabble called *duplicate* which was invented in Belgium in 1972 and is extremely popular in Europe enjoying a considerable media coverage. *Duplicate* is sometimes played in British Scrabble Clubs though the traditional game is paramount.

Only one word-game specifically limits you to a particular dictionary and this game is called Dixit® which is played to the *Collins Minigem Dictionary*, supplied at the time of purchase. Whilst the television version of Countdown® limits contestants to words found in *The Concise Oxford* the boxed game of Countdown has no such restraint.

As previously mentioned, any type of word is grist to the crossword mill but when playing word-games you will find that all sorts of inhibiting factors and anomalies exist. As an example consider using in the various games the following 'animal' words: aardvark, woodworm and rother.

aardvark This word may be played in Dixit, Kan-U-Go®, Countdown and Scrabble (in the USA); sometimes in Lexicon® not at all in UK championship Scrabble and as Sylabex® is limited to 6 and 9-letter words the occasion would not arise.

woodworm Only in USA Scrabble can this word be played with total authority, it is invalid in UK championship Scrabble, a Dixit player may have doubts and in all the other games including Scrabble at home it can (under certain circumstances) be played with total assurance.

rother This word may be played in Sylabex, Lexicon, Kan-U-Go, Countdown (at home) and Scrabble (at home) but not in official UK or USA Scrabble, Dixit or Countdown (on TV).

It becomes even more confusing when you consider the plural forms of these words as some games permit plurals, some ban them completely and one only allows them under certain circumstances.

These anomalies arise because of the limitations imposed by the rules of the various games and the way these words are presented and defined in the different dictionaries.

aardvark *Chambers* defines this as a foreign word, the *Concise Oxford* as a word of foreign origin; whilst both *Collins Minigem* and the *OSPD* (the *Official Scrabble Players' Dictionary*) make no mention of the word's etymology.

woodworm *Chambers* hyphenates this word; *Collins Minigem* has it hyphenated but only because it occurs at the end of a line of type (*Collins Gem* clearly shows it to be an unhyphenated word); the *Concise Oxford* and the *OSPD* clearly show it to be an unhyphenated word.

rother This word does not appear in *Collins Minigem*, the *Concise Oxford* or the *OSPD* and it appears in *Chambers* as a 'Shakespeare emendation'.

A word-game player therefore needs to consider how his preferred pastime treats the different categories of words before attempting to become an expert by increasing his word power, which *Pears Word-Puzzler's Dictionary* is specifically designed to encourage.

CATEGORIES OF WORDS

Abbreviations As, by definition, an abbreviation is not a word so abbreviations cannot be used in any game. However, certain abbreviations eventually become words (such as *Raf* the slang word for the Royal Air Force) and these can then be treated on their own merits.

Archaic words Perfectly valid for all games but some could be challenged if used on the television version of Countdown.

Colloquial words A 'grey' category as it has a tendency to shade into slang and, unless the dictionary you are using clearly defines the difference this will always be a problem. Colloquial words, however, are valid for all games.

Dialect words Perfectly valid for all games except the national Scrabble championship of Singapore where *Chambers* is the official reference.

Digraphs and letter-sounds A digraph is two letters expressing one sound as, for example, *ar* (the letter *r*) and *es* (the letter *s*). Digraphs describing an individual letter are permitted in American Scrabble but not in UK championship Scrabble. Some digraphs and letter sounds are words in their own right such as *el*, *es* and *zed* all of which describe a shape of the form of the specified letter and, as genuine words in their own right, are valid for UK Scrabble. None of the crossword-type games impose any restriction upon the use of digraphs so players must use their own judgement in this respect.

Foreign words Not valid for Lexicon, Scrabble or Sylabex but quite acceptable for Kan-U-Go, Dixit or Countdown providing such words appear in the English dictionary you are using for reference. UK championship Scrabble treats words limited in use to overseas Commonwealth countries as 'foreign' even though English is the recognized tongue of that country.

It is important to note the difference between a word of foreign origin but which has now been Anglicized and a word in common English usage which is defined as being foreign. The former are now perfectly proper English words and valid for all games, the latter only valid for games named above. *Chambers*, for example, shows the difference very clearly by the type of brackets used and the positioning of a bracketed word within an individual definition. For example: (Fr.) meaning French and appearing in round brackets immediately following the headword means that the word is French and therefore foreign. [Fr.] in square brackets at the end of the headword's definition means that the word was originally French but is now an English word and, as such, perfectly valid.

Hyphenated words These are a bone of contention for all games. The example of *wood-worm* has already been given but now consider *sea-eagle*.

Sea-eagle is the form in which this word is listed in both *Chambers* and the complete *Oxford English* dictionaries whereas another leading authority, *Funk and Wagnalls*, prefers this as two individual words, *sea eagle*.

Hyphenated words, therefore, cannot be assumed to be a single word even though *woodworm* would be valid for all word-games providing that you were not using *Chambers* or any other dictionary which chooses to hyphenate this word. As *Chambers* is both a leading authority and a specified game reference so you will discover examples of hyphenated word ambiguities given throughout this book where *Chambers* is at odds with other authorities or even with itself!

Hyphenated words are specifically excluded from Scrabble and, whilst not mentioned in the rules of the other games, must be the subject of your own judgement as to their acceptability for play.

Obscene words Perfectly valid for all games so long as no other rule is infringed.

Obsolete words Perfectly valid for all games and only specifically excluded from the television version of Countdown and UK championship Scrabble. UK championship Scrabble includes words defined as having only ever having been known to be used by Shakespeare, Spenser and/or Milton as falling within this category. To assist both Scrabble players and players of other games who may wonder why their smaller dictionary ignores such a word (they only appear in the larger classic dictionaries) these are shown in this book with the suffix (**obs.**).

Plurals Valid for Scrabble, Countdown and Sylabex without question. Only permitted in Kan-U-Go where the *S* (or *ES*) is already in play and a word is linked to that letter.

By definition words such as *mice*, *men* or *oxen* are invalid for Lexicon, Dixit and Kan-U-Go as plurals are specifically barred.

Proper nouns, etc. As the rules of Scrabble specifically state that you cannot use words 'starting with a capital letter' and as all the listed words in the *Official Scrabble Players' Dictionary* are in capitals so, theoretically, you cannot play Scrabble in the USA! Obviously common sense is called for in interpreting this rule.

Countdown, Lexicon and Dixit specifically bar proper nouns and Sylabex specifically bars proper names – but, what of proper adjectives?

The most sensible attitude is that adopted by championship Scrabble and that is to bar all words that require a capital letter except where that word also has an alternative meaning for which a lower case initial letter is perfectly acceptable. To assist games-players, hundreds of examples of these words are given in this book and if you appreciate that DAISY is both a girl's name (invalid) and a flower (valid) then this concept is quite clear. Thus the FLORA section of this book has the flower listed as **daisy** and the PERSONAL NAME—GIRLS' NAMES section has the person listed as **Daisy***, the asterisk denoting an alternative meaning for this word which validates it for games play.

Scottish English Perfectly valid for all games and only the Singapore Scrabble championship specifically excludes such words. Gaelic is not the same as Scottish English and should be treated as a language foreign to English.

Shortened forms *Ad* is a shortened form of the word *advertisement* which is now accepted as a word in its own right. Language is never static thus to argue that, as *ad* was originally an abbreviated form, it should be invalid today is the same as saying that, as *tomato* was originally a Nahuatl Red Indian word, so it too should be invalid on the grounds of being foreign.

Slang Not valid for Dixit, Sylabex or Countdown but perfectly acceptable for all other games.

Welsh Welsh, being a Celtic language and so foreign to English, is the same as a 'foreign' language in games terms. To illustrate the examples of valid and invalid Welsh words consider these two non-vowel examples; *cwm* and *crwth*—defined in GEOGRAPHICAL TERMS and MUSIC respectively. *Cwm* is a Welsh word used in English and consequently invalid for those games which bar foreign words. *Crwth* is a word of Welsh origin now Anglicized and so valid for all games.

Words in a phrase A word which appears only in a phrase, such as *carne* in *chilli con carne*, is invalid for championship Scrabble but no such stricture is applied to the other games. You must use your own judgement as to the acceptability of such a word.

Chilli and *con* are both words in their own right but, unless your dictionary defines *carne* as an independent word, you would be more in keeping with the spirit of your game if you disallowed it.

Word derivation not given in dictionary Another perennial problem for all word games is how to treat words derived from others but which are not specified in that form by the dictionary. For example: the word *form* is given and defined but what about *un*form, *re*form, form*s*, form*ed*, form*ing*, *un*form*ed*, *re*form*ed*, etc. where that particular form is not given?

With USA Scrabble the answer is simple – if it is not in the *OSPD* then it can't be played. On the other hand, the television version of Countdown accepts that a dictionary only gives some of the examples of words prefixed by *un* or *re* and has a far more liberal attitude. Equally it accepts that the various suffixed formations are also rarely given. UK championship Scrabble comes somewhere between these extremes. It will only accept a prefixed form if it is listed in the reference dictionary but permits all sensibly formed adjectival comparatives and super- latives together with all normal verb forms and plurals. The other games do not mention these points in their rules thus leaving a player in the dark as what attitude to adopt.

How, then, should one approach this problem? As the *OSPD* has been produced specifically for word-play then only a dictionary of that ilk can be taken as a final authority. As the television version of Countdown has an expert referee in attendance so it can afford liberality – a luxury which could lead to dispute at home. The best thing to do, therefore, is to decide in advance how you will treat such words and then stick to that decision.

Words requiring apostrophes Only Scrabble specifically bars them but to use them in other games is to strain the rules to breaking point. For example, one could argue that whilst *cats* (the plural of *cat*) cannot be played in some of the word games, *cat's* (that which belongs to the *cat*) is valid. To counter such a legalistic argument challenge the player of such a move to discover *cat's* listed as such in the dictionary. Should he come up with *cat's-tail* you have the basis of a brand new game called Argument!

With Word for Word® none of these considerations arise as you are given full rein to play any word without restrictions – even having 'part-words' where necessary. However, Word for Word addicts will find that the ready access given by *Pears Word-Puzzler's Dictionary* to words of a specified number of letters is a valuable aid to scoring points in this crossword-type game.

As all players of all games wish to have defined limits (for example, there is nothing in the rules of Word for Word to prevent your opponent literally making up his own nonsense words) so you may decide to impose your own limitations. If so then the examples of word categories quoted above should be helpful in this respect.

Finally, the format of this book will be equally valuable for other word-games (such as Word Mastermind®) where the emphasis is upon words of a specified number of letters.

WORD POWER

This is, of course, the key to success in all word games and many players are daunted by the apparent encyclopaedic knowledge of their opponents. This book is intended to help you become a word-game champion no matter which is your particular favourite pastime. Sylabex players, for example, will be pleased to discover that *Pears Word-Puzzler's Dictionary* increases by twenty per cent the number of words available to play in that delightful card game. The rules permit you to play words other than those given in the published list and so you will discover that both the APPENDIX to this book and STRANGERS are particularly happy hunting grounds. Whilst you will naturally peruse the 6-letter word lists don't overlook 5-letter words such as *carse* in GEOGRAPHICAL TERMS which, pluralized as *carses*, is perfect for your game.

Whilst it is possible with Sylabex to discover every possible word available for play and to commit all these to memory the same is not true for any of the other word games so that other means have to be sought to achieve expertise without attempting to memorize every word in the complete *Oxford English* or any other great, classic dictionary.

Many people don't play words which they already know simply because they either confuse the rules of one game with another and, for example, don't play plurals in a game which permits them or, fail to appreciate that hundreds of seemingly proper nouns have an alternative meaning which validates their use for play. PERSONAL NAMES and TOWNS AND CITIES (Great Britain) are sections which have been specially annotated for just this purpose as they are an especially fertile field for this endeavour. Equally, you can successfully challenge an opponent if you are aware of a word being designated 'foreign', 'hyphenated', 'obsolete', etc. (*see* FOR WORD-GAME PLAYERS).

But, for the crossword-type game player, it is the 2-letter words which will turn him or her from a 'rabbit' into a 'tiger'. These words are utterly invaluable in creating a link to a word already in play and a knowledge of the valid 2-letter words is an essential factor of success.

Let us assume that you are playing one of these games, it permits plurals, and you are using *Chambers Twentieth Century Dictionary* as your official reference. Imagine that only the word TAENIAE (which means ribbons or fillets) has been played and you have created the 7-letter word STEALER but can't, of course, make a tangential link with the 's' on the end of TAENIAE as that word is already a plural. How do you play it?

Amazing as it may seem the answer is to put it directly above the existing word:

STEALER
TAENIAE

as ST, TA, EE, AN, LI, EA and RE are all valid for play.

On the other hand, if your reference dictionary was the *Official Scrabble Players' Dictionary* then you would have to make an anagram of STEALER and place it below TAENIAE as follows:

TAENIAE
ELATERS

due to the differences in 2-letter word validity. (STEALER, ELATERS and TAENIAE being valid words in both dictionaries.)

Pears Word-Puzzler's Dictionary has carefully selected all 92 of the 2-letter words which would be valid for normal word-game play, out of the approximate 250 2-letter words which can be discovered in the various English dictionaries. Hence words such as *aa* (a type of volcanic lava) and *xi* (the Greek letter) have been ignored whilst esoteric gems such as *ky* and *zo* will be found listed in FAUNA-ANIMALS.

Having mastered these 2-letter words the aspiring word-game champion should then pay particular attention to those 3-letter words which consist of an existing 2-letter word plus another letter; once again the purpose being that of creating a link.

Three-letter words are especially valuable in another connection which, surprising as it may seem, includes the game of Countdown. Three-letter words are often syllables in much longer words and if you wish to create a mental library then *Ing* (the Norse hero) should certainly be on your mental shelf.

By having rapid access to 2- and 3-letter words with *Pears Word-Puzzler's Dictionary* so you can, after confirming the rules of your preferred game, relate these to your own particular reference dictionary and quickly achieve 'tiger' status – you will find that it is not necessary to attempt to memorize larger words as the 'syllable method' will make these sought-after words reasonably apparent.

WORD-PUZZLE CREATION

Only the crossword rivals the *word-search* puzzle in popularity and, whilst you may find that creating a crossword is not so simple, you now have the perfect book for devising your own *word-search* square.

As *Pears Word-Puzzler's Dictionary* enlists all the words of an individual subject together so the chief problem in creating this type of puzzle has been overcome. Professional *word-search* compilers think of a subject, try and think of as many relevant words as they can, then (using graph paper for convenience) weave the results into a square – filling in the gaps with any old letters. Now all *you* need do is find the graph paper, use a little of your own ingenuity, and you have not only a new pastime but you could well find that you have devised a puzzle good enough for one of the many magazines which specialize in this type of puzzle.

On the other hand you may care to devise a crossword; if so, then those awkward little gaps which have you struggling to find (say) four suitable letters (either a word or a set of initials) will no longer be a problem.

FOR GENERAL REFERENCE

Finally, you may wish to use this book as a work of general reference and the CONTENTS reveal the range of subjects covered, some of which are in considerable depth.

NOTES FOR THE READER

When using this dictionary be sure to check the beginning of each section for any particular points relating to that section. Some symbols are used only in certain sections and are given at the start of those sections, but the following symbols are found throughout:

*indicates that the word has an alternative meaning which validates its use for most word games subject to other strictures such as the use of plurals, etc.

(obs) (obs.) obsolete. If placed against the **headword** then the word is invalid. If placed within the definition then that particular *meaning* is invalid but NOT the word.

(f) (f) foreign or otherwise invalid for certain word games.

Where a word appears in italics further useful information is available in the same section under that word.

ABBREVIATIONS

Abbreviations used in this book are of two distinct types: standard and specific.

Standard abbreviations are those encountered in everyday literature and which feature as entries in the dictionary under the individual subject. These are especially relevant to the crossword solver as they are frequently used as syllables in anagrams.

Specific abbreviations are those found only in this book and have relevance only to the section or chapter in which they appear. For convenient cross-reference they have been italicized.

Abbreviations and full stops: The modern tendency is to ignore full stops with abbreviations though both forms are correct. However, certain conventions have arisen so that the use of a stop *effectively* imparts a different meaning. For example:
Am americium
Am. America
Br bromine
Br. brother
Where this is encountered with a *standard abbreviation* it is shown in the text. The *specific abbreviations* used mirror the same conventions applying to the use of stops.

ACCENTS

In the convention of crosswords and word-games accents have been largely ignored.

THE
DICTIONARY

THE ARTS

ART

atk artwork (of various kinds)
MAd Modern Art, dehumanized, totally abstract
MAdx Modern Art, dehumanized experimentally up to a point
MAx Modern Art, experimental but with recognizable forms
mvt movement or school
Ptg a painting
ptg act of painting

2/3

op *op art*
hue colour: tint
mat dull gold/white border
sit to pose or model

4

body opacity of paint/pigment
boss a raised ornament
bust head (and breast) sculpture
chic artistic skill
Dada *MAd mvt* 1916–c.1920
daub (to paint) a coarse *Ptg*
draw to make a picture of
etch draw on glass, metal, etc.
icon (1) carved/painted portrait
icon (2) *Ptg*/mosaic of Christ (etc.)
ikon *icon* (1) (2)
limn to draw or paint
oils oil paints or painting
size weak glue
tone colour: tint or shade
wash to cover with thin coat

5

batik a method of cloth design
burin (1) a copper engraving chisel
burin (2) individual style of using (1)

cameo gem with relief carved figure
draft *study*
easel artist's work-support frame
Fauve one who produced *Fauvism*
gesso plaster surface for painting
grave to engrave on hard surface
japan a glossy black lacquer
magot a small grotesque figure
model one posing for artist
mount card surrounding picture
mural a wall painting
op art *MAx* producing optical effects
pieta see RELIGIOUS TERMS (p.346)
prime to apply *primer*
print printed picture: engraving
putto young (winged) boy in art
rebus punningly pictured name
scene picture of place/action
sculp to carve/engrave/sculpture
secco painting on dry plaster
shade (1) a variety/degree of colour
shade (2) a hue mixed with black
shade (3) dark part of picture
shade (4) to mark with colour gradation
sketch (to make) outline drawing
study a preliminary art work
throw form on potter's wheel
tondo a circular *Ptg*/carving
vertu erroneous form of *virtu*
virtu objects of art/antiquity

ART

6

barock *baroque*
bosses plural of *boss*
canvas coarse cloth for painting
cubism *MAdx* using geometric figures
cubist one who produces *cubism*
design a drawing or sketch
ectype a reproduction or copy
emboss to cover with *bosses*
enamel (1) a glossy type of paint
enamel (2) to use (1)
flambe of a Chinese type of glaze
fresco *true fresco: dry fresco*
ground the artwork surface
Kitcat a portrait 36″ × 28″
limner a portrait painter
mobile suspended wind-blown *atk*
mosaic pieced-together *atk* (marble, etc.)
niello a method of ornamenting metal
pastel (1) artist's (coloured) chalk
pastel (2) work produced with (1)
pastel (3) of soft colour
pinxit (f) . . . . . . painted (this)
pop art *Ptg* of poster/comic strip imagery
primer preparatory coat of paint
reflex of *Ptg* with an illuminated part
relief *atk* with raised projection
rococo florid (tasteless) *atk*
school artists following same discipline
sculpt to sculpture
sketch (1) a preliminary drawing
sketch (2) the act of (1)
statue a representation in the round
studio an artist's workroom
uncial of a form of manuscript writing
versal an illuminated letter

camaieu *cameo:* monochrome *Ptg*
cartoon *study:* comic/satirical *atk*
carving act/art of sculpture
collage picture from pasted scraps
diptych a pair of hinged pictures
draught usually *draft*
drawing (1) art of lineal representation
drawing (2) a work of (1)
emblema an inlaid ornament
etching (1) art of engraving
etching (2) a work of (1)
excudit (f) . . . . . . struck, forged (etc.) (this)
faience glazed coloured earthenware
Fauvism 2-dimensional *MAx* (early 20th C.)
Fauvist one who produced *Fauvism*
glazing (1) adding a gloss to *biscuit*
glazing (2) modifying colours in *ptg*
gouache matt-surfaced watercolour *Ptg*
linocut (1) design cut in linoleum
linocut (2) print taken from (1)
lunette a crescent-shaped ornament
montage an assembled picture
palette artist's colour mixing board
pigment paint: colouring matter
scumble (1) to soften the effect
scumble (2) colour/work of (1)
shading see *shade* (1) (2) (3) (4)
stabile immobile suspended *atk*
stipple (1) to engrave/paint/draw in dots
stipple (2) work/effect produced by (1)
tableau a picture
tachism *MAd mvt* mid 20th C.
tempera *Ptg* produced from egg + paint
tessera individual *mosaic* piece
woodcut (1) engraving cut on wood
woodcut (2) impression taken from (1)

7

art deco decorative style 1920/30
atelier an artist's studio
barocco *baroque*
baroque bold, vigorous to *rococo*
Bauhaus German *school* (1919/33)
biscuit unglazed pottery
bottega (f) an artist's studio

8

abstract *MAd*
acrolith wooden statue + stone extremities
anaglyph (1) low relief ornament
anaglyph (2) stereoscopically viewed picture

aquatint a mode of copper etching
art autre post w.w.II *mvt* inc. *tachism*
damaskin *damascene*
diaglyph *intaglio*
dry-point (1) copper-plate engraving needle
dry-point (2) work/impression from (1)
figurine small carved/moulded figure
frottage (1) rubbing for texture effect
frottage (2) *atk* produced from (1)
graffiti plural of *graffito*
graffito an illicit (pathetic) *mural*
hatching shading in fine lines
intaglio gem with hollowed-out figure
luminist *luminarist*
majolica glazed/enamelled earthenware
makimono long picture on silk roll
monotint single tint drawing/*ptg*
penumbra light/shade blending
plein-air of open air painting
portrait likeness of real person
repousse raised in relief
sea-piece *seascape*
seascape *Ptg/ptg* of sea scene
statuary of/suitable for sculpture
tachisme *tachism*
tapestry an ornamental textile
tesserae plural of *tessera*
trecento Italian 14th C. art
triptych three hinged pictures
vignette a small embellishment

9

alla prima (f) single layer of pigment *ptg*
aquarelle water-colour *ptg*
aquatinta *aquatint*
arabesque (1) of/like Arabian designs
arabesque (2) Spanish-Moorish ornament
bas-relief low relief sculpture
calligram *calligramme*
cerograph (1) an *encaustic (1) Ptg*
cerograph (2) waxed plate engraving
cloisonne decorated with enamel compartments
colourist painter

damascene gold (etc.) inlaid on steel
damaskeen *damascene*
damasquin *damascene*
distemper a mode of *ptg* in *size*, etc.
dry fresco mural on partly dry plaster
emblemata plural of *emblema*
encaustic (1) *ptg* in melted wax (ancient method)
encaustic (2) having colours burned in
grisaille mural imitating *bas-relief*
grotesque an extravagant ornament
landscape *Ptg/ptg* of countryside
mahlstick *maulstick*
marquetry inlaid with various wood
maulstick artist's hand-resting stick
mezzotint (1) a copperplate engraving method
mezzotint (2) impression taken from (1)
miniature (1) manuscript illumination
miniature (2) *Ptg* on ivory (etc.) small scale
oleograph print imitating oil *Ptg*
sculpture (1) the act of (stone) carving
sculpture (2) *atk* produced from (1)
serigraph a silk-screen print
statuette a small statue
still-life inanimate object *Ptg*
stretcher a *canvas* stretching device
symbolism use of symbols in art
symbolist one using *symbolism*
tailpiece engraving/design on page
tenebrist painter like Caravaggio
vorticism *MAdx mvt* British
woodblock *woodcut* (1) (2)
xylograph *woodcut* (1) (2)

10

art nouveau decorative art (c.1890–1910)
caricature exaggerated/distorted likeness
damasceene *damascene*
kinetic art art encompassing movement
lithograph a print from stone
luminarist (1) one who paints luminously

ART

luminarist (2) *plein-airist:* impressionist
mezzotinto *mezzotint* (1) (2)
monochrome picture in one colour
nightpiece (1) *Ptg* of a night scene
nightpiece (2) *Ptg* for artificial light viewing
pietra-dura inlaid work with hard stones
silhouette shadow-outline picture
silk-screen a stencil process
surrealism *MAx* French (from c.1919)
tessellate to pave with *tesserae*
true fresco mural on damp plaster

calligraphy artistic/fine penmanship
chinoiserie (f) Chinese decoration/objects, etc.
fresco secco *dry fresco*
life drawing drawing from (nude) life
oil-painting *Ptg/ptg* in oil paints
plein-airist a *plein-air* painter
pointillism *ptg* by individual dots
primitivism primitive art
tessellated paved with *tesserae*

12/13/14

11

alto-rilievo high relief sculpture
battle-piece picture of a battle
calligramme a design using letters

palette-knife colour mixing tool
impressionism realistic school of *ptg*
Pre-Raphaelite 19th C. school of *ptg*
action painting American *tachism*
pavement artist one chalking on pavement

DRAMA AND ENTERTAINMENT

Also see MUSIC p. 38

(h) historical
chr character
pf performance
pfr(s) performer(s)
T/a Theatre auditorium
T/s Theatre (back) stage area

2

MC master of ceremonies
no Japanese (religious dance) drama

3

act (1) to perform: a *pf*
act (2) main division of a play
bit *bit-part*
box small seated enclosure in *T/a*
cue hint to perform
die *die the death*

dry *dry up*
dub add fresh sound-track to
fly raise/lower scenery
gag interpolation by actor
god occupant of gods' seat
ham overact: one who overacts
hit (1) an effective remark
hit (2) a successful play/film, etc.
mug to grimace
mum (1) to act in a dumb show
mum (2) to act as a *mummer*
noh *no*
pan (1) severely criticize *pf/pfr*
pan (2) camera panorama effect
pas a step: a dance
pit groundfloor *T/a*: occupants of
rag theatre curtain
rep repertory theatre
run period of *pf* life
set (1) company performing dance
set (2) a series of dance figures
set (3) a set scene
tap *tap-dancing*

4

book libretto, play text
boom microphone/camera rod
call pre-*pf* summons
camp theatrical, exaggerated
cast (1) to appoint actor(s)
cast (2) company of actors
dame panto comic lead (male)
diva popular female singer
Emmy the TV *Oscar* (USA)
epic large-scale film
feed to supply a *cue*
film (1) a (narrative) motion picture
film (2) act of making (1)
flat movable stage scenery
foil minor contrast *pfr*
fool jester *(h)*
gods (1) *T/a* gallery seating
gods (2) occupants of (1)
grid scenery/lighting framework *T/s*
hero (melodrama) male lead
hwyl inspired oratory
iron theatre safety curtain
lead (*pfr* of) chief role
line (1) part of *lines*
line (2) a *bingo* objective
live unrecorded: actual *pf*
mask (1) grotesque face covering *(h)*
mask (2) *masque* (1) (2)
mike abbr. for microphone
mime (1) *farce* inc. mimicry *(h)*
mime (2) a play without dialogue
mime (3) actor in (1) or (2)
movy *movie*
mute actor without *lines*
part (1) a character in a *play* (1)
part (2) persona assumed by actor
play (1) performed literary work
play (2) to perform
plot the play/film story
prop a theatrical property
role *part* (1)
rush unedited film print
shot a unit of *film* (2)
show an entertainment
skit a dramatized burlesque
sock (1) shoe worn in comedy *(h)*
sock (2) comedy *(h)* see *buskin*
spot spotlight: TV (etc.) appearance

star a leading performer
take *shot*
tour travel with a play (etc.)
turn variety *pf/pfr*
wing (1) side of stage
wing (2) scenery set at (1)

5

actor one who acts
ad. lib. use own words
angel a financial backer
apron stage projecting into *T/a*
aside words supposedly secret
bingo popular gambling entertainment
clown buffoon: act buffoonishly
comic (1) of/pertaining to *comedy*
comic (2) actor of droll parts
dance movement with measured step
drama dramatic literature/
  entertainment
dry up forget one's *lines*
enact perform
exode (1) concluding part of play *(h)*
exode (2) farce or afterpiece
extra a (crowd-scene) film *mute*
farce extravagantly humorous comedy
flies space above *T/s*
flyer one-off *bingo* card
foyer public room leading to *T/a*
heavy (1) of serious/grave roles
heavy (2) major/minor villain
house (1) audience: auditorium: *pf*
house (2) *full house* (2)
lines words of an actor's *part* (1)
mimer *mime* (3)
mimic one who (exaggeratedly)
  imitates
movie *film* (1)
on cue just at the right moment
opera see MUSIC (p. 41)
Oscar the Film Industry award
panto pantomime
piece dramatic composition
props *prop* plural: *property-man*
radio sound broadcasting
revue (topical/musical) *show*
scene (1) the stage *(h)*
scene (2) place of action in play

DRAMA AND ENTERTAINMENT

scene (3) scenery suggesting (2)
scene (4) a division of act/play
scene (5) dramatic incident in (4)
slate *pan* (1) unsparingly
stage (1) theatre: theatrical calling
stage (2) platform for acting upon
stall individual armed seat in *T/a*
stunt difficult showy *pf*
telly television
usher *T/a* worker
wings usual form of *wing* (1) (2)

6

action movement of events
august maladroit circus clown
ballet (1) pantomimic dancing exhibition
ballet (2) music/performing troupe for (1)
barker fairground/circus tout
big top main circus tent (USA)
boards the stage
busker an itinerant *pfr*
buskin (1) shoe worn in tragedy *(h)*
buskin (2) tragedy *(h)* see *sock*
chorus (1) band of singers, dancers
chorus (2) *Greek chorus*
chorus (3) a person acting as (2)
chorus (4) a company of singers
chorus (5) that sung by (4)
chorus (6) a general refrain
cinema (1) *cinematograph*
cinema (2) building where (1) is shown
circle gallery in *T/a*
circus (1) building for games *(h)*
circus (2) tent/building for entertainment
circus (3) company/show in (2)
circus (4) a display (tennis/flying, etc.)
claque body of hired applauders
comedy (1) pleasant humorous drama
comedy (2) drama with happy ending
[1] **corpse (1)** lose *part* (2) in laughter
[1] **corpse (2)** cause other to (1)

[1] Games players note: *corpse* may only be used as a NOUN

dancer one skilled in *dance*
encore (1) a call for repeat
encore (2) item given in response to (1)
feeder one supplying *feed*
fly-man worker in the *flies*
jester joker: court-fool *(h)*
kabuki popular Japanese drama, etc.
kinema *cinema* (1) (2)
make up (1) to adjust one's appearance
make up (2) apply facial paint/powder
masque (1) a masked spectacle *(h)*
masque (2) dramatic form of (1) *(h)*
motley variegated: jester-like
mummer actor in folk-play
nautch *pf* by *nautch-girls*
number part of (musical) show
on tour *tour*
parody a burlesque imitation
patter rapid, glib talk
player an actor
prompt supply forgotten words
puppet manipulated doll/image
ring up raise stage curtain
screen (1) to make *film* (1)
screen (2) display, exhibit *film* (1)
script broadcasting text: *scenario*
serial film (etc.) in instalments
singer one who sings
sketch short entertainment scene
stager actor
stalls *T/a* ground floor area
stooge *feeder:* stage butt
studio film/TV workshop
talkie *film* (1) with sound-track
troupe a company of *pfrs*
walk on a small part actor
warm up pre-broadcasting *pf*

7

acrobat rope-dancer: tumbler
actress feminine of *actor*
auguste *august*
balcony (1) gallery above dress-circle (UK)
balcony (2) dress-circle (USA)
benefit *pf* for charity (etc.)
bit-part small acting *part* (1)
buffoon (low/vulgar) jester

cabaret (1) restaurant with *variety*
cabaret (2) *pf/pfr* at (1)
call-boy prompter's attendant
cartoon filmed drawings
catcall a sound-effect instrument
channel TV/radio frequency/company
charade an acted riddle
chorine a chorus-girl
circuit a group of theatres (etc.)
close-up detailed film-shot
commere feminine of *compere* (1)
compere (1) master of *pf* ceremonies
compere (2) to act as (1)
coryphe *coryphee*
dresser male/female *pf* valet
effects sound/lighting devices
farceur writer/actor of *farce*
filmdom *the cinema*
film fan devotee of the cinema
film set *set* (3) for *film* (2)
gallery (1) upper circle seating
gallery (2) occupants of (1)
Guignol chief French puppet
heroine (melodrama) female *lead*
ingenue (f) naive young female *pfr*
juggler dexterous throwing *pfr*
leg-show *pf* with female display
leotard *pfr's* skin-tight garment
long run *hit* (2)
matinee afternoon (unfashionable) *pf*
musical *see* MUSIC (p. 44)
on-stage on public view
overact overdo the *pf* of
pageant (1) dramatic *pf (h)*: stage *(h)*
pageant (2) a series of tableaux
perform act: display *pf* skills
Pierrot* white-faced buffoon
playboy a boy actor
playlet a short play
preview pre-public *pf*
recital (1) narration
recital (2) (solo) musical *pf*
resting out of work
revival renewed *pf* of play (etc.)
scenery theatrical hangings (etc.)
showbiz show business
showman exhibitor/owner of show
stagery theatrical contrivances
stand in (stunt) deputy

starlet a young film actress
tableau *tableau vivant*
tragedy elevated drama
trailer sample of new *film* (1)
trouper (1) member of *troupe*
trouper (2) an experienced actor
tumbler athletic display *pfr*
upstage (1) rear of stage
upstage (2) disadvantage fellow *pfr*
variety music-hall entertainment
vent act ventriloquist's act
villain (melodrama) *chr* lead
western Wild West film

8

animator *cartoon* artist
audition (a) trial *pf*
backdrop *back-cloth*
bioscope cinema (projector) *(h)*
burletta musical farce
camp it up consciously act *camp*
carnival fair-like entertainment
chat show TV 'interview' *pf*
coliseum *colosseum*
comedian writer/actor of *comedy* (1)
   (2)
conjuror stage magician
coryphee (f) a (male) ballet dancer
danseuse a (female) ballet dancer
director directs film acting
dumb-show *pantomime* (1)
duologue dialogue for two
epilogue (1) speech at *pf* conclusion
epilogue (2) speaker of (1)
epilogue (3) TV concluding piece
fan dance tantalizing erotic solo *pf*
farceuse feminine of *farceur*
fauteuil a theatre-stall
festival a season of plays (etc.)
figurant a ballet dancer
filmgoer regular film patron
filmland *the cinema*
film star popular film *pfr*
high camp absurd extravagant *camp*
libretti a plural of *libretto*
libretto text of an opera (etc.)
live show actual unrecorded show
location site for filming

31

DRAMA AND ENTERTAINMENT

newscast news (TV) broadcast
newsreel news (TV) film
off-stage hidden from T/a view
parterre *pit* (under gallery)
playbill bill announcing a play
playbook (1) printed play
playbook (2) a book of plays
playgirl feminine of *playboy*
play-goer regular theatre patron
premiere (f) (1) leading actress (etc.)
premiere (f) (2) first *pf* of play (etc.)
producer (1) *film* (2) chief executive
producer (2) directs stage acting
prologue (1) action preceding *chorus (2)*
prologue (2) speech before a play
prologue (3) speaker of (2)
prompter (1) *stage-manager*
prompter (2) one who prompts
quiz show questionable entertainment!
rehearse train by practice
ring down lower stage curtain
scenario (film) skeletal outline
set piece (1) standing *scenery*
set piece (2) elaborately prepared *pf*
show bill bill announcing a show
showgirl decorative female *pfr*
side-show subordinate exhibition
smash-hit great *hit* (2)
stage-box *box* over proscenium
star-turn (1) the chief item
star-turn (2) *pfr* of (1)
stripper a strip-tease *pfr*
subtitle translation on film (1)
take a bow acknowledge applause
telecast television broadcast
Thespian* (1) of/pertaining to *tragedy*
Thespian* (2) (tragedy) actor
typecast (1) *cast* (1) naturally
typecast (2) *cast* (1) in similar role
wardrobe room having *pf* costumes

9

announcer news/item reader (TV, etc.)
arabesque a ballet posture
back-cloth item of scenery
backstage behind the scenes
ballerina female ballet-dancer

bandstand structure for band
bandwagon band's car in parade
barnstorm to travel & present *pf*
bingo club club for bingo (etc.)
boxkeeper *T/a* attendant
box-office (1) ticket sales office
box-office (2) *pf* commercial quality
broadcast radio/TV *pf*
burlesque (1) a 'send-up' *pf*
burlesque (2) (USA) *vaudeville* (+ strip-tease)
cameraman film/TV photographer
character personality created for play
clip-joint overcharging night-club
colosseum Vespasian's *amphitheatre (h)*
Columbine* sweetheart of *Harlequin*
coryphaei plural of *coryphaeus*
double act a pair of (comedy) *pfrs*
downstage near the footlights
dramatics study of drama
dramatist a writer of plays
dramaturg (f) production assistant
drop-scene a drop-curtain
entrechat type of ballet leap
figurante *figurant*
flash-back scene of the past
floor show night-club entertainment
folk-dance traditional native dance
full house (1) *pf* with all seats taken
full house (2) a full *bingo* card
greenroom *pfrs* retiring-room
Harlequin* a *pantomime* (2) *chr*
impresari a plural of impresario
limelight (1) brilliant stage lighting *(h)*
limelight (2) glare of publicity
love scene romantic *scene* (5)
low comedy slapstick, farcical comedy, etc.
melodrama crude sensational drama
melodrame *melodrama*
monodrama one-man play
monologue one person dialogue
music-hall a variety theatre
night-club late night entertainment
on the road on *tour*
panel game radio/TV guessing *pf*
Pantaloon* a *pantomine* (2) *chr*
pantomime (1) dumb-show/*mime* (2) *(h)*

pantomine (2) (1) plus *harlequinade (h)*
pantomime (3) Roman actor in (1) *(h)*
pantomime (4) Christmas entertainment
pas de deux two-person dance
performer one who performs
Pierrette feminine of *Pierrot*
pirouette (to) spin on tiptoe
playhouse theatre
prompt-box box for *prompter* (2)
puppeteer manipulator of puppets
slapstick (1) a sound-effect lath
slapstick (2) clownish comedy
soap opera (TV) emotional serial
soliloquy speech to oneself
soubrette (1) maid-servant in comedy
soubrette (2) a female singer
spotlight (1) light of emphasis
spotlight (2) figuratively in (1)
stage-door actors' theatre entrance
stage-hand worker in *T/s*
stage left left as facing *T/a*
stage-name actor's professional name
stage-play play intended for stage
strip club club with *strip-tease*
tap-dancer *pfr* of *tap-dancing*
the cinema (1) films in general
the cinema (2) film as an art form
the cinema (3) the film industry
the method *method acting*
the movies *the cinema* (1) (3)
title-role role of play's title
torch-song 1930s love song
tragedian actor of *tragedy*
usherette feminine of *usher*

10

afterpiece minor piece after play
apron-stage *apron*
auditorium spectator's area
choreology study of ballet (history)
chorus-girl female in *chorus* (1)
comedienne feminine of *comedian*
comedietta short comic piece
comic opera opera of amusing nature
commercial (1) sponsored radio/TV (USA)
commercial (2) radio/TV advert (UK)

continuity (1) complete *scenario*
continuity (2) writer of (1)
coryphaeus leader of chorus
crowd scene (film) scene of crowd
denouement unravelling of plot
disc jockey (radio) records announcer
dramaturge playwright
dramaturgy theatrical art
fantoccini marionettes
first night opening night of *pf*
footlights lights on stage front
hippodrome (1) (chariot) racecourse *(h)*
hippodrome (2) circus: variety theatre
horror film film of fear
horse opera Wild West film
impresario opera co. manager
in the round viewed from all sides
in the wings off-stage
legitimate legitimate drama
librettist writer of *libretti*
marionette puppet on strings
newscaster *newsreader*
newsreader news reader (TV, etc.)
one act play short play
on location at site for filming
opera-house theatre for opera
persona muta operatic *mute*
playwright a writer of plays
prompt-book *pf* copy of script
prompt-copy *prompt-book*
prompt-side (1) *stage left* (UK)
prompt-side (2) *stage right* (USA)
proscenium (1) stage curtain and framework
proscenium (2) front part of stage
puppet-show show with puppet *pfrs*
rave notice enthusiastic press review
repertoire total of *pf* stock
repetiteur *pf* coach/tutor
ring-master circus MC
screenplay full text for film
screen test filming audition
silent film film without sound
sound-track film-sound recording
stage-craft theatrical expertise
stage-fever a passion to be a *pfr*
stage right right as facing *T/a*
strip-tease seductive undressing *pf*
sword-dance dance with sword(s)

tap-dancing foot tapping *pf* dance
tear-jerker over sentimental (film)
television (sound &) picture broadcasting
travelogue film/talk on travel
understudy (1) *pfr's* deputy
understudy (2) learn *pfr's* part
vaudeville (1) popular topical song *(h)*
vaudeville (2) play with songs/dances
vaudeville (3) variety (especially USA)
walk on part small part

Passion-play drama of Christ
protagonist chief actor
Punchinello Punch (puppet)
show-stopper great song/moment of *pf*
stage-effect theatrical effect
stage-fright pre-*pf* nerves
stage-struck severe *stage-fever*
Terpischore the muse of song/dance
tragedienne tragic role actress
tragi-comedy comedy with tragic overtones
ventriloquy *ventriloquism*

11

accompanist supporting musical *pfr*
balletomane enthusiast for ballet
black comedy (1) thesis of despair
black comedy (2) dreadful events comedy
broadcaster one who broadcasts
cap and bells mark of a jester
cliffhanger tense, exciting adventure
comic relief humorous bit in tragedy
commentator broadcaster who comments
cutting room film editor's workroom
documentary film of real-life
dress-circle first gallery in *T/a*
equilibrist *pfr* of balancing tricks
exeunt omnes (f) all leave stage
feature film long main film
film theatre *cinema* (2)
funambulist rope walker/dancer
grease paint *pfr's* make up
Greek chorus commentating *pfrs*
illusionist a stage magician
in character in harmony with *part* (1)
iron curtain *iron*
kitchen-sink sordid 'real-life' drama
legerdemain sleight-of-hand
light comedy *comedy* (1)
make one's bow leave the stage
matinee idol popular *pfr*
miracle play religious drama *(h)*
nautch-girls Indian dancing women
opera bouffa (f) 18th C. comic opera
opera bouffe funny/farcical opera

12

academy award *Oscar*
amphitheatre circus-like theatre
choreography art of (ballet) dancing
dramaturgist *playwright*
exotic dancer strip-tease *pfr*
first-nighter habitual *first night* patron
Grand Guignol short horror play
harlequinade buffoonery section
method acting personally living the part
morality-play vice/virtue personified *(h)*
Pepper's ghost reflection device
principal boy actress as pantomime hero
Punch* and Judy* puppet show
run of the play duration of *pf* run
scene-shifter *stage-hand*
silver screen cinema screen
stage manager supervisor of *T/s* activity
stage whisper 'secret' audible in *T/a*
top of the bill main *pfr/pf*

13/14/15

bastard prompt reversed *prompt-side*
tableau vivant living picture
ventriloquism voice projection illusion
proscenium arch stage 'picture frame'
tableaux vivants plural, *tableau vivant*

LITERATURE AND PROSODY

c/f consisting of
lg long and/or stressed syllable
sh short and/or unstressed syllable

3

dit a poem
lay a short narrative poem
ode an addressed poem
pun a play on words
tag (1) a trite (Latin) quotation
tag (2) a moral to a story

4

bard a (Celtic) poet
copy matter for printing
ditt *dit*
duan a division of a poem
epic (of) long narrative poem
epos an epic poem
foot division of line of poetry
form structural unity
gest tale of adventure/romance
iamb *iambus*
idyl *idyll*
pean *paean*
play see DRAMA (p. 29)
plot the story
poem a composition in verse
poet author of a *poem*
quip a short clever remark
rime *rhyme*
rune *futhork* letter: *canto*
saga old Icelandic prose tale
tale a (fictitious) story
tome a big book or volume

5

blurb a publisher's puff
canto a division of a long poem

codex a manuscript volume
ditty a little (sung) poem
elegy serious/pensive poem
epode a kind of lyric poem
essay a written composition
fable (1) tale with non-human speakers
fable (2) tale to instruct/amuse
fable (3) *plot* of an *epic*
folio a book (see MEASUREMENT, p. 216)
geste *gest*
gloss (word) explanation
gnome a pithy sententious saying
haiku a type of Japanese poem
hokku *haiku*
iambi (1) a plural of *iambus*
iambi (2) see *iambuses* (2)
idyll a short pictorial poem
Iliad (1) Homer's epic on Troy
Iliad (2) a long (woeful) story
index a list of prohibited books
lyric poetry expressing emotion
maxim pithy saying: proverb
metre syllable relationship in poetry
motif a theme or subject
novel a fictitious prose narrative
paean a *lyric* to a god
poesy poetry collectively/in abstract
prose all writing not in verse
quote (1) originally to divide (chapters, etc.)
quote (2) to refer to: to cite
rhyme sound identity (jingle mingle)
roman medieval romance: *novel*
runic of/pertaining to *rune*
stich a line of verse/prose
story a (fictitious) narrative
triad (1) a group of 3 stories (Welsh lit.)
triad (2) a group of 3 stanzas
verse (1) a line of metre: stanza
verse (2) short division of a chapter

6

Adonic verse, *dactyl + spondee*
Alcaic verse style of Alcaeus
annals historical records
author original writer of a book
ballad a simple narrative poem
cesura *caesura*
choree *trochee*
dactyl *foot (c/f lg, sh, sh)*
dipody a double *foot*
epopee epic poetry: an epic poem
gnomae a plural of *gnome*
haikai Japanese informal verse/prose
heroic epic verse
iambic (1) of/pertaining to *iambus*
iambic (2) *c/f iambi/iambuses*
iambus *foot (c/f sh, lg)*
ledden (obs.) language, dialect, speech
legend (1) a story of a saint's life
legend (2) a traditional story
legend (3) untrue/unhistorical story
memoir usually *memoirs*
monody a mournful ode or poem
poetic (1) of/pertaining to *poetry*
poetic (2) *poetics*
poetry the art of the poet
rondel a verse-form
satire ridicule of folly/vice
saying *maxim*
sonnet a 14 line poem
stanza subdivision of a poem
tenson verse competition
theses plural of *thesis*
thesis an essay on a theme
verser a writer of verse

eclogue a short pastoral poem
elegist a writer of elegies
epigram short pithy (satirical) poem
epistle letter: letter-form verse
fantasy fictional story
fiction the novel
futhark *futhork*
futhore *futhork*
futhork ancient Germanic alphabet
georgic a poem on husbandry
glosses plural of *gloss*
Homeric (1) of/pertaining to Homer
Homeric (2) in heroic/epic style
Leonine* a kind of Latin verse
lexicon a word-book/dictionary
measure a unit of verse
memoirs historic/biographic material
novella tale, short story/novel
novelle a plural of *novella*
Odyssey* Homer's epic poem
odyssey a tale of wandering
poetess female poet
poetics the criticism of poetry
poetise to write as a poet
poetize *poetise*
prosody the study of versification
romance a tale of chivalry
sapphic (1) of/pertaining to Sappho
sapphic (2) verse style of Sappho
spondee *foot (c/f lg, lg)*
the book the Bible
tragedy a sad story
trilogy a group of 3 novels
trochee *foot (c/f lg, sh)*
virelay an old French lyric form
western novel set in Wild West

7

agonist the chief character
apology *apologia*
ballade various types of poem
Byronic of style of Byron
caesura pause in line of verse
choreus *choree*
classic great writer or work
codices plural of *codex*
couplet a pair of rhyming lines
distich *couplet*

8

acrostic an acronym-like poem
anapaest *foot (c/f sh, sh, lg)*
apologia written defence/vindication
balladry ballads: ballad-making
doggerel worthless verses
folktale traditional story
glossary a collection of *glosses*
iambuses (1) a plural of *iambus*
iambuses (2) iambic (satirical) verse
limerick humorous 5 line verse

Pindaric of (supposed) manner of Pindar
quatrain stanza of four lines
rhapsody an (instalment of) epic
thriller a sensational story
who-dun-it *whodunnit*

prosodian one skilled in *prosody*
prosodist *prosodian*
saga novel *roman fleuve*
terza-rima an Italian verse form
Vergilian *Virgilian*
Virgilian in the manner of Virgil
whodunnit a crime mystery novel

9

anthology a collection of poems
biography individual's life-history
criticism the art of judging
decastich a 10 line poem
dime novel a cheap (sensational) novel
dithyramb a hymn-like short poem
ditrochee a trochiac *dipody*
free verse (1) verse defying metrical laws
free verse (2) verse-form rhythmic prose
hexameter a verse of six feet
hexastich poem/stanza of six lines
minor poet genuine but not great poet
monometer a verse of one measure
monorhyme a series of rhyming lines
monostich poem of one line
novelette a short (trite) novel
poetaster a petty poet
poeticule a petty poet
pot-boiler (1) work for essential cash
pot-boiler (2) a writer of (1)

10

amphibrach *foot (c/f sh, lg, sh)*
amphimacer *foot (c/f lg, sh, lg)*
bestseller (1) commercially successful book
bestseller (2) writer of (1)
blank verse unrhymed verse *c/f* 5 feet
gay science poetry (from 'gai saber' Fr.)
ghost-writer one writing in another's name
roman a clef novel of real people
short story prose under 10,000 words

11

Gothic novel psychological horror-story
roman a these novel propounding thesis
roman fleuve novel of family history

MUSIC

Also see RELIGIONS, RELIGIOUS AND ECCLESIASTICAL TERMS (p. 344), and DRAMA AND ENTERTAINMENT (p. 28).

NOTES
A,B,C,D,E,F,G also used as prefixes such as 'A flat', 'B sharp', etc.

ABBREVIATIONS
Explanations of terms are given in following section.
note The asterisk* indicates that an abbreviation is also a word, usually with a totally different meaning, and valid for most word games.

1

f *forte*
p *piano* (1)

2

D.C. *da capo*
D.S. *dal segno*
ff *fortissimo*
fp *forte-piano*
fz *forzato*
mf *mezzo-forte*
M.M. Maelzel's metronome
mp *mezzo-piano*
Op* *opus*
pp *pianissimo*
rf *rinforzato*
sf *sforzato* (sforzando)
T.S. *tasto solo*
U.C. *una corda*
V.S. *volte subito*

3

cal. *calando*
dim.* *diminuendo*
fff *fortississimo*

leg.* *legato*
ppp *pianississimo*
ped.* *pedal*
rfz *rf*
rit.* *ritardando*
sfp *sforzato-piano*
sfz *sf*
ten.* *tenuto*

4

anim. *animato*
arco. *arco saltando*
a tem. *a tempo*
marc.* *marcato*
pizz. *pizzicato*
rall. *rallentando*
rinf. *rf*
sost. *sostenuto*

5/7

accel. *accelerando*
ad*lib.* *ad libitum*
cresc. *crescendo*
smorz. *smorzando*
decresc. *decrescendo*

WORDS AND TERMS

comp. composition
mus. music or musical
in. instrument (musical)
m/in. musical instrument
m/ins musical instruments

2

do 1st note *sol-fa* scale
fa 4th note of scale
gu rude kind of violin
la 6th note of scale
me *mi*
mi 3rd note of scale
re 2nd note of scale
si 7th note *Aretinian scale*
so 5th note of scale
te *ti*
ti *sol-fa* substitute for *si*
ut the Aretinian *do*

3

air (chief, upper) melody, tune
alt a high tone
bar measure of musical time
bis a direction for repetition
bop *bebop*
bow a rod with horsehair
cue a hint
doh *do*
duo *duet* (1) (3)
fah *fa*
gju *gu*
gue *gu*
hum closed mouth singing
jig a lively dance
key (1) lever, piston-end on *m/ins*
key (2) a system of tones
kit a small pocket violin
lah *la*
lay a lyric: a song
pop currently popular music
rag ragtime music
ray *re*

run a definite sequence
sax *saxophone*
soh *so*
sol *so*
tie a sustentation symbol
vox voice
zel an Oriental cymbal

4

alto (1) counter tenor: contralto
alto (2) viola
aria an air or melody
band a body of musicians
bard a strolling minstrel
base *bass* (obs.)
bass (1) low or grave part of *mus.*
bass (2) a deep voiced male singer
bass (3) a bass-toned instrument
beat (1) marking time with a baton
beat (2) *beat music*
bell (1) *m/in.* giving a ringing sound
bell (2) the sound of (1)
bell (3) orifice of wind *in.*
bind *tie*
clef a symbol denoting pitch
coda concluding *mus.* passage
drum (1) a percussion instrument
drum (2) to play (1)
duan a division of a *canto*
duet (1) *mus.* composition for two
duet (2) performance of (1)
duet (3) performers of (1)
echo a soft toned organ
fife (1) a small type of flute
fife (2) to play (1)
flat (1) relatively low
flat (2) below the right pitch
flat (3) black key on a piano
flat (4) sign for semitone lower
flat (5) (4) as played
flat (6) (5) in key-signature
flat (7) an insipid passage
fret ridge on stringed *in.*
glee an unaccompanied song
gong suspended percussion *in.*

harp (1)   plucked string *in.*
harp (2)   to play (1)
high   acute in pitch: loud
horn   a (brass) wind *in.*
hymn   a song of praise
jazz   type of US Negro folk *mus.*
jota   a Spanish dance
juba   a Negro rustic dance
koto   Japanese silk-stringed *in.*
lead   prime guide as *lead singer*, etc.
lied   a German art-song
lilt (1)   a cheerful song or air
lilt (2)   to perform (1)
lute (1)   an old stringed *in.*
lute (2)   to play (1)
lyre   a harp-like instrument
mode (1)   division of an octave
mode (2)   old *mus.* time division
mood   *mode* (2)
mort   a hunting flourish
mute (1)   device for subduing sound
mute (2)   to employ (1)
neum   *neume*
note (1)   mark representing sound
note (2)   a piano (etc.) key
note (3)   sound of (1)
note (4)   song of bird
note (5)   tune (obs.): music (poetic)
oboe (1)   a woodwind *in.*
oboe (2)   an organ stop
opus   a musical composition
part   voice/*in.* in concerted *mus.*
peal (1)   a loud sound
peal (2)   a continuous production of (1)
peal (3)   a set of bells
peal (4)   a chime or carillion
peal (5)   to resound/give forth (2)
pean   *paean*
pipe (1)   a *mus.* wind instrument
pipe (2)   a part of (1)
pipe (3)   to play (1)
pipe (4)   the note of a bird
pipe (5)   a (high) voice
pipe (6)   a boatswain's whistle
pipe (7)   to lead by (1)
port (1)   an instrumental tune
port (2)   a bagpipe composition
reed (1)   *pipe* (1)
reed (2)   vibrating tongue of *m/in.*
reel   a (Celtic) tune and dance

rest (1)   *m/in.* prop or support
rest (2)   interval of *mus.* silence
rock   a simple form of jazz
root   fundamental note of chord
slur (1)   perform smoothly
slur (2)   perform to one syllable
slur (3)   a *mus.* written symbol
soli   plural of *solo*
solo   voice/*in.* solitary passage
song   sung words: melody: *note* (4)
stop (1)   to limit vibration
stop (2)   a fret on lute/guitar
stop (3)   device for altering pitch/tone
stop (4)   a set of organ pipes
stop (5)   mechanism which operates
   (4)،
time   rhythm, tempo
toll   to sound as a bell
tone (1)   the character of a sound
tone (2)   a Gregorian psalm-tune
trio (1)   *mus.* composition for three
trio (2)   the performers of (1)
trio (3)   a division of various *mus.*
   pieces
tuba (1)   a Roman straight trumpet
tuba (2)   the *bombardon*
tuba (3)   a low-pitched brass *in.*
tuba (4)   an organ stop
tune   tone: melody, air
turn   an ornament of 4 notes
vamp   to improvise inartistically
vina   an Indian stringed *in.*
viol   a type of early violin
vivo   lively
wind   the orchestral wind *ins*
wood   the orchestral woodwind *ins*

5

arses   plural of *arsis*
arsis   vocal elevation
assai   very
banjo   *m/in.* of guitar kind
basso   *bass* (2)
baton   a conductor's staff
bebop   a variety of jazz (c. 1940)
blues   slow sad (Negro) music
bones   hand-held rattles
bongo   small Cuban drum

brass   orchestral brass *m/ins*
breve   an obsolescent *mus.* note
bugle   a type of trumpet
canon   a species of *mus.* composition
canto   part carrying melody
carol   Christmas song/hymn
cello   *violoncello*
chant   a song: to sing: church *mus.*
chime   harmony of bells
choir   a chorus of singers
chord (1)   harmonious union of notes
chord (2)   a *m/in.* string
corno   the French horn
crook   part of a wind *in.*
croon   sing/hum in undertone
crowd   the *crwth* (obs.)
crwth   a Welsh stringed *in.*
dance   *mus.* for dancing
dirge   funeral song/hymn
ditty   a song: a sung poem
dolce   sweet music: organ stop
drone (1)   a deep humming sound
drone (2)   bagpipe bass-pipe
duett   duet (1) (2) (3)
dumka (1)   a lament
dumka (2)   a slow movement/piece
duple   two beats to a bar
elegy   a song of mourning
etude   training/testing *mus.* piece
flute (1)   a *mus.* pipe with fingerholes
flute (2)   an organ stop
forte   loud
fugue   a type of *mus.* composition
galop   lively dance (tune)
gamba   *viola da gamba*
gamut   the complete (Aretinian) scale
gigue   a lively dance form
grace   *grace note*
grave   low in pitch
knell   the sound of a bell
largo   broad and slow
lento   slow(ly): slow passage
lyric   of a *lyre*: song
major (1)   semitone greater than minor
major (2)   involving a *major third*
march   (style of) marching *mus.*
metre   musical time
minim   note = two crotchets
minor   semitone less than major
minor   involving a *minor third*

molto   very, much
motet   anthem, church cantata
motif   figure, subject, leitmotif
naker   a *kettledrum*
nebel   a Hebrew harp
neume   notes sung to one syllable
nonet   *comp.* for nine performers
octet   group of/*comp.* for eight
opera (1)   musical drama
opera (2)   plural of *opus*
organ   a keyboard wind *in.*
paean   song of thanksgiving/triumph
pause   continuance of note/rest
pavan (obs.)   Spanish dance (music)
pedal (1)   a lever on a *piano* (2)
pedal (2)   a *pedal-organ*
piano (1)   soft, softly: soft passage
piano (2)   *pianoforte*
piper   player of a (bag)pipe
pitch   acuteness of sound
polka   Bohemian dance tune
primo   first part in duet/trio
quill   *plectrum: mus.* pipe
rebec   *rebeck*
regal   a small portable organ
rondo (f)   a type of *mus.* composition
round   dance tune: sung canon
sanko   *sancho*
sansa   *zanza*
scale   see *sol-fa: Aretinian scale*
scena (1)   an operatic scene
scena (2)   aria following recitative
score   arranged music
segno   start/end repetition sign
senza   without
shake   *trillo*
shalm   *shawm*
sharp   key/note/symbol raised semitone
shawm   oboe-like *m/ins*
sitar   Hindu plucked-string *in.*
sixth (1)   a musical interval
sixth (2)   a combination of two tones
slide   gliding from one note to next
snare   a type of drum
sol-fa   scale superseding Aretinian
stave   *mus.* staff: stanza, verse
strad.   *Stradivarius*
strum   to play haphazardly
suite   a sequence of (e.g.) dance-tunes
swell(1)   an organ device

swell (2) *diminuendo* following *crescendo*

swing *swing-music*

tabor a small type of drum

tacet is silent

tempo time: speed and rhythm

tenor (1) type of male voice

tenor (2) *m/in.* matching (1) in tone

theme a short melody

third (1) a musical interval

third (2) a note during (1)

thrum repeat in sing-song

tibia an ancient flute

tonal of tone: according to key

tonic (1) of/pertaining to tone

tonic (2) a key-note

triad a chord of three notes

trill a tremulous sound

trite 3rd string of a lyre

trope a short *cadence*

trump (1) a trumpet: to trumpet

trump (2) a Jew's harp

tuner (1) one who tunes *ins*

tuner (2) one who sings/makes *mus.*

tuner (3) device on an organ

tutti (1) all (performers)

tutti (2) a passage for (1)

valse waltz: to waltz

viola a tenor fiddle

volta (1) an old type of dance

volta (2) turn, time

volte plural of *volta* (1) (2)

waits out-door Christmas singers

waltz (1) a type of dance

waltz (2) dancing (1)

waltz (3) music for (1)

wrest a piano-tuning instrument

zanza an African *m/in.*

zinke an old cornet-like *m/in.*

6

accent stress on a note

adagio slow(ly): a slow movement

anthem a song of praise, gladness

arioso in the manner of an aria

atabal a Moorish *kettledrum*

a tempo in time

atonal not referred to any scale

aubade a sunrise song

ballad (1) orig. song accompanying dance

ballad (2) popular (scurrilous) song

ballad (3) slow, sentimental song

ballat *ballad* (1) (2) (3)

bolero Spanish dance and tune

burden (1) bourdon or bass

burden (2) part of song, repeated

chanty *shanty*

cither the Tirolese *zither*

citole a medieval stringed *in.*

cornet (1) *cornett*

cornet (2) an organ stop

cornet (3) a treble bass valve *in.*

cymbal a hollow brass plate-like *in.*

da capa a performance instruction

damper a *mute* (1)

diesis major/minor semitone difference

ditone an interval in ancient Greek *mus.*

duetto duet (1) (2) (3)

eighth an *octave* (1)

euouae a Gregorian cadence

euphon type of glass harmonica

fiddle violin or violin-like *m/in*

figure a group of notes

finale final part of *mus.* composition

flugel a grand piano

fugato fugue-like

giusto suitable: regular: strict

guitar a fretted *m/in.*

intone chant/read in *mus.* tones

jingle (1) thin, paltry verse

jingle (2) a tambourine part

legato smooth(ly)

lieder plural of *lied*

manual keyboard played by hand

medley *mus.* pot-pourri

melody air, tune: music

minuet (1) dance (music) in triple measure

minuet (2) a sonata movement in (1)

monody song for one voice

octave (1) interval of 12 semitones

octave (2) note 8 above/below another

octave (3) the 8 notes of (2)

octave (4) an organ stop

off-key out of tune

phrase a short group of notes

plagal of a Gregorian mode
presto very quick
quaver half a crotchet
rebeck medieval viol-like *in.*
rhythm regular recurrence
rubato in modified/distorted rhythm
sancho a W. African guitar
sennet (obs.) stage *mus.* flourish
shanty a sailor's song
sittar *sitar*
solito in the usual manner
slogan correct meaning of *slughorn*
sonata a *mus.* composition
spinet harpsichord-like *in.*
syrinx Pan-pipes
tabour *tabor*
tam-tam a (orchestral) gong
tenuto sustained
timbal a *kettledrum*
timbre quality of a sound
tirade a run between two notes
tom-tom any primitive drum
treble (1) in the treble
treble (2) high-pitched: soprano, etc.
trillo a shake
tucket (obs.) a trumpet flourish
tune up putting *m/ins* in tune
tymbal *timbal*
unison identity of pitch
upbeat an unaccented beat
veloce with great rapidity
ventil an organ valve
vielle a *hurdy-gurdy*
violin bowed 4 string *m/in.*
vivace lively
warble (1) sing quaveringly
warble (2) sweet bird song
zither a stringed *in.*
zufolo a small flute

7

agitato agitated
allegro with brisk movement
amoroso tender
andante moderately slow even
    expression
animato animatedly
arietta a little aria/air

ariette (f) *arietta*
bagpipe a wind *in.*
ballade a form of instrumental *mus.*
bandore an Elizabethan stringed *in.*
baryton *barytone*
bassoon a woodwind *in.*
bazooka a slide wind *in.*
bitonal using two *mus.* keys
bourdon (1) refrain of a song
bourdon (2) *drone* (2)
bourdon (3) an organ bass stop
bravura (1) spirit, dash in execution
bravura (2) a florid air
burthen *burden* (1) (2)
cadence modulation: rhythm, etc.
cadenza an outstanding virtuoso
    passage
calando gradually slower and quieter
calypso a W. Indian folk song
cantata concert-aria: short oratorio
canzone madrigal-like song
canzoni plural of *canzone*
celesta a keyboard *in.*
celeste a type of soft pedal on piano
cembalo (1) a *dulcimer* (1)
cembalo (2) a keyboard version of (1)
chamade *mus.* call for parley/surrender
chanson a song
cithara ancient Greek lyre
cithern *cither: gittern*
cittern *cither*
concert *mus.* harmony/entertainment
cornett an old woodwind *in.*
Cremona* a kind of violin
cremona erroneous form of *cromorna*
csardas a Hungarian dance (music)
czardas faulty spelling of *csardas*
descant an accompanying melody
dichord an ancient lute
epicede a funeral ode
fagotto a bassoon
fanfare a flourish of trumpets
fermata a pause
flutina a kind of accordion
forzato *sforzando*
furioso with fury
gavotte a dance and music
gittern a kind of guitar
gravity lowness of pitch
G-string the thinnest *mus.* string

harmony agreeable *mus.*: *mus.* in general
hautboy an *oboe*
keynote the fundamental note
lullaby a cradle-song
maestro an eminent composer/conductor
mandola a large mandoline
mandora *mandola*
marimba an African xylophone
mazurka Polish dance (music)
measure a bar of *mus.*: (slow) dance
mediant third tone of a scale
melisma song: tune: melodic embellishment
musical (1) of/pertaining to music
musical (2) successor to *mus.* comedy
natural (1) tone neither sharp nor flat
natural (2) keyboard white key
ocarina a musical toy
pandora (1) ancient Eastern lyre
pandora (2) *bandore*
Pianola a 'self-playing' piano
pibroch a form of bagpipe *mus.*
piccolo (1) a small flute
piccolo (2) an organ stop
piffero (1) an Italian bagpipe
piffero (2) a crude oboe
posaune the trombone
prelude preliminary passage, etc.
ragtime form of us Negro *mus.*
refrain *burden* (2), *bourdon* (1)
reprise repeated *mus.* passage
ripieno supplementary
romance romantic music
rondeau *rondo*
rondino (f) a short *rondo*
rosalia a type of repetition
roulade melodic embellishment
sackbut (1) an old trombone-like *in.*
sackbut (2) *sambuca*
sambuca an ancient harp-like *in.*
saxhorn a brass wind *in.*
scherzo a lively *mus.* passage
schisma a division in *mus.*
sciolto free
secondo (f) lower part in duet
serpent an obs. brass wind *in.*
seventh a (semi)tone less than an octave

sistrum ancient Egyptian rattle
skiffle a type of jazz folk-music
soprano (1) treble, the highest voice
soprano (2) part for/singer with (1)
sordino a mute or damper
spinnet *spinet*
stopped see *stop* (1)(2)(3)(4)(5)
stretta a coda in quicker time
stretto part of a fugue
strophe a song in a Greek play
taborin type of small drum
tambour a drum: the bass drum
theorbo a large bass lute
timbrel an ancient *tabor*
timpani plural of *timpano*
timpano an orchestral *kettledrum*
tipping a way of playing flute, etc.
toccata a sort of *fantasia*
tremolo (1) a tremulous effect
tremolo (2) device on organ producing (1)
triplet a group of three notes
trumpet (1) a powerful wind *in.*
trumpet (2) to play (1)
trumpet (3) an organ-reed stop
ukelele *ukulele*
ukulele a small guitar
upright upright-piano
vibrato a throbbing effect
violone a bass viol
zithern *zither*
zuffolo *zufolo*

8

archlute a large bass lute
arpeggio rapidly played chord
autoharp a kind of zither
bagpipes usual form of *bagpipe*
baritone (1) deep-toned male voice
baritone (2) singer with (1)
barytone (1) *baritone* (1) (2)
barytone (2) a viola da gamba-like *m/in.*
barytone (3) a kind of saxhorn
bass clef the F clef
bass drum the large drum
bass horn an old wind *in.*
bass tuba *bombardon*

bass viol *viola da gamba*
berceuse a cradle song
canzonet a type of *canzone*
carillon (1) a set of bells
carillon (2) a melody played on (1)
castrati plural of *castrato*
castrato castrated male singer
cavatina a short operatic air
chaconne old dance (music)
cheville stringed *in.* peg
clarinet a wind *in.*
clavicin harpsichord
concerto composition in sonata form
con fuoco (f) with fire
couraute old dance (music)
cromorna a krummhorn (stop)
crotchet half a *minim*
dal segno replay from a marked point
diapason (1) a whole octave
diapason (2) a bass part
diapason (3) compass of tones
diapason (4) a standard of pitch
diapason (5) an organ stop
diaphone an organ stop
diatonic using natural *mus.* scales
doloroso (f) in a soft, pathetic manner
dominant fifth note above tonic
downbeat an accented beat
drumhead skin of a drum
dulcimer (1) hammered string *in.*
dulcimer (2) ancient Jewish bagpipes
eleventh an octave and a fourth
ensemble a group of musicians
entr'acte interval music
falsetto forced voice above natural
fandango old Spanish dance (music)
fantasia free form *mus.* composition
folkrock folk-music in rock form
folk-song traditional song
folk-tune traditional music
forzando *sforzando*
galliard a 16th/17th C. dance
hornpipe (1) an old Welsh *m/in.*
hornpipe (2) sailors' dance (music)
interval tonal pitch difference
Jew's-harp v. small lyre-shaped *in.*
jongleur a wandering minstrel
keyboard a range of levers in *m/in.*
knackers castanets
ligature a tie or slur

madrigal an unaccompanied song
mandolin *mandoline*
melodeon a small reed organ
mirliton a toy reed pipe
moderato at moderate speed
modulate to change key
monotone single unvaried tone
movement a major division
musicale a *mus.* social gathering
nocturne a dreamy (piano) *comp.*
operetta short light *mus.* drama
oratorio (Biblical) story set to *mus.*
ostinato a ground-bass
overtone a harmonic
overture an instrumental prelude
Pan-pipes fastened reeds *m/in.*
plectrum a string-plucking device
polyphon *polyphone*
post-horn a postman's horn
recorder a fipple-flute
register (1) an organ stop
register (2) compass of voice or *m/in.*
rhapsody irregular emotional *mus.*
  piece
ricercar forerunner of *fugue*
rigadoon jig-like dance (music)
saraband slow Spanish dance (music)
semitone half a *tone* (1)
serenade (1) symphonic-like *comp.*
serenade (2) nocturnal open air
  performance
serenade (3) to perform (1) or (2)
serenata (1) *serenade* (1)
serenata (2) a pastoral cantata
sforzato *sforzando*
smorzato *smorzando*
spiccato half staccato
staccato with each note detached
sticcado a kind of xylophone
sticcato *sticcado*
symphony (1) obs. name for various
  m/ins
symphony (2) harmony of sound
symphony (3) an orchestral *comp.*
tabourin *taborin*
tamboura an Eastern guitar-like *in.*
trendody ode/song of lamentation
triangle a percussion *in.*
trombone a brass wind *in.*
tympanum a drum (head)

una corda one string, *soft pedal*
virginal a spinet
virtuosi plural of *virtuoso*
virtuoso highly skilled musician
vocalist a singer
woodwind a wind-*in.* of wood
zambomba a simple Spanish *m/in.*

9

accordion bellows and keyboard *m/in.*
ad libitum (f) freedom of play
allemande (1) a suite movement
allemande (2) Swabian/German dance
allemande (3) a dance movement
andantino slower/quicker than *andante*
arabesque a type of *mus. comp.*
bagatelle a piece of light *mus.*
balalaika a Russian guitar-like *m/in.*
banjulele a small banjo
barcarole (like) a gondolier's song
beat music popular rhythmic *mus.*
bombardon a low pitched brass *in.*
brass band band of (mainly) brass
cacophony dischord of sound(s)
castanets hard clicking shells
charivari rough music, cats' concert
chromatic of melodic notes
clarionet *clarinet*
coach-horn *post-horn*
conductor director of orchestra
contralto (1) lowest female *mus.* voice
contralto (2) part for/singer of (1)
crescendo increasing in loudness
dead-march (military) funeral *mus.*
death-bell the passing bell
decachord an old stringed *in.*
dissonant without harmony
dithyramb ancient Greek hymn
drumstick stick for beating drum
Dulcitone a keyboard *in.*
euphonium the brass saxhorn
extempore composed/performed impromptu
flageolet a small fipple-flute
folk-music traditional native *mus.*
fortissimo very loud
gallopade a quick dance (music)
generator a fundamental tone

glissando a *mus.* effect
grace note an embellishing note
harmonica (1) musical glasses
harmonica (2) a hammer struck *m/in.*
harmonica (3) *mouth organ* (1)
harmonium a reed-organ
imbroglio an ordered confusion
larghetto (a) somewhat slow (movement)
leger-line *ledger-line*
mandoline a guitar-like *in.*
metronome a timing device
mezza voce with medium volume, tone
modulator a tonic sol-fa chart
monochord (1) an acoustical instrument
monochord (2) a *clavichord*
monochord (3) a *tromba marina*
obbligato important *mus.* accompaniment
octachord (1) an eight-stringed *in.*
octachord (2) series of eight tones
orchestra a large company of musicians
pastorale a pastoral *mus. comp.*
pitchfork a tuning fork
pitchpipe a tuning pipe
pizzicato played by plucking
polonaise a Polish dance (music)
polyphone a lute-like *in.*
prick-song (obs.) written music: descant
quadrille a dance (music)
reed-organ the American organ
ricercare *ricercar*
ricercata *ricercar*
roundelay song with a refrain
saxophone a reeded wind *in.*
semibreve half a *breve*
semi-grand a type of *piano* (2)
septimole a group of seven notes
seraphine a keyboard *m/in.*
sforzando forced, strongly accented
siciliana Sicilian pastoral dance (music)
signature an indication of key
smorzando gradual fading away
soft pedal a tone reducing device
solfeggio (f) a sol-fa exercise
sostenuto sustained
syncopate to alter the rhythm
tablature an old *mus.* notation

tailpiece part of a fiddle
tasto solo bass without harmony
tenor-clef the C clef
tessiture ordinary compass of voice
variation change in key, tempo, etc.
voluntary *mus.* played at will
vox humana an organ stop
xylophone a hammer struck *m/in.*

10

affettuoso tender, tenderly
allegretto somewhat brisk
bandmaster conductor of a band
barcarolle *barcarole*
basset horn richest, softest wind *in.*
cantillate to chant, intone
canzonetta a little *cansone*
chitarrone a large lute-like *in.*
clarichord *clavichord*
clavichord an old keyboard *in.*
coloratura florid vocal passages
comic opera opera of amusing nature
concertina a bellows *m/in.*
concertino a short concerto
contrabass *double-bass*
cor anglais a type of oboe
dance-music *mus.* arranged for dancing
demi-ditone a minor third
diminuendo letting the sound die away
dolcemente softly and sweetly
double-bass a large stringed *in.*
double-flat a flat note flattened
embouchure wind *in.* mouthpiece
flugelhorn a kind of keyed bugle
fortepiano 18th C. name for early
    piano
forte-piano loud then immediately
    soft
fortissimo louder than forte
French horn an orchestral horn
grand opera opera without dialogue
grand piano a large piano
ground-bass constantly repeated bass
    part
harmonicon *harmonica* (3): *orchestrion*
harpsichord twitched-string keyboard
    in.

hurdy-gurdy a hand-organ
hypodorian *Aeolian mode*
intermezzo (1) *entr'acte*
intermezzo (2) a short movement
kettledrum a percussion *in.*
ledger-line an added short line
light opera *operetta*
major third interval of four semitones
mezzo-forte moderately loud
mezzo-piano moderately soft
minor third interval of three semitones
minstrelsy (1) art of a minstrel
minstrelsy (2) a body of minstrels
minstrelsy (3) music
minstrelsy (4) a collection of songs
mouth music unaccompanied song
mouth organ (1) an oral metallic reed
    in.
mouth organ (2) *Pan-pipes*
musicology the study of music
opera seria (f) *grand opera*
ophicleide an up-dated *serpent*
pentachord (1) a five stringed *m/in.*
pentachord (2) a series of five notes
percussion the struck *m/ins*
pianissimo very soft
pianoforte keyed hammer-struck *m/in.*
piano-organ barrel-organ-like piano
prima donna leading female singer
recitative speech-like song
rinforzato reinforced, suddenly
    accented
ritardando with diminishing speed
ritornello prelude, refrain
semiquaver half a quaver
sourdeline a small bagpipe
Stradivari *Stradivarius*
strathspey a Scottish dance (tune)
string-band (1) a band of stringed *ins*
string-band (2) string section of
    orchestra
tambourine a type of small drum
tarantella a Neopolitan dance (tune)
tetrachord (1) a four stringed *m/in.*
tetrachord (2) a series of four sounds
tin whistle penny whistle, flageolet
tonic sol-fa adapted *sol-fa*
tuning fork instrument of known
    pitch
vibraphone a hammer-struck *m/in.*

11

accelerando gradually increasing in speed
aeolian harp wind operated *m/in.*
Aeolian* mode a Greek *mus.* mode
barrel-organ a mechanical *m/in.*
clairschach the old Celtic harp
contrabasso *contrabass*
counterbase *contrabass*
decrescendo (f) *diminuendo*
fipple-flute the 'English flute'
orchestrina orchestra imitating *in.*
orchestrion orchestra imitating *in.*
quarter-note *crotchet: quarter-tone*
quarter-tone half a semitone
rallentando becoming slower: slowing
rock and roll *rock*
violoncello the 'cello
volte subito turn over the page quickly

arco saltando a quick staccato
boogie-woogie a type of jazz
chamber music *mus.* suitable for a room
concert grand a grand piano
concert pitch a standard of pitch
corno inglese (f) *cor anglais*
counter-tenor highest alto male voice
glockenspiel hammers and bells *in.*
mezzo-soprano (1) low soprano voice
mezzo-soprano (2) singer with/part for (1)
penny whistle tin whistle, flageolet
philharmonic loving music
Stradivarius *m/in.* made by Stradivari
tromba marina an obs. viol
viola da gamba a bass viol

13/14

fortississimo as loud as possible
pianississimo as soft as possible
Aretinian scale *ut·re·mi·fa·so·la·si·ut*
demi-semiquaver half a *semiquaver*

12

acciaccatura a short *appoggiatura*
appoggiatura a *grace note*

GEOGRAPHY

ABBREVIATIONS

IVR international vehicle registration symbol
note words indicated* may be valid for play in word games.

1

A Austria *(IVR)*
B Belgium *(IVR)*
C Cuba *(IVR)*
D Germany *(IVR)*
E east: English: Spain *(IVR)*
F France *(IVR)*
H Hungary *(IVR)*
I Italy *(IVR)*
J Japan *(IVR)*
K Khymer Republic *(IVR)*
L Luxembourg *(IVR)*
M Malta *(IVR)*
N north: northern: Norway *(IVR)*
O Ohio
P Portugal *(IVR)*
Q Quebec: Queensland
R Romania *(IVR)*
S south: southern: Sweden *(IVR)*
T Thailand *(IVR)*
U Uruguay *(IVR)*
V Vatican City *(IVR)*
W west: Welsh
Z Zambia *(IVR)*

2

AL Albania *(IVR)*
Al. Alabama
Am.* America
Ar. Arabic
BA Buenos Aires
BC British Columbia
BG Bulgaria *(IVR)*
BH British Honduras *(IVR)*

BS Bahamas *(IVR)*
CB Cape Breton
CH Switzerland (also *IVR*)
Ch. China
CI Channel Islands: Ivory Coast *(IVR)*
CL Sri Lanka *(IVR)*
CO Colombia *(IVR)*
Co. county
CP Cape Province (S. Africa)
CR Costa Rica *(IVR)*
Ct. Connecticut
CY Cyprus *(IVR)*
DC District of Columbia
DK Denmark *(IVR)*
DY Dahomey *(IVR)*
DZ Algeria *(IVR)*
EC Ecuador *(IVR)*
Ed. Edinburgh (in university degrees)
EI East Indies
ET Egypt *(IVR)*
Fa.* Florida
FL Liechtenstein (also *IVR*)
Fr. France: French
Ga. Georgia
GB Great Britain (also *IVR*)
GH Ghana *(IVR)*
Gk Greek
GR Greece *(IVR)*
Gr. Greek
HK Hong Kong (also *IVR*)
Ia. Iowa
Id.* Idaho
IR Iran *(IVR)*
Ir. Irish
IS* Iceland *(IVR)*
Is.* island(s)
It.* Italian

ABBREVIATIONS

IW Isle of Wight
JA Jamaica *(IVR)*
KL Kuala Lumpur
Ks. Kansas
Ky.* Kentucky
LA* Los Angeles
La.* Louisiana
LB Liberia *(IVR)*
LI* Long Island
LS Lesotho *(IVR)*
MA* Morocco *(IVR)*
MC Monaco *(IVR)*
Md. Maryland
ME* Middle East
Me.* Maine
Mi.* Mississippi
Mo.* Missouri
MS Mauritius *(IVR)*
Mt (mt) mount
Mx Middlesex
NA* N. America: Dutch Antilles *(IVR)*
NB New Brunswick: North
    Britain/British
N.C. North Carolina
N.D. North Dakota
NE north-east: New England
N.H. New Hampshire
NI Northern Ireland
N.J. New Jersey
NL Holland *(IVR)*
N.M. New Mexico
N.O.* New Orleans
NW north-west
NY New York (city or state)
NZ New Zealand (also *IVR*)
Or.* Oregon
PA* Panama *(IVR)*
Pa.* Pennsylvania
PE Peru *(IVR)*
Pg. Portugal: Portuguese
PL Poland *(IVR)*
PQ Province of Quebec
PR Puerto Rico
Pr. Provencal
PY Paraguay *(IVR)*
RA Argentina *(IVR)*
RH Haiti *(IVR)*
RI Rhode Island: Indonesia *(IVR)*
RL Lebanon *(IVR)*
RM Malagasy Republic *(IVR)*

RU Burundi *(IVR)*
SA S. Africa: S. America: S. Australia
S.C. South Carolina
SE south-east
SF Finland *(IVR)*
SN Senegal *(IVR)*
St* Strait
SU Soviet Union (also *IVR*)
SW south-west
SY Seychelles *(IVR)*
TG Togo *(IVR)*
TN Tunisia *(IVR)*
TR Turkey *(IVR)*
TT Trinidad and Tobago *(IVR)*
UK United Kingdom
UN* United Nations
US* United States
Ut.* Utah
Va. Virginia
VN Vietnam *(IVR)*
Vt. Vermont
WA West Africa: Western Australia
WD Dominica, Windward Is. *(IVR)*
WG Granada, Windward Is. *(IVR)*
WL St Lucia, Windward Is. *(IVR)*
WS Western Samoa *(IVR)*
Wy. Wyoming
YU* Yugoslavia *(IVR)*
YV Venezuela *(IVR)*
ZA South Africa *(IVR)*
ZR Zaire *(IVR)*
ZW Zimbabwe *(IVR)*

3

ACP African, Caribbean and Pacific
ACT* Australian Capital Territory
ADN People's Democratic Republic of
    Yemen *(IVR)*
AFG Afghanistan *(IVR)*
Ala.* Alabama
AND* Andorra *(IVR)*
Ark.* Arkansas
Arm.* Armenian: Armoric (of
    Brittany)
AUS Australia, Papua, New Guinea
    (IVR)
Boh.* Bohemia: Bohemian
Bol. Bolivia

BRN Bahrain *(IVR)*
BRU Brunei *(IVR)*
BUR* Burma *(IVR)*
Cal. California
Cam.* Cambridge
CAR* Central African Republic
CDN Canada *(IVR)*
Col.* Colorado
Cop.* Coptic
CSA Confederate States of America
Cym. Cymric
Dan.* Danish
DDR East Germany (also *IVR*)
Del. Delaware
DMZ demilitarized zone
DOM Dominican Republic *(IVR)*
Dom. Dominion
Dor.* Doric
EAK Kenya *(IVR)*
EAT* Tanzania *(IVR)*
EAU* Uganda *(IVR)*
EAZ Tanzania *(IVR)*
ENE* east-north-east
Eng. England: English
ESE east-south-east
Fla. Florida
GBA Alderney, CI *(IVR)*
GBG Guernsey, CI *(IVR)*
GBJ Jersey, CI *(IVR)*
GBM Isle of Man *(IVR)*
GBZ Gibraltar *(IVR)*
GDR German Democratic Republic
Geo.* Georgia
Ger. German
Gib.* Gibraltar
GLC Greater London Council
GUY* Guyana *(IVR)*
HKJ Jordan *(IVR)*
HWM high water mark
IDN same as *IND*
IFS* Irish Free State (1922–37)
Ill.* Illinois
IND India *(IVR)*
Ind. Indiana: India (poetic)
IOM Isle of Man
IOW Isle of Wight
IRL Ireland *(IVR)*
IRQ Iraq *(IVR)*
Isl. island
IVR International Vehicle Registration

Kan. Kansas
Ken.* Kentucky
LAO Laos *(IVR)*
LAR* Libya *(IVR)*
LCC London County Council (now *GLC*)
MAL Malaysia *(IVR)*
Man.* Manitoba
MEX Mexico *(IVR)*
Mex. Mexico: Mexican
Mon. Monmouthshire
Mor. Morocco
msl mean sea-level
Mts (mts) mountains
Neb.* Nebraska
Nev. Nevada
NNE north-north-east
NNW north-north-west
NSW New South Wales
NWT North-west Territory (Canada)
NYC New York City
Ont. Ontario
Ore.* Oregon
PAK Pakistan *(IVR)*
Pal.* Palestine
Pan.* Panama
PEI Prince Edward Island
Pen.* Pennsylvania
Que. Quebec
RCA Central African Republic *(IVR)*
RCB Congo *(IVR)*
RCH Chile *(IVR)*
RIM* Mauretania *(IVR)*
RMM Mali *(IVR)*
ROK* Korea *(IVR)*
RSA Republic of South Africa
RSM San Marino *(IVR)*
RSR Rhodesia (now zw) *(IVR)*
RWA Rwanda *(IVR)*
SGP Singapore *(IVR)*
SME Surinam *(IVR)*
SRI Holy Roman Empire (see HISTORY, p. 111)
SSW south-south-west
SWA South West Africa *(IVR)*
Ten.* Tennessee
Ter. Territory
Tex. Texas
UAR United Arab Republic
Uru. Uruguay

51

ABBREVIATIONS

USA United States of America (also *IVR*)
Vat.* Vatican
WAG* Gambia *(IVR)*
WAL Sierra Leone *(IVR)*
Wal. Walloon
WAN* Nigeria
Wis. Wisconsin
WNW west-north-west
W. Va. West Virginia
Wyo. Wyoming

4

Alas.* Alaska
Alba. Alberta
Alta. Alberta
Amer. American
Arab.* Arabic
Ariz. Arizona
Beds* Bedfordshire
Belg. Belgium: Belgian: Belgic
Braz. Brazil: Brazilian
Bret. Breton (also see *Arm.*)
Brit.* Britain: British: Briton
Bulg. Bulgaria: Bulgarian
Camb. Cambridge
Cant.* Canterbury
CCCP see *USSR*
Celt.* Celtic
Chal.* Chaldee: Chaldaic
Ches. Cheshire
Chin.* China: Chinese
Colo. Colorado
Conn.* Connecticut
Corn.* Cornwall
Edin. Edinburgh
Flor. Florida
geog. geography
geol. geology
Glam.* Glamorganshire
Glos. Gloucestershire
Irel. Ireland
Leic. Leicestershire
Leip. Leipzig
Lond. London
Mass.* Massachusetts
Mers. Merseyside
Mich. Michigan

Mont. Montana: Montgomeryshire
N. Dak.* North Dakota
Nebr. Nebraska
Neth. Netherlands
New M. New Mexico
N. Mex. New Mexico
Norf. Norfolk
Okla. Oklahoma
Oreg. Oregon
Oxon. Oxfordshire
Penn. Pennsylvania
Pers. Persian
Sask. Saskatchewan
Scot.* Scotland: Scottish
S. Dak.* South Dakota
Tays. Tayside
Tenn. Tennessee
Terr. Territory
USSR Union of Soviet Socialist Republics
Vict. Victoria
Warw. Warwickshire
Wash.* Washington

5

Berks* Berkshire
Bucks* Buckinghamshire
Calif.* California
Cambs Cambridgeshire
Cards* Cardiganshire
Chald. Chaldee: Chaldaic
Cleve.* Cleveland
Hants Hampshire (orig. Hantshaving)
Herts Hertfordshire
Humbs. Humberside
Hunts* Huntingdonshire
Lancs Lancashire
Leics Leicestershire
Lincs Lincolnshire
Manit. Manitoba
Notts* Nottinghamshire
Salop* Shropshire
RSFSR Russian Soviet Federated Socialist Republic
Wilts* Wiltshire
Worcs. Worcestershire
Yorks* Yorkshire

6/7/8/9

Ind. Ter. Indian Territory
Is.* of Sc. Isles of Scilly
Staffs* Staffordshire
Strath.* Strathclyde

W. Isles* Western Isles
Benelux Belgium, Holland, Luxembourg
Gtr. Mches Greater Manchester
Northumb. Northumberland
Northants Northamptonshire

GEOGRAPHICAL TERMS

Also see MEASUREMENT (p. 210)

2

ea (1) river: running water
ea (2) drainage canal in Fens
pa Maori settlement

3

ait *eyot*
alp a high mountain (pasture)
bay coastal inlet
ben a mountain peak
bog marsh
cay *key*
col a mountain pass
cop a hilltop
cru (f) vineyard (or, group of)
cwm (f) *coomb* (1) and (2)
dam (1) a water-flow restraint
dam (2) a mill stream
den cave: narrow valley
dub a pool of foul water
dun a hill
eau *ea* (1) and (2)
erf (f) a small piece of ground
fen morass or bog
feu piece of tenanted land
gap pass in mountain ridge
gat (1) opening between sandbanks
gat (2) *strait*
geo gully, creek
gio *geo*
goe *geo*
hag (1) broken ground in a bog

hag (2) pool, hole in bog
hag (3) high firm place in bog
how a hollow: low hill
key low island or reef
kop (f) hill, usu. round-topped
law (1) a (rounded/conical) hill
law (2) low, see *lawland*
lay *lea*
lea meadow (pasture/arable)
lee *lea*: river (obs.)
ley *lea*
lin (1) waterfall, cascade pool
lin (2) ravine
low (1) (of latitude) equatorial
low (2) hill: tumulus
lug a perch or rod of land
map plan of geog. features
mir Russian village community
nab a hilltop: promontory
nek (f) *col*
pah *pa*
pan a hollow in the ground
pap a round conical hill
pen (1) a small enclosure
pen (2) W. Indian farm/plantation
pen (3) dam or weir
pow (1) a slow-moving stream
pow (2) small creek at river mouth
puy a small volcanic cone
ras a headland
ria a normal drowned valley
rig *ridge*
rip a stretch of broken water
sea small ocean: saline lake
spa a mineral spring
tel a hill in Arab lands
tor a rocky height
urn source of river (poetic)

GEOGRAPHICAL TERMS

vae *voe*
via a way, road
vly (f) *vlei* (1) (2)
voe bay, creek
way passage, road, street, track
wud *wood*

4

bank (1) mound, ridge: acclivity
bank (2) margin of river, lake, etc.
beck brook
berg hill, mountain: iceberg
bill a sharp promontory
bore violent tidal river flood
burn small stream, brook
cape waterside headland
carr (copse in) boggy ground
cave hollow place in rock
city (large) high-ranking town
comb *coomb* (1) (2)
cove sea inlet, bay
crag (1) a rough steep rock
crag (2) shelly deposit in sand
dale low ground between hills
dean dene (1)
dell (arboreal) deep hollow
deme a Greek township
dene (1) a small valley
dene (2) *dune*
dike *dyke*
doab land-strip between rivers
dorp a (Dutch) village
down (1) a treeless upland
down (2) *dune*
duar Arab (tented) village
dump (1) deep hole in river bed
dump (2) a pool
dune low hill of (marine) sand
eddy reverse current (wind/water)
eger *bore*
farm land/water used for live produce
fell upland moorland
fief land held in fee
firn granular glacial snow
flat plain: water-covered land
floe a field of floating ice
flow (1) morass: quicksand
flow (2) a sea basin or sound

fohn *foehn*
ford wading point of river, etc.
fork branch/tributary of river
foss (1) a waterfall
foss (2) a canal
foss (3) ditch, moat, trench
ghat Indian mountain pass
gill (1) small ravine, wooded glen
gill (2) a brook
glen narrow valley with stream
gore triangular piece of land
grip small ditch, trench
gulf (1) indentation in coast
gulf (2) deep place: abyss: whirlpool
haaf deep-sea fishing ground
hagg *hag* (1) (2) (3)
hide see MEASUREMENT (p. 215)
hill mound: inclined road
holm river islet: riverside land
holt a wood: woody hill
hope (1) upper end of mt valley
hope (2) *coomb* (1)
howe *how*
inch (1) an island
inch (2) a riverside meadow
isle an island
kaim *esker*
kame *esker*
khor dry watercourse: ravine
kill stream, brook, river
kith native land
knap hillock, hill crest
kyle a narrow strait
laer (f) *laager*
lade a mill stream
lake (large) inland body of water
laky of a lake
lair pasture
land (1) solid portion of global surface
land (2) country: district: nation
land (3) real estate: earth: soil
lane (1) narrow road or street
lane (2) channel: sluggish stream
lare *lair*
leat a water trench
leet *leat*
linn *lin* (1) (2)
loan *lane* (1): field passage
loch arm of the sea: lake
lock section of a canal**

lode (1)   vein of metallic ore
lode (2)   a reach of water
lode (3)   an open ditch
loss   *loess*
mead   meadow
meer   *mere* (obs.)
mere   pool or lake
mesa   table-shaped hill
mete   a boundary or limit
mire   deep mud
mole   a massive breakwater
moor   heath: wide untilled land
moss   bog: boggy ground
mote   a mound: tumulus
muir   moor
mull   a promontory
naze   a headland or cape
neap   of tides *(neaptide)*
ness   a headland
noup   *crag* (1): steep headland
pass (1)   narrow mountain passage
pass (2)   defile
path   course, route, footway
pays   country (Fr)
peak   mountain summit
plat   flat place/region
plot   small piece of ground
pole   end of earth's axis
pond (1)   small (artificial) lake
pond (2)   stretch between canal locks
pond (3)   the Atlantic Ocean
pool (1)   small body of still water
pool (2)   deep part of a stream
port   (town with) harbour
quag   a boggy place
quay   a landing place
race   land or water track
rack   a shallow ford
raik   pasture
rake   track: pasture
rand   ridge overlooking valley
rean   a *rhine*
reef (1)   chain of water-surface rocks
reef (2)   a shoal or bank
reef (3)   gold bearing lode, vein
reef (4)   non-valuable mine ground
reen   a *rhine*
rill   a very small brook
riva   cleft in rock
road   highway

rock   large mass of stone
rode   *road* (obs.)
scar (1)   bare place on hill face
scar (2)   a cliff
scar (3)   a reef in the sea
shaw   a small wood
sike   *syke*
sill   a bed of rock
slap   a hill pass
slob   a mud flat
spit   strip of land running into sea
spur   branch of hill range
stew   fish pond: oyster bed
sudd   temporary (natural) dam
sump   bog, pool, puddle
tarn   a small mountain-lake
tell   *tel*
toft   homestead: hillock
torr   *tor*
town   an urban community
trod   track, path
tump   hillock: clump
vale   valley: world (fig.)
vega (1)   low fertile plain
vega (2)   Cuban tobacco-field
vill   township (hist.): village (poetic)
vlei (f) (1)   wet season lake (Africa)
vlei (f) (2)   swamp (USA)
wadi (1)   dry bed of a torrent
wadi (2)   a river valley
wady   *wadi* (1) (2)
ward   division of a town/city
wave   ridge on sea surface
wear   *weir*
weel   whirlpool
well   a (mineral) spring
wick (1)   creek
wick (2)   village, town: farm
wold   open tract of country
wood   a collection of trees
wynd   narrow lane in town
zila   an Indian district
zone   region
zupa   Serbian village confederation

5

abyss (1)   bottomless gulf
abyss (2)   depths of the sea

GEOGRAPHICAL TERMS

alley passage, narrow lane, etc.
aldea (f) Spanish village/hamlet
antar (obs.) a cave
arete a sharp ridge
arish *arrish*
atlas a book of maps
atoll a coral island
bayou (f) marshy offshoot of river
bight a wide bay
brook a small stream
canal an artificial watercourse
canon *canyon*
carse alluvial river-side plain
cauld dam in stream: weir
chart marine/hydrographical map
chasm yawning or gaping hollow
chine a ravine
cleve hillside
cliff (1) high steep rock
cliff (2) steep side of mountain
clift *cliff* (1) (2)
clime country, region, tract
close a small field
coast the seashore
combe *coomb* (1) (2)
coomb (1) deep little wooded valley
coomb (2) hollow in a hillside
craig *crag* (1) (2)
creek (1) small inlet, bay
creek (2) small river/brook
crest summit of hill/wave
croft small farm
delta river-mouth alluvial deposit
delve a cave (obs.)
donga gully
dovar *duar*
dowar *duar*
downs upland tract of pasture
drift (1) a heap of driven snow
drift (2) water-driven floating material
drift (3) slow current caused by wind
drift (4) cattle track, drove road
duchy territory of a duke
eager *bore*
eagre *bore*
erven (f) plural of *erf*
esker ridge of sand/gravel
field tillage/pasture/sports-ground
fiord *fjord*
fjord long narrow rock-bound inlet

firth (1) *frith* (1) (2)
firth (2) an arm of the sea
fleet shallow creek: bay: brook
flume (1) artificial waterway
flume (2) ravine occupied by torrent
force *foss* (1)
fosse *foss* (2)
fount a spring of water
frith (1) wooded country
frith (2) coastal river-mouth
ghaut *ghat*
ghyll *gill* (1) (2)
glade open space in wood
glaur *mire*
globe (representative sphere of) earth
gorge a ravine
grike (1) a fissure in limestone
grike (2) deep valley, ravine
gripe *grip*
grove (1) a small wood
grove (2) an avenue of trees
gryke *grike* (1) (2)
gulch ravine, gully
gully water channel: ditch: ravine
gulph *gulf* (2)
gurge (obs.) whirlpool
guyot submarine mountain
halse pass, defile: connecting ridge
haugh riverside meadow, flat
hause halse
haven ship shelter: harbour
hawse *halse*
heath barren open country
heuch *heugh*
heugh crag: ravine
hithe small haven: river port
hurst a wood, grove (1)
hythe *hithe*
ice-cap ice covering a convexity
ice-pan a slab of floating ice
inlet small bay or opening
islet a little isle
Karoo S. African pastoral tableland
karst rough limestone country
kloof a mountain ravine
kopje older form of *koppie*
knoll (1) round hillock
knoll (2) the top of a hill
knowe *knoll* (1)
kraal S. African native village

lahar mud-lava
lande French forested sandy tract
lathe a division of Kent
laund glade, grassy place
lease pasture
leaze pasture
ledge a shelf of rocks
levee riverside embankment
llano vast S. American steppe
loess a loamy deposit
logan a rocking stone
lough Irish *loch*
mains a home farm
march a border district
marsh wet land: morass, fen, swamp
meith land mark: boundary
motte *mote*
mound hillock: a heap
mount (1) mountain
mount (2) small hill, mound
mouth downstream end of river
Munro (Scottish) mt over 3,000 ft
nulla *nullah*
oasis fertile spot in desert
ocean global saline surface
pampa *pampas*
piste beaten (snow) track
plage a fashionable beach
plain an extent of level land
plump a cluster of trees
point a cape or headland
polar of, pertaining to the poles
poles *pole* (N. pole: S. pole)
poort (f) a mountain pass
power an influential state
rapid *rapids*
reach a stretch of stream
rhine ditch, water course
ridge (1) strip of arable land
ridge (2) a hill range
river a large stream of water
roost a tidal race
salse a mud volcano
sands sea beach: desert
sault waterfall: rapid
scarp an *escarpment*
scaur *scar* (1) (2) (3)
scree cliff debris
serac part of former glacier
shelf shoal: sandbank

shore (1) land bordering sea, etc.
shore (2) a sewer
slack (1) a cleft between hills
slack (2) a boggy place
slade (1) a little valley, dell
slade (2) low moist ground
sloot (f) *sluit*
sluit (f) a narrow water-channel
sound a strait
stank ditch: pool: dam
state nation/constituent part of
steep a precipitous place
stray a common
swale shady spot: marshy place
swamp (1) wet spongy land
swamp (2) (USA) tree covered *swamp* (1)
sward grassy surface of land
swire hollow between two hills
taluk subdivision of district
thorp village, hamlet
tilth cultivated land
tract a region, area
villa *vill*
viver fish-pond
weald open (wooded) country

6

Alpine* of the Alps
alpine *Alpine*: of any mountain
arbour a bower of trees
arctic of the N. Polar region
arrish a stubble field
arroyo (1) rocky ravine
arroyo (2) dry water-course
boreal of the north
callow an alluvial flat
canada narrow canyon
canton a territorial division
canyon deep gorge, ravine
circar *sircar*
cirque *corrie*
cleuch *clough*
cleugh *clough*
clough ravine, valley
colony external territorial unit
common a tract of open land
corrie mountain recess

GEOGRAPHICAL TERMS

coteau (f) hilly upland area
county count's domain: shire
course a water channel
crater (1) mouth of volcano
crater (2) hole where meteor fell
cuesta a hill ridge
defile a long narrow pass
desert desolate or barren tract
dingle a dell
domain estate, territory
empery empire, power
empire group of states
escarp (1) scarp or steep slope
escarp (2) escarpment
eyalet a division of Turkey
forest (1) large arboreal tract
forest (2) hunting reserve
geyser hot water spring
glacis a gentle slope
graben a rift valley
greave a thicket (obs.)
groyne a breakwater
gulley *gully*
hamlet a small village
herbar (obs.) *arbour*
inland interior: remote from sea
jungle dense tropical forest
Karroo *Karoo*
kingle very hard rock
koppie a low hill
krantz (f) precipice
laager an encampment
lagoon a shallow lake
lallan Scottish lowland
leasow pasture, to pasture
lochan *lakelet*
maidan an open space
meadow rich pasture land
menhir ancient standing stone
morass soft wet ground: marsh
moulin shaft in glacier
nullah ravine: water-course
oblast province, district
orient the east
ostium river mouth
padang a field
pampas S. Amer. vast treeless plain
parano S. Amer. plain
parish small administrative unit
petary a peat bog

polder low-lying reclaimed land
rapids very swift part of river
ravine deep narrow gorge
region part of larger unit
Riding* part of Yorks., other counties
rillet a small rill
rivage bank, shore (poetic)
runlet *runnel*
runnel a small brook
seaway (1) a way by sea
seaway (2) a heavy sea
seaway (3) regular ocean route
seaway (4) inland major waterway
seiche a lake 'tide'
sierra a mountain range
sircar province, district
sirkar *sircar*
skerry a reef of rock
sleech a mud flat
slough (1) a hollow filled with mud
slough (2) a marsh
slough (3) backwater, marshland creek
spinny small clump of trees
steppe dry, grassy (treeless) plain
strait narrow waterway
strand (1) sea/lake margin
strand (2) rivulet, gutter
strath broad valley
stream (1) inland natural waterway
stream (2) a marine current
street paved house-lined road
suburb district adjoining a town
thorpe *thorp*
tropic of Cancer: of Capricorn
tundra a frozen Arctic plain
valley (1) elongated hollow between hills
valley (2) stretch watered by river
vennel a lane
volost a soviet rural district
warren (1) game-breeding ground
warren (2) densely populated slum
warren (3) a maze of narrow passages

7

alluvia plural of *alluvium*
austral southern
bergfall a rock fall

58

bogland *bog*
channel (1) the bed of a stream
channel (2) a strait or narrow sea
channel (3) a navigable passage
channel (4) groove, furrow: gutter
channel (5) gravel
cistern natural/artificial reservoir
clachan a small village
commune (1) small town (France)
commune (2) agricultural community
compass direction finding instrument
contour outline of equal character
current flow of water/air
cutting road/rail excavation
enclave territory within foreign
   territory
eparchy modern Greek province
equator 0° latitude
erupius an arm of the sea
estuary tidal part of river
eustacy changes in shore-line level
eustasy *eustacy*
exclave *enclave* of another state
Foss Way see *Fosse Way*
foss way Roman road with a *foss* (3)
fluvial of/pertaining to rivers
geodesy large scale earth measurement
geogony science of earth formation
geology science of earth history
glacier mass of mountain ice
habitat the local physical environment
harbour natural/artificial ship haven
highway public road
hillock a small hill
hilltop summit of a hill
hommock *hummock* (1) (2)
hornito oven-shaped *fumarole*
hummock (1) hillock
hummock (2) pile/ridge of ice
hundred see MEASUREMENT (p. 218)
iceberg huge mass of floating ice
ice-fall (1) a fall of ice
ice-fall (2) steep broken part of glacier
ice-floe large sheet of floating ice
icepack drift ice packed together
insular (1) belonging to an island
insular (2) surrounded by water
isthmus narrow neck of land
kingdom (ex-) monarchical state
lakelet a little lake

lawland Scottish lowland
leasowe *leasow*
lowland low (relative) land
low tide tide at lowest ebb
midland middle part of territory
montane mountainous
moraine glacial debris
moshava Israeli agric. settlement
norland the north country
norward northward
oceanic of/formed by (etc.) the ocean
orology the study of mountains
pelagic *oceanic*
pightle *croft*, small enclosure
plateau a tableland
prairie grassy treeless plain
rivered watered by rivers
riveret small river
riviera warm coastal region
rivulet a small river
salt-pan natural salt-pit
salt-pit large evaporation depression
satrapy a satrap's province
savanna *savannah*
sea-bank the sea shore
sea-gate outlet to the sea
sea-lane a navigable passage
sea-line coastline: sea-horizon
sea-loch an arm of the sea
seamark a mark of tidal limit
sea-mile see MEASUREMENT (p. 219)
seaport marine port/harbour
sea-road a shipping route
sea-room safe ship-manoeuvring space
seaside neighbourhood of the sea
sea-wall wall to keep out sea
seaward towards the sea
spinney *spinny*
spur-way a bridle road
stickle steep, rapid: a rapid
straits a *strait*
thalweg profile of river-bed
thicket dense mass trees/shrubs
thwaite piece of reclaimed land
torrent (1) a rushing stream
torrent (2) a variable mt stream
torrent (3) abounding turbulent flow
tropics earth's surface central region
village rural parish inhabited area
volcano eruptive mountain

GEOGRAPHICAL TERMS

wavelet a little wave
waymark a guide post
wayside border of path, road, etc.

8

affluent tributary stream
alluvial of/pertaining to *alluvium*
alluvium matter deposited by river (etc.)
altitude a high point
antipole the opposite pole
brooklet a little brook
burnside ground beside a burn
cadastre public register of land
cataract water-spout: waterfall
crevasse (1) a cleft in a glacier
crevasse (2) a breach in waterway
district a defined territorial part
dominion a self-governing colony
effluent an outflowing stream
eminence a rising ground
environs outskirts of a city
foothill an adjacent minor elevation
footpath a pedestrian track
foreland a headland
fossette a small *foss*
Fosse Way Exeter–Lincoln Roman Rd
fosse way see *foss way*
frontier a country's border
fumarole volcanic gas hole
headland (1) point of land running into sea
headland (2) border of a field
headrace race leading to water-wheel
highland a mountainous district
highroad a chief public road
high tide high water
hillside the slope of a hill
homeland (1) native land, fatherland
homeland (2) mother-country
interior remote part: inland
landmark (1) any conspicuous feature
landmark (2) any land-boundary mark
landslip action/mass of fallen rock
landward towards the land
latitude angular distance from equator
littoral (1) of the seashore
littoral (2) space between high/low tide

littoral (3) strip of land beside (2)
low water low tide
mainland principal/larger land
monticle *monticulus*
moorland a tract of moor
mountain (1) a very high hill
mountain (2) wild pasture land (Eire)
neaptide tide of minimum amplitude
occident the west
oreology *orology*
oriental eastern
post-town town with post office
province part of empire/state
quagmire wet boggy ground
quicksand treacherous sandy area
republic non-monarchical state
river-bed channel of river flow
riverway river as a waterway
savannah tract of level land
sea-beach sand/gravel sea border
seaboard land bordering the sea
sea-chart a chart of the sea
sea-cliff cliff fronting the sea
seacoast land adjacent to the sea
sea-floor bottom of the sea
sea-front land, etc. fronting the sea
sea-level mean surface level
sea-marge margin of the sea
seamount submarine mountain
sea-power powerful maritime nation
seaquake marine earthquake
seashore land bordering the sea
sea-water water of/from the sea
sheading an Isle of Man district
snowline limit of perpetual snow
swelchie whirlpool
toparchy a toparch's territory
townland *township*
township (1) village
township (2) a farm (Scotland)
township (3) block of public land (USA)
township (4) site/settlement (Austr.)
township (5) county sub-division (USA)
tricklet a little *rill*
water-gap mt gap containing stream
waterway (1) stretch of navigable water
waterway (2) a water-route
woodland land covered in trees
zastruga a snow ridge
zastrugi plural of *zastruga*

9

acclivity an upward slope
antarctic of the S. Polar region
antipodes diametrically opposite points
backwater (1) water held by dam
backwater (2) pool detached from river
backwater (3) swell caused by ship
backwoods forest beyond cleared area
Cisalpine on this (Roman) side of Alps
Cispadane Roman side of river Po
coastline shoreline
continent (1) a great division of land mass
continent (2) a bank or shore
coral-reef a reef of coral
declivity a downward slope
floodtide the rising tide
fluviatic of/formed by rivers
foothills usual form (plural) of *foothill*
Highlands* the N.W. of Scotland
High* Street* main shopping street
Holarctic of the northern region
land-flood inundation by water
landslide *landslip*
longitude length
marshland marshy country
monticule *monticulus*
orography description of mountains
peneplain all but a plain
peninsula all but an island
precipice high vertical cliff
river-bank bank of river
river-flat piece of alluvial land
river-head the source of a river
river-wall wall confining river
salt-marsh land, subject to sea flood
shoreline land/water boundary
shoreward landward
stewartry territory of a steward
subalpine at the foot of the Alps
tableland plateau
tidal wave a great wave
tributary stream running into another
wapentake *hundred*
waterfall perpendicular descent of water
water-gate floodgate: street
water-head (1) source of a stream
water-head (2) region of *water-head* (1)

water-head (3) dammed-up body of water
water-line *water-level*
watershed line separating two river-basins
waterside shore of sea, lake, etc.

10

cismontane on this side of mts
cispontine on this side of bridges
confluence rivers' meeting-place
county seat US county town
county town admin. town of county
equatorial of/pertaining to the equator
escarpment precipitous side of hill
fluviatile of/formed by rivers
frigid zone polar-circle region
hemisphere half of the earth
hinterland inland region
land-locked cut off from the sea
land-spring shallow intermittent spring
market-town town with a market
meridional southern
metropolis capital of country/county, etc.
monticulus a little elevation
no-man's-land disputed waste region
occidental of the west, western
palatinate province of a palatine
plantation (1) colony
plantation (2) estate planted with cash-crop
plantation (3) large estate (USA)
promontory headland
river-basin region drained by river
river-drift old alluvia of river
river-front land facing river
river-mouth downstream end of river
spring-tide tide of maximum amplitude
torrid zone the tropical belt
water-bound detained by floods
water-break a piece of broken water
water-flood an inundation
waterfront water-facing land
water-level still water surface level
water-plane a canal without locks
waterquake *seaquake*
watersmeet streams' meeting-place

wilderness uncultivated uninhabited area

11

Archipelago* the Aegean Sea
archipelago a group of islands
bergschrund a crevasse
circumpolar of/round the pole
Cisatlantic on this side of Atlantic
continental of a continent
conurbation an aggregation of towns
coral island an island of coral
country town town in rural area

equinoctial of equatorial regions
morning-land the east
mountainous of mountains
mountain-top top of mountain
river-bottom marginal alluvial land
septentrion (obs.) north
transalpine opposite of *Cisalpine*
transandean *transandine*
transandine beyond the Andes
transmarine across/beyond the sea
trout-stream stream with trout
ultramarine overseas
watercourse natural/artificial stream
water-meadow flood-fertilized meadow
water-splash a shallow ford

GREAT BRITAIN

note
This section embraces the whole of the United Kingdom only in respect of towns and cities as both Northern Ireland and Eire share certain geographical features such as rivers and mountains. All non-urban Irish features are listed in the REST OF THE WORLD section, commencing page 89.

ALTERNATIVE PLACE NAMES
(including rivers, hills, bays, etc.)

To determine the alternative name match the reference number, i.e. the first entry in the 11 letter words is '**1 Bawden Rocks 12/3**' thus continuing to the 12 letter words the third entry reads '**3 Man and his man 11/1**'. Similarly the 'rivers' Thames and Isis have corresponding references.

4

1 **Park 5/1**

5

1 **Pairc 4/1**
2 **Scaur 8/7**

6

1 **An Torc 14/1**
2 **Bac Mor 12/2**
3 **Ifield 10/15**

7

1 **Glen Mor 9/4**

2 **Heisker 14/6**
3 **Old Peak 10/16**
4 **St Mary's 11/10**
5 **Shroton 14/4**

8

1 **Bala Lake 9/6**
2 **Bell Rock 8/6**

3 Ben Attow 10/2
4 Broad Bay 10/8
5 Hebrides 12/9
6 Inchcape 8/2
7 Kippford 5/2
8 Lanherne 12/8
9 Moorland 14/7
10 River Cam 9/13
11 River Dee 15/1
12 River Lea 8/13
13 River Lee 8/12

9

1 Ardersier 12/1
2 Carn Ealer 15/2
3 Deil's Dike 10/4
4 Glen Albyn 7/1
5 Ligger Bay 9/10
6 Llyn Tegid 8/1
7 Loch Sealg 9/8
8 Loch Shell 9/7
9 Ness Point 10/10
10 Perran Bay 9/5
11 Porth-mawr 12/10
12 River Isis 11/15
13 River Rhee 8/10

10

1 Bait Island 13/4
2 Beinn Fhada 8/3
3 Blencathra 10/14
4 Celtic Dike 9/3
5 Forvie Ness 11/8
6 Hell's Mouth 11/12
7 Kelton Hill 10/11
8 Loch a Tuath 8/4
9 Looe Island 15/4

10 North Cheek 9/9
11 Rhonehouse 10/7
12 River Creed 11/7
13 River Trent 11/14
14 Saddleback 10/3
15 Singlewell 6/3
16 South Cheek 7/3

11

1 Bawden Rocks 12/3
2 Bideford Bay 13/1
3 Coombe Island 11/9
4 Crocketford 11/11
5 Duchray Hill 12/4
6 East Chaldon 14/2
7 Greeta River 10/12
8 Hackley Head 10/5
9 Neave Island 11/3
10 Newton Haven 7/4
11 Ninemile Bar 11/4
12 Porth Neigwl 10/6
13 Port Nessock 12/6
14 River Piddle 10/13
15 River Thames 9/12
16 Sibertswold 13/5
17 The Foreland 13/2

12

1 Campbelltown 9/1
2 Dutchman's Cap 6/2
3 Man and his man 11/1
4 Mealna Letter 11/5
5 Old West River 14/8
6 Port Logan Bay 11/13
7 St Alban's Head 13/3
8 Vale of Mawgan 8/8

9 Western Isles 8/5
10 Whitesand Bay 9/11

13

1 Barnstaple Bay 11/2
2 Handfast Point 11/17
3 St Aldhelm's Head 12/7
4 St Mary's Island 10/1
5 Shepherdswell 11/16

14

1 Boar of Badenoch 6/1
2 Chaldon Herring 11/6
3 Forty Foot Drain 15/5
4 Iwerne Courtney 7/5
5 Little Don River 14/9
6 Monarch Islands 7/2
7 Northmoor Green 8/9
8 River Great Ouse 12/5
9 The Porter River 14/5

15

1 Black Water of Dee 8/11
2 Carn an Fhidhlier 9/2
3 New Bedford River 16/1
4 St George's Island 10/9
5 Vermunden's Drain 14/3

16

1 Hundred Foot Drain 15/3

ISLES, 'ISLES' AND ISLANDS (inland and marine)

note Most common form of name given (i.e. **Skye** is enlisted under **Isle of Skye***)
therefore to find possible crossword answers also look in columns:
    4 letters higher **Isle**
    6 letters higher **Isle of: Island**
    8 letters higher **Island of**
(*the Ordnance Survey gives '*Island* of Skye')
    Also see ALTERNATIVE PLACE NAMES (p. 62).

3	Godag	Samson
	Gruna	Sanday
Hoy	Gunna	Scares
Soa	Hunda	Staffa
	Huney	Switha
	Islay	Tresco
4	Lamba	
	Langa	
Coll	Linga	
Eday	Luing	7
Eigg	Lundy	
Fara	Lunga	Egilsay
Herm	Pabay	Gometra
Iona	Scarp	Heisker
Isay	Shuna	Oronsay
Jura	Swona	St Agnes
Muck	Tiree	St Kilda
Oxna	Vaila	St Mary's
Papa		Zetland
Rhum		
Rona	6	
Sark		
Soay	Duslic	8
Ulva	Erraid	
Unst	Fetlar	Alderney
Uyea	Fladda	Anglesey
Yell	Flotta	Cheynies
	Grunay	Colonsay
	Gruney	Fair Isle
	Housay	Flat Holm
5	Jersey	Guernsey
	Jethou	Hebrides
Barra	Orkney	Lady Isle
Eorsa	Pabbay	Maisgeir
Faray	Raasay	Mingulay
Fidra	Rumble	St Helen's
Filla		

9

Belle Isle
Calf of Man
East Linga
Eilean Mor
Eynhallow
Giltarump
Gluss Isle
Horse Isle
Isle of Ely
Isle of Ewe
Isle of Man
Isle of May
Isle Ristol
North Uist
Papa Stour
Rat Island
Rumblings
Runnymede
South Uist
Steep Holm
The Smalls

10

Bait Island
Eilean Mora
Ellen's Isle
Holm Island
Holy Island
Isle Martin
Isle of Dogs
Isle of Noss
Isle of Skye
Looe Island
Muckle Ossa
Nave Island
Papa Little
Rysa Little
Salt Island
Small Isles
Sunk Island

11

Barry Island

Brother Isle
Burgh Island
Gigha Island
Holme Island
Horse Island
Isle of Grain
Isle of Harty
Isle of Lewis
Isle of Oxney
Isle of Wight
Longa Island
Neave Island
Read's Island
Rough Island
St Mary's Isle
Sheep Island
Shuna Island
Soyea Island
Sully Island
Summer Isles
The Skerries

12

Black Islands
Bottle Island
Caldey Island
Canvey Island
Drake's Island
Farne Island
Flannan Isles
Horsea Island
Horse Islands
Horsey Island
Island Davarr
Island of Bute
Island of Mull
Isle of Nibbon
Isle of Purbeck
Isle of Thanet
Isle of Walney
Oldany Island
Orisay Island
Ornish Island
Potton Island
Priest Island
Puffin Island

Stack Islands
Western Isles

13

Foulney Island
Great Mew Stone
Hayling Island
Inner Hebrides
Island of Arran
Island of Danna
Island of Fleet
Isle of Sheppey
Isles of Scilly
Mullion Island
Orkney Islands
Outer Hebrides
Portsea Island
Rabbit Islands
St Mary's Island
St Ninian's Isle
St Serf's Island
Staffin Island

14

Barrel of Butter
Brownsea Island
Cardigan Island
Foulness Island
Island of Stroma
Isle of Portland
Little Colonsay
North Ronaldsay
St Clement's Isle
St Patrick's Isle
South Ronaldsay

15

St George's Island

16

Bishops and Clerks

LAND AND MARINE FEATURES

cv cave, cavern
hd headland, point
int inlet, bay, creek
lk lake
lo. loch (including marine)
m marine/estuary channels, etc.
mt hill(s), mount, mountain(s), fell, ben
op. open space (moorland, heathland, etc.)
pen. peninsula
sbk sandbank
rk rock outcrop, fissure, column, etc.
val. valley, dale, glen, etc.
wf waterfall

6

Alwhat *(mt)*
Cat Law *(mt)*
Corn Du *(mt)*
Loch Ba
Mam Tor *(mt)*
No Ness *(hd)*
Odness *(hd)*
Pillar *(mt)*
Red Nab *(hd)*
The Bin *(mt)*
Tor Bay

7

Ape Dale
Ben Hope
Bow Fell
Box Hill
Dog Fall *(wf)*
Glen Dhu
Glen Roy
Gott Bay
High Tor *(mt)*
Loch Awe
Loch Bee
Loch Bog *(lo.)*
Loch Eye

Lop Ness *(hd)*
Mam Soul *(mt)*
Odin Bay
Old Peak *(hd)*
Old Wick *(hd)*
Oss Mere *(lk)*
Pen Caer *(pen.)*
Pig's Bay
Red Tarn *(lk)*
Rest Bay
Snowdon *(mt)*
The Galt *(hd)*
The Nore *(sbk)*
Win Hill

8

Bala Lake
Beer Head *(hd)*
Ben Nevis
Broad Law *(mt)*
Bull Hole *(m)*
Dovedale *(val.)*
Fife Ness *(hd)*
Goat Fell
Great Dod *(mt)*
Grim Ness *(hd)*
Hare Ness *(hd)*
Hay Bluff *(mt)*

Hog's Back *(mt)*
Holy Loch
Land's End *(hd)*
Largo Bay
Loch Doon
Loch Fell *(mt)*
Loch Muck
Loch Ness
Lose Hill
Mad Wharf *(sbk)*
Mull of Oa *(hd)*
Noup Head *(hd)*
Nun's Cave
Ord Point *(hd)*
Pen Brush *(hd)*
Polly Bay
Poole Bay
Port Jack *(int)*
Rams Ness *(hd)*
Ranny Bay
Ray Creek
Red Point *(hd)*
Rose Ness *(hd)*
Rubha Mor *(hd)*
Rue Point *(hd)*

9

Aira Force *(wf)*

Bay of Work
Ben Arthur
Black Head *(hd)*
Calf Sound *(m)*
Colwyn Bay
Crag Point *(hd)*
Dollar Law *(mt)*
Dungeness *(hd)*
Earl's Seat *(mt)*
Fairy Glen
Farr Point *(hd)*
Glen Livet
Great Rhos *(mt)*
Grey Friar *(mt)*
Hellvellyn *(mt)*
High Raise *(mt)*
Hope's Nose *(hd)*
Linn of Dee *(wf)*
Loch Leven
Loch Loyal
Ness of Ork *(hd)*
New Forest
Over Water *(lk)*
Papa Sound *(m)*
Porth Iago *(int)*
Quey Firth *(int)*
Rede's Mere *(lk)*
Ross Point *(hd)*
Rubha Dubh *(hd)*
Scapa Flow *(m)*
The Rivals *(mt)*
The Saddle *(mt)*
The Wrekin *(mt)*
Yell Sound *(m)*
Zone Point *(hd)*

10

Baggy Point *(hd)*
Beachy Head *(hd)*
Blanch Fell
Blowup Nose *(hd)*
Bodmin Moor
Brown Willy *(mt)*
Cow and Calf *(rk)*
Far Out Head *(hd)*
Firth of Tay *(m)*
Fitful Head *(hd)*
Girdle Fell

Girdle Ness *(hd)*
Glen Eagles
Head of Work *(hd)*
Horse Sound *(m)*
Little Ossa *(rk)*
Loch Lomond
Lynn of Lorn *(m)*
Nell's Point *(hd)*
Ness of Huna *(hd)*
North Downs *(mt)*
Nose's Point *(hd)*
Pass of Leny
Pass of Lyon
Peak Cavern
Plym Forest
Point of Air *(hd)*
Pools of Dee
Porth China *(int)*
Porth Diana *(int)*
Reay Forest
Rogan's Seat *(mt)*
Rogie Falls *(wf)*
Ross of Mull *(pen.)*
Selsey Bill *(hd)*
St Mary's Bay
South Downs *(mt)*
The Cobbler *(mt)*
The Needles *(hd)*
The Pennies *(mt)*
Wookey Hole *(cv)*

11

Appin of Dull *(val.)*
Bottom Flash *(lk)*
Chesil Beach
Chicken Head *(hd)*
Fingal's Cave
Five Sisters *(mt)*
Kinder Scout *(mt)*
Kyles of Bute *(m)*
Linn of Muick *(wf)*
Lizard Point *(hd)*
Menai Strait *(m)*
Mendip Hills
Ness of Sound *(hd)*
Norton Creek *(m)*
Old Man of Hoy *(rk)*
Old Man of Mow *(rk)*

One Tree Hill
Ossian's Cave
Pap of Glencoe *(mt)*
Point of Knap *(hd)*
Point of Ness *(hd)*
Point St John *(hd)*
Port Groudle *(int)*
Porth Colman *(in)*
Prawle Point *(hd)*
Priest's Nose *(hd)*
Proud Giltar *(hd)*
Prussia Cove
Rob Roy's Cave
Royal Forest
St Bride's Bay
St John's Head *(hd)*
St Magnus Bay
St Mary's Loch
Scafell Pike *(mt)*
Solway Firth *(m)*
Startup Hill

12

Bay of Holland
Bay of Ireland
Blue John Mine *(cv)*
Cannock Chase *(op.)*
Cheddar Gorge
Cuillin Hills
Derwent Water *(lk)*
Falls of Lora *(wf)*
Firth of Clyde *(m)*
Firth of Forth *(m)*
Forest of Dean
Forest of Deer
Lochan nan Cat *(lo.)*
Maclean's Nose *(hd)*
Malvern Hills
Ness of Brough *(hd)*
Ness of Litter *(hd)*
Ogmore Forest
Peak District
Point of Sleat *(hd)*
Point of Stoer *(hd)*
Rheidol Falls *(wf)*
St Mary's Haven *(int)*

13

Brecon Beacons *(mt)*
Brother's Water *(lk)*
Chiltern Hills
Coniston Water *(lk)*
Cotswold Hills
Cromarty Firth *(m)*
Devil's Beef Tub *(mt)*
Falls of Clyde *(wf)*
Falls of Conon *(wf)*
Frenchman's Bay
Gog Magog Hills
Grey Mare's Tail *(wf)*
Head of Holland *(hd)*

Menteith Hills
Mull of Kintyre *(hd)*
Nelly Ayre Foss *(wf)*
Old Man of Storr *(rk)*
Pass of Brander
Pass of Glencoe
Paviland Caves
Pennyhole Bay
Pentland Firth *(m)*
Pentland Hills
Quantock Hills
Robin Hood's Bay
Rob Roy's Prison *(cv)*
St Trudwal's Bay
The Chancellor *(mt)*

Vale of Belvoir

14

Bay of the Tongue
Cleveland Hills
Great Ormes Head *(hd)*
Manifold Valley
Pendennis Point *(hd)*
Peppermill Dam *(lk)*
Salisbury Plain
Sherwood Forest
The Devil's Point *(mt)*

RIVERS

Normally prefixed **River** except where shown by either:
    (R) when **River** follows the name or
    (Z) when the given name is complete
    ● indicates a Derbyshire underground river
note Many rivers have the same name but listed duplications refer only to cases
where the word **River** is a suffix for one and a prefix for the other.
    Also see ALTERNATIVE PLACE NAMES (p. 62).

1

E

2

Ba
Og

3

Add
Aln
Alt
Ant
Ash
Awe
Axe
Ayr

Bay *(R)*
Box
Cam
Can
Cur
Cwm
Ddu
Dee
Doe
Don
Eau
Ely *(R)*
Esk
Ewe
Exe
Eye
Fal
Gam
Hiz
Irk
Irt

Kym
Lea
Lee
Len
Lew
Loy
Nar
Neb
New
Noe
Ock
Ord *(R)*
Ore
Ose *(R)*
Pib
Ray
Rea
Red *(R)*
Rha
Rib
Roy

Rue	Char	Lair
Rye	Chet	Lark
Sid	Claw	Leam
Sow	Clun	Leen
Taw	Cole	Ling
Tay	Coll	Liza
Ter	Coln	Lugg
Til	Cona *(R)*	Lune
Tud	Cree	Lyne
Ure	Culm	Lyon
Usk	Dane	Maun
Ver	Dart	Meig
Wey	Dean	Meon
Wye	Deer	Mint
Yar	Dell *(R)*	Mite
Ydw	Dhoo	Mole
Yeo	Dibb	Nene
Yox	Doon	Ness
	Dore	Nidd
	Dorn	Nith
4	Dove	Ogau
	Dyke	Oich
Abel	Earn	Oude
Adur	Ebbw	Ouse
Afan	Eden	Pang
Aire	Ehen	Pant
Alan	Elwy	Pean
Alde	Erme	Penk
Alne	Fiag	Plym
Alun	Fyne	Pont
Alyn	Gain	Quin
Aran	Gaur	Rede
Aray	Gele	Rhee
Aros *(R)*	Gelt	Rhiw
Arun	Glen	Roch
Avan	Gloy	Ruel
Avon	Gour	Sand
Bain	Gowy	Sark
Bank	Hart	Seph
Bewl	Hope	Shin
Bran	Hull	Slea
Bray	Idle	Soar
Brit	Inny	Sorn
Brue	Isis	Sowe
Bude	Isla	Spey
Bure	Ivel	• Styx
Burn	Keer	Taff
Cain	Kenn	Tale
Cale	Kent	Tame
Cary	Lael	Tavy

69

Tees
Teme
Tern
Test
Thet
Till
Tone
Tove
Tyne
Ugie
Urie
Wear
Went
Wick *(R)*
Wolf
Wyre
Yare

5

Abbey
Allen
Alwen
Alwin
Amber
Anker
Annan
Anton
Ardle
Arnol
Arrow
Ashop
Avill
Barle
Beult
Bidno
Bleng
Blyth
Bogie
Bovey
Braen
Brain
Brant
Brede
Brent
Brett
Bride
Brock

Broom
Brora
Camel
Carey
Chess
Churn
Clown
Clwyd
Clyde
Clyst
Colne
Conon
Corfe
Corve
Cothi
Cover
Crane
Creed
Craig *(R)*
Dalch
Deben
Delph
Devon
Divie
Dovey
Druie
Duich *(R)*
Duisk *(R)*
Dutch *(R)*
Ebble
Einig
Ellen
Eskin
Fleet
Forsa
Forth
Fowey
Frome
Gairn
Garry
Gisla *(R)*
Glass
Glyme
Gress *(R)*
Greta
Gryfe
Gwash
Hamra *(R)*
Hayle
Inver

Ithon
Kerry
Knaik
Laver
Laxay
Leach
Leven
Livet
Lochy
Lodon
Loyne
Lussa *(R)*
Mease
Meden
Moors *(R)*
Muick
Naver
Neath
Nethy
Ogwen
Orchy
Orrin
Otter
Ouzel
Oykel
Peris
Perry
Polly
Roach
Roden
Roman *(R)*
Runie
Ryton
Sence
Seven
Sheaf
Shiel
Shira
Smite
Snail
Solva
Spean
Sprint
Stort
Stour
Stree
Swale
Swift
Tamar
Tarff

Teign
Teith
Tiddy
Tirry
Torne
Trent
Truim
Tweed
Under *(R)*
Waver
Wiske
Worfe
Worth
Wylye
Yarty
Yealm
Ythan

6

Affric
Almond
Alport
Averon
Beauly
Blithe
Blythe
Bollin
Borgie
Bourne
Brathy
Calder
Callop *(R)*
Chater
Cocker
Colwyn
Conder
Conway
Coquet
Corran *(R)*
Corris
Coulin
Crouch
Darwen
Dearne
De Lank *(R)*
Duddon
Eamont

Eidart
Enrick
Ericht
Evelix
Ey Burn *(Z)*
Eynort *(R)*
Farrar
Feshie
Finnan
Foyers
Gilpin
Glaven
Granta
Greeta *(R)*
Grudie
Grudie *(R)*
Hamble
Hepste
Hodder
Humber
Hurich
Irvine
Irwell
Itchen
Keekie
Kelvin
Kennet
Killin
Kingie
Kintra *(R)*
Laggan
Leadon
Ledbeg *(R)*
Liever
Loanan
Lochay
Loddon
Lossie
Loxley
Lydden
Lynher
Mallie
Mashie
Medina
Medway
Meoble
Mersey
Monnow
Mudale
Nadder

Nethan
Orwell
Ossian
Ottery
Piddle
Quaich
Quoich
Ribble
Riccal
Roding
Rother
Seaton
Severn
Skerne
Teviot
Thames
Thurne
Thurso
Tromie
Trothy
Tummel
Turret
Waldon
Weaver
Wensum
Wharfe
Witham
Wreake
Yarrow

7

Afon Wen
Baldwin
Bellart
Brittle
By Brook *(Z)*
Cannich
Cassley
Ceiriog
Chelmer
Churnet
Cladich *(R)*
Coiltie
Coupall
Derwent
Deveron
Dionard

Dochart	**8**	West Onny
Douglas		Whaplode *(R)*
Drolsay	Ale Water *(Z)*	Wheelock
Drynoch	Attadale	
Dudwell	Barbreck *(R)*	
Elchaig	Beaulieu *(R)*	**9**
Erewash	Birk Beck *(Z)*	
Esragan	Bladnoch	Arkle Beck *(Z)*
Etherow	Breamish	Babingley *(R)*
Falloch	Cherwell	Black Burn *(Z)*
Feehlin	Claggain *(R)*	East Allan
Fiddich	Clywedog	Ewe's Water *(Z)*
Garnock	Coladoir *(R)*	Gala Water *(Z)*
Geiraha	Cuckmere *(R)*	Glen Golly *(R)*
Gipping	Dessarry	Great Ouse
Hart Burn	Dye Water *(Z)*	Halladale *(R)*
Haultin	East Onny	Helmsdale
Henmore	Erradale	Kiachnish
Hergest *(R)*	Evenlode	Kype Water *(Z)*
Irthing	Eye Water *(Z)*	Little Don
Kanaird	Farigaig	Lymington *(R)*
Kinloch *(R)*	Foulness	Misbourne
Kirkaig	Freshney	Raven Beck *(Z)*
Laxdale	Glenmore *(R)*	Rule Water *(Z)*
Laxford	Gruinard *(R)*	Sgitheach
Lednock	Hertford	Skinsdale
Lostock	Hindburn	Sligachan
Loughor	Isbourne	South Tyne
Lowther	Kilennan *(R)*	The Porter *(R)*
Luineag	Lambourn	Traligill
Mallart *(R)*	Lyvennet	Varragill
Meavaig *(R)*	Manifold	Water of Ae *(Z)*
Moidart	Moriston	West Allen
Okement	North Esk	Whitelake
Old West *(R)*	Old Croft *(R)*	
Parrett	Park Burn *(Z)*	
Pattack	Petteril	**10**
Poulter	Rea Brook *(Z)*	
Rheidol	Romesdal	Applecross
Rivelin	Rye Water *(Z)*	Back Stream *(Z)*
Roeburn	Skirface	Barbon Beck *(Z)*
Scaddle	South Esk	Barrisdale
Snizort	Stiffkey	Black Water *(Z)*
Tarbert	Strathby	Blackwater
Toscaig	Thrushel	Blackwater *(R)*
Wampool	Torridge	Blane Water *(Z)*
Waveney	Torridon	Burn of Lyth *(Z)*
Welland	Wansbeck	Crooked Oak
Wenning	Washburn	Hinnisdale
Winster	West Dart *(R)*	Little Dart *(Z)*

CONSTRUCTIVE FORMATION OF PLACE NAMES GB/UK

Little Ouse *(R)*	**Luther Water** *(Z)*	**Rotten Calder** *(Z)*
Mouse Water *(Z)*	**Old River Don** *(Z)*	**Ruchill Water** *(Z)*
New Bedford *(R)*	**Pendle Water** *(Z)*	**Ruthven Water** *(Z)*
Rankle Burn *(Z)*	**Piddle Brook** *(Z)*	**Saddell Water** *(Z)*
Twenty Foot *(R)*	**Prosen Water** *(Z)*	
	Quoich Water *(Z)*	

11

12

14/15

Burn of Ample *(Z)*		**Black Cat Water** *(Z)*
Calder Water *(Z)*	**Ashford Water** *(Z)*	**Glenderamackin**
Devil's Brook *(Z)*	**Corriemulzie** *(R)*	**Little Guinard** *(R)*
Devil's Water *(Z)*	**Potrail Water** *(Z)*	**Blackwater of Dee** *(Z)*

CONSTRUCTIVE FORMATION OF PLACE NAMES

CONJUNCTIONS (variously hyphenated)

1	by	3	de la	of the
	Da		Dubh	on the
a'	in	an t	en le	super
e	la	cum	near	under
o'	le	is y	next	
t	of	mon	over	
y	on	na h	tal y	7
	na	nam	upon	
	St	nan		next the
2	Ti	the		upon the
	ty		5	
Am	ym	4		
an	yn		by the	
a'r	yr	an da	in the	

PREFIXES (small word)

1	2	3	Hoe	Out
			Hoo	Pen
A'	An	All	Key	Red
Y	Ha	Cwm	Lea	Rye
	No	Dry	Lee	Taf
	St	Dun	Low	Tal
	Ty	Eas	Lye	The
	Up	Geo	Mid	Tir
	Yr	Gob	Moy	Toa
		Ham	New	Tom
				Tor

SUFFIXES

2	-bury	-sham	-stone
	-coln	-shaw	-troon
-by	-cote	-shot	-trose
-on	-cott	-side	-ville
	-dale	-town	-water
	-dean	-tree	-worth
3	-down	-well	
	-fast	-wich	6
-all	-font	-wick	
-den	-ford	-wood	-ampton
-der	-gate	-wydd	-bourne
-don	-glen	-wyth	-bridge
-end	-gwyn		-brooke
-ham	-hall		-caster
-ing	-horn	5	-castle
-ley	-hunt		-church
-low	-kirk	-aston	-cliffe
-nau	-land	-burgh	-ingdon
-sea	-loch	-combe	-ingham
-son	-lock	-cross	-ington
-tan	-mere	-field	-philly
-ted	-mont	-firth	-shiels
-ton	-moor	-forth	-thorpe
-way	-more	-grove	-worthy
-wen	-nach	-haven	
-wyl	-nell	-holme	
-wyn	-ness	-house	7
	-nish	-hurst	
	-nock	-kelly	-borough
4	-over	-leigh	-chester
	-pool	-mouth	-hampton
-bane	-port	-nauld	-ingbury
-beck	-quay	-stead	-ingford
-burn	-rick	-stoke	-minster

TOWNS AND CITIES – LOCATION GUIDE

Subsequent sections of this chapter will refer back to the bracketed *specific* abbreviations used below. These abbreviations are to be found against the most commonly used form of the county or region in question though it may have a longer or shorter form (i.e. 'Co. Durham' is selected in preference to 'County Durham' or 'Durham').

The Local Government Acts of 1972 (England and Wales) and 1973 (Scotland) altered virtually every county or regional boundary as well as giving rise to new names. Both old and new names are listed below as follows:

(1) Names in CAPITALS with a suffixed, bracketed abbreviation are (wholly) new counties with new names.

(2) Names in **lower case** with a suffixed, bracketed abbreviation are old counties still fully operational though boundary changes (may) have been effected.

(3) Names with no suffixed abbreviation are no longer legal entities.

(**W**) now part of Wales.

ENGLISH COUNTIES

Also see GEOGRAPHICAL ABBREVIATIONS (p. 49).

4

AVON *(A)*
Beds *(Bd)*
Kent *(K)*

5

Berks *(Bk)*
Bucks *(Buk)*
Devon *(Dv)*
Essex *(Ex)*
Hants *(Hp)*
Herts *(Hf)*
Hunts
Notts *(No)*
Salop *(Sp)*
Wilts *(Wl)*

6

Dorset *(Do)*
Staffs *(St)*
Surrey *(Su)*

7

CUMBRIA *(Cu)*
Holland
Lindsey
Norfolk *(Nf)*
Rutland
Suffolk *(Sf)*

8

Cheshire *(Ch)*
Co. Durham *(CD)*
Cornwall *(Cw)*
Kesteven
Somerset *(Sm)*

9

CLEVELAND *(Cl)*
Isle of Ely
Middlesex
Northants *(Na)*

Yorkshire

10

Cumberland
Derbyshire *(Db)*
East Riding
East Sussex *(ES)*
HUMBERSIDE *(Hb)*
Huntingdon
Lancashire *(La)*
MERSEYSIDE *(M)*
West Riding
West Sussex *(WS)*

11

East Suffolk
ISLE OF WIGHT *(IW)*
North Riding
Oxfordshire *(Ox)*
TYNE AND WEAR *(TW)*
Westmorland

West Suffolk

Herefordshire
WEST YORKSHIRE *(WY)*

SOUTH YORKSHIRE *(SY)*
Worcestershire

12

Lincolnshire *(Li)*
Warwickshire *(Ww)*
WEST MIDLANDS *(WM)*

14

15/17/18/20

Gloucestershire *(Gl)*
GREATER
   MANCHESTER *(GM)*
Soke of Peterborough
HEREFORD AND
   WORCESTER *(HW)*

Cambridgeshire *(Cb)*
Leicestershire *(Le)*
(W) Monmouthshire
NORTH YORKSHIRE *(NY)*
Northumberland *(Nu)*

13

GREATER LONDON *(GL)*

WELSH COUNTIES

(E) includes Monmouthshire

5

CLWYD *(Cy)*
DYFED *(D)*
Flint
(E) GWENT *(Gt)*
POWYS *(P)*

Denbigh
GWYNEDD *(Gw)*
Anglesey
Cardigan
Pembroke

Caernarvon
Carmarthen
Montgomery

9/10

6/7/8

Brecon

Glamorgan
Merioneth

12/13/14

MID GLAMORGAN *(MG)*
WEST GLAMORGAN *(WG)*
SOUTH GLAMORGAN *(SG)*

SCOTTISH REGIONS AND FORMER COUNTIES

3/4/5/6

Ayr
Fife *(F)*
Banff
Moray
Nairn
Argyll
Lanark

7

Berwick
BORDERS *(B)*
CENTRAL *(C)*
Kinross
LOTHIAN *(L)*
Peebles
Selkirk

TAYSIDE *(T)*
Wigtown

8

Aberdeen
Dumfries
GRAMPIAN *(G)*

HIGHLAND *(H)*   **Midlothian**   13/15/19
Roxburgh   **Perthshire**
                        Sutherland   **Kirkcudbright**
                                                    Stirlingshire
9   **Ross and Cromarty**
                                                    DUMFRIES AND
Caithness   GALLOWAY *(DG)*
Dunbarton
Inverness   11

                        Clackmannan
10   **East Lothian**
                        STRATHCLYDE *(SC)*
Kinkardine   **West Lothian**

NORTHERN IRELAND COUNTIES
(The traditional six counties)

6/9/11   **Armagh** *(Ah)*   **Fermanagh** *(F)*
                        Co. Down *(Dn)*   **Londonderry** *(Ld)*
Antrim *(Am)*   **Tyrone** *(Ty)*

ISLANDS

Also see ISLES, 'ISLES', ISLANDS (p. 64).

Orkney *(O)*   **Isle of Man** *(IM)*   **Isles of Scilly** *(IS)*
Shetland *(S)*   WESTERN ISLES *(WI)*

TOWNS AND CITIES – ENGLAND
(including Isle of Man, Isle of Wight, Isles of Scilly)

To locate check specific abbreviation in the LOCATION GUIDE (i.e. **Ely** *(Cb)* = Ely, Cambridgeshire).

+ indicates other inhabited place in *another county* having the same name (i.e. **Eye** *(Sf)* + = Eye in Suffolk with a smaller place or places having the same name).

A number (i.e. **Newton** 114) means that there are at least 114 places in Great Britain called Newton or which include Newton as part of their name.

Popular shortened forms as well as some of the full titles have been included (i.e. Hull and Kingston-upon-Hull).

note The asterisk* indicates that the place name is also a word valid for most word games.

3

Ely *(Cb)*
Eye* *(Sf)*+
Rye* *(ES)*
Wem* *(Sp)*

4

Acle *(Nf)*
Bath* *(A)*
Bude *(Cw)*
Bury* *(GM)*+
Deal* *(K)*
Dent* *(Cu)*
Diss* *(Nf)*
Eton *(Bk)*
Holt* *(Nf)*+
Hove* *(ES)*
Hull* *(Hb)*
Hyde *(GM)*+
Leek* *(St)*
Looe *(Cw)*
Lydd *(K)*
Peel* *(IM)*
Ryde *(IW)*
Shap *(Cu)*
Ware* *(Hf)*+
Yarm *(Cl)*
York* *(NY)*

5

Abram *(GM)*
Acton* *(GL)*+
Alton *(Hp)*+
Amble* *(Nu)*
Bacup *(La)*
Blyth *(Nu)*
Calne *(Wl)*
Chard* *(Sm)*
Cheam *(GL)*
Colne *(La)*+
Cowes *(IW)*
Crewe *(Ch)*
Crook* *(CD)*
Derby* *(Db)*
Dover* *(K)*
Egham *(Su)*
Epsom *(Su)*
Filey *(NY)*
Fowey *(Cw)*
Frome *(Sm)*
Goole *(Hb)*
Hawes *(NY)*
Hedon *(Hb)*
Hurst* *(GM)*+
Hythe* *(K)*+
Leeds *(WY)*
Leigh *(GM)*+
Lewes *(ES)*
Louth *(Li)*
Luton *(Bd)*+
March* *(Cb)*

Olney *(Buk)*+
Otley *(WY)*+
Poole *(Do)*+
Ripon *(NY)*
Rugby* *(Ww)*
Selby *(NY)*
Stoke* *(St)*+
Stone* *(St)*+
Thame *(Ox)*
Tring *(Hf)*
Truro *(Cw)*
Wells* *(Sm)*+
Wigan* *(GM)*

6

Alford *(Li)*+
Alston *(Cu)*+
Arnold *(No)*+
Barnet *(GL)*
Batley *(WY)*
Battle* *(ES)*+
Bawtry *(SY)*
Bedale *(NY)*
Belper *(Db)*
Bodmin *(Cw)*
Bognor *(WS)*
Bolton *(GM)*+
Bootle *(M)*+
Boston* *(Li)*
Bungay *(Sf)*
Burton* 43

Buxton *(Db)*+
Church* *(La)*
Clowne *(Db)*
Cobham *(Su)*+
Cromer *(Nf)*+
Darwen *(La)*
Dudley *(WM)*+
Durham *(CD)*
Ealing *(GL)*
Eccles *(GM)*+
Epping *(Ex)*
Exeter *(Dv)*+
Goring* *(Ox)*
Hanley *(St)*
Harlow *(Ex)*
Harrow* *(GL)*
Havant *(Hp)*
Heanor *(Db)*
Hexham *(Nu)*
Howden *(Hb)*+
Ilford *(GL)*+
Ilkley *(WY)*
Jarrow *(TW)*
Kendal *(Cu)*
Leyton *(GL)*
London
Ludlow *(Sp)*
Lynton *(Dv)*
Lytham *(La)*
Maldon *(Ex)*
Malton *(NY)*
Marlow *(Buk)*
Masham *(NY)*
Morley *(WY)*+
Nelson* *(La)*+
Neston *(Ch)*+
Newark *(No)*+
Newent *(Gl)*
Newlyn *(Cw)*
Newton* 114
Oakham *(Le)*
Oldham *(GM)*
Ossett *(WY)*
Oundle *(Na)*
Oxford *(Ox)*
Pewsey *(Wl)*
Pinner* *(GL)*
Pudsey* *(WY)*
Putney *(GL)*
Ramsey *(IM)*+

Redcar *(Cl)*
Repton *(Db)*
Ripley *(Db)*+
Romsey *(Hp)*
St* Ives *(Cw)*+
Seaham *(CD)*
Seaton 13
Selsey *(WS)*+
Settle* *(NY)*
Strood *(K)*
Stroud* *(Gl)*
Sutton 83
Thirsk *(NY)*
Thorne *(SY)*
Totnes *(Dv)*
Walton 36
Weston 61
Whitby *(NY)*+
Widnes *(Ch)*
Wilton *(Wl)*+
Witham *(Ex)*
Witney *(Ox)*
Wooler *(Nu)*
Yeovil *(Sm)*

7

Alnwick *(Nu)*
Andover *(Hp)*
Appleby *(Cu)*+
Arundel *(WS)*
Ashford *(K)*+
Aylsham *(Nf)*
Bampton *(Dv)*+
Banbury *(Ox)*
Barking* *(GL)*
Beccles *(Sf)*
Bedford *(Bd)*
Berwick *(Nu)*+
Bewdley *(HW)*
Bexhill *(ES)*
Bilston *(WM)*+
Bourton 12
Brandon 8
Bristol *(A)*
Brixham *(Dv)*
Bromley *(GL)*+
Burnham 16
Burnley *(La)*

Burslem *(St)*
Caistor *(Li)*
Catford *(GL)*+
Charing* *(K)*
Chatham *(K)*
Cheadle *(St)*+
Cheddar *(Sm)*
Chesham *(Buk)*
Chester *(Ch)*
Chorley *(La)*+
Clacton *(Ex)*
Clifton 34
Crawley *(WS)*+
Croydon *(GL)*+
Datchet *(Bk)*
Dawlish *(Dv)*
Devizes *(Wl)*
Dorking *(Su)*
Douglas *(IM)*+
Dursley *(Gl)*
Enfield *(GL)*+
Evesham *(HW)*
Exmouth *(Dv)*
Fareham *(Hp)*
Farnham *(Su)*+
Feltham *(GL)*
Glossop *(Db)*
Gosport *(Hp)*
Grimsby *(Hb)*
Halifax *(WY)*
Hampton *(GL)*+
Harwich *(Ex)*
Haworth *(WY)*
Helston *(Cw)*
Heywood *(GM)*
Hitchin *(Hf)*
Honiton *(Dv)*
Hornsea *(Hb)*
Hornsey *(GL)*
Horsham *(WS)*
Ipswich *(Sf)*
Keswick *(Cu)*+
Kington *(HW)*
Lancing* *(WS)*
Ledbury *(HW)*
Leyburn *(NY)*
Lincoln *(Li)*
Malvern *(HW)*
Margate *(K)*
Matlock *(Db)*

Molesey *(Su)*
Moreton 21
Morpeth *(Nu)*
Mossley *(GM)*+
Newbury *(Bk)*+
Newport *(IW)*+
Norwich *(Nf)*
Oldbury *(WM)*
Padstow *(CW)*
Penrith *(Cu)*
Prescot *(M)*+
Preston *(La)*+
Rainham *(GL)*+
Reading* *(Bk)*
Redhill *(Su)*
Redruth *(Cw)*
Reigate *(Su)*
Retford *(No)*
Romford *(GL)*
Royston *(SY)*
Rugeley*(St)*
Runcorn *(Ch)*
St* Neots *(Cb)*
Salford *(GM)*+
Saltash *(CW)*
Sandown *(IW)*
Seaford *(ES)*
Shifnal *(Sp)*
Shipley *(WY)*+
Silloth *(Cu)*
Skipton *(NY)*
Spilsby *(Li)*
Staines *(Su)*
Stanley *(CD)*+
Sudbury *(Sf)*+
Sunbury *(Su)*
Swanage *(Do)*
Swindon *(Wl)*+
Swinton *(SY)*+
Taunton *(Sm)*
Telford *(Sp)*
Tetbury *(Gl)*
Thaxted *(Ex)*
Tilbury* *(Ex)*
Torquay *(Dv)*
Twyford *(Bk)*+
Ventnor *(IW)*
Walsall *(WM)*
Waltham 11
Wantage *(Ox)*

Wareham *(Do)*
Warwick *(Ww)*+
Watchet* *(Sm)*
Watford *(Hf)*+
Wembley *(GL)*
Windsor *(Bk)*+
Winslow *(Buk)*
Wisbech *(Cb)*
Worksop *(No)*

8

Abingdon *(Ox)*
Alfreton *(Db)*
Alnmouth *(Nu)*
Amesbury *(Wl)*
Ampthill *(Bd)*
Bakewell *(Db)*
Barnsley *(SY)*+
Beverley *(Hb)*
Bicester *(Ox)*
Bideford *(Dv)*
Blackrod *(GM)*
Bolsover *(Db)*
Brackley *(Na)*
Bradford *(WY)*+
Brampton *(Cu)*+
Bridport *(Do)*
Brighton *(ES)*+
Bromyard *(HW)*
Camborne *(Cw)*
Carlisle *(Cu)*
Caterham *(Su)*
Chertsey *(Su)*
Clevedon *(A)*
Coventry *(WM)*
Crediton *(Dv)*
Daventry *(Na)*
Debenham *(Su)*
Deptford *(GL)*+
Dewsbury *(WY)*
Egremont *(Cu)*+
Fakenham *(Nf)*
Falmouth *(Cw)*
Grantham *(Li)*
Hadleigh *(Sf)*+
Hailsham *(ES)*
Halstead *(Ex)*+
Hastings* *(ES)*+

Hatfield *(Hf)*+
Helmsley *(NY)*
Hereford *(HW)*
Herne Bay* *(K)*
Hertford *(Hf)*
Hinckley *(Le)*
Holbeach *(Li)*
Hugh Town* *(IS)*
Ilkeston *(Db)*
Keighley *(WY)*
Kingston 32
Lavenham *(Sf)*
Liskeard *(Cw)*
Longtown *(St)*+
Lynmouth *(Dv)*
Maryport *(Cu)*+
Midhurst *(WS)*
Minehead *(Sm)*
Nantwich *(Ch)*
Newhaven *(ES)*+
New* Mills* *(Db)*+
Nuneaton *(Ww)*
Ormskirk *(La)*
Oswestry *(Sp)*
Penzance *(Cw)*
Pershore *(HW)*
Peterlee *(CD)*
Petworth *(WS)*
Plaistow *(GL)*+
Plymouth *(Dv)*
Ramsgate *(K)*
Redditch *(HW)*
Richmond *(GL)*+
Ringwood *(Hp)*
Rochdale *(GM)*
Rothbury *(Nu)*
St* Albans *(Hf)*
St* Helens *(M)*+
Saltburn *(Cl)*+
Sandwich* *(K)*
Sedbergh *(Cu)*
Shanklin *(IW)*
Shipston *(Ww)*
Sidmouth *(Dv)*
Skegness *(Li)*
Sleaford *(Li)*+
Southend *(Ex)*+
Spalding *(Li)*
Stafford *(St)*
Stamford *(Li)*+

Stanhope *(CD)*+
Stanwell *(Su)*
Staveley *(Db)*+
Stratton *(Cw)*+
Surbiton *(GL)*
Swaffham *(Nf)*
Tamworth *(St)*
Thetford *(Nf)*+
Thornaby *(Cl)*
Tiverton *(Dv)*+
Tunstall *(St)*+
Uckfield *(ES)*
Uxbridge *(GL)*
Wallasey *(M)*
Wallsend* *(TW)*
Wanstead *(GL)*
Westbury *(Wl)*+
Wetherby *(WY)*
Weymouth *(Do)*
Woolwich *(GL)*
Worthing *(WS)*+
Yarmouth *(IW)*+

9

Aldeburgh *(Sf)*
Aldershot *(Hp)*
Ambleside *(Cu)*
Ashbourne *(Db)*
Ashburton *(Dv)*
Avonmouth *(A)*
Axminster *(Dv)*
Aylesbury* *(Buk)*
Blackburn *(La)*+
Blackpool *(La)*+
Blandford *(Do)*
Bracknell *(Bk)*
Braintree *(Ex)*
Brentford *(GL)*
Brentwood *(Ex)*
Brighouse *(WY)*
Broughton 33
Cambridge *(Cb)*+
Carnforth *(La)*
Chingford *(GL)*
Clay* Cross* *(Db)*
Clitheroe *(La)*
Congleton *(Ch)*
Cranbrook *(K)*

Crewkerne *(Sm)*
Cricklade *(Wl)*
Cuckfield *(WS)*
Dartmouth *(Dv)*
Devonport* *(Dv)*
Doncaster *(SY)*
Droitwich *(HW)*
Dronfield *(Db)*
Dunstable *(Bd)*
Ellesmere *(Sp)*
Faversham *(K)*
Fleetwood *(La)*
Gateshead *(TW)*
Godalming *(Su)*
Gravesend *(K)*
Greenwich *(GL)*
Guildford *(Su)*
Harrogate *(NY)*
Haslemere *(Su)*
Haverhill *(Sf)*
Holmfirth *(WY)*
Immingham *(Hb)*
Kettering *(Na)*
King's* Lynn *(Nf)*
Kingswear *(Dv)*
Lancaster *(La)*
Leicester *(Le)*
Lichfield *(St)*
Liverpool *(M)*
Long* Eaton *(Db)*
Lowestoft *(Sf)*
Lyme Regis *(Do)*
Maidstone *(K)*
Mansfield *(No)*
Melbourne *(Db)*+
Middleton *(GM)*+
Newcastle *(TW)*+
Newmarket* *(Sf)*+
New* Romney *(K)*
Northwich *(Ch)*
Penistone* *(SY)*
Pen-y-ghent *(NY)*
Pickering *(NY)*
Rochester *(K)*
Ross-on-Wye* *(HW)*
Rotherham *(SY)*
St* Austell *(Cw)*
Salisbury *(Wl)*+
Sevenoaks *(K)*
Sheerness *(K)*

Sheffield *(SY)*
Sherborne *(Do)*+
Southgate *(GL)*+
Southport *(M)*
Southwall *(No)*+
Southwold *(Sf)*
Stevenage *(Hf)*
Stockport *(GM)*
Stokesley *(NY)*
Stourport *(HW)*
Stratford *(GL)*+
Tavistock *(Dv)*
Tenterden *(K)*
Tideswell *(Db)*
Todmorden *(WY)*
Tonbridge *(K)*
Towcester *(Na)*
Tynemouth *(TW)*
Ulverston *(Cu)*
Upminster *(GL)*
Uppingham *(Le)*+
Uttoxeter *(St)*
Wainfleet *(Li)*
Wakefield *(WY)*
Weybridge *(Su)*
Wimbledon *(GL)*
Wincanton *(Sm)*
Wokingham *(Bk)*
Woodstock *(Ox)*+
Worcester *(HW)*
Wymondham *(Nf)*+

10

Accrington *(La)*
Altrincham *(GM)*
Barnstaple *(Dv)*
Beaminster *(Do)*
Bedlington *(Nu)*
Bellingham *(GL)*+
Billericay *(Ex)*
Birkenhead *(M)*
Birmingham *(WM)*
Bridgnorth *(Sp)*
Bridgwater *(Sm)*
Bromsgrove *(HW)*
Buckingham *(Buk)*
Canterbury* *(K)*
Carshalton *(GL)*

Castletown *(IM)*
Chelmsford *(Ex)*
Cheltenham *(Gl)+*
Chichester *(WS)*
Chippenham *(Wl)*
Chulmleigh *(Dv)*
Colchester *(Ex)*
Cullompton *(Dv)*
Darlington *(CD)*
Dorchester *(Do)*
Dukinfield *(GM)*
Eastbourne *(ES)+*
Folkestone *(K)*
Gillingham *(K)+*
Gloucester *(Gl)*
Halesworth *(Sf)*
Hartlepool *(Cl)*
Heathfield *(ES)+*
Horncastle *(Li)*
Hornchurch *(GL)*
Hungerford *(Bk)+*
Hunstanton *(Nf)*
Huntingdon *(Cb)*
Ilfracombe *(Dv)*
Kenilworth *(Ww)*
Launceston *(Cw)*
Leamington *(Ww)*
Leominster *(HW)*
Maidenhead* *(Bk)*
Malmesbury *(Wl)*
Manchester *(GM)*
Mexborough *(SY)*
Middlewich *(Ch)*
Nailsworth *(Gl)*
Nottingham *(No)*
Okehampton *(Dv)*
Pangbourne *(Bk)*
Pontefract *(WY)*
Portishead *(A)*
Portsmouth *(Hp)*
Potters* Bar* *(Hf)*
St* Leonards *(ES)+*
Saxmundham *(Sf)*
Shepperton *(Su)*
Sheringham *(Nf)*
Shrewsbury *(Sp)*
Stowmarket *(Sf)*
Sunderland *(TW)+*
Teddington *(GL)*
Teignmouth *(Dv)*

Tewkesbury *(Gl)*
Thamesmead *(GL)*
Torrington *(Dv)*
Trowbridge *(Wl)*
Warminster *(Wl)*
Warrington *(Ch)+*
Washington *(TW)+*
Wednesbury *(WM)*
Wellington* *(Sm)+*
Whitchurch 13
Whitehaven *(Cu)*
Whitstable *(K)*
Whittlesey *(Cb)*
Willenhall *(WM)*
Winchelsea *(ES)*
Winchester *(Hp)*
Windermere *(Cu)*
Wirksworth *(Db)*
Withernsea *(Hb)*
Wolsingham *(CD)*
Woodbridge *(Sf)+*
Workington *(Cu)*

11

Basingstoke *(Hp)*
Berkhamsted *(Hf)*
Biggleswade *(Bd)*
Bognor Regis *(WS)*
Bournemouth *(Do)*
Bridlington *(Hb)*
Buntingford *(Hf)*
Cleethorpes *(Hb)*
Cockermouth *(Cu)*
East* Retford *(No)*
Glastonbury *(Sm)*
Guisborough *(Cl)*
Haltwhistle *(Nu)*
High* Wycombe *(Buk)*
Leytonstone *(GL)*
Lostwithiel *(Cw)*
Ludgershall *(Wl)*
Lutterworth *(Le)*
Mablethorpe *(Li)*
Manningtree *(Ex)*
Market* Rasen *(Li)*
Marlborough *(Wl)*
Much* Wenlock *(Sp)*
New* Brighton 7

Newton* Abbot* *(Dv)*
Northampton *(Na)*
Petersfield *(Hp)*
Pocklington *(Hb)*
Rawtenstall *(La)*
Scarborough *(NY)*
Shaftesbury *(Do)*
Southampton *(Hp)*
South* Molton *(Dv)*
Stalybridge *(GM)*
Stourbridge *(WM)*
Swadlincote *(Db)*
Wallingford *(Ox)*
Walthamstow *(GL)*
Westminster *(GL)*
Woodhall Spa* *(Li)*

12

Attleborough *(Nf)*
Chesterfield* *(Db)*
Christchurch *(Do)+*
Gainsborough *(Li)*
Great* Malvern *(HW)*
Huddersfield *(WY)*
Loughborough *(Le)*
Macclesfield *(Ch)*
Milton Keynes *(Buk)*
North* Shields* *(TW)*
North* Walsham *(Nf)*
Peterborough *(Cb)*
South* Shields* *(TW)*
Stoke*-on-Trent *(St)*

13

Barnard Castle* *(CD)*
Bishop's* Castle* *(Sp)*
Boroughbridge *(NY)*
Brightlingsea *(Ex)*
Burton* on Trent *(St)*
Bury* St* Edmunds *(Sf)*
Chipping* Ongar *(Ex)*
East* Grinstead *(WS)*
Godmanchester *(Cb)*
Great* Yarmouth *(Nf)*
Higham Ferrers *(Na)*
Kidderminster *(HW)*

Kirkby Stephen *(Cu)*
Knaresborough *(NY)*
Littlehampton *(WS)*
Lytham St* Annes *(La)*
Market* Deeping *(Li)*
Market* Drayton *(Sp)*
Melton* Mowbray *(Le)*
Middlesbrough *(Cl)*
Northallerton *(NY)*
Saffron* Walden *(Ex)*
Shepton Mallet* *(Sm)*
Wolverhampton *(WM)*

14

Ashby de la* Zouch *(Le)*
Bishop* Auckland *(CD)*
Bishops* Waltham *(Hp)*

Chipping* Norton *(Ox)*
Hemel Hempstead *(Hf)*
Kirkby Lonsdale *(Cu)*
Market* Bosworth *(Le)*
Stockton-on-Tees* *(Cl)*
Stony* Stratford *(Buk)*
Tunbridge Wells* *(K)*
Wellingborough *(Na)*
Wootton Bassett *(Wl)*

15

Ashton-under-Lyne *(GM)*
Barrow-in-Furness *(Cu)*
Burnham-on-
    Crouch* *(Ex)*
Burton upon Trent *(St)*

Chapel* en* le
    Frith* *(Db)*
Leighton Buzzard* *(Bd)*
Sutton Coldfield *(WM)*
Weston-super-Mare* *(A)*

16

Berwick upon
    Tweed* *(Nu)*
Bishop's* Stortford *(Hf)*
Kingston upon
    Hull* *(Hb)*
Littlestone-on-Sea* *(K)*
Stratford upon
    Avon *(Ww)*
Welwyn Garden* City*
    (Hf)

TOWNS AND CITIES – WALES

3/4

Usk *(Gt)*
Bala *(Gw)*
Mold *(Cy)*
Rhyl *(Cy)*

5

Chirk* *(Cy)*
Conwy *(Gw)*
Flint* *(Cy)*
Neath* *(WG)*
Risca *(Gt)*
Tenby *(D)*

6

Amlwch *(Gw)*
Bangor *(Gw)*
Brecon *(P)*
Conway *(Gw)*
Penryn *(Gw)*

Ruabon *(Cy)*
Ruthin *(Cy)*+

7

Cardiff *(SG)*
Cwmbran *(Gt)*
Denbigh *(Cy)*
Maesteg *(MG)*
Newport *(Gt)*+
Newtown *(P)*+
Rhymney *(MG)*
St* Asaph *(Cy)*
Swansea *(WG)*
Wrexham *(Cy)*

8

Aberdare *(MG)*
Abergele *(Cy)*
Barmouth *(Gw)*
Bridgend *(MG)*+
Caerleon *(Gt)*

Cardigan* *(D)*
Chepstow *(Gt)*
Hawarden *(Cy)*
Holyhead *(Gw)*
Holywell *(Cy)*+
Kidwelly *(D)*
Knighton *(P)*+
Lampeter *(D)*
Llanrwst *(Gw)*
Monmouth *(Gt)*
Pembroke* *(D)*
Pwllheli *(Gw)*
Rhayader *(P)*
Talgarth *(P)*
Tredegar *(Gt)*
Tregaron *(D)*

9

Aberaeron *(D)*
Aberdovey *(Gw)*
Beaumaris *(Gw)*
Criccieth *(Gw)*
Dollgellau *(Gw)*

Fishguard *(D)*   Carmarthen *(D)*   Abertillery *(Gt)*
Llandudno *(Gw)*   Llandovery *(D)*   Aberystwyth *(D)*
Pontypool *(Gw)*   Llangollen *(Cy)*   Builth Wells* *(P)*
Porthcawl *(MG)*   Llanidloes *(P)*
Welshpool *(P)*   Montgomery *(P)*
                         Presteigne *(P)*

                                                   13/16

10   11   Haverfordwest *(D)*
                                                   Merthyr Tydfil *(MG)*
Caernarvon *(Gw)*   Abergavenny *(Gt)*   Llandrindod Wells* *(P)*

TOWNS AND CITIES – SCOTLAND
(including Orkney, Shetland and Western Isles)

dE   district of Edinburgh
dG   district of Glasgow

3   Kelso *(B)*   Rothes *(G)*
                         Leith *(dE)*   Thurso *(H)*
Ayr *(Sc)*   Nairn *(H)*   Wishaw *(Sc)*+
Uig *(WI)*   Perth *(T)*
                         Troon *(Sc)*+

4   7
                         6
Alva *(C)*   Airdrie *(Sc)*
Barr *(Sc)*+   Alford *(G)*   Brechin *(T)*
Duns* *(B)*   Beauly *(H)*   Brodick *(Sc)*
Elie *(F)*   Biggar *(Sc)*   Carluke *(Sc)*
Oban *(Sc)*   Buckie* *(G)*   Culross *(F)*
Wick* *(H)*+   Crieff *(T)*   Cumnock *(Sc)*
                         Dollar* *(C)*   Douglas *(Sc)*+
                         Dunbar *(L)*   Fairlie *(Sc)*+
5   Dundee *(T)*   Falkirk *(C)*
                         Dunoon *(Sc)*   Galston *(Sc)*
Alloa *(C)*   Forfar *(T)*   Glasgow *(Sc)*
Annan *(DG)*   Forres *(G)*   Gorbals *(dG)*
Banff *(G)*   Girvan *(Sc)*   Gourock *(Sc)*
Beith *(Sc)*   Hawick *(B)*   Granton *(dE)*
Crail *(F)*   Huntly *(G)*   Kilsyth *(Sc)*
Cupar *(F)*   Irvine *(Sc)*   Kinross *(T)*
Denny *(C)*   Lanark *(Sc)*   Larbert *(C)*
Elgin *(G)*   Lauder* *(B)*   Lerwick *(S)*
Ellon *(G)*   Leslie *(F)*   Macduff *(G)*
Govan *(dG)*   Moffat *(DG)*   Maybole *(Sc)*
Keith *(G)*   Rosyth *(F)*   Melrose *(B)*

Paisley* *(Sc)*
Peebles *(B)*
Polmont *(C)*
Portree *(H)*
Renfrew *(Sc)*
Selkirk *(B)*
Tarbert *(WI)+*
Tayport *(F)*
Tranent *(L)*
Turriff *(G)*

8

Aberdeen *(G)*
Arbroath *(T)*
Armadale *(L)*
Banchory *(G)*
Blantyre *(Sc)*
Burghead *(G)*
Cromarty *(H)*
Dalkeith *(L)*
Dingwall *(H)*
Dufftown *(G)*
Dumfries *(DG)*
Dunblane *(C)*
Earlston *(B)*
Eyemouth *(B)*
Fortrose *(H)*
Greenock *(Sc)*
Hamilton *(Sc)*
Jedburgh *(B)*
Kinghorn *(F)*
Kirkwall *(O)*
Langholm *(DG)*
Loanhead *(L)+*
Markinch *(F)*
Montrose *(T)*
Muirkirk *(Sc)*
Neilston *(Sc)*
Newburgh *(F)+*
Newmilns *(Sc)*
Penicuik *(L)*
Rothesay *(Sc)*
Stirling *(C)*
Ullapool *(H)*
Whithorn *(DG)*

9

Aberfeldy *(T)*
Ardrossan *(Sc)*
Buckhaven *(F)*
Callander *(C)*
Dumbarton *(Sc)*
Edinburgh *(L)*
Inverurie *(G)*
Inverness *(H)*
Johnstone *(Sc)+*
Kilmacolm *(Sc)*
Kingussie *(H)*
Kirkcaldy *(F)*
Leadhills *(Sc)*
Lochgelly *(F)*
Lockerbie *(DG)*
Mauchline *(Sc)*
Milngavie *(Sc)*
Peterhead *(G)*
Pitlochry *(T)*
Port* Ellen *(Sc)*
Prestwick *(Sc)*
Riccarton *(Sc)*
St* Andrews *(F)*
Saltcoats *(Sc)+*
Stranraer *(DG)*
Thornhill *(DG)+*
Tobermory *(Sc)*

10

Anstruther *(F)*
Ardrishaig *(Sc)*
Auchinleck *(Sc)*
Ballantree *(Sc)*
Carnoustie *(T)*
Coatbridge *(Sc)*
Coldstream *(B)*
Dalbeattie *(DG)*
East* Linton *(L)*
Galashiels *(B)*
Glenrothes *(F)*
Kilmarnock *(Sc)*
Kilwinning *(Sc)*
Kirriemuir *(T)*

Lennoxtown *(Sc)*
Lesmahagow *(Sc)*
Linlithgow *(L)*
Livingston *(L)*
Milnathort *(T)*
Motherwell *(Sc)*
Pittenweem *(F)*
Portobello *(dE)*
Rutherglen *(Sc)*
Stonehaven *(G)*
Strathaven *(Sc)*

11

Blairgowrie *(T)*
Campbeltown *(Sc)*
Cumbernauld *(Sc)*
Dunfermline *(F)*
Ecclefechan *(DG)*
Fort* William *(H)*
Fraserburgh *(G)*
Helensburgh *(Sc)*
Invergordon *(H)*
Lossiemouth *(G)*
Musselburgh *(L)*
Portpatrick *(DG)*
Prestonpans *(L)*

12

Auchterarder *(T)*
East* Kilbride *(Sc)*
Innerleithen *(B)*
North* Berwick *(L)*
Tillicoultry *(C)*

13

Auchtermuchty *(F)*
Castle* Douglas *(DG)*
Dalmellington *(Sc)*
Inverkeithing *(F)*
Kirkcudbright *(DG)*
Kirkintilloch *(Sc)*
Newton* Stewart *(DG)*

TOWNS AND CITIES – NORTHERN IRELAND

5/6

Derry　*(Ld)*
Larne　*(Am)*
Newry　*(Dn)*
Omagh　*(Ty)*
Antrim　*(Am)*
Comber*　*(Dn)*
Lurgan　*(Am)*

7

Belfast
Caledon　*(Ty)*
Fintona　*(Ty)*
Gilford　*(Dn)*
Glenarm　*(Am)*
Lisburn　*(Am/Dn)*

8

Dungiven　*(Ld)*
Portrush　*(Am)*

Strabane　*(Ty)*

9

Ballymena　*(Am)*
Banbridge　*(Dn)*
Bushmills　*(Am)*
Coleraine　*(Ld)*
Cookstown　*(Ty)*
Dungannon　*(Ty)*
Moneymore　*(Ld)*
Newcastle　*(Dn)+*
Portadown　*(Ah)*
Rostrever　*(Dn)*

10

Ballyclare　*(Am)*
Ballymoney　*(Am)+*
Donaghadee　*(Dn)*
Markethill　*(Ah)*
Portaferry　*(Dn)*

Saintfield　*(Dn)*
Tanderagee　*(Ah)*

11

Ballycastle　*(Am)*
Ballygawley　*(Ty)*
Crossmaglen　*(Ah)*
Downpatrick　*(Dn)*
Enniskillen　*(F)*
Londonderry　*(Ld)*
Magherafelt　*(Ld)*
Portglenone　*(Am)*
Randalstown　*(Am)*

12/13/14

Castlewellan　*(Dn)*
Hillsborough　*(Dn)*
Stewartstown　*(Ty)*
Carrickfergus　*(Am)*
Newtown* Stewart　*(Ty)*

VILLAGES, HAMLETS AND LOCALITIES

A selection of 'cryptic' potential, *all* in Great Britain.

　(Word-game players: note some surprisingly valid words together with some oddly invalid words.)

3

		4
Aby*	**Kew**	**Acre***
Ash*	**Law***	**Back***
Bow*	**Old***	**Bale***
Box*	**Par***	**Ball***
Elm*	**Ram***	**Bank***
Ham*	**Raw***	**Bare***
Hem*	**Row***	**Bean***
Hoe*	**Sea***	**Beer***
How*	**Van***	**Boot***

Bray*
Burn*
Coat*
Crow*
Dawn*
Dial*
Doll*
Drum*
Dull*
Edge*
Fern*
Gang*
Hive*
Hole*
Hope*
Jump*
Lake*
Ogle*
Over*
Pale*
Pant*
Paul*
Pill*
Pool*
Rake*
Rash*
Reed*
Ripe*
Rise*
Rock*
Rode*
Rope*
Rose*
Salt*
Sand*
Seal*
Shop*
Stow*
Tone*
Week*
Wing*
Wool*

Bride*
Brook*
Broom*
Bugle*
Bunny*
Cargo*
Cleat*
Clive
Combs*
Coven*
Crank*
Cross*
Delph*
Drift*
Eagle*
Egypt
Fence*
Fleet*
Golly*
Greet*
Hatch*
Knock*
Largo*
Loans*
Loose*
Paris
Plush*
Potto*
Press*
Racks*
Raise*
Ridge*
River*
Salem
Shelf*
Shute
Slack*
Stank*
Steep*
Swell*
Swine*
Walls*
Worth*

Barrow*
Bicker*
Bisley
Canada*
Canton*
Cawdor
Cowbit
Dallas
Dublin
Dunlop
Gotham
Lionel*
Martin*
Ostend
Pity* Me*
Saline*
Scales*
Stakes*
Staple*
Street*
Tongue*
Tumble*
Twenty*

7

America
Arcadia
Bassett
Bohemia
Bottoms*
Bowling*
Calgary
Charles
Cold* Ash*
Cooling*
Cowling*
Docking*
Duck* End*
Dunkirk
Dunning*
Everton
Foxhole*
Glencoe
Holland*
Ireland
Letters*
Mucking*
Mumbles*

5

Angle*
Babel
Booze*
Brawl*

6

Anchor*
Badger*
Barley*

GB/UK   VILLAGES, HAMLETS, ETC.

New* York*
Patrick*
Shirley
Slickly*
Stanley
Sticker*
Stilton
Toronto
Winston
Yelling*

8

Barnacle*
Black* Dog*
Boundary*
Catbrain
Cromwell
Dial* Post*
Edge* Hill*
Farewell*
Flushing*
Frog* Pool*
Normandy
Red* Roses*
Rhodesia
Scotland
Seething*
Upton End*
Waterloo
Wide* Open*

9

Badminton*
Baker's* End*
Ballygown
Bethlehem
Bishopric*
Blackboys
Black* Pill*
Botany* Bay*
Bow* Street*
Brig* o' Turk

Churchill
Clock* Face*
Crow's* Nest*
Gibraltar
Hole's* Hole*
Mark* Cross*
Mousehole
Much* Birch*
Palestine
Small* Dole*
Watergate

10

Allhallows
Amen* Corner*
Charleston
Crossroads*
Dog* Village*
Donkey* Town*
Duck's* Cross*
Fairy* Cross*
Four* Throws*
Georgetown
High* Street*
Littleover
New* Zealand
Over* Wallop*
Peak* Forest*
Row*-of*-Trees*
Sebastopol
Shop* Street*
Westward* Ho*
Wookey Hole*

11

Above* Church*
Barber* Booth*
Bolton Percy
Broadbottom
Burton* Agnes
Collier's* End*

Curry* Mallet*
Edith Weston
Great* Coates
Little* Worth*

12

Bowling* Green*
Countess* Wear*
Devil's* Bridge*
Great* Snoring*
Indian Queens*
Little* London
Mavis* Enderby
Philadelphia

13

Cross* o'th' Hands*
Heart's* Delight*
Hole*-in*-the*-Wall*
Little* Comfort*
Little* Snoring*
Margaret Marsh*
Plain* Dealings*

14

Halfpenny* Green*
Lower* Slaughter*

15

Constable* Burton*
Cricket* St* Thomas
Sixpenny* Handley

16

Barton* in* the* Beans*

REST OF THE WORLD

CONTINENTS

Abbreviations shown are those used in subsequent sections.

Asia
Africa *Afr.*
Europe *Eur.*
America see *North/South America*
Oceania *Oc.*
Antarctica *Ant.*
Australasia see *Oceania*
North America■ *N/Am.*
South America *S/Am.*
Gondwanaland primeval land-mass

(■ including Central America)

COUNTRIES AND CAPITALS
(with continent in brackets followed by capital or capitals)

Carib. Caribbean Island(s)

3

USA *(N/Am.)* Washington D.C.

4

Chad *(Afr.)* N'Djamena
Cuba *(Carib. N/Am.)* Havana
Eire *(Eur.)* Dublin
Fiji *(Oc.)* Suva
Iran *(Asia)* Tehran
Iraq *(Asia)* Baghdad
Laos *(Asia)* Vientiane
Mali *(Afr.)* Bamako
Oman *(Asia)* Muscat
Peru *(S/Am.)* Lima
Togo *(Afr.)* Lome
USSR *(Eur./Asia)* Moscow

5

Benin *(Afr.)* Porto Novo
Burma *(Asia)* Rangoon
Chile *(S/Am.)* Santiago
China *(Asia)* Peking (Beijing)
Congo *(Afr.)* Brazzaville
Egypt *(Afr.)* Cairo
Gabon *(Afr.)* Libreville
Ghana *(Afr.)* Accra
Haiti *(Carib. N/Am.)* Port-au-Prince
India *(Asia)* New Delhi
Italy *(Eur.)* Rome
Japan *(Asia)* Tokyo
Kenya *(Afr.)* Nairobi
Libya *(Afr.)* Tripoli/Benghazi
Macao *(Asia)* Macao City
Malta *(Eur.)* Valletta
Nauru *(Oc.)* no capital

Nepal *(Asia)* Katmandu
Niger *(Afr.)* Niamey
Qatar *(Asia)* Doha
Spain *(Eur.)* Madrid
Sudan *(Afr.)* Khartoum
Syria *(Asia)* Damascus
Tonga *(Oc.)* Nuku'alofa
Yemen *(Asia)* Sana
Zaire *(Afr.)* Kinshasa

6

Angola *(Afr.)* Luanda
Belize *(N/Am.)* Belmopan
Bhutan *(Asia)* Thimbu
Brazil *(S/Am.)* Brasilia
Brunei *(Asia)* Bandar Seri Begawan
Canada *(N/Am.)* Ottawa
Cyprus *(Asia)* Nicosia
France *(Eur.)* Paris
Gambia *(Afr.)* Banjul
Greece *(Eur.)* Athens
Guiana *(S/Am.)* Cayenne
Guinea *(Afr.)* Conakry
Guyana *(S/Am.)* Georgetown
Israel *(Asia)* Jerusalem
Jordan *(Asia)* Amman
Kuwait *(Asia)* Kuwait
Malawi *(Afr.)* Lilongwe
Mexico *(N/Am.)* Mexico City
Monaco *(Eur.)* Monte Carlo
Norway *(Eur.)* Oslo
Panama *(N/S/Am.)* Panama City
Poland *(Eur.)* Warsaw
Russia see *USSR*
Rwanda *(Afr.)* Kigali
Sweden *(Eur.)* Stockholm
Taiwan *(Asia)* Taipei
Turkey *(Eur./Asia)* Ankara
Tuvalu *(Oc.)* Funafuti
Uganda *(Afr.)* Kampala
Zambia *(Afr.)* Lusaka

7

Albania *(Eur.)* Tirana
Algeria *(Afr.)* Algiers
America see *USA*

Andorra *(Eur.)* Andorra
Austria *(Eur.)* Vienna
Bahamas *(Carib. N/Am.)* Nassau
Bahrain *(Asia)* Manama
Belgium *(Eur.)* Brussels
Bermuda *(N/Am.)* Hamilton
Bolivia *(S/Am.)* La Paz/Sucre
Burundi *(Afr.)* Bujumbura
Denmark *(Eur.)* Copenhagen
Ecuador *(S/Am.)* Quito
Grenada *(Carib. S/Am.)* St George's
Holland *(Eur.)* Amsterdam
Hungary *(Eur.)* Budapest
Iceland *(Eur.)* Reykjavik
Ireland see *Eire*
Jamaica *(Carib. N/Am.)* Kingston
Lebanon *(Asia)* Beirut
Lesotho *(Afr.)* Maseru
Liberia *(Afr.)* Monrovia
Morocco *(Afr.)* Rabat
Namibia *(Afr.)* Windhoek
Nigeria *(Afr.)* Lagos
Reunion *(Afr.)* St Denis
Romania *(Eur.)* Bucharest
St Lucia *(Carib. S/Am.)* Castries
Senegal *(Afr.)* Dakar
Surinam *(S/Am.)* Paramaribo
Tunisia *(Afr.)* Tunis
Uruguay *(S/Am.)* Montevideo
Vietnam *(Asia)* Hanoi

8

Barbados *(Carib. S/Am.)* Bridge-town
Botswana *(Afr.)* Gaborone
Bulgaria *(Eur.)* Sofia
Cameroon *(Afr.)* Yaoundé
Colombia *(S/Am.)* Bogota
Djibouti *(Afr.)* Djibouti
Dominica *(Carib. S/Am.)* Roseau
Ethiopia *(Afr.)* Addis Ababa
Honduras *(N/Am.)* Tegucigalpa
Hong Kong *(Asia)* Victoria
Kiribati *(Oc.)* Tarawa
Malaysia *(Asia)* Kuala Lumpur
Mongolia *(Asia)* Ulan Bator
Pakistan *(Asia)* Islamabad
Paraguay *(S/Am.)* Asuncion

COUNTRIES AND CAPITALS

Portugal *(Eur.)* Lisbon
Sri Lanka *(Asia)* Colombo
Tanzania *(Afr.)* Dar es Salaam
Thailand *(Asia)* Bangkok
Zimbabwe *(Afr.)* Harare

9

Argentina *(S/Am.)* Buenos Aires
Australia *(Oc.)* Canberra
Costa Rica *(N/Am.)* San Jose
Gibraltar *(Eur.)* no capital
Greenland *(N/Am.)* Godthaab
Guatemala *(N/Am.)* Guatemala City
Indonesia *(Asia)* Jakarta
Kampuchea *(Asia)* Phnom Penh
Mauritius *(Afr.)* Port Louis
Nicaragua *(N/Am.)* Manegua
St Vincent *(Carib. S/Am.)* Kings-
town
San Marino *(Eur.)* San Marino
Singapore *(Asia)* Singapore
Swaziland *(Afr.)* Mbabane
Venezuela *(S/Am.)* Caracas

10

El Salvador *(N/Am.)* San Salvador
Guadeloupe *(Carib. S/Am.)* Pointe a
Pitre
Ivory Coast *(Afr.)* Abidjan
Luxembourg *(Eur.)* Luxembourg
Madagascar *(Afr.)* Tananarive
Martinique *(Carib. S/Am.)*
Fort-de-France
Mauritania *(Afr.)* Nouakchott
Mocambique *(Afr.)* Maputo
Montserrat *(Carib. S/Am.)* Plymouth
New Zealand *(Oc.)* Wellington
North Korea *(Asia)* Pyongyang
Puerto Rico *(Carib. N/Am.)* San
Juan
Seychelles *(Afr.)* Victoria
South Korea *(Asia)* Seoul
Upper Volta *(Afr.)* Ouagadougou
Yugoslavia *(Eur.)* Belgrade

11

Afghanistan *(Asia)* Kabul
Bangladesh *(Asia)* Dacca
East Germany *(Eur.)* East Berlin
New Hebrides *(Oc.)* Vila
Netherlands see *Holland*
Philippines *(Asia)* Manila
Saudi Arabia *(Asia)* Riyadh
Sierra Leone *(Afr.)* Freetown
South Africa *(Afr.)* Cape
Town/Pretoria
Switzerland *(Eur.)* Berne
Vatican City *(Eur.)* no capital
West Germany *(Eur.)* Bonn

12

Faroe Islands *(Eur.)* Thorshavn
Guinea Bissau *(Afr.)* Bissau
New Caledonia *(Oc.)* Noumea
St Kitts-Nevis *(Carib. S/Am.)*
Basseterre
Western Samoa *(Oc.)* Apia

13

Cayman Islands *(Carib. N/Am.)*
Georgetown
Comoro Islands *(Afr.)* Moroni
Ellsworth Land *(Ant.)* no capital
Liechtenstein *(Eur.)* Vaduz
Queen Mary Land *(Ant.)* no capital
Queen Maud Land *(Ant.)* no capital
Southern Yemen *(Asia)* Aden
Virgin Islands *(Carib. N/Am.)*
Charlotte Amalie
Western Sahara *(Afr.)* El Aaiun

14

Czechoslovakia *(Eur.)* Prague
Papua New Guinea *(Oc.)* Port
Moresby
Solomon Islands *(Oc.)* Honiara
Somali Republic *(Afr.)* Mogadishu

15/16

Falkland Islands *(S/Am.)* Stanley
Equatorial Guinea *(Afr.)* Malabo

17/18

Antigua and Barbuda *(Carib. S/Am.)*
St John's

Dominican Republic *(Carib. N/Am.)*
San Domingo
Trinidad and Tobago *(Carib. S/Am.)*
Port of Spain
United Arab Emirates *(Asia)* no capital

FEDERAL STATES, USA
With capitals (and nicknames in brackets)

note Except for Rhode Island the nickname is prefixed 'The' and suffixed 'State'.

4

Iowa Des Moines (Hawkeye)
Ohio Columbus (Buckeye)
Utah Salt Lake City (Beehive)

5

Idaho Boise (Gem)
Maine Augusta (Pinetree)
Texas Austin (Lone Star)

6

Alaska Juneau
Hawaii Honolulu (Aloha)
Kansas Topeka (Sunflower)
Nevada Carson City (Sagebrush)
Oregon Salem (Beaver)

7

Alabama Montgomery (Cotton)
Arizona Phoenix (Apache)
Florida Tallahassee (Everglade)
Georgia Atlanta (Cracker)
Indiana Indianapolis (Hoosier)
Montana Helena (Treasure)
New York Albany (Empire)
Vermont Montpelier (Green

Mountain)
Wyoming Cheyenne (Equality)

8

Arkansas Little Rock (Wonder or
Bear)
Colorado Denver (Centennial)
Columbia the Federal District
Delaware Dover (Diamond)
Illinois Springfield (Prairie)
Kentucky Frankfort (Bluegrass)
Maryland Annapolis (Cockade or Old
Line)
Michigan Lansing (Wolverine)
Missouri Jefferson City (Ozark or
Show Me)
Nebraska Lincoln (Tree Planter)
Oklahoma Oklahoma City (Sooner)
Virginia Richmond (Old Dominion)

9

Louisiana Baton Rouge (Pelican or
Creole)
Minnesota St Paul (Gopher)
New Jersey Trenton (Garden)
New Mexico Santa Fe (Sunshine)
Tennessee Nashville (Volunteer)
Wisconsin Madison (Badger)

10

California Sacramento (Golden)
Washington Olympia (Evergreen)

11

Connecticut Hartford (Nutmeg)
Mississippi Jackson (Bayou)
North Dakota Bismarck (Flickertail)
Rhode Island Providence (Little
Rhody)
South Dakota Pierre (Coyote)

12

New Hampshire Concord (Granite)
Pennsylvania Harrisburg (Keystone or
Quaker)
West Virginia Charleston (Panhandle)

13

Massachusetts Boston (Bay)
North Carolina Raleigh (Tarheel)
South Carolina Columbia (Palmetto)

MAJOR CITIES

With few exceptions metropolitan area populations exceed 500,000.
Cities in CAPITALS are either national or federal state capitals as indicated.
    ASSR Autonomous Soviet Socialist Republic within USSR
    SSR Soviet Socialist Republic within USSR
    For other cities see COUNTRIES AND CAPITALS (p. 89), FEDERAL STATES, USA (p. 92)
and BIBLICAL PLACES (p. 326).

3

UFA Bashkir *ASSR*

4

Agra India
Cali Colombia
Gary Indiana (USA)
KIEV Ukrainian *SSR*
Kobe Japan
LIMA Peru
Lodz Poland
L'vov USSR
Omsk USSR
OSLO Norway
RIGA Latvian *SSR*
ROME Italy
Sian China
Xian *Sian*
Zibo *Tzepo*

5

ACCRA Ghana
Akita Japan
AMMAN Jordan
CAIRO Egypt
Chiba Japan
DACCA Bangladesh
DELHI India
Essen W. Germany
Gorki USSR
Gorky *Gorki*
Haifa Israel
HANOI Vietnam
Izmir Turkey
Jilin *Kirin*
Jinan *Tsinan*
KABUL Afghanistan
Kirin China
KAZAN Tartar *ASSR*
Kyoto Japan
LAGOS Nigeria
Lille France

Lyons France
Miami Florida (USA)
Milan Italy
MINSK Belorrussian (*SSR*
Omaha Nebraska (USA)
Osaka Japan
PARIS France
PATNA Bihar (India)
PERTH Western Australia
QUITO Equador
RABAT Morocco
SEOUL S. Korea
SOFIA Bulgaria
Tampa Florida (USA)
TOKYO Japan
Tulsa Oklahoma (USA)
TUNIS Tunisia
Turin Italy
Tzepo China
Wuhan China

Naples Italy
Newark New Jersey (USA)
OTTAWA Canada
PEKING *BEIJING*
PRAGUE Czechoslovakia
Saigon *Ho Chi Minh City*
Suchow China
Suzhow *Suchow*
Swatow China
SYDNEY New South Wales (Aust.)
TAIPEI Taiwan
TEHRAN Iran
Toledo Ohio (USA)
Tsinan China
VIENNA Austria
WARSAW Poland
ZAGREB Croatia (Yugoslavia)
Zurich Switzerland

7

ALGIERS Algeria
ATLANTA Georgia (USA)
BAGHDAD Iraq
BANGKOK Thailand
BEIJING China
Buffalo New York (USA)
Calgary Alberta (Canada)
CARACAS Venezuela
Chicago Illinois (USA)
Cologne W. Germany
Cordoba Argentina
Detroit Michigan (USA)
Guiynag *Kweiyang*
Hamburg W. Germany
HANOVER Lower Saxony (W. Ger.)
Houston Texas (USA)
Irkutsk USSR
IZHEVSK Udmurt *ASSR*
Kananga Zaire
Karachi Pakistan
Kharkov USSR
Kunming China
Lanchow China
Lanzhow *Lanchow*
Leipzig E. Germany
LUCKNOW Uttar Pradesh (India)
Mashhad Iran
Memphis Tennessee (USA)

6

Aleppo Syria
ANKARA Turkey
ATHENS Greece
BERLIN EAST/West Germany
BOGOTA Colombia
BOMBAY Maharashtra (India)
BOSTON Massachusetts (USA)
BREMEN Land (W. Germany)
Dallas Texas (USA)
Dayton Ohio (USA)
Denver Colorado (USA)
DUBLIN Eire
Durban S. Africa
FRUNZE Kirghiz *SSR*
Fushun China
HARARE Zimbabwe
HAVANA Cuba
IBIDAN Western Prov. (Nigeria)
Inchon S. Korea
Indore India
LISBON Portugal
MADRAS Tamil Nadu (India)
MADRID Spain
MANILA Philippines
MOSCOW USSR
Nagoya Japan

NAIROBI Kenya
Nanjing *Nanking*
Nanking China
New York New York (USA)
Norfolk Virginia (USA)
Oakland California (USA)
Okayama Japan
Phoenix Arizona (USA)
Qingdao *Tsingtao*
Qiqihar *Tsitsihar*
RANGOON Burma
St Louis *Missouri* (USA)
SAN JOSÉ Costa Rica
San José California (USA)
Sapporo Japan
Saratov USSR
Seattle Washington (USA)
Seville Spain
Shantou *Swatow*
Taiyuan China
Tbilisi USSR
TORONTO Ontario (Canada)
Wroclaw Poland
Wuchang *Wuhan*

Montreal Ottawa (Canada)
Nanchang China
Paterson New Jersey (USA)
Portland Oregon (USA)
PRETORIA South Africa
RICHMOND Virginia (USA)
San Diego California (USA)
SANTIAGO Chile
SAO PAULO Sao Paulo (Brazil)
Shanghai China
Syracuse New York (USA)
Tangshan China
TASHKENT Uzbek *SSR*
Thonburi Thailand
Tianjing *Tientsin*
Tientsin China
Tsingtao China
WINNIPEG Manitoba (Canada)

9

AHMADABAD Gujarat (India)
AMSTERDAM Holland
Baltimore Maryland (USA)
Barcelona Spain
BUCHAREST Romania
Changchun China
Chengchow China
Cleveland Ohio (USA)
Fort Worth Texas (USA)
Frankfurt West Germany
Hamamatsu Japan
Hiroshima Japan
Hyderabad India
Hyderabad Pakistan
Karaganga USSR
Kuang-chou *Kuangchow*
Kuangchow China
Leningrad USSR
Makeyevka USSR
MELBOURNE Victoria (Aust.)
NASHVILLE Tennessee (USA)
PHNOM-PENH Kampuchea
Pittsburg Pennsylvania (USA)
PYONGYANG North Korea
Rochester New York (USA)
SINGAPORE Singapore
STOCKHOLM Sweden

8

ADELAIDE South Australia
Auckland New Zealand
BELGRADE Yugoslavia
BRISBANE Queensland (Aust.)
BRUSSELS Belgium
BUDAPEST Hungary
CALCUTTA West Bengal (India)
CAPE TOWN South Africa
Changsha China
COLUMBUS Ohio (USA)
CURITIBA Parana (Brazil)
EDMONTON Alberta (Canada)
Hamilton Ontario (Canada)
Hang-chou *Hangchow*
Hangchow China
HARTFORD Connecticut (USA)
HELSINKI Finland
Istanbul Turkey
Jabalpur India
Katowice Poland
KINSHASA Zaire
Kweiyang China

STUTTGART Baden-Württemburg (W. 11
Ger.)
Tsitsihar China
Vancouver Brit. Columbia (Canada)
Volgograd USSR
Yaroslavl USSR
Zhengzhou *Chengchow*

11

BUENOS AIRES Argentina
GUADALAJARA Jalisco (Mexico)
Krasnoyarsk USSR
KUALA LUMPUR Malaysia
Minneapolis Minnesota (USA)
Springfield Massachusetts (USA)
Vladivostok USSR

10

12

ADDIS ABABA Ethiopia
Alexandria Egypt
Birmingham Alabama (USA)
Chittagong Bangladesh
Cincinnati Ohio (USA)
COPENHAGEN Denmark
DUSSELDORF N. Rhine-Westphalia (W.
Ger.)
Greensboro' North Carolina (USA)
Jersey City New Jersey (USA)
Kitakyushu Japan
Los Angeles California (USA)
Louisville Kentucky (USA)
MEXICO CITY Mexico
MONTEVIDEO Uruguay
New Orleans Louisiana (USA)
Providence Rhode Island (USA)
San Antonio Texas (USA)
Sverdlovsk USSR
WASHINGTON USA
Youngstown Ohio (USA)

Ciudad Juarez Mexico
Higashiosaka Japan
INDIANAPOLIS Illinois (USA)
Jacksonville Florida (USA)
Johannesburg South Africa
OKLAHOMA CITY Oklahoma (USA)
Philadelphia Pennsylvania (USA)
RIO DE JANEIRO Guanabara (Brazil)
SALT LAKE CITY Utah (USA)
San Francisco California (USA)

13/14

BELO HORIZONTE Minas Gerais (Brazil)
GUATEMALA CITY Guatemala
Ho Chi Minh City Vietnam
San Bernardino California (USA)
Dnepropetrovsk USSR
Fort Lauderdale Florida (USA)

MARINE NOMENCLATURE (inc. UK)

With a few exceptions indexing ignores prefixes and suffixes.
art. artificial waterway
br. arm or branch of (larger marine unit)
c/w coastal water of
lake inland sea or saline lake
lkd landlocked but with outlet to oceans
// dividing waterway between
∞ connecting waters between

3

Lim Fjord Denmark, *North Sea* ∞ *Kattegat*
Red Sea N.E. Africa // S.W. Asia

4

Aden, Gulf of *br. Arabian Sea*
Aral Sea lake, USSR
Azov, Sea of *lkd*, European USSR
Bass Strait Australia // Tasmania
Cook Strait North // South Is., N.Z.
Dead Sea lake, Israel/Jordan
Foxe Basin Canada // Baffin Island
Foxe Channel *Foxe Basin* ∞ *Hudson Strait*
Java Sea Java // Borneo
Kara Sea *br. Arctic Ocean*
Kiel Canal *art., North Sea* ∞ *Baltic Sea*
Oman, Gulf of *Hormuz Str.* ∞ *Arabian Sea*
Palk Strait N. Sri Lanka // India
Riga, Gulf of *c/w* Estonia, Latvia
Ross Sea *br. Antarctic Ocean*
Savu Sea Sumba Is. // Timor
Siam, Gulf of *br. South China Sea*
Suez Canal *art. Suez G* ∞ *Med.*
Suez, Gulf of *br. Red Sea*

5

Aqaba, Gulf of *br. Red Sea*

Banda Sea *c/w* Indonesian Islands

Banda Sea *c/w* Indonesian Islands
Black Sea *lkd*, USSR/Balkans/Turkey
Cabot Strait Nova Scotia // Newfoundland
Cerem Sea *c/w* Indonesian Islands
China Sea *East/South China Sea*
Coral Sea Australia // New Hebrides
Davis Strait Greenland // Baffin Island
Dover, Strait of Dover // Calais
False Bay inlet Cape of Good Hope
Irish Sea GB // Ireland
James Bay *br. Hudson Bay*
Japan Current *Kuroshio*
Japan, Sea of Asia // Japan
Kerch Strait *Azov* ∞ *Black Sea*
Korea Bay *br. Yellow Sea*
Korea Strait *E. China Sea* ∞ *Sea of Japan*
Lions, Gulf of *c/w* S. France
Minch, The Lewis // Scotland
Minch, The Little Harris // Skye
North Channel Ulster // S.W. Scotland
North Sea east GB // Europe
Sound, The *Kattegat* ∞ *Baltic Sea*
Sunda Strait Java // Sumatra
Timor Sea Australia // Indonesia
White Sea *br. Barents Sea*

6

Aegean Sea *br.* E. *Mediterranean*
Alaska, Gulf of *c/w* Alaska, USA
Arctic Ocean North Polar Ocean
Baffin Bay Canada // Greenland

Baltic Sea *lkd*, northern Europe
Bengal, Bay of *br. Indian Ocean*
Bering Sea *br. N. Pacific Ocean*
Bering Strait USSR // Alaska, USA
Biscay, Bay of *c/w* W. France/N. Spain
Bitter Lakes part of *Suez Canal*
Celtic Sea *Atlantic ∞ Bristol Channel*
Chihli, Gulf of *br. Yellow Sea*
Darien, Gulf of *br. Caribbean: c/w* C. America
Dogger Bank *North Sea* sandbank
Flores Sea *Java Sea ∞ Arafura Sea*
German Ocean *North Sea*
Hormuz, Strait of *Persian G. ∞ G. of Oman*
Hudson Bay *lkd* sea, N.E. Canada
Hudson Strait *Hudson Bay ∞ Atlantic*
Indian Ocean 3rd great ocean
Inland Sea *Korea Strait ∞ Pacific*
Ionian Sea Greece // Sicily
Laptev Sea *br. Arctic Ocean*
Mannar, Gulf of N.W. Sri Lanka // India
Mexico, Gulf of N. *br Caribbean Sea*
Norton Sound *br. Bering Sea, c/w* Alaska
Panama Canal *art., Caribbean ∞ Pacific*
Putrid Sea *Sivash Sea*
Salton Sea lake, California, USA
Sivash Sea Crimean lagoon
Tasman Sea Australia // Tasmania
Torres Strait Australia // New Guinea
Wadden Sea N. Holland // West Frisians
Yellow Sea *br. East China Sea*

7

Andaman Sea *c/w* S. Burma
Arabian Sea *br. Indian Ocean*
Arafura Sea *c/w* northern Australia
Barents Sea *br. Arctic Ocean*
Boothia, Gulf of Canadian Arctic
Bothnia, Gulf of *br. Baltic Sea*
Bristol Bay *br. Bering Sea c/w* Alaska
Bristol Channel Wales // s.w. England
Caspian Sea lake, USSR
Celebes Sea *Sula Sea ∞ Molucca Sea*

Dampier Strait West Irian // Waigeo Is.
English Channel S. England // N. France
Finland, Gulf of *br. Baltic Sea*
Florida Strait Florida // Bahamas
Fonesca, Gulf of *br. Pacific, c/w* Honduras
Formosa Strait South ∞ East China Seas
Galilee, Sea of lake, Israel
Hauraki Gulf *c/w* N. Is., N. Zealand
Makasar Strait Borneo // Celebes
Malacca Strait Sumatra // Malaya
Marmara, Sea of *Bosphorus ∞ Dardanelles*
Molucca Sea *Celebes Sea ∞ Pacific*
Okhotsk, Sea of *br. Pacific,* N.E. Asia
Pacific Ocean greatest ocean
Persian Gulf *br. Arabian Sea*
Tartary, Gulf of seas of *Japan ∞ Okhotsk*
Tsugaru Strait Hokkaido // Honshu (Japan)
Weddell Sea *br. Antarctic Ocean*

8

Adriatic Sea Italy // Yugoslavia
Amundsen Gulf *br. Beaufort Sea,* Canada
Amundsen Sea *br. Antarctic Ocean*
Atlantic Ocean 2nd largest ocean
Balkhash Lake lake, USSR
Beaufort Sea *br. Arctic Ocean*
Bismarck Sea *c/w* N. Papua New Guinea
Bosporus *Black Sea ∞ Sea of Marmara*
Canaries Current cold stream, *Atlantic*
Cardigan Bay *br. St George's Channel*
Clarence Strait Darwin // Melville Is. (Australia)
Delaware Bay Delaware River ∞ *Atlantic*
Hebrides, Sea of *Little Minch ∞ Atlantic*
Hwang Hai *Yellow Sea*

Kattegat *Skagerrak ∞ Great Belt/Sound*
Kuroshio warm stream, W. *Pacific*
Ligurian Sea N. Corsica // Monaco
Martaban, Gulf of *c/w* Rangoon, Burma
Sargasso Sea stillwater zone, *Atlantic*
Shelikof Strait Alaska // Kodiak Island
Tiberius, Lake *Sea of Galilee*
Tongking, Gulf of *c/w* N. Vietnam
Viscount Sound Canadian Arctic

9

Antarctic Ocean South Polar waters
Belle Isle Strait Quebec // Newfoundland
Caribbean Sea *br. Atlantic*; West Indies *c/w*
East China Sea *br. Pacific;* W. China *c/w*
Gibraltar, Strait of *Mediterranean ∞ Atlantic*
Great Belt *Baltic Sea ∞ Kattegat*
Greenland Sea *br. Arctic Ocean*
Lancaster Sound Canadian Arctic
St Vincent, Gulf of *c/w* Adelaide, Australia
Skagerrak *North Sea ∞ Kattegat*
Zuider Zee Former marine area, Holland

10

California Current cold stream, *Pacific*
California, Gulf of *br. Pacific c/w* Mexico
Coronation Gulf Canadian Arctic
Gennesaret, Lake *Sea of Galilee*
Golden Gate *San Francisco Bay ∞ Pacific*
Gulf Stream warm current, *Atlantic*
Ijsselmeer reclaimed from *Zuider Zee*
South China Sea Vietnam // Philippines
Tyrrhenian Sea Sardinia // Italy

11

Bab-al-Mandab *Red Sea ∞ Indian Ocean*
Carpentaria, Gulf of *br. Arafura Sea,* Australia
Dardanelles European // Asian Turkey

12/13

East Siberian Sea *br. Arctic Ocean*
San Francisco Bay *Pacific* inlet, West USA
Azouskoye More *Sea of Azov*
Mediterranean Sea S. Europe // N. Africa

SIGNIFICANT RIVERS

'River' is normal prefix except as follows:
   (1) Rud and Rio mean 'river' and the name is therefore complete. Equally, various Chinese names are complete.
   (2) see **(R)**/*(R)* below.
AUST. Australia
Aus. Austria
(b) forms part boundary between
Cz Czechoslovakia
d/w dry in winter
ev eventually disappears by evaporation
m length of course in miles
NSW New South Wales, Australia
(R)/*(R)* 'River' is usually suffix
SSR Soviet Socialist Republic within USSR
Swz Switzerland
tr. tributary of
Ukr. Ukrainian *SSR*
USSR(W) European or Western USSR
Yg Yugoslavia
zz subject to change in course
   (60m) mileage for largest British river of same name
note Where continent is given river flows through two or more countries.

2

Ob 2,600m Siberia, USSR
Po 405m North Italy

3

Ain 121m *(tr. Rhone)* France
Bug (R) *Southern Bug*
Bug *Western Bug*
Chu 500m Kazakh *SSR*
Dee 20m Louth, Eire
Don 1,222m (82m) *USSR(W)*
Ems 280m W. Germany
Fly 800m Papua, New Guinea
Fox *tr. Illinois* USA
Han 800m *(tr. Yangtze)* China
Hay 350m Alberta, Canada
Ili c.750m *(tr. Yangtze)* China/USSR
Inn 320m *(tr. Danube) Swz/Aus*

Kan c.550m South China
Lek 40m branch of *Neder Rijn*
Lot 272m *(tr. Garonne)* France
Min (1) Fukien, South China
Min (2) Szechwan, North China
Oka (1) 500m *(tr. Angara)* Siberia
Oka (2) 950m *(tr. Volga)* Russia
Pit California, USA
Red (R) (1) *Song-koi*
Red (R) (2) 1,600m *tr. Mississippi*
Red (R) (3) *Red River of the North*
San 276m *(tr. Vistula)* Poland
Tom 440m *(tr. Ob)* Siberia
Uso Central Italy, Caesar's *Rubicon?*
Wei c.500m *(tr. Yellow)* China

4

Aare 181m *(tr. Rhine) Swz*
Adda 150m *(tr. Po)* Italy

RIVERS

Amur 1,767m Siberia *(b)* China
Aras 550m Turk./Iran *(b)* USSR
Beas *tr. Sutlej* Punjab, India
Bias *Beas*
Cher 200m *(tr. Loire)* France
Coco 300m Honduras/Nicaragua
Drau *Drava*
Drin 180m *Yg*/Albania
East (R) 16m New York City
Ebro 580m N.E. Spain
Eder *tr. Fulda*, W. Germany
Eger *Ohre*
Elbe 725m East *(b)* W. Germany
Enns 112m *(tr. Danube) Aus.*
Erne 72m N. Ireland/Eire
Gila 650m *(tr. Colorado)* USA
Isar 163m Austria/W. Germany
Juba 545m Somalia
Juca 250m East Spain
Kama 1,260m *(tr. Volga)* USSR(W)
Kemi 300m N.E. Finland
Kern E. California, USA
Kosi *tr. Ganges*, India
Kura 940m Turkey/USSR
Kymi 90m Finland
Labe *Elbe*
Lech 177m *(tr. Danube)* Europe
Lena 2,800m Siberia, USSR
Liri 105m Central Italy
Maas *Meuse* in Holland
Main 304m *(tr. Rhine)* W. Germany
Meta 750m *(tr. Orinoco)* S. America
Napo 550m *(tr. Amazon)* S. America
Neva 46m via Leningrad, N. USSR(W)
Nile (1) 4,145m N.E. Africa
Nile (2) *Blue N./Black N./White N.*
Nisa *Eastern Neisse/Western Neisse*
Oder 540m Poland *(b)* E. Germany
Odra *Oder* in Poland
Ohio 980m *tr. Mississippi*
Ohre 140m Bohemia, *Cz*
Oise 186m *(tr. Seine)* France
Prut 360m *(tr. Danube)* Europe
Ravi 450m *(tr. Chenab)* India
Rock 285m *tr. Mississippi*
Ruhr 145m *(tr. Rhine)* W. Germany
Salt (R) 240m *(tr. Gila)* Arizona
Sava 580m *(tr. Danube) Yg*
Seim 300m *(tr. Desna) Ukr.*
Sele South Italy

Suir 85m to Waterford, Eire
Svir 125m between lakes, USSR(W)
Tana 500m Kenya
Tarn 235m *(tr. Garonne)* France
Tisa c.600m *(tr. Danube)* Europe
Toce 54m N. Italy
Tone Japan
Umea 250m Sweden
Vaal 500m *(tr. Orange)* S. Africa
Waal arm of *Rhine*, Holland
Yalu China *(b)* N. Korea
Yana 1,000m Siberia, USSR
Yuan 400m *(tr. Yangtze)* China

5

Adige 225m N. Italy
Adour 207m S.W. France
Aisne 150m *(tr. Oise)* France
Aldan 1,767m *(tr. Lena)* USSR
Benue 870m *(tr. Niger)* W. Africa
Boyne 80m Eire
Cauca 600m *(tr. Magdalena)* Colombia
Congo now *Zaire*
Cross 400m S.E. Nigeria
Desna 740m *(tr. Dnieper)* USSR(W)
Dnepr *Dnieper*
Donau *Danube*
Douro 485m Spain/Portugal
Drava 450m *(tr. Danube) Aus./Yg*
Drina 300m *(tr. Sava) Yg*
Duero *Douro* in Spain
Dvina *Northern D./Western D.*
Eider 125m W. Germany
Giuba *Juba*
Gogra *Ghaghara*
Grand (R) (1) 250m Michigan, USA
Grand (R) (2) + *Green (R)* form
  Colorado
Green (R) 730m Utah, USA
Havel 221m *(tr. Elbe)* E. Germany
Indus 1,800m Tibet/Pakistan
Isere *tr. Rhone* S.E. France
Jacui 350m S. Brazil
Jalon *tr. Ebro*, Spain
James 340m Virginia, USA
Jumna 850m *(tr. Ganges)* India
Jurua (R) 2,000+m *(tr. Amazon)* S.
  America

Kabul c.300m *(tr. Indus)* Asia
Karun 470m s.w. Iran
Kasai 1,200+m *(tr. Zaire)* Africa
Kizil 700m Turkey
Lagan 35m N. Ireland
Lippe 110m *(tr. Rhine)* W. Germany
Loire 625m France
Marne c.325m *(tr. Seine)* France
Mesta c.175m Bulgaria/Greece
Minho 170m Spain *(b)* Portugal
Narew c.270m *(tr. Vistula)* Europe
Negro *Negro Rio/Rio Negro*
Netze *Notec*
Niger 2,600m W. Africa
North (R) 300m Kwangtung S. China
Notec 140m *(tr. Warta)* Poland
Onega 400m N. *USSR(W)*
Peace 1,050m *(tr. Slave)* Canada
Pearl (R) (or Canton*(R)*) *Chu-Kiang*
Pecos 926m *(tr. Rio Grande)* USA
Piave 125m N.E. Italy
Plate Argentina *(b)* Uruguay
Purus 2,100m *(tr. Amazon)* S. America
Rance Brittany, France
Rhone 507m *Swz*/France
Saale 225m *(tr. Elbe)* E. Germany
Saone 282 *(tr. Rhone)* France
Segre c.170m *(tr. Ebro)* Spain
Seine 473m via Paris, France
Sepik 500m New Guinea
Shari to Lake Chad, Africa
Shire 370m *(tr. Zambezi)* Africa
Siret 280m *(tr. Danube)* Romania
Slave (R) 1,260m downstream *Mackenzie*
Snowy 270m *NSW*/Victoria
Sobat 500m *(tr. White Nile)* Africa
Somme 116m N.E. France
Spree 227m *(tr. Havel)* E. Germany
Tagus Spain/Portugal
Tamar (45m) Tasmania, Australia
Tapti 450m W. India
Tarim *Tarim He*
Terek 370m N. Caucasia, USSR
Tiber 220m via Rome, Italy
Tinto 65m s.w. Spain
Tisza *Tisa*
Tobol 500m *(tr. Irtysh)* Siberia
Torne 320m Sweden *(b)* Finland

Vitim 900m *(tr. Lena)* Siberia
Volga 2,325m *USSR(W)*
Volta *White Volta*
Warta 450m *(tr. Oder)* Poland
Weser 330m W. Germany
White 690m *tr. Mississippi*
Xingu 1,200m *(tr. Amazon)* Brazil
Yonne 180m *(tr. Seine)* France
Yukon 2,000m Canada/Alaska
Zaire c.3,000m Equatorial Africa

6

Amazon 4,195m South America
Angara 1,300 *(tr. Yenisey)* Siberia
Atbara 790m *(tr. Nile)* Ethiopia/Sudan
Balsas 500m Mexico
Barito (R) c.275m Borneo
Barrow 120m to Waterford, Eire
Brazos 950m Texas, USA
Canton (R) (or Pearl *(R)*) *Chu-Kiang*
Caroni *tr. Orinoco*, Venezuela
Chenab 900m *(tr. Sutlej)* Punjab
Chiapa 200m Guatemala/Mexico
Chubut 400m Argentina
Clutha (R) 200m S. Is., New Zealand
Cunene *Kunene*
Danube 1,725m s.E. Europe
Donets 650m *(tr. Don)* USSR(W)
Fraser 850m Brit. Columbia, Canada
Gambia 700m Senegal/Gambia
Glomma 250m Norway
Harlem 8m New York City
Huai-Ho *Hwai-Ho*
Hudson 350m New York State
Hwai-Ho 765m ZZ *(tr. Yangze)* China
Irtysh 1,850m *(tr. Ob)* Siberia, USSR
Iscaro 50m *(tr. Adige)* Italy
Jhelum *tr. Indus*, Punjab
Jordan 230m Israel/Jordan
Kansas 170m *(tr. Missouri)* USA
Kolyma 1,600m Siberia, USSR
Kunene 750m Angola
Laggan *Lagan*
Liao-ho c.1,000m China
Liffey 50m to Dublin, Eire
Limmat 80m *(tr. Aare)* Swz
Lufira + *Lualaba* form *Zaire*

Mamore 1,200m *(tr. Amazon)* S. America
Manych 300m *(tr. Don)* USSR(W)
Mekong 2,500m Tibet to Vietnam
Moldau *Vitava*
Morava (1) 212m *(tr. Danube)* Aus.
Morava (2) 350m *(tr. Danube)* Yg
Muonio Finland *(b)* Sweden
Murray 2,310m inc. *Darling, AUST.*
Neckar 240m *(tr. Rhine)* W. Germany
Neisse *Eastern N./Western N.*
Nelson 1,450m inc. *Saskatchewan*
Nestos *Mesta* in Greece
Nisava 100+m *(tr. Morava)* Yg
Ogooue 500m Gabon/Congo
Olenek 1,350m Siberia, USSR
Orange 1,300m South Africa
Ottawa 625m *(tr. St Lawrence)* Canada
Parana 2,050m *tr. Rio de la Plata*
Platte 1,400m *North + South Platte*
Pregel 125m Poland
Pripet 350m *(tr. Dnieper)* USSR(W)
Rufiji 450m Tanzania
Sabine 585m Texas/Louisiana, USA
St John 450m Canada *(b)* USA
Sambre 110m *(tr. Meuse)* Europe
Sarthe 165m *(tr. Loire)* France
Scioto 250m *(tr. Ohio)* Ohio, USA
Segura 180m to Guardamar, Spain
Sereth 450m *(tr. Danube)* Europe
Severn 350m (215m) Ontario, Canada
Shilka 345m *(tr. Amur)* Siberia
Sutlej 1,000m *(tr. Indus)* Pakistan
Ticino 150m *(tr. Po)* Swz/Italy
Tigris 1,150m to *Euphrates* (s.w. Asia)
Ubangi 1,400m *(tr. Zaire)* Africa
Ussuri *tr. Amur,* China *(b)* USSR
Vienne 220m *(tr. Loire)* France
Vilyni 1,500m *(tr. Lena)* Siberia
Vitaza c.260m *(tr. Elbe)* Cz
Wupper 40m *(tr. Rhine)* W. Germany
Yakima 208m *(tr. Columbia)* USA
Yapura 1,500m *(tr. Amazon)* S. America
Yellow (R) *Hwang-Ho*

7

Alabama *tr. Tombigbee* USA

Bandama c.200m Ivory Coast
Chambal 550m *(tr. Jumna)* India
Conchos 350m *(tr. Rio Grande)* Mexico
Damodar (R) Bihar, India
Darling 1,702m *(tr Murray)* NSW
Derwent 30m (60m) Tasmania AUST.
Detroit 25m USA *(b)* Canada
Dnieper 1,400m Ukraine SSR
Durance 217m *(tr. Rhone)* France
Emscher 55m *(tr. Rhine)* W. Germany
Feather N. Carolina USA
Fitzroy 350m *d/w* W. AUST.
Gallego 110m N.E. Spain
Garonne 450m S.W. France
Glommen *Glomma*
Guapore 1,900m *(tr. Mamore)* Brazil
Hari-Rud 650m Afghan./Iran
Helmand c.850m Afghanistan
Helmund *Helmand*
Hooghly 160m arm of *Ganges*
Humbolt 300m *ev* Nevada, USA
Hwang-Ho c.3,000m *zz* China
Javarti *tr. Amazon,* Peru *(b)* Brazil
Kanawha *tr. Ohio* W. Virginia, USA
Kerulen 785m Mongolia/China
Krishna 850m S. India
Kristna *Krishna*
Lachlan 920m *tr. Murrumbidgee*
Limpopo 1,000m Southern Africa
Lualaba c.500m downstream *Zaire*
Madeira c.2,000m *(tr. Amazon)* Brazil
Meurthe *tr. Moselle,* France
Moselle 328m *(tr. Rhine)* Europe
Narmada 800m Central India
Niagara 35m Canada *(b)* USA
Orinoco 1,480m Venezuela
Orantes 250m Lebanon/Syria/Turkey
Pechora 1,120m N. USSR(W)
Potomac 290m Virginia *(b)* Maryland, USA
Pripyat *Pripet*
Rubicon *Fiumicino? Uso?* Italy
St John's 350m Florida, USA
Salinas 140m California, USA
Salween 1,800m Tibet to Burma
Salzach 130m *(tr. Inn)* Austria
San Juan (1) 90m Nicaragua *(b)* Costa Rica
San Juan (2) 400m *(tr. Colorado)* USA

Segovia 300m Honduras *(b)* Nicaragua
Shannon 224m Eire
Sheksna 100m N. *USSR(W)*
Sittang 610m Burma
Song-Koi c.800m China/Vietnam
Sungari 1,150m *(tr. Amur)* N.E. China
Tarim He Central China
Trinity 500m Texas, USA
Tsangpo 850m *Brahmaputra* in Tibet
Ucayali *Amazon* headstream, Peru
Vistula 660m Poland
Waikato 264m N. Is., N. Zealand
Warrego 400m *(tr. Darling)* AUST.
Yangtze 3,500m Tibet/China
Yarkand 500m *(tr. Tarim)* China
Yenisey 3,300m Siberia, USSR
Zambesi 2,200m S.E. Africa

8

Araguaia 1,000m *(tr. Tocontins)* Brazil
Arkansas 1,459m *tr. Mississippi*
Berezina 380m *(tr. Dnieper)* USSR(W)
Blue Nile meets *White Nile* at
  Khartoum
Canadian *(R)* 900m *(tr. Arkansas)* USA
Charente S.W. France
Cheyenne 500m *tr. Missouri*
Chindwin 500m *(tr. Irrawaddy)* Burma
Chu-Kiang 110m China/Hong Kong
Colorado (1) 530m Argentina
Colorado (2) 970m Texas
Colorado *(R)* 1,450m West USA
Columbia 1,400m W. Canada/USA
Dalalven 325m Sweden
Delaware *(R)* 315m New England, USA
Diamante 200m *(tr. Salado)* Argentina
Dniester 870m Ukraine SSR
East Main *(R)* 270m Quebec, Canada
Gatineau 300m *(tr. Ottawa)* Canada
Ghaghara 600m *(tr. Ganges)* India
Godavari 900m India
Guadiana 510m Spain *(b)* Portugal
Kentucky 1,250m *(tr. Ohio)* USA
Klondike 100m *(tr. Yukon)* Canada
Kootenai *Kootenay*
Kootenay 450m *(tr. Columbia)* Canada
Kzyl Orda Kazakh SSR

Mahanadi 520m India
Missouri 2,464m *tr. Mississippi*
Negro Rio (1) Argentina
Negro Rio (2) c.950m *(tr. Amazon)*
  Brazil
Okovango 1,000m Angola/Botswana
Pachitea 320m Peru
Paraguay 1,200m South America
Parnaiba 750m Brazil
Pei-kiang *North (R)*
Putumayo 1,000m *(tr. Amazon)* S.
  America
Rio Bravo *Rio Grande* (2)
Rio Negro 500m *(tr. Uruguay)* S.
  America
Saguenay 110m *(tr. St Lawrence)*
  Canada
St Claire 85m Canada *(b)* USA
Savannah 450m Georgia/S. Carolina,
  USA
Syr Dar'ya 1,500m Central USSR
Tennessee 782m *(tr. Ohio)* USA
Thompson 280m *(tr. Fraser)* BC,
  Canada
Wanganui 160m N. Is., New Zealand

9

Allegheny 325m *(tr. Ohio)* USA
Black Nile *Atbara*
Churchill formerly Hamilton *R.*,
  Canada
Crocodile *(R)* *Limpopo*
Des Moines 550m *tr. Mississippi*
Dimbovita *Dambovitta*
Euphrates 1,780m to *Shatt-al-Arab*
Fiumicino Central Italy, Caesar's
  Rubicon?
Indigirka 1,100m Yakut ASSR
Irrawaddy 1,250m Burma
Mackenzie 2,500m Canada
Macquarie 600m *(tr. Darling)* NSW
Magdalena 1,000m Colombia
Muskingum 240m *(tr. Ohio)* Ohio, USA
Neder Rijn 40m *Rhine* distributary,
  Holland
Rio Branco 350m *(tr. Rio Negro)* S.
  America

RIVERS

Rio Grande (1) 650m headstream of *Parana*
Rio Grande (2) c.1,885m USA *(b)* Mexico
St Maurice 325m *(tr. St Lawrence)* Canada
Tocantins 1,600m Central Brazil
Tombigbee 409m Mississippi State, USA
White Nile 500m Lake No to Khartoum
Wisconsin 600m *(tr. Mississippi)*, USA
Yarkant He *Yarkand*
Zeravshan 460m *ev* Tadzhik/Uzbek *SSR*

10

Black Volta 750m Upper Volta/Ghana
Blackwater (R) 90m Eire
Courantyne 450m Guyana
Cumberland (R) 690m *(tr. Ohio)* USA
Dambovitta 150m *(tr. Danube)* Romania
Fort George 550m Quebec, Canada
Great Whale (R) 250m Quebec, Canada
Sacramento 390m California, USA
St Lawrence 2,100m Canada *(b)* USA
San Joaquin 320m California, USA
Schuylkill 130m *(tr. Delaware)* USA
Shenandoah 170m *(tr. Potomac)* USA
Western Bug tr. *Vistula, USSR(W) (b)* Poland
White Volta 950m West Africa

11

Bahr-el-Azraq *Blue Nile*
Brahmaputra 1,800m Himalayas/Asia
Eastern Nisa *Eastern Neisse*
Guadalaviar 130m E. Spain
Madre de Dios tr. *Madeira*

Peru/Bolivia
Mississippi 3,860m inc. *tr.*, USA
Monongahela + *Allegheny* form *Ohio*
North Platte 680m *(tr. South Platte)* USA
Shatt-al-Arab final 120m *Tigris/Euphrates*
Southern Bug 533m Ukrainian *SSR*
South Platte Nebraska, see *Platte*
Western Nisa *Western Neisse*

12

Guadalquivir 350m S. Spain
Murrumbidgee 1,350m *(tr. Murray)* AUST.
Sao Francisco 1,600m Brazil
Saskatchewan Canada see *Nelson*
Ukrainian Bug *Southern Bug*
Victoria Nile *Nile* headwater stretch
Western Dvina c.635m Latvian *SSR*

13

Eastern Neisse 120m *(tr. Oder)* Poland
Glatzer Neisse *Western Neisse*
Lausitzer Nisa *Eastern Neisse*
Little Bighorn (R) 90m Wyoming/Montana
Northern Dvina 465m *USSR(W)*
Rio de la Platte *Plate*
Western Neisse 140m *(tr. Oder)* Europe

15/16/18

Lausitzer Neisse *Eastern Neisse*
Rio Grande de Norte *Rio Grande* (2)
Red River of the North 650m USA/Canada

VARIOUS
(Mountains, Freshwater Lakes, Islands, etc.)

Prefixes/suffixes variously included.
 eEp extreme Easternmost point of
 eNp extreme Northernmost point of
 eNEp extreme North-Easternmost point of
 eSp extreme Southernmost point of
 hd headland
 mt mount or mountain
 mt/r mountain range
 pen. peninsula
 rg region
 SSR Soviet Socialist Republic within USSR
 vo. volcano
 wf waterfall

3

Cos Aegean island, Greece
Kos *Cos*
Rif *mt/r*, Morocco
Yap Pacific isle (Carolines) USA

4

Alps *mt/r*, Europe
Bled glacial lake, Yugoslavia
Cook *mt* 12,349ft, *Southern Alps*
Gobi desert, China/Mongolia
Jura *mt/r*, Switzerland/France
Meru *mt* 14,953ft, Tanzania
Riff *Rif*
Rigi *mt* 5,905ft, Switzerland
Tana *lake*, source Blue Nile

5

Andes great *mt/r*, S. America
Askja *vo.*/lake/lava plain, Iceland
Atlas *mt/r*, N.W. Africa
Eiger *mt* 13,042ft, *Bernese Oberland*
Ghats *Eastern/Western Ghats*
Irazu *vo.* 11,268ft, Costa Rica
Kaffa *mt*/forest *rg*, Ethiopia

Negev desert *rg*, Israel
Tarai marsh/jungle *rg*, Nepal/India
Urals *mt/r*, European/Asian USSR
Yorke *pen.*, South Australia

6

Ararat *mt* 16,945ft, Turkey
Cho Oyo *mt* 26,967ft, Nepal/Tibet
Cradle *mt* 8,069ft, Tasmania
Elbert *mt* 14,431ft, *Rockies*, USA
El Ghor depression Israel/Jordan
Honshu main island, Japan
Kasbek *mt* 16,549ft, *Caucasus*
Kazbek *Kasbek*
Khyber pass in *Hindu Kush*
Kun Lun *mt/r*, Tibet/China
Kyushu large island, Japan
La Futa pass, *Apennines*
La Sila massif, S. Italy
Lhotse *mt* 27,890ft, Nepal/Tibet
Lop Nor marsh, China
Makalu *mt* 27,824ft, Nepal/Tibet
Pindus *mt/r*, Albania/Greece
Punjab plains *rg*, India/Pakistan
Rainer *mt*, 14,530ft, Washington, USA
Sahara great desert, N. Africa
Santis *mt* 8,216ft, Switzerland
Taunus *mt/r*, West Germany

Turfan depression, China
Zagros *mt/r*, Iran

7

Aletsch glacier, Switzerland
Balkans *mt/r*, Bulgaria
Cape Cod *pen.*, Massachusetts, USA
El Misti *mt* 19,166ft, S. Peru
Everest *mt* 29,028ft, Nepal/Tibet
Gris-Nez cape, N.E. France
Hoffman *mt* 8,108ft, *Sierra Nevada* (2)
Kara-Kum desert, USSR
Klamath *mt/r*, California/Oregon, USA
Kwen Lun *Kun Lun*
Lapland *rg*, N. Scandanavia/USSR
Lebanon *mt/r*, Lebanon/Syria
Nanling *mt/r*, S. China
Nan Shan *mt/r*, part of *Kun Lun*
Orizaba *mt* 18,701ft, Mexico
Rockies *Rocky Mountains*
Shikoku smallest major island, Japan
Sudetes *mt/r*, Czechoslovakia/Poland
The Skaw cape, *eNp* Denmark
Tibesti *mt/r*, Libya/Chad
Timarum *mt* 10,539ft, Lebanon
Zealand Danish island (inc.
  Copenhagen)

8

Alcatraz island, San Francisco Bay
Altamira caves, Spain
Ardennes hilly, wooded *rg*, Benelux
Bad Lands infertile *rg*, S. Dakota, USA
Bogdo Ula massif, Sinkiang, China
Caucasus *mt/r*, European USSR
Cotopaxi *vo.* 19,613ft, Ecuador
Demavend *mt* c.18,600ft, Iran
Durmitor *mt* 8,245ft, *Dinaric Alps*
Dust Bowl *rg* of eroded plains, USA
East Cape (1) *eNEp* Asia
East Cape (2) *eEp* New Zealand
Eldorado radium mine, Canada
Feldberg *mt* 4,905ft, *Black Forest*
Grimaldi caves, N.W. Italy
Hokkaido Large island, Japan
Iron Gate rapids on river Danube

Issyk Kul *mt* lake 2,400sq.m.,
  Tien-Shan
Jungfrau *mt* 13,642ft, *Bernese
  Oberland*
Kalahari southern African desert
Krakatoa volcanic island, Sunda Strait
Lake Chad 50,000sq.m., Africa
Lake Como 56sq.m., N. Italy
Lake Erie shallowest *Great Lake*
Manna Kea *vo.* 13,823ft, Hawaii
Manna Loa *vo.* 13,675ft, Hawaii
Mulhacen *mt* 11,420ft, *Sierra Nevada*
  (1)
Pegu Yoma *mt/r*, Burma
Poyang Hu lake 1,800sq.m., China
Pyrenees *mt/r*, France/Spain
St Helena British island, Atlantic
Sokhondo *mt* 8,230ft, *Yablonovy*
Tien Shan *mt/r*, Central Asia
Vesuvius *vo.* c.3,890ft, S. Italy

9

Aconcagua *mt* 22,835ft, *Andes*
Aniakckak *vo.* S.W. Alaska, USA
Annapurna massif 26,492ft, Nepal
Apennines *mt/r*, Italy
Bolan Pass Pakistan to Afghanistan
Catskills *mt/r*, New York, USA
Clear Cape *eSp* Eire (Clear Island)
Dolomites *mt/r*, N.E. Italy
Dukla Pass crosses *Carpathians*
Furka Pass Switzerland
Gomal Pass Pakistan to Afghanistan
Great Lake (1) Tasmania, Australia
Great Lake (2) one of 5 *Great Lakes*
Grey Range *mt/r*, Queensland,
  Australia
Himalayas vast *mt/r*, Asia
Hindu Kush *mt/r*,
  Afghanistan/Pakistan
Jebel Kesl *mt* 6,594ft, *Saharan Atlas*
Lake Huron 23,010sq.m., *Great Lake*
Lake Onega 3,765sq.m., European
  USSR
Lenin Peak *mt* 23,382ft, USSR
Main Range *mt/r*, West Malaysia
Marmolade *mt* 11,000ft, *Dolomites*
Mont Blanc *mt* 15,784ft, *Alps*

Moscow Sea artificial lake, USSR
Mount Eddy 9,038ft *Klamath*
Tirich Mir *mt* 25,426ft, *Hindu Kush*
Tongariro *vo.*, N. Is., New Zealand
Weisshorn *mt* 14,707ft, *Alps*
Yablonovy *mt/r*, Siberia, USSR
Zardeh Kuh *mt* 14,921ft, *Zagros*
Zugspitze *mt* 9,735ft, *Bavarian Alps*

10

Angel Falls *wf* 3,212ft drop, Venezuela
Beerenberg *vo.*, Jan Mayen Island,
   Norway
Black Hills *mt/r*, S. Dakota, USA
Castle Peak 14,115ft, *Elk Mountains*
Chimborazo *mt* 20,610ft, Ecuador
Coast Range *mt/r*, Pacific coast, USA
Devil's Isle ex penal colony, S.
   America
Elgon Mount 14,100ft, Kenya/Uganda
Golden Horn *pen.*, Bosporus, Turkey
Graian Alps *mt/r*, France/Italy
Great Atali *mt/r*, Mongolia/Siberia
Great Atlas *mt/r*, part of *Atlas*
Great Lakes (5) 4 form US/Canada
   border
Hispaniola island, Haiti/Dominican
   Republic
Horney Peak *mt* 7,420ft, *Black Hills*
Jebel Aissa *mt* 7,350ft, *Saharan Atlas*
Jebel Aurès *mt* 7,644ft, *Saharan Atlas*
Julian Alps *mt/r*, Switzerland/France
Lake Geneva 223sq.m., Switzerland
Lake Pepius 1,400sq.m., Estonian *SSR*
Lough Neagh 153sq.m., Northern
   Ireland
Mato Grosso plateau, Brazil
Matterhorn *mt* 14,678ft, Switzerland
Monte Corno *mt* 9,583ft, Italy
Mount Adams 12,470ft, Washington,
   USA
Mount Athos 6,670ft, Greece
Mount Halla *vo.*, Cheju Island, S.
   Korea
Mount Kenya *vo.* 17,040ft, Kenya
Okefenokee swamp, Georgia/Florida,
   USA
Serra do Mar *mt/r*, Brazil

Shipka Pass crosses *Balkans*
Susten Pass Switzerland
Tanganyika large African lake
Tarim Basin depression, China
Thal Desert Pakistan
Thar Desert India/Pakistan
Tung Ting Hu lake 2,500sq.m., China
Wetterhorn *mt* 12,165ft, Switzerland
Wilkes Land featureless plateau,
   Antarctic

11

Alaska Range *mt/r* USA
Barrow Point *hd*, *eNp* USA (Alaska)
Black Forest *Schwarzwald*
Brenner Pass Italy to Austria
Brooks Range *mt/r*, N. Alaska, USA
Carpathians *mt/r*, E. Europe
Che-ling Pass crosses *Nanling*
Cottian Alps *mt/r* France/Spain
Daryal Gorge *Caucasus*, Georgian *SSR*
Death Valley arid *rg*, California, USA
Dinaric Alps *mt/r* Yugoslavia/Albania
Dismal Swamp morass, south-west USA
Glittertind *mt* 8,140ft, S. Norway
Grand Canyon Arizona, USA
Grand Combin *mt* 14,164ft,
   Switzerland
Kanchipuram *mt* 28,146ft,
   Nepal/Sikkim
Kilimanjaro *mt* 19,340ft, Tanzania
Lake Ontario 7,500sq.m. *Great Lake*
Lough Corrib 68sq.m., Eire
Mammoth Cave Kentucky, USA
Meiling Pass crosses *Nanling*
Mount Carmel 1,818ft, N.W. Israel
Mount Delphi Euboea Island, Greece
Mount Elbruz 18,463ft, *Caucasus*
Mount Katmai *vo.* 7,000ft, Alaska,
   USA
Pennine Alps part of (Swiss) *Alps*
Rann of Kutch desert *rg*,
   India/Pakistan
Schwarzwald *mt*/forest *rg*, W.
   Germany
Selwyn Range *mt/r*, Queensland,
   Australia
Sierra Madre two *mt/rs*, Mexico

Stelvio Pass Italy to Switzerland
Swabian Alps *mt/r*, Germany
Yellowstone lake/National Park, USA

12

Appalachians parallel *mt/rs*, USA
Barbary Coast east N. Africa
Bavarian Alps *mt/r*, West Germany
Cape Farewell *eSp* Greenland
Darling Downs plateau, Queensland, Australia
Dauphine Alps *mt/r*, S.E. France
Eastern Ghats *mt/r*, S. India
Eisenerz Alps *mt/r*, Austria
Elk Mountains *mt/r*, Colorado, USA
Gran Paradiso *mt* 13,320ft, *Graian Alps*
Holy Mountain *Mount Athos*
Ida Mountains *mt/r*, N.W. Turkey
Jebel Toubkal *mt* 13,578ft, *Atlas*
Lake Michigan 23,900sq.m., *Great Lake*
Lake Superior 32,000sq.m., *Great Lake*
Lake Victoria 26,000sq.m., Africa
Mount Kaufman *Lenin Peak*
Mount Kinbalu 13,455ft, Borneo
Mount Olympus 9,753ft, Greece
Mount Palomar 6,126ft, California
Mount Whitney 14,898ft *Sierra Nevada* (2)
Niagara Falls *wf*, Canada/USA
Reindeer Lake 2,500sq.m., Canada
Saharan Atlas *Atlas mt/r* in Algeria
Sierra Morena *mt/r*, Spain
Sierra Nevada (1) *mt/r*, Spain
Sierra Nevada (2) *mt/r*, California, USA
Southern Alps *mt/r*, N.Is., New Zealand
Victoria Falls *wf*, R. Zambezi, Zaire
Western Ghats *mt/r*, S. India

13

Arabian Desert eastern Egypt
Atacama Desert north Chile
Carrantuchill *mt* 3,414ft, Kerry, Eire

Crows Nest Pass crosses Canadian *Rockies*
Cumberland Gap *mt/r* gap, Kentucky, USA
Flinders Range *mt/r*, South Australia
Goodwin-Austen *mt* (K2) 28,250ft, Tibet/China
Great Bear Lake 14,000sq.m., Canada
Gross Glockner *mt* and pass, Austria
Harz Mountains *mt/r*, E/W Germany
Mount Gargarus 5,797ft, *Ida Mountains*
Mount of Olives east of Jerusalem
Pripet Marshes 18,000sq.m. *rg*, USSR
Semmering Pass across *Alps*, Austria
Table Mountain 3,549ft, S. Africa
Tasman Glacier S.Is., New Zealand
Western Desert Egypt

14

Altai Mountains *mt/r*, Mongolia
Australian Alps part Gr. Dividing Range, Australia
Cape of Good Hope *hd*, S. Africa
Great St Bernard *mt* and pass, Switzerland
Great Slave Lake 11,000sq.m., Canada
Green Mountains part of *Appalachians*
Magnet Mountain Southern *Urals*
Mount Communism 24,590ft, *Pamir Mountains*
Mount Koskiusko 7,310ft, *Alps*, Austria
Mount Mansfield 4,393ft *Green Mountains*
Mount Parnassus Greece (Delphic oracle site)
Ozark Mountains Oklahoma/ Arkansas, USA
Pamir Mountains plateau, central Asia
Rocky Mountains vast *mt/r*, Alaska to Mexico
Sayan Mountains *mt/r*, USSR/China
Snowy Mountains part of *Australian Alps*
Tatra Mountains part of *Carpathians*
Yaila Mountains Ukrainian *SSR*

Yellowhead Pass crosses *Rockies*,
  Canada

15

Bernese Oberland alpine *rg*,
  Switzerland
Great Rift Valley 3,000m, Asia/Africa
Little St Bernard *mt* and pass, *Graian
  Alps*
Macdonnell Range *mt/r*, Australia
Mount Lofty Range *mt/r*, South
  Australia

Mount Washington 6,288ft,
  Appalachians
San Andreas Fault geol. factor,
  California
Sierra Pacaraima *mt/r*,
  Brazil/Venezuela

16

Craters of the Moon volcanic scenic *rg*,
  Idaho
Kicking Horse Pass crosses *Rockies*,
  Canada

HISTORY

IMPERIAL MONARCHS
(names, titles, dynasties)

Aus. Austrian (1804–1918)
Ch. Chinese (2697BC–1911AD)
emp. emperor or empress regnant
eRm Eastern Roman (Byzantine 393–1453)
dy. dynasty
Ger. German (1871–1918)
HRm Holy Roman (European 800–1806)
Ind. Indian (British monarchs 1876–1947)
Pers. Persian (550BC–1980AD)
Rm Roman (27BC–393AD)
Rus. Russian (1462–1918)
wRm Western Roman (393–480)

3

Han *Ch. dy.* 206BC–220AD
Leo various *eRm emp.*
Sui *Ch. dy.* 381–618AD
Yin *Ch. dy.* 1766–1122BC
Zoe joint *eRm emp.* 1042

4

Anne *Rus. emp.* 1730/40
Ch'in *Ch. dy.* 255–206BC
Chou *Ch. dy.* 1122–255BC
czar *title Rus.* emperor
Geta *Rm emp.* 211AD
Hsia *Ch. dy.* 2205–1766BC
Ivan various *Rus. emp.*
John various *eRm/wRm emp.*
Karl *Aus. emp.* 1916/18
Ming *Ch. dy.* 1368–1644
Nero *Rm emp.* 54–68AD
Otho *Rm emp.* 68AD
Otto various *HRm. emp.*
Paul *Rus. emp.* 1796–1801
P'u-yi *Ch. emp.* 1908–1911

shah title *Pers. emp.*
Sung *Ch. dy.* 960–1279
T'ang *Ch. dy.* 618–907
tsar *czar*
Yuan *Mongol*
Zeno *eRm emp.* 474–491

5

Basil various *eRm emp.*
Boris *Rus. emp.* 1598–1605
Cyrus first *Pers. emp.*
Ducas *eRm dy.* 1059–81
Franz *Aus. emp.* 1804–35
Galba *Rm. emp.* 68AD
Guido *HRm emp.* 887–894
Irene *eRm emp.* 797–802
Isaac various *eRm emp.*
Jimmu first *Jap. emp.* c.660BC
Kao Ti founded *Han dy.*
Kavad various *Pers. emp.*
Nerva *Rm emp* 96–98
Niger joint *Rm emp.* 193
Peter various *Rus. emp.*
Rurik *Rus. dy.* 1462–1598

IMPERIAL MONARCHS

Saxon *HRm emps* 918–1024
Shang *Yin*
Titus *Rm emp.* 79–81
Wen Ti founded *Sui dy.*

6

Alexis *Rus. emp.* 1645–76
Arnulf *HRm emp.* 896–899
Avitus *wRm emp.* 455–456
Caesar title *Rm emp.* (also reflected by czar, shah, etc.)
Ch'ing *Manchu*
Conrad various *HRm emp.*
Darius various *Pers. emp.*
Decius *Rm emp.* 249–251
Gallus *Rm emp.* 251–253
Jovian *Rm (eRm) emp.* 363–4
Julian *Rm (eRm) emp.* 361–3
Justin various *eRm emp.*
kaiser title *Ger. emp.*
Lothar various *HRm emp.*
Manchu *Ch. dy.* 1644–1911
mikado title Japanese *emp.* (European term)
Mongol *Ch. dy.* 1206–1368
Phocas *eRm emp.* 602–10
Probus *Rm emp.* 276–82
Rudolf various *HRm* emp.
Rupert *HRm emp.* 1400–10
Salian *HRm emps* 1024–1138
Sophia *Rus.* regent 1682–9
Tafari *Haile Selassie*
Tai Tsu *Jenghiz Khan*
Trajan *Rm emp.* 98–117
Wenzel *HRm emp.* 1376–1400
Wu Wang founded *Chou dy.*
Xerxes various *Pers. emp.*

7

Amorian *eRm dy.* 820–67
Angelus *eRm dy.* 1185–1204
Carinus joint *Rm emp.* 284
czarina title *Rus.* empress
Florian *Rm emp.* 276
Godunov *Rus. dy.* 1598–1613
Hadrian *Rm emp.* 117–38

Leonine *eRm dy.* 457–518
Leopold various *HRm emp.*
Marcian *eRm emp.* 450–7
Maximus *wRm emp.* 455
Michael *Rus. emp.* 1613–45
Pahlevi *Pers. dy.* 1925–1980
Romanov *Rus. dy.* 1613–1917
Romulus *wRm emp.* 475–6
Severus *wRm emp.* 461–5
Shih Tsu *Kublai Khan*
Tacitus *Rm emp.* 275–6
Vassili *Rus. emp.* 1505–33

8

Arcadius *Rm (eRm) emp.* 395–408
Augustus first *Rm emp* 27BC–14AD
Aurelian *Rm emp.* 270–5
Berengar *HRm emp.* 915–18
Caligula *Rm emp.* 37–41
Claudius *Rm emp.* 41–54
czarevna daughter *czar*: wife *czarevich*
czaritza *czarina*
Domitian *Rm emp.* 81–96
Hapsburg *HRm dy.* 1438–1806
Honorius *wRm emp.* 393–423
Isaurian *eRm dy.* 717–820
Iturbide Mexican *emp.* 1822–3
Lascarid *eRm dy.* 1204–58
Majorian *wRm emp.* 457–61
Matthais *HRm emp.* 1612–19
Napoleon French *emps* 1804–14: 1852–70
Nicholas *Rus. emps* 1825–55: 1894–1917
Octavius *Augustus*
Olybrius *wRm emp.* 472–3
padishah *shah: kaiser-i-Hind*
Pertinax joint *Rm emp.* 193
Phraates various *Pers. emp.*
Theodora *eRm emp.* 1042, 1055–6
Theodore various *eRm/Rus. emp.*
Tiberius *Rm emp.* 14–37
Timur Beg *Tamberlaine*
tsarevna *czarevna*
tsaritsa *czarina*
Victoria *Ind. emp.* 1876–1901

9

Alexander various *Rus. emp.*
Athemius *wRm emp.* 467–72
Bonaparte *Buonaparte*
Catherine *Rus. emp.* 1725–7: 1762–96
Comnenian *eRm dy.* 1081–1185
czarevich a son of *czar*
Elizabeth *Rus. emp.* 1741–62
Ferdinand various *Aus./HRm emp.*
Frederick various *HRm emp.*
Heraclian *eRm dy.* 610–717
Heraclius *eRm emp.* 610–41
Justinian *eRm dy.* 518–610: various *emp.*
Sigismund *HRm emp.* 1410–37
Tamerlane *Tamburlaine*
tsarevich *czarevich*
Vespasian *Rm emp.* 68–79
Vitellius *Rm emp.* 68

10

Androchius various *eRm emp.*
Barbarossa *HRm emp.* 1152–90
Buonaparte French *dy. Napoleon*
czarevitch *czarevich*
Diocletian *Rm emp.* 284–305
Elagabalus *Rm emp.* 218–22
Kaiser Bill (William III) *Ger. emp.*
Kublai Khan *Ch. emp.* 1260–94
Leo the Wise (Leo VI) *eRm emp.* 886–912
Macedonian *eRm dy.* 867–1059
Maximilian Mexican: *HRm emp.*
Nicephorus various *eRm emp.*
Theodosian *eRm dy.* 379–457
Theodosius various *e/wRm emp.*
Theophilus *eRm emp.* 829–42
tsarevitch *czarevich*

11

cesarevitch eldest son of *czar*
cesarewitch *cesarevitch*
Charlemagne first *HRm emp.* 800–14
Constantine various *Rm/eRm emp.*
Constantius various *wRm emp.*
Franz Joseph *Aus. emp.* 1848–1916

Heracleonas *eRm emp.* 641
Jenghiz Khan *Ch. emp.* 1206–27
Julius Nepos *wRm emp.* 473–80
kaiser-i-Hind title *Ind. emp.*
Mithridates *Pers. emp.* 123–90BC
Palaeologan *HRm dy.* 1258–1453
Philippicus *eRm emp.* 711–13
Shih Huang Ti founded *Ch'in dy.*
Tamberlaine *Pers.* (Mongol) *emp.* died 1405
tsesarevitch *cesarevitch*
Valentinian various *Rm/wRm emp.*

12

Antonius Pius *Rm emp.* 138–61
Hohenstaufen *HRm dy.* 1138–1410
Hohenzollern *Ger. dy.* 1871–1918
Ivan the Great *Rus. emp.* 1462–1505
Leo the Chazar *eRm emp.* 775–80
tsesarevitch *cesarevitch*

13

Adolf of Nassau *HRm emp.* 1292–8
Charles the Fat *HRm emp.* 882–7
Constantinius *Rm(eRm) dy.* c.309–78
Haile Selassie last Ethiopian *emp.*
Henry the Black *HRm emp.* 1037–56
Henry the Saint *HRm emp.* 1002–24
Louis the Child *HRm emp.* 899–901
Louis the Pious *HRm emp.* 814–40
Peter the Great *Rus. emp.* 1682–1725

14

Charles the Bald *HRm emp.* 875–81
Conrad the Salic *HRm emp.* 1024–37
Didius Julianus joint *Rm emp.* 193
Henry the Fowler *HRm emp.* 918–36
Leo the Isaurian *eRm emp.* 717–40
Marcus Aurelius *Rm emp.* 161–80

15

Ivan the Terrible *Rus. emp.* 1533–84
Louis of Provence *HRm emp.* 901–11
Septimus Severus *Rm emp.* 193–211

MONARCHS AND ENGLISH ROYAL HOUSES (Dynasties)

Also see WARRIORS (p. 125)

3

Ali of the Hejaz
Ida Bernica (Northumbria)
Ine Wessex
Zog Albania

4

Abel Denmark
Anna East Anglia
Anne England
Coel Wessex
Cnut *Canute*
Dubh Scotland
Edwy England
Elle Northumbria
Eric Norway: Sweden: Denmark
Erik Norway
Inge Norway: Sweden
John England: Portugal: France, etc.
Juan Castile/Leon
Karl Hungary
Knut Denmark
Luis Spain
Luiz Portugal
Mary England: Scotland
Nils Denmark
Octa Kent
Offa Mercia
Oisc Kent
Olaf Norway: Sweden: Denmark
Oswy Mercia: Bernica (Northumbria)
Otto Bavaria: Greece
Paul Greece
Saul Biblical
York (House of) 1461–1485

5

Aelle Deria (Northumbria)
Anjou (House of) *Plantagenet*
Carol Rumania
Cearl Mercia
Chaka Zulu
David Scotland: Biblical
Diniz Portugal
Edgar Scotland
Edred England
Egric East Anglia
Eocha Scotland
Henry England: France
Idris Libya
James Scotland: England/Scotland
Louis France: Poland
Milan Serbia
Oscar Sweden
Osred Northumbria
Osric Northumbria
Peada Mercia
Pedro Portugal
Penda Mercia
Peter Yugoslavia
Pybba Mercia
Rufus William II, England
Tudor (House of) 1485–1603

6

Albert Belgium
Arthur legendary British
Beorna East Anglia
Birger Sweden
Canute England
Cedric (House of) 802–1016: 1042–1066
Cenred Mercia
Creoda Mercia

Cynric Wessex
Donald Scotland
Duncan Scotland
Edmund England
Edward England
Egbert England
Farouk Egypt
George England: Greece
Godwin (House of) 1066
Haakon Norway
Harold England
Indulf Scotland
Joseph Portugal
Leszek Poland
Ludeca Mercia
Ludwig Bavaria
Lulach Scotland
Manoel Portugal
Orange (House of) joint 1689–94: 1694–1702
Oswald East Anglia
Philip France: Spain
Salote Queen of Tonga
Sancho Portugal
Stuart (House of) 1603–49: 1660–94: 1702–14
Sverre Norway
Waclaw Poland
Wiglaf Mercia

7

Alfonso Spain
Alfrith Northumbria
Amadeus Spain
Casimir Poland
Ceawlin Wessex
Charles England: Spain
Cuilean Scotland
Cullean Scotland
Denmark (House of) 1016–1042
Eadbald Kent: Mercia
Elfwald East Anglia
Enrique Castile/Leon
Eric Lam Denmark
Eystein Norway
Francis France
Hanover (House of) 1714–1901
Hengest Kent

Juliana Holland
Kenneth Scotland
Macbeth Scotland
Malcolm Scotland
Mieszko Poland
Michael Rumania
Redwald East Anglia
Richard England
Solomon Biblical: Zulu
Stenkil Sweden
Stephen England
Tarquin Ancient Rome
Umberto Italy
Victoria England
William England: Holland
Windsor (House of) 1910 – (adopted 1917) formerly Saxe-Coburg-Gotha

8

Abdullah Jordan
Bolesaw Poland
Boudicca Ancient British
Cetewayo Zulu
Coelwulf Mercia
Coenwulf Mercia
Eardwulf Northumbria
Ecgfrith Northumbria
Eorpwald East Anglia
Ethelred England
Gustavus Sweden
Isabella Castile
Margaret Scotland/Norway/Sweden
Normandy (House of) 1016–1154
Seaxburg Wessex
Sihanouk Cambodia
Wulfhere Mercia

9

Alexander Scotland
Athelstan England
Beornwulf Mercia
Brian Boru Ireland
Cunobelin Ancient British
Elizabeth England
Ethelhere East Anglia
Ethelwald East Anglia

MONARCHS AND ENGLISH ROYAL HOUSES

Ethelwulf England
Frederick Prussia: Sweden
Ferdinand Portugal: Aragon
Hugh Capet France
Lancaster (House of) 1399–1461:
  1470–71
Old Rowley Charles II, England
Sigismund Poland
Wenceslas Bohemia
Wladislaw Poland

10

Bloody Mary Mary, England
Donald Bane Scotland
Gorm the Old Denmark
Maximilian Bavaria
Olaf Hunger Denmark
Skjoldungs, the (House of) *Denmark*
Tribhuvana Nepal
The Sun King Louis XIV, France
Wilhelmina Holland

11

Coeur de Lion Richard I, England
Constantine Greece: Scotland
Emund the Old Sweden
Inge the Good Sweden
John Balliol Scotland
Maria the Mad Portugal
Plantagenet (House of) 1154–1399

12

Bluff King Hal Henry VIII, England
Eric Kipping Denmark
Lady of Norway *Margaret*
Lady of Sweden *Margaret*

13

Alfonso the Fat Portugal
Ananda Mahidol Thailand
Ethelwald Moll Northumbria
Good Queen Bess Elizabeth I, England
Louis-Philippe France
Magnus the Good Norway
Pedro the Cruel Castile/Leon
Victor Amadeus Sardinia

14

Alfonso the Wise Castile/Leon
Alfred the Great England
Brandy-faced Nan Anne, England
Edward the Elder England
Magnus Barelegs Norway
Pedro the Severe Portugal
Robert the Bruce Scotland
Stephen Bathory Poland
Svein Forkbeard Denmark
Uther Pendragon legendary British
Victor Emmanuel Italy
William the Lion Scotland

POPES AND ANTIPOPES

ap antipope ('Pope' as uncanonical prefix to name)
app antipopes
bl beatified ('Blessed' or 'Bl' as prefix to name)
p pope
pp popes
ss saints
st saint ('Saint', 'St' or 'S' as prefix to name)
note (1) Only one antipope (St Hippolytus) was canonized; all other saints refer to the legitimate pope.
(2) numbers refer to totals e.g. Leo 13 popes, 4 of whom have been canonized.

3

Leo 13*pp*: 4*ss*

4

John 23*pp*: 2*app*: *st*
Paul 6*pp*: *st*
Pius 12*pp*: 3*ss*

5

Conon *p*
Donus *p*
Felix 3*pp*: 2*ap*: 3*ss*
Gaius *p, st*
Lando *p*
Linus *p, st*
Peter *p, st*
Soter *p, st*
Urban 8*pp*: *st*: 2*bl*

6

Adrian 6*pp*: *st*: *English pope*
Agatho *p, st*
Albert *ap*
Fabian *p, st*
Julius 3*pp*: *st*
Lucius 3*pp*: *st*
Marcus *p, st*

Martin 5*pp*: *st*
Philip *ap*
Sixtus 5*pp*: 3*ss*
Victor 3*pp*: 2*app*: *bl*
Xystus St Sixtus I

7

Anteros *p, st*
Clement 14*pp*: 3*app*: *st*
Damasus 2*pp*: *st*
Gregory (1) 16*pp*: 2*app*: 5*ss*
Gregory (2) chant (Gregory 1)
  calendar (Gregory XIII)
Hyginus *p, st*
Marinus 2*pp*
Paschal 2*pp*: 2*app*: *st*
Ronanus *p*
Sergius 4*pp*: *st*
Stephen 3*pp*: *st*
Ursinus *ap*
Zosimus *p, st*

8

Agapetus 2*pp*: *st*
Anicetus *p, st*
Benedict 15*pp*: 3*app*: 2*ss*
Boniface 9*pp*: *ap*: 2*ss*
Caliztus 3*pp*: *ap*: *st*
Eugenius 3*pp*: *st*: *bl*

POPES AND ANTIPOPES

Eulalius *ap*
Eusebius *p, st*
Formosus *p*
Gelasius 2*pp*: *st*
Hilarius *p, st*
Honorius 4*pp*: *ap*
Innocent 13*pp*: *ap*: 2*ss*: *bl*
John Paul current and previous *pp*
Liberius *p, st*
Nicholas 5*pp*: *ap*: *st*
Novation *ap*
Pelagius 2*pp*
Pope Joan mythical female pope
Pope John John XXIII
Sabinian *p, st*
Siricius *p, st*
Theodore 2*pp*: *ap*
Vigilius *p*
Vitalian *p, st*

Miltiades *p, st*
Pontianus *p, st*
Severinus *p*
Silverius *p, st*
Sisinnius *p*
Sylvester 3*pp*: *ap*: *st*
Symmachus *p, st*
Theodoric *ap*
Zacharius *p, st*

10

Anastasius 4*pp*: *ap*: *st*
Hildebrand *Gregory the Great*
Hippolytus *ap, st*
Laurentius *ap*
Simplicicus *p, st*
Telephorus *p, st*
Valentinus *p*
Zephyrinus *p, st*

9

Adeodatus 2*pp*
Alexander 8*pp*: *ap*: *st*
Anacletus *p*: *ap*: *st*
Black Pope see RELIGIOUS TERMS
   (p. 350)
Celestine 5*pp*: *ap*: 2*ss*
Cornelius *p, st*
Deusdedit *p, st*
Dionysius *p, st*
Dioscorus *ap*
Evaristus *p, st*
Hormisdas *p, st*
Marcellus 2*pp*: *st*

11

Christopher *ap*
Constantine *p*: *ap*
English Pope Nicholas Breakspear
Eleutherius *p, st*
Eutychianus *p, st*
Leo the Great St Leo I
Marcellinus *p, st*

15

Gregory the Great St Gregory VII

PRESIDENTS

(USA where dated and unspecified)

3

Abe *Lincoln*
Bru Cuba
F.D.R. *Roosevelt, Franklin Delano*
Ike *Eisenhower*

J.F.K. *Kennedy*
L.B.J. *Johnson, Lyndon Baines*
Roy Haiti

4

Amin, Idi Uganda
Brum Uruguay
Coty France
Daza Bolivia
Diaz Mexico
Frei Chile
Ford, Gerald 1974–77
Gill Paraguay
Jack *Kennedy*
Khan, Ayub Pakistan
Khan, Yahya Pakistan
Pena Argentina: Paraguay
Polk, J. Knox 1845–49
Rhee, Syngman South Korea
Roca Argentina
Taft, William Howard 1909–13
Tito Yugoslavia
Toro Bolivia

5

Adams, John 1797–1801
Adams, John Quincy 1825–29
Benes Czechoslovakia
Davis, Jefferson The Confederacy
Grant, Ulysses S. 1869–77
Hayes, Rutherford B. 1877–81
Jerry *Ford*
Jimmy *Carter*
Mitre Argentina
Montt Chile
Nixon, Richard Milhous 1968–74
Palma Guatemala
Pando Bolivia
Pardo Peru
Peron Argentina
Pieck East Germany
Plaza Ecuador
Prado Peru
Simon Haiti
Sucre Bolivia
Swart South Africa
Teddy *Roosevelt, Theodore*
Tildy Hungary
Tyler, John 1841–45
Ulate Costa Rica

6

Arthur, Chester A. 1881–85
Auriol France
Balewa Nigeria
Blanco Bolivia
Branco Brazil
Cabste Latvia
Carnot France
Carter, James 1977–81
Castro Portugal: Venezuela
Doumer France
Dupont Rhodesia
Flores Ecuador
Franco Paraguay
Hoover, Herbert C. 1929–33
Joseph, Archduke Hungary
Juarez Mexico
Lebrun France
Lincoln, Abraham 1861–65
Miklas Austria
Mobutu Congo
Monroe, James 1817–25
Nasser Egypt/UAR
Neguib Egypt
Ojukwu Biafra
Pierce, Franklin 1853–57
Prasad India
Somoza Nicaragua
Taylor, Zachary 1849–50
Truman, Harry S. 1945–53
Tubman Liberia
Vargas Brazil
Wilson, Woodrow 1913–21

7

Ataturk Turkey
Auguste Haiti
Barrios Guatemala
Batista Cuba
Carrera Guatemala
Carrion Ecuador
Harding, Warren G. 1921–23
Jackson, Andrew 1829–37
Johnson, Andrew 1865–69
Johnson, Lyndon Baines 1963–69
Kennedy, John Fitzgerald 1961–63
Madison, James 1809–17

Masaryk Czechoslovakia
Neichev Bulgaria
Nkrumah Ghana
Papa Doc *Duvalier*
Pierrot Haiti
Smetona Lithuania
Tshombe Katanga
Ulmanis Latvia

8

Ben Bella Algeria
Big Daddy *Amin*
Buchanan, James 1857–61
Childers, Erskine Eire
Coolidge, Calvin 1923–29
Cosgrave Irish Free State
de Gaulle France
de Nicola Italy
De Valera Eire
Duvalier Haiti
Figueres Costa Rica
Fillmore, Millard 1850–53
Garfield, James 1881
Gonzalez Chile: Mexico: Paraguay
Harrison, Benjamin 1889–93
Harrison, W. H. Mar.–Apr. 1841
Kasavubu Congo
Kenyatta Kenya
Makarios, Archbishop Cyprus
McKinley, William 1897–1901
O'Higgins Chile
Pompidou France
Sikorski, General Free Polish Forces
Simon Sam Haiti
Trujillo Dominican Republic
Van Buren, Martin 1837–41

Victoria Mexico

9

Bjornsson Iceland
Cleveland, Grover 1885–89: 1893–97
De la Plaza Argentina
Jefferson, Thomas 1801–09
Roosevelt, Franklin Delano 1933–45
Roosevelt, Theodore 1901–09
Santa Anna Mexico
Santa Cruz Bolivia and Peru
Sun Yat-sen China
Villaroel Bolivia

10

Buonaparte, Louis Napoleon France
Christophe, 'King' Haiti
Dessalines, 'Emperor' Haiti
Eisenhower, Dwight David 1952–61
Hindenburg Germany
Santa Maria Chile
Washington, George 1789–97

11

Boumedienne Algeria
Sanclemente Columbia
Tricky Dicky *Nixon*

13

Chiang Kai-shek China

PRIME MINISTERS OR EQUIVALENT HEADS OF ADMINISTRATIONS

(United Kingdom where unspecified)

2

Nu, U Burma

3

Law *Bonar Law*
Lee Singapore
Saw, Ang Burma, murdered 1947
Saw, U Burma, murdered Ang Saw

4

Avon, Earl of *Eden*
Bach Austria 1852–59
Beck Austria 1906–08
Blum France
Bute, Earl of 1762–63
Cook Australia 1913–14
Eden, Sir Anthony 1955–57
Figl Chancellor, Austria 1945–53
Grey, Earl 1830–1834
Holt Australia, drowned 1967
Home, Earl of *Douglas-Home*
Meir, Mrs Golda Israel
More, Sir Thomas Lord High
   Chancellor
Nagy, Imre Hungary
Nash New Zealand 1957–60
Peel, Sir Robert 1834–5: 1841–6
Pitt, William 1783–1801: 1804–06
Reid Australia 1904–5
Tojo Japanese War Leader
Ward N. Zealand 1906–11: 1928–30

5

Botha first S. African PM 1910

Bruce Australia 1923–29
Debre France
Derby, Earl of 1866–68
Ender Austrian Chancellor
Heath, Edward 1970–74
Kei-ki *Yoshinobu*
Laval France 1935–6
Lenin chairman of Council, USSR
Lyons Australia 1931–39
Malan, Dr South Africa
Nehru, Pandit India
North, Lord 1770–82
Price, George Belize
Smith, Ian Rhodesia
Smuts, General South Africa
Spaak Belgium
Stoph premier, East Germany
Yugov premier, Bulgaria

6

Abbott Canada 1891–92
Attlee, Clement (Earl) 1945–1951
Barton first PM Australia 1901–03
Borden Canada 1911–20
Brandt Chancellor, West Germany
Brooke, Sir Basil *Brookeborough*
Curtin Australia 1941–45
Deakin Australia 1903–4: 1905–08:
   1909–10
Dubcek Party Secretary,
   Czechoslovakia
Erhard Chancellor, West Germany
Fisher Australia 1908–9: 1910–13:
   1914–15
Hitler, Adolf Chancellor, Germany
Hughes Australia 1915–23
O'Neill, Capt. Terence Northern
   Ireland
Pelham, Hon. Henry 1743–54

PRIME MINISTERS ETC.

Savage New Zealand 1935–40
shogun title, Japanese leader
Stalin chairman of Council, USSR
Wilson, Sir Harold 1964–70: 1974–76
Wolsey, Cardinal Lord High
    Chancellor
Zahedi, General Iran

7

Asquith, Herbert Henry 1908–16
Baldwin, Stanley 1923–24: 1924–29:
    1935–37
Balfour, Arthur James 1902–05
Canning, George 1827
Chatham, Earl of 1766–68
Gomulka party secretary, Poland
Grafton, Duke of 1768–70
Holland New Zealand 1949–57
Mazarin, Cardinal first minister,
    France
Menzies Australia 1934–41: 1949–66
Otomaro, Otomo first shogun 794AD
Papagos Greece
Pearson Canada 1963–68
Russell, Lord John 1846–52
Salazar, Dr Portugal 1932–68
Schuman France
Shastri, Jan India
Tshombe Congo (see PRESIDENTS,
    p. 120)
Vorster South Africa
Walpole, Sir Robert first PM
Whitlam, Gough Australia, sacked by
    Gov. Gen.

8

Abdullah, Sheikh premier, Kashmir
Aberdeen, Earl of 1852–55
Adenauer chancellor, West Germany
Bismarck 'The Iron Chancellor',
    Germany
Bonar Law, Andrew 1922–23
Bulganin chairman of Council, USSR
Cromwell, Thomas Lord High
    Chancellor
Disraeli, Benjamin 1868: 1874–80

Goderich, Viscount 1827–28
Kerensky premier, Russia
Malenkov chairman of Council, USSR
Menderes premier, Turkey
Mussadeq, Dr Iran
Perceval, Spencer 1809–12
Portland, Duke of 1783: 1807–09
Rosebery, Earl of 1894–95
Songgram, Pibul Thailand
Strijdom South Africa
SuperMac Macmillan
Verwoerd, Dr South Africa
Yoritomo powerful shogun 1192AD

9

Ben Gurion Israel
Callaghan, James 1976–79
Chou En-lai first communist PM China
Churchill, Sir Winston 1940–45:
    1951–55
Gladstone, William Ewart 1868–74:
    1880–05: 1886: 1892–4
Grenville, George 1763–65
Grenville, Lord William 1806–07
Karamanlis Greece
Khruschev chairman of Council, USSR
Liverpool, Earl of 1812–27
Macdonald first PM Canada 1867–73
MacDonald, James Ramsey 1924:
    1929–35
Macmillan, Harold 1957–63
Melbourne, Viscount 1834: 1835–41
Newcastle, Duke of 1754–56
Pelletier Minister of State, Monaco
Pilsudski Poland 1918–19: 1926–35
Richelieu, Cardinal first minister,
    France
Salisbury, Marquis of 1885–6:
    1886–92: 1895–1902
Shelburne, Earl of 1782–83
St Laurent Canada 1948–57
Yoshinobu last shogun 1866–67

10

Devonshire, Duke of 1756–57
Paderewski Poland 1919–21

Palmerston, Viscount 1855–8: 1859–65
Pig-iron Bob Sir Robert *Menzies*
Rockingham, Marquis of 1765–66:
  1782
Smigly-Rydz Poland 1935–39
Wellington, Duke of 1828–30: 1834
Wilmington, Earl of 1741–43

11

Chamberlain, Arthur Neville 1937–40
Diefenbaker Canada 1957–63
Douglas-Home, Sir Alexander
  (Alec) 1963–4
Lloyd George, David 1916–22
Robespierre Revolutionary France

12

Beaconsfield, Earl of *Disraeli*

Mendes-France France
Pitt the Elder *Chatham*
Seyss-Inquart Austrian chancellor,
  Mar. 1938

13

Brookeborough, Lord Northern
  Ireland
Mackenzie King Canada 1921–30:
  1935–48
Von Metternich Austria 1809–48

14/15/17

Pitt the Younger *Pitt*
Chichester-Clark Northern Ireland
Campbell-Bannerman, Sir
  Henry 1905–08

STATESMEN AND POLITICIANS

British where unspecified.

3

Fox, Charles James 1749–1806 Whig
Lee, Viscount gave Chequers to nation
Lie, Trygve UN secretary general
  1946–52
Pym, John 1584–1643 anti-Charles I

4

Cato, Marcus Porcius 234–149BC,
  Roman
Coke, Sir Edward jurist and rival to
  Bacon
Hill, Sir Rowland founded penny post
  d. 1879
Hogg the Hailsham family name
King, Martin Luther USA negro rights
  leader

Long, Huey Pierce 1893–1935, USA
Mann, Tom 1856–1941, Labour
Root, Elihu 1845–1937, USA
Rusk, Dean USA foreign affairs
Vane, Sir Henry 1613–62 anti-Charles I
Webb, Sydney 1859–1947, Labour

5

Adams, Samuel 1722–1803, USA
Astor, Viscountess 1879–1938, MP
Bacon, Sir Francis served Elizabeth
  I/James I
Beria, Lavrenti 1889–1953, USSR
Bevan, Aneurin (Nye) architect
  National Health Service
Bevin, Ernest foreign secretary
  1945–51
Burke, Edmund Whig MP and writer

STATESMEN AND POLITICIANS

Ciano, Galeazzo 1903–44, Italian
Cimon 512–449BC, Greek
Essex, Earl of served Elizabeth I
Herzl, Theodore 1806–1904, founder Zionism
Malik, Yakov Soviet diplomat
Marat, Jean Paul French Revolutionary
Nenni, Pietro Italian Socialist
Thant, U UN secretary general, 1962–72

6

Albert, Prince consort and advisor d. 1861
Bright, John radical orator 1811–89
Butler, R. A. pro-welfare state Tory
Carson, Edward opponent Irish home rule
Cicero, Marcus Tullius 106–43BC, Roman
Cripps, Sir Stafford 'austerity' chancellor
Curzon, Marquess foreign secretary 1919–24
Danton French Revolutionary
Darvitt, Michael MP Irish nationalist d. 1906
Dulles, John Foster USA secretary of state 1953–9
Gandhi, Mahatma Indian patriot, killed 1948
Gordon, Lord anti-papal agitator d.1793
Hardie, James Keir early Labour leader
Jowitt, Earl 1885–1957 lord chancellor
Kidric, Boris 1912–53, Yugoslav
Maxton, James 1885–1946, Labour
Thorez, Maurice 1900–64, French communist
Wilkes, John 1727–97, Whig
Wilkie, Wendell 1892–1944, USA

7

Addison, Joseph 1672–1719, Whig

Arundel, Thomas 1353–1414, archbishop
Collins, Michael Irish leader, killed 1922
Grattan, Henry 1746–1820, Irish
Gromyko, Andrei Soviet foreign minister
Haldane, Viscount 1856–1928, Liberal
Halifax, Earl of 'appeasement' foreign secretary
Kellogg, Frank Billings 1856–1937, USA
Kennedy, Robert Francis USA attorney general
Litinov, Maxim 1876–1952, USSR
Luthuli, Albert 1899–1967, Zulu
Molotov Soviet diplomat
Parnell, Charles Stuart 1846–91, Irish leader
Trotsky, Leo Soviet revolutionary, killed 1940

8

Burghley, Lord lord high treasurer 1572/98
Damocles Syracusan flatterer 5th C. BC
Franklin, Benjamin early USA statesman
Harcourt, Sir William Liberal, revised death duties
Harriman, Averell USA foreign affairs
Hastings, Warren administrator in India d. 1818
Lansbury, George 1859–1940 Labour
Le Duc Tho N. Vietnamese diplomat
Morrison, Herbert deputy PM (Lord M. of Lambeth)
O'Connell, Daniel 1775–1847 Irish leader
Pericles c.490–429BC, Athenian
Plimsoll, Samuel 1824–98, Liberal
Waldheim, Kurt UN secretary general
Woodcock, George TUC general secretary 1960–9

9

Bondfield, Margaret minister of labour 1929–31

Bottomley, Horatio politician and swindler
Clarendon, Earl of chancellor to Charles II
Gaitskell, Hugh Labour leader 1955–63
Henderson, Arthur 1863–1935, Labour
Kissinger, Henry USA secretary of state
Vyshinski, Andrei Soviet jurist-diplomat

10

Alcibiades c.450–404BC, Athenian
Bernadotte, Count Swedish UN official
Birkenhead, Earl lord chancellor 1919–22
Talleyrand 1754–1838, French
Templewood, Viscount 1880–1959, Tory

11

Beaverbrook, Lord minister of aircraft production

Chamberlain, Joseph 1836–1914, Liberal/Tory
Castlereagh, Viscount 1769–1822, foreign secretary
Demosthenes 385–322BC, Greek orator
Li Hung Chang 1823–1901, Chinese
Machiavelli, Niccolo 1467–1527, Florentine
Wilberforce, William anti-slavery campaigner

12

Chesterfield, Earl of 1604–1773 (4th Earl)
Hammarskjold Dag UN secretary general 1953–61

13/14

Chateaubriand, Vicomte de 1768–1848, French
Northumberland, Duke of 1502–53

WARRIORS OF LAND, SEA AND AIR

Military and/or British where unspecified.

3

Auk, The *Auchinleck*
Cid, El *Diaz*, Rodrigo
Lee, Robert E. 1807–70, Confederate general
Ney, Michel 1769–1815, Marshal, France

4

Bock, Col.-General 1880–1945, German
Diaz, Rodrigo c.1035–99, Spanish knight

Diaz, Marshal 1861–1928, Italian
Giap, General Vietnam, present day
Haig, Earl 1861–1928, field marshal
Hood, Viscount 1724–1816, admiral
Howe, Earl 1726–1799, admiral
Juin, Marshal 1888–1967, French
Maud, General 1864–1917
Ross *Lawrence*
Shaw *Lawrence*
Slim, Viscount 1891–1970, field marshal
Togo, Admiral 1847–1934, Japanese
Tojo, General 1884–1948, Japanese
York, Sgt USA, awarded Medal of Honor

WARRIORS

5

Balbo, Marshal 1896–1940, Italian
Blake, Robert 1598–1657,
general/admiral
Botha, General 1862–1919, S. African
Bulow, General 1846–1921, German
Clive, Robert 1725–74
Conde 1621–86, Louis II, France
Dayan, Moshe Israel
De Wet, General 1854–1922, S. African
Drake, Sir Francis c.1545/96, admiral
'G.I. Joe' the American soldier
Henry V 1387–1422
Hobbs, General 1864–1938, Australian
Horne, General 1861–1929
Ismay, Lord 1887–1964, general
Jones, John Paul 1747–92 (Scots) USA
sailor
Keyes, Lord 1872–1945, admiral
Kluck, General 1846–1934, German
Kluge, Field Marshal 1882–1944,
German
Kundt, General 1860–1939, Bolivian
Limbu, L/Cpl VC Malaysia 1965
(Nepalese)
Milne, Lord 1866–1948, field marshal
Monty *Montgomery*
Tilly, Count von 1559–1632, Holy
Roman Empire
'Tommy' the British soldier
Upham, Capt. VC and bar W.W.II (N.
Zealander)
Wolfe, James 1727–59, general
Ypres, Earl of *French*

Darlan, Admiral 1881–1942, French
Eugene, Prince 1663–1776, Holy
Roman Empire
French, Field Marshal 1852–1925
Gibson, Guy 'Dam Buster' VC
Giraud, General 1879–1949, French
Gordon, 'Chinese' 1833–85, soldier,
governor
Hannah, Sgt W.W.II RAF VC
Hipper, Admiral 1863–1932, German
Joffre, Marshal 1852–1931, French
Monash, General 1865–1931,
Australian
Nelson, Horatio 1758–1805, viscount,
admiral
Nimitz, Admiral 1885–1964, USA
Patton, General 1885–1945, USA
Paulus, Field Marshal d. 1957,
German
Petain, Marshal 1856–1951, French
Plumer, Viscount 1857–1932, field
marshal
Pompey Roman naval commander
Quanah Comanche chief
Rob Roy 1671–1734, Scots freebooter
Rommel, Erwin 1891–1944, German
field marshal
Rupert, Prince 1619–82, served
England
Ruyter, Michael 1607–76, Dutch
admiral
Scipio 237–183BC, Roman general
Tedder, Lord 1890–1967, marshal of
the RAF
Wavell, Lord 1883–1950, field marshal
Xerxes c.519–465BC, Persian
Zhukov, Marshal 1896–1974, Russian

6

Alaric 376–410, Visigoth
Anders, General 1872–1970, Polish
Beatty, Earl 1871–1936, admiral
Bishop, Air Marshal 1894–1956,
Canadian VC
Blamey, Field Marshal 1884–1951,
Australian
Borgia, Caesar 1476–1507, Italian
general
Caesar, Gaius Julius 102–44BC, Roman
Cronje, General 1835–1911, S. African

7

Allenby, Viscount 1861–1936, field
marshal
Blucher, Gebhard von 1742–1819,
Prussian
Bolivar, Simon 1783–1830, S. America
Budenny, Marshal 1853–1926, Russian
Cadorna, General 1850–1928, Italian
Chakmak, Marshal 1876–1950,
Turkish

Charles XII 1682–1718, Sweden
Cochise Chiricahua Apache chief
Dempsey, General 1896–1969
Dowding, Lord 1882–1970, air chief marshal
Fritsch, Col.-General 1880–1939, German
Goering, Hermann 1893–1946, German field marshal
Hunyadi, John Corvinus c.1387–1456, Hungarian
Jackson, General 1824–63, Confederacy
Jackson, Warrant Officer RAF VC W.W.II
Lyautey, Marshal 1854–1934, French
Mannock, Major W.W.I air ace, VC
Manoury, General 1847–1934, French
Metaxes, General 1871–1941, Greek
Methuen, Lord 1845–1932, field marshal
Nivelle, General 1856–1924, French
Papagos, Marshal 1883–1955, Greek
Roberts, Earl 1832–1914, general, VC
Sarrail, General 1856–1929, French
Tirpitz, Grand Admiral 1849–1930, German
Turenne, Vicomte de 1611–75, French
Wallace, Sir William c.1272–1305, Scot
Warwick, Earl of 'the Kingmaker' c.1428–71
Weygand, General 1867–1965, French
Wingate, F. R. 1861–1953, general
Wingate, Orde 1903–44, major general

8

Alexeiev, General 1857–1918, Russian
Avarescu, General 1859–1938, Rumanian
Badoglio, Marshal 1871–1956, Italian
Birdwood, Lord 1865–1951, field marshal
Cheshire, Gp. Capt. W.W.II RAF VC
Chetwode, Lord 1869–1950, field marshal
Cromwell, Oliver 1599–1658
Degoutte, General 1866–1938, French
Freyberg, Viscount 1890–1963, general

Gallieni, General 1849–1916, French
Geronimo Apache leader d. 1909
Gokhayeh *Geronimo*
Graziani, Marshal 1882–1955, Italian
Gustavus VI 1594–1632, Sweden
Hamilton, General 1853–1947
Hannibal c.247–183BC, Carthaginian
Ironside, Lord 1880–1959, field marshal
Jellicoe, Earl 1859–1935, admiral
Kondylis, General 1879–1936, Greek
Krylenko, General 1885–1938, Russian
Lawrence (of Arabia) 1888–1935, Lt. Colonel
Marchand, General 1863–1934, French
Marshall, General 1880–1959, USA
Napoleon 1769–1821, French
Red Baron, The *Richtofen*
Samsonov, General 1859–1914, Russian
Sikorski, General 1881–1943, Polish
Speakman, Sgt Korean War VC
Timur Beg *Tamerlane*
Wolseley, Viscount 1833–1913
Xenophon 444–359BC, Greek

9

Alexander, Earl 1891–1969, field marshal
Brussilov, General 1853–1926, Russian
Churchill, John *Marlborough*
Desert Fox, The *Rommel*
Dundonald, Earl 1852–1935, general
Fairchild, General 1894–1950, USAF
Garibaldi, Giuseppe 1807–82, Italian
Kitchener, Earl 1850–1916, field marshal
MacArthur, General 1880–1964, USA
Mackensen, Field Marshal 1849–1945, German
Marseille, Oberleutnant W.W.II air ace, German
Montgomery, Viscount (of Alamein), field marshal
Pilsudski, Marshal 1867–1935, Polish
Richtofen, Rittmeister W.W.I air ace, German

WARRIORS

Rundstedt, Field Marshal 1875–1953, German
Spartacus d. 71BC, Thracian rebel
Stillwell, General 1883–1946, USA
Tamerlane *Tamberlaine*
Tolbukhin, Marshal 1894–1949, Russian
Trenchard, Viscount 1873–1956, marshal of the RAF
Wellesley, Sir Arthur *Wellington*

10

Alanbrooke, Viscount 1883–1963, field marshal
Auchinleck, Field Marshal 1884–1981
Belisarius c.505–565, Byzantine
Crazy Horse Oglala Sioux Chief
Cunningham, Viscount 1883–1963, admiral
Eisenhower, General 1890–1969, USA
Falkenhayn, General 1861–1922, German
Hindenburg, Field Marshal 1847–1934, German
Kesselring, Field Marshal 1885–1960, German
Kretschmer, Kapitan U-boat commander, W.W.II
Ludendorft, General 1865–1937, German
Malinovski, Marshal 1898–1967, Russian
Mannerheim, Marshal 1867–1948, Finnish
Mountevans, Lord 1881–1957, admiral
Sokolovski, General 1897–1968, Russian
Timoshenko, Marshal 1895–1970, Russian
Voroshilov, Marshal 1881–1954, Russian
Washington, George 1732–99, USA

Wellington, Duke of 1769–1852, 'Iron Duke'

11

Jenghiz Khan 1162–1227, Mongol
Marlborough, Duke of 1650–1722
Milhailovich, General 1893–1946, Yugoslav
Mountbatten, Earl (of Burma), admiral of the fleet
Rennenkampf, General 1897–1968, Russian
Sitting Bull Hunkpapa Sioux chief d. 1890
Tamberlaine 1335–1405, Mongol
Wallenstein, Albrecht von 1583–1634, Holy Roman Empire

12

Attila the Hun c.400–453
Estegarribia, General 1888–1940, Paraguayan
Ghenghiz Khan *Jenghiz Khan*
Nikolaievich, Grand Duke 1856–1929, Russian

13

Bor-Komorowsky, General d. 1966, Polish
Carton de Wiart, Lt. Gen. 1880–1963
Peter the Great 1672–1725, Russian tsar

15/17

Hereward the Wake last Saxon leader
Alexander the Great 356–323BC, Greek
Frederick the Great 1712–86, Prussia

WRITERS, ARTISTS, COMPOSERS, ENGINEERS, SCIENTISTS, ETC.

Unspecified single-person entry is British.

3

Bax, Sir Arnold composer
Cox, David painter
Fry, Christopher poet/dramatist
Gay, John poet/lyricist
Ged, William printer/inventor
Low, Sir David cartoonist
Ohm, Georg Simon German physicist
Poe, Edgar Allen American poet/writer
Ray, John naturalist

4

Abel, Sir Frederick military chemist
Adam, Robert architect
Airy, Sir George astronomer royal
Arne, Thomas Augustine composer
Bach, Johann Sebastian German composer
Baer, Karl Ernst von German naturalist
Bede, The Venerable historian
Bell, Alexander Graham inventor
Benz, Karl German motor engineer
Berg, Alban Austrian composer
Best, Charles Herbert Canadian physiologist
Bode, Johann Ehlert German astronomer
Bone, Sir Muirhead official war artist
Bull, John composer
Byrd, William composer
Cato, Marcus Porcius writer/statesman (Rome)
Coke, Sir Edward legal writer
Colt, Samuel American inventor
Cuyp, Albert Dutch painter
Davy, Sir Humphry chemist
Doré, Gustave French artist

Etty, William artist
Eyck, Jan van Flemish painter
Faed Thomas: John (painters)
Ford, Henry American motor pioneer
Gide, André French writer
Gill, Eric sculptor, engraver
Goya Spanish painter
Gray, Thomas poet
Hahn, Otto German scientist
Hale, George Ellery American astronomer
Hals, Frans painter
Hood, Thomas poet
Howe, Elias American inventor
Hugo, Victor French poet/dramatist/novelist
Hunt, Holman artist
Hunt, Leigh poet/essayist
Hyde, Douglas Irish poet/historian/President
John, Augustus painter/etcher
Jung, Carl Gustav Swiss psychiatrist
Kent, William painter/architect, etc.
Klee, Paul Swiss artist
Koch, Robert German bacteriologist
Lamb, Charles essayist
Lely, Sir Peter Dutch painter
Mann, Thomas German writer
Mond, Ludwig German chemist
More, Sir Thomas writer/statesman/saint
Nash, John architect
Nash, Paul official war artist
Oman, Sir C. W. historian
Otto, Nikolaus August German engineer
Ovid Latin poet
Pope, Alexander poet/writer
Read, Sir Herbert poet
Rops, Felicien Belgian artist
Ross, Sir Ronald physician

WRITERS, ARTISTS, ETC.

Sadi *Saadi*
Sand, George French writer
  (Armandine Lucie Dupin)
Shaw, George Bernard Irish dramatist
Snow, Lord C. P. physicist/novelist
Watt, James engineer/inventor
Wolf, Hugo Austrian song-writer
Wren, Sir Christopher architect
Zola, Emile French novelist
Zorn, Anders Leonhard Swedish
  sculptor

5

Acton, Lord historian
Adams, John Couch
  mathematician/astronomer
Adler, Alfred Austrian psychiatrist
Aesop (of Phrygia) semi-legendary
  fabulist
Arago, Dominique French
  astronomer/physicist
Asser traditional biographer of Arthur
Auden, W. H. poet
Bacon, Roger alchemist
Baird, John Logie television pioneer
Baker, Sir Herbert architect
Bakst, Leon Russian painter
Banks, Sir Joseph amateur scientist
Barry, Sir Charles architect
Bizet, Georges French composer
Black, Joseph chemist
Blake, William poet/artist
Bliss, Sir Arthur composer
Bloch, Ernest composer
Blunt, Wilfred poet/political writer
Boito, Arrigo Italian poet/composer
Boyle, Robert scientist
Brahe, Tycho Danish astronomer
Broch, Herman Austrian novelist
Bruch, Max German composer
Burns, Robert (Rabbie) poet
Byron, Lord poet
Camus, Albert French writer
Canal, Antonio *Canaletto*
Clare, John poet
Corot, Jean Baptiste French painter
Crome, John painter
Curie, Marie Polish scientist

Dante Italian epic poet
Defoe, Daniel writer
Degas, Edgar French painter
Dewar, Sir James scientist
Donne, John poet
Doyle, Sir Arthur Conan novelist
Drury, Alfred sculptor
Dumas, Alexandre novelist: (son)
  dramatist
Durer, Albrecht German
  painter/engraver
Dyson, Sir George composer/writer
Elgar, Sir Edward composer
Eliot, George *Evans*
Ellis, Havelock writer on sex
Euler, Leonhard Swiss mathematician
Evans, Mary Ann (Marion) novelist
  (George Eliot)
Falla, Manuel Spanish composer
Fauré, Gabriel Urbain French
  composer
Fermi, Enrico Italian nuclear physicist
Field, John Irish composer
Freud, Sigmund Moravian psychiatrist
Frost, Robert American poet
Fuchs, Leonard German naturalist
Gluck, C. W. German composer
Gogol, N. V. Russian
  novelist/dramatist
Gorky, Maxim Russian writer
Gosse, Sir Edmund poet
Gower, John poet
Grieg, Edvard Hagerup Norwegian
  composer
Grimm, The Brothers German
  folk-lorists
Grote, George historian
Grove, Sir George musicologist
Guido, Reni Italian painter
Hafiz Persian lyrical poet
Hardy, Thomas novelist/poet
Harty, Sir Hamilton composer
Haydn, Franz Joseph Austrian
  composer
Heine, Heinrich German-Jewish poet
Henry, Joseph American physicist
Hertz, Heinrich Rudolf German
  physicist
Holst, Gustav Theodore composer
Homer epic poet (Greek?)

Hooke, Robert physicist/architect
Ibsen, Henrik Norwegian playwright/poet
James, Henry American novelist
Jokai, Mor Hungarian novelist
Jones, Inigo architect
Joule, James Prescott physicist
Joyce, James Irish author
Kafka, Franz German-Jewish writer
Keats, John poet
Leech, John humorist/artist
Lewis, Sinclair American novelist
Lippi, Fra Filippo Italian artist
Liszt, Franz Hungarian composer
Lorca, Federico Garcia Spanish poet
Lyell, Sir Charles geologist
Manet, Edouard French painter
Maxim, Sir H. S. American inventor
Mehul, Etienne Nicolas French composer
Milne, A. A. writer
Monet, Claude French painter
Moore, George Irish novelist
Morse, Samuel American inventor
Nobel, Alfred Bernhard Swedish inventor
Orpen, Sir William painter
Osler, Sir William Canadian physician
Ouida novelist (Louise de la Ramee)
Papin, Denis French physicist/inventor
Pepys, Samuel diarist
Plato Greek philosopher/writer
Pound, Ezra American poet/writer
Powys, John Cowper writer
Prior, Matthew poet
Ranke, Leopold von German historian
Ravel, Maurice French composer
Rilke, Rainer Maria German lyric poet
Rodin, Auguste French sculptor
Saadi Persian poet (Muslin Addin)
Sachs, Hans German poet
Sachs, Julius von German botanist
Salda, Frantisek Czech essayist/poet
Scott, Sir Walter novelist/poet
Smith, Adam economist
Soddy, Frederick chemist
Sousa, John Philip American composer
Steen, Jan Dutch painter
Steer, Philip Wilson painter

Stowe, Harriet Beecher American writer
Swift, Jonathan satirist
Synge, John Millington Irish poet
Tasso, Torquato Italian epic poet
Twain, Mark American writer (S. L. Clemens)
Unwin, Sir Raymond architect
Verdi, Giuseppe Italian composer
Verne, Jules French writer
Volta, Alessandro Italian physicist
Waley, Arthur orientalist/translator
Watts, Isaac hymn-writer
Waugh, Evelyn author
Weber, C. M. F. E. von German composer
Weill, Kurt German composer
Wells, H. G. author
White, Patrick Australian novelist
Wilde, Oscar Irish author/dramatist
Woolf, Virginia writer
Wyatt, Sir Thomas poet
Yeats, W. B. Irish poet/playwright
Young, Thomas physicist/Egyptologist

6

Adrian, Lord physiologist
Alcott, Louisa May American author
Ampère, André Marie French physicist
Argand, Aimee Swiss physician/inventor
Aristo, Ludovico Italian poet
Arnold, Matthew poet, critic
Austen, Jane author
Ayrton, William Edward inventor
Balzac, Honore de French novelist
Barham, Richard Harris wrote as 'Thomas Ingoldsby'
Barrie, J. M. author/dramatist
Bartók, Béla Hungarian composer
Belloc, Hilaire author/historian
Berlin, Irving Russian-born composer
Bernal, John Desmond Irish physicist
Brecht, Bertold German dramatist/poet
Breton, André French poet
Bridie, James author/dramatist

WRITERS, ARTISTS, ETC.

Brontë (sisters) Charlotte: Emily: Anne (authors)
Brooke, Rupert poet
Bunsen, Robert Wilhelm German chemist
Bunyan, John writer
Burney, Fanny writer
Butler, Samuel verse-satirist
Camden, William historian
Canova, Antonio Italian sculptor
Canton, John physicist
Chares Greek sculptor
Chopin, Frederic François Polish composer
Conrad, Joseph Polish novelist
Cooper, James Fenimore American novelist
Cowper, William poet
Crabbe, George narrative poet
Dalton, John chemist/mathematician
Darwin Erasmus: Charles (scientists)
Daudet, Alphonse French writer
Dawber, Sir Guy architect
Delius, Frederick composer
Diesel, Rudolf German inventor
Dryden, John poet/dramatist
Dvořák, Antonin Czech composer
Edison, Thomas Alva American inventor
Erlich, Paul German bacteriologist
Evelyn, John diarist
Fildes, Sir Luke painter/woodcut-designer
Finsen, Niels Ryberg Danish physician
Florey, Lord pathologist
Fokker, Anthony Dutch aircraft engineer
Fowler, Sir John engineer
France, Anatole French writer
Franck, Cesar Belgian composer
Fulton, Robert American engineer
Galton, Sir Francis founder of eugenics
Gesner, Conrad Swiss naturalist
Giotto Florentine artist
Glinka, M. I. Russian composer
Gounod, Charles François French composer
Graves, Robert author/poet
Greene, Graham novelist

Greuze, Jean Baptiste French artist
Halevy, Ludovic French playwright
Hallam, Henry historian
Halley, Edmond astronomer royal
Hamsun, Knut Norwegian author
Handel, George Frederick German composer
Harris, Joel Chandler American author
Harvey, William physician
Hesiod Greek poet
Holden, Sir Isaac inventor
Holmes, Oliver Wendell American author
Horace Roman satirist/poet
Hughes, Thomas novelist
Huxley, Aldous author
Huxley, Sir Julian biologist/writer
Huxley, T. H. biologist
Ingres, J. A. D. French painter
Irving, Washington American essayist
Jacobs, W. W. novelist
Jenner, Edward physician
Jerome, Jerome K. author
Jonson, Ben poet/dramatist
Keller, Helen American author
Kepler, Johann German astronomer
Keynes, Lord economist
Kodaly, Zoltan Hungarian composer
Krylov, I. A. Russian writer
Lassus, Orlandus Flemish composer
Lavery, Sir John Irish painter
Lennon, John ballad-writer
Le Sage, Alain Rene French author/dramatist
Lister, Lord surgeon
London, Jack American writer
Lowell, Robert American poet
Lytton, Lord novelist/playwright
Mahler, Gustav Austrian composer
Malory, Sir Thomas writer
Manson, Sir Patrick physician
Mendel, Gregor Johann Austrian botanist
Millet, Jean François French painter
Milton, John poet
Morris, William poet/craftsman
Mozart, Wolfgang Amadeus Austrian composer
Napier, John mathematician

Nernst, Walther Herman German scientist
Newman, Cardinal writer
Newton, Sir Isaac scientist
O'Casey, Sean Irish dramatist
O'Neill, Eugene American playwright
Orwell, George satirist (Eric Arthur Blair)
Palmer, Samuel painter/etcher
Pascal, Blaise French mathematician/inventor
Pavlov, Ivan Petrovich Russian physiologist
Piazzi, Giuseppe Italian astronomer
Pindar Greek lyric poet
Pinero, Sir Arthur Wing dramatist
Pitman, Sir Isaac inventor
Planck, Max German mathematical physicist
Proust, Marcel French novelist
Racine, Jean French poet/dramatist
Rameau, Jean Philippe French composer
Rennie, John civil engineer
Renoir, Pierre Auguste French painter
Robbia, Luca Della Florentine sculptor
Romney, George artist
Rubens, Sir Peter Paul Flemish painter
Ruskin, John author/art critic
Sauger, Frederick scientist
Sankey, Ira David American composer
Sappho poetess of Lesbos
Sardon, Victorien French dramatist
Sartre, Jean-Paul French philosopher/dramatist, etc.
Sidney, Sir Philip poet/writer
Singer, Isaac Merritt American engineer
Sisley, Alfred painter
Sloane, Sir John architect
Smiles, Samuel writer
Spence, Sir Basil architect
Steele, Sir Richard essayist
Stoker, Bram Irish author
Tallis, Thomas composer
Teresa, St (of Avila) writer
Thales Greek scientist
Thomas, Dylan poet
Titian Venetian painter
Turner, J. M. W. painter

Undset, Sigrid Norwegian novelist
Valery, Paul French poet/essayist
Villon, François French poet
Virgil Roman epic poet
Wagner, Richard German composer
Waller, Edmund poet
Wallis, Sir Barnes scientist/inventor
Walton, Izaak writer
Walton, Sir William composer
Wesley, Charles hymn-writer
Wright, Frank Lloyd American architect
Wright (brothers) Wilbur: Orville (air pioneers)
Yukawa, Hideki Japanese physicist

7

Aldrich, Henry composer/theologian/architect
Alfieri, Count Italian poet/dramatist
Anouilh, Jean French playwright
Apelles Greek painter
Banting, Sir Frederick Canadian physician
Beckett, Samuel dramatist/novelist
Behring, Emil von German bacteriologist
Bellamy, Edward American author
Bellini Jacopo: Gentile: Giovanni (painters)
Bellini, Vincenzo Italian operatic composer
Bennett, Arnold author
Berlioz, Hector Swiss composer
Bernard, Claude French physiologist
Blunden, Edmund poet
Bonnard, Pierre French painter
Borodin, Alexander Russian composer
Boswell, James writer
Bowdler, Thomas 'bowdlerizer'
Brahman, Joseph inventor
Braille, Louis French inventor
Brennan, Louis Irish inventor
Bridges, Robert poet laureate
Britten, Benjamin composer
Buchner, Edward German chemist
Caedmon poet
Carlyle, Thomas writer
Carroll, Lewis *Dodgson*

WRITERS, ARTISTS, ETC.

Cellini, Benvenuto Italian sculptor/goldsmith
Celsius, Anders Swedish physicist/astronomer
Cezanne, Paul French artist
Chagall, Marc Russian artist
Chaucer, Geoffrey poet
Chekhov Anton Russian dramatist
Cocteau, Jean French writer/artist
Colette French writer
Collins, William Wilkie novelist
Compton, Arthur Holly American physicist
Cousins, Samuel mezzotint engraver
Crookes, Sir William physicist
Daimler, Gottlieb German inventor
Da Vinci, Leonardo *Leonardo*
Debussy, Claude French composer
Dickens, Charles novelist
Dodgson, Charles writer (Lewis Carroll)
Dowland, John composer
Eastman, George American inventor
Epstein, Sir Jacob sculptor
Faraday, Michael experimental physicist
Fitzroy, Robert meteorologist
Flaxman, John sculptor
Flecker, James Elroy poet
Fleming, Sir Alexander bacteriologist
Fleming, Sir Ambrose scientist
Furniss, Harry caricaturist
Galileo Italian scientist
Galvini, Luigi Italian physician
Gilbert, Sir Alfred sculptor/goldsmith
Gilbert, W. S. librettist
Gillray, James caricaturist
Grahame, Kenneth writer
Gregory, James mathematician
Hazlitt, William essayist/critic
Herbert, George poet
Herrick, Robert lyric poet
Hogarth, William engraver/painter
Hokusai, Katsushika Japanese artist
Holbein, Hans father: son (painters)
Hopkins, Gerard Manley poet
Hoppner, John painter
Housman, A. E. poet
Huggins, Sir William astronomer
Huygens, Christian Dutch scientist/astronomer
Hypathia Greek woman mathematician
Ireland, John composer
Israels, Joseph Dutch painter
Janáček, Leos Czech composer
Jimenez, Juan Ramon Spanish lyric poet
Johnson, Dr Samuel lexicographer
Juvenal Roman poet
Kneller, Sir Godfrey painter
Leacock, Stephen Canadian humorist
Leighton, Lord painter
Lesseps, Ferdinand de French engineer
Lippman, Gabriel French physicist
Lutyens, Sir Edwin architect
Macadam, John inventor
McLuhan, Marshall Canadian author
Malraux, André French novelist
Manzoni, Alessandro Italian novelist
Marconi, Guglielmo Italian inventor
Marlowe, Christopher dramatist
Marryat, Capt. Frederick author
Marvell, Andrew poet
Masters, Edgar Lee American poet
Matisse, Henri French painter
Maugham, W. Somerset writer
Mauriac, François French writer
Maxwell, James Clark physicist
Millais, Sir John Everett artist
Mistral, Frederick French poet
Moliere French playwright
Morland, George painter
Murdock, William inventor
Murillo, B. E. Spanish painter
Nasmyth, James inventor
Oersted, Hans Christian Danish physicist
Pasteur, Louis French chemist
Patmore, Coventry poet
Peacock, Thomas Love novelist
Phidias Greek sculptor
Picasso, Pablo Ruiz Spanish painter
Piccard, Auguste Swiss physicist/adventurer
Piccard, Jacques son of Auguste Piccard, adventurer
Poussin, Nicholas French painter
Ptolemy (of Alexandria) astronomer/cartographer

Puccini, Giacomo Italian composer
Purcell, Henry composer
Pushkin, Alexander Russian writer
Rackham, Arthur artist/illustrator
Raphael Italian artist
Ricardo, David political economist
Rolland, Romain French author
Röntgen, W. K. von German scientist
Rossini, G. A. Italian composer
Rostand, Edmond French dramatist
Sargent, John Singer American painter
Sassoon, Siegfried poet/writer
Scheele, Carl Wilhelm Swedish
  chemist
Shelley, Percy Bysshe poet
Shirley, James dramatist
Sickert, Walter Richard artist
Sitwell, Edith poet
Sitwell, Osbert poet/critic
Sitwell, Sacheverell poet/critic
Smeaton, John engineer/inventor
Smetana, Bedrich Czech composer
Snyders, Frans Flemish painter
Southey, Robert poet/historian
Spencer, Herbert philosopher/writer
Spencer, Sir Stanley artist
Spenser, Edmund poet
Stephen, Sir Leslie writer/biographer,
  etc.
Strauss, Eduard (son) Viennese
  composer
Strauss, Johann (father) Viennese
  composer
Strauss, Johann (son) Viennese
  composer
Strauss, Josef (son) Viennese
  composer
Strauss, Richard German composer
Symonds, John Addington author
Tactitus, Gaius Cornelius Roman
  historian
Tartini, Giuseppe Italian
  violinist/composer
Telford, Thomas engineer
Teniers, David elder: younger
  (painters)
Tenniel, Sir John illustrator
Terence Berber poet/dramatist
Thierry, Augustin French historian
Thomson, James poet: essayist

Thoreau, Henry David American
  essayist
Tolstoy, Count Leo Russian writer
Toynbee, Arnold historian
Tyndale, John Irish physicist
Unamuno, Miguel de Spanish writer
Van Dyck, Sir Anthony Flemish
  painter
Van Gogh, Vincent Dutch painter
Vermeer, Jan Dutch painter
Vernier, Pierre French inventor
Vivaldi, Antonio Venetian composer
Wallace, Alfred Russel naturalist
Wallace, Edgar novelist/playwright
Walpole, Horace writer
Watteau, Jean Antoine French painter
Webster, Noah American
  lexicographer
Wharton, Edith American novelist
Wheeler, Sir Charles sculptor
Whitman, Walt American poet
Whittle, Sir Frank jet pioneer
Zosimus first known alchemist

8

Anacreon Greek lyric poet
Andersen, Hans Christian Danish
  writer
Angelico, Fra Italian painter
Angstrom, Anders Swedish physicist
Appleton, Sir Edward physicist
Avogadro, Amedeo Italian physicist
Barbusse, Henri French writer
Beerbohm, Sir Max caricaturist
Bessemer, Sir Henry inventor
Boethius Roman scientific writer
Brangwyn, Sir Frank artist
Brewster, Sir David physicist
Brindley, James canal builder
Browning Elizabeth Barrett: Robert
  (poets)
Bruckner, Anton Austrian composer
Campbell, Thomas poet
Chambers, Sir William architect
Cimarosa, Domenico Italian composer
Congreve, William dramatist
Crompton, Samuel inventor
Day Lewis, C. poet laureate

WRITERS, ARTISTS, ETC.

De la Mare, Walter poet/novelist
Edelinck, Gerard Flemish engraver
Einstein, Albert German-Jewish
  mathematical physicist
Falconer, Hugh botanist/
  palaeontologist
Faulkner, William American novelist
Ferguson, James astronomer
Fielding, Henry novelist
Firdansi Persian poet
Flaubert, Gustave French novelist
Fletcher, John dramatist
Forester, C. S. novelist
Franklin, Benjamin American
  inventor/statesman
Gershwin, George American composer
Goodyear, Charles American inventor
Harrison, John inventor
Herschel, Sir William German-born
  astronomer
Jacquard, Joseph Marie French
  inventor
Josephus, Flavius Jewish historian
Kauffman, Angelica Anglo-Swiss
  painter
Kingsley, Charles novelist
Korolyov, Sergei Russian space
  scientist
Kreisler, Fritz Austrian
  violinist/composer
Lagerlof, Selma Swedish novelist
Landseer, Sir Edwin painter
Langland, William poet
Lawrence, D. H. poet/novelist
Lawrence, Sir Thomas painter
Leonardo Italian artist/genius
Linnaeus Swedish botanist
Macneice, Louis poet/playwright
Mercator, Gerhardus Flemish
  geographer
Meredith, George novelist/poet
Michelet, Jules French historian
Millikan, Robert Andrews American
  physicist
Munkacsy, Michael von Hungarian
  painter
Munnings, Sir Alfred painter
Palgrave, Sir Francis historian
Palladio, Andrea Italian architect
Perugino, Pietro Italian artist

Petrarch, Francesco Italian poet
Phillips, Stephen poet
Pissarro, Camille French painter
Plutarch Greek biographer
Polybius Greek inventor
Prichard, James Coles ethnologist
Rabelais, François French satirist
Reynolds, Sir Joshua painter
Robinson, W. Heath
  cartoonist/illustrator
Rossetti, Dante Gabriel poet/painter
Rousseau, Henri French painter
Schiller German dramatist/poet
Schubert, Franz Peter Austrian
  composer
Schumann, Robert German composer
Scriabin, Alexander Russian composer
Sgambati, Giovanni Italian
  pianist/composer
Sheridan, Richard Brinsley dramatist
Sibelius, Jean French composer
Sidgwick, Henry philosopher/writer
Sinclair, Upton American novelist
Smollett, Tobias George novelist
Stendhal French novelist (M. H.
  Beyle)
Suckling, Sir John poet/invented
  cribbage
Sullivan, Sir Arthur Irish composer
Telemann, Georg Phillipp German
  composer
Tennyson, Alfred, Lord poet
Traherne, Thomas poet
Trollope, Anthony novelist
Tulsi Das Indian poet
Turgenev, Ivan Sergeyvich Russian
  novelist
Vanbrugh, Sir John
  architect/playwright
Verlaine, Paul French poet
Voltaire French philosopher/writer
Whistler, James American artist
Whittier, John Greenleaf American
  poet

9

Aeschylus founder Greek tragic drama
Arkwright, Sir Richard inventor

Beardsley, Aubrey black and white artist
Beethoven, Ludwig van German composer
Berzelius, Jons Jakob Swedish chemist
Blackmore, R. D. novelist
Blackwood, Algernon novelist
Boccaccio, Giovanni Italian author
Canaletto Italian artist
Carissimi, Giacomo Italian composer
Cavendish, Henry scientist
Cervantes, Miguel de Spanish novelist/dramatist
Cockcroft, Sir John nuclear physicist
Coleridge, Samuel Taylor poet/critic
Constable, John painter
Corneille, Pierre French dramatist
Delaroche, Paul French painter
Donatello Italian sculptor
Donizetti, Gaetano Italian composer
Du Maurier, George writer
Dunstable, John composer
Edgeworth, Maria Irish novelist
Euripides Greek tragic dramatist
Flamsteed, John first astronomer royal
Goldsmith, Oliver Irish poet/dramatist/novelist
Greenaway, Kate artist
Hauptmann, Gerhart German dramatist/novelist
Hawthorne, Nathaniel American author
Hemingway, Ernest American novelist
Herodotus Greek historian
Hindemith, Paul German composer
Kokoschka, Oscar Austrian painter
Mackenzie, Sir Compton writer
Mansfield, Katherine N. Zealand writer
Masefield, John poet laureate
Mechnicov, Ilya Russian biologist
Mestrovic, Ivan Yugoslav sculptor
Montaigne, Michel de French essayist
Newcomen, Thomas inventor
Nicholson, Sir William artist
Offenbach, Jacques German-Jewish composer
Pasternak, Boris Russian poet/writer
Priestley, J. B. novelist/playwright
Priestley, Joseph chemist

Prokofiev, S. S. Russian composer
Quasimodo, Salvatore Italian poet
Rembrandt Dutch painter
Santayana, George American philosopher/poet
Scarlatti, Alessandro Italian composer
Sholokhov, Mikhail Russian novelist
Sophocles Athenian dramatist
Spofforth, Reginald writer of glees
Stevenson, Robert engineer
Stevenson, Robert Louis writer
Sudermann, Hermann German writer
Swinburne, A. C. poet
Thackeray, William Makepeace novelist
Trevelyan, G. M. historian
Velasquez Spanish painter
Wodehouse, P. G. writer
Wycherley, William dramatist

10

Apollonius (1) mathematician (2) poet
Archimedes Greek mathematician
Bartolozzi, Francesco Italian engraver
Baudelaire, Charles Pierre French poet
Blackstone, Sir William writer on law
Botticelli, Sandro Italian painter
Cartwright, Edmund inventor
Chesterton, G. K. writer
Conscience, Hendrik Henri Flemish novelist
Copernicus, Nicholas Polish astronomer
Cruikshank, William caricaturist
Democritus Greek scientific thinker
Drinkwater, John poet/playwright
Fahrenheit, Gabriel Daniel German physicist
FitzGerald, Edward poet
Flammarion, Camille French astronomer
Galsworthy, John novelist/playwright
Hargreaves, James inventor
La Fontaine, Jean de French poet/fabulist
Longfellow, Henry Wadsworth American poet

WRITERS, ARTISTS, ETC.

Lope de Vega Spanish writer
MacDiarmid, Hugh poet
Maupassant, Guy de French writer
Mendeleyev, D. I. Russian chemist
Metastasio, Pietro Italian librettist
Modigliani, Amedo Italian
  painter/sculptor
Monteverdi, Claudio Italian composer
Mussorgsky, Modest Petrovitch
  Russian composer
Palestrina, G. P. da Italian composer
Paracelsus Swiss physician
Pirandello, Luigi Italian dramatist
Praxiteles Greek sculptor
Pythagoras Greek
  philosopher/mathematician
Richardson, Samuel author
Rutherford, Lord physicist
Saint-Saëns, C. C. French composer
Schoenberg, Arnold Austrian
  composer
Senefelder, Alois Bavarian inventor
Stephenson, George engineer
Stephenson, Robert engineer
Stravinsky, Igor Russian composer
Strindberg, Johan August Swedish
  writer
Sutherland, Graham artist
Tarkington, Booth American author
Theocritus Greek poet
Thucydides Greek historian
Tintoretto Venetian painter
Torricelli, Evangelista Italian physicist
Trevithick, Richard engineer/inventor
Tweedsmuir, Lord novelist
Watson-Watt, Sir Robert physicist
Westmacott, Sir Richard sculptor
Wheatstone, Sir Charles physicist
Wordsworth, William poet

11

Abercrombie, Sir Patrick architect
Anaximander Greek
  philosopher/geographer
Apollinaire, Guillaume French poet
Bartolommeo, Fra Italian painter
Dostoyevsky, Feodor Russian novelist
Hippocrates (of Chios) mathematician

Hippocrates (of Cos) physician
Le Corbusier Swiss architect
Leoncavallo, Ruggiero Italian
  composer
Mendelssohn, Felix German composer
Nostradamus physician/astrologer
Omar Khayam Persian
  poet/mathematician
Rachmaninov, S. V. Russian composer
Rothenstein, Sir William painter
Shakespeare, William epic
  dramatist/poet
Sienkiewicz, Henryk Polish novelist
Szymanowski, Karol Polish composer
Tchaikovsky, Peter Ilyich Russian
  composer
Thorwaldsen, Bertel Danish sculptor

12

Aristophanes Greek dramatist/comic
  poet
Friese-Greene, William inventor
Gainsborough, Thomas painter
Michelangelo Italian
  painter/sculptor/poet, etc.
Schiaparelli, G. V. Italian astronomer
Solzhenitsyn, Alexander Russian
  novelist
Westinghouse, George American
  engineer

13

Ortega y Gasset, José Spanish essayist
Pliny the Elder Roman naturalist
Shostakovitch, Dimitri Russian
  composer

14

Rimsky-Korsakov Russian composer

15

La Rochefoucauld, Duc de French
  writer

Leonardo da Vinci *Leonardo*
Pliny the Younger Roman writer
Toulouse-Lautrec, Henri de French
  painter
Vaughan Williams, Ralph composer

17
Teilhard de Chardin French
  Jesuit/scientist

LAND BATTLES

Also see SIEGES (p. 147)

3

Acs 1849
Teb *El Teb*
Ulm 1805

4

Alma 1854
Caen 1944
Ceva 1796
Dego 1796
Ivry 1590
Jena 1806
Laon 1814
Lens 1648
Lodi 1796
Metz 1870
Mons 1914
Naas 1798
Nive 1813
Novi 1799: 1800
Soor 1745: 1866
Tara 1798
Wawz 1831
Zama 202BC
Zela 47BC

5

Adowa 1896
Aisne 1914: 1917: 1918
Alamo, The 1836
Allia 390BC
Anjou 1421

Anzio 1944
Boyne, The 1690
Bulge, The *Ardennes*
Buxar 1764
Crecy 1346
Crete 1941
Delhi 1803: 1804: 1857
Douro 1809
Dreux 1592
Dunes 1658
El Teb 1884
Eutaw 1781
Eylau 1807
Gorey 1798
Hanau 1813
Ipsus 301BC
Kalka 1224
Kazan 1552
Khart 1829
Kolin 1757
Largs 1263
Lewes 1264
Ligny 1815
Lipau 1434
Lissa *Leuthen*
Maida 1806
Marne, The 1914: 1918
Morat 1476
Mudki 1845
Munda 45BC
Muret 1213
Narva 1700
Nedao 454
Ormuz 1622
Parma 1734
Patay 1429
Pavia 1525

LAND BATTLES

Rieti 1821
Sedan 1870
Selby 1644
Sesia, The 1524
Spurs, The *Guinegatte*
Stoke 148
Tours 732
Ucles 1809
Valmy 1792
Varna 1444
Vilna 1831
Wavre 1815
Worth 1870
Ypres 1914: 1915: 1917: 1918
Zenta 1697

6

Alford 1645
Aliwal 1846
Angora 1402
Arbela 331BC
Arcole 1796
Argaum 1803
Arklow 1798
Arnhem 1944
Arques 1589
Aspern 1809
Assaye 1803
Atbara, The 1898
Auneau 1587
Barnet 1471
Baylen 1808
Beauge *Anjou*
Berlin 1945
Boxtel 1794
Braila 1773
Busaco 1810
Camden (USA) 1780: 1781
Cannae 216BC
Citate 1854
Dieppe 1942
Dunbar 1296: 1650
Euslin 1899
Famars 1793
Gujrat 1849
Harlaw 1411
Hexham 1464
Himera 408BC

Ingogo 1881
Ingour 1855
Jarnac 1569
Kalisz 1706
Kohima 1942
Konieh 1832
Kurdia 1795
Landen 1693
Lioppo 1860
Lonato 1796
Lutzen 1632: 1813
Majuba 1881
Margus 285: 505
Mincio 1796: 1814
Minden 1759
Mohacs 1526: 1687
Mukden 1905
Multan 1848
Nachod 1866
Najara 1367
Narvik 1940
Naseby 1645
Nesbit 1402
Novara 1849
Obidos 1808
Oporto *Douro*
Orthez 1814
Ortona 1943
Oulart 1798
Pinkie 1547
Plevna 1877(3)
Podoll 1866
Prague 1757
Rivoli 1797
Rocroi 1643
Rolica 1808
Sadowa 1866
Sangro 1943
Shiloh 1862
Suakin 1888
Tarbes 1814
Thabor 1799
Torgau 1760
Towton 1461
Tudela 1808
Wagram 1809
Warsaw 1656: 1794(2): 1831: 1939:
    1943: 1944
Ximena 1811
Yermuk 636

Zurich 1799

7

Aboukir 1799: 1801
Abu Klea 1885
Alarcos 1185
Albuera 1811
Almansa 1707
Antioch 1098
Asunden 1520
Atlanta 1864
Aughrim 1691
Badajoz 1812
Bapaume 1871
Barrosa 1811
Bassano 1796
Bautzen 1813
Belmont 1899
Bitonto 1734
Borisov 1812
Brechin 1452
Breslau 1757
Brienne 1814
Bull Run 1861: 1862
Carrhae 53BC
Cassano 1705: 1799
Cassino 1944
Chalons 451
Colenso 1899
Corinth (Miss. USA) 1862
Corunna 1809
Coutras 1587
Craonne 1814
Czaslau 1742
Devizes 1643
Dresden 1813
Dunkirk *Dunes*: 1940
Eckmuhl 1809
Enghein 1692
Essling *Aspern*
Evesham 1265
Falkirk 1298: 1746
Fleurus 1622: 1690: 1794
Fornovo 1495
Glencoe (S. Africa) 1899
Grochow 1831
Hasbain 1408
Herrera 1837

Idstadt 1850
Kilsyth 1645
Klissow 1702
Kossovo 1389: 1448
Krasnoi 1812
Leipzig 1813
Leuctra 371BC
Leuthen 1757
Libenau 1866
Lincoln 1141: 1217
Magenta 1859
Magnano 1799
Marengo 1800
Milazzo 1860
Mockern 1813: 1814
Mohilev 1812
Mondovi 1796
Newburn 1640
Newbury 1643: 1644
New Ross 1798
Orleans 1429: 1870
Ourique 1139
Panipat 1526: 1556: 1761
Plassey 1757
Plataea 479BC
Polotzk 1812
Poltava 1709
Preston 1648: 1715
Pultusk 1806
Raucoux 1746
Ravenna 1512
Redinha 1811
Rio Seco 1808
Sagunto 1811
Saintes 1242
Sakaria, The 1921
Salerno 1943
Sempach 1386
Seneffe 1674
Skalitz 1866
Sobraon 1846
Thapsus 46BC
Tournai 1794
Trebbia 281BC: 1799
Vilagos 1521
Vimiero 1808
Vitebsk 1812
Vitoria 1813
Vouille 507
Waitzen 1849

LAND BATTLES

Winwaed 654
Zallaca 1086

8

Aiznadin 633
Albufera 1812
Almenara 1710
Antietam 1862
Ardennes 1944
Assandun 1016
Ayacucho 1824
Bastogne 1944
Beresina 1812
Bir Hakim 1942
Blenheim 1704
Blumenau 1866
Borodino 1812
Bouvines 1214
Castalla 1813
Cawnpore 1857(3)
Chatalja 1912
Chippewa 1814
Clontarf 1014
Courtrai 1302
Culloden 1746
Custozza 1848: 1866
Drumelog 1679
Edgehill 1642
Edington 878
Fair Oaks 1862
Flushing 1809
Fontenoy 1745
Formigny 1450
Gembloux 1578
Gitschin 1866
Hastings 1066
Hatfield 632
Homildon 1402
Inkerman 1854
Jemappes 1792
Katzbach 1813
Kulikovo 1380
Kumanovo 1912
Laffeldt 1747
Landshut 1809
Langport 1645
Langside 1568
Lansdown 1643

Lauffeld 1746
Liaoyang 1904
Liegnitz 1760
Magnesia 190BC
Malvalli 1799
Mantinea 418: c.367: 295: 242: 207BC
Marathon 490BC
Metaurus 207BC
Moliwitz 1741
Monastir 1912
Nantwich 1644
Nivelles 1813
Omdurman 1898
Palestro 1859
Palo Alto 1846
Pelusium 525BC
Placenza 1746
Poitiers 1356
Pyramids, The 1798
Pyrenees, The 1813
Rossbach 1757
Roverodo 1796
St Albans 1455: 1461
Saratoga 1777
Seidlitz 1831
Seminara 1503
Simancas 936
Smolensk 1812: 1941
Soissons 486
Sorauren 1813
Spion Kop 1900
Standard, The 1138
Syracuse 413BC
Szegedin 1849
Talavera 1809
Talikota 1565
Toulouse 1814
Truellas 1793
Valeggio 1848
Valtezza 1821
Volturno 1860
Waterloo 1815
Wurschen 1813
Zorndorf 1758

9

Agincourt 1415

Agnadello 1509
Akhalzikh 1828
Auerstadt 1806
Aylesford c.455
Balaklava 1854
Benevento 1266
Big Bethel 1861
Borghetto 1796
Brentford 1642
Castlebar 1798
Cerignola 1503
Cerisoles 1454
Chaeronea 338BC: 86BC
Chalgrove 1643
Dennewitz 1813
Dettingen 1743
Dorylaeum 1097
el Alamein 1942
Elchingen 1805
Espierres 1794
Friedland 1807
Gaugamela *Arbela*
Hochkirch 1758
Hochstadt *Blenheim*
Kissingen 1866
La Bicocca 1522
Laingsnek 1881
Lexington 1775: 1861
Lincelles 1793
Lippstadt 1632
Manzikert 1071
Marignano 1515: *Pavia*: 1859
Millesimo 1796
Moeskirch 1800
Morgarten 1315
Oltenitza 1853
Otterburn 1388
Oudenarde 1708
Pelekanon 1326
Pharsalia 48BC
Pirmasens 1793
Porto Novo (S. India) 1781
Ramillies 1706
Rathmines 1649
Ruremonde 1794
Salamanca 1812
Saragossa 1710: 1809
Schwechat 1870
Sedgemoor 1685
Solferino 1859

Steenkirk 1692
Tchernaya 1855
Trautenau 1866
Valteline 1812
Vauchamps 1814
Vimy Ridge 1917
Wakefield 1460
Wandiwash 1760
White Oaks *Mechanicsville*
Worcester 1642: 1651
Wurtzburg 1796
Zullichau 1759

10

Adrianople 323: 378: 1829
Alexandria 1801: 1882
Argentario 378
Aspromonte 1862
Austerlitz 1805
Bennington 1777
Blore Heath 1459
Brandywine 1777
Brunanburh c.937
Bunker Hill 1775
Calatafimi 1860
Carporetto 1917
Castillion 1453
Cedar Creek 1864
Chatanooga 1863
Chateaudun 1870
Chelbreiss 1798
Cold Harbor 1864
Dannevirke 1331: 1848
Donnington (Glos.) 1645
Drummossie *Culloden*
Dungan Hill 1647
Fehrbellin 1675
Firozshahr 1845
Germantown 1777
Gettysburg 1863
Goose Green 1982
Gravelotte 1870
Guinegatte 1513
Injim River 1951
Koniggratz *Sadowa*
Kunersdorf 1759
Lule Burgas 1912
Lundy's Lane 1814

LAND BATTLES

Lutzelburg 1758
Maharajpur 1843
Malplaquet 1709
Maserfield 641
Milli Duzov 1829
Moncontour 1569
Montebello 1796: 1805
Montenotte 1796
Mount Tabor 1799
Neerwinden 1793
Nordlingen 1634: 1645
Ostrolenka 1831
Paardeberg 1900
Port Arthur 1894
Quatre Bras 1815
Rosebecque 1382
Saint-Denis 1567
Santa Lucia 1848
Shrewsbury 1403
Solway Moss 1542
Stone River *Murfreesboro*
Strasbourg 1870
Tannenburg 1410: 1914
Tel-el-Kebir 1882
Tewkesbury 1471
Tinchebray 1106
Wilderness 1864

11

Bannockburn 1314
Briars Creek 1779
Castelnuovo 1796
Castiglione 1796
Champaubert 1814
Chickamauga 1863
Chilianwala 1849
Clifton Moor 1745
Gross Beeren 1813
Guadalajara 1937
Halidon Hill 1333
Hennersdorf 1745
Hohenlihden 1800
Isandlhwana 1879
Kesselsdorf 1745
Kirk-Kilisse 1912
Langensalza 1866
Marston Moor 1644
Modder River 1899

Montinirail 1814
Mookerheede 1574
Northampton 1460
Pfaffendorf 1760
Philiphaugh 1645
Port Stanley 1982
Prestonpans 1745
Rheinfelden 1638
Rietfontein 1899
Rorke's Drift 1879
Saint-Dizier 1814
Sheriffmuir 1715
Tagliacozzo 1268
Villafranca 1812
Vinegar Hill 1798
White Plains 1776

12

Arcis-sur-Aube 1814
Atherton Moor 1643
Carberry Hill 1567
Chickahominy 1862
Elandslaagte 1899
Flodden Field 1513
Great Meadows 1754
Munchengratz 1866
Murfreesboro 1862: 1863
Neville's Cross 1346
Saint-Antoine 1652
Saint-Quentin 1557: 1871
Sarantoporon 1912
Seringapatam 1791: 1792
Villaviciosa 1710
Williamsburg 1862

13

Bosworth Field 1485
Cynoscephalae 190BC
Killiecrankie 1689
'Knightsbridge' (N. Africa) 1942
Little Bighorn 1876
Magersfontein 1899
Milvian Bridge 312
Mons Badonicus c.500
Navas de Tolosa 1212
Newtownbutler 1689

Nicholson's Nek 1899
Northallerton *Standard, The*
Passchendaele 1917
Spottsylvania 1864
Stow-on-the-Wold *Donnington*
White Mountain 1620
White Oak Swamp 1862
Yenidje Vardar 1912

14

Bothwell Bridge 1679
Chateau Thierry 1814: 1918
Cropredy Bridge 1644
Fredericksburg 1862: *Chancellorsville*
Fuentes de Onoro 1811

Hohenfriedburg 1745
Mechanicsville 1862
Mortimer's Cross 1461
Pusan Perimeter 1950

15

Resasca de la Palma 1846
Teutoburger Wald 9AD

16

Chancellorsville 1863
Gross Jaegerndorf 1757
Linlithgow Bridge 1526

NAVAL BATTLES

4

Acre 1840
Java 1942
Nile, The 1798
Oran 1940
Yalu 1894

5

Cadiz 1587
Dover 1652: 1653
Downs, The 1666
Hango 1714
Lagos 1759
Lissa 1866
Samos 1824
Sirte 1942
Sluys 1340
Texel 1653

6

Armada (destruction of) 1588
Lemnos 1913

Malaga 1704
Malaya 1941
Manila 1898
Midway 1942
Narvik 1940
Saints, The 1782
Sinope 1853
Ushant 1778: 1794

7

Actium 31BC
Altmark (boarding of) 1940
Coronel 1914
Dunkirk 1666
Harwich 1666
Jutland 1916
La Hogue 1692
Lepanto 1571
Matapan 1941
Messina 1676
Minorca 1756
Salamis 430BC
Taranto 1940

NAVAL BATTLES

8

Aix Roads 1809
Bismarck (sinking of) 1941
Coral Sea 1942
Dannoura 1185
Dominica *Saints, The*
Itamarca 1640
Japan Sea 1904
Navarino 1827
Portland 1653
Quiberon 1759
Rosas Bay 1809
Santiago 1898
Tchesine 1770
Tsu Shima 1905

9

Algeciras 1801
Cartagena 1588
Champlain 1814
Dungeness 1652
Negapatam 1782
St Vincent 1693: 1780: 1797
Santa Cruz 1657: 1797
Trafalgar 1805
Yellow Sea 1904(2)
Zeebrugge 1918

10

Aboukir Bay *Nile, The*
Beachy Head 1690
Camperdown 1797
Copenhagen 1801: 1807

Dogger Bank 1781: 1915
Falkland Is. 1914
Guadeloupe *Saints, The*
Heligoland 1914
New Orleans 1862
River Plate, The 1939

11

Aegospotami 404BC
Basque Roads *Aix Roads*
Bismarck Sea 1943
Newport News *Hampton Roads*
Passaro Cape 1718
Pearl Harbor 1941

12

Gibraltar Bay 1782
Hampton Roads 1862
Southwold Bay 1672

13

Aegadean Isles 241BC
Chesapeake Bay 1781
Lake Champlain 1814
North Foreland 1653: 1666(2)
Philippine Sea 1944
South Atlantic 1982

14

Cape Finisterre 1747(2): 1805
Macassar Strait 1942

SIEGES

4

Acre 1189–91: 1799: 1832: 1840
Bonn 1689: 1703
Como 1127
Coni 1691: 1744
Kars 1855
Kehl 1796–7
Metz 1552–3: 1870
Mons 1691: 1709: 1746: 1792
Nice 1705
Riga 1700: 1710
Rome 1527: 1849
Sico 1822
York 1644

5

Arras 1640
Breda 1625: 1793
Cadiz 1812
Calvi 1794
Capua 211BC: 1501: 1799
Conde 1676: 1793: 1794
Corfu 1536: 1716–18
Cumae 553
Delhi 1857
Douay 1710
Gaeta 1707: 1734: 1860–61
Genoa 1684: 1747: 1800
Ghent 1706
Glatz 1622: 1742: 1807
Herat 1837–8: 1856
Leith 1560
Liege 1468: 1702: 1914
Lille 1708: 1792
Lyons 1793
Mainz 1689: 1793
Malta 1565: 1798: 1800: 1940–42
Namur 1692: 1695
Padua 1509
Paris 885–6: 1594: 1870–71
Pavia 1525: 1655

Rouen 1419: 1449: 1591
Thorn 1703
Tunis 1270: 1535
Turin 1640: 1706
Xeres 1262
Ypres 1648: 1794

6

Alesia 52BC
Amiens 1597
Ancona 1799
Bataan 1942
Berlin (blockade) 1948–49
Bilbao 1835: 1874: 1937
Burgos 1812: 1813
Calais 1347: 1558: 1596: 1940
Candia 1667–69
Chalus 1199
Cracow 1702: 1794
Danzig 1734: 1793: 1807: 1813–14
Dublin 1170: 1500: 1649
Exeter 1136
Gerona 1808–09
Ismail 1770: 1790
Janina 1913
Landau 1702: 1703: 1793
Lerida 1647: 1707: 1810
Leyden 1574
Madrid 1936–39
Malaga 1487
Mantua 1796–97
Naples 1495: 1799: 1806
Olmutz 1741: 1758
Ostend 1601–04: 1706: 1745: 1798
Peking (legations) 1900
Plevna 1877
Prague 1741–44
Quebec 1759
Rheims 1359
Rhodes 1306–09: 1480: 1522
Tobruk 1941: 1942
Toledo 1936

SIEGES

Toulon 1707: 1793
Vannes 1342
Venice 1849
Verdun 1792: 1916
Vienna 1529: 1683: 1848
Warsaw 1831: 1939: 1944
Xativa 1246: 1707
Zurich 1544

7

Algiers 1682–83: 1816: 1830
Almeida 1810
Antwerp 1584–85: 1832: 1914
Avignon 1226
Badajoz 1385: 1396: 1542: 1705: 1811: 1812
Baghdad 1258
Berwick 1296: 1333: 1481
Bethune 1710
Bologna 1506: 1796: 1799
Brescia 1512: 1849
Breslau 1807
Brisach 1638
Chester 1643–46
Chillon 1536
Chitral 1895
Corinth 1205: 1209
Cordova 1012
Cremona 1702
Dresden 1756: 1760: 1813
Dunkirk 1646: 1793
Granada 1491–92
Haarlem 1572–73
Komaron 1849
La Motte 1634
Leipzig 1547: 1642
Lucknow 1857
Messina 1282: 1719: 1848
Orleans 1428–29: 1563
Quesnay 1793–94
Scutari 1913
Seville 1248
Tortosa 1810–11
Tournai 1340: 1513: 1581: 1667: 1709: 1792
Zutphen 1586

8

Belgrade 1456: 1521: 1717: 1789
Besancon 1668: 1674
Bordeaux 1451: 1453
Bouchain 1711
Boulogne 1544
Brussels 1695: 1746
Budapest 1541: 1686: 1944–45
Chartres 1568
Drogheda 1649
Flushing 1809
Harfleur 1415
Kandahar 1521: 1839–42
Khartoum 1884–85
Limerick 1651: 1690–91
Mafeking 1899: 1900
Mannheim 1793
Numantia 134–133BC
Olivenza 1811
Pamplona 1813
Richmond (Va. USA) 1864–65
Rochelle 1573: 1628
Roxburgh 1460
Saguntum 219BC
Smolensk 1611: 1812
Temesvar 1716
Toulouse 844: c.848: 1229
Valencia 1812

9

Algeciras 1342–44
Barcelona 1471: 1697: 1705: 1706: 1714
Belle Isle 1761
Bois-le-Duc 1601: 1603: 1794
Bomarsund 1854
Cartagena 1706: 1873–74
Charleroi 1672: 1690
Cherbourg 1418: 1758
Compiegne 1430
Edinburgh 1093: 1296
Famagusta 1571
Gibraltar 1704: 1779: 1782–83
Gottingen 1760
Groningen 1594: 1678
Jerusalem c.1400BC: 588BC: 70AD: 637: 1099
Kimberley 1899–1900

Ladysmith 1899–1900
Leningrad 1941–43
Luxemburg 1795
Magdeburg 1631: 1806
Montargis 1427
Montauban 1621
Oudenarde 1705
Perpignan 1542: 1642
Saragossa 1710: 1808: 1809
Silistria 1854
Stralsund 1715
Tarragona 1813
Vicksburg 1863

10

Adrianople 1912–13
Charleston (USA) 1780: 1863–65
Colchester 1648
Copenhagen 1658: 1801: 1807
Gloucester 1643
Heidelberg 1688
Landrecles 1712: 1794
Maestricht 1579: 1673: 1703: 1748:
1793–94
Montevideo 1807: 1814
Phalsbourg 1814: 1815: 1870
Port Arthur 1904
Romorantin 1356
Sebastopol 1854–55: 1941–42
Stalingrad 1942

Strasbourg 1870
Therouanne 1303: 1479: 1513
Thionville 1792

11

Dien Bien Phu 1954
Londonderry 1689
Pondicherry 1748
Schweidnitz 1762: 1807

12

Bergen-op-Zoom 1588: 1622: 1747:
1814
Fredrikshald 1718
Phillipsburg 1644: 1676: 1688: 1734:
1799–1800
Saint-Quentin 1557
San Sebastian 1813
Seringapatam 1792: 1799
Valenciennes 1677: 1793: 1794
Westerplatte 1939

13/14/15

Ciudad Rodrigo 1810: 1812
Constantinople 1453
Edinburgh Castle 1571

TREATIES

3

Abo 1743

4

Caen 1081
Lauf 1453
Lodi 1454
Riga 1920: 1921
Rome 1957

5

Alton 1101
Arras 1482
Athis 1305
Baden 1714
Basle 1499
Blois 1504: 1505
Breda 1667
Brest 1435
Delft 1428
Hague 1625: 1716: 1790

8

Aranjuez 1752
Augsburg 1686
Barwalde 1631
Belgrade 1739
Boulogne 1550
Bretigny 1360
Brussels 1516: 1522: 1948
Cherasco 1631
Escorial 1733
Esinburg 1664
Gandamak 1879
Guerande 1365
Khaeroed 1613
Murzsteg 1903
Nijmegen 1678–79
Pretoria 1881
Pyrenees 1659
Roskilde 1658
Roxburgh 1332
St Claire 911
Stolbova 1617
Tarascon 1291
Tientsin 1858
Uccialli 1889
Valencay 1813
Waitangi 1840

9

Aberdaron 1406
Algeciras 1906
Amsterdam 1717
Aquisgram 1749
Barcelona 1493: 1529
Bromsebro 1645
Bucharest 1886
Compiegne 1624
Dordrecht 1489
Edinburgh 1560
Luneville 1801
Newcastle 1334
Picquigny 1475
Pressburg 1490: 1626: 1805
St Germain 1331: 1570: 1679
Salisbury 1289
Saragossa 1529

Stockholm 1720: 1724: 1959
Vancelles 1556
Vincennes 1330

10

Dusseldorf 1624
Gerstungen 1074
Montebello 1175
Nicolsburg 1866
San Germano 1230
San Stefano 1878
Schonbrunn 1805
Shrewsbury 1267
Versailles 1756: 1783: 1919–20
Washington 1846: 1949
Westphalia 1648(2)

11

Altranstadt 1706
Campo Formio 1797
Furstenberg 1373
Northampton 1328
Passarowitz 1718
Reichenbach 1790
Shimonoseki 1895
Tordesilhas 1494
Vereeniging 1902
Villafranca 1859
Wallingford 1153
Westminster 1654: 1716: 1756
Zsitva-Torok 1606

12

Antananarivo 1895
Bretton Woods 1944
Grosswardein 1538
Hampton Court 1562
Herrenhausen 1725
Hubertusberg 1763
St Petersburg 1805
San Idlefonso 1796
Wusterhausen 1726

13

Aix-la-Chapelle 1668: 1748
Clayton-Bulwer 1850
Fontainebleau 1785

14

Charlottenburg 1723

Constantinople 1479: 1573: 1724: 1889: 1897
Fredericksborg 1720
Frederickshamn 1809

15

Cateau Cambresis 1559
Kuchuk Kainardji 1774

WILD WEST (people and places)

Also see LAND BATTLES (p. 139) for Civil War, etc.; LANGUAGES (p. 189) for Red Indian tribes and locations; WARRIORS (p. 125) for Civil War generals and Red Indian chiefs; YCLEPT (p. 153) for former names of locations.

4

Bean, Roy saloonkeeper-judge, Texas
Cody, Buffalo Bill owner, Wild West Show
Earp (brothers) James: Morgan: Virgil: Wyatt
Ford, Bob killed Jesse James
Horn, Tom gunfighter

5

Boone, Daniel frontiersman
James (brothers) Frank: Jesse

6

Bonney, William H. *Billy the Kid*
Carson, Kit trapper
Custer, George Armstrong glorymongering cavalry officer
El Paso town in Texas
Hardin, John Wesley notorious gunfighter
Hickok, James Butler 'Wild Bill', lawman
Oakley, Annie 'Little Sure Shot'
Parker, Isaac Charles 'the hanging judge'

7

Abilene town in Texas
Allison, Clay Texas gunfighter
Cassidy, Butch leader of *Wild Bunch*
Clanton (Ike: Billy) fought at *O.K. Corral*
Garrett, Pat sheriff, shot *Billy the Kid*
Guthrie town in Oklahoma
Liberty town in Montana
Lincoln (county) scene of 'War'
Maledon, George 'prince of hangmen'
Rosebud (creek) scene of Indian battle
Siringo, Charles Angelo *Pinkerton* agent
Wichita town in Kansas
Younger (brothers) Bob: Cole: Jim: John

8

Boot Hill cemetery
Holliday, Doc notorious gunfighter
Lawrence town in Kansas
O.K. Corral scene of gunfight *(Earp)*
Tilghman, Bill lawman

9

Bent's Fort trading post on R. Arkansas
Dodge City town in Kansas
Fort Smith town in Arkansas
Fort Worth town in Texas
Lexington town in Montana
Masterson, Bat lawman
Pinkerton detective agency
Quantrill, William Clarke Confederate guerilla leader
Rio Grande (river) US/Mexico boundary
Tombstone town in Arizona
Wild Bunch, The outlaw gang

10

Belle Starr bandit queen
Black Hills, The area in Dakota
Cattle Kate gun-toting rustler queen
Clearwater, River scene of Indian battle

Dalton Gang Bob: Emmett: Gratton (brothers)
Doolin Gang outlaws
Northfield town in Minnesota
Poker Alice railroad gambler
soiled dove 'lady of the evening'
Wells Fargo express company
Yazoo Strip region of land scandal

11

Big Nose Kate *soiled dove*
Billy the Kid notorious gunfighter
Coffeyville town in Kansas
Sundance Kid member of *Wild Bunch*
Wounded Knee (creek) scene of Indian battle

12/13

Salt Lake City Mormon foundation
Chisholm Trail cattle-driving route

YCLEPT
(former names and designations of places)

note Boundary changes make some definitions approximate.
Also see BIBLICAL PLACES (p. 326).

3

An-i Ho-tung, China
Bec Vienna
Edo Tokyo
Ezo Hokkaido, Japan
Goa India (part of)
Gur Rask, Iran
Oea Tripoli, Libya

4

Acre *Ptolemais*

Aden South Yemen (part of)
Aela Aqaba, Jordan
Amid Digarbakir, Turkey
Asir Saudi Arabia (part of)
Bone Annaba, Algeria
Buda Twin city to Pest (Budapest)
Deva Chester
Dwyr Dover
Elne Perpignan, France
Gaul France
Guns Doszeg, Hungary
Hail Saudi Arabia (part of)
Isca Caerleon, Wales
Java Indonesia (part of)

Kasi Varanasi, India
Kent an English Kingdom c.449–860
Masr Cairo
Nedj Saudi Arabia
Pest twin city to Buda (Budapest)
Siam Thailand
Tver Kalinin, USSR
Tyre Sur, Lebanon
Urci Almeria, Spain
Wien Vienna
Yedo Tokyo
York Toronto

5

Agram Zagreb, Yugoslavia
Alban A Scottish kingdom
Annam Vietnam (part of)
Aquae *Aquae Sextiae*
Ariha Jericho, Jordan
Aulon Vlone, Albania
Baden part of Germany
Bornu, Kingdom of split
  Nigeria/Cameroons, etc.
Chepe Cheapside, London
Cirta Constantine, Algeria
Congo (Kinshasa) Zaire
Congo, River River Zaire
Dagon Rangoon, Burma
Deira, Kingdom of *Northumbria* (part
  of)
Delos Mikra Dili
Emesa Homs, Syria
Emona Ljubljana, Yugoslavia
Erech Uruk, Iraq
Essex an English kingdom
Eylan Bagrationovsk, USSR
Gades Cadiz
Ghent capital of *Flanders*
Goree Dakar, Senegal
Halab Aleppo, Syria
Hejaz Saudi Arabia (part of)
Hesse Germany (part of)
Iceni British tribe of Boudicca
Ilium Troy, Turkey
Ister, River River Danube
Kedah Malaysia (part of)
Kyoto capital of Japan till 1868
Liger, River River Loire

Lorch Linz, Austria
Lydda Lod, Israel
Meath an Irish kingdom
Morea Peloponnese, Greece
Ninus Nineveh, Iraq
Pagan capital of Burma 849–1287
Papia Pavia, Italy
Prima *Scupi*
Scupi *Uskub*
Sidon Saida, Syria
Suran Da Nang, Vietnam
Tgras, River River Dniester
Thorn Torun, Poland
Thule (possibly) Fair Isle
Tyana Bor, Turkey
Uskub Skopje, Yugoslavia
Wadai Chad (part of)
Ypres Ieper, Belgium

6

Acadia Nova Scotia
Africa Tunisia
Al Quds Jerusalem
Ambian Amiens, France
Apulum *Gyulafehervar*
Aragon a Spanish kingdom
Azotus Ashdod, Israel
Berger Mons, Belgium
Beroea *Halab*
Biafra (1967–70) part of Nigeria
Borneo Malaysia (part of)
Bosnia Yugoslavia (part of)
Brecia Wroclaw, Poland
Canton Guangzhou, China
Cathay China
Ceylon Sri Lanka
Cracow capital of Poland 1320–1609
Cyrene Shahhat, Libya
Danzig Gdansk, Poland
Delphi Kastri
Dubris Dover
Edessa Urfa, Turkey
Fustat Cairo
Glevum Gloucester
Hadria Atri, Italy
Hamwih Southampton
Iberus, River River Ebro
Istria Yugoslavia (part of)

Johore Malaysia (part of)
Kachan Quang Nam, Vietnam
Kaukab Belvoir, Israel
Latvia USSR (part of)
Liampo Ningpo
Lindum Lincoln
Loango split Congo/Angola etc.
Malaya Malaysia (part of)
Mercia an English kingdom c.500–874
Moscow (Grand Duchy) Russia
Newton Hartford, Conn., USA
Nicaea Iznik, Turkey
Orchoe Uruk, Iraq
Peking Beijing
Perlis Malaysia (part of)
Persia Iran
Prague Praha, Czechoslovakia
Ragusa Dubrovnik, Yugoslavia
Ratuma Rouen
Saigon Ho Chi Minh City, Vietnam
Salona Amfissa, Greece
Saxony Germany (part of)
Serbia Yugoslavia (part of)
Smyrna Izmir, Turkey
Sussex an English kingdom
   c.477–c.685
Tanais, River River Don
Tarsus Tarsus Cayi, Turkey
Thebes Karnak, Egypt
Tilsit Sovetsk, USSR
Tingis Tangiers
Tolosa Toulouse
Treves Trier, W. Germany
Ulster an Irish kingdom
Vernyy Alma-Ata, USSR
Viadua, River River Oder
Wahran Oran, Algeria
Wessex the eventual kingdom of
   England

7

Akhtiar *Sevastopol*
Alsatia (nickname) Whitefriars,
   London
Antioch Antakya, Turkey
Arelate Arles, France
Armenia USSR (part of)
Ash Sham Damascus, Syria

Assyria former Middle East empire
Avignon papal 1309–77; antipapal
   1378–1408
Aynthia former capital of *Siam*
Babylon former Middle East empire
Bactria (Persian Province) Afghanistan
   (part of)
Batavia Djakarta, Indonesia
Bavaria Germany (part of)
Benares Varanasi, India
Bernica, Kingdom of *Northumbria*
   (part of)
Bohemia Czechoslovakia (part of)
Breslau Wroclaw, Poland
Castile a Spanish kingdom
Celebes Indonesia (part of)
Cherson *Kherson*
Coimbra capital of Portugal 1139–1260
Cologne Koln
Corcyra Corfu, Greece
Croatia Yugoslavia (part of)
Danelaw Danish territory in England
Dimashq Damascus, Syria
Durazzo Durres, Yugoslavia
Eritrea Ethiopia (part of)
Estonia USSR (part of)
Etruria Tuscany
Felsina Bologna, Italy
Formosa Taiwan
Goshen, Land of Boer republic 1882–4
Hanover Germany (part of)
Icosium Algiers, Algeria
Illyria Greek Adriatic colonies
Illyria, Kingdom of Napoleonic
   creation (see *Istria*)
Ipaygia Calabria, Italy
Karmona Cordoba, Spain
Katanga 1960–63 Congo (part of)
Kerkira Corfu, Greece
Kherson *Akhtiar*
Leghorn Livorno, Italy
Lepanto Navpaktos, Greece
Limonum Poitiers, France
Livonia split Estonia/Latvia
Lucayos Bahamas
Lutetia Paris
Maeonia Lydia, Asia Minor
Moravia Czechoslovakia (part of)
Munster an Irish kingdom
Nanking a former capital of China

Navarre alternate French/Spanish province
Olisipo Lisbon
Ostland Nazi-occupied Baltic area
Parthia *Persia* (part of)
Pototsk Baltic state 10th C.–1307
Prussia Germany/Poland (parts of)
Rutland Leicestershire (part of)
Salamis Famagusta, Cyprus
Salonae Split, Yugoslavia
Sardica *Serdica*
Serdica Sofia, Bulgaria
Spalato Split, Yugoslavia
Stabrok Georgetown, Guyana
Stettin Szczecin, Poland
Ticinum Pavia, Italy
Tourane Da Nang, Vietnam
Treveri Trier, W. Germany
Vistula, River River Wista

8

Akkerman Belgorod-Dnestrovskiy
Aquincum *Buda + Pest*
Ariminum Rimini, Italy
Armorica Brittany
Auckland former capital N. Zealand
Avaricum Bourges, France
Bathurst Banjul, Gambia
Belgrade Beograd
Bosporus Karadenzi, Bogazi
Caerleon Chester
Caer-luel Carlisle
Cambodia Kampuchea
Carthage ancient Phoenecian city
Cawnpore Kampur, India
Caesarea (1) Cherchell, Algeria
Caesarea (2) Kayseri, Turkey
Caesarea (3) Har Qesari, Israel
Chemnitz Karl-Marx-Stadt, E. Germany
Dalmatia (ancient) Yugoslavia (approx)
Dalmatia (modern) Yugoslavia (part of)
Dalriada part of County Antrim
Dunaburg Dvinsk, USSR
Eboracum York
Eburacum York

El-Kahira Cairo
Flanders Belgium (part of)
Florence an Italian republic
Golconda India (part of)
Hispalis Seville
Hispania Spain/Portugal
Kelantan Malaysia (part of)
Kiaochow Tsingtao, China
Lapurdum Bayonne, France
Leucosia Nicosia, Cyprus
Lugunum Lyon, France
Magnesia Manisa, Turkey
Mahratta *Central Provinces*
Massalia Marseilles
Moldavia Yugoslavia (part of)
Monastir Bitola, Yugoslavia
Nemausus Nimes, France
Nemessos Limassol, Cyprus
New Sarum Salisbury, Wilts
Pannonia Illyricum (part of) see *Illyria*
Panormus Palermo, Sicily
Pax Iulia Beja, Portugal
Pictones Poitiers, France
Rhodesia (ex S. Rhodesia) Zimbabwe
Roskilde capital of Denmark till 1443
Sardinia an Italian kingdom
Segontia Caernarvon, Wales
Slovakia Czechoslavakia (part of)
Togoland split Ghana/Togo
Tonking Vietnam (part of)
Vivarium Squillance, Italy
Wa States see *Shan States*
Zanzibar Tanzania (part of)
Zululand S. Africa (part of)

9

Abyssinia Ethiopia
Amarapure former capital of Burma
Antigonea Nicaea
Auschwitz Oswiecim, Poland
Barcelona capital, Republican Spain 1937–9
Bethlehem Beit-Lahm
Brunswick Braunschweig, W. Germany
Burdigala Bordeaux, France

Byzantium *Contantinople*
Chalcedon (1) Kadikoy, Turkey
Chalcedon (2) Uskadar, Turkey
Chungking capital of China 1941/5
Connaught an Irish kingdom
Epidamnus Durres, Yugoslavia
Firuzabad Rask, Iran
Fort Garry Winnipeg
Gold Coast Ghana
Indo-China Vietnam
Karlsburg Alba Julia, Romania
Kaupangen Trondheim, Norway
Khanbalik *Peking*
Krung Thep Bangkok, Thailand
Laodiceia Beirut, Lebanon
Lithuania USSR (part of)
Lusitania Portugal/Spain (part of)
Maracanda Samarkand, USSR
Nyasaland Malawi
Oil Rivers Nigeria
Palestine (ancient) Ottoman Empire
  (part of)
Palestine (modern) Israel
Petrograd Leningrad
Phoenicia Lebanon/Syria (parts of)
Pressburg Bratislava, Czechoslovakia
Ptolemais *St Jean d'Acre*
Rotomagus Rouen, France
Salisbury Harare, Zimbabwe
Saragossa Zaragoza, Spain
Thang Long Hanoi, Vietnam
Trajeatum Utrecht, Holland
Transvaal S. Africa (part of)
Tsaritsin *Stalingrad*
Turkestan (Chinese) Sinkiang
Turkestan (Russian) various Soviet
  Socialist Republics
Vindobona Vienna
Visurgis, River River Weser
Wallachia Rumania (part of)
Zuider Zee Yssel Meer

10

Adrianople Edirne, Turkey
Alexandria (1) Arbil, Iraq
Alexandria (2) Eski Stambul, Turkey
Alexandria (3) Ghanzi, Afghanistan

Alexandria (4) Herat, Afghanistan
Alexandria (5) Kandahar, Afghanistan
Alexandria (6) Egypt: extant
Antiocheia (1) Adana, Turkey
Antiocheia (2) (Antioch) Antakya,
  Turkey
Antiocheia (3) Gerasa, Jordan
Antiocheia (4) Mallus, Turkey
Antiocheia (5) Mary, Iran
Antiocheia (6) Nusaybin, Turkey
Antiocheia (7) (Tarsus) Tarsus Cayi,
  Turkey
Antiocheia (8) Urfa, Turkey
Antiocheia (9) Yalvac, Turkey
Basutoland Lesotho
Cape Colony Cape Province
Constantia Famagusta, Cyprus
Durovernum Canterbury
East Anglia an English kingdom
Fort Nassau Albany, New York, USA
Fort Orange Albany, New York, USA
Gotenhafen 1939–45 Nazi Gdynia
Griqualand S. Africa (part of)
Heliopolis Baalbeck, Lebanon
Hellespont Dardanelles
Holmgaard Novgorod, USSR
Justiniana Prima
Klaarwater Griquatown, *Griqualand*
Madagascar Malagasy
Mamecestre Manchester
Montenegro Yugoslavia (part of)
Negroponte Chalcis, Greece
Niger Coast Nigeria
Pax Augusta Badajoz, Spain
Port Arthur Lushun, China
Quinnipiac New Haven, Conn., USA
Sevastopol Sebastopol, USSR
Shan States (+ Wa States) Burma
Singidunum Belgrade
Stalinabad Dushanbe, USSR
Stalingrad Volgograd, USSR
Stellaland a Boer republic 1882–4
Tanganyika Tanzania (part of)
Third Reich Nazi Germany
Thunder Bay Fort William, Ontario
Tikhon'kaya Birobidjan, USSR
Verulamium St Albans
Westphalia a Napoleonic kingdom
  1807–14
Yerba Buena San Francisco

YCLEPT

11

Albertville Kalemie, Zaire
Ammochostos Famagusta, Cyprus
Aquisgranum *Aix-la-Chapelle*
Borysthenes, River River
  Dnepr/Dnieper
Bourbonnais Allier, France
Brandenburg *Prussia* (as electorate)
Camulodunum Colchester
Chersoneus *Cherson*
Christiania Oslo
Cochin China *Indo-China*
Durcortorum Rheims
Dutch Guiana Surinam
Eastern Nedj (W. Nedj) *Nedj*
Hierosolyma Jerusalem
Hippo Regius *Bone*
Julia Romula Seville
Kerak of Moab Karak, Jordan
Koenigsburg Kalingrad, USSR
Lotharingia, Kingdom of Lorraine
Luguvallium Carlisle
Mare Nostrum Mediterranean Sea
Mashonaland Zimbabwe (part of)
Mesopotamia Iraq
Middle Congo Congo (Brazzaville)
Moguntiacum Mainz, W. Germany
Northumbria an English kingdom
Pataliputra Patna, India
Philomelium Aksehir, Turkey
St Jean d'Acre Akko, Israel
Samarobriva *Ambian*
Strathclyde a Scottish kingdom
Sunda Kalapa Djakarta, *Java*
Telo Martius Toulon
Transjordan Jordan
Upper Canada Ontario (1791–1867)
Vichy France Southern France 1940–45
Western Nedj see *Eastern Nedj*

12

Aquae Sextiae Aix-en-Provence
Argentoratum Strasbourg, France
Bechuanaland Botswana
Belgian Congo *Congo* (Kinshahsa)
Caesarodunum Tours, France
Durocortorum Reims/Rheims, France

Ekaterinburg Sverdlovsk, USSR
French Guinea Guinea
Hippo Zarytis Bizerta, Tunisia
Land of Goshen *Goshen*
Legerceastre Leicester
Leopoldville Kinshasa, Zaire
Matabeleland Zimbabwe (part of)
Medehamstede Peterborough
New Amsterdam New York
Newfoundland Canada (part of)
Nombre de Dios Porto Bello, Panama
Philadelphia (1) Alasehir, Turkey
Philadelphia (2) Amman, Jordan
St Petersburg *Petrograd* (1914–24)
Second Empire France, 1852–71
Stanleyville Kisangani, Zaire
Streoneshalh Whitby
Tenochtitian Mexico City (Aztec
  period)
Thessalonika Salonica
Tripolitania Libya
Victoriahavn Narvik

13

Aix-la-Chapelle Aachen, West
  Germany
Alexandra Land Northern Territory,
  Australia
Banda Oriental Uruguay
Borbetomagnus Worms
British Guiana Guyana
Caesaragusta *Saragossa*
Dionysiopolis Balchik, Bulgaria
Ekaterinoslav Dniepropetrovsk
El Iskandariya Alexandria, Egypt
Fort Amsterdam New York, USA
Fort Prudhomme Memphis, Tennessee
Fredrickshald Halden, Norway
Galica-Volhyia Ukraine
Gyulafehervar *Karlsburg*
Hadrianopolis Edirne, Turkey
Indian Country Oklahoma (see
  LANGUAGES, p. 191)
Medina Majerit Madrid
Nijni Novgorod Gorki
Northworthige Derby
Ottoman Empire Turkey, Middle East,
  Balkans

Pontus Euxinus Black Sea
Sinus Arabicus Red Sea
Venta Belgarum Winchester

14

Bohemia-Moravia Nazi protectorate
 1939–45
Castile and Leon a Spanish joint
 kingdom
Ciudad Trujillo Santo Domingo
 (1936–61)
Congo Free State Zaire
Congo (Kinshahsa) Zaire
Constantinople Istanbul
Crocodilopolis Patara, Egypt
Elisabethville Lubumbashi, Zaire
Fort St Frederic Crown Point, Quebec
Fort Washington Cincinnati
Geramicopolis Ermenek, Turkey
Hesse-Darmstadt a German republic
 1919–33
Irish Free State Eire (1922–37)
Kingdom of Illyria see *Illyria*
La Ville d'Etroit Detroit
Mare Germanicum North Sea
Novum Castellum Neuchatel

Olnets Province Soviet Karelia
Red River Colony Manitoba
Russian America Alaska
Van Dieman's Land Tasmania
Weimar Republic post w.w.i Germany

15

Aelia Capitolonia Jerusalem
Aurelia Aquensis Baden-Baden
Baile Atha Cliath Dublin
Brighthelmstone Brighton
British Honduras Belize
Canakkale Bogazi Dardanelles,
 Turkey
Dutch East Indies Indonesia
United Provinces Uttar Pradesh

16

Batavian Republic Holland 1795–1806
Calleva Atrebatum Silchester
Central Provinces Madhya Pradesh
German East Africa *Tanganyika*
Southern Rhodesia *Rhodesia*

HOME AND AWAY

Apart from the FOOD AND DRINK section (p. 170) the emphasis is given to the less usual, foreign or historical aspects of the individual subjects with many slang and dialect words.

tf type of
vr various

BUILDINGS

Also see RELIGIOUS TERMS (p. 344) and GEOGRAPHICAL TERMS (p. 53).

3

cot cottage (poetic)
cub cattle pen
hut small/mean house
inn public house
ken a (disreputable) house
lat an isolated pillar (India)
mew original singular of *mews*
pit a (castle) prison
pub public house, inn
sty pig-pen
suk souk, E. market place
suq *suk*
won to dwell: a dwelling (obs.)

4

bawn house fortification: cattle pen
bema Greek orator's rostrum
byre cowhouse
coop prison: fowl pen
fank a sheepfold
grot grotto (poetic)
hong Chinese warehouse
kayf cafe (vulgar spelling)
khan a caravanserai
mews stable-house(s)
pawn gallery: covered walk
pile a tall building
quod prison

tana Indian police/military station
tilt tent: hut
xyst *xystus*
yett gate, door (Scotland)
yurt Siberian skin tent
zeta small room, closet

5

agger Roman military mound
bazar *bazaar*
bothy humble cottage: hut
broch *tf* circular castle
choky prison: toll-station
dacha Russian county house
fonda (f) a Spanish tavern
hovel small/wretched dwelling: hut
igloo dome-shaped snow house
kasba Arab castle/fortress
kiosk an Eastern garden pavilion
kraal S. African native hut
meuse *mews*
mewes new plural of *mews*
minar a tower
qanat an underground tunnel
serae *khan*
tanna *tana*
tepee Red Indian skin tent
thana *tana*
torii Japanese temple gateway
yamen mandarin's residence

yourt *yurt*

6

bagnio Oriental prison: brothel
bailey (1) outer wall of castle
bailey (2) court within (1)
barton a farmyard
bazaar (shop aping) Eastern market
bedlam a lunatic asylum
biggin a house
bothie *bothy*
cabana small tent-like cabin
camera vaulted/private chamber
casbah *kasba*
donjon castle central tower
durbar an audience chamber
godown Eastern warehouse/
  storeroom
gopura Indian temple-gate tower
grotto (imitation) cave
insula *vr* Roman buildings
kasbah *kasba*
kermis a fair in Low Countries
loggia covered open arcade
loggie a plural of *loggia*
nurhag *nuraghe*
parpen stone wall: bridge parapet
pharos a lighthouse
posada an inn
serail seraglio
serdab an underground chamber
soffit a ceiling
tannah *tana*
tavern inn
teepee *tepee*
thanah *tana*
thanna *tana*
tholus round building: dome (etc.)
turret a small tower
vallum a rampart
vintry wine store/shop
wigwam Red Indian hut
xystos *xystus*
xystus covered portico: open
  colonnade
zareba Sudanese stockade
zenana India/Persia women's
  apartments

7

alcazar (f) palace: fortress: bazaar
bastion *tf* fortified tower
choltry caravanserai: assembly shed
citadel a city fortress
dovecot a pigeon-house
emporia a plural of *emporium*
kibitka Central Asian felt tent
kremlin a citadel
loggias *loggie*
marquee a large tent
mastaba ancient Egyptian tomb
mirador belvedere, watch-tower
nuraghe Bronze Age tower
nuraghi a plural of *nuraghe*
nurhags *nuraghi*
ponceau small bridge: culvert
propyla plural of *propylon*
schloss German castle/palace
thannah *tana*

8

abattoir a public slaughterhouse
barbette *vr tf* gun platform
choultry *choltry*
cockloft room under roof
cromlech a stone circle
dog-house a dog kennel
dove-cote *dovecot*
dry-stove *tf* dry heat hothouse
emporium a big shop
entrepot storehouse: bonded
  warehouse
entresol low, minor storey
frontage front part of building
hostelry an inn
hothouse heated building for plants
log cabin hut built of logs
log house log cabin: prison (USA)
magazine (military) storehouse
martello coastal circular fort
mortuary temporary place for dead
orangery orange tree hothouse
pavilion tent: *vr tf* building
pothouse an ale house
propylon (temple) gateway
refinery place for refining

BUILDINGS

seraglio (1) Muslim women's quarters
seraglio (2) a Turkish palace
shamiana large tent: canopy
slop-shop ready-made clothes shop
smeltery a place for smelting
tap-house a tavern
tea house oriental house for tea
windmill mill powered by wind
workshop room/shop for work
ziggurat Babylonian temple tower
zikkurat *ziggurat*

9

belvedere roof pavilion: summer-house

bridewell house of correction
calaboose (f) prison
gate-house building at/over a gate
lazaretto a place of quarantine
prytaneum Ancient Greek town hall
shamianah *shamiana*
trattoria an Italian restaurant

10/11/12

panopticon *tf* prison: exhibition room
Texas* tower offshore radar tower
zenodochium guest/reception house
Bailey* bridge a prefabricated bridge
caravanserai caravan stopping-place

CLOTHING, MATERIALS AND ORNAMENTATION
(including fabrics used in furnishing)

Also see RELIGIOUS TERMS (p. 344).
o/gmt outer garment
note Plural forms of natural pairs rarely given (i.e. boots indexed as boot).

2

DB double breasted (abbreviation)
es a link of dignitary's collar
gi *gie*
oo wool
os outsize (abbreviation)
SB single breasted (abbreviation)

3

aba Syrian camel hair *o/gmt*
abb woof-/weft-yarn
bib chest apron for child
boa woman's scarf-like *o/gmt*
box cricketer's protective 'cod-piece'
bra brassiere
cap (1) brimless covering for head
cap (2) woman's light head-dress
ess *es*

fez Egyptian red conical cap
gie judo/karate costume
jiz *gizz*
kid glove/shoe of kidskin
kip young animal skin
lap flap: clout (S. Africa)
lei (Hawaiian) garland
mac *macintosh*
mob negligé: mob-cap
obi Japanese woman's sash
rag garment
rep a corded cloth
rug wig (theatrical slang)
sox slang spelling of socks
taj crown: Dervish's cap
tam *Tam o' Shanter*
tog a garment
wig artificial covering of hair
zip toothed-metal clothes fastener

4

abba *aba*
baft a coarse fabric
boot foot and lower leg shoe
capa a Spanish cloak
cape a sleeveless cloak
caul head net/cover
clog wooden-soled shoe
coif *vr tf* head covering
cowl a cap or hood
drag transvestite clothing
duds poor/ragged clothes
felt unwoven fabric
frog an ornamental fastening
gamp an umbrella
garb dress: to clothe
gaud ornament: finery
gear clothes: armour
gimp (trimming of) *tf* yarn
gizz wig (Scotland)
gown loose flowing *o/gmt*
gymp *gimp*
haik Arabic *o/gmt*
hide larger animal skins
hose covering for legs and feet
hyke *haik*
jump a short coat
kell head-dress: hairnet
kepi French military cap
kilt man's short pleated skirt
lamé fabric with metal threads
lawn fine linen
leno thin muslin-like fabric
mack *macintosh*
maud Scottish shepherd's plaid
mino Japanese (hemp) raincoat
mitt mitten
muff hand/foot cylinder
muil *mule* (Scotland)
mule a loose slipper
ouch a brooch
pelt raw hide
poke poke-bonnet
pump *tf* light shoe
quiz a monocle
repp *rep*
ruff starched neck frill
sack *vr tf* women's clothing
saga plural of *sagum*

sari Hindu woman's *o/gmt*
sash (1) waist/shoulder band
sash (2) a turban cloth
slip woman's undergarment
sock (1) see DRAMA AND ENTERTAINMENT
  (p. 29)
sock (2) half-hose
spat *tf* gaiter
tace *tasse*
tapa paper-mulberry bark
toga Roman *o/gmt*
toge *toga*
topi solar hat: pith helmet
tutu ballet dancer's skirt
vamp front part of shoe
veil *vr* facial coverings
vest (1) garb: robe: waistcoat (etc.)
vest (2) undershirt: bodice facing
weed a garment
wrap *wrapper*
yarn spun thread
zona a girdle

5

abaya *aba*
acton warrior's padded jacket
amice cloak: wrap: furred hood
apron cloth/leather front cover
beret (Basque) flat cap
budge lambskin fur
burga *burka*
burka Arabic woman's *o/gmt*
busby hussar's fur hat
caxon *tf* wig
chaps *chaparajos*
choli under-sari blouse
clout piece of patching cloth
crape thin silk (black) fabric
crash coarse strong linen
crepe a *crape*-like fabric
curch *tf* head covering
cymar (1) woman's
  dress/undergarment
cymar (2) *chimer*
Derby* *tf* hat: *tf* strong boot
dhoti Hindu loin-cloth
dicky a false shirt front
drill *drilling*

CLOTHING ETC.

ducks coarse cloth garment
fichu three-cornered hat
flare a skirt shape
frock sailor's jersey: military coat
gilet waistcoat: bodice
grego hooded jacket/cloak: overcoat
g-suit anti-blackout protective garb
haick *haik*
hards coarse flax/hemp
ihram Moslem pilgrimage garb
jabot a lace frill
jemmy an overcoat
jumps stays: clothes
jupon sleeveless jacket: petticoat
kanzu E. African long white *o/gmt*
lapje *lap*
Levis* denim trousers/*o/gmts*
manta a cloak
manto *manteau*
modii plural of *modius*
mufti plain/civilian clothing
mutch woman's close cap
pagri turban: head-scarf
palla Roman woman's mantle
parka windproof hooded *o/gmt*
parki *parka*
pelta a light *buckler*
pilch cloak
plaid a shoulder cloth
primp to dress fussily
romal a head-cloth
rumal *romal*
sabot French wooden shoe
sagum Roman military cloak
saree *sari*
scarf (1) a light decorative band
scarf (2) military/official sash
scarf (3) veil: necktie: muffler: cravat
shako *tf* military cap
shift smock: chemise: shirt (etc.)
slang a watch chain
smock loose protective *o/gmt*
stays a stiff corset
stuff (woollen) cloth
talma loose cloak/cape
tamin thin worsted stuff
tammy *Tam o' Shanter*
tanga a string-like bikini
tappa *tapa*
tasar *tusser*

tasse piece of skirt armour
terai *tf* sun hat
topee *topi*
tower woman's high head-dress
tozie a shawl
tunic Roman undergarment
visor movable facial armour
vitta headband: strap: sash
vizor *visor*
volet back of head veil
weeds widow's mourning apparel
weedy clad in *weeds*

6

abolla Roman military cloak
achkan Indian knee-length coat
afghan a heavy knitted shawl
albert a short watch-chain
anarak *anorak* (1) (2)
Angola of/pertaining to *Angora*
Angora* mohair: *tf* silky wool
anorak (1) Greenlander's fur coat
anorak (2) hooded waterproof *o/gmt*
banian Indian jacket/gown, etc.
banyan *banian*
barret flat cap: biretta
basque a short-skirted jacket
beaver part of facial armour
berret *beret*
bertha a woman's falling collar
berthe *bertha*
biggin child's cap/hood: nightcap
bikini woman's very reduced
   swimwear
blazer a light sporting jacket
boater a straw hat
bobwig a bob-tailed wig
bodice stiffened (inner) garment
bolero a jacket-like bodice
bootee woman's/child's shoe
bowler *tf* stiff felt hat
brogue a stout shoe
burkha *burka*
bustle skirt-shape contrivance
byrnie mail-coat: breastplate
byssus Biblical 'fine linen'
caftan Turkish/Persian *o/gmt*
calash woman's over-cap hood

164

calico (Indian) cotton cloth
calpac *kalpak*
camese *camise*
camise usual Arab shirt
camlet wool and goat's hair cloth
capote long *tf* cloak/mantle
casque helmet: head covering
cestus (1) (Aphrodite's) girdle
cestus (2) ancient boxing glove
chatta an umbrella
chimer a long sleeveless tabard
chinos (f) US twilled cotton trousers
chintz *tf* printed cotton
chopin high clog/*patten*
claque an opera hat
cloche woman's close-fitting hat
coatee short close-fitting coat
corium leather armour
cravat (man's) neckcloth
crepon silk/nylon *crepoline*
cyprus *cypress*
damask (silk) figured material
dhooti *dhoti*
diadem crown: headband
diaper baby's nappy (USA)
dickey *dicky*
dimity a stout white cotton
dirndl Alpine bodice and skirt
dolman Turkish robe: woman's mantle
domino hooded cloak: mask
faille *tf* silk/rayon fabric
fedora *tf* felt hat
ferret narrow silk/cotton ribbon
flares wide-bottomed trousers
flossy overdressed
gaiter ankle covering
garter stocking support band
guimp *gimp*
gurrah coarse Indian muslin
gusset (1) part of chainmail armour
gusset (2) inserted piece in garment
haique *haik*
harden fabric from *hards*
herden *harden*
hogger a footless stocking
hurden *harden*
infula Roman headband
insole inner sole of shoe
jampot clergyman's high collar
jemima elastic-sided boot

jerkin jacket: waistcoat
jersey (1) finest part of wool
jersey (2) woollen upper garment
joseph women's caped overcoat
jubbah long loose Muslim *o/gmt*
jumper (1) woman's knitted upper garment
jumper (2) an overall
jumper (3) a pinafore dress (USA)
kabaya a loose tunic
kaftan *caftan*
kalpak Turk/Tartar felt cap
kersey a coarse woollen cloth
kimono Japanese long robe
kincob a rich silk fabric
kirtle gown: outer petticoat
lappet a little lap or flap
lappie *lap*
linsey linen and wool cloth
livery distinctive garb
loafer a casual shoe
lorica a leather corslet
madras Negro head-scarf
mantle cloak: loose *o/gmt*
mantua woman's loose gown
merino a fine dress fabric
mesail a (two-part) *visor*
mezail *mesail*
mitten (1) a fingerless glove
mitten (2) boxing glove
mob-cap woman's indoor cap
modius Roman god's head-dress
moggan a footless stocking
mohair cloth of Angora goathair
moreen stout corded stuff
morian an open helmet
muslin *tf* cotton fabric
nebris *tf* Greek skirt
nutria coypu fur
panama hat made in Ecuador
panton a slipper
parkee *parka*
patten wooden shoe (obs.)
peplos ancient Greek robe
peruke a wig
pileus a Roman felt cap
pompom hairy ornament: woolly ball
pompon *pompom*
poncho S. American cloak

CLOTHING ETC.

7

puttee wound-cloth legging
puttie *puttee*
raglan *tf* overcoat (sleeve)
ratine *tf* rough dress-fabric
reefer short DB jacket
regale singular of *regalia*
rig out furnish with complete dress
romper *rompers*
ruffle frill: ruff
russel *tf* ribbed material
russet homespun cloth/dress
sacque sham-French *sack*
salade *sallet*
sallet *tf* light helmet
sarong Malay unisex skirt
sateen a satin-like material
sequin a spangle
serape Mexican riding-blanket
shoddy recycled cloth
shorts short trousers
slacks long loose trousers
smalls underclothes: small clothes
sunhat hat with shady brim
tabard (1) peasant's overcoat (hist.)
tabard (2) knight's coat (hist.)
tabard (3) herald's coat: woman's
  o/gmt
tamine *tamin*
tartan woollen checkered stuff
taslet *tasse*
tasset *tasse*
tettix a hair ornament
tippet cape: hangman's rope
tonnag a shaped neck shawl
topper top hat
toupee (part) wig
toupet *toupee*
trilby a soft felt hat
tucker bosom-covering cloth
turban wound-cloth headdress
tusser fawn-coloured silk dress
tuxedo dinner jacket (USA)
ulster long loose overcoat
velvet *tf* silk fabric
visite woman's short cloak
vizard a mask
wampun Red Indian shell beads
weeper *vr* mourning items
whites white attire
zoster Greek waist-belt

baboosh *babouche*
babuche *babouche*
baldric warrior's belt/sash
bandana *tf* coloured handerkchief
bandeau hair/hatband
bashlyk Russian (military) hood
bauchle a badly-worn shoe
belcher *tf* coloured handkerchief
bloomer *tf* woman's complete outfit
blucher a leather half-boot
bottine *vr tf* lady's boot
brasset *brassard*
brocade *tf* silk stuff
buckler a small shield
buckram stiffened fabric
burnous Arabic hooded mantle
calpack *kalpak*
cambric fine white linen/cotton
capuche *tf* cloak/hood
chapeau hat
chechia cylindrical skull-cap
chemise woman's skirt/smock/shift
chimere *chimer*
chlamys man's short cloak
chopine *chopin*
civvies civilian clothes
clobber gear: shoemaker's paste
cockade rosette hat-badge
coronet small crown (nobility)
corsage (1) bodice/waist of dress
corsage (2) bouquet worn at (1)
corslet (1) *curiass*
corslet (2) combined corset and bra
curiass breastplate (and backplate)
cypress a *crape*-like material
delaine *tf* light dress material
dornick *tf* stout figured linen
doublet man's upper garment
drabbet a coarse linen fabric
drawers underpants, knickers
epaulet shoulder badge/ornament
ermelin ermine, stoat's white fur
falsies brassiere pads/padding
filabeg *filibeg*
filibeg long kilt/dress/petticoat
flannel a soft woollen cloth
flounce hanging strip on dress
fustian *tf* coarse twilled cotton fabric

galloon *tf* lace: tape-like trimming
gantlet *gauntlet*
genappe a smooth worsted yarn
gingham *tf* cotton cloth
grogram silk and mohair coarse cloth
G-string narrowest possible decency
  wear
gumboot a rubber boot
gym slip schoolgirl's belted pinafore
Hessian* *tf* long boot
hessian jute cloth
hip-belt 14th C. sword belt
holland a coarse linen fabric
Homburg *tf* man's hat
hosiery hose collectively
jaconet *tf* cotton fabric
layette baby's complete outfit
legging a lower leg covering
leghorn *tf* straw hat
leotard (dancer's) skin-tight garment
lockram a coarse linen
Mae* West* pneumatic life-jacket
maillot tights: swimsuit
manteau woman's loose gown
mantlet woman's small cloak
minever *miniver*
miniver a white fur
mittens see *mitten*: handcuffs
monocle a single eyeglass
montero Spanish huntsman's cap
morrian *morian*
muffler a scarf
nacaret orange-red coloured fabric
nankeen buff coloured cotton cloth
négligé easy undress
oilskin (1) oiled waterproofed fabric
oilskin (2) garment made of (1)
organza transparently thin material
orleans worsted-cotton fabric
overall a protective garment
paisley (1) fabric with Paisley pattern
paisley (2) item made with (1)
paletot a loose overcoat
pelisse military cloak: woman's mantle
pallium a Roman mantle
panoply complete armour
periwig (to dress with) a wig
partlet (obs.) neck cover: ruff: shirt
pierrot woman's low-cut basque
placket breast/back plate armour

puggree *pagri*
puggery *pagri*
pyjamas Indian's light trousers
raiment clothing
ratteen *ratine*
regalia insignia: special garb
rompers child's play garb
sarafan Russian woman's cloak
sarsnet *sarsenet*
satinet (1) a thin satin
satinet (2) a cotton-woollen cloth
scarlet red cloth/garment
singlet an undershirt
soubise 18th C. cravat
spangle small glittering piece
spencer wig: overcoat: undergarment
sporran an ornamental pouch
stammel *tf* woollen cloth
Stetson a 'cowboy hat'
surcoat medieval *o/gmt*
surtout close-bodied frock-coat
tarbush *tarboosh*
topknot piece of added hair
tricorn three-cornered hat
tussore *tusser*
uniform distinctive common garb
vandyke deeply cut collar
wet suit cold-water wear
whittle a woollen shawl
worsted fine wool fabric
wrapper woman's loose *o/gmt*
yashmak Muslim woman's veil

8

accoutre to dress/equip (warrior)
aigrette (egret) plume: jewel-spray
babouche Oriental heelless slipper
babushka (Russian) triangular
  headscarf
baldrick *baldric*
balmoral bonnet: petticoat: boot
bandanna *bandana*
barathea worsted (and silk) fabric
basquine Basque outer petticoat
bearskin (1) skin of bear
bearskin (2) shaggy overcoat cloth
bearskin (3) Guardsman's high fur
  hat

CLOTHING ETC.

black cap death-sentencing cap
bloomers *bloomer* trousers: knickers
bone-lace lace woven with bobbins
bongrace broad-brimmed hat/bonnet
bootikin boot for gout/torture
brassard part of arm armour
brassart *brassard*
breeches trousers ending below knee
buckskin (1) deer/sheepskin
buckskin (2) a strong twilled cloth
burganet 16th C. helmet
burgonet *burganet*
burnouse *burnous*
bycocket 15th C. peaked cap
calyptra a Greek veil
camisole (1) a sleeved jacket
camisole (2) woman's jacket/morning
  gown
camisole (3) a loose under-bodice
capeline (1) archer's iron skullcap
capeline (2) a light woollen hood
cardigan knitted woollen jacket
cashmere (1) Kashmir goat wool
cashmere (2) shawl, etc. made of (1)
chaperon *tf* hood/cap
chenille a velvet-like material
cingulum a girdle
cod-piece male display appendage
corduroy a ribbed fustian
corselet *corslet* (1) (2)
culottes a divided skirt
dalmahoy a bushy bobwig
drilling stout twilled linen/cotton
dungaree coarse Indian calico
en* tout* cas *tf* parasol-umbrella
Fair* Isle* *tf* knitwear design
fillabeg *filibeg*
flannels casual trousers
florence *Florentine*
frippery tawdry finery
frou-frou elaborate trimmings
furbelow flounce: superfluous
  ornament
gauntlet iron glove: long glove
glad rags best/dress clothes
gossamer any very thin material
half hose socks
himation Ancient Greek *o/gmt*
hipsters trousers from the hip
jackboot a high cavalry boot

jirkinet a woman's bodice
jodhpurs riding-breeches/boots
kaffiyeh Bedouin head shawl
kalyptra Greek woman's veil
kerchief square piece of cloth
knitwear knitted clothing
lingerie women's underclothing
mackinaw short heavy woollen coat
mantelet *mantlet*
mantilla small mantle: veil
mocassin *moccasin*
moccasin Red Indian shoe
moleskin (1) skin of mole
moleskin (2) superior *tf* fustian
monokini (f) topless bikini
nankeens breeches made of
  nankeen
negligee (1) 18th C. loose gown
negligee (2) woman's (flimsy)
  dressing-gown
negligee (3) (red coral) necklace
nightcap cap worn in bed
opera hat collapsible top hat
organdie fine muslin
overalls (1) protective clothing
overalls (2) cavalryman's trousers
pabouche a slipper
pantable *pantofle*
pantofle slipper: overshoe
pauldron shoulder-plate armour
pelerine woman's tippet/cape
philabeg *filibeg*
philibeg *filibeg*
pinafore loose dress-covering
plimsoll rubber-soled canvas shoe
pouldron *pauldron*
puggaree *pagri*
rag trade garment trade
sarcenet *sarsenet*
sarsenet thin tissue of silk
slipslop a loose sandal
sombrero broad-brimmed hat
stephane ancient Greek head-dress
tarboosh *fez*
tarboush *tarboosh*
tricorne *tricorn*
vambrace forearm armour
vestiary of/pertaining to clothes ·
wristlet a wrist band/strap
zuchetta *zucchetto*

9

astrakhan M. East lambskin
bandoleer (ammunition) shoulder belt
bandolier *bandoleer*
bengaline a light *tf* fabric
billycock a hard felt hat
bombasine *vr tf* worsted fabric
bombazine *bombasine*
brassiere 'Bristol fashion'
buckskins breeches/suit of buckskin
Chantilly silk/linen lace
chaperone *chaperon*
cheong-sam sexy Chinese dress
corduroys trousers of *corduroy*
crepoline light *crape*-like material
crinoline (1) horsehair and flax fabric
crinoline (2) a hooped petticoat
décolleté of low-cut dress
dungarees overalls of *dungaree*
epaulette *epaulet*
forage-cap military undress cap
full-dress of state/ceremonial dress
gabardine *gaberdine*
gaberdine (Jew's) loose cloak: coat: twill fabric
garibaldi woman's loose blouse
georgette thin silk stuff
glengarry a Highlander's cap
habergeon sleeveless mail-coat
habiliment attire
head-dress covering for head
huckaback towelling cloth
Inverness of cloak/cape/overcoat
loin-cloth cloth covering loins
macintosh a waterproof overcoat
millinery women's headgear, etc.
moleskins trousers (etc.) of *moleskin* (2)
muffin-cap man's small cap
newmarket a close-fitting coat
pantalets *tf* woman's trousers: ruffle
pantoffle *pantofle*
pantoufle *pantofle*
petersham a heavy greatcoat
phillabeg *filibeg*
phillibeg *filibeg*
plus-fours baggy knickerbockers
polonaise bodice and skirt *o/gmt*
pourpoint medieval quilted doublet

redingote woman's long DB overcoat
Sam Browne officer's belt and strap
satinette *satinet*
sheepskin sheep's skin/leather
Sloppy* Joe* large loose sweater
sou' wester large waterproof hat
steenkirk loosely worn lace cravat
trousseau a bride's outfit
velveteen fustian, imitation velvet
wide-awake low wide-brimmed hat
zucchetto a skull-cap

10

Balbriggan (1) a knit cotton fabric
Balbriggan (2) underclothing of (1)
Berlin* wool fine worsted
boiler suit workman's overall
buff-jerkin strong military coat
bush jacket light belted jacket
chaparajos cowboy's protective leggings
chatelaine ornamental chains
crinolette a small crinoline
cummerbund waist belt/sash
dishabille undress (garment)
espadrille rope-soled shoe
Eton collar (1) broad starched collar
Eton collar (2) woman's jumper collar
Eton jacket boy's black dress-coat
florentine a durable silk fabric
fustanella Greek man's white kilt
grasscloth *vr* coarse cloths
habiliment attire
kerseymere finest twilled cloth
mackintosh *macintosh*
mousseline fine French muslin
needlecord *tf* cotton material
nightdress nightgown (etc.)
night-shift *nightdress*
nightshirt man's sleeping shirt
opera cloak an elegant cloak
Oxford bags very wide trousers
pantaloons *vr tf* trousers
piccadilly *tf* man's collar
pith helmet a solar pith hat
poke-bonnet projecting-front bonnet
riding-boot high boot for riding
riding-hood woman's hood for riding

CLOTHING ETC.

roquelaure man's short cloak
scratch-wig a part wig
seersucker thin crinkly fabric
trench-coat short waterproof coat
trousseaux plural of *trousseau*
tusser-silk *tusser*

pickelhaube German spiked helmet
spatterdash a long gaiter
Tam* o' Shanter *tf* Scot's cap
torchon lace peasants' bobbin lace
windcheater pullover: anorak

11

battledress *tf* military uniform
chapeau-bras three-cornered hat
cheesecloth a loose woven cloth
crash-helmet (driver's) safety hat
deerstalker sportsman's cap
Dolly* Varden woman's muslin dress
dreadnaught *dreadnought*
dreadnought thick cloth (garment)
farthingale *tf* crinoline
flannelette flannel-like cotton
Honiton lace *tf* lace
Kendal-green forester's cloth
leatherette imitation leather
mantonniere chin/throat armour
mousquetair woman's cloak: collar
neckerchief kerchief for the neck
nettle-cloth nettle-fibre cloth
nightingale an invalid garment
Phrygian cap *tf* conical cap

12

antigropelos waterproof leggings
calceamentum red silk sandal
camiknickers knickers and *camisole* (3)
chesterfield a long overcoat
crêpe-de-chine *crape*-like fabric
dinner jacket tailless dress coat
donkey jacket *tf* strong jacket
Easter* bonnet woman's festive hat
evening dress formal evening wear
galligaskins wide hose: leggings
handkerchief (1) nose-wiping cloth
handkerchief (2) *neckerchief*
kletterschue *tf* climbing boots
lumber jacket (1) man's (belted) jacket
lumber jacket (2) woman's cardigan
monkey jacket close-fitting jacket
morning dress formal day wear (men)
Paisley* shawl a Scottish shawl
shirtwaister a tailored dress
wedding dress a bride's dress

FOOD AND DRINK

For cereals, fruit, vegetables, fish, etc. see NATURAL HISTORY (p. 229).
For various anatomical features also see MEDICINE (p. 363).
note Crossword answers 6 upwards ignore pie, soup, etc. as suffix where the descriptive phrase can be readily constructed from previously indexed data. This includes NATURAL HISTORY items, i.e. apple pie/jam/tart/pudding, etc. and drinks such as cider-cup, gin and it, whisky and soda, Scotch whisky. The only ignored suffix in *word construction* is -ade (lemon*ade*).

2
it Italian vermouth

3
-ade suffix *mineral water* (2)
ale *tf* strong bitter beer

ava *kava*
bap *tf* breakfast roll
bub strong drink
bun *tf* sweet cake
cha tea: rolled tea
cob *cobloaf*
cup a wine mixed beverage

dop Cape brandy
dry unsweet (non-fruity wine)
fat solid animal/vegetable oil
ghi *ghee*
gin distilled grain/malt spirit
ham (hog's) dried salted thigh
ice ice cream: frozen confection
jam conserve of boiled fruit
mum wheatmeal beer
nog eggnog (etc.)
ort a meal fragment
pap child's soft food
pat small lump of butter
peg a brandy and soda
pie crust-covered food
poi Hawaiian taro root dish
pop ginger beer: champagne (etc.)
rob a fruit syrup
rum distilled sugar-cane spirit
rye distilled rye spirit (whisky)
sec dry (of wines)
sey part of beef carcase
soy a thick soy-bean sauce
tea an infusion of tea leaves
vin (f) wine

4

agar a seaweed jelly
arak *arrack*
Asti an Italian white wine
baba rum syrup soaked cake
bard game-cooking pig fat
barm fermenting liquor froth
beef ox/horse flesh
beer malt liquor
bock (f) a strong German beer
Brie a soft white cheese
bull rinsed-barrel drink
cake (1) baked dough: small loaf
cake (2) any flattened baked mass
cake (3) sweetened bread-like
  confection
char *cha*
chop mutton/pork with a rib
chou a cream bun
chow *chow-chow*
Coke* Coca-Cola
cola cola-flavoured soft drink

curd (1) acid thickened milk
curd (2) cheese part of milk
Edam *tf* Dutch cheese
fine ordinary French brandy
fino a dry sherry
fizz champagne: cocktail effervescence
flam *flawn*
flan flat open tart
flip hot beer and spirits
fool stewed fruit dish
game wild animal flesh
ghee clarified (buffalo) butter
gill ground ivy infused ale
grog (naval) rum and water
grub to eat: food
hard of (very) alcoholic drink
hash (1) to hack/mince/chop
hash (2) that which has been (1)
hash (3) mixed dish
hock (1) meat cut from leg
hock (2) white Rhenish
junk salt meat
kava narcotic pepper drink
kola *cola*
lard (1) rendered hog fat
lard (2) to smear/enrich with (1)
lard (3) stuff with bacon/pork
lard (4) garnish, strew
lean not fat (meat)
loaf bread: conical sugar mass
malt (1) processed grain
malt (2) malt liquor
marc fruit refuse in wine
mash (1) crushed malt and hot water
mash (2) mixed food
mash (3) mashed potatoes
mead fermented honey drink
meal (1) food taken at one time
meal (2) ground, powdered grain
meat (1) anything eaten as food
meat (2) edible animal flesh
mild lesser hop-flavoured ale
milk mammalian white fluid
mull to warm, spice (etc.) wine
mush *meal* (2) boiled in water
must new wine: unfermented juice
neat undiluted (alcohol)
olio a savoury mixed dish
ouzo an aniseed liqueur
pâté a blended meat paste

FOOD AND DRINK

pone maize bread/cake (USA)
pork swine flesh
port a Portuguese fortified wine
puff puff pastry cake/biscuit
purl warmed, spiced ale
raki Levantine/Greek spirit
roll small loaf: spiral cake
rosé a pinkish wine
roux butter and flour thickening
ruby red wine
rusk small hard toast cake
sack a Spanish wine
sago pith of *vr* palms
sake Japanese rice beer: alcohol
saki *sake*
salt (1) a fundamental taste
salt (2) chloride of sodium
samp maize porridge
slaw cabbage salad
soda soda water
soft of non-alcoholic drink
soss dish of sloppy food
soup stewed liquid food
stew dish of stewed food
stum *must*
suet *tf* animal fat
tack food
tart uncovered pastry dish
tass a small drink
tent deep red Spanish wine
tiff (1) stale/sour/thin liquor
tiff (2) a sip: a dram
tiff (3) to sip/drink/lunch
tift *tiff* (1) (2) (3)
veal calf meat
whet an appetizer, meal stimulant
whey watery part of milk
whig *whey*: sour- /butter-milk
wine (1) fermented juice of grapes
wine (2) fermented *vr* fruit juice
wort unfermented malt
yill ale (Scotland)

5

aspic savoury meat jelly
assai assai palm fruit drink
bacon swine's salted back and sides
bagel (f) a hard leavened roll

bever a snack
bingo brandy
bohea black tea
bombe (ice cream) dessert
brawn a meat preparation
brose *tf* oat/peasemeal food
broth *tf* soup
brule (f) cooked with brown sugar
bully canned/pickled beef
butty sandwich (Lancs., etc.)
bumbo *tf* cocktail
cabob kebab
caboc cream cheese in oatmeal
candy a sugar sweetmeat
chack a snack (Scotland)
chump thick end of mutton loin
cider *hard cider*: *sweet cider*
cocoa powdered cacao seed (drink)
congo *congou*
cream top of the milk
crumb (1) a morsel (of bread)
crumb (2) soft part of bread
Cupid* *tf* jam tart (USA)
curry a mixed spice dish
Derby* an English cheese
dough unbaked flour mass
fagot *faggot*
filet (f) undercut of beef
flamm *flawn*
flaun *flawn*
flawn a custard: a pancake
flour finely ground (wheat) *meal* (2)
fudge a soft sweetmeat
gigot a leg of mutton
Gouda a Dutch cheese
gravy cooked meat juices
grits coarsely ground grain
grout coarse meal
gruel thin oatmeal
gumbo okra soup/dish
halva a Turkish sweetmeat
honey nectar of flowers
hooch *hootch*
hyson fine *tf* green tea
icing coat with/of sugar
Irish whiskey
jelly anything gelatinous
jemmy a baked sheep's head
joint a cut piece of meat
julep US mint and spirit drink

kabab *kebab*
kabob *kebab*
kebab skewered meat dish
kebob *kebab*
kefir fermented milk drink
kenno cheese for natal gossips
kvass rye-beer
lager a light beer
lolly *lollipop* (1) (2): *lollipops*
lunch midday meal: snack: slice
Mâcon a burgundy
manna SEE NATURAL HISTORY: FLORA
marge margarine
matza *matzo*
matzo unleavened bread (wafer)
mebos (f) salted/sugared dried apricots
Médoc a French wine
mince minced meat: mincemeat
mobby sweet-potato drink
Mocha a Red Sea coffee
morat a honey drink
Nantz brandy
nappy strong ale
negus wine and hot spiced water
noyau *tf* liqueur
pasta processed flour dough
patty a little pie/cake
pekoe a scented black tea
perry pear cider
pilau a savoury rice dish
pilaw *pilau*
pilow *pilau*
pizza an Italian dish
plonk (cheap) wine
punch (alcoholic) mixed drink
puree pulped, sieved food
quaff (to drink) a draught
roast (1) cook, bake
roast (2) a (beef) joint
salad cold vegetable dish
salmi a (game) ragout
sauce (1) a food dressing
sauce (2) vegetables: stewed fruit (USA)
scone *tf* flat (round) plain cake
shchi cabbage soup
short (1) *neat*: small spirit drink
short (2) crisp, flaky (pastry)
sirup *syrup* (1) (2)
skirt meat midriff
sling an American drink

snack a light repast
souse pickled meat
speck fat: bacon: blubber
spice aromatic pungent vegetable
steak slice of meat/fish
still non-effervescent (drink)
stock simmered meat/bone liquor
stout extra strong porter
sugar a sweet carbohydrate
swats new ale (Scotland)
sweet (1) a fundamental taste
sweet (2) sweet dish: sweetmeat
syrup (1) non-fermented boiled sugar
syrup (2) any thick sweet liquid
taffy *toffee*
tafia a variety of rum
tansy tansy-flavoured pudding/cake
toast (1) (to) brown bread
toast (2) to half melt (cheese)
toast (3) to drink to
toddy (1) fermented palm juice
toddy (2) spirit and hot water mixture
Tokay a Hungarian sweet wine
toffy *toffee*
tonic tonic water
tripe part of (cow's) stomach
viand an article of food
Vichy a mineral water
vifta *vivda*
vivda dried meat (Shetland Is.)
vodka Russian rye/potato spirit
wafer thin crisp cake/biscuit
yeast fungi used in brewing, etc.

6

alegar sour wine (vinegar)
arrack an Eastern spirit
batter a cooking paste
Beaune a French red wine
biffin cake of flattened apple
bitter (1) a fundamental taste
bitter (2) *tf* ale
bonbon a sweetmeat
borsch Russian beetroot soup
brandy spirit distilled from wine
brunch *br*eakfast-l*unch* compromise
bubbly champagne
burger *hamburger*

FOOD AND DRINK

burgoo sailor's dish: picnic stew
butter churned cream
canape bread with *dainty*
canary a Canary Island wine
cassis blackcurrant drink/flavouring
cat-lap any thin/despised drink
catsup ketchup
caudle a warm sweet drink
cecils fried minced meat balls
cheese a food from *curd* (2)
claret dark red *Bordeaux*
coffee drink from coffee beans
Cognac a French brandy
collop (fried) slice of meat
comfit a sweetmeat
compot preserved/stewed fruit
congee *conjee*
congou *tf* black tea
conjee boiled rice water
cookie bun (Scotland): biscuit (USA)
cooper stout and porter mixture
corned granulated: salted
crusta cocktail in sugared glass
cuscus *couscous*
cutlet (1) meat with a rib
cutlet (2) food in shape of (1)
dainty a delicacy
dinner day's chief meal
éclair cake long in shape
eggnog eggs and hot liquor drink
entrée a dinner dish
faggot ball of pig entrails (etc.)
fillet rolled, boned meat/fish
flitch salted, cured side of hog
fodder cattle food: food
fondue *tf* sauce: *tf* soufflé
fumado a smoked fish
gammon ham/adjacent parts
gateau a fancy cake
geneva gin
giblet made of *giblets*
gimlet a spirit and lime juice
grappa *tf* brandy
Graves* red/white French wine
greens green vegetables
haggis a Scottish dish
halvah *halva*
haslet (hog's) entrails
hootch (1) Red Indian fermented
  dough
hootch (2) whiskey
hootch (3) illicit spirit
hot dog hot sausage sandwich
hotpot *tf* mutton and vegetable stew
humbug a sweet confection
jujube lozenge: see FLORA (p. 273)
jumbal thin, crisp, sweet cake
jumble *jumbal*
junket (1) flavoured curds and cream
junket (2) feast, picnic, etc.
kephir *kefir*
kirsch *kirschwasser*
kumiss fermented mares' milk
kummel cumin-flavoured liqueur
leaven dough-rising ferment
lights animal lungs
liquor (1) any liquid
liquor (2) alcoholic drink
Lisbon Portuguese wine
Malaga a Spanish white wine
maslin mixed grain
matzah *matzo*
matzas *matzot*
matzoh *matzo*
matzos *matzot*
matzot a plural of *matzo*
mobbie *mobby*
mousse a whipped cream dish
muffin a soft porous cake
muscat *muscatel*
mutton sheep's flesh
nocake Red Indian meal
noodle *tf* (egg) paste
nougat a sweet confection
Oliver* *Bath Oliver*
omelet fried beaten-egg pancake
oolong green flavoured black tea
oolung *oolong*
orgeat almond and sugar syrup
oxymel honey and vinegar
oxtail soup/stew ingredient
paella *tf* stew
panada *tf* bread dish: *tf* sauce
panary of/pertaining to bread
parkin oatmeal and treacle biscuit
pastry (1) paste/dough articles
  collectively
pastry (2) crust of pies, tarts (etc.)
pastry (3) a small cake
perkin parkin

pickle (1)   a preserving liquid
pickle (2)   food item in (1)
pickle (3)   a grain of corn
pickle (4)   to eat sparingly
pilaff   *pilau*
pillau   *pilau*
piment (obs.)   spiced sweetened wine
polony   *tf* dry sausage
pomace   crushed cider apples
porter   a dark malt liquor
posset   a diabetic drink
potage   thick soup
poteen   illicit Irish whiskey
pulque   Mexican fermented sap
quiche   a savoury tart
ragout   highly seasoned stew
rasher   thin slice of bacon
relish (1)   (characteristic) flavour
relish (2)   appetizer: condiment
salame   *tf* Italian sausage
salami   plural of *salame*
sallad   *salad*
sallat   *salad*
saloop   salep/sassafras drink
samshu (1)   Chinese rice/millet spirit
samshu (2)   any *tf* spirit
Scotch*   whisky
sea-pie   sailor's baked meat dish
shandy   beer and lemonade/ginger-beer
sherry   a Spanish fortified wine
shorts   *short* plural: bran
shtchi   *shchi*
simnel   Christmas/Easter cake
skilly   thin gruel
sorbet   sherbet: water-ice
sowans   *sowens*
sowens   a Scottish oat dish
spirit   a distilled liquid
sponge   leavened dough
squash   a fruit-juice drink
stingo   strong malt liquor
strunt   spiritous liquor (Scotland)
sundae   a mixed confection
supawn   *suppawn*
supper   late meal
swiper   bad/spoilt beer: small beer
swipes   *swiper*
tartar   *tartare sauce*
tidbit   *titbit*
tiffin (f)   *tiffing* (2)

tipper   *tf* ale
titbit   a choice delicacy/item
toffee   a sweetmeat
trifle   a mixed confection
umbles   (deer's) entrails
viands   food
waffle   *tf* batter cake
wallop   beer
wastel   bread of finest flour
whisky   a malt spirit
yaourt   *yoghurt*
zythum   ancient Egyptian beer

7

absinth   wormwood liqueur
alcohol   an intoxicating liquor
alicant   a Spanish wine
aniseed   *anisette*
bannock   *tf* oatmeal cake
banquet (1)   a feast
banquet (2)   a separate course
Bath* bun   a rich sweet bun
biltong (f)   sun-dried lean meat
biscuit (1)   thin unleavened crisp cake
biscuit (2)   a soft round cake (USA)
bitters   bitter herb/root drink
bortsch   *borsch*
bouilli   boiled/stewed meat
bourbon   maize whiskey
brioche   sponge cake/roll
brisket   the breast
calipee   turtle's yellowish belly
caramel   sugar substance: sweetmeat
carcake   *tf* Shrove Tuesday cake
castock   a cabbage stock
catawba   an American red wine
catchup   ketchup
Chablis   a dry white *Burgundy*
chapati   Indian unleavened bread
charqui   sun-dried beef strips
Cheddar   an English cheese
chowder   fish/clams, vegetables dish
chupati   *chapati*
chutney   an E. Indian condiment
cobbler   iced sweet alcoholic drink
cobloaf   rounded/mis-shapen loaf
compote   *compot*
confect   a sweetmeat

FOOD AND DRINK

cordial fruit-flavoured drink
cracker a thin crisp biscuit
crowdie (1) meal and water: *brose*
crowdie (2) cheese-like milk
  preparation
crumpet unsweetened griddle cake
custard flavoured milk and eggs
  composition
custock *castock*
dariole a shell of pastry
dejeune *déjeuner*
dessert a final sweet course
egg-flip an alcoholic mixed drink
fondant a soft sweetmeat
fritter a fried piece
gelatin *gelatine*
giblets entrails
gin fizz a fizzy gin drink
glucose grape-sugar
gnocchi a small dumplings dish
goulash *tf* stew
Gruyere Swiss wholemilk cheese
halavah *halva*
hoe cake Indian meal cake (USA)
kebbock a cheese (Scotland)
kebbuck *kebbock*
ketchup a tomato sauce
koumiss *kumis*
lasagna *lasagne*
lasagne a baked pasta dish
liqueur a strong sweet *liquor* (2)
mace ale mace-flavoured ale
Madeira sherry: cake
malmsey a strong sweet wine
manchet finest wheat bread
Marsala Sicilian sherry-like wine
Martini* vermouth (cocktail)
mashlam *maslin*
mashlim *maslin*
mashlin *maslin*
mashlum *maslin*
matzahs *matzot*
matzoth *matzot*
meltith meal (Scotland)
mineral *mineral water* (1) (2)
oatcake hard cake of oatmeal
oatmeal *meal* (2) of oats
olycook (f) *olykoek*
olykoek (f) *tf* doughnut (USA)
Orvieto an Italian white wine

pabulum any *tf* food
pace egg an Easter egg
pale ale *tf* bitter ale
pancake thin fried batter
pannage swine's forest food
parfait *tf* frozen dessert
pemican *pemmican*
persico fruit kernel cordial
pigment *piment*
pikelet tea cake: crumpet: muffin
pilsner a light beer
pink gin gin with Angostura bitters
pink tea women's tea party (USA)
polenta an Italian porridge
popcorn heated maize
potable fit to drink: beverage
potheen *poteen*
pottage *potage*: boiled vegetables
praline sugar coated kernel
prawlin *praline*
pretzel a crisp salted biscuit
pudding (1) savoury food in a skin
pudding (2) sausage: entrails
pudding (3) flour cased fruit/meat
  (etc.)
pudding (4) soft *tf* sweet dish
ramakin *ramekin*
ramekin a baked dish
rarebit incorrect *(Welsh) rabbit*
ratafia (1) almond flavouring essence
ratafia (2) fruit kernel liqueur/cordial
ratafia (3) almond biscuit/cake
ravioli small savoury pasta cakes
red wine red coloured wine
retsina Greek resin-flavoured wine
Rhenish Rhine wine
risotto *tf* rice dish
rissole fried minced food ball
rosolio a raisin cordial
rum baba *baba*
samshoo *samshu* (1)
sapsago a hard green cheese
sausage meat in edible tube
saveloy a highly seasoned sausage
savoury (1) of good savour/relish
savoury (2) savoury course/dish
schnaps *hollands*
seafood shellfish: any marine edible
seltzer a (Prussian) mineral water
sherbet fruit drink (powder): *sorbet*

shicker strong drink
sirloin (upper part) loin of beef
sloe-gin a sloe liqueur
soubise an onion sauce
soufflé a light (egg) dish
stengah a peg of whisky and soda
Stilton an English cheese
stinger *stengah*
strudel very thin pastry cover
suppawn maize porridge
surloin sirloin
swizzle a compound drink
tabasco hot pepper sauce
tapioca sago and potato starch
tartare *tartare sauce*
tartlet a little tart
tequila a Mexican *liquor* (2)
terrine a casserole
tiffing (1) sipping
tiffing (2) lunch: light repast
Tom* trot *tf* toffee
twankay *tf* green tea: gin
venison deer meat
vinegar condiment, pickling medium
wassail a salutation drink
whiskey whisky from USA/Ireland
yoghurt fermented-milk food
zakuska a snack: *whet*

8

absinthe *absinth*
advocaat egg liqueur: egg and rum drink
agar-agar *agar*
ale-berry bread and ale beverage
anisette anise seed liqueur/cordial
aperitif (f) *aperitive*
Bakewell see entries at 12, 15
bechamel *tf* white sauce
beeswing tartar crust in old port
beverage any drink
black tea simple dried tea
Bordeaux a French wine
bouillon a strong broth
breaskit brisket (Scotland)
bucellas a Portuguese white wine
burgundy a French (red) wine
calipash greenish turtle-jelly

chapatti *chapati*
Cheshire an English cheese
chop-suey a US Chinese dish
chow-chow food: Chinese mixed condiment
chow-mein (1) fried noodles
chow-mein (2) meat and vegetable dish with (1)
chupatti *chapati*
ciderkin an inferior cider
club soda soda water
Coca*-Cola* a carbonated soft drink
cocktail *vr* (alcoholic) concoctions
cole-slaw cabbage salad
confetti sweetmeats
confetto (f) singular of *confetti*
conserve (sugar) preserved fruit
consommé a clear soup
corn pone *pone* (USA)
couscous (1) granulated wheat flour
couscous (2) Arabic rice and meat dish with (1)
cracknel a light brittle biscuit
daiquiri rum-based cocktail
déjeuner (f) breakfast/lunch
doughnut fried dough cake
Drambuie a Scotch liqueur
dripping fat from cooking meat
dumpling *tf* thick pudding/paste mass
eau* de vie* brandy
espresso pressure-made coffee
fish-meal *meal* (1) (2) of fish
flapjack biscuit: apple-puff: pancake
florence *tf* meat pie
flummery blancmange: *sowens* (etc.)
gelatine a foodstuff glue
gin-sling flavoured gin and cold water
green tea steam-withered tea
hardbake almond toffee
highball (f) whiskey and soda (USA)
hollands Dutch gin
hotchpot *hotchpotch*
hydromel honey and water beverage
ice cream iced cream (substitute)
julienne (1) *tf* clear soup
julienne (2) shredded foodstuff
kedgeree Indian rice dish
kickshaw *kickshaws*
kromesky *tf croquette*
loblolly thick gruel

177

FOOD AND DRINK

lollipop (1) sugar and treacle
  sweetmeat
lollipop (2) sweetmeat on a stick
luncheon *lunch*
macaroni *tf* pasta
macaroon almond biscuit
marzipan a sweet almond paste
mashloch *maslin*
matzoths *matzot*
meringue *tf* crisp cake/covering
mishmash *hotchpotch*
molasses a thick sugar treacle
mountain mountain grape wine
muscadel *muscatel*
muscatel *vr* rich spicy wines
napoleon brandy: iced cake
nightcap a nocturnal drink
noisette meat: nutlike sweet
omelette *omelet*
Parmesan an Italian cheese
parritch porridge (Scotland)
pemmican Red Indian meat dish
persicot *persico*
pilsener *pilsner*
porridge boiled oatmeal
potation drinking: draught: liquor
preserve preserved fruit: jam
quenelle a forcemeat ball
ramequin *ramekin*
red biddy red wine and meths drink
resinata a Greek white wine
Riesling a dry white wine
roly-poly *tf* dough pudding
rosoglio *rosolio*
rum-shrub a rum liqueur
St* Julien a red Bordeaux
sandwich food in bread slices
sangaree W. Indian wine drink
Sauterne *Sauternes*
schiedam *hollands*
schnapps *hollands*
seasoner *seasoning*
seedcake cake with caraway seeds
semolina hard wheat particles
sillabub curdled cream dish
slapjack (f) flapjack: griddle-cake
  (USA)
slivovic *slivovitz*
small ale *tf* unhopped ale
souchong fine *tf* black tea

spare rib swine's rib
stuffing *vr* savoury ingredients
sukiyaki a Japanese dish
switchel treacle-beer
syllabub *sillabub*
tequilla *tequila*
thridace thickened lettuce juice
turnover a small pie
umble-pie pie of *umbles*
verjuice juice of unripe fruit
vermouth wormwood flavoured wine
water-ice frozen fruit juice
white-pot a baked Devon dish
yoghourt *yoghurt*
[1]**zwieback** rusk: spiced toast

9

antipasto (f) an (Italian) *whet*
appetiser *whet*
appetizer *whet*
aqua vitae (f) alcohol
baba* au rum* *baba*
bacharach a Rhenish wine
barmbrack a currant bun
beestings post-calving milk
black beer *tf* German beer
breakfast first meal of day
bridecake a wedding cake
Camembert a soft rich cheese
cassareep W. Indian sauce ingredient
cassaripe *cassareep*
casserole *vr* cooked dishes
cassonade unrefined sugar
cassoulet bean and meat stew
champagne a sparkling white wine
charlotte a cooked apple dish
chipolata a small sausage
crackling roast pork rind
cracknels fried pork-fat pieces
croquette a savoury fried cake
dandyfunk *dunderfunk*
Derby* sage *tf* Christmas cheese
Easter* egg festive (artificial) egg
entrecôte steak cut between ribs
entremets between-courses *dainty*

[1] Games players note: unlike the 1977
    edition the latest *Chambers* has *Zwieback*.

forcemeat   seasoned chopped meat
fricassee   *tf* white meat dish
galantine   cold jellied meat
Genoa* cake   *tf* fruit cake
grenadine (1)   a (pomegranate) syrup
grenadine (2)   veal/poultry fillets
hamburger (1)   a large sausage
hamburger (2)   beef cake (in a bun)
hard cider   alcoholic apple drink
hermitage   a French wine
hippocras   spiced wine
humble pie   pie of deer's umbles
Irish stew   *tf* mutton and vegetable stew
kickshaws   a fantastical dish
Leicester   an English cheese
lemon curd   lemon, eggs, butter paste
lobscouse   *tf* stew/hash
lollipops   sweetmeats in general
macédoine   a jellied medley
madeleine   small shell-shaped cake
Manhattan   an American cocktail
margarine   a vegetable butter
marmalade   a citrus fruit jam
mayonaise   *mayonnaise* (1) and (2)
mincemeat (1)   meat chopped small
mincemeat (2)   dried fruit chopped
   small
moonshine   illicit liquor
muscadine   *muscatel*
muscovado   unrefined sugar
nutriment   food
pettitoes   pig's trotters
pot-pourri   *olla podrida*
pound cake   *tf* sweet cake
provender   (dry) food (for animals)
raised pie   pie unsupported by dish
Roquefort   a French cheese
saccharin   an intensely sweet substance
Sally* Lunn   a sweet tea cake
Sauternes   a French white wine
schnitzel   a veal cutlet
Scotch* egg   egg in sausage meat
seasoning   relish additive
shortcake   shortbread: layered cake
   (USA)
slivovica   *slivovitz*
slivovitz   a dry plum brandy
slivowitz   *slivovitz*
small beer   weak beer
soda water   carbon-dioxide charged
   water
sour-crout   *sauerkraut*
sourdough   leaven
spaghetti   cord-like pasta
stirabout (f)   porridge
succotash   green corn stew
sugar-plum   a boiled sweet
sweetmeat   a sugar confection
Swiss roll   rolled thin, filled cake
Tarragona   a Spanish port-like wine
the cratur   whisky (Scotland); whiskey
   (Ireland)
tipsy cake   wine and almond cake
vol*-au-vent*   *tf* pie
warden pie   warden pear pie
white meat (1)   milk/butter/egg food
white meat (2)   poultry, rabbit, veal, etc.
white wine   clear/yellowish wine
wholemeal   entire wheat grains meal
youghourt   *yoghurt*

10

barley-bree   strong ale: whisky
barley-broo   *barley-bree*
Bath* Oliver*   *tf* biscuit
Beaujolais   a French red wine
beefburger   *hamburger*
blancmange   *tf* milk jelly
blanquette (f)   white sauce ragout
bloody Mary   vodka and tomato juice
breadstuff   bread
brown stout   *tf* porter
butter-milk   milk after churning
cannelloni   *tf* stuffed pasta
cappuccino   coffee with little milk
Chambertin   a red burgundy
Chartreuse (1)   a brandy liqueur
Chartreuse (2)   mould of
   rice/blancmange
cheesecake   sweet (cheese) confection
Chelsea bun   *tf* fruit bun
cockyleeky   *cockieleekie*
comestibles   food
confection   a sweetmeat
Constantia   a S. African sweet wine
cracklings   non-tallow suet
dunderfunk   a baked ship's biscuit
Eccles cake   a Lancashire cake

FOOD AND DRINK

Fanny* Adams tinned mutton
frangipane *frangipani*
frangipani a cream-filled pastry
fricandeau larded slice of veal
genevrette a wild fruit wine
gingersnap gingerbread biscuit
girdle cake griddle cake
Gloucester an English cheese
Gorgonzola a blue cheese
heather ale a Scottish liqueur
hodgepodge *hotchpotch*
hotchpotch (1) mutton and vegetable broth
hotchpotch (2) any random (food) mixture
iron ration emergency concentrated food
Jamaica rum a full-bodied rum
jugged hare hare stewed with wine
Lancashire an English cheese
manzanilla very dry light sherry
maraschino Dalmatian cherry liqueur
marc brandy brandy from *marc*
mayonnaise (1) egg-based sauce
mayonnaise (2) cold dish with (1)
Mickey* Finn a doped drink
minestrone a *tf* thick soup
numble pie *humble pie*
on the rocks ice in a drink (US)
rumfustian *tf negus*
Russian tea tea with lemon
saccharine *saccharin*: of sugar
salmagundi a mixed dish
salmagundy *salmagundi*
sauerkraut fermented cabbage dish
shortbread a brittle crumbling cake
spitch-cock spit, boiled eel
sustenance nourishment
sweet cider unfermented apple drink
tanglefoot (f) whiskey: any spirit (USA)
tonic water aerated quinine water
usquebaugh whisky
vermicelli very slender macaroni

11

aguardiente (1) Spanish/Portuguese brandy
aguardiente (2) any spirituous liquor

amontillado a slightly sweet sherry
Apollinaris a *mineral water* (1)
Athole brose honey/whisky mixture
Banbury cake *tf* mince-pie
barley-broth *barley-bree*
Benedictine *tf* liqueur
black velvet champagne and stout
bonne-bouche a delicious morsel
Bristol milk sherry
brown George a hard biscuit
cockaleekie *cockieleekie*
crappit-head *crappit-heid*
crappit-heid stuffed haddock's head
frankfurter a small smoked sausage
gingerbread *tf* treacle cake
griddle cake pancake
hors d'oeuvre *whet*
Irish coffee coffee, cream and whiskey
John* Collins a gin cocktail
lemon cheese *lemon curd*
marshmallow *tf* sweetmeat
mountain-dew whisky
Niersteiner a Rhine wine
olla-podrida a Spanish hash/stew
Pomfret* cake *Pontefract cake*
profiterole small filled cake puff
Rudesheimer a Rhenish white wine
Scotch* broth *tf* vegetable broth
scuppernong a N. Carolina wine
smörgåsbord Swedish-style dishes
Steinberger a Rhenish white wine
tutti*-frutti (ice) fruit confection
Welsh* rabbit cheese (and ale) on toast
Wensleydale an English cheese

12

Bakewell tart a false *Bakewell pudding*
butterscotch *tf* butter toffee
cheeseburger hamburger and molten cheese
cockieleekie fowl and leek soup
Cornish pasty true ½ fruit ½ vegetable
hasty pudding *tf* porridge
kirschwasser wild cherry liqueur
maid of honour *tf* cheesecake
merrythought fowl's wishbone
mineral water (1) *vr* natural

springwaters
mineral water (2) aerated soft drink
mulligatawny E. Indian curry soup
pumpernickel German rye bread
shepherd's pie meat and potato dish
sweet-and-sour a Chinese sauce
tartare sauce mayonnaise
water biscuit a thin plain biscuit
Welsh* rarebit *Welsh rabbit*

13

bouillabaisse *tf* fish chowder
Chateaubriand* a thick fillet steak
chili* con* carne a Mexican pepper
 dish
cobbler's punch hot beer and spirit
 drink
cottage cheese a soft white cheese
fine Champagne* *tf* brandy
liebfraumilch (f) a German wine

prairie oyster a hangover drink
Scotch* collops minced beef
toad-in-the-hole sausage in batter

14

mock-turtle soup imitation turtle soup
pate* de fois gras (f) goose liver paste
petticoat-tails small shortbread cakes
Pontefract cake a liquorice sweetmeat
Scotch* woodcock egg and anchovies
 on toast
Turkish delight a gelatinous sweetmeat

15

Bakewell pudding an 'upside down'
 pastry
Devonshire cream clotted cream
eggs in moonshine an egg dish

FURNITURE AND FURNISHINGS

For fabrics see CLOTHING, MATERIALS AND ORNAMENTATION (p. 162).
 For various types of barrel also see MEASUREMENT (p. 217).

2

da a heavy Burmese knife
po chamber pot
yu precious jade

3

cap a wooden drinking-bowl
cog *cogie*: *cogue*
cub a chest
dah *da*
dan coal box: tub
dop a drink container
jag a (saddle-) bag
kid a small tub
kip a bed
nef table utensils (etc.)

pad *ped*
ped pannier, hamper
pig *tf* brush: *vr* earthenware
rip a wicker basket
sye milk strainer: sieve
tat E. Indian hempen matting
tot a drinking cup
urn *vr tf* vessel: ballot box
van a winnowing basket

4

buat *bowat*
coop a wicker basket
corf miner's basket: lobster cage
dixy *dixie*
etna vessel for heating liquids
etui a small case

FURNITURE AND FURNISHINGS

ewer   a large water jug
jack   leather pitcher/bottle
kang   large Chinese water jar
mull   a snuffbox
pock   *poke*
poke   bag/pouch
pouf   a large hassock
skep   basket: beehive
tass   a drinking cup
trug   flat wooden fruit-basket
zarf   ornamental cup-holder
zurf   *zarf*

5

billy   an Australian teapot
bowat   a lantern
bowet   *bowat*
cabas   work basket/reticule
cogie   small wooden bowl
cogue   *tf* barrel
cruse   earthenware pot: cup, bottle
cylix   *tf* two-handled cup
Derby*   *tf* porcelain
dilli   *dilly-bag*
dilly   *dilly-bag*
diota   ancient two-handled vase
dixie   military cooking vessel
dolia   plural of *dolium*
dolly   washing-tub implement
etuee   *etui*
joram   *jorum*
jorum   a large drinking bowl
keeve   a large tub
kieve   *keeve*
kylix   *cylix*
peggy   *dolly*
peter   a safe
pokal   ornamental drinking vessel
punka   (palm leaf/mechanical) fan
quern   a stone *handmill*
scull   a shallow basket
skull   *scull*
Spode*   *tf* bone-ash porcelain
stean   stone/earthenware vessel
steen   *stean*
stein   (hinged lidded) beer mug
tazza   shallow vessel: bowl
tazze   plural of *tazza*

6

bicker   a (wooden) vessel
caster   *castor*
castor   a sprinkling vessel
coggie   *cogie*
dolium   *tf* Roman earthenware jar
fingan   *tf* coffee cup
finjan   *fingan*
hydria   large Greek water-vase
kirbeh   skin for holding water
lagena   a narrow-necked bottle
mocock   Red Indian box/basket
mocuck   *mocock*
muffin   a small plate
noggin   small mug: wooden cup
pallet   mattress: couch: bed
petara   travelling box: clothes basket
piggin   pail: bowl: *vr* vessels
pipkin   small (earthenware) pot
pitara   *petara*
pithos   large Greek wine-jar
posnet   *tf* small cooking-pot
pottle   strawberry basket
pouffe   *pouf*
Primus*   portable cooking stove
punkah   *punka*
punnet   small chip-basket
purdah   a (screening) curtain
quaich   *tf* Scottish drinking-cup
quaigh   *quaich*
quarry   square slab: *quarrel*
rumkin   *tf* drinking vessel (obs.)
rummer   a large drinking-glass
sconce   an Oxford mug
shippo   Japanese cloisonné ware
tassie   a small cup (Scotland)
teapoy   small table: tea caddy
trivet   three-legged pot/stand
tureen   large soup dish
valise   travelling/kit bag
wisket   a basket

7

cricket   a low stool
cylices   plural of *cylix*
hassock   a stuffed stool
Ottoman   *vr tf* seat

pitarah *petara*
platter large plate/dish
potiche *tf* Oriental vase
quarrel square tile:*quarrel-pane*
ramakin *ramekin*
ramekin a baking dish
samovar a Russian tea-urn
scuttle basket: coal vessel
scyphus a Greek drinking-cup
skippet a flat box
stamnos Greek short-necked jar
terrine earthenware jar: *tureen*
Toby* jug man-shaped beer mug
whatnot shelving furniture

8

dilly-bag Australian rush/bark bag
gallipot small glazed pot
[1]**hand-mill** coffee/pepper mill, etc.
jeroboam large bowl/bottle
kalamdan Persian writing-case
lekythos narrow-necked Greek flask
monteith a large (silver) bowl
pancheon an earthenware pan
panchion *pancheon*
pembroke *tf* small table
pomander perforated perfume
  container
qalamdan Persian writing-case
ramequin *ramekin*
solander a book-like box

9

banquette *vr tf* long bench
blackjack a large (leather) jug
davenport (1) small writing desk
davenport (2) a large sofa
devonport *davenport* (1)
lachrymal a bottle for tears
muffineer dish: *castor*

palampore flowered chintz bedcover
palempore *palampore*
paillasse *palliasse*
palliasse a straw mattress
papeterie a stationery case
porrenger *porringer*
porringer small soup/porridge dish
posset cup cup/bowl for posset
pounce box dusting powder sprinkler
Worcester* fine china

10

batalia pie convent-embroidered
  items
crown Derby* *tf* 18th C. porcelain
mousseline very thin glassware
pouncet-box *pomander: pounce box*
queen's ware cream-coloured
  Wedgwood
quernstone *quern*
Victoriana Victorian era items

11

brown George *tf* earthenware vessel
Chippendale *tf* furniture design
Hepplewhite *tf* furniture design
Moses basket a portable cot
portmanteau *tf* large travelling bag
quarrel-pane diamond-shaped glass
  pane

12

antimacassar a chair covering
chesterfield a heavily padded sofa
lachrymal urn *lachrymal*
portmanteaus *portmanteaux*
portmanteaux a plural of *portmanteau*
Windsor chair *tf* strong wooden chair

[1] Games players note: to discover *handmill*
(without hyphen) in *Chambers* see *quern*.

GAMES

2

E O 18th C. gambling game
go a Japanese game

3

gin gin rummy
loo *tf* card game
maw an old card game
nap *napoleon*
nim an old game
pam nap-like card game
pit a noisy card game
put nap-like card game
tag *tig*
taw marbles: a large marble
tig children's touching game

4

brag *tf* poker
camp old form of football
crib *cribbage*
dibs children's catching game
I spy children's word game
loto lotto
ludo *tf* board game
main *hazard*
mora finger guessing game
polo *tf* horseback hockey
pool *vr* billiard-table games
putt *put*
ruff an old card game
skat *tf* card game
solo a whist variant
sumo Japanese wrestling
vint bridge-like card game

5

bandy ball game: ice game

craps dice gambling game
fives *tf* walled-court ball game
gleek an old card game
jacks five stones, knuckle-bones, *dibs*
lotto (small scale) bingo
lurch an old table game
maris *merils*
merel *meril*
meril a counter in *merils*
monte a gambling card game
morra *mora*
poker a gambling card game
prize a match (i.e. prize-fight)
rummy *vr* card games
skeet *tf* clay-pigeon shooting
snobs jacks, five stones, *dibs*
spoof hoaxing game: card game
tarok *tarot*
tarot special (divination) card game
trump *ruff*

6

aikido a Japanese combative sport
boston *tf* card game
casino *tf* card game
crambo a rhyming game
ecarte *tf* card game
fan-tan a Chinese gambling game
gobang a Japanese game
hazard an old dicing game
karate Japanese combative sport
kung fu Chinese unarmed combat
merell *meril*
merils a rustic game
morals *merils*
morris *merils*
pelota Basque fives-like game
piquet *tf* card game
quinz *tf* card game
raffle an old dicing game
savate foot and hand boxing
shinny *shinty*
shinty a hockey-like game

tennis (1) close/court/real/royal-
tennis (2) lawn- (derived from (1))
wraxle to wrestle

7

bezique *tf* card game
canasta *tf* card game
coon-can *tf* card game
croquet a lawn ball game
jackpot *tf* poker
karting go-kart racing
Lexicon* a word card game
mah-jong *mah-jongg*
merrels *merils*
matador a domino game
muggins *tf* dominoes: *tf* card game
pachisi Indian ludo-like game
pallone an Italian ball game
peevers *hop-scotch*
pontoon *tf* card game
primero an old card game
tenpins tenpin bowling

8

ball-game US football/baseball (etc.)
biathlon skiing and shooting sport
cribbage *tf* card game
korfball *tf* Dutch basketball
lacrosse a team ball game
leap-frog children's leaping game
mah-jongg old Chinese table game
miracles *merils*
Monopoly* a board game
napoleon *tf* card game
ninepins traditional skittles
pastance pastime
petanque a French bowling game
Ping*-Pong* table tennis
roly-poly an old ball game
sardines *tf* hide and seek
teetotum a gambling game

9

blackjack *tf* card game

black pool a precursor of snooker
cut-throat *tf* 3-player bridge
[1] **hop-scotch** children's outdoor game
jingo-ring children's dancing game
lanterloo earlier form of *loo*
level-coil an old Christmas game
motocross motor scrambling
newmarket *tf* card game
nineholes a ball game
quadrille *tf* card game

10

five stones jacks, *dibs*
[2] **jack-straws** spillikins
lansquenet *tf* card game
pentery-web word puzzle game
philippina *philopoena*
philippine *philopoena*
philopoena nut-eating forfeit game
real tennis *tennis* (1)
shove groat *shovel-board*
shuffle-cap money-in-cap game
trou-madame *troll-my-dame*
[3] **volley-ball** a ball game

11

close tennis *tennis* (1)
post and pair an old card game
shovel-board a coin-pushing game
troll-my-dame old *tf* bagatelle

---

[1] Games players note: hyphenated in *Chambers*, other authorities prefer it as one word.
[2] Games players note: unhyphenated as one word in some dictionaries and optionally hyphenated in others; it is hyphenated in *Chambers*.
[3] Games players note: *Collins Gem* gives it as an unhyphenated word; *Funk and Wagnalls* either unhyphenated or as two separate words; the *Concise Oxford* and *Chambers* as hyphenated. It does not appear at all in *Collins Minigem*, the *Official Scrabble Players' Dictionary* or the *Complete Oxford*.

12

shuffle-board *shovel-board*
troll-my-dames *troll-my-dame*

knur and spell north England outdoor
  game

TRANSPORT

3

cab *vr tf* public vehicle
car manned part of airship
cat *tf* coal/timber vessel
cog ship: cockboat
dak (travelling) mail post
dow *dhow*
gig a light carriage
hoy large-one-decked boat
LEM Lunar Excursion Module
tub a clumsy ship/boat

4

biga (f) a two-horse chariot
brig *tf* sailing ship
buck body of a cart
buss small Dutch fishing vessel
chay vulgar 'singular' of chaise
dawk *dak*
dhow an Arab sailing vessel
dory a surf-riding boat
dray strong cart: timber sledge
duck *tf* military amphibious vehicle
ekka small one-horse carriage
grab an Eastern coasting vessel
junk Chinese sailing vessel
kago Japanese basketwork
  palanquin
koff small Dutch sailing vessel
pink a small sailing ship
pram (1) Dutch lighter: dinghy:
  barge
pram (2) milkman's hand-cart
prau Malay sailing/rowing boat
prow forepart of ship: *prore*
pulk *pulka*
punt *tf* flat-bottomed boat
saic a Levantine vessel

shay *chay*
sled a (small) sledge
snow a brig-like vessel
wain wagon
yawl *vr* small boats

5

bigae (f) plural of *biga*
blimp *tf* small airship
brake *break*
break a long wagonette
canoe a paddled *skiff*
copor alcohol supply ship
dingy *dinghy*
kaiak *kayak*
kayak Eskimo sealskin canoe
ketch small two-masted vessel
palki a palanquin
pinky *pink*
praam *pram* (1)
prahu *prau*
prore a ship (poetic): *prow*
pulka Laplander's sledge
quant to punt
saick *saic*
sedan (1) *sedan-chair*: litter
sedan (2) large saloon car
skiff a small light boat
sloop light-boat: *tf* cutter
smack coaster, fishing vessel
taube *tf* German monoplane
tonga a light Indian vehicle
umiak Eskimo woman's boat
xebec small three-masted vessel
yatch light fast sailing vessel
zabra Spanish coastal vessel
zebec *xebec*

6

bateau (Canadian) river boat
berlin *tf* covered carriage
calash light low-wheeled carriage
carack *carrack*
chaise a light open carriage
cooper *coper*
cutter *vr tf* small vessel
dennet a light gig
dingey *dinghy*
dinghy rowing/collapsible small boat
droger W. Indian sailing vessel
dromon *dromond*
fiacre hackney-coach: cab
galley (1) oar and sail vessel
galley (2) Roman/Greek warship
galley (3) large open rowing boat
gay-you an Anamese boat
gharri an Indian cart
gharry *gharri*
halser *hawser*
hawser a small cable
hooker Dutch vessel: fishing-smack
kafila camel train, caravan
litter a stretcher
lorcha junk-rigged European boat
masula *masoolah*
oomiak *umiak*
palkee *palki*
pinkie *pink*
pulkha *pulka*
pulwar a Ganges light boat
puteli flat-bottomed Ganges craft
randan *tf* rowing boat
saique *saic*
sampan a Chinese boat
sandal a N. African boat
settee a Mediterranean boat
sleigh a sledge
tartan a Mediterranean vessel
wherry light boat: barge
whiskey a light gig
zebeck *xebec*

birlinn Scottish chief's barge
britska *britzka*
britzka *tf* open carriage
cacolet military mule-litter
capsule self-contained (part)
   spacecraft
caravel *tf* light sailing ship
cariole open carriage: light cart
caroche a (grand) carriage
carrack a large ship of burden
carract *carrack*
carreck *carrack*
catboat smooth-water rigged boat
dogcart *tf* small horse-cart
drogher *droger*
dromond swift medieval warship
felucca *tf* sailing vessel
galliot old Dutch cargo boat
galloon a galleon
hackery Indian bullock-cart
kibitka Russian covered wagon/sledge
mitisko *xebec*-like coaster
nacelle *car* of a balloon
norimon a Japanese palanquin
oomiack *umiak*
patamar Bombay coastal vessel
pedicab hooded tricycle
phaeton *tf* open carriage
pinnace *vr* small boats
polacca a Mediterranean vessel
Pullman railway saloon/sleeping car
ricksha *rickshaw*
shandry N. England light cart
stanhope *tf* light open carriage
tartane *tartan*
trawler *tf* fishing vessel
trireme an ancient *tf* gallery
trishaw *tf* tricycle-rickshaw
tumbrel *vr tf* cart
tumbril *tumbrel*
voiture a carriage
volante *tf* horse (-drawn vehicle)
whiskey *whisky*

8

britzska *britzka*
buckcart *tf* cart
cabriole earlier form of *cab*

7

bateaux plural of *bateau*
berline driver-partitioned car

TRANSPORT

clarence *tf* four-wheeled carriage
cockboat (ship's) small boat
gallivat a large Malay boat
Irish car a jaunting car
mackinaw flat-bottomed lake-boat
masoolah Indian oared surf-boat
massoola *masoolah*
montaria a Brazilian *monoxylon*
rickshaw (motor) cycle hooded
   carriage
rockaway an American carriage
tartarna small covered wagon
trimaran boat with three hulls
wherries plural of *wherry*
zeppelin cigar-shaped airship

9

britschka *britzka*

jollyboat ship's boat
monoxylon canoe from single log
palankeen *palanquin*
palanquin a light litter
peter-boat *tf* fishing boat: dredger
privateer 'legal pirate's' ship

10

black Maria* prison van
brigantine a two-masted vessel
chapel cart Whitechapel cart
chuck-wagon food wagon
jinricksha *rickshaw*
jinrikisha *rickshaw*
montgolfier a fire-balloon
paddy wagon *black Maria*
shandrydan *shandry: chaise*
veteran car pre-1916 car

LANGUAGES

Languages do not respect international boundaries and consistently borrow words from each other. Individual languages are defined below in one of two ways according to circumstances. Two United Kingdom examples (English and Manx) will show why. English is international and is the first-choice tongue in many different countries thus its given definition is one of linguistic technicality. On the other hand, by 1969, there remained only one person for whom Manx was his first choice so Manx is defined geographically. Manx and Cornish (extinct by 1771) are both being revived whilst many languages are 'dead'. Dead languages are also geographically defined. Technically English is a Major language of the Western Germanic branch of the Germanic sub-group of the Indo-European family of languages. Manx is Gaelic of the Goidelic branch of the Celtic sub-group of the same Indo-European family. Cornish (with Welsh and Breton) belongs to the Brythonic branch of Celtic. Many of the languages listed in the second section can be similarly traced in the section below thus providing a guide to their historical stem.

FAMILY, SUB-GROUP, BRANCH, SUB-BRANCH

3

Gur branch of *Western Sudanic*
Kwa branch of *Western Sudanic*
Tai *Sino-Tibetan* sub-group

5

Bantu branch of *Benue-Congo*
Indic branch of *Indo-Iranian*
Maban small Sudan/Chad family
Mande branch of *Western Sudanic*
Mayan N. American Indian family
Munda northern/central India family
Oghuz *Southwestern Turkic*
Ugric branch of *Finno-Ugric*
Yuman N. American Indian family

6

Altaic Turkish and Asiatic family

Baltic *Indo-European* sub-group
Berber *Afro-Asiatic* sub-group
Celtic *Indo-European* sub-group
Chadic *Afro-Asiatic* sub-group
Finnic branch of *Finno-Ugric*
Italic *Indo-European* sub-group
Manchu *Southern Tungusic*
Nubian branch of *Eastern Sudanic*
Papuan a New Guinea/Islands family
Siouan N. American Indian family
Slavic *Indo-European* sub-group
Tanoan N. American Indian family
Turkic *Altaic* sub-group
Uralic Europe's other major family
Zunian N. American Indian family

7

Adamawa branch of *Adamawa-Eastern*
Aramaic branch of *Semitic*
Caddoan N. American Indian family
Eastern branch of *Adamawa-Eastern*

FAMILY, SUB-GROUP, ETC.

Iranian branch of *Indo-Iranian*
Keresan N. American Indian family
Khoisan non-Bantu Southern African family
Kipchak *Northwestern Turkic*
Miao-Yao *Sino-Tibetan* sub-group
Nilotic branch of *Eastern Sudanic*
Romance *Indo-European* sub-group
Saharan Saharan family
Samoyed *Uralic* sub-group
Semitic *Afro-Asiatic* sub-group
Sinitic *Sino-Tibetan* sub-group
Zoquean N. American Indian family

8

Chagatai *Southeastern Turkic*
Cushitic *Afro-Asiatic* sub-group
Dagestan *Caucasian* sub-group
Egyptian *Afro-Asiatic* sub-group
Ethiopic branch of *Semitic*
Germanic *Indo-European* sub-group
Goidelic branch of *Celtic*
Hellenic *Indo-European* sub-group
Penutian N. American Indian family
Salishan N. American Indian family
Tungusic *Altaic* sub-group
Wakashan N. American Indian family

9

Algonkian N. American Indian family
Brythonic branch of *Celtic*
Caucasian a Russian family, few written
Chari-Nile eastern African family
Dravidian mainly southern India family
Indo-Aryan *Indic* sub-branch
Iroquoian N. American Indian family
Mongolian *Altaic* sub-group
Mon-Khymer s.e. Asian family
Musdogean N. American Indian family

10

Artificial manufactured language

Athapascan N. American Indian family
Australian Australian Aborigine family
Benue-Congo *Niger-Congo* sub-group
Canaanitic branch of *Semitic*
Finno-Ugric *Uralic* sub-group
Indonesian *Malayo-Polynesian* sub-group
Melanesian *Malayo-Polynesian* sub-group
Niger-Congo largest African family
Polynesian *Malayo-Polynesian* sub-group
Uto-Aztecan N. American Indian family

11

Afro-Asiatic Red Sea region family
Eskimo-Aleut Arctic regions family
Ge-Pano-Carib C./S. American Indian family
Independent various unclassified languages
Indo-Iranian *Indo-European* sub-group
Micronesian *Malayo-Polynesian* sub-group
Nilo-Hamitic *Eastern Nilotic*
North Arabic branch of *Semitic*
Oto-Manguean N. American Indian family
Sino-Tibetan China and neighbours' family

12

Austronesian *Malayo-Polynesian*
Indo-European the largest family
Macro-Sudanic *Chari-Nile*
Paleo-Asiatic eastern Siberian family
Scandinavian *Northern Germanic*
Tibeto-Burman *Sino-Tibetan* sub-group
West Atlantic branch of *Western Sudanic*

13

Eastern Slavic branch of *Slavic*
Hamito-Semitic *Afro-Asiatic*
Macro-Chibchan C./S. American
   Indian family
Western Slavic branch of *Slavic*

14

Adamawa-Eastern *Niger-Congo*
   sub-group
Central Sudanic *Chari-Nile* sub-group
Eastern Nilotic *Nilotic* sub-branch
Eastern Sudanic *Chari-Nile* sub-group
Southern Slavic branch of *Slavic*
Western Nilotic *Nilotic* sub-branch
Western Sudanic *Niger-Congo*
   sub-group

15

Southern Nilotic *Nilotic* sub-branch
Western Germanic branch of
   Germanic

16

Andean Equatorial C./S. American
   Indian family
Eastern Caucasian *Caucasian*
   sub-group
Malayo-Polynesian Indian/Pacific
   Oceans' family
Northern Germanic branch of
   Germanic
Northern Tungusic branch of *Tungusic*
Southern Tungusic branch of *Tungusic*
Western Caucasian *Caucasian*
   sub-group

17

Southern Caucasian *Caucasian*
   sub-group

18

Northeastern Turkic branch of *Turkic*
Northwestern Turkic branch of *Turkic*
Southeastern Turkic branch of *Turkic*
Southwestern Turkic branch of *Turkic*

MAJOR/MINOR LANGUAGES, SIGNIFICANT DIALECTS, ETC.

m.l.   minor language
official   legal language of
For words in CAPITAL LETTERS, see preceding section.

2

Ga Accra plains region, Ghana
Ge (Indian) Amazon valley, Brazil
Ho *m.l.* (MUNDA family) India
Wa *m.l.* China/Burma border
Wu 50 million speakers, China
Yi 3 million speakers, China

3

Edo Mid-Western state, Nigeria
Ewe Ghana and Togo
Fox (Red Indian) eastern Iowa
Fur Darfur province, Sudan
Ibo (KWA) 8 million speakers, Nigeria
Ido simplified *Esperanto* (1901)

MAJOR/MINOR LANGUAGES

Ijo Niger River delta, Nigeria
Ket *m.l.* Yenisei River, Siberia
Kru Liberian coast
Kui ½ million speakers, C. India
Lak *m.l.* (DAGESTAN sub-group), USSR
Lao (TAI) official language of Laos
Luo Lake Victoria area, Kenya
Mam (Maya Indian) Guatemala
Meo (MIAO-YAO) Vietnam/Lagos etc.
Min *Fukienese*
Mon ancient Burmese (extant Burma/Thailand)
Suk (SOUTHERN NILOTIC) Kenya
Tiv central Nigeria
Twi (KWA) important language, Ghana
Ute (Red Indian) Utah/Colorado
Vai Liberia/Sierra Leone border
Yao (MIAO-YAO) Tanzania/Vietnam etc.

4

Afar Eritrea, Ethiopia
Agni southeast Ivory Coast
Ainu unique, almost extinct, Japan
Alur northwest Uganda
Amoy 30 million speakers, China
Anyi *Agni*
Avar (DAGESTAN) Caucasian *m.l.*
Bari near Uganda border, Sudan
Beja (CUSHITIC) Sudan/Ethiopia
Bodo (TIBETO-BURMAN) Assam, India
Bubi Equatorial Guinea
Cham (INDONESIAN)
     Vietnam/Cambodia
Chin Chin Hills, Burma
Chol (Maya Indian) Mexico
Cree (Red Indian) Canada
Crow (Red Indian) Montana
Cuna (MACRO-CHIBCHAN) Panama
Dyak Borneo aboriginal
Efic near Calabar, Nigeria
Enga (PAPUAN) Papua New Guinea
Erse *Gaelic*
Even (TUNGUSIC) Siberia
Fang
     (BANTU) Cameroon/Guinea/Gabon
Fula *Fulani*
Garo (TIBETO-BURMAN) Assam, India
Geez ancestor of all ETHIOPIC

Gheg northern Albanian dialect
Gisu (BANTU) S.E. Uganda
Gola Guinea/Sierra Leone/Liberia
Gold *Nanai*
Hehe (BANTU) Tanzania
Hopi (Red Indian) Arizona
Hova Madagascar
Igbo *Ibo*
Ijaw *Ido*
Iron *Ossetian* dialect
Kate (PAPUAN) Papua New Guinea
Kawa *Wa*
Kiga *Chiga*
Kiro *Pidgin English*, Sierra Leone
Komi (FINNIC) north eastern USSR
Lahu (TIBETO-BURMAN) China
Lisu (TIBETO-BURMAN) China
Lolo (TIBETO-BURMAN) *Yi*
Loma Guinea/Liberia/Sierra Leone
Lozi (BANTU) Zaire
Luba (BANTU) Zaire
Maba (MABAN) Chad
Madi (CENTRAL SUDANIC) Uganda
Mari (FINNIC) central European USSR
Manx Isle of Man
Maya language of Maya civilization
Mayo (Red Indian) Mexico
Mbum (ADAMWA) Cameroon/Chad
Miao (MIAO-YAO) southern China
Mixe (ZOQUEAN) Mexico
More *Mossi*
Moso *Nakhi*
Motu *Pidgin English*, Papua
Nuer south Sudan
Nung (TAI) China
Nupe Nigeria
Odul *Yukagir*
Pedi *Northern Sotho*
Pima (Red Indian) Arizona
Puyi (TAI) China
Saho (CUSHITIC) Eritrea, Ethiopia
Sara (CENTRAL SUDANIC) Chad
Shan (TAI) north Burma
Sibo (MANCHU) of *Manchu* origin
Sora *Savara*
Susu (MANDE) S.W. Guinea
Taal Cape Dutch
Teda (SAHARAN) Chad
Teso (NILO-HAMITIC) Uganda
Tewa (Red Indian) New Mexico

Thai (TAI) Thailand
Tiwa Taos/Isleta Red Indians, USA
Toro (BANTU) S.W. Uganda
Tosk Southern Albanian dialect
Towa Jemenez Red Indians, USA
Tulu (DRAVIDIAN) Mangalore, India
Tung (TAI) China
Tupi (ANDEAN-EQUATORIAL) Brazil
Urdu (INDIC) of *Sanskrit* origin
Uvea (POLYNESIAN) Wallis Islands
Xosa *Xhosa*
Yuma (Red Indian) Arizona
Zulu (BANTU) South Africa
Zuni (Red Indian) New Mexico

5

Aleut Aleutian/Commander isles,
   USA/USSR
Attic Greek dialect
Banda (EASTERN) Central African
   Republic
Bassa (KWA) coastal Liberia
Batak (INDONESIAN *m.l.*) Sumatra
Baule (KWA) Ivory Coast
Bemba (BANTU) Zambia
Bhili (INDIC) west central India
Bikol (INDONESIAN) Philippines
Caddo (Red Indian) Oklahoma
Carib (GE-PANO-CARIB) Honduras etc.
Chewa *Chinyanja*
Chiga (BANTU) Uganda
Creek (Red Indian) Oklahoma
Croat *Croatian*
Cufic Islamic writing style
Czech (WESTERN
   SLAVIC) Bohemia/Moravia
Dayak *Dyak*
Digor *Ossetian* dialect
Dinka south Sudan
Dogra N.W. India
Doric distinct *Greek* dialect
Duala (BANTU) Duala city, Cameroon
Dutch (WESTERN
   GERMANIC) international
Dyola (WEST ATLANTIC) Senegal
Dyula (MANDE) Mali
Enets (SAMOYED) Northern USSR
Erzya a *Mordvin* dialect

Fanti (KWA) Ghana
Farsi *Persian*
Fulbe *Fulani*
Galla (CUSHITIC) Ethiopia/Kenya
Ganda (BANTU) Buganda, Uganda
Gbaya (EASTERN) Central African
   Republic
Gondi (DRAVIDIAN) India
Grebo (KWA) Liberia
Greek (HELLENIC) Greece/Cyprus
Gumbo (French creole) West Indies
Gurma (GUR) Togo
Haida (Red Indian) Canada
Hakka *Chinese* dialect 20 million
   speakers
Hatsa (KHOSIAN) Tanzania
Hausa (CHADIC) Nigera/Niger etc.
Hindi (INDIC) of *Sanskrit* origin
Idoma Benue-Plateau, Nigeria
Ionic distinct *Greek* dialect
Iraqi *Arabic* dialect, Iraq
Irish (GOIDELIC) Eire
Jarai (INDONESIAN) Vietnam
Kabre (GUR) Togo
Kamba (BANTU) Kenya
Karen south Burma
Khasi (MON-KHYMER) Khasi Hills, India
Khmer Cambodia (official)
Kiowa (Red Indian) Oklahoma
Kissi (WEST ATLANTIC) Liberia/Sierra
   Leone
Kiwai (PAPUAN) Papua New Guinea
Kongo (BANTU) Kikongo
Korku (MUNDA) India
Kumyk (KIPCHAK) Volga delta, USSR
Ladin Alto Adige Italy
   (Rhaeto-Romantic)
Lamut *Even*
Lango (NILOTIC) Uganda
Latin ancestor of ROMANCE languages
Lenca (MACRO-CHIBCHAN) Honduras
lingo despised or not understood
Lunda (BANTU) Angola/Zaire/Zambia
Lwena (BANTU) Angola/Zambia
Makua (BANTU) north Mozambique
Malay (INDONESIAN) Malaysia and Far
   East
Mansi *Vogel*
Maori (POLYNESIAN) New Zealand
Masai (NILO-HAMITIC) Kenya/Tanzania

Mende (MANDE) Sierra Leone
Mongo (BANTU) central Zaire
Mossi (GUR) Upper Volta
Muong (INDEPENDENT) north Vietnam
Nakhi (TIBETO-BURMAN) S. China
Nanai (MANCHU) China/USSR
Nandi (SOUTHERN NILOTIC) Kenya
Nivkh (PALEO-ASIATIC) USSR
Nkole (BANTU) Uganda
Nogai (KIPCHAK) USSR
Norse *Norwegian*: Old Norwegian
Nyoro (BANTU) Uganda
Omaha (Red Indian) Nebraska
Oraon *Kurukh*
Oriya (INDIC) Eastern India
Osage (Red Indian) Oklahoma
Oscan (ITALIC) virtually extinct, Italy
Otomi (OTO-MANGUEAN) Mexico
Palau (MICRONESIAN) Palau Island
Pokot *Suk*
Rhade (INDONESIAN) Vietnam
Rundi (BANTU) Burundi
Salar (CHAGATAI) China
Sango *lingua franca* Central African
   Republic
Serer (WEST ATLANTIC) Senegal
Shluh (BERBER) southern Morocco
Shona (BANTU) Zimbabwe
Sioux (Red Indian) Midwest USA
Sotho (BANTU) *Southern Sotho*
Swazi (BANTU) Swaziland/S. Africa
Tamil (DRAVIDIAN) India/Ceylon/
   Malaysia
Tatar (KIPCHAK) widely dispersed USSR
Tavgi *Nganasan*
Temne (WEST ATLANTIC) Sierra Leone
Tibbu *Teda*
Tigre (ETHIOPIC) Eritrea, Ethiopia
Tonga (BANTU) south Zambia
Uiger (CHAGATAI) China/USSR
Uzbek (CHAGATAI) USSR/Afghanistan
Venda (BANTU) Transvaal, S. Africa
Vogel (UGRIC) western Siberia
Welsh (BRYTHONIC) Wales
Wolof (WEST
   ATLANTIC) Senegal/Gambia
Xhosa (BANTU) South Africa
Yabim (MELANESIAN) northern New
   Guinea
Yakut (TURKIC) N/E Siberia

Yurak *Nenets*
Zande Sudan/Zaire border
Zoque (ZOQUEAN) Mexico

6

Acholi (NILOTIC) Uganda
Aeolic distinct *Greek* dialect
Apache (Red Indian) Arizona
Arabic (NORTH ARABIC) official UN
   (1974)
Aranda (AUSTRALIAN) central Australia
Arawak (ANDEAN EQUATORIAL) S.
   America
Arunta *Aranda*
Aymara (ANDEAN
   EQUATORIAL) Bolivia/Peru
Bahnar (KHYMER) south Vietnam
Balkar (KIPCHAK) USSR
Bariba (GUR) Dahomey
Basque (INDEPENDENT) France/Spain
Bihari (INDIC) 3 similar languages
Brahui (DRAVIDIAN) Baluchistan,
   Pakistan
Breton (CELTIC) Brittany, France
Bribri (MACRO-CHIBCHAN) Costa Rica
Buryat (MONGOLIAN) Southern Siberia
Chagga Mt. Kilimanjaro, Tanzania
Chokwe (BANTU) Angola
Chuang (TAI) largest ethnic minority
   China
Coptic liturgical, from ancient
   Egyptian
Creole *pidgin* as mother tongue
Cymric *Welsh*
Dakota *Sioux*
Danish Denmark/Greenland/Faroes
   (official)
Dargin (DAGESTAN) Caucasus region,
   USSR
Djerma south west Niger
Eskimo Greenland/Canada/Alaska/Si-
   beria
Evenki (NORTHERN TUNGUSIC) Eastern
   USSR
Fantee *Fanti*
Fijian (MELANESIAN) Fiji
French (ROMANCE) Official UN

Fulani (WEST ATLANTIC) N. Nigeria/Guinea, etc.
Gaelic (CELTIC) *Irish, Scottish*
German (WESTERN GERMANIC) international
Gilyak *Nivkh*
Guaymi (MACRO-CHIBCHAN) Panama
Gurage (ETHIOPIC) Ethiopia
Hebrew (CANAANITIC) Israel (official), international
Herero (BANTU) S.W. Africa
Hsiang *Chinese* dialect 15 million speakers
Ibibio near Calabar, Nigeria
Jivaro (ANDEAN EQUATORIAL) Peru/Ecuador
Jonkha (TIBETO-BURMAN) Bhutan
Kabyle (BERBER) Algeria
Kachin extreme north Burma
Kalmuk *Kalmyk*
Kalmyk (MONGOLIAN) Volga delta, USSR
Kanuri (SAHARAN) Nigeria
Kazakh (KIPCHAK) USSR/China
Kekchi (Maya Indian) Guatemala/Honduras
Khanty (UGRIC) Western Siberia
Khymer *Khmer*
Kikuyu (BANTU) largest Kenya tribe
Kirgiz (KIPCHAK) China border USSR
Kituba Kongo *creole* Congo
Korean (INDEPENDENT) Far East inc. Japan/USSR
Koryak (PALEO-ASIATIC) Kamchatka, USSR
Kpelle (MANDE) Liberia
Kurukh (DRAVIDIAN) central India
Ladino *Spanish* variety, Turkey/Israel
Lahnda a *Punjabi* dialect, Pakistan
Lepcha (TIBETO-BURMAN) Sikkim
Lotuko near Uganda border, Sudan
Lushei (TIBETO-BURMAN) Assam, India
Luvale Lewena
Magyar *Hungarian*
Manchu (MANCHU) extinct Chinese language
Marind (PAPUAN) West Irian, New Guinea
Mbundu (BANTU) Umbundu/Kimbundu, Angola

Micmac (Red Indian) Nova Scotia
Mixtec (OTO-MANGUEAN) Mexico
Mohave (Red Indian) Arizona
Mohawk (Red Indian) USA/Canada
Moksha A *Mordvin* dialect
Mongol *Mongolian*
Navaho most important Red Indian language
Navajo (Navaho) Arizona, N. Mexico, Utah
Nenets (SAMOYED) Northernmost USSR
Nepali (INDIC) Nepal
Niuean (POLYNESIAN) Nieu Island
Nootka (Red Indian) Vancouver Island
Nubian (NUBIAN) Sudan
Nyanja *Chinyanja*
Ojibwa (Red Indian) USA/Canada
Oneida (Red Indian) N.Y. State/Wisconsin
Ostyak *Khanty*
Paiute (Red Indian) Western USA
Pakhto Pathan *Pashto*
Papago (Red Indian) Arizona
Pashto (IRANIAN) Afghanistan/Pakistan
patois illiterate or provincial dialect
Pawnee (Red Indian) Oklahoma
pidgin simplified additional language
Polish (WESTERN SLAVIC) Poland
Pushtu *Pashto*
Quiche *Maya*
Romaic vernacular modern *Greek*
Romany (INDIC) the Gypsy language
Ruanda *Kinyarwanda*
Samoan (POLYNESIAN) Samoa
Savara (MUNDA) Orissa, India
Selkup (SAMOYED) western Siberia
Seneca (Red Indian) New York State
Senufo (GUR) Ivory Coast/Mali
Shawia (BERBER) Algeria
Sidamo (CUSHITIC) S.W. Ethiopia
Sindhi (INDIC) Pakistan/India
Slovak Slovakia, Czechoslovakia
Somali (CUSHITIC) Somalia (official)
Strine comic Australian-English
Sukuma (BANTU) Tanzania
Syriac (ARAMAIC) liturgical
Tacana (GE-PANO-CARIB) Bolivia
Tartar *Tatar*
Telugu (DRAVIDIAN) S./E. India
Thonga (BANTU) Mozambique

MAJOR/MINOR LANGUAGES

Tongan (POLYNESIAN) Tonga
Tsonga *Thonga*
Tswana *Western Sotho*
Tuareg *Tamashek*
Tungus *Evenki*
Tuscan Tuscany, Italy
Udmurt (FINNIC) north eastern USSR
Votyak *Udmurt*
Yakima (Red Indian) Washington State
Yapese (MICRONESIAN) Yap Island
Yaunde (BANTU) Cameroon
Yoruba (KWA) Nigeria

7

Adangme (KWA) Accra plains, Ghana
Amharic (ETHIOPIC) Ethiopia
Arapaho (Red Indian) Oklahoma/Wyoming
Baining (PAPUAN) New Britain
Balante (WEST ATLANTIC) Guinea-Bissau
Baluchi (IRANIAN) Iran/Pakistan
Bambara (MANDE) Mali
Bashir (KIPCHAK) Southern Urals, USSR
Bengali (INDIC) of *Sanskrit* origin
Burmese (TIBETO-BURMAN) majority of Burma
Bushman (KHOISAN) Kalahari Desert (Africa)
Cabecar (MACRO-CHIBCHAN) Costa Rica
Carrier (Red Indian) Fraser River, Canada
Catalan Spain/France: Andorra (official)
Chechen EASTERN CAUCASIAN *m.l.*
Chiluba *Luba*
Chinese (SINITIC) official UN
Choctaw (Red Indian) Oklahoma/Mississippi
Chontal (Maya Indian) Mexico
Chukchi (PALEO-ASIATIC) N/E Siberia
Chuvash (TURKIC) Volga region USSR
Cornish (CELTIC) Cornwall, England
Dagbane *Dagomba*
Dagomba (GUR) Ghana
English (WESTERN GERMANIC) official UN

Faroese similar to *Old Norse (m.l.)*
Finnish Finland (official)/Sweden/USSR
Flemish Flanders, northern Belgium
Foochow Northern-*Fukienese*
Frisian *(m.l.)* northern Holland
Guarani (ANDEAN-EQUATORIAL) Paraguay
Hadzapi *Hatsa*
Hamitic languages of Ham (Biblical) origin
Hittite language of Hittites (Biblical)
Huastec (Maya Indian) Mexico
Hurrian ancient Mesopotamia
Iberian ancient Spanish CELTIC
Ilocano (INDONESIAN) Philippines
Italian (ROMANCE) international
Itelmen (PALEO-ASIATIC) USSR
Kalmuck *Kalmyk*
Kannada *Kanarese*
Kashmiri (INDIC) Kashmir
Keresan (Red Indian) New Mexico
Khakass (NORTHEASTERN TURKIC) USSR
Kikongo Zaire/Angola/Congo-Brazzaville
Kirghiz (KIPCHAK) near China, USSR
Kirudni Rundi
Klamath (Red Indian) Oregon
Konkani *Marathi* dialect, Goa
Kurdish (IRANIAN) Turkey/Iraq/Iran, etc.
Lappish (FINNIC *m.l.*) Laplanders
Latvian (BALTIC) Latvia, USSR
Lettish *Latvian*
Lingala Zaire/Congo-Brazzaville
Luganda *Ganda*
Lugbara (CENTRAL SUDANIC) Uganda
Makonde Mozambique/Tanzania
Malayan *Malay*
Malinke (MANDE) Senegal/Gambia etc.
Maltese (NORTH ARABIC) Malta
Maranao (INDONESIAN) Philippines
Marathi (INDIC) of *Sanskrit* origin
Mazahua (OTO-MANGUEAN) Mexico
Mazatec (OTO-MANGUEAN) Mexico
Meithei (TIBETO-BURMAN) Assam, India
Miskito (MACRO-CHIBCHAN) Nicaragua
Mordvin (FINNIC) European Russia
Murngin (AUSTRALIAN) north Australia
Nahuatl the Aztec language
Naskapi (Red Indian) northern Quebec

Nauruan (MICRONESIAN) Nauru Island
Orokolo (PAPUAN) Papua New Guinea
Palaung north of Mandalay, Burma
Panjabi *Punjabi*
Prakrit any vernacular INDIC, India
Persian (IRANIAN) Iran/Afghanistan
Punjabi (INDIC) India/Pakistan
Quechua the Inca language
Riffian (BERBER) north Morocco
Russian (EASTERN SLAVIC) official UN
Sandawe (KHOSIAN) Tanzania
Santali only written MUNDA, India
Serbian Serbo-Croatian (CYRILLIC
  alphabet)
Sesotho (BANTU) the Sotho languages
Shilluk Upper Nile province, Sudan
Shuswap (Red Indian) Fraser River,
  Canada
SEMITIC languages of Shem (Biblical)
  origin
Sinhala *Sinhalese*
Songhai near Timbuktu, Mali
Soninke (MANDE) Mali/Mauritania
Sorbian (WESTERN SLAVIC) East
  Germany
Spanish (ROMANCE) Official UN
Swahili (BANTU) Tanzania/Kenya (both
  official)
Swedish Sweden (official): Finland
Tadzhik (IRANIAN) Chinese border USSR
Tagalog renamed *Pilipino* 1962
**Tarasco (North American
  Indian)** Mexico
Tibetan (TIBETO-BURMAN) Tibet/Nepal
Tlingit (Red Indian) Alaska
Totonac (N. American Indian) Mexico
Trukese (MICRONESIAN) Truk Island
Tuamotu (POLYNESIAN) Tuamotu
  Archipelago
Tumbuka (BANTU) Malawi
Turkana (NILO-HAMITIC) Malawi
Turkish (OGHUZ) Turkey/Cyprus etc.
Turkmen (OGHUZ) USSR/Afghanistan
Tzeltal (Maya Indian) Mexico
Tzotzil (Maya Indian) Mexico
Visayan (INDONESIAN) Philippines
Wendish *Sorbian*
**Yiddish (WESTERN
  GERMANIC)** European Jews
Yucatec *Maya*

Yukagir (PALEO-ASIATIC) USSR
Zapotec (OTO-MANGUEAN) Mexico

8

Achinese (INDONESIAN) Sumatra
Akkadian oldest known SEMITIC
Albanian Albania/Yugoslavia
Armenian
  (INDO-EUROPEAN) international
Assamese (INDIC) Assam, India
Assyrian (ARAMAIC) *Akkadian* dialect
Balinese (INDONESIAN) Bali
Buginese (INDONESIAN *m.l.*) Celebes
Chaldean Biblical
Chamorro (MICRONESIAN)
  Guam/Marina Is.
Cheremis *Mari*
Cherokee (Red Indian) Oklahoma
**Cheyenne (Red
  Indian)** Oklahoma/Montana
Chingpaw *Kachin*
Chippewa *Ojibwa*
Comanche (Red Indian) Oklahoma
Croatian *Serbo-Croatian* (ROMAN
  alphabet)
Delaware (Red Indian) Oklahoma
Esquimau *Eskimo*
Estonian (FINNIC) Estonia, USSR
Etruscan pre-Roman Italy
Fanakalo Zulu *pidgin*, S. Africa
Flathead (Red Indian) Montana
Friulian Italy/Yugoslavia
  Rhaeto-Romantic
Galician Portuguese dialect, Spain
Georgian the only major CAUCASIAN
GOIDELIC ancient Gael (Goidel)
Gujarati (INDIC) of *Sanskrit* origin
Hawaiian *(m.l.)* Hawaii
Hellenic *Greek*
Hispanic *Spanish*
Illyrian ancient Albanian coastal
Japanese (INDEPENDENT) Japan
Javanese (INDONESIAN) Java
Karachai (KIPCHAK) Caucasus, USSR
Karanese (DRAVIDIAN) S./W. India
Kashmiri (INDIC) Kashmir
Kwakiutl (Red Indian) northern

Vancouver
Ligurian pre-ITALIC, Italy
Lillooet (Red Indian) Fraser River, Canada
Livonian almost extinct, Baltic USSR
Lusation *Sorbian*
Madurese (INDONESIAN) Java/Madura
Malagasy (INDONESIAN) Madagascar, Africa
Malgache *Malagasy*
Mandarin *Chinese* dialect, 650 million speakers
Mosquito Miskito
Nez Perce (Red Indian) Idaho
Nganasan (SAMOYED) northernmost Russia
Nimboran (PAPUAN) West Irian, New Guinea
Nyamwezi (BANTU) Tanzania
Nyancole *Nkole*
Okanagan (Red Indian) British Columbia
Ossetian (IRANIAN) Caucasus Mts. USSR
Phrygian Phrygia, Asia Minor
Pilipino (INDONESIAN) Philippines (official)
Ponapean (MICRONESIAN) Ponape Island
Old Norse the Viking language
Quechuan *Quechua*
Romansch official Swiss Italian *Rhaeto-Romantic*
Rumanian only East European ROMANCE
Sanskrit (INDIC) ancient, classical, sacred
Scottish (GOIDELIC) Scotland
Seminole (Red Indian) Florida
Shoshone (Red Indian) Western USA
Tahitian (POLYNESIAN) Tahiti (Society Is.)
Taki-Taki Surinam *Pidgin English*
Tamashek (BERBER) Tauregs, N. Africa
Teutonic primitive GERMANIC
Thibetan Tibetan
Thompson (Red Indian) Fraser River, Canada
Thracian ancient INDO-EUROPEAN, Balkans
Tigrinya (ETHIOPIC) Ethiopia

Turcoman *Turkmen*
Turkoman *Turkmen*

9

Afrikaans (WESTERN GERMANIC) S. Africa
Blackfoot (Red Indian) USA/Canada
Bulgarian (SOUTHERN SLAVIC) Bulgaria
Cambodian *Khmer*
Cantonese *Chinese* dialect 45 million speakers
Cape-Dutch early *Afrikaans*
Castilian literary *Spanish*
Chickasaw (Red Indian) Oklahoma
Chilcotin (Red Indian) Chilcotin River, Canada
Chinantec (OTO-MANGUEAN) Mexico
Chinyanja (BANTU) Malawi/Zambia
Chipewyan (Red Indian) Canada
Chungchia *Puyi*
Cuneiform earliest known writing
Esperanto (ARTIFICIAL) devised 1887
Fox and Sac Fox/Sac Red Indians
Fukienese *Chinese* dialect, 45 million speakers
Hottentot (KHOSIAN) South West Africa
Hungarian (UGRIC) Hungary and neighbours
Icelandic similar to *Old Norse*
Kabardian WESTERN CAUCASIAN *m.l.*
Kamchadal now called *Itelmen*
Kiswahili *Swahili*
Low German northern *German*
Malayalam (DRAVIDIAN) extreme S. India
Maldivian (INDIC) Maldive Islands
Marquesan (POLYNESIAN) Marquesas Islands
Moldavian (ROMANCE) Moldavia, USSR
Mongolian (MONGOLIAN) Mongolia/China/USSR
Norwegian (NORTHERN GERMANIC) Norway
Pampangan (INDONESIAN) Philippines
Provencal decaying classic, S. *French*
Saramacca Surinam English-*Creole*
Sardinian (ROMANCE) Sardinia
Sinhalese (INDIC) Sri Lanka (official)

Slovenian Slovenia, Yugoslavia
(official)
Sundanese (INDONESIAN) Java
Tamazight (BERBER) central Morocco
Tocharian historic INDO-EUROPEAN,
central Asia
Tokharian *Tocharian*
Tsimshian (Red Indian) British
Columbia
Ukrainian (EASTERN SLAVIC) 35 million
speakers
**Winnebago (Red
Indian)** Wisconsin/Nebraska

10

Anglo Saxon *Old English*
Assiniboin (Red Indian) USA/Canada
Azerbaijan *Azerbaijani*
Burushaski (INDEPENDENT) N./W.
Kashmir
Cakchiquel (Maya Indian) Guatemala
**Circassian (WESTERN
CAUCASIAN)** USSR/Turkey
Devanagari formal Indian alphabet
Gilbertese (MICRONESIAN) Gilbert
Islands
Glagolitic liturgical alphabet, Dalmatia
High German southern, standard
German
Hindustani form of *Hindi*
Indonesian (INDONESIAN) Indonesia
Kara-Kalpak (KIPCHAK) Soviet central
Asia
Karamojong N.E. Uganda
Lithuanian (BALTIC) Lithuania, USSR
Macedonian Macedonia, Yugoslavia
(official)
Nicobarese (KHMER) Nicobar Is., Bay
of Bengal
Occidental (ARTIFICIAL) scientific
purpose
Old English *English* to approximately
1100AD
Papiamento a Spanish *creole* (Antilles)
Police Motu simplified *Motu*
Portuguese Portugal/Brazil (both
official)
Rajasthani (INDIC) various Indian

dialects
Rarotongan (POLYNESIAN) Cook Island
Singhalese *Sinhalese*
Tarahumara (Red Indian) Mexico
Vietnamese (INDEPENDENT) Vietnam

11

Anglo-Norman Norman dialect
Azerbaijani (OGHUZ) USSR/Iran
Belorussian USSR near Poland
Interlingua (ARTIFICIAL) 20th C.
invention
Kinyarwanda (BANTU) Rwanda/Zaire
Old Prussian extinct BALTIC language
Marshallese Marshall Islands
Modern Greek began approx. 9th C.

12

French Creole West Indies etc.
Letzeburgesh *Luxembourgian*
lingua-franca international jargon
Mingangkabau (INDONESIAN) Indonesia
Norman French medieval Norman
Northumbrian *Anglo-Saxon* dialect
Western Sotho Botswana *(Sesotho)*

13

Arcado-Cyprian distinct *Greek* dialect
Luxembourgian *German* dialect
Middle English approx. 1100/1500AD
Northern Sotho Transvaal *(Sesotho)*
Ostyak-Samoyed *Selkup*
Passamaquoddy (Red Indian) Maine
Pidgin English New Guinea *lingua
franca*
Serbo-Croatian Yugoslavia
Southern Sotho S. Africa *(Sesotho)*
Yenisei-Ostyak *Ket*

14

Classical Greek pre *Modern Greek*
Rhaeto-Romantic Swiss/north Italy
dialects

WORDS AND TERMS FROM FOREIGN LANGUAGES

ANGLO-EUROPEAN WORDS

Foreign words appear in crosswords usually in one of three ways:

(1) As cryptic syllables such as *'the German'* with the German word for THE as part of a longer word. *'A French'*, *'an Italian'* or *'in Spanish'* being similar examples.

(2) Where the word is common to both English and another language but has a totally different meaning (i.e. *cola*, Spanish for *glue*).

(3) As a word with acceptable international currency (i.e. *Frau, senora, signora*). This section is designed to meet all three contingencies and, in consequence, has a format unlike the rest of the dictionary. In determining the answer match your clue to the *given word* and the *description* contains the possible solution. The order is strictly alphabetical without reference to number of letters.

note (1) In the convention of crosswords and word-games accents are ignored and therefore not given.

(2) Where German and other languages use the same noun the German practice of a capital letter is taken (i.e. aunt).

Fr French
Ger German
It Italian
Sp Spanish

CLUES	ANSWERS	CLUES	ANSWERS
a (an) *Fr* un, une		*It* quasi	
Ger ein, eine		**alone** *It/Sp* solo	
It un, una, uno		**already** *Sp* ya	
Sp un, una		**among** *Ger* unter	
acorn *Fr* gland		*It* fra	
act *Ger* Tat		**and** *Fr* et	
advice *Ger* Rat		*Ger* und	
after *Fr* apres (que)		*It* e,ed	
against *Sp* contra		*Sp* e,y	
age *Ger* Alter		**animal** *Ger* Tier	
ago *It* fa		**ant** *It* formica	
air *Ger* Luft		**any** *Fr* d,d(e)(es)(u), en,tout	
It aria		**apple** *Fr* pomme	
aisle *Ger* Gang		**arm** *Fr* armer, bras	
all *Fr* tout		**as** *Fr* aussi, comme, en	
almost *Ger* fast		*It* come	

200

ANGLO-EUROPEAN WORDS

FOREIGN WORDS

CLUES	ANSWERS

Sp como, tan
asparagus *Fr* asperges
at *Fr* a, sur
  Ger an, in, um
  It a, in
  Sp a, en
aunt *Fr/Ger* Tante
away *Fr* absent, loin
  It via
bacon *Fr* lard
bare *Fr* nu
bath *Fr* bain
  Ger Bad
battery *Fr* pile
bear *Fr* ours, porter, supporter
  Ger Bar
beard *Ger* Bart
beast *Ger* Tier
beautiful *Fr* belle, beau
beaver *Fr/Sp* castor
bed *Fr* lit
bee *It* ape
beer *Ger* Bier
beg *Ger* bitten
beneath *Ger* unten, unter
bench *Ger* Bank
between *It* fra
big *Ger* gross
bird *Sp* ave
black *Fr* noir
  It nero
  Sp negro
blackbird *Fr* merle
  Ger Star
blade *Fr* lame
  It lama
blank *Ger* leer
blanket *Sp* manta
blister *Ger* Blase
blood *Fr* sang
board *Sp* junta
boarding house *Fr/Sp* pension
boat *Ger* Boot
bond *Ger* Band
bone *Fr* os
book *Fr* livre
border *Fr* bord
  Ger Rand

CLUES	ANSWERS

boredom *Fr* ennui
boss *Fr/Sp* patron
  Ger Chef
bottom *Fr* fond
bound *Fr* bond
bow *Ger* Bug
boy *Fr* garcon
bread *Fr* pain
  It pane
  Sp pan
breast *It* petto
bridge *Fr* pont
bright *Ger* hell
brute *Ger* Tier
bull *It/Sp* toro
burden *Ger* Last
but *Fr* mais, sinon
  Ger aber
  It me
butter *It* burro
butterfly *Fr* papillon
by *Fr* avant, par, pres
  Ger bei, mal, uber, vor
  It per, presso
  Sp por
cabbage *Ger* Kohl
  Sp col
cake *Fr* gateau
calf *Ger* Wade
call *Fr* cri, crier
cape *Fr* cap
  Ger Kap
  It capo
  Sp cabo
cardboard *Fr/Sp* carton
carriage *Fr* port
case *Fr* cas
  Ger Fall
castle *Fr* chateau
  Ger Schloss
  It castello
  Sp castillo
cat *Fr* chat
cathedral *Ger* Dom
cellar *Fr* cave
chap *Fr* type
  Sp chico
charge *Fr* charge(r), imputer, prix

FOREIGN WORDS   ANGLO-EUROPEAN WORDS

CLUES   ANSWERS   CLUES   ANSWERS

Sp cargo
cheerful *Fr* gai
cheese *Fr* fromage
cherry *Ger* Kirsche
chest *It* petto
chicken *It*/*Sp* pollo
child *Fr* enfant
 Ger Kind
 It bambino
 Sp nino
Christmas *Fr* Noel
church *Fr* eglise
city *Fr* ville
 Ger Stadt
 It citta
 Sp ciudad
clean *Ger* rein
clover *Ger* Klee
coarse *Ger* grob
coast *Fr* cote
 It/*Sp* costa
cock *Fr* coq
 It/*Sp* gallo
coffee *Fr*/*Sp* cafe
cold *Fr* froid, rhume
collar *Fr* col
colonel *Ger* Oberst
comma *Sp* coma
cool *It*/*Sp* fresco
corner *Fr* coin
cost *Fr* prix
 Sp costa
council *Ger* Rat
counsel *Ger* Rat(schlag)
country *Fr* campagne, pays
courage *Ger* Mut
cousin *Ger* Vetter
crash *Fr* fracas
crazy *Fr* fou, folle
 Sp loco
creek *Ger* Bach
crest *Fr* Crete
cross *Fr* crosier, croix, traverser
crown *It*/*Sp* corona
crude *Fr* brut
cry *Fr* cri, crier
cup *Fr*/*Ger* Tasse
custom *It* costume

dad *Fr* papa
 Ger Vati
 It babbo
 Sp papa
dance *Fr* bal, danse, danser
darling *Fr* cheri
 Ger Liebling
daughter *Fr* fille
day *Fr* jour, journee
 Ger Tag
 Sp dia
dead *Fr* mort
 Ger tot
death *Ger* Tod
deck *Fr* jeu (de cartes), pont
deed *Ger* Tat
deep *Fr* grave
degree *Ger* Grad
deposit *Fr* deposer, depot
devil *Sp* diablo
dew *Ger* Tau
dice *Fr* des
diet *Fr* regime
dirty *Fr* sale
dish *Fr* mets
 Sp plato
dismal *Ger* duster
distress *Ger* Not
do *Ger* tun
 It fare
doctor *Sp* medico
dog *Fr* chien
 Ger Hund
 It cane
dream *Sp* sonar
dreary *Ger* ode
during *Fr* pendant
dysentery *Ger* Ruhr
eagle *Ger* Adler
earth *It* terra
east *Fr*/*It* est
eastern *Fr*/*Sp* oriental
edge *Fr* bord
 Ger Rand
egg *Fr* oeuf
 Ger Ei
end *Fr* fin, finir, terminer
 It fine

ANGLO-EUROPEAN WORDS

CLUES   ANSWERS

entry *Fr* article
establish *Fr* fonder
Europe *Ger/It/Sp* Europa
even *It* piano
every *Fr* tout
evil *Fr* mal, mauvais
     It male
     Sp mal, malo
except *It* salvo
faint *Ger* matt
fair *Fr* beau, blond, passable
fairy *Fr/Ger* Fee
faith *Sp* credo, fe
far *Fr* loin
fat *Ger* dick
father *Fr* pere
     It/Sp padre
fellow *Fr* type
     It persona
field *Fr* champ, domaine
file *Fr* dossier, lime
fine *Fr* fin
firm *Ger* fest, Firma
flame *Sp* llama
flat *It/Sp* piano
flax *Fr* lin
     It/Sp lino
flesh *Fr* chair
flight *Fr* fuite, vol
floor *Ger* Stock
     It piano
flower *Sp* flor
fly *Sp*[1] mosca, volar
fold *Fr* pli, plier
follower *Fr* partisan
fool *Fr* sot
     Sp tonto
foolish *Sp* bobo
foot *Fr* pied
     Ger Fuss
     Sp pie
for *Fr* car, pour
     Ger denn, fur
     It per, perche
     Sp par, para, porque

[1] For the various names of the famous 'Spanish fly' see INSECTS (p. 257).

CLUES   ANSWERS

forehead *Fr* front
fort *It* forte
found *Fr* fonder
frank *It/Sp* franco
free *It* gratis
fresh *It/Sp* fresco
friend *Fr* ami
     Sp amigo
from *Fr/Sp* de
     Ger aus, von
     it da
funny *Fr* drole
further *Sp* adicional, mas
garlic *Fr* ail
gate *Ger* Tor
gay *Fr* gai
gem *It* gemma
gentle *Sp* suave
give *It* dare
     Sp dar
glory *It/Sp* gloria
glue *Sp* cola
go *Fr* aller
     Sp ir
goal *Fr* but
     It/Sp meta
goat *It* capra
God *Fr* Dieu
     Ger Gott
     It Dio
     Sp Dios
gold *Fr* or
good *Fr* bon
     Ger gut
     Swedish bra
grade *Fr* annee, grade, note
     Ger Note, Rang
grave *Ger* ernst, Grab
great *Ger* gross
greatness *Fr* grandeur
green *Fr* vert
grim *Ger* hart
gross *Fr* brut, gros, grosse
guardian *Sp* tutor
gulf *Ger* Golf
gypsy *Fr* bohemien
half *Fr* demi, moite
     Ger halb, Halfte

FOREIGN WORDS   ANGLO-EUROPEAN WORDS

CLUES   ANSWERS   CLUES   ANSWERS

It meta, mezzo
Sp medio, mitad
hall *Fr* corridor, salle
Ger Gang
hand *Fr* main
It/Sp mano
handsome *Fr* belle, beau
hard *Fr* difficile, dur
Ger hart
hardship *Ger* Not
harsh *Fr* apre, dur
It aspro, rude
hat *Fr* chapeau
Ger Hut
hate *Fr* hair
he *Fr* il, lui
Ger er
It esso
Sp el
head *Fr* chef, mener, tete
It capo, testa
hearth *Ger* Herd
heel *Fr/Sp* talon
hell *Fr* enfer
It inferno
her *Fr* elle, la, lui, sa, son, ses
Ger ihr, ihrer, sie
It il suo, i suoi, la, le(i), la sua, la sue
Sp la, se
herb *Ger* Kraut
here *Fr* ici
It qui
hero *Ger* Held
hers/his *Fr* la sienne, le sien, sa, ses, son
It il suo, i suoi, la sua, le sue
Sp el suyo, la(s) suya(s), los suyos, su
Ger (hers) ihr(e)(em)(en)(er) (es)
(his) sein(e)(em)(en)(er) (es)
hide *Ger* Fell
high *It/Sp* alto
him *Fr* le, lui
Ger ihm, ihn, seiner
It lo, lui

Sp le, lo
his see *hers/his*
hole *Fr* trou
Ger Loch
horn *Fr* cor, corne (d'auto)
hour *It* ora
Sp hora
how *Fr* comment
Ger wie
It come
hunger *It* fame
hurl *Fr* lancer
hyphen *Fr* trait d'union
I *Fr* je, moi
Ger ich
It io
Sp yo
if *Fr/Sp* si
Ger ob, wenn
It se
in *Fr* dans, pendant
Ger bei, in
It dentro, durante, in
Sp en
infant *It* bambino
into *Fr* dans
iron *Fr* fer
juice *Fr* jus
key *Fr* clef
kidney *Fr* rein
kind *Ger* Art
It gentile, specie
king *Fr*[2] roi
Ger[2] Konig
It[2] re
Sp[2] rey
kiss *Fr* baiser
lady *Fr/Ger* Dame
It signora
Sp dama
lake *Fr* lac
Ger See
large *Ger* gross
late *Fr* en retard, feu, tard
law *Fr* droit, loi

[2] For names of various foreign kings see MONARCHS (p. 114).

ANGLO-EUROPEAN WORDS   **FOREIGN WORDS**

CLUES   ANSWERS   CLUES   ANSWERS

leap *Fr* bond, sauter   **mere(ly)** *Ger* bloss
left *Ger* link, Linke, links   **merry** *Fr* gai
level *It* livello, piano   *It* allegro
light *Ger* hell, leicht, Licht   **middle** *Fr* milieu
like *Fr* aimer, comme, semblable   *It* mezzo
lily *Fr* lis   **might** *Fr* puissance
linen *Sp* lino   **mighty** *Fr* puissant, vaste
link *Fr* lien   **Miss** *Fr* Mademoiselle, Mlle
lion *Sp* leon   *Ger* Fraulein
little *Fr* petit, (un) peu (de)   *It* (la) signorina
         Ger Klein, wenig   *Sp* (la) senorita, srita
         It piccolo, poco   **miss** *Fr* rater, regretter
live *It/Sp* vivo   **Mistress (Mrs)** *Fr* Madame, Mme
living *Fr* vie   *Ger* Frau
load *Ger* Last   *It* (la) signora
loaf *Fr* pain   *Sp* (la) senora, sra
         It pane   **mistress** *Fr* maitresse
log *Sp* leno   **mode** *Ger* Art
lonely *Fr* desert, solitaire   **money** *Fr*[3] argent
         Sp solo   *Ger*[3] Geld
look *Fr* aspect, regard(er)   *It*[3] denaro
loose *Ger* locker   *Sp*[3] dinero
loud *Fr* fort   **monkey** *Fr* singe
         It forte   *Sp* mono
lung *Ger* Lunge   **month** *Sp* mes
mad *Sp* loco   **moon** *Fr* lune
maid *Fr* bonne   *Ger* Mond
major *Sp* mayor   *It/Sp* luna
male *Sp* macho   **morale** *Ger* Mut
man *Fr* homme   **more/most** *Sp* mas
         Ger Mann   **moss** *Fr* mousse
         Sp hombre   *Ger* Moos
manly *It* virile   **moth** *Fr* mite
map *Fr* carte   **mother** *Fr* mere
margin *Fr* bord, marge   *Ger* Mutter
married *Fr* marie   *It/Sp* madre
mast *Fr* mat   **motley** *Ger* bunt
master *It* maestro, padrone   **Mr (Mister)** *Fr* Monsieur, M.
         Sp amo, maestro   *Ger* Herr
me *Fr* me, moi   *It* (il) signore
         Ger mich, mir   *Sp* (el) senor, sr
         It/Sp me, mi   *Yiddish* her
meadow *Fr* prairie   **Mrs** see *Mistress (Mrs)*
meaning *Fr* sens   **murder** *Ger* Mord
measure *Ger* Mass, messen   **mustard** *Fr* moutarde
medical *It/Sp* medico
medium *It* mezzo   [3] For various foreign currencies see
menu *Fr* carte   CURRENCY (p. 221).

205

FOREIGN WORDS

CLUES ANSWERS

my *Fr* ma, mes, mon
 Ger mein(e)(em)(en)(er)(es)
 It il mio, i miei, la mia, le mie
 Sp mi(a)(o)(s)(as)(so)
nail *Sp* clavo, una
naked *Fr* nu
name *Fr* nom
 It nome
 Sp nombre
nap *Sp* siesta
native *Sp* natural
object *Fr* but, objet, opposer
of *Fr* de
 Ger von
 It di
 Sp de
 Yiddish fun
old *Fr* vieil, vielle, vieux
 Ger alt
on *Fr* sur
 Ger auf
 It su
 Sp en
or *Fr* ou
 Ger oder
 It o
 Sp o, u
pace *Fr* train
 Ger Tempo
palace *Fr* palais
parents *Sp* padres
parson *Fr* cure
past *Fr* passe
pat *Fr* tape, taper
peace *It* pace
peanut *Sp* mani
per *Fr* par
 Ger fur
 Sp por
person *It/Sp* persona
physical *Sp* corporal, fisico
piano *It* pianoforte
pink *Fr* rose
pitch *Fr* lancer, poix
place *Fr* lieu, poser
plate *Ger* Teller
platform *Fr* quai
plead *Fr* supplier

CLUES ANSWERS

plus *Sp* mas
poison *Ger* Gift
pole *Ger* Pol, Stange
 It palo, polo
policy *Fr* police
polite *Fr* poli
pool *Fr* mare
poor *Fr* pauvre
 Ger arm
pope *It/Sp*[4] papa
powerful *Fr* puissant
praise *Ger* Lob
 It lode
pretty *Fr* joli
price/prize *Fr* prix
prompt *It/Sp* pronto
punch *Fr* coup
pure *Ger* rein
purpose *Fr* but
puzzle *It* enigma
queen *Fr* reine
 Ger Konigen
 It regina
 Sp reina
queer *Fr* bizarre
quiet *Ger* still
rank *Fr* rang
rate *Fr* tarif, taux, train
read *Sp* leer
red *Fr* rouge
 Ger rot
regal *Sp* real
rehearsal *Ger* Probe
report *Fr* rapport
revenge *It* vendetta
Rhine *It* Reno
river *Sp* rio
room *Fr* piece, place
 It stanza
rough *It* aspro, scabro
royal *Sp* real
rudder *Sp* timon
rum *Sp* ron
safe *It* salvo
salt *Fr* sel

[4] For names of popes see POPES AND
ANTIPOPES (p. 117).

CLUES	ANSWERS	CLUES	ANSWERS
It sale		*Ger* bald, fruh	
Sp sal		*It* presto	
sample *Ger* Muster		*Sp* pronto	
sand *Fr* sable		**soul** *Sp* alma	
Sp arena		**sound** *Sp* sano, sonar	
satin *Ger* Atlas		**south** *Fr/It* sud	
saw *Ger* Sage		*Sp* sur	
say *Fr/It* dire		**speech** *Fr* discours, parole	
screw *Fr* vis		**staff** *Ger* Personal, Stab	
sea *Fr* mer		**star** *Ger* Stern	
Ger Meer		*It* stella	
It mare		**start** *Fr* commencement	
Sp mar		**steady** *Fr* ferme, lieu	
senior *Sp* mayor		**stick** *Ger* Stock	
session *Fr* seance		**stock** *Fr* actions, provision	
settler *Fr* colon		**stocking** *Sp* media	
shade *Fr* ombre, store		**stone** *Fr* pierre	
Sp cortina, sombra		**stout** *Fr* corpulent, fort	
shallow *Fr* plat		*Ger* stark	
she *Fr* elle		**stove** *Ger* Herd, Ofen	
Ger sie		**street** *Fr* rue	
It/Sp ella		**strong** *Fr* fort	
shepherd *Sp* pastor		*Ger* stark	
ship *It* nave		*It* forte	
shock *Fr* choc, choquer		**such** *It* tale	
shop *Fr* boutique		**summer** *It* estate	
short *Fr* court		**sun** *It* sole	
It breve		*Sp* sol	
shower *Fr* averse, douche		**sway** *Fr* balancer, empire, se	
shrewd *Fr* fin		**Sweden** *Fr* Suede	
silver *Fr* argent		**sword** *Fr* epee	
since *Ger* da, seit		**table** *Fr* table, tableau	
single *It/Sp* solo		**tail** *Sp* cola	
sir *Fr* monsieur		**tall** *It/Sp* alto	
Ger Herr		**tap** *Fr* robinet, taper	
It signore		**tardy** *Ger* spat	
Sp senor		**taste** *Fr* gout, gouter	
skin *Ger* Fell, Haut		*It* gusto	
shirt *Ger* Rock		**tea** *Fr* the	
slang *Fr* argot		*Ger* Tee	
Slavic *Fr* slave		*It/Sp* te	
slender *Fr* mince		**teacher** *Sp* maestro	
slow *Fr* lent, tardif		**tell** *Fr* dire, raconter	
snail *Fr* escargot		**than/that** *Fr/Sp* que	
snake *Fr* serpent		**thick** *Ger* dick	
so *Ger* also, auch, damit, so		**thing** *Fr* chose	
song *Ger* Lied		**thus** *Ger* also, so	
soon *Fr* bientot, tot		**tip** *Fr* bout	

FOREIGN WORDS

CLUES   ANSWERS

to *Fr* a, en, pour
   Ger nach, um, zu
   It a, in, per
   Sp a, hasta, para
today *Sp* hoy
tone *Fr/Ger* Ton
tooth *Fr* dent
torment *Ger* Qual
tour *It* giro
tower *Fr* tour
trace *Ger* spur
trade *Ger* Handel
transit *Ger* Transport
trifle *Fr* bagatelle
type *Fr* genre
ugly *Fr* laid
view *Sp* vista
vision *It/Sp* vista
Wales *Sp* Gales
wall *Ger* Wand
wasp *It* vespa
water *Fr* eau
well *Ger* gut, nun
what *Ger* was
where *It* dove
whether *Ger* ob

ANGLO-EUROPEAN WORDS

CLUES   ANSWERS

white *It* bianco
   Sp blanco
who *It* che, chi
wide *It* largo
wife *Fr* femme
   Ger Frau
willow *Sp* sauce
wind *Fr* vent
wine *Fr* vin
   It/Sp vino
with *Fr* avec
   Ger mit
   It/Sp con
within *Fr* dans
without *Fr* sans
   Sp sin
woman *Fr/Ger* see *wife*
   It donna
word *Fr* mob
   Ger Wort
world *Ger* Welt
wrong *Fr/Sp* mal
   It male
year *Fr* an
yes *Fr* oui, si
   Ger ja, doch
   It/Sp si

(FRENCH, GERMAN) DAYS, MONTHS, NUMBERS

Sunday dimanche/Sonntag
Monday lundi/Montag
Tuesday mardi/Dienstag
Wednesday mercredi/Mittwoch
Thursday jeudi/Donnerstag
Friday vendredi/Freitag
Saturday samedi/Samstag

January janvier/Januar
February fevrier/Februar
March mars/Marz
April avril/April
May mai/Mai
June juin/Juni
July juillet/Juli

August aout/August
September septembre/September
October octobre/Oktober
November novembre/November
December decembre/Dezember

1 un: une/eins
2 deux/zwei
3 trois/drei
4 quatre/vier
5 cinq/funf
6 six/sechs
7 sept/sieben
8 huit/acht
9 neuf/neun

10 dix/zehn
11 onze/elf
12 douze/zwolf
13 treize/dreizehn
14 quatorze/vierzehn
15 quinze/funfzehn
16 seize/sechzehn
17 dix-sept/siebzehn
18 dix-huit/achtzehn
19 dix-neuf/neunzehn
20 vingt/zwanzig
21 vingt et un/einundzwanzig
22 vingt-deux/zweiundzwanzig
intermediate 20–3, etc./3 and 20, etc.
30 trente/dreissig
40 quarante/vierzig

50 cinquante/funfzig
60 soixante/sechzig
70 soixante-dix/siebzig
80 quatre-vingts/achtzig
90 quatre-vingt-dix/neunzig
100 cent/hundert
101 cent un/hundert und eins
200 deux cents/zweihundert
201 deux cent un/ '200' und eins
1000 mille/(ein)tausend
1001 mille un/tausend und eins
2000 deux mille/zweitausend
2001 deux mille un/'2000' und eins
1,000,000 un million/eine Million
billion un milliard/eine Milliarde

MEASUREMENT

ABBREVIATIONS

note The asterisk* indicates that the abbreviation is also a word, usually with a totally different meaning, and valid for most games.

1

A Ampere: high class: angstrom: atomic
a are: acre: afternoon: year
B black (on lead pencils)
B magnetic flux density
C electrical capacitance
°C degrees Celsius or centigrade
₵ centi-: cent: centime
c cent(s): cedi(s) (Ghana currency unit): circa
D electric flux (displacement)
d day: diameter: degree: penny
E exa- (million million million)
e nat. log. base: conic section eccentricity
F Fahrenheit: farad
f farthing: fathom: foot: forte: folio
f frequency
G Gauss: giga- (thousand million)
G constant of gravitation
g gram(me)
g acceleration of gravity
H hard (on lead pencils)
h hour: hecto- (hundred)
h height: Planck's constant
ℏ Dirac's constant
I electric current
i imaginary square root of −1
J joule
j imaginary square root of −1
K Kelvin: kelvin: Kochel: Kirkpatrick

k kilo-(thousand)
L lambert: lumen: learner: pound
L inductance: luminance
l litre: latitude: pound
l length
M thousand
m thousand: metre: mile: noon
m mass
N newton: Avogadro number: neper
n noon: nano- (thousand million)
P poise: peta- (thousand million million)
P power
p new penny (pence): pico-(million millionth)
Q electric charge: quality
q farthing: quintal
R rand:rontgen: Reaumer
S square: stokes: Schmieder: siemens
s second(s)
$ dollar
T tesla: tera- (million million)
t tonne
t time
U universal (movie grading): upper class
V volt
V electric potential difference
v velocity: volume
W watt
X movie grading (18+ only)
Y yen (Japanese currency)
y year: yard

AA movie grading (adult accompaniment)
AC before Christ: alternating current
AD* in the year of the Lord
ad* before the day: after date
ae.* of his age: aged
AH* in the year of Mohammed
Ah* ampere hour
AM* before noon: in year of World
am* before noon
an.* anno (in the year): ante (before)
AQ achievement quotient
ar in the year of the reign
AS* in the year of salvation
AU angstrom
av lived (so many) years
BB double black (on lead pencils)
BC before Christ
be* bill of exchange
bl barrel
bp boiling point
br bank rate: branch
bu. bushel(s)
ca circa (about)
cc cubic centimetre(s)
cd candella
cf. confer (compare)
cg centigram(me)(s)
c.g. centre of gravity
Ci curie
cl centilitre(s): class
CM common metre
cm centimetre(s): metric carat
cp candle-power: compare
cr. crown
c/s cycles per second (hertz)
ct cent: carat
cu. cubic
da* deca- (ten)
dB decibel
D/D days after date
dd days after date
dg decigram(me)(s)
dl decilitre(s)
dm decimetre(s)
dr dead reckoning: dram
D/S days after sight
ds days after sight

eV electron volt
ff folios
fl. florin
fm fathom
fo. folio
fp freezing point
Fr franc: Friday
fr franc
ft foot: feet
gm gram(me)
gr. grain
gs guineas
gu.* guinea
ha* hectare: this year
HB hard black (on lead pencils)
HE* horizontal equivalent
hf half
hl hectolitre(s)
HP horsepower
hp horsepower
hr hour
Hz hertz (cycles per second)
id.* the same
in* inch(es)
IQ Intelligence Quotient
iq the same as
IU international unit
kg kilogram(me)(s)
km kilometre(s)
kn knot
kr kreutzer (coin): krone (coin)
kW kilowatt
lb pound
LM long metre
lm lumen
ln natural logarithm
Lr lira (Italian currency)
lx lux
mg milligram(me)(s)
MJ megajoule(s)
ml millilitre(s)
mm millimetre(s)
mo* month
mp melting point
MS milestone
M/S months (after) sight
ms millisecond(s): months (after) sight
mv muzzle velocity
ns nanosecond(s)
OM old measurement

ABBREVIATIONS

OS outsize
Pa* pascal
pa* past: per annum
p/e price/earnings ratio
Pf pfennig (German currency)
pH pH-value
PM (pm) afternoon
pr. pair
ql as much as you please
qq quartos
qr quarter
qt quantity: quart(s)
qv as much as you will
Rd rand (S. African currency)
rd rutherford
Rs rupees
SD standard deviation
SF signal frequency
SI the metric system
SL South latitude
SM Short Metre
Sq. square
sq. square
St* stokes
st.* stone
SU strontium unit
tc tierce
tf till forbidden
Tu. Tuesday
UT* Universal Time
vd various dates: vapour density
VE Victory in Europe (1945)
VJ Victory over Japan (1945)
vy various years
Wb weber
wg wire gauge
wk week
wt weight
Xm. Christmas
yd yard
Yn yen (Japanese currency)
yr year

3

ADC advise duration (and) charge
aet. of his age: aged
alg. algebra
alt.* altitude

amp.* ampere
amt amount
amu atomic mass unit
Apr. April
AUC in the year of the city
Aug. August
bal. balance
BBB triple black (on lead pencils)
bef. before
BeV billion electron-volt(s)
bhp brake horse-power
BOD* biochemical oxygen demand
Btu British thermal unit
bus.* bushel(s)
BWV catalogue of Bach's works
cal calorie
CAN* customs assigned number
Can.* canto
car.* carat
cat.* catalogue
cen. central: century
CET Central European Time
cgs centimetre-gramme-second
cir. circa (about)
Cod.* codex
c.o.g.* centre of gravity
cos* cosine
cot* cotangent
CPI consumer price index
cpp current purchasing power
CST Central Standard Time
cub.* cubic
cur.* current (this month)
cwt hundredweight(s)
Dec. December
DIN* German Industrial Standards
Dnr dinar (Yugoslav currency)
doz. dozen
dpm disintegrations per minute
dwt pennyweight
dyn dyne
eod every other day
EST Eastern Standard Time
est. estimated
esu electrostatic unit
ETA estimated time of arrival
ETD estimated time of departure
ext. extinct: extra
Feb. February
FPS foot-pound-second

fth fathom
fur.* furlong(s)
fut. future
gal.* gallon(s)
gen.* genus: gender
GeV giga-electron-volts(s)
Gld guilder (Dutch currency)
hhd hogshead
HWM high water mark
inf. infra (below)
Jan. January
Jul. July
Jun. June
kWh kilowatt-hour
lat.* latitude
log* logarithm
lon. longitude
Mar.* March
max. maximum
med. middle
MeV mega-electron-volt(s)
MEZ Central European Time
MKS metre-kilogram-second
MKK Markka (Finnish currency)
MLR minimum lending rate
mod.* modern
mol mole
mos* months
mpg miles per gallon
mph miles per hour
MSF medium standard frequency
msl mean sea level
MST mountain standard time
mth month
NNI noise and number index
Nov. November
obs. obsolete
Oct. October
oct. octavo
par.* parallel
per.* period
Pes. peseta (Spanish currency)
PST Pacific Standard Time
pwt pennyweight
qid four times a day
qto quarto

qty quantity
rad.* radian: radix (root)
r.a.m.* relative atomic mass
rev* revolution
rms root-mean-square
RPI retail price index
rpm revolutions per minute
rps revolutions per second
RRP recommended retail price
Sat.* Saturday
sec* secant: second: section
sin* sine
stp standard temperature and pressure
SWG standard wire gauge
tan* tangent
tid* thrice a day
USW ultrasonic waves: ultrashort waves
VAr volt-ampere(s)-reactive
vel. velocity
vol.* volume
wpm words per minute
ZPG zero population growth
ZST Zone Standard Time

4

APRC in the year of Rome
cosh* hyperbolic cosine
coth* hyperbolic cotangent
curt* current (this month)
diam. diameter
fthm fathom
inst. the present month
kilo* kilogram(me): kilometre
Linn. Linnaean
long.* longitude
MKSA metre-kilogram-second-ampere
morn.* morning
Pent.* Pentecost
prox. next month
Reau Reaumur's thermometric scale
sech hyperbolic secant
temp.* temperature: in the time of
Tues. Tuesday
Xmas Christmas

ASSORTED WEIGHTS AND MEASURES

adp avoirdupois
msr measure
wt weight

note (1) For standard abbreviations used see ABBREVIATIONS (p. 210).
(2) Vessels mentioned as units of measure.
(3) Many of the units listed are legally obsolete.
(4) Answers 8 upwards exclude the units prefixed 'imperial', 'half', 'quarter', 'cubic', and 'square'.

2

as a Roman (12 oz)lb
em a printer's measure
en half of an *em*
li Chinese distance unit (⅓ mile)
mu (f) Greek letter-symbol for *micron*

3

amp *ampere*
are SI land unit (100 sq. metres)
bar units of atmospheric pressure
bel *msr* of noise intensity
cab Hebrew dry *msr* (nearly 3 pints)
cog *cogue*
cor Hebrew (roughly 11 bushels)
cos *coss*
day space between mullions of a window
ell a cloth measure
erg SI unit of work
fly a boxing *wt* prefix
hin Hebrew liquid *msr* (about 4 or 6 quarts)
kat ancient Egyptian unit of *wt*
keg a small *cask*
kin Chinese/Japanese lb *(catty)*
lea yarn (80yd worsted: 120 cotton: 300 linen)
log Hebrew (approx. pint)
lux one *lumen* per sq. metre
mho obs. unit of electrical conductance

mil millilitre (pharmacy)
mna *mina* (1)
net *(gross) – (tret+tare+cloff)*
nth to an unlimited degree
ohm unit of electrical resistance
oke Turkish (about 2⅘lbs)
rod 5½ yards *(perch, pole, rood)*
tod wool (about 28lbs)
ton (1) *msr* of capacity *tonnage*
ton (2) 2240lb
ton (3) 100 mph/runs/£'s, etc.
ton (4) a great weight
tot (1) to add up or total
tot (2) *dram* (4)
tun (1) a large *cask*
tun (2) 216 gallons of ale
tun (3) 252 gallons of wine
tun (4) ton (1)
vat a large vessel or tank
wey a dry-goods *wt* (variable)

4

acre 4840 sq. yards
bale a bundle of goods
bath Hebrew (approx. 6 gallons)
boll grain *msr* (variable)
butt (1) a large *cask*
butt (2) 126 gallons of beer
butt (3) 108 gallons of sherry
cade a barrel or *cask* (for fish)
cask *barrel, msr* of capacity
comb *coomb*
cord *msr* of cut wood (128 cu. ft)

coss Indian (approx 1¾ miles)
coth hyperbolic cotangent
cran freshly landed herring (37½ gal.)
darg a day's work
demy pre-SI paper size (approx. A2)
dram (1) *drachma*
dram (2) ¹⁄₁₆th oz *adp*
dram (3) ⅛th oz (apothecaries)
dram (4) a small *msr* of alcohol
drop *msr* of medicament
drum a bundle (Australia)
dyne *cgs* unit of force
epha *ephah*
feet plural of *foot*
fold see *twofold,threefold*
foot 12″ (length of man's foot)
gage *gauge* (4)
gill a small *msr* (variable)
gram SI unit of mass
half one of two equal parts
hand (1) horse *msr* (4″)
hand (2) division of bunch of bananas
hank yarn *msr* (variable with type)
hard quality of lead in pencil
hide variable unit of land area
inch twelfth of a *foot* (2.54 cm)
khat *kat*
kilo *kilogram*, etc.
knot a nautical mile per hour
koss *coss*
last a load, cargo (variable)
link ¹⁄₁₀₀th surveyor's chain (7.92″)
load variable specific quantity
maze *mease*
mile Roman mile: *statute mile*
mina (1) a Greek *wt*
mina (2) Hebrew *wt* of money
mole atomic/molecular/ionic etc. *msr*
muid (1) an old French *msr* of capacity
muid (2) *hogshead*
muid (3) 3 bushels (S. Africa)
nail 2¼″
nett *net*
obol Greek *wt* ⅙th *drachma*
omer Hebrew dry *msr* (¹⁄₁₀ *ephah*)
pace (1) space between feet, walking (30″ approx)
pace (2) Roman, double *pace (1)*
pair a set of two equal or like things

palm a handsbreadth (3″ or 4″)
peck (1) dry goods *msr* (2 gal.: ¼ *bushel*)
peck (2) an indefinite great amount
pica a size of type (12 *point*)
pint (1) imperial (liquid or dry) = 568cc
pint (2) USA (liquid) = 473cc
pint (3) USA (dry) = 551cc
pipe *cask/butt* of wine (usu. 105 gal)
pole (1) *rod, perch, rood*
pole (2) 30¼ square yd
pood Russian (approx 36lbs *adp*)
post a size of writing paper
raik *rake*
rake amount carried at one journey
ream 20 quires (paper)
reel length of wound material
rood (1) linear/square *rod, pole, perch*
rood (2) ¼ acre (40 square *poles*)
root mathematical factor of quantity
rotl a variable Levantine *wt*
sack *msr* of capacity (variable)
seam pack-horse load: cartload
seer Indian *wt* (variable)
span (1) maximum extent of stretched hand
span (2) 9″
span (3) of bridges, aeroplanes, etc. (variable)
step (1) *pace (1)*
step (2) a small space
step (3) a short journey
step (4) a degree of a scale
step (5) coincidence in speed and phase
tael *liang* (Chinese ounce)
tare *wt* of vessel/wrapping/container
tola Indian unit of *wt* (11.66 gm)
tret purchasers' wastage allowance
tron system of public *msr wts*
troy precious metal (12 oz = lb)
unit base subdivision or base
vara Sp. American linear *msr* (variable)
volt MKSA unit of electromotive force
warp four herrings/oysters, etc.
watt MKS unit of power
yard 3ft, 36″ (0.9144 metres)

5

anker old N. European (variable) liquid *msr*

ardeb Egyptian dry *msr* (5½ bushels)

asses plural of *as*

bigha Indian (½ to ⅔ acre)

black quality of lead in pencil

brace a pair or couple

cable ¹⁄₁₀th nautical mile (approx 200yds)

candy Indian *wt* (approx 500lbs)

carat a unit of *wt* for gems

catty *kin*, approx 1¾lb *adp*

chain 100 *links*, 22yds

cloff wholesale purchasing *wt* allowance

clove old (variable) *wt* wool, cheese

codex a *volume* of manuscript

cogue a round wooden vessel

coomb *msr* of capacity (4 bushels)

count (1) size of roofing slate (20″×10″)

count (2) number indicating size of yarn

crown a size of paper

cubit length, elbow to tip of middle finger

curie radioactivity quantity/time *msr*

cycle recurring series of changes

ephah Hebrew (10 ephah = *homer*)

farad a unit of electrical capacitance

folio (1) a folded paper size

folio (2) a book size

folio (3) a number of words for computation

gauge (1) a standard of measure

gauge (2) diameter/calibre/width *msr*

gauge (3) distance between wheels or track

gauge (4) relative position of a ship

gauss cgs magnetic flux density unit

gerah smallest Hebrew *wt*

grain (1) a very small quantity

grain (2) smallest British *wt*

gross (1) whole (see *net*)

gross (2) main bulk

gross (3) 12 dozen (see *great gross*)

hertz electrical unit of frequency

homer *cor*

joule MKS unit energy, work, heat

kandy *candy*

karat *carat*

leash a set of three (esp. animals)

liang *tael* Chinese approx 1½ oz

libra Roman pound (£ money = lb weight)

litre SI unit of capacity

livre old French weight (approx lb)

lumen (1) a unit of luminous flux

lumen (2) the cavity of a tube

lumen (3) space within cell-wall (botany)

maise *mease*

maize *mease*

maneh *mina* (2)

maund (usually) 20 = *candy*

mease 5 *'hundreds'* of herrings (c.500/630)

meter (1) a gauge or apparatus for *msr*

meter (2) USA spelling of *metre*

metre (1) poetry/music regulator

metre (2) SI fundamental unit of length

metre (3) SI fundamental unit of mass

minim (1) a least part

minim (2) apothecaries' *msr* (¹⁄₆₀th fld *drachm*)

minim (3) apothecaries' *wt* (*grain*)

neper unit for expressing ratio (volts, etc.)

oboli plural of *obolus*

octet a group of 8 (electrons, etc.)

ounce (1) 480 *grains* (2): ¹⁄₁₆th lb *adp*: ¹⁄₁₂th lb *troy*

ounce (2) a very small quantity

perch (1) *rod, pole, rood* (5½yds)

perch (2) a navigation mark

perch (3) stonework (24¾ or 25 cubic ft)

picul Chinese *wt* (approx 60 kg)

pinch a small quantity

plate over ¼″ (see *sheet*)

plumb weighted line, *msr* of vertical

point (1) a place in a scale, cycle, etc.

point (2) a unit in scoring, judging, etc.

point (3) a unit of type measurement

point (4) a division of the compass

point (5) ¹⁄₁₀₀th of a *carat*

poise non-SI *cgs* unit of viscosity

pound (1) 7000 grains (16 oz *adp*)

pound (2) 5760 grains (12 oz *troy*)

proof a standard strength of spirit
pugil *pinch* (originally, a handful)
quart ¼ *gallon*, 2 pints
quire paper (1/20th of a *ream*)
quota a proportional share
royal (1) writing paper 19″×24″
royal (2) printing paper 20″×25″
royal (3) book (see *royal octavo*)
score (1) a notch in a tally
score (2) a reckoning, account, ground
score (3) a set of twenty
score (4) 20 or 21 pounds
score (5) a fixed number of coal tubs (20/26)
sheet structural material under ¼″ thick
shock 3 *score*
skein standard length (thread/yarn)
stere timber *msr* (cubic metre)
stoke *stokes*
stone (1) 14lbs *avp* standard *msr*
stone (2) 24lbs wool: 22lbs hay, etc.
stook a *shock* of sheaves
tesla unit of magnetic flux density
therm 100,000 thermal units
tithe a tenth part
toise old French *msr* (6.395ft)
token *msr* of handpress work
tonne metric ton (1000 kg)
truss (1) 56lb old hay, 60lb new
truss (2) 36lb straw
verst Russian *msr* (approx ⅔ mile)
weber MKS unit of magnetic flux
yojan Indian *msr* (approx 5 miles)

6

ampere MKS unit of current
arroba Iberian *wt* (approx 25lbs)
arshin (1) Russian *msr* (approx 28″)
arshin (2) Turkey (1) metre (legal) (2) approx 30″
assize (1) to set or fix quantity/price of
assize (2) statute on weight/measure, etc.
bantam a boxing *wt* prefix
barrel (1) wooden vessel, contents, capacity
barrel (2) 36 imperial gallons ale/beer

bovate *oxgang*
bundle a definite measure/quantity
bushel dry *msr*, 8 gallons
candie *candy*
cantar *kantar*
central 100lbs
chopin (1) French, approx. a *pint*
chopin (2) Scots, approx. a *quart*
degree (1) a unit of temperature
degree (2) relative position
degree (3) 1/360th of a revolution
degree (4) 60 geographical miles
degree (5) a grade or step
double (1) twofold: twice as much, etc.
double (2) roofing slate 13″×6″
drachm *drachma*
fathom (1) reach of outstretched arms
fathom (2) nautical *msr*, 6 feet
fathom (3) timber *msr*, 216 cubic feet
firkin (1) brewing, a ¼ *barrel*
firkin (2) 56lbs butter
firlot Scottish dry *msr*, ¼ *boll*
fother (1) load, quantity, cartload
fother (2) lead, 19½cwt
gallon (1) Imperial 277.4 cubic inches
gallon (2) USA 231 cubic inches
gramme *gram*
gunter *Gunter's chain: Gunter's scale*
kantar Turkey/Egypt, etc. approx. 1 cwt
kelvin (1) SI unit of temperature
kelvin (2) kilowatt-hour
kilerg 1000 *ergs*
league (1) nautical, 1/20th degree
league (2) 3 nautical miles (3.456 miles)
league (3) Roman, 1.376 miles
league (4) French, 2.764 miles
league (5) Spanish, 4.214 miles
megohm a million *ohms*
micron one millionth of a *metre*
mikron *micron*
minima plural of *minimum*
minion print type size
minute (1) extremely small
minute (2) 1/60th of a *degree* (3)
minute (3) distance traversed in 60 secs
moiety (1) half: one of two parts
moiety (2) a small share
morgen (1) Holland, S. Africa, USA approx. 2 acres

WEIGHTS AND MEASURES

morgen (2) Norway, Denmark, Prussia ⅔ acre
newton SI unit of force
noggin *dram* (4)
obolus *obol*
octane see *octane number*
octant (1) arc, ⅛th of circle circumference
octant (2) sector, ⅛th of circle
octant (3) a position 45° from another
octave (1) a set of eight
octave (2) cask, ⅛th of a *pipe*
octavo a size of paper
octett *octet*
oxgang ⅛th of a *carucate*
oxgate *oxgang*
oxland *oxgang*
parsec approx. 19 billion miles
pascal an SI unit of pressure
pocket ½ sack of wool
pottle ½ gallon
quarto a size of paper
quotum *quota*
rotolo Italian *rotl*
second ⅟₆₀th of a *minute* (2)(3)
shekel Hebrew *wt* (approx. 14 grams)
stater ancient Greek *pound*
stokes cgs unit of kinematic viscosity
suttle *wt* after deduction of *tare*
talent ancient unit of (variable) *wt*
terset verse, group of 3 lines
thrave (1) 2 *stooks*
thrave (2) two dozen
thrave (3) a good number
tierce ⅓ *pipe*
yojana *yojan*

7

acreage area in acres
arsheen *arshin*
arshine *arshin*
boiling collection, set (colloquial)
brevier a printer's type size
candela unit of luminous intensity
Celsius *centigrade*
centner *hundredweight* (usually 50 kg)
chalder Scots dry *msr*, 16 *bolls*
codices plural of *codex*

coulomb 96,500 coulombs = *faraday*
cruiser a boxing *wt* prefix
cubitus a *cubit* (varying 18″ to 22″)
decibel ⅟₁₀th of a *bel*
drachma ancient Greek *wt*
ellwand a measuring rod
faraday an electrolysis unit
feather a boxing *wt* prefix
furlong 40 *poles*, ⅛th *mile*
hectare 100 *acres*
hundred (1) fish quantity (approx. 100)
hundred (2) a division of land
hundred (3) *great* or *long hundred*
kilobar 1000 *bars*
kiloton explosive force *msr*
lambert a unit of brightness
leaguer old Dutch liquid *msr* (obs.)
long-oil a *msr* of *oil length*
long ton *ton (2)*
maxwell *cgs* unit of magnetic flux
measure (1) size, standard or unit
measure (2) an instrument or vessel
measure (3) a portion or proportion
measure (4) a unit of verse
measure (5) paper width (total of *ems*)
mileage distance in miles
minimal least size, amount, degree
minimum least quantity, degree
minimus a being of the smallest size
modicum (1) a small amount
modicum (2) small man (obs.): woman (obs.)
octette *octet*
outsize very large garment
pailful as much as fills a pail
per cent in the hundred
pH value (1) expression of acidity
pH value (2) expression of alkalinity
quarter (1) fourth part of *cwt*
quarter (2) 8 bushels
quarter (3) part of a corpse
quarter (4) fourth part of shield
quarter (5) a cardinal point of compass
quinary fivefold: by/in fives: etc.
quintal (1) *hundredweight*
quintal (2) 100 kilograms
Reaumur of thermometer (scale) 80°bp
rontgen unit of X-ray dose
scruple (1) a small weight/quantity
scruple (2) 20 grains (apothecaries' *wt*)

sea-mile geographical or nautical mile
siemens SI term replacing *mho*
stadium Greek *msr* (606¾ English feet)
stature body height
ternary in/of/based on, three
ternion a section of book-paper
threave *thrave*
tonnage ship's carrying capacity
twafald in a doubled-up position
twifold *twofold*
twofold (1) in two divisions
twofold (2) twice as much
twoline a print *msr* of depth
twyfold *twofold*
virgate land *msr* (usually 30 acres)

8

angstrom a unit of wavelength
carucate *msr* of ox-ploughed land
centiare hundredth of an *are*
chaldron coal (36 heaped bushels)
decagram ten grammes
decigram tenth of a *gram*
desyatin *dessiatine*
elephant a size of paper
foolscap a size of paper
hogshead (1) 52½ imperial gallons
hogshead (2) beer, 54 gallons
hogshead (3) claret, 46 gallons
hogshead (4) tobacco (USA) 750 to 1200lbs
imperial (1) paper 22″ × 30″: USA 23″ × 33″
imperial (2) slates 33″ × 24″
kilogram SI unit of mass
kilowatt 1000 *watts*
latitude global *msr* (E/W axis)
milliare thousandth of an *are*
millibar 1000 dynes per sq. cm
mutchkin Scots (¾ imperial, ¼ Scots pint)
nanogram microscopically small *wt*
parasang Persian (approx 3 to 4 miles)
puncheon *cask* (70 to 120 gallons)
roentgen *rontgen*
quadrant ¼ of a circle
quartern ¼ peck/stone/lb/pint

ship-load actual/possible load of ship
short-oil a *msr* of *oil length*
short ton (USA/Canada) 2,000lbs
spoonful recipe/remedy *msr*
tolldish *msr* of toll in mill
yardland *virgate*
yardwand *yardstick* (1)

9

amplitude (1) extent of vibratory movement
amplitude (2) heavenly body, angular distance
centigram hundreth part of a *gram*
decilitre tenth of a *litre*
decimetre tenth of a *metre*
flyweight boxer of 8st or less
foot-pound unit of mass height energy
freight ton 40 cubic ft cargo space
hectogram 100 grams
Irish acre 7840 sq. yds (obs.)
Irish mile 2240 yds (obs.)
isometric having equality of *msr*
kilohertz *msr* of sound/radio frequency
kilometre 1000 metres (approx ⅝ mile)
light-year *msr* of galactic distance
long dozen 13 (same as baker's: devil's)
long metre *msr* of verse
luminance *msr* of surface brightness
megacycle a million *cycles*
megadeath unit of nuclear casualties
megajoule 3.6 megajoules = *kilowatt hour*
metric ton *tonne* (0.984 ton)
milestone a mark of distance
[1]**milligram** thousandth of a *gram*
net weight see *net*
nonpareil a printer's type size
oil length oil/resin ratio
Roman mile 1000 double paces (1,611yds)
Scots mile 1,976yds (obs.)
small pica a printer's type size
threefold (1) in three divisions

---

[1] Games players note: Whilst *milligram* is in common usage it is not specifically listed in *Chambers*.

WEIGHTS AND MEASURES

threefold (2) three times as much
wire gauge diameter of wire
yard of ale quantity of ale
yardstick (1) a stick 3ft long
yardstick (2) figurative standard of *msr*

10

ampere hour *msr* of electric current by time
ampere-turn *msr* of electricity in coil
barleycorn half an inch
barrel-bulk 5 cubic feet
centesimal hundredth: centigrade thermometer
centigrade having a hundred degrees
centilitre hundredth of a litre
centimeter *centimetre*
centimetre hundredth of a metre
dead-weight (1) unrelieved weight
dead-weight (2) heavy and oppressive burden
dead-weight (3) difference in ship's displacement
decagramme *decagram*
decigramme *decigram*
demy quarto paper 8¾″ × 11¼″
dessiatine Russian land *msr* (2.7 acres)
dessyatine *dessiatine*
dry measure bulk *msr* of grain etc.
Fahrenheit thermometer scale (212 bp – 32 fp)
fifty-fifty *half-and-half*
fluid ounce liquid measure
freight ton 40 cubic feet
great gross 12 *gross* (12×12×12)
hectolitre 100 *litres*
hectometre 100 *metres*
hectostere 100 *steres*
kilogramme *kilogram*
microfarad millionth of a *farad*
millesimal thousandth
[2]**millilitre** thousandth of a litre
[2]**millimetre** thousandth of a metre
  Mohs's scale mineral hardness scale

[2] Games players note: Whilst *millilitre* and *millimetre* are in common usage they are not specifically listed in *Chambers*.

round dozen 12
rutherford unit of radioactive disintegration
short metre a *msr* of verse
super-royal of paper, larger than *royal*
two or three a few
yard of land *virgate*

11

acre-breadth 22 yards
avoirdupois *wt* system, 16 ozs = lb
baker's dozen 13 (also long d., devil's d.)
ballad metre a *msr* of verse
binary scale has radix of 2
cable-length *cable*
candle-power *msr* of illumination
centigramme *centigram*
common metre a *msr* of verse
devil's dozen 13 (also baker's d., long d.)
half-and-half equal share
heavyweight the heaviest boxing *wt*
hectogramme *hectogram*
kilocalorie 1000 *calories*
lightweight boxing *wt* 9st–9st 9lb (amateur 9st 7lb)
long-hundred (1) six *score* (also great h.)
long-hundred (2) 33 *warps* (also great h.)
megawatt day unit of nuclear energy
metric carat 200 milligrams (see *carat*)
pennyweight 24 grains *troy wt*
register ton 100 cubic feet
royal octavo book size (6¼″ × 10″)
statute mile 1,760 yards (1.61 km)

12

kilowatt hour *msr* of energy by time
octane number % by volume (motor fuel)
Scottish acre 6150.4 sq. yds (obs.)

CURRENCY

• indicates coins formerly used in weighing
note Crossword answers 9 upwards will normally have prefix such as 'half', 'two', 'silver' or 'gold'.

2

• **as** Roman copper coin

3

bob shilling (slang)
cob Spanish-American dollar
dam Indian copper coin (obs.)
ecu 5 fr. France
joe *joey*
lat Latvian franc
lei plural of *leu*
lek Albanian monetary unit
leu Rumanian franc
lev Bulgarian franc
lew *lev*
ley *leu*
mil proposed (Cyprus) £1/1000
• **mna** *mina*
öre Denmark, Norway, Sweden
pie India 3 pie = *pice* (obs.)
ree Portuguese money of account
sen Japanese, 100 = *yen*
sol French, 20 = *livre* (obs.)
sou French 5 cent. piece
sov (colloquial) sovereign
won Korean coin
yen Japanese monetary unit

4

anna 16 annas = *rupee* (obs.)
buck USA dollar
cash small Eastern coin
cent 1/100 various currencies
coin metallic money
dime USA 10 cents

doit Dutch ½ farthing
joey 4d piece/3d piece (obs.)
lakh 100,000 rupees
lira Italian monetary unit
lire a plural of *lira*
mail ½ penny (obs.)
mark (1) *reichsmark*: Deutsche mark
mark (2) *markka*
merk Scottish mark (13/4d) (obs.)
• **mina** Greek 100 drachmas
mite very small (old Flemish)
obol (1) Charon's ferry fee (Greek 1½d)
obol (2) English ½d (obs.)
para small Turkish coin
peso (1) Spanish 5-*peseta* piece
peso (2) Mexican dollar
peso (3) C./S. America various
pice ¼ *anna* (see *new pice*)
quid (slang) £1, formerly *guinea*
rand S. African monetary unit
real (1) ¼ *peseta*
real (2) Portugal/Brazil (obs.)
reis plural of *real* (2)
rial *ryal*
ryal old English gold coin
• **tael** Chinese money of account
yuan Chinese monetary unit

5

angel old English gold coin
asper small Turkish coin (obs.)
• **asses** plural of *as*
bekah Hebrew ½ shekel (Bible)
belga former Belgian currency unit
brass (slang) money
colon El Salvador: Costa Rica
conto Portugal: Brazil

CURRENCY

crown English 5/- (25p)
daric coin of Darius, Persia
dinar (1) various Arabic countries
dinar (2) Yugoslavian franc
ducat Europe gold: Italy silver
eagle USA gold coin 10$
franc France, Belgium, Switzerland, etc.
groat English silver 4d (obs.)
krona Sweden, 100 öre
krone (1) Denmark: Norway
krone (2) Austria and Germany (obs.)
lepta plural of lepton
liard old French farthing
libra Roman pound (£): Peru
livre French £ till 1795
louis old French gold coin
• maneh mina
mohur Persian, Indian gold coin (obs.)
noble old English gold coin (6/8d)
obang old Japanese coin
pagod pagoda
pence a plural of penny
• penny originally 240 = £
plack Scottish ⅓ penny (obs.)
• pound 240d, 100p
royal ryal
ruble Russian monetary unit
rupee India, Pakistan, Ceylon
sceat old English coin
scudi plural of scudo
scudo Italian silver coin (obs.)
semis ½ as
soldi plural of soldo
soldo former Italian coin
sucre Ecuador, monetary unit
• sycee Chinese silver ingots
• tical Siamese coin (obs.)
toman Persian gold coin (obs.)
unite English £ later 22/-
zloty Polish monetary unit

6

aureus Roman gold coin
balboa Panama monetary unit
bawbee Scots ½d, originally 3d
bezant Byzantine gold coin
condor Chilean gold coin

copeck kopeck
copper coin or coins
cowrie shell-money, Pacific
decime tenth of a franc (obs.)
dollar thaler, various countries
escudo various countries
florin (1) ancient Florentine gold coin
florin (2) UK tenth of a £
forint Hungarian monetary unit
gilder guilder
gourde Haiti, monetary unit
guinea English gold 21/- (obs.)
gulden Hungary: Holland
heller Austria and Czech. (obs.)
kopeck 100 = ruble
kronen plural of krone (2)
kroner plural of krone (1)
kronor plural of krona
lepton Greek coin: biblical mite
markka mark of Finland
nickel USA ½ dime
pagoda former Indian coin
peseta Spanish franc
qintar 100 = lek
rouble ruble
sceatt sceat
sequin old Italian gold coin
• shekel Hebrew coin (biblical)
solidi plural of solidus
sovran sovereign
• stater ancient Greek coin
stiver Dutch penny
• talent ancient, Biblical
tanner (slang) 6d (obs.)
tester old English coin
teston various old coins
thaler German dollar (obs.)

7

bolivar Bolivian monetary unit
carolus Charles I gold coin
centavo Portugal: Brazil
centime France etc. 100 = franc
cordoba Nicaragua, monetary unit
crusado a Portuguese coin
• drachma Greek franc
guilder gulden: old gold coin
jacobus James I gold coin

manilla W. African bracelet-money
markkaa plural of *markka*
milreis Brazil and Portugal (obs.)
moidore Portuguese gold coin (obs.)
new pice 100 = *rupee*
pennies a plural of *penny*
pfennig German 100 = *mark*
piastre *cob*: 100 = Turkish £
pistole Spanish: Scottish (obs.)
quarter 25 cents USA
quetzal Guatemalan dollar
sextans Roman 6 = *as*
solidus old name for *bezant*
testern *tester*
testoon Portuguese, Italian *teston*
testril *tester*
unicorn old Scottish gold coin

kreutzer Austria and S. Germany
  (obs.)
louis d'or *louis*
maravedi Spanish copper coin (obs.)
napoleon Napoleon gold coin
new franc France 1960/63
new pence plural *new penny*
new penny 100 = £
pfenning *pfennig*
picayune USA (obs.): trifle
pistolet *pistole*
quadrans 4 = *as*
sceattas plural *sceat*
sesterce 2½ (later 4) *asses*
shilling 12d (obs.): 5p
sixpence 6d and 2½p (obs.)
testrill (obs.) *tester*

8

9

cruzeiro Brazilian monetary unit
denarius Roman silver coin
didrachm a double *drachma*
doubloon Spanish gold coin (obs.)
ducatoon Venetian silver *ducat*
farthing ¼ of a *penny* (d)
florence Edward III gold florin
groschen Austria: Germany
johannes John V, Portugal, coin

boliviano Bolivian dollar
didrachma a double *drachma*
sovereign English gold pound

10

reichsmark German mark 1924/48

TIME

(*Ch.*) Chinese year
note Chinese years are lunar based and only approximate to given definitions.
(Chinese New Year begins at 11 pm on the night of the first new moon in
Aquarius.) Full names recur every 60 years.

2

Ab a Hebrew month
mo (slang) moment

day 24 hours: period of light
eon *aeon*
era an *age*
May month of goddess Maia
yug *yuga*

3

age great division of time

4

Abib *Nisan*

TIME

Adar a Hebrew month
aeon a vast *age*
dawn daybreak
hour division of *day*
Ides 8th day after *Nones*
July month of Julius Caesar
June month of goddess Juno
Lent period pre-Easter
morn morning
noon midday
term relative period of time
week seven days
year twelve months
yuga a Hindu world *age*

5

April first month of spring
calpa *kalpa*
cycle repeating (quality of) period
epact lunar/solar year comparative
  excess
epoch a reference date
fasti Roman legal business day
hiems (obs.) winter
horal hourly
Iyyar a Hebrew month
kalpa Hindu, immense time period
March the month of Mars
month *lunar month*: *calendar month*
night hours of darkness
Nisan a Hebrew month
Nones 5th (or 7th) of a month
reign period of (royal) rule
Sebat *Shebat*
Sivan a Hebrew month
teens youth, 13–19
Tisri a Hebrew month
watch a division of night

6

annual yearly
August month of Augustus Caesar
autumn the third season
curfew restricted period
Diwali Hindu festival
Easter Christian festival

ferial non-feast or fast day
Fire Ox (*Ch.*) 1937:1997
Friday day of goddess Frig
heyday period of full bloom
Judica Passion Sunday
Kisleu *Kislev*
Kislev a Hebrew month
Lammas feast of first fruits
May day first day of May
mensal monthly
midday noon
minute division of an hour
modern present time
moment very short time
Monday day of the moon
morrow the following day
season any particular period
second division of a minute
Shebat a Hebrew month
spring the first season
summer the second season
Sunday day of the sun
sunset beginning of night
Tammuz a Hebrew month
Tebeth a Hebrew month
Veadar Hebrew intercalary month
vernal pertaining to spring
vesper evening
whilom formerly, once
winter the fourth season
Wood Ox (*Ch.*) 1925:1985

7

ancient of former times
antique ancient
bedtime time for sleep
betimes early: seasonable
Beltane ancient Celtic festival
by and by in due course
calends Roman first day of month
century 100 years
Chislev *Kislev*
daytime daylight period
diurnal of the day
dog days period of star Sirius
Earth Ox (*Ch.*) 1949:2009
equinox equal day/equal night

etesian periodical
evening close of daytime
fast day day of restraint
fete day festival day
Fire Dog (*Ch.*) 1946:2006
Fire Rat (*Ch.*) 1936:1996
half-day half working day
harvest crop-gathering time
[1]**Hock-day** sex held sex to ransom
holiday originally *holy day*
holy day religious festival day
January month of god Janus
jubilee time of jubilation
Lady Day 25th March
lustrum period of 5 years
Metal Ox (*Ch.*) 1901:1961
new moon initial waxing moon
October originally 8th month
quartan every fourth day (incl.)
quintan every fifth day (incl.)
Ramadan Muslim diurnal-fasting
  month
regency term of regent
rent day day to pay rent
Sabbath a holy rest day
sundown evening
sunrise morning
tea time time for tea
tertian every third day (incl.)
Thammuz (obs.) *Tammuz*
triduum period of 3 days
Tuesday day of god Tyr
wartime period of war
Water Ox (*Ch.*) 1913:1973
Wood Dog (*Ch.*) 1934:1994
Wood Rat (*Ch.*) 1924:1984

8

aestival of the summer
annually every year
antedate pre true-date
anterior before
biannual 2 yearly: ½ yearly

---

biennial of or lasting 2 years
birthday anniversary of birth
bi-weekly twice a week: fortnightly
calendar list: record: almanac
carnival pre-Lent festival
day by day daily
December originally 10th month
doomsday day of doom
Earth Dog (*Ch.*) 1958: 2018
Earth Rat (*Ch.*) 1948: 2008
eternity eternal duration
eventide evening
February month of expiation
Fire Boar (*Ch.*) 1947: 2007
forenoon later morning
Georgian 1714–1830
gloaming twilight, dusk
half-year six months
hebdomad a week
hibernal of winter
high noon exactly noon
Hock-tide 2nd Monday/Tuesday after
  Easter
Hogmanay last day of year
Holy Week week before Easter
interval interim period
leap year has intercalary day
Lord's Day Sunday
menology calendar of Greek saints
Metal Dog (*Ch.*) 1910: 1970
Metal Rat (*Ch.*) 1900: 1960: 2020
midnight 12 o'clock at night
natal day day of birth
noontide midday
November originally ninth month
Passover annual Jewish feast
Ramadhan *Ramadan*
Saturday day of god Saturn
semester university ½ year course
sennight week
Stone Age Palaeolithic: Neolithic
Thursday day of god Thor
tomorrow immediate morrow
twilight post-sunset: pre-sunrise
vacation holiday
Water Dog (*Ch.*) 1922: 1982
Water Rat (*Ch.*) 1912: 1972
Wood Boar (*Ch.*) 1935: 1995
Yuletide Christmas season
zero hour exact moment of launch

---

[1] See *Hock Monday, Hock Tuesday,
  Hock-tide*.

9

Adar Sheni *Veadar*
aforetime former or past time
afternoon between noon and evening
afterward *afterwards*
antelucan before dawn
bi-monthly twice monthly or every 2 months
Boxing Day December 26th
Candlemas 2nd February
centenary a century
Christmas December 25th
civil year calendar year
decennary period of 10 years
Earth Boar (*Ch.*) 1935: 1995
Easter Day Easter Sunday
Edwardian 1901–1910
Ember-days 3 fast-days each quarter
Ember-week contains 3 *Ember-days*
Fire Horse (*Ch.*) 1906: 1966
Fire Sheep (*Ch.*) 1907: 1967
Fire Snake (*Ch.*) 1917: 1977
Fire Tiger (*Ch.*) 1926: 1986
fortnight two weeks
Hallowmas 1st November
Halloween eve of *Hallowmas*
hodiernal of the present day
honeymoon first weeks after marriage
indiction a 15-year cycle
legal year *calendar year*
Low Sunday first Sunday after Easter
lunar year 12 lunar months (354 days)
lunch-time period for lunch
market-day fixed day for market
Martinmas 11th November
matutinal of the morning
menstrual monthly
Metal Boar (*Ch.*) 1911: 1971
midsummer middle of summer
mid-winter middle of winter
Neolithic late Stone Age
nightfall beginning of night
night-tide night-time
night-time time of night
noviciate *novitiate*
novitiate period of being novice
octennial of or lasting 8 years
overnight all night
peacetime time of peace

premature before time, unduly early
quarterly once a quarter
quotidian daily, everyday
September 9th (orig. 7th) month
septenium seven years
sexennial of or lasting 6 years
solar year 365 days 5hr. 48min. 46sec.
Thargelia ancient Athenian festival
Thermidor a French Revolutionary month
triennial of or lasting 3 years
trimester 3 months
Victorian 1837–1901
Water Boar (*Ch.*) 1923: 1973
Wednesday day of god Woden
Wood Horse (*Ch.*) 1954: 2014
Wood Sheep (*Ch.*) 1955: 2015
Wood Snake (*Ch.*) 1905: 1965
Wood Tiger (*Ch.*) 1914: 1974
yesterday day last past
yestereve yesterday evening

10

afterwards in later time
All-Hallows *Hallowmas*, All Saints Day
antecedent prior
beforehand before the time
beforetime in former time
bimestrial of 2 months' duration
centennial once in or lasting 100 years
Childermas Innocents' day, 28th December
days of yore olden times
dinner time period for dinner
Earth Horse (*Ch.*) 1918: 1978
Earth Sheep (*Ch.*) 1919: 1979
Earth Snake (*Ch.*) 1929: 1989
Earth Tiger (*Ch.*) 1938: 1998
fence month close season
Fire Dragon (*Ch.*) 1916: 1976
Fire Monkey (*Ch.*) 1956: 2010
Fire Rabbit (*Ch.*) 1927: 1987
fiscal year 12-month accounting
Good Friday Friday before Easter
Hebrew year *a lunisolar year*
Hock Monday men held women to ransom

isochronal of equal time
Julian year 365¼ days
lunar cycle *Metonic cycle*
lunar month *synodic month*
Metal Horse (*Ch.*) 1930: 1990
Metal Sheep (*Ch.*) 1931: 1991
Metal Snake (*Ch.*) 1941: 2001
Metal Tiger (*Ch.*) 1950: 2010
Michaelmas 29th September
Middle Ages 5th–15th centuries
millennium 1000 years
occasional now and then
oftentimes frequently
Palm Sunday Sunday before Easter
quarter-day first or last day of quarter
Sexagesima 2nd Sunday before Lent
Shrovetide days preceding Ash Wednesday
solar month one twelfth of *solar year*
springtide time of spring
springtime *springtide*
summer time time of summer
synchronal coinciding in time
Theban year Egyptian year (365¼ days)
thereafter after that reference
vespertine of the evening
Water Horse (*Ch.*) 1942: 2002
Water Sheep (*Ch.*) 1943: 2003
Water Snake (*Ch.*) 1953: 2013
Water Tiger (*Ch.*) 1902: 1962
wedding day day of marriage
Whit Monday follows *Whitsunday*
Whitsunday 7th Sunday after Easter
winter-tide winter
winter-time winter
Wood Dragon (*Ch.*) 1904: 1964
Wood Monkey (*Ch.*) 1944: 2004
Wood Rabbit (*Ch.*) 1915: 1975
working day day of employment

11

All Fools' Day April 1st
All Souls' Day November 2nd
anniversary (annual) recurrence/celebration
bank-holiday English general holiday
bicentenary of 200 years

Black Monday Easter Monday
Black Friday *Good Friday*
closing time end of licensed period
Earth Dragon (*Ch.*) 1928: 1988
Earth Monkey (*Ch.*) 1908: 1968
Earth Rabbit (*Ch.*) 1939: 1999
Elizabethan 1558–1603
everlasting endless
Fire Rooster (*Ch.*) 1957: 2017
hebdomadary weekly
Hock Tuesday women held men to ransom
interregnum period of breach
jubilee year year of *jubilee*
judgment-day final judgment of mankind
leisure time free from employment
Metal Dragon (*Ch.*) 1940: 2000
Metal Monkey (*Ch.*) 1920: 1980
Metal Rabbit (*Ch.*) 1951: 2011
natural year *solar year*
New Year's Day first day of year
New Year's Eve last day of year
Passion-week Holy-week
prehistoric before extant record
pudding-time (obs.) the right moment
Tudor period 1485–1558 (or 1603)
twelvemonth a year
Water Dragon (*Ch.*) 1952: 2012
Water Monkey (*Ch.*) 1932: 1992
Water Rabbit (*Ch.*) 1903: 1963
Whitsuntide season of Pentecost
Wood Rooster (*Ch.*) 1945: 2005
yesternight last night

12

All Saints' Day 1st November
antediluvial of *antediluvian*
antediluvian pre Noah's Flood
antemeridian before noon
ante meridiem (f) before noon
Ascension Day Holy Thursday
Ash Wednesday first day of *Lent*
bicentennial once in or lasting 200 years
calendar year 12 calendar months
carbon dating prehistoric-organism test

TIME

Christmas Day December 25th
Christmas Eve December 24th
duodecennial occurring every 12 years
Easter Sunday follows 1st full moon
 post 21st March
Earth Rooster (*Ch.*) 1909: 1969
Holy Thursday 10 days before
 Whitsunday
Metal Rooster (*Ch.*) 1921: 1981
Metonic Cycle 19-year lunar cycle
Midsummer day 24th June, quarter
 day
old fashioned out of date
Palaeolithic old Stone Age
Platonic year a cycle of years
Plough Monday old rural festival
post-diluvial of *post-diluvian*
post-diluvian after Noah's Flood
post-meridian after noon
post-prandial after dinner
Quadragesima first Sunday of *Lent*
quinquennial of or lasting 5 years
red-letter day special day
Rogation Days 3, pre *Ascension Day*
Rogation Week week of *Rogation Days*
sidereal time based on Aries
sidereal year 365 days 9min. 9.6sec.
stellar month 27.3217 days

synodic month 29.5306 days
tercentenary 300-year anniversary
tropical year *solar year*
Twelth-night last night of *Yuletide*
Water Rooster (*Ch.*) 1933: 1993

13

All-hallowmass *All-Saints' day*
All-hallowtide *All-Hallows* season
April Fools' Day 1st April
calendar month as on calendar
financial year *fiscal year*
golden jubilee 50 years
lunisolar year adjusted *embolistic year*
Shrove Tuesday day before *Ash
 Wednesday*
silver jubilee 25 years
tropical month 27.3216 days

14

Chinese New Year lunisolar based
embolistic year 13 lunar months
Maundy Thursday day before *Good
 Friday*

NATURAL HISTORY

FAUNA – ANIMALS

note (1) 'Obvious' creatures such as cat, dog, etc. are deliberately omitted.
(2) Many hyphenated words are optional forms.

2

ai three-toed *sloth*: fish
ky cows
ox bull, castrated for draught (*oxen*)
zo *zho*

3

bat small flying mammal
bok (f) S. African *antelope*
cob short-legged horse
cub a *whelp*
cur a worthless dog
dam beast's mother
doe female deer
dso *zho*
dzo *zho*
elk large deer
elt a young *sow*
gib castrated cat
gnu a large *antelope*
hog swine
kid a young goat
kob African water-*antelope*
nag a horse
pad a working elephant
roe a species of deer
sai the capuchin monkey
sow a female pig
teg sheep in second year
tit titmouse; horse
tod a fox
tup a ram
wat hare (obs.)
yak Tibetan ox (*oxen*)
zho Tibetan yak/cattle hybrid

4

anoa the *sapi-utan*
atoc *atok*
atok a species of *skunk*
barb swift horse
boar the male swine
buck male deer/rabbit
cain hen, paid as tax
cavy guinea pig
colt young horse
cony a rabbit
coon the *raccoon*
dieb African jackal
eyra S. American wild cat
fawn a young deer
foal a young horse
gaur Indian ox (*oxen*)
hack poor quality horse
hart adult male deer
hind red deer female
ibex mountain wild goat
jade a worthless nag
[1]**joey** baby kangaroo
jomo *zho*
kine cattle
kudu an African *antelope*
lynx bobtailed wildcat
mare female horse
mink type of *weasel*
mohr an African *gazelle*
moke a donkey
mole a small *insectivore*

---

[1] Games players note: providing that your game permits foreign words then *joey* in this sense is valid. It is also an English slang word for a coin (see page 221), a category which validates it for other games.

FAUNA – ANIMALS

mona an African monkey
mule hybrid ass/horse
neat a *bovine* animal
nout *nowt*
nowt cattle
Oryx* a genus of *antelope*
oxen male/female draught cattle
paca the spotted *cavy*
paco *llama*
pard the leopard
peba S. American *armadillo*
pika the tailless hare
puma cougar, large cat
quey a heifer
roan horse of mixed colour
runt smallest of litter
Rusa* a genus of deer
saki S. American monkey
skug squirrel
tahr Himalayan wild goat
tegg *teg*
urus the *aurochs*
urva crab-eating *mongoose*
vole *rodent*
zebu Asian ox (*oxen*)
zobo *zho*

5

addax African *antelope*
aguti S. American *rodent*
ariel kind of *gazelle*
bidet a nag
biped two-footed
bongo African *bushbuck*
brock badger
Bruin fictional bear
burro donkey
caple horse
capul *caple*
civet cat-like *carnivore*
coati American *raccoon*
coney rabbit
coypu S. American *rodent*
crone an old ewe
cuddy donkey
daman the Biblical *cony*
dhole Indian wild dog
dingo Australian wild dog

drill W. African *baboon*
dsomo *zho*
dzomo *zho*
eland S. African *antelope*
Felis cat genus
filly a young *mare*
fitch *polecat*
gayal Indian ox (*oxen*)
genet *civet*-like *carnivore*
goral Asian goat-*antelope*
grice a little pig
hinny stallion/she-ass hybrid
hutia hog-rat
hyena carrion-feeding *carnivore*
Hyrax* *marmot*-like genus
Indri *lemur* genus
izard Pyrenean *ibex*
jocko chimpanzee
kaama *hartebeest*
koala bear-like *marsupial*
kyloe Hebridean cow/bull
lemur monkey-like animal
llama S. American pack animal
loris E. Indian *lemur*
magot Barbary ape
Manis *pangolin* genus
manul Asian wild cat
morse the *walrus*
okapi giraffe-like animal
oribi small *antelope*
otary external-eared seal   ·
ounce snow leopard
pekan N. American *marten*
Phoca* seal genus
pongo *anthropoid* ape
potto *kinkajou*
punch short-legged horse
rasse a small *civet*
Ratel* badger-like genus
royal twelve-point stag
sable arctic *marten*
saiga Asian *antelope*
sajou capuchin monkey
sasin Indian *antelope*
screw broken-winded horse
serow Asian goat/*antelope*
shoat young *hog*
shrew mouse-like *insectivore*
skunk an odorous *Mustela*
sloth sluggish arboreal *edentate*

Sorex* the *shrew* genus
spado castrated animal
staig stag
Talpa* *mole* genus
tapir large odd-toed *ungulate*
tatou giant *armadillo*
tayra large S. American *weasel*
urial Himalayan wild sheep
urson Canadian *porcupine*
vison American *mink*
vixen she-fox
waler Australian horse in India
whelp puppy, etc.
yapok S. American water-*opossum*
zerda *fennec*
zibet Asiatic *civet*
zizel ground squirrel
zoril *zorro*
zorro S. American fox

6

agouta rat-like *insectivore*
agouti S. American *rodent*
aliped wing-footed animal
alpaca domesticated *llama*-like beast
angora Turkish goat
argali Asian wild sheep
aye-aye squirrel-like *lemur*
baboon large monkey
bandar *rhesus* monkey
bayard a bay horse
beeves cattle, *oxen*
bovine pertaining to cattle
bronco half-tamed horse
brumby (f) wild horse
bharal Himalayan blue sheep
burhel *bharal*
castor beaver
Castor* beaver genus
cayuse (f) Red Indian pony
chacma large S. African *baboon*
coaiti spider monkey
cosset hand-reared lamb
cougar *puma*
coyote *prairie-wolf*
curtal (obs.) horse, etc. with docked tail
dassie S. African *marmot*
desman Russian aquatic *insectivore*
dickey an ass

dik-dik various E. African *antelopes*
dzeren Asian *antelope*
ermine stoat in winter
farrow litter of pigs
fennec African fox
fox-bat a fruit *bat*
Galago a *lemur* genus
garran *garron*
garron small horse
gerbil desert-dwelling *rodent*
gibbon long-armed ape
gopher various burrowing animals
grison S. American *weasel*: monkey
grivet African monkey
guenon various long-tailed monkeys
hackee *chipmunk*
heifer young cow
hogget a yearling sheep
howler S. American monkey
impala large African *antelope*
jackal dog-like *carnivore*
jaguar leopard-like cat
jennet small Spanish horse
jerboa desert *rodent*
kalong large fruit *bat*
kelpie Scottish horse-ghost
koodoo African *antelope*
langur the *entellus* monkey
lionel small lion
lionet young lion
malkin a hare
margay spotted tiger-cat
marmot a burrowing stoat
marten *weasel*-like animal
mawkin hare
merino Spanish sheep
morkin accidentally dead animal
musk ox Canadian ox (*oxen*)
nilgai large Indian *antelope*
ocelot a small leopard
onager Asian wild ass
oorial Himalayan wild sheep
pallah *impala*
porker a young *hog*
possum Australian *herbivore, opossum*
pygarg Biblical deer (possibly *addax*)
quagga extinct wild ass
racoon *raccoon*
reebok S. African *antelope*
rhesus Indian monkey

FAUNA – ANIMALS

roarer diseased roaring horse
rodent mammal with prominent
  incisors
rother (obs.) ox, cow
sambar large Indian deer
sambur *sambar*
sea-ape otter: shark: *manatee*
sea-cow *walrus*
serval tiger-cat
simian ape-like
sorrel horse: 3rd-year buck
suslik ground squirrel
taguan E. Indian *flying squirrel*
tapeti Brazilian rabbit
tarpan extinct Russian wild horse
teledu Javanese stinking badger
tenrec large Madagascan *insectivore*
theave a young ewe
Tupaia tree-*shrew* genus
vermin obnoxious fauna
vervet African monkey
vicuna wild *llama*
walrus carnivorous marine animal
wapiti large N. American deer
weasel small furtive *carnivore*
wether castrated ram
wivern a fictitious monster
wombat (*marsupial*) *opossum*
wow-wow Japanese silver *gibbon*
wyvern *wivern*
yapock S. American water-*opossum*
zorino S. American fox

7

acouchy type of *agouti*
antbear S. American ant-eater
aurochs extinct wild ox (*oxen*)
banting E. Indian wild ox (*oxen*)
bighorn Rocky Mountain goat or
  sheep
blesbok S. African *antelope*
bonasus bison
brocket stag in 2nd year
broncho half-tamed horse
Bubalis* *hartebeest* genus
Bubalus buffalo genus
bullock castrated bull: *ox*
bush-cat the *serval*
caracal Persian *lynx*

caribou American reindeer
cervine relating to deer
Cetacea genus of various whales
chamois goat-like *antelope*
cheetah unique type of big cat
Cheviot short-woolled sheep
chimera fabulous monster
Colobus* almost-thumbless monkey
  genus
courser swift horse: running bird
dasypod an *armadillo*
Dasypus a genus of armadillos
dasyure carnivorous *marsupial*
dolphin a whale-like mammal
draft-ox draught-*ox*
eanling a young lamb
Echidna* a genus of monotremes
epizoon symbiotic animal
ermelin *ermine*
fatling animal fed for early slaughter
finback a *rorqual*
fitchet *polecat*
fitchew *fitchet*
foumart *polecat*
fur-seal sea-bear
gazelle small *antelope*
gelding castrated horse
gemsbok (f) S. African *antelope*
genette *civet*-like *carnivore*
glutton a northern *weasel*
grampus whale
griffin an imaginary animal: unraced
  pony
griffon *griffin:* dog
grizzly Rocky Mountain bear
guanaco wild *llama*
hackney carriage horse
huanaco wild *llama*
jacchus S. American *marmoset*
jackass rabbit: bird: fish
keitloa two-horned *rhinoceros*
kidling young *kid*
klipdas the Cape *hyrax*
lambkin a little lamb
lemming *vole*-like *rodent*
leveret hare in first year
libbard leopard
linsang Asian *civet*-like animal
Macacus *macaque* genus
macaque a type of monkey

mammoth   extinct hairy elephant
manatee   Atlantic sirenian (*Sirenia*)
markhor   Asian wild goat
marmose   small S. American *opossum*
meerkat   ground squirrel: *lemur*
minever   *miniver*
miniver   *ermine*
molerat   name for several rodents
Mormops   leaf-nosed *bat* genus
mouflon   Corsican wild sheep
muntjak   Oriental small deer
musk-rat   *musquash*
mustang   American feralized horse
Mustela   the *marten* genus
Mycetes*   *howler* monkey genus
Mylodon*   a genus of *sloth*
narwhal   kind of tusked whale
Nasalis   proboscis monkey genus
noctule   the great *bat*
nylghau   large Indian *antelope*
opossum   American *marsupial carnivore*
palfrey   lady's saddle-horse
panther   large leopard: *puma*
pardale (obs.)   small *pard*
peccary   *hog*-like animal
polecat   a large type of *weasel*
potoroo   *marsupial* rat-kangaroo
pricket (obs.)   *buck* in 2nd year
Procyon   *raccoon* genus
raccoon   small bear-like animal
rorqual   finback whale
sagouin   a titi monkey
saimiri   a squirrel monkey
sapajou   a capuchin monkey
sassaby   the bastard *hartebeest*
Sciurus   squirrel genus
sheltie   Shetland pony
siamang   the largest *gibbon*
Sirenia   an aquatic mammal order
soliped   uncloven-hoofed animal
sondeli   Indian musk-*shrew*
sounder   herd of swine: young *boar*
souslik   ground squirrel
sumpter   packhorse
tamarin   small squirrel monkey
thiller   shaft-horse
twinter   2-year-old sheep
Viverra   *civet* genus
wart-hog   African wild *hog*

wistiti   a *marmoset*
zamouse   W. African buffalo
zorille   African *skunk*-like animal
zorillo   a S. American *skunk*

8

aardvark (f)   S. African ant-eater
aardwolf (f)   *hyena*-like *carnivore*
antelope   hollow-horned *ruminant*
Bactrian   two-humped camel
behemoth   Biblical animal (hippopotamus?)
bontebok   S. African *antelope*
bush-baby   small S. African *lemur*
²**bush-buck**   small S. African *antelope*
cachalot   sperm whale
cacholot   *cachalot*
capybara   largest living *rodent*
chimeara   a fabulous monster
chipmuck   *chipmunk*
chipmunk   N. American squirrel
civet-cat   cat-like *carnivore*
Cotswold   a breed of sheep
Cricetus   hamster genus
demi-wolf   wolf/dog hybrid
dormouse   squirrel-like mouse
duckbill   an aquatic monotreme
edentate   naturally toothless animal
entellus   an Indian monkey
Galloway   small strong horse
hedgepig   hedgehog
hylobate   a *gibbon*
kinkajou   *raccoon*-like animal
lamantin   the *manatee*
mandrill   large W. African *baboon*
mangabey   white-eyelid monkey
marmoset   very small American monkey
Mastodon*   genus of extinct elephant
milch-cow   dairy cow
mongoose   Indian *civet*
moufflon   Corsican wild sheep
musk deer   a hornless deer
musquash   large *vole*-like *rodent*

² Games players note: *bush-buck* is the form
  in which this word appears in *Chambers*
  even though other authorities prefer
  bushbuck.

FAUNA – ANIMALS

pangolin scaly ant-eater
Physeter sperm whale
platypus the *duck-bill*
porkling a young pig
porpoise short-nosed *dolphin*
Rodentia the *rodent* order
ruminant cud-chewing animal
sapi-utan Celebes wild ox
sea-otter N. Pacific otter-like animal
serotine small reddish *bat*
suricate S. African *civet*
talapoin a small green monkey
tiger-cat middle-sized wild cat
Ungulata order of hoofed animals
viscacha heavy-built burrowing *rodent*
wallaroo kangaroo
wanderoo Celonese *langur*
warrigal *dingo*: wild horse
weanling newly-weaned young
yeanling lamb: kid
yearling year-old animal

9

armadillo an American *edentate*
bandicoot largest species of rat
barbastel hairy-lipped *bat*
blackbuck common Indian *antelope*
blue whale largest living animal
carnivore flesh-eating animal
catamount various wild cats
chickaree an American red squirrel
deer-mouse American mouse
delundung weasel-cat of Java
Didelphys American *opossum* genus
dromedary one-humped camel
dziggetai Asian wild ass
flying fox a large *bat*
Glyptodon gigantic fossil
grimalkin an old cat
ground-hog woodchuck: *aardvark*
guinea-pig the *cavy*
herbivore grass/vegetation eater
honey-bear the *kinkajou*
ichneumon crocodile-egg-eating
  mongoose
leviathan Biblical animal (crocodile?)
malt-horse brewery horse
marsupial pouched animal

monoceros a one-horned animal
mouse-deer *chevrotain*
orang-utan arboreal ape
pachyderm thick-skinned animal
pack-horse load-bearing horse
pademelon a small wallaby
padymelon *pademelon*
percheron French draught-horse
petaurist a flying *phalanger*
phalanger *marsupial* with webbed toes
porcupine large spiny *rodent*
prongbuck male *pronghorn*
pronghorn American *antelope*-like
  ruminant
quadruman four-handed primate
quadruped four-footed animal
rearmouse *reremouse*
reremouse a *bat*
rosmarine a *walrus* (obs.)
sapi-outan *sapi-utan*
shearling sheep between 1st and 2nd
  shearings
silver fox an American fox
Southdown breed of sheep
springbok S. African *antelope*
stud-horse a breeding stallion
thylacine Tasmanian 'wolf'
tree-shrew squirrel-like *shrew*
water-buck various antelopes
water-vole water-rat
white-bear polar bear
wolverene American *glutton*
wolverine *wolverene*
woodshock the *pekan*
yongling a young animal
zoophagon a *carnivore*

10

angwantibo small W. African *lemur*
animalcule microscopic animal
anthropoid man-like animal
camelopard the giraffe
catarrhine pertaining to certain
  monkeys
chevrotain small, deer-like animal
chinchilla *rodent*
Chinchilla* cat: rabbit
cockatrice a fabulous monster

cottontail USA rabbit
diphyodont mammal with 2 sets of teeth
Dolichotis genus of long-eared rodents
fallow deer small type of deer
fieldmouse various mice
hartebeest large S. African *antelope*
hippogriff fabulous animal
paddymelon *pademelon*
pichiciago small S. American *armadillo*
pilot-whale a type of whale
pine-marten rare British *marten*
prairie-dog gregarious burrowing *marmot*
raccoon-dog *raccoon*-like wild dog
rhinoceros a large *ungulate*
rightwhale the Greenland whale
river-horse *hippopotamus*
rock-badger the Cape *hyrax*
rock-rabbit a *hyrax*
Ruminantia *ungulate* cud-chewing division
shrewmouse a *shrew*
starveling a lean, weak animal
vampire-bat blood-sucking *bat*
wildebeest (f) a *gnu*

11

barbastelle hairy-lipped *bat*
cardophagus donkey (thistle-eater)
digitigrade animal that walks on its toes
douroucouli a night-ape
flying lemur an *insectivore*
Grevy's zebra largest wild equid
grizzly bear Rocky Mountain bear
Insectivora small insect-eating mammals
jumping-deer black-tailed American deer
kangaroo-rat American *rodent*
killer whale the *grampus*
Megatherium gigantic extinct ground *sloth*
Monotremata lowest order of mammals
mountain-cat wild cat
orang-outang *orang-utan*

pipistrelle the commonest British *bat*
prairie-wolf the coyote
sea-elephant the elephant-seal
snow leopard the ounce
wishtonwish N. American prairie-dog

12

Barbary sheep N. African wild sheep
elephant seal large inflatable-nosed seal
flitter-mouse a *bat*
harvest mouse corn-nesting mouse
hippotamus a large African *ungulate*
klipspringer small S. African *antelope*
mountain-hare small species of hare
mountain-lion the *puma*
Pachydermata non-ruminating *ungulate*
pouched mouse small *marsupial*
rhesus monkey an Indian monkey
Shetland* pony small hardy pony
spider-monkey an American monkey
tree-kangaroo a tree-climbing kangaroo

13

carriage horse carriage-drawing horse
Chapman's zebra a plains-dwelling zebra
Galeopithecus so-called flying *lemur*
laughing hyena carrion-feeding *carnivore*
Parry's wallaby a type of wallaby
polyprotodont *marsupial* suborder
ring-tail coati American *raccoon*
Semnopithecus an ape genus
Tasmanian wolf a wolf-like *dasyure*

14

Burchell's zebra Orange Free State zebra

flying squirrel squirrel with parachute-skin
laughing hyaena *laughing hyena*
snow-shoe rabbit American hare
Tasmanian devil a ferocious *dasyure*
Tasmanian tiger striped *Tasmanian wolf*

15

Bennett's wallaby large Tasmanian wallaby
flying phalanger marsupial with parachute-skin
sabre-tooth tiger a fossil *carnivore*
Thomson's gazelle long-horned *gazelle*

FAUNA–BIRDS

2

ka *kae*

3

Ara a parrot genus
auk of *Alcidae*
cob male swan
daw jackdaw
emu very large, akin to *cassowary*
fum *phoenix*
kae jackdaw
kea sheep-killing parrot
mew gull
moa gigantic extinct bird
pen female swan
pie magpie
ree female ruff *(sandpiper)*
roc fabulous gigantic bird
ruc *roc*
tui parson-bird

4

Anas* a duck genus
Asio an owl genus
Aves* birds
barb pigeon
Bubo* an owl sub-family
chat genus akin to thrush
coot type of water-fowl
Crax the *curassow* genus
dodo extinct flightless bird

emeu *emu*
erne eagle
eyas unfledged hawk
fung *phoenix*
guan noisy game-bird
hern heron
ibis akin to *spoonbill*
Jynx* *wryneck* genus
kaka a N. Zealand parrot
kite a rapacious hawk
knot *snipe*-like shore bird
koel (f) cuckoo
loon various diving birds
lory various parrots
mina *myna*
myna akin to starling
nyas *eyas*
Otis *bustard* genus
Pavo peacock genus
pern *honey-buzzard*
Pica* magpie genus
piet *pyot*
poot *poult*
pyat *pyot*
pyot magpie
rail any of genus Rallus
rhea S. African ostrich
roch *rotch*
rock Plymouth Rock fowl
ruff kind of *sandpiper*: pigeon
rukh *roc*
runt breed of pigeon
rype *ptarmigan*
shag the green cormorant
skua a genus of gulls
smee various ducks

smew duck
sora short-billed *rail*
sore hawk of first year (obs.)
taha weaver-bird
teal of *Anas*
tern akin to gull
tody green sparrow
wavy snow-goose
Xema fork-tailed gull genus
yunx of *Jynx*

5

agami S. American *crane*
Ardea heron/*bittern* genus
biddy fowl
booby type of *gannet*
Buteo *buzzard* genus
capon castrated cock
colin Virginian *quail*
crake crow: raven: *corncrake*
crane large wading bird
diver various birds
egret various white heron
eider fine-downed duck
galah Australian *cockatoo*
glede *kite*
grebe freshwater *diver*
harpy large S. American eagle
hobby small falcon species
jager *skua*
junco *reed-bunting*
Larus principal gull genus
macaw of *Ara*
madge barn owl: magpie
mavis song-thrush
merle blackbird
miner *oven-bird*
monal *monaul*
murve of *Alcidae*
mynah *myna*
nandu *rhea*
noddy akin to *tern*
ornis *avifauna*
ousel *ouzel*
ouzel blackbird
owlet young owl
pewit *peewit*
Picus woodpecker genus

pipit lark-like genus
Pitta* *ant-thrush* genus
poker *pochard*
poult chicken
quail small partridge genus
reeve *ree*
rotch little *auk*
ryper plural of *rype*
saker falcon species (female)
scape *snipe*
serin species of canary
snipe long-billed, marsh dwellers
solan *gannet*
spink chaffinch
stilt akin to *avocet*
stint *dunlin*
terek *sandpiper*
twite mountain *linnet*
umbre *umbrette*
urubu S. American vulture
wader various wading birds
wavey *wavy*
whaup *curlew: whimbrel*

6

avocet a *wader*
avoset *avocet*
auklet small *auk*
barbet bristly-beaked bird
bonxie the great *skua*
bulbul Persian nightingale
chauna large spur-winged bird
chough red-legged crow: jackdaw
(obs.)
chukor an Indian partridge
condor large S. American vulture
corbie raven: crow
Corvus* crow genus
coucal a bush-bird genus, etc.
culver dove: pigeon
curlew akin to *woodcock*
cushat *ring-dove*
cygnet young swan
darter akin to cormorant
dipper *water-ouzel: dabchick*
drongo of Dicuridae family
ducker a diving-bird
dunlin small *sandpiper*

eaglet young/small eagle
elanet *kite*
elf owl tiny, single-species genus
fulmar akin to *petrel*
gambet *redshank*
gander male goose
gannet of Sulidae family
garrot various ducks
gentoo Falkland Is. penguin
godwit *plover*
gooney *albatross*
goslet Eastern dwarf goose
grakle *grackle*
haglet *hacklet*
hareld northern sea duck
hoopoe crested, mentioned in Bible
jabiru large Brazilian stork
jacana long-toed swamp bird
jaeger *jager*
kakapo almost flightless owl-parrot
lanner kind of falcon (female)
Leipoa* *mound-bird* genus
linnet a finch
loriot *golden oriole*
martin of swallow genus
Mergus a diving-bird genus
merlin small falcon species
Merops *bee-eater* genus
missel *missel-thrush*
monaul Himalayan pheasant
mopoke a N. Zealand owl
motmot akin to kingfisher
musket male *sparrow-hawk*
nandoo *nandu*
Nestor *kea* genus
oriole akin to crow
osprey the fish hawk
ox-bird *dunlin*
pavone of *Pavo*
peahen female pea-fowl
pecker woodpecker
peewit *lapwing*
petrel akin to *Albatross*
plover the Charadriidae family
pochard pockard, diving-duck
pouter type of pigeon
puffin of *Alcidae*
pullet young hen
queest *cushat*
Quelea* a weaver-bird genus

red-cap goldfinch
roller akin to kingfisher
rotche *rotch*
scamel (obs.) bar-tailed *godwit*
scoter a duck genus
sea-cob seagull
sea-maw *sea-mew*
sea-mew seagull
sea-pie *oyster-catcher*
shrike impales victims on thorns
siskin type of finch
smeath *smee*
smeeth *smee*
strich (obs.) *screech-owl*
sultan purple *coot*
tarcel *tercel*
tarsal *tercel*
tarsel *tercel*
tassel *tercel*
tercel a male hawk
tococo (f) *oven-bird*
tomtit blue or other tit
toucan various, immense-beaked
towhee various American finches
turbit type of pigeon
Turdus thrush genus
turtle turtle-dove
tystie black *guillemot*
wigeon *widgeon*
willet *tattler*
xenops (f) *oven-bird*
yaffle *tattler*
ynambu very large *tinamou*
zoozoo *wood-pigeon*

7

Apteryx* kiwi genus
Alcidae marine diving-bird family
babbler akin to thrush
barn owl a buff-coloured owl
bat hawk crepuscular bat raptor
bittern akin to heron
bluecap blue *titmouse*
boobook an Australian owl
bullbat (f) *night-hawk*
bunting finch akin to *crossbill*
Buphaga genus akin to starling
bustard akin to *crane/rail*

buzzard large bird of prey
cariama *seriema*
catbird akin to thrush
cheeper young game bird
chewink *red-eyed towhee*
colibri *humming-bird*
Columba pigeon genus
corella an Australian *cockatoo*
Cotinga* bright-plumaged birds genus
courlan various, akin to *rail*
cowbird *cow blackbird*
creeper small, runs up trees
cropper pigeon with large crop
Dorking breed of poultry
dottrel *dotterel*
dovekie an *auk*
dun-bird female *pochard*
dunnock hedge-sparrow
emu wren small Australian bird
fantail pigeon: various others
fern owl *nightjar*
gadwall type of duck
gobbler turkey-cock
gorcock *red grouse* cock
gorcrow carrion-crow
goshawk short-winged hawk
gosling a young goose
grackle of *Icterus*: hill *myna*
greyhen female *blackcock*
greylag common wild goose
grey owl *tawny owl*
hacklet *kittiwake: shearwater*
halcyon kingfisher
harrier type of hawk
hawk owl diurnal owl
hoatzin stink-bird
hornbill casque-billed, akin to *hoopoe*
ice-bird little *auk*: sea dove
Icterus* yellow bird genus
jacamar any of Galbulidae family
Jacobin a hooded pigeon
kamichi horned *screamer*
kestrel small falcon species
killdee type of ringplover
kinglet fire-crested wren
lapwing *plover*
leghorn small breed of fowl
mallard male common wild duck
manakin various small birds
marabou adjutant-bird

martlet *martin*
moorhen *water-hen: moorfowl*
mudlark various birds
oil-bird akin to *goatsucker*
ortolan bunting, table delicacy
Oscines the song-birds
oven-tit *willow-warbler*
Pandion *osprey* genus
Partlet traditional proper name for hen
percher any perching bird
Phaeton tropic-bird genus
phoenix fabulous Chinese bird
pinnock hedge-sparrow: blue-tit
pintado *petrel: pigeon: guinea fowl*
pintail a duck
pochard a red-headed duck
poe-bird *parson-bird*
poy-bird *parson-bird*
puttock *buzzard: kite* (obs.)
quetzal C. American long-tailed bird
rainbow type of *humming-bird*
redpoll akin to *linnet*
redwing type of thrush
rosella a *parakeet*
rotchie *rotch*
ruddock redbreast
sakeret male *saker*
sawbill *merganser: motmot*
scooper *avocet*
sea crow *skua: chough*: cormorant, etc.
sea-fowl any sea-bird
sea-hawk *skua*
seriema *crane*-like bird
sirgang green jay-like bird
skimmer sea-skimming bird
squacco small crested heron
staniel *kestrel*
stanuel *staniel*
stanyel *staniel*
sunbird various, akin to *honey-eater*
tanager various, akin to finches
tarrock various sea-birds
tassell *tercel*
tattler akin to *snipe*
tiercel *tercel*
tinamou partridge-like bird
titlark a *pipit*
titling meadow *pipit*: hedge-sparrow
Totanus *redshank* genus
touraco *plantain-eater*

tumbler type of pigeon
vulturn Australian *brush-turkey*
waxbill various, akin to weaver-bird
waxwing of *Passeriformes*
whooper type of swan
widgeon type of duck
wimbrel *whimbrel*
witwall green woodpecker
wrybill twisted bill, akin to *plover*
wryneck akin to woodpecker

8

aasvogel (f) S. African vulture
Accentor* hedge-sparrow genus
adjutant large *crane*
aigrette *egret*
alcatras pelican, *albatross*, *gannet*, etc.
amadavat akin to weaver-bird
arapunga *campanero*
avifauna birds of same region
bee-eater eats bees, akin to kingfisher
bell-bird *campanero: honey-eater*
blackcap type of warbler
bluewing an American *teal*
boatbill type of heron
boattail *grackle*
bobolink *troupial*, sings 'Bob Lincoln'
bob-white *quail*, sings 'Bob White'
brancher young hawk
caracara several vulture-like hawks
cargoose crested *grebe*
churn-owl *nightjar*
cockatoo large crested parrot
curassow large, turkey-like
cursores running birds
dabchick little *grebe*
dandy-hen bantam
didapper *dabchick*
Dinorsis a *moa* genus
dipchick *dabchick*
dotterel *plover*
duck-hawk *moor-buzzard*
dun-diver *merganser*
eagle owl huge owl
estridge (obs.) ostrich
gairfowl *garefowl*
garefowl the *great auk*
garganey *summer-teal*

great auk extinct c.1844
grosbeck hawfinch
guachero *oil-bird*
hangbird *Baltimore oriole*
hangnest *hangbird*
hernshaw young heron
heronsew *hernshaw*
hickwall green woodpecker
hoactzin *hoatzin*
killdeer *killdee*
kingbird tyrant-flycatcher
lanneret male *lanner*
laverock lark
lorikeet small *lory*
lyre-bird male's tail lyre-shape
marabout *marabou*
megapode *mound-bird*
moorcock *moorfowl*
moorfowl *red* or *black grouse*
nightjar of Caprimulgidae family
Notornis* flightless-rail genus
nuthatch akin to tit
[3]**oven-bird** builds oven-shaped nest
ox-pecker African weaver-bird
paitrick partridge
peesweep *peewit*
peetweet (f) spotted *sandpiper*
pigmy owl sparrow-size owl
popinjay parrot
puff-bird akin to *barbet*
raddocke (obs.) *ruddock*
redshank red-legged *sandpiper*
redstart an American warbler
ring-dove wood pigeon
(ring-tail)* female hen-*harrier*
rock-bird *puffin*, etc.
rock-dove a pigeon
Scops owl tiny owl genus
screamer *chauna: seriema*
shelduck female *sheldrake*
shoebill *whale-head*
snowy owl white, ground-nesting owl
stallion *staniel* (obs.)
Struthio ostrich genus
Tantalus* wood-*ibis* genus

[3] Games players note: *oven-bird* is the form in which this word appears in *Chambers* even though other authorities prefer *ovenbird*.

tawny owl species with sensitive hearing
tercelet *tercel*
thrasher American *mocking-bird*
thresher *thrasher*
throstle *mavis*
titmouse tit
troopial *troupial*, any of *Icteridae*
troupial bird famous for song
umbrette *hammerkop*
Waldrap *hermit ibis*
water-hen various birds
wheatear akin to *chat*
whimbrel akin to *curlew*
whip bird akin to *chat*
whinchat type of *chat*
whistler fabulous, fatal to hearer
wood-chat species of *shrike*
woodcock genus akin to *snipe*
wood-lark arboreal, sings on wing
yeldring *yoldring*
yeldrock *yoldring*
yoldring *yellow-hammer*
zopilote *urubu*

9

Aepyornis gigantic wingless fossil
albatross large gliding seabird
ant-thrush various ant-eating birds
bald eagle symbol of USA
beccaccia (f) *woodcock*
beccafico garden-warbler, table delicacy
beefeater *ox-bird*
bergander *sheldrake*
blackcock male *blackgrouse*
blackgame *blackgrouse*
bower-bird bower-making bird
brambling akin to chaffinch
cachalote (f) an *oven-bird*
campanero note like church bell
cassowary genus akin to *emu*
chatterer *wax-wing: cotinga*
chickadee American *titmouse*
cinclodes (f) an *oven-bird*
cockatiel small, crested, parrot
columbine dove-like
corncrake type of *rail*

crossbill crossed-mandible finch
dandy-cock bantam
fieldfare species of thrush
fig-pecker *beccafico*
firecrest *kinglet*
francolin a partridge genus
friarbird featherless-headed *honey-eater*
frogmouth *mopoke*
gallinule water-hen
gerfalcon large falcon
gier-eagle vulture (Bible)
goldcrest golden-crested bird
golden-eye northern sea-duck
goldspink goldspink
goosander of *Mergus*
gowdspink *goldspink*
guillemot of *Alcidae*
guinea-hen guinea-fowl: turkey (obs.)
gyrfalcon *gerfalcon*
hammerkop (f) akin to stork
heathbird *black grouse*
heathcock *black grouse*
heronshaw *hernshaw*
honey-bird *honey-eater: honey-guide*
Icteridae *Icterus* family
Jenny* wren traditional proper name added
jerfalcon *gerfalcon*
kittiwake species of gull
little owl antiphonal singing species
lorrikeet a small *lory*
mallemuck *fulmar*
merganser any of genus *Mergus*
mollymawk albatross
mound-bird creates large nest-mounds
nighthawk *goat-sucker*
ossifrage *osprey: bald eagle*
paraquito *parrakeet*
par(r)akeet small long-tailed parrot
parroquet *parrakeet*
peregrine species of falcon
phalarope coot-footed wader
ptarmigan type of grouse
razorbill razorbilled *auk*
red grouse retains colour in winter
ring-ousel *ouzel*
sandpiper various *snipe/plover*
scrub-bird akin to *lyre-bird*
sea-parrot puffin

sheldrake a large duck
sheldduck female *sheldrake*
shellduck *sheldduck*
shielduck *sheldduck*
shoveller type of duck
skunk-bird *bobolink*
snakebird *darter: wryneck*
spoonbill has spoon-shaped bill
stilt-bird *stilt*
stonechat notes like clicking stones
stone-hawk *merlin*
storm-bird *petrel*
talegalla *brush turkey*: purple *coot*
thickhead various fly-catcher/*shrike*
thick-knee *stone-curlew*
tiercelet *tercel*
trochilus *crocodile-bird*
Trochilus* a *humming-bird* genus
trumpeter swan: pigeon: *crane*-like
varied tit paper-carrying fortune teller
whale-head whale-headed stork
wheat-bird chaffinch
widow-bird various weaver-birds
wind-hover kestrel
woodspite green woodpecker
wyandotte breed of domestic fowl

10

aberdevine *siskin*
bluebreast *bluethroat*
bluethroat akin to nightingale
brant-goose *brent-goose*
brent-goose small wild goose
bufflehead a diving duck
burrow-duck *bergander*
butler-bird *bobolink*
canvas-back N. American duck
chiff-chaff small warbler
crested owl a small-eared species
crow-shrike piping crow
dickcissel disputed *troupial*
Didunculus tooth-billed pigeon genus
ember goose great northern *diver*
eyas-musket unfledged male hawk
fishing owl fish-eating owl
flycatcher various avian insectivores
goatsucker *nightjar*
gooney-bird *albatross* on land

greenfinch green-coloured finch
greenshank a large *sandpiper*
hermit ibis has a revolting smell
honey-eater Australian honey-sucker
honey-guide 'guides' to honey
  (African)
hoodie-crow hooded crow
kookaburra laughing jackass
marsh-robin *towhee*
meadow-lark *troupial*
moth-hunter *goatsucker*
mottled owl species with different-sized
  ears
night-heron nocturnal heron
night-raven (obs.) bird of ill-omen
nutcracker akin to crow
oropendola (f) *troupial*
parson-bird N. Zealand honey-bird
pratincole akin to *plover*
regent-bird a *bower-bird*
rock-pigeon rock-dove
sacred ibis now extinct in Egypt
sand-grouse akin to pigeon
sandmartin sand-nesting *martin*
screech owl insect-hunting species
sea-swallow *tern: storm petrel*
shearwater sea-skimming bird
solan goose *gannet*
summer-teal of *Anas*
tailor-bird nest of sewn-leaves
water-ousel an *ouzel*
wattle-bird *honey-eater*
weasel-coot female *smew*
whydah-bird *widow-bird*
willow-wren *willow-warbler*
wonga-wonga white-faced pigeon
wood pigeon ring-dove
yaffingale *tattler*
zebra finch Australian weaver-bird

11

accepitrine pertaining to hawks
blackgrouse a British species
brush turkey a *mound bird*
butcher-bird *shrike*
Crag-chillia *tococo*
dragoon-bird umbrella-bird
fallow-finch *wheatear*

frigate bird large tropical sea-bird
Grallatores wading birds
ground robin *towhee*
humming-bird small, rapid flight
laughing owl a ground-nesting species
leaf-scraper an *oven-bird*
leather-head *friarbird*
mockingbird mimic, akin to thrush
moorbuzzard *marsh-harrier*
Muscovy duck type of duck
Procellaria *petrel* genus
pterodactyl bird-like fossil reptile
reed-bunting black-headed *bunting*
reed-warbler nests on reeds
scrub-turkey a *mound bird*
shelldrake *sheldrake*
shieldrake *sheldrake*
snow-bunting British winter visitor
sparrow-hawk *goshawk*-like falcon
stone-curlew stone-plover
stone-plover a large *plover*
storm petrel smallest of all sea-birds
tassell-gent (obs.) male *peregrine* falcon
tree-creeper small, insect-hunter
whitethroat various, akin to *blackcap*
wood-swallow *shrike*-like *flycatcher*
yellow-ammer *yellow-hammer*

12

burrowing owl a terrestrial-dwelling
species
cardinal-bird large American finch
cow blackbird cattle-accompanying
bird
falcon-gentil *falcon-gentle*
falcon-gentle female *peregrine*
golden oriole *oriole*
green sparrow *humming bird*
honey-buzzard eats bee/wasp larvae
marsh harrier *harrier* frequenting
marshes
missel-thrush eats mistletoe berries
mourning-dove plaintive-noted pigeon
painted quail genus akin to *quail*
sage-thrasher mountain *mockingbird*
scissor-tail American *flycatcher*

sedge warbler common British
warbler
stone-chatter *stonechat*
stormy petrel *storm petrel*
tassel-gentle (obs.) *tercel-gentle*
tercel-gentle male *peregrine* falcon
tercel-jerkin male *gerfalcon*
umbrella-bird of *Cotinga*
water-wagtail pied-wagtail
whip-poor-will *nightjar*
whooping-swan *whooper*
yellow-hammer (yellow) finch

13

barnacle-goose believed hatched from
barnacles
crocodile-bird feeds *inside* reptile's
mouth
horned screamer S. American bird
mocking-thrush *thrasher*
oyster-catcher *sea-pie*
Passeriformes sparrow-like perching
order
red-eyed towhee large finch
secretary-bird snake-eating raptor
stream-creeper *oven-bird*
turkey buzzard an American vulture
willow-warbler small European bird
yellow-bunting *yellow-hammer*

14

Baltimore oriole *Icterus*
bird of paradise beautiful plumage,
akin to crow
foliage-gleaner *oven-bird*
Manx shearwater very harsh
vocalization
ornate tinamous non-gregarious
species
owlet-frogmouth owl-like *nightjar*
plantain-eater coarse-banana eater
rhinoceros-bird *beefeater: hornbill*
Robin* redbreast traditional proper
name added

FAUNA – DOGS

3

lym (obs.) *lyam-hound*
pom *Pomeranian*
pug small, short-haired
toy often lap-dog

4

chow Chinese breed
peke *Pekinese*
rach scent-hunter
tike cur
tyke *tike*
wolf possible dog ancestor

5

boxer akin to *bulldog*
brach hunting bitch
cairn a *terrier*
colly *collie*
corgi small Welsh breed
dhole Indian wild dog
dingo Australian wild dog (feral?)
husky Eskimo sled-dog
laika various small Finnish breeds
pi-dog *pariah*
rache *rach*
spitz *Pomeranian*

6

Afghan* ancient hound breed
bandog leashed (ferocity/watchdog)
barbet kind of *poodle*
basset hound
beagle small hound
borzoi long-legged hound
cocker cocker spaniel

collie sheep dog
coyote *prairie-wolf*
gun dog hunting-party dog
jackal wild carnivore
jowler heavy-jawed hound
pariah an ownerless cur
poodle originally large sporting dog
pug-dog *pug*
ranger ground-beater
ratter rat killer
saluki silky-haired greyhound
setter dog that sets
shough shaggy lap-dog
talbot extinct breed of hound
teckel *dachshund*
toy dog very small pet dog

7

basenji barkless hunting dog
bird-dog *retriever*
bouvier (f) sheepdog
bulldog courageous breed (orig. bull-baiters)
bush-dog small wild dog
clumber breed of *spaniel*
griffon coarse-haired *terrier*
harrier hare hunter
lurcher greyhound cross
Maltese *Maltese dog*
mastiff thick-set watchdog
pie-dog *pi-dog*
pointer game dog
pye-dog *pi-dog*
samoyed *Pomeranian*
sapling young greyhound
showghe (obs.) *shough*
spaniel hunting dog
starter game dog
terrier small hunter
tumbler rabbit catcher (obs.)
whippet small greyhound cross
wolf-dog wolf cross: wolf hunter

8

Airedale large *terrier*
Alsatian German sheep dog
chow-chow *chow*
coachdog *Dalmatian*
demi-wolf wolf cross
Derby* dog racecourse stray
Doberman Doberman pinscher
elkhound large Norwegian breed
foxhound fox hunter (pack)
keeshond Dutch *spitz*-type
Labrador sporting dog
malamute Arctic sled-dog
papillon *toy* spaniel
Pekinese dwarf *pug-dog*
sealyham short-legged *terrier*
springer kind of *spaniel*
turnspit roasting-spit worker
water-dog any water-game dog
water-rug kind of water-dog

9

badger-dog hound
boarhound powerful, wild-boar hunter
buckhound small *staghound*
chihuahua smallest dog
dachshund *badger-dog*
Dalmatian spotted, carriage attendant
deerhound large rough-coated
  greyhound
Eskimo dog powerful, double-coat
  breed
lime-hound *lyam-hound*
lyam-hound bloodhound
lyme-hound *lyam-hound*
Molossian a kind of *mastiff*
retriever breed: game retriever
St* Bernard very large Swiss breed
schnauzer German *terrier*
staghound Scottish deerhound
wolf-hound wolf hunter
yellow-dog a mongrel

10

Bedlington long-bodied *terrier*

bloodhound keen-scented hunter
fox-terrier fox hunter
Iceland dog shaggy white dog
Maltese dog very small *spaniel*
otter-hound otter hunter
Pomeranian cross from *Eskimo dog*
raccoon dog night-hunting wild dog
toy spaniel Blenheim: *King Charles*
Welsh* corgi *corgi*

11

Afghan* hound royal hunting dog
basset-hound large, badger-hunter
bull-mastiff *bulldog/mastiff* cross
bull-terrier *bulldog/terrier* cross
carriage dog a coach dog
King* Charles black-and-tan coated
  toy spaniel
prairie-wolf a small *wolf*
Skye terrier small, long haired

12

cairn terrier fox hunter
Golden* jackal possible dog ancestor
Gordon setter hunting dog
Irish spaniel *water spaniel*
Irish terrier wiry reddish-brown coat
Newfoundland large intelligent breed
water spaniel liver coloured (game
  dog)

13

affenpinscher small *griffon*
Boston* terrier *bulldog/bull-terrier*
  cross
Dandie Dinmont* rough-coated *terrier*
Sussex spaniel golden-liver or brown
  coat

14

Cape* hunting dog wild, pack-hunter
clumber spaniel lemon-and-white coat

German* shepherd *alsatian*
Simenian jackal Ethiopian *jackal*

15

Aberdeen terrier coarse-haired *terrier*

Airedale terrier large *terrier*
Blenheim spaniel red-and-white coat
German* police dog *alsatian*
golden retriever hunting dog
miniature poodle *toy dog*

FAUNA – FISH

2

ai *ayu*
id freshwater *carp*

3

asp Russian food-fish
ayu cormorant-caught food-fish
bib *pout*
dab small flatfish
gar *garfish*
ged pike
ide *id*
orc fierce sea-monster
ray of Elasmobranchii
red *rummy-nosed tetra*
roe fish eggs
tai Japanese *sea-bream*

4

apod *apode*
barb various, akin to *carp*
bass *sea-perch*
blay *bleak*
bley *blay*
brit young herring
carp slender freshwater fish
chad *shad*
char akin to salmon
chub small fat *carp*
chum *keta*
coho Pacific salmon

cusk torsk: *burbot*
dace akin to *carp*
dare *dace*
dart *dace*
dory akin to mackerel
drum *croaker*
file *file-fish*
goby small *sucker*
grig *sand-eel*
hake of *Gadus*
huso great *sturgeon*
jack young pike: *horse-mackerel*
kelt just-spawned salmon, etc.
keta *dog-salmon*
ling of *Gadus*
luce pike
milt male soft *roe*
mort 3-year-old salmon
Naso *unicorn-fish* genus
opah *kingfish*
orfe type of *id*
parr young salmon
peal *grilse*
pope *ruff*
pout of *Gadus*
redd fish-spawn
rudd *red-eye*
ruff akin to *perch*
scad *horse-mackerel*
scar *scarfish*
scup *porgy*
shad akin to herring
snig immature eel
sole eliptical flatfish
tope small shark species
tuna *tunny:* N. Zealand eel
tusk *torsk*

5

ablet bleak
allis a *shad* species
angel *angel-fish*
apode fish without ventral fins
bleak small white riverfish
brassy bib or *pout*
bream various *carp*/mackerel
brill akin to *turbot*
capon herring
charr *char*
cisco *lake herring*
cobia *sergeant-fish*
cohoe *coho*
Doras overland-walking genus
dorse small cod
elops genus akin to *tarpon*
elver young eel
flake *dogfish* (trade name)
Gadus the cod genus
gaper *sea-perch*
gibel Prussian *carp*
guppy *millions*
hound small shark family
lance *launce*
loach small riverfish
moray type of eel
Mugil *mullet* genus
murry *moray*
nurse shark: *dogfish*
perai *piranha*
Perca spiny-finned freshwater genus
perch of *Perca*
pirai *piranha*
platy cross-breedable aquarium fish
pogge *armed bullhead*
porgy various *sea-bream*
powan Lochs Lomond/Eck whitefish
roach akin to *carp*
roker *thornback*
ruffe *ruff*
saith *coalfish*
Salmo salmon and trout genus
saury akin to *garfish*
sewen Welsh sea-front *grilse*
sewin *sewen*
skate *ray*
smelt of *Salmo*
smolt young river-salmon

snoek *snook*
snook *cobia: robalo: garfish*
Solen* razor-fish genus
sprat small, herring-like
tench akin to *carp*
tetra popular aquarium fish
togue Great Lake *char*
torsk *burbot*
trout of *Salmo*
tunny large, akin to mackerel
twait species of *shad*
whiff akin to *turbot*
zeige (f) akin to *carp*

6

alevin a young fish
allice *allis*
Anabas* *climbing-perch* genus
angler various angling fish
barbel akin to *carp*
belone *sea-pike*
bichir (f) primitive, freshwater fish
big-eye a nocturnal fish
blenny a genus of slimy fishes
bonito various *tunny*
bounce lesser spotted *dogfish*
bowfin N. American freshwater fish
braise *porgy*
braize *braise*
bumalo *Bombay duck*
burbot freshwater cod
caplin *capelin*
Caranx* *scad* genus
caribe *piranha*
caviar *roe* of *sturgeon*
cheven *chub*
chevin *cheven*
Clupea herring genus
comber *gaper*
conger a large eel
darter small, akin to *perch*
Diodon a *globe-fish* genus
Dipnoi the lungfishes
doctor *sea-surgeon*
dorado *coryphene*
dun-cow *shagreen ray*
ellops kind of *sturgeon*
finnac *finnock*

FAUNA – FISH

finnan kind of smoked haddock
garvie *sprat*
Gobius *goby* genus
goramy large freshwater food-fish
grilse salmon on first return
groper *grouper*
gunnel *butter-fish*
gurami *goramy*
gurnet *gurnard*
Labrus *wrasse* genus
launce a *sand eel*
lawyer *bowfin*
madtom (f) of *Ictaluridae*
mahsir *mahseer*
marlin akin to *swordfish*
meagre *drum*
megrim *scald-fish*
milter a male fish
minnow akin to *carp*
morgay *bounce*
mullet small palatable fish
murray *moray*
murrey *moray*
piraya *piranha*
pollan Loch Neagh whitefish
porgie *porgy*
poulpe poulp
rapfen (f) *asp*
redeye akin to *roach*
remora *sucking fish*
robalo pike-like fish
ruffin (obs.) *pope*
saithe *coalfish*
samlet young salmon
sardel akin to *sardine*
sauger small *pike-perch*
saurel *scad*
Scarus *parrot-wrasse* genus
sea-ape *thresher shark*
sea-bat various wing-finned fish
sea-cat *catfish*: weaver-fish
sea-dog *dogfish*
sea-eel *conger*
sea-fox *thresher shark*
sea-owl *lumpsucker*
sephen *sting-ray*
shanny smooth *blenny*
shiner various small fish
sucker akin to *carp*
tarpon gigantic, akin to herring

tautog of *Labrus*
Trygon *sting-ray* genus
turbot large flatfish
twaite *shad*
ulicon *eulachon*
ulikon *eulachon*
vendis *vendace*
weever poisonous, akin to *mullet*
wrasse *perch*-like (often cleaners)
zingel akin to *perch*

7

alewife akin to herring
anchovy small, akin to herring
bat-fish have wing-like fins
bergylt of *Scorpaena*
bluecap year-old salmon
bluefish large, voracious
brassie bib or *pout*
bummalo *Bombay duck*
capelin akin to *smelt*
catfish *wolf-fish*, etc.
cavally *horse-mackerel*
chagrin old form of *shagreen*
cichlid any of *Cichlidae*
croaker of *Sciaenidae*
crucian the German *carp*
crusian *crucian*
dogfish small shark
dolphin *dolphin-fish*
dun-fish cured codfish
eelfare brood of young eels
eelpout *burbot*
escolar has spectacled appearance
findram (obs.) *finnan*
finnack *finnock*
finnock young *sea-trout*
garfish the bony pike
garpike *garfish*
garvock *sprat*
goldeye N. American freshwater fish
gourami *goramy*
grindle (f) *bowfin*
grouper various *bass*-like fish
grunter various grunting fish
gudgeon of *Gobius*
gurnard grunts when taken
gwiniad Bala Lake whitefish

gwyniad *gwiniad*
halibut large flatfish
herling *finnock*
homelyn spotted *ray*
holibut *halibut*
jawfish (f) akin to *weever*
jewfish various large fish
keeling codfish
lampern *river lamprey*
lamprey primitive jawless fish
logfish (f) *barrelfish*
mahseer large Indian riverfish
merling (obs.) *whiting*
morwong Australian food-fish
mud-fish mud-burrowing fish
muraena *moray:* moray genus
oar-fish *ribbon-fish*
old wife various fish
Pegasus* a *sea-horse* genus
pig-fish various *grunters*
piranha ferocious riverfish
pollack akin to cod
pollock *pollack*
pomfret various fishes
pompano various fishes
quinnat King salmon
rice eel bubble-nest builder
rock-cod various fishes
sand-eel sand-burrowing eel
sardine young *pilchard*
Scomber mackerel genus
sculpin of *Cottidae*
sea-bass various marine *perch*
sea-dace *bass*
sea-pike pike-like marine fish
sea-wife akin to *wrasse*
sea-wolf *wolf fish*
Silurus *sheat-fish* genus
skegger young salmon
skipper *saury pike*
skulpin *sculpin*
snapper various fish
sockeye chief N. Pacific salmon
spawner adult female fish
speldin *spelding*
spot-fin *bowfin*
spur-dog type of shark
sterlet small *sturgeon*
sun-fish *opah: basking shark,* etc.
topknot small, akin to *turbot*

torgoch *red-bellied char*
torpedo of *Elasmobranchii*
tubfish various *gurnard*
ulichon *eulachon*
vaagmar (f) dealfish
vendace small whitefish
whiting small, akin to cod
Xiphias common *swordfish* genus

8

albacore large *tunny*
albicore *albacore*
Anableps* air/water-sighted genus
Anguilla common eel genus
arapaima largest (4 cwt) freshwater
  fish
band-fish various ribbon-shaped fish
'basilisk' *Jenny Hanniver*
billfish (f) various *swordfish*, etc.
blueback *sockeye*
bluefish large voracious fish
boarfish akin to *horse-mackerel*
bony pike garfish
bullhead (1) *father lasher* (2) *naked*
  catfish
cat shark various sharks
coalfish cod
corkwing kind of *wrasse*
Cottidae sculpin family
cow shark type of shark
chimaera akin to shark
Cyprinus *carp* genus
dragonet *goby*
drumfish of *Sciaenidae*
eagle-ray large *sting-ray*
eulachon *candle-fish*
file-fish of Balistes genus
flounder various flatfish
forktail various fish
foxshark thresher
frog-fish various fish
gillaroo an Irish trout
gilt-head various fish
goatfish *red mullet*
goldfish akin to *carp*
graining *dace*
grey-fish *dogfish* (trade name)

FAUNA – FISH

hair-tail whiplike-tailed fish
hardhead *menhaden: gurnard*, etc.
Holostei order of primitive fish
hornbeak *garfish*
John* Dory* akin to mackerel
kingfish large seafish
klipfish (f) *scaled blenny*
lumpfish clumsy seafish
[1]**lung-fish** fish with lungs
lyre-tail a *killifish*
menhaden oily, akin to herring
millions small, rapid breeders
monkfish *angel shark*
moon-fish *opah*
pickerel young pike
pilchard small, herring-like
pipefish akin to *seahorse*
red mumea (f) *snapper*
rock-cook small-mouthed *wrasse*
rock-fish various sea-bed dwellers
rockling small, akin to cod
roncador various 'snorers'
rosy barb N. Indian *barb*
sail-fish *basking shark: swordfish*
salmonet *samlet*
sardelle *sardel*
scarfish a *parrot-wrasse*
Scopelus luminous-spotted marine
genus
sea-adder *pipefish*: marine stickleback
sea-bream of *Spiridae*
sea-devil *devil-fish*
'sea eagle' *Jenny Hanniver*
seahorse *hippocampus*
sea-hound *dogfish*
sea-perch a bass
sea-robin a *gurnard*
sea-snipe *snipe-fish*
sea-stick herring, cured at sea
sea-swine *ballan-wrasse*
sea-trout salmon-trout
shagreen ray or sharkskin
snake-eel eel without tail-fin
Sparidae spiny-finned fish family
sparling *smelt*

[1] Games players note: *lung-fish* is the form in which this word appears in *Chambers* (and the *Oxford English*) even though other authorities prefer *lungfish*.

spelding dried fish (esp. haddock)
speldrin *spelding*
spirling *sparling*
sting-ray type of *ray*
stonecat (f) of *Ictaluridae*
sturgeon large primitive fish
surf-fish various *perch*-like fish
tarwhine Australian *sea-bream*
toadfish various toad-like fish
trevally various *horse-mackerel*
troutlet a little trout
wolf-fish *bass*
X-ray fish of *Characinidae*

9

anchovies plural of *anchovy*
angel-fish shark: tropical riverfish
blackfish salmon after spawning
black goby *rock-fish*
black ruff type of *ruff*
blind barb Congolese *barb*
blue shark a *grey shark*
bull-trout salmon-trout
bummaloti *bummalo*
Chaetodon* tropical fish genus
choupique *bowfin*
Cichlidae *angel-fish* family
conger-eel large marine eel
Coregonus herring-like salmon genus
coryphene *dolphin-fish* genus
cramp fish *torpedo*
cuckoo ray type of *ray*
devil-fish *angler*
dog-salmon Pacific salmon
ghost fish *glass catfish*
globe-fish various expanding fish
goldfinny *goldsinny*
goldsinny *corkwing*
golomynka oily fish, in Lake Baikal
green-bone *garfish: blenny*
grey shark species source of vitamin A
hippodame (obs.) *seahorse*
horn shark various sharks
hornyhead of *Cyprinidae*
houndfish *dogfish*
jaculator *archer-fish*
killifish (f) family incl. *annual fish*
mako shark fierce shark

neon tetra of *Characinidae*
pike-perch has pike-like jaws
pilot-fish accompanies ships, sharks
porbeagle harmless shark
red mullet type of *mullet*
rock-perch *scorpion-fish*
sand-pride small *river lamprey*
saury pike water-leaping fish
scaldfish smooth *sole*
Scorpaena *scorpion-fish* genus
sea-dragon *seahorse*
sea-lawyer shark
sea-salmon *coalfish*
sheat-fish gigantic European riverfish
snipe-fish *trumpet-fish*
spearfish kind of *swordfish*
speldring *spelding*
stargazer an upward-looking fish
stingaree (f) *sting-ray*
sting-bull *weever*
sting-fish *weever*
stockfish unsalted dried *hake*, etc.
stonefish *scorpion-fish*
surmullet species of *red mullet*
sweetlips (f) *perch*-like, thick-lipped
swordfish upper jaw 'sword'
sword-tail small Cyprinodont
thornback a *ray*
tiger barb striped *barb*
tittlebat *stickleback* (childish word)
troutling a little trout
trumpeter large N. Zealand food-fish
wobbegong *carpet shark*

10

alpine char of *Salmo*
amberjacks (f) akin to *scad*
Amblyopsis mammoth cave blindfish
angel shark *ray*-like sharks
annual fish rainy-season lifespan
archer-fish spits at insect prey
Arctic* char *alpine char*
barracouta *snoek*
barrelfish (f) *rudder-fish*
beacon fish of *Characinidae*
bitterling symbiotically-cared eggs
black bream marine food-fish
black molly of *Mollienesia*

black shark akin to *barb*
black widow of *Characinidae*
Bombay duck small, akin to salmon
bony-tongue primitive 'air breather'
brown trout of *Salmo*
butter-fish various slimy fish
candle-fish oily, dried and used as candle
Cestracion Port Jackson shark
chum salmon *dog-salmon*
coelacanth of great antiquity
common carp ancient fertility symbol
Cyprinidae *carp* family
demoiselle akin to *wrasse: tiger shark*
dragon-fish *dragonet*
elfin shark grotesque shark
fingerling *parr*
flutemouth akin to *stickleback*
flying barb a leaping *barb*
German* carp *carp* without barbels
golden barb C. Indian *barb*
golden orfe akin to *carp*
grey mullet *perch*-like
jewel tetra type of *tetra*
lemon shark type of shark
lumpsucker clumsy seafish
mirror carp large scales on flanks
'monkeyfish' *Jenny Hanniver*
mud-skipper 'air breathing' *goby*
pigmy shark smallest (10½″ max.) shark
pink salmon small Canadian salmon
Polypterus *Crossopterygian* genus
pufferfish self-inflating fish
rabbit-fish herring: *chimaera*, etc.
'ray monster' *Jenny Hanniver*
red herring cured, dried herring
red piranha a *piranha*
ribbon-fish long slender fish
rock salmon *wolf-fish* (trade name)
rock turbot *wolf-fish* (trade name)
rudder-fish *pilot fish*
sand-launce *launce*
sand-sucker the rough *dab*
Sciaenidae noise-producing family
Scombresox *skipper* genus
sea-leopard *wolf-fish* skin
sea-poacher *pogge*
sea-surgeon ·spiny-finned fish
sea-swallow flying fish

FAUNA – FISH

sheath-fish *sheat fish*
silver-fish various white fish
square-tail preys on jellyfish
striped drum of *Sciaenidae*
tiger shark voracious striped shark
triple-tail tropical, *perch*-like
whale shark largest shark
white beam akin to *carp*
yellow-tail *rainbow runner*
zebra shark striped *carpet shark*

11

Amazon* molly female-only species
Atlantic cod important food fish
anemone fish shelters among lethal
  tentacles
bellows-fish akin to *pipe-fish*
brown meagre largest of *Sciaenidae*
carpet shark various sharks
cleaner fish various parasite-feeders
common skate member of 100 species
  genus
crucian carp akin to *goldfish*
dolphin-fish brilliant death colours
electric eel akin to *carp*
fishing-frog *devil-fish*
gattorugine (f) *Tompot blenny*
goblin shark *elfin shark*
hippocampus small, horse-like fish
  genus
Ictaluridae a small freshwater catfish
  family
Jack* Dempsey *cichlid*
lake herring of *Coregonus*
lantern-fish luminous marine fish
Mollienesia the molly genus
Moorish* idol akin to *surgeon-fish*
prickleback *stickleback*
pumpkinseed (f) aquarium *sun-fish*
salmon-trout of *Salmo*
sea-hedgehog a *globe-fish*
sea-scorpion *scorpion-fish*
shagreen ray thick-skinned *ray*
smooth hound type of shark
soldier-fish *squirrel-fish*
speckled cat *bowfin*
stickleback small, spiny-backed
striped bass a *'rock-fish'*

sucking-fish has adhesive disc
surgeon-fish has blade-like keel
trumpet-fish *bellows-fish*
two-spot barb Sumatran *barb*
unicorn-fish has curious conical horn

12

alligator gar *garpike*
Antarctic cod akin to icefish
ballan wrasse British *wrasse*
basking shark often motionless
beaked salmon of *Salmo*
blind cave barb African eyeless fish
bramble shark alligator *dogfish*
brook lamprey British *lamprey*
Characinidae *dorado/piranha* family
climbing perch air breather
common blenny shanny-out-of-water
'crucifixfish' skull of certain *catfish*
cuckoo wrasse pretty-coloured *wrasse*
cucumber-fish lives inside sea
  cucumbers
deep-red tetra type of *tetra*
dwarf gourami air breather
father lasher *sculpin*
fighting-fish pugnacious male
frilled shark primitive, elongated shark
glass catfish transparent *catfish*
golden salmon *dorado*
great pointer great white shark
Johnny* darter male defends eggs
lesser weever *weever*
long rough dab akin to *halibut*
Malayan angel aquarium fish
miller's thumb *sculpin*
mosquito-fish akin to tooth-carp
naked catfish of *Ictaluridae*
parrot-wrasse of *Scarus*
piked dogfish *spur-dog*
²Prussian carp *carp* without barbels
rainbow trout of *Salmo*
red swordtail *platy* crossbreed
requiem shark *grey shark*
river lamprey British *lamprey*

² Games players note: as the phrase *prussian blue* is the only form in which the word *prussian* is shown in *Chambers* without a capital letter so its validity for play is extremely doubtful.

sail-fin molly of *Mollienesia*
scaled blenny live-bearing *blenny*
scorpion-fish usually poisonous
sergeant-fish akin to mackerel
silver salmon N. Pacific salmon
sleeper shark any Arctic shark
squirrel-fish face vaguely like squirrel
sucking loach aquarium 'cleaner'
thornback ray common British *ray*
Tompot blenny largest British *blenny*
wagtail platy *platy* crossbred
white piranha a large *piranha*
Zambesi shark estuary and river shark

13

armed bullhead bony-plated fish
black-ruby barb Ceylonese *barb*
black sea bream *black bream*
black bullhead akin to *catfish*
brown bullhead *naked catfish*
bronze catfish type of *catfish*
buffalo sucker has terminal mouth
Burnett salmon Australian *lungfish*
butterfly-fish various fish
cardinal tetra of *Characinidae*
catfish madtom (f) of *Ictaluridae*
checkered barb Sumatran *barb*
Chinook* salmon akin to *coho*
climbing perch capable of leaving water
Cornish sucker a clingfish
deep-sea angler female absorbs tiny male
greater weever *weever*
horse-mackerel a family of various fish
Indian catfish air breather
Jenny* Han(n)iver skate's head con trick
Japanese Hi-goi golden *carp*
leafy seahorse seaweed-skin disguise
luminous shark *sleeper shark*
mackerel shark permanently cruises
mailed catfish air breather
mermaid's-purse egg case of *skate*, etc.
Midwater shark small shark
pepper catfish *leopard catfish*
porcupine-fish spiky, akin to *puffer-fish*
rainbow runner akin to *horse-mackerel*

rainbow wrasse a cleaner
smooth dogfish *hound*
thresher shark 'long-tailed' shark
yellow surgeon a *surgeon-fish*

14

African catfish air breather
Atlantic salmon British salmon
anadromous fish marine river-breeders
bottle-nosed ray a European *ray*
Crossopterygii nearly extinct species subclass
Cutter's* cichlid eggs have stalks
Elasmobranchii cartilaginous-skeleton class
emperor snapper warm-water shore fish
glowlight tetra of *Characinidae*
great blue shark large *grey shark*
Greenland shark *sleeper shark*
humpback salmon *pink salmon*
humpback sucker sharply-keeled back
leopard catfish type of *catfish*
long-nosed skate type of *skate*
long-nose sucker type of *sucker*
orange chromide a *cichlid*
red-bellied char type of *char*
spotted cichlid 'kiss' in courtship
spotted dogfish type of shark
steelhead trout N. Pacific trout
sucking catfish aquarium 'cleaner'
viviparous barb lays eggs
yellow bullhead *naked catfish*
zebra killifish type of *killifish*

15/16/17

armoured catfish type of *catfish*
black rudder-fish *barrelfish*
butterfly blenny a *blenny*
electric catfish can discharge 350 volts
great white shark most dreaded man-eater
hammerhead shark oddly-shaped shark
labyrinthfishes air breathers
marbled bullhead *naked catfish*

peacock flounder tropical Atlantic flatfish
Quillback sucker type of *sucker*
rummy-nosed tetra small Amazon River fish
scaleless blenny a *blenny*

spotted wolf-fish largest blenoid
Spanish mackerel a 'club mackerel'
blockhead cichlid has head-lump
catadronomous fish freshwater marine-breeder
shanny-out-of-water a *blenny*

FAUNA – INSECTS AND ARACHNIDS

3

bot *botfly* maggot
dor kind of *dung-beetle*
lak *lakh*
nit egg or young of *louse*
pug *pug-moth*
sow *sow-bug*

4

bott *bot*
cleg *gadfly*: horse-fly
dart *dart-moth*
dorr *dor*
frit small wheat-destructive fly
goat *goat-moth*
grig cricket: *grasshopper*
grub an insect *larva*
lakh (100,000) *lak-insect*
lice plural of *louse*
mawk *maggot*
pupa stage between *larva* and *imago*
puss *puss-moth*
tick blood-sucking acarid
zimb *dipteran*, cattle pest

5

acari plural of *acarus*
aphid sucks plant juices
aphis *aphid*, of *Homoptera*
borer any boring insect
brize *gadfly*: *botfly*
Cimex* bed-bug genus
comma butterfly

Culex* gnat genus
drake *Ephemera*
drone male honey-bee
eggar *egger*
egger moth from egg-shaped *cocoon*
emmet ant
eruca (f) caterpillar
imago final 'perfect' stage
larva immature active state
louse wingless parasite
midge small gnat-like fly
Musca house-fly genus
pupae plural of *pupa*
Pulex flea genus
Tinea* clothes-moth genus
Vespa* common wasp genus

6

acarus mite
ant cow *aphis*, ant's 'dairy' creature
aphids plural *aphid/aphis*
botfly horse intestine larval parasite
breese *brize*
breeze *brize*
burnet *burnet moth*
caddis larva of *caddis-fly*
chafer a beetle
chigoe flea under toe-nail
chigre *chigoe*
chinch bed-bug (USA)
cicada very noisy, of *Homoptera*
cicala *cicada*
Coccus* a genus of *Hemiptera*
cocoon egg-nest: stage-chamber
Cynips a *gall-wasp* genus
day-fly *mayfly*

dog-bee *drone*
dor-bug *cockchafer* (USA)
dor-fly *dor*
earwig of *Dermaptera/Forficula*
elater *skipjack beetle*
Epeira* common garden spider (etc.) genus
epizoa plural of *epizoon*
gadfly blood-sucking cattle pest
graine *silkworm* eggs
hopdog *tussock-moth* caterpillar
hop-fly hop-infesting greenfly
hopper *grasshopper*
hornet large kind of wasp
jigger *chigoe*
lappet *lappet moth*
larvae plural of *larva*
locust highly destructive migrators
looper *pug-moth* caterpillar
maggot legless *grub*
mantid forelegs in 'prayer'
Mantis* the *mantid* genus
may-bug *cockchafer*
mayfly *Ephemera*
mygale bird-catching spider
saw-fly has saw-like ovipositor
scarab *dung-beetle*, sacred
sow-bug a *wood-louse*
sphinx a hawk moth
Termes a *termite* genus
Thecla hair-streak butterfly genus
[1]Thrips* minute black insect genus
Tipula* *daddy-long-legs* genus
tsetse *tsetse-fly*
veneer *veneer-moth*
weevil of *Rhynchophera*

beet-fly *larvae* feed on beet
boat fly back-swimming *water-bug*
buzzard blundering insect
caddice *caddis*
chigger *chigoe*
cornfly *gout-fly*
culicid gnat
Diptera two-winged insects
dog-tick dog pest
duck-ant Jamaican *termite*
epeirid of *Epeira*
epizoon skin-surface dweller
firefly luminous beetle
gall-fly *gall-wasp*
goutfly wheat-boring fly
grayfly (obs.) unknown insect
hexapod six-footed creature
hop-flea hop-infesting beetle
hornbug (f) *stag-beetle*
katydid akin to *grasshopper*
ladybug *ladybird*
ladycow *ladybird*
ladyfly *ladybird*
lamp-fly *glow-worm? firefly?*
Papilio* *swallow-tail* butterfly genus
pismire ant
pug-moth small type of moth
rose-bug rose-eating beetle
sand-fly *midge*: moth-like midge
Stylops a parasite genus
termite ant-like social insect
Tortrix* a moth genus
Vanessa* *red admiral* genus
wax-moth *bee-moth*
wood-ant forest ant: destructive *termite*

7

8

ant-lion *larva* trap ants
army ant migratory carnivore
aphides *aphids*
bee-moth *larvae* feed on young bees

[1] Games players note: *thrip*, an erroneous 'singular' form, is valid for play. The correct plural of an individual *thrips* is either *thrips* or *thripses*. Both *thrip* and *thrips* are valid for all games; *thripses* only for those games which permit plural forms.

arachnid of *Arachnida*
corn-moth akin to clothes-moth
cornworm *corn-weevil*
crane-fly *daddy-long-legs*
dart-moth a cutworm moth
dipteran of *Diptera*
dog-louse dog pest
drake-fly *drake*
Ephemera* very short adult life
flesh-fly *larvae* feed on flesh
froth fly *larvae* live in cuckoo spit

FAUNA – INSECTS AND ARACHNIDS

fruit-fly used in heredity experiments
gall-gnat eggs cause plant galls
gall-wasp eggs cause plant galls
glow-worm female beetle and *larva* luminous
goat-moth larval goat-like smell
greenfly *aphid*
Hexapoda insects
Isoptera *termite* genus
lace-wing *lace-wing fly*
ladybird pretty, little round beetles
longhorn *longicorn beetle*
meal-worm beetle *larva* in granaries
mealy-bug hot-house pest
mosquito female blood-suckers
multiped *woodlouse* (obs.)
myriapod of *Myriapoda*
night-fly night-flying fly: moth
pedipalp *whip-scorpion*
puss-moth thick-bodied, hairy
queen-ant fertile female ant
queen-bee fertile female bee
sand-flea *chigoe*
sheep-ked blood-sucking wingless fly
silkworm *larva* of *silkworm moth*
skipjack *skipjack beetle*
stone-fly underwater larval stage
symphile symbiotic ant-guest
Tenebrio* *meal-worm beetle* genus
thief ant smallest ant
water-bug various pond dwellers
wheat-fly various wheat-destructive flies
white ant *termite*
woodlice various arboreal creatures
wood-mite various arboreal mites
wood-tick various arboreal ticks
wood-wasp *gall-wasp*
[2]**wood-worm** wood-boring *larva*

9

amazon-ant slave-raiding ant
Anopheles* germ-carrying *mosquito* genus

[2] Games players note: *wood-worm* is the form in which this word appears in *Chambers* although other authorities prefer *woodworm*.

Arachnida order of spiders, scorpions, mites, etc.
auger-worm *goat-moth* larva
brimstone common yellow butterfly
bumble-bee large wild bee
caddis-fly of *Trichoptera*
cantharis *Spanish fly*
chrysalis *pupa*: pupa-case
churr-worm *fen-cricket*
Cicindela *tiger-beetle* genus
clavicorn clavate-antennaed beetle
cochineal *Coccus*, source of red-dye
cockroach a common insect
corn-borer moth, maize pest
crab-louse infests pubic hair
dor-beetle *dor*
driver ant *army ant*
dumbledor *bumble bee*: brown *cockchafer*
dwarf blue world's smallest-known butterfly
forest fly horse pest
Forficula common earwig genus
gall-midge gall-making *midge*
ghost-moth of ghostly-white appearance
golden-eye lace-wing moth
grass-moth small, frequents grass
Hemiptera ½ leathery ½ membranous wings order
Homoptera alike-wings order
humble-bee *bumble-bee*
ichneumon *ichneumon-fly*
lac-insect found in teeming numbers
large blue British butterfly, extinct 1980
Lomechusa symphile, beetle
longicorn *longicorn beetle*
milk-weed great *monarch* butterfly
millipede of *Myriapoda*
multipede woodlouse (obs.)
Myriapoda multi-legged class
orange-tip a butterfly
orb-weaver type of spider
plant-lice plural of *plant-louse*
sheep-lice plural of *sheep-ked*
sheep-tick *sheep-ked*
sinoekete *synoecete*
small blue smallest British butterfly
sugar-mite infests unrefined sugar

synoecete indifferently tolerated ant-guest
tailor ant leaf-sewn nest builder
tarantula (1) *wolf spider*, venomous, Italy
tarantula (2) bird-catching spider, USA
tarantula (3) non-venomous spider, Africa
tarantula (4) large harmless spider, Australia
tsetse-fly causes sleeping-sickness
tumble-bug a *dung beetle*
turnip-fly *larva* infests turnips
warble-fly akin to *botfly*
wax-insect wax-secreting insect
wheat-moth *larva* devour stored wheat
winged ant ant at reproductive stage
wood-borer various arboreal *larvae*
woodlouse various, including *termite*
worker-ant sterile female ant
worker-bee sterile female bee

10

bark-beetle various bark-tunnellers
bird-spider bird-catching spider
black-widow very poisonous spider
blister-fly *Spanish fly*
bluebottle a large fly
boll-weevil *larvae* infest cotton-bolls
bombardier acrid-fluid-firing beetle
burnet moth fore-wings red-spotted
cabbage-fly *maggot* injures cabbage roots
canker-worm plant-eating *larva*
carpet-moth carpet-eating moth
cheese-mite breeds in cheese
cockchafer *buzzard*, beetle
Coleoptera the beetle order
cornflower *bluebottle*
corn-weevil *corn-moth* larva
death-watch a 'ticking' beetle
deer botfly female, world's fastest fly
Dermaptera order of earwigs
dolphin-fly a black *aphis*
Drosophila* *fruit-fly* genus
dung-beetle dwells in dung
fen-cricket *mole-cricket*
fritillary various butterflies

frog-hopper *froth fly*
hairstreak a butterfly
Hessian* fly a *wheat-fly*
lantern fly lantern-shaped jaw
lappet moth caterpillar has lappets
leaf-hopper various plant-juice suckers
leaf-insect wings imitate leaves
musk-beetle attar of roses smell
Neuroptera a former order of insects
Orthoptera* the *cockroach* order
Phylloxera* genus akin to *greenfly*
pine-beetle various, attack pine-trees
pine-chafer a *pine-beetle*
plant-louse *aphid*
red admiral a popular butterfly
rose-beetle *rose-bug*
rose-chafer *rose-bug*
saltigrade a jumping spider
sand-hopper *sand-flea*
Scaraebeus the *scarab* genus
sheep-louse *sheep-ked*
silver-fish *springtail*
soldier ant *army ant*
Spanish fly traditional aphrodisiac
springtail various insect-like creatures
stag beetle males have 'antlers'
tumble-dung *tumble-bug*
turnip-flea *turnip-fly*
veneer-moth a *grass-moth*
wolf spider the infamous *tarantula*
woolly-bear hairy caterpillar (various moths)

11

balm-cricket *cicada*
black-beetle *cockroach*
cabbage-moth *larva* feeds on cabbage
cabbage-worm moth/butterfly *larva*
cantharides plural of *cantharis*
click-beetle upside-down makes noise
codling-moth causes 'worm-eaten' apples
coprophagan *dung-beetle*
emperor moth large British moth
froth-hopper *froth fly*
grasshopper akin to *locust* and cricket
Hymenoptera 4 transparent wings order

lace-wing fly gauzy wings, golden eyes
Lepidoptera butterfly and moth order
mole-cricket burrows, mole-like legs
money-spider supposed to bring luck
painted lady thistle-butterfly
scale insect of *Homoptera*
scorpion-fly male has upturned abdomen
stick-insect twig-like insect
swallow-tail largest native British butterfly
tiger-beetle carnivore
Trichoptera hairy-winged order
tussock-moth caterpillar has hair 'tussocks'
vine-fretter vine-infesting insect
walking twig *stick insect*
water-beetle swimming beetle
water-spider an aquatic spider

water-strider various, long-legged
whip-scorpion of *Arachnida*
white admiral akin to *red admiral*
wood-engraver type of beetle

13

blister-beetle *cantharis*
daddy-long-legs long-legged fly
diamond beetle a beautiful *weevil*
fiddler spider *brown-recluse*
goliath-beetle bulkiest of all insects
house-longhorn timber-destructive beetle
leaf-cutter ant cultivates own fungus-food
leather-jacket *crane-fly* grub
purple emperor large British butterfly

12

brown-recluse most-poisonous spider
button spider highly poisonous
buzzard-clock *cockchafer*
cabbage-white a butterfly
carpenter bee excavates nest in wood
cheese-hopper fly, breeds in cheese
cinnabar moth large red moth
diadem spider common garden spider
great monarch largest British butterfly visitor
ground beetle akin to *tiger-beetle*
hawk-head moth fastest moth, 33 mph
ichneumon-fly parasitic wasp
legionary ant *army ant*
money-spinner *money-spider*
Rhynchophora beetles with snouts
silkworm moth scents female 6½ miles
walking-stick *stick insect*
walking-straw *stick insect*
water-boatman a *water-bug*

14

cardinal spider 5″ leg span
Colorado beetle infamous potato pest
comma butterfly 'commas' on wings
death's-head moth death's-head hawk moth
great owlet moth has 12″ wingspan
Hercules beetle 6½″ body length
meal-worm beetle adult *meal-worm*
skipjack beetle a clip-beetle

15

brown cockchafer type of beetle
funnel-web spider highly poisonous
golden orb-weaver catches birds in 12′ web
Indian atlas-moth has 12″ wingspan
longicorn beetle 3″ body, 10½″ + antennae

FAUNA – MOLLUSCS, FOSSILS, SHELLS, ETC.

3

Mya a *mollusc* genus
Uca a *crab* genus

4

clam edible *shellfish*
Clio shell-less *Pteropoda*
crab decapod crustacean
slug a land *mollusc*
spat *shellfish* spawn
Unio freshwater pearl-*mussel* genus

5

Bulla* bubble-shell genus
chank of *Gasteropoda*
conch *chank*, shell as trumpet
gaper of *Mya*
krill phosphorescent shrimps
Murex* gasteropod genus, yields
   purple dye
Nassa *dog-whelk* genus
poulp octopus
prawn shrimp-like crustacean
Sepia* *cuttlefish* genus
snail terrestrial gasteropod
Solen* razor-fish *genus*
squid any decapodan cephalopod
Venus* venus-shell genus
whelk various gasteropods
zooid individual of Polyzoa

6

buckie *shellfish*
cockle large *bivalve* mollusc

cowrie gasteropod, used as money
cuttle of *Sepia*
dodman *snail*
isopod tightly clinging gasteropod
Loligo common *squid* genus
medusa *jellyfish*
muskle (obs.) *mussel*
mussel marine/freshwater *shellfish*
oyster edible *shellfish*
partan the edible *crab*
quahog *clam*, of Venus
sea-ear an ear-shell
sea-egg *sea-urchin*
sea-pen marine polyp colony
shrimp small edible crustacean
sponge an aquatic animal
Triton* large-gasteropod genus
urchin *sea-urchin*

7

abalone *sea-ear*
acaleph *jellyfish*
asterid *starfish*
bivalve shell in two halves
Cidaris* a *sea-urchin* genus
copepod minute crustacean
decapod ten-limbed
   crustacean/cephalopod
echinus *sea-urchin*
fiddler *fiddler-crab*
lobster large edible crustacean
mollusc limbless invertebrate
pandore esteemed *oyster* variety
Patella* limpet genus
Sabella* a *sea-worm* genus
sea-hare of *Gasteropoda*
sea-star *starfish*
sea-worm any marine worm
Terebra* a gasteropod genus

FAUNA – MOLLUSCS, FOSSILS, SHELLS

8

ammonite a fossil cephalopod
amphipod a small crustacean
Asterias *crossfish* genus
barnacle a *cirripede*
calamary *squid*
crawfish *crayfish*
crayfish freshwater *lobster*
dog-whelk small *whelk*
lancelet one of the lowest vertebrates
sea-acorn acorn-shell
sea-mouse a *chaetopod*
starfish akin to *sea-urchin*

9

Brachyura crabs
cone shell of *Gasteropoda*
Crustacea aquatic *Arthropoda*
chaetopod bristle-crawling worm
cirripede a degenerate crustacean
crossfish *sea-urchin*
devil crab *velvet crab*
fishlouse crustacean parasite
jellyfish jelly-bodied creature
nemertine worm-like marine animal
Pteropoda swimming *Gasteropoda*
razor-clam *razor-fish*
razor-fish a *bivalve* mollusc
sea-nettle *jellyfish*
sea-sleeve *cuttlefish*
sea-spider of *Arthropoda*
sea-squirt primitive marine animal
sea-urchin slimy, spherical animal
shellfish any shelled marine
  invertebrate
tuckshell type of *mollusc*
waterflea various, minute crustacean
woodlouse *isopod* crustacean

10

Arthropoda segmented bodies, jointed
  appendages
auger-shell of *Terebra*
Brachiopoda class akin to worms, etc.
cuttlebone internal shell of *cuttlefish*
cuttlefish cephalopod, ejects black ink
periwinkle edible gasteropod
razor-shell *razor-fish*
ribbonworm a *nemertine*
sandhopper small crustacean
sandsaucer sea-snail's egg mass
sea-blubber *jellyfish*
velvet crab *velvet-fiddler*
venus-shell animal and shell

11

brittle-star akin to *sea-urchin*
Cephalopoda highest class of *mollusc*
fiddler crab male has enlarged claw
Gasteropoda a *mollusc* class
oyster-shell shell of *oyster*
sea-crawfish *sea-crayfish*
sea-crayfish spiny *lobster*
sea-cucumber akin to *sea-urchin*
sea-hedgehog *sea-urchin*
Stomatopoda the *mantis shrimp* order

12

Branchiopoda *Crustacea* subclass
mantis shrimp legs near mouth
sea-butterfly of *Pteropoda*

13

dog-periwinkle *dog-whelk*
mermaid's glove largest British *sponge*
velvet-fiddler velvety swimming *crab*

FAUNA – REPTILES AND AMPHIBIANS

3

asp poisonous snake, Cleopatra's supposed killer
boa any large constrictor
eft newt, terrestrial larval stage

4

apod limbless animal
boma *boa* or *anaconda*
Bufo* toad genus
emys freshwater terrapin
gila a venomous lizard
Hyla *tree-frog* genus
Rana* frog genus

5

Agama lizard genus
Anole *chameleon*-like reptile
Anura tailless amphibians
Apoda limbless amphibians
aspic *asp*
Draco dragon-lizard
Elaps *coral-snake* genus
gecko lizard
guana any large lizard
Hydra* mythical monster
krait deadly rock snake
mamba large deadly snake
skink African lizard
Racer* a *Coluber* snake
varan a *monitor*

6

Anguis *blind-worm* genus
aspick *asp*
caiman *cayman*
cayman an *alligator*
dipsas non-venomous snake

garial slender-snouted crocodile
iguana a *monitor*
karait *krait*
moloch harmless spiny lizard
mugger Indian crocodile
'red eft' *red spotted newt*
Ridley species of turtle
Sauria reptile order
taipan deadliest Australian snake
womas Australian constrictor
worral *monitor*
worrel *worral*

7

agamoid thick-tongued lizard
Aglossa tongueless frog
Ajolote a *worm-lizard*
axolotl larval *mole-salamander*
Caudata tailed amphibia
Coluber* non-venomous snake genus
gharial *garial*
hicatee freshwater tortoise
Hylidae *tree-frogs*
Lacerta a lizard genus
langaha wood-snake
monitor very large lizard
oak toad American toad
Ophidia order of snakes
paddock toad or frog
rattler rattlesnake
sand boa a constrictor
tuatara 'living fossil' lizard
Urodela tailed amphibia
Varanus *monitor* genus
Xenopus *clawed frog* genus
Zonurus lizard genus

8

anaconda gigantic water-*boa*
Arum* frog a white frog
basilisk monster; lizard

FAUNA – REPTILES AND AMPHIBIANS

bullfrog a large frog
cerastes a horned viper
Chelonia a reptile order
Cook's boa a constrictor
dinosaur any extinct huge reptile
hiccatee *hicatee*
jararaca a venomous snake
matamata S. American river turtle
moccasin venomous *pit viper*
platanna pregnancy-test frog
pit viper bodyheat-detecting snake
rosy boa a constrictor
sea-snake venomous marine snake
slow worm a legless lizard
terrapin water tortoise
tree-frog toad-like arboreal frog
wood frog dead-leaf dweller

9

alligator crocodile-like reptile
Aistopoda a fossil-amphibian order
blindworm legless lizard
boomslang large *tree snake*
box turtle hinged-shell turtle
bull snake a 'bellowing' constrictor
Cape* cobra S. African snake
chameleon colour-changing lizard
file snake a *wart snake*
galliwasp W. Indian lizard
ghost frog peculiar S. African frog
ground boa a constrictor
hairy frog male has a fur-like skin
hamadryad large venomous snake
king cobra snake-only diet
king snake a constrictor
kloof frog adhesive-fingered frog
Iguanodon *dinosaur*
mole viper slender African adder
mud turtle thick-skinned turtle
ophidians snakes
Pelodytes a frog genus
pipe snake non-venomous snake
puff adder thick venomous snake
ring-snake English grass snake
rubber boa a constrictor
sheep frog a 'bleating' frog
tommygoff (f) *fer-de-lance*
Trachodon a *dinosaur*

tree snake arboreal snake
tree viper African viper
wart snake rough-skinned snake
warty newt aquatic only for mating
whip-snake various whip-like snakes
worm snake burrowing snake

10

bandy-bandy small venomous snake
black mamba the fastest snake
black snake various types of snake
blind snake burrowing snake
bushmaster big venomous snake
chamaeleon *chameleon*
clawed frog pregnancy-test frog
cockatrice fabulous monster
copperhead venomous snake
coral-snake small venomous snake
Cotylosaur an extinct reptile
crag lizard S. African lizard
Crocodylia crocodile order
death-adder venomous Australian
  snake
Diplodocus extinct biped reptile
edible frog European delicacy
eyed lizard Spanish lizard
fer-de-lance a *pit-viper*
glass snake a legless lizard
green mamba arboreal *mamba*
hellbender large American
  salamander
horned frog bizarre toad-like frogs
horned toad a lizard
loggerhead a large sea-turtle
long mugger a crocodile
megalosaur gigantic *dinosaur*
musk turtle a small turtle
natterjack European running toad
night adder primitive viper
pteranodon largest-ever flying
  creature
puff adder highly venomous African
  snake
racerunner (f) a lizard
rainbow boa a constrictor
rock python large Australasian
  constrictor
salamander newt-like amphibian

sand lizard a lacertid
sidewinder a rattlesnake
smooth newt aquatic only for mating
star tortoise Asiatic tortoise
tiger snake Australian snake
whip lizard S. African lizard
worm-lizard little-known reptile

11

banded krait venomous Asian snake
black cayman huge *caiman*
bush squeaker a frog
carpet viper venomous desert snake
cottonmouth *water moccasin*
crested newt European newt
diamondback (f) a rattlesnake
flying gecko arboreal lizard
forest cobra arboreal snake
Gaboon viper a *puff adder*
garter snake a harmless snake
gila monster a venomous lizard
green iguana colour fades in captivity
green lizard European lizard
green turtle basis of turtle soup
Gymnophonia *Apoda*
Indian cobra Asiatic cobra
Kemp's* Ridley a turtle
leather-back the *leathery turtle*
leopard frog American frog
midwife toad male nurses eggs
Nile monitor a lizard
Oligokyphus mammal-like *dinosaur*
Olive* Ridley a turtle
Papua turtle thick-skinned turtle
pterodactyl extinct flying reptile
royal python a constrictor
snake-lizard a lizard
spotted Rana* a frog
Stegosaurus a *dinosaur*
Surinam toad a tongueless frog
thirst snake small inoffensive snake
thorny devil a *Moloch*
thread snake burrowing snake
triceratops a *dinosaur*
water lizard 3ft. lizard
white dragon Chinese *salamander*

12

Anguid lizard snake-like lizard
brontosaurus a *dinosaur*
caiman lizard big lizard
coal tortoise carrion feeder
flat tortoise S. African tortoise
flying dragon arboreal lizard
grey tree-frog incredibly immobile frog
Komodo dragon a 9ft. *monitor*
marine iguana seaweed-eating lizard
pond tortoise web-footed tortoise
pterodactyle *pterodactyl*
sunbeam snake a harmless snake
wood tortoise carrion-feeder

13

Cheirotherium *labyrinthodont*
Cuba crocodile length to 7ft.
frilled lizard semi-arboreal lizard
giant tortoise longest-living tortoise
Greek tortoise a tortoise
green tree-frog N. American frog
hog-nosed snake non-venomous snake
marsupial frog *tree frog*
Nile crocodile length to 33ft.
Nyika squeaker a frog
red-banded frog a walking frog
Russell's viper deadly Indian snake
Siam crocodile like *Cuba crocodile*
spade-foot toad toad with digging foot
tyrannosaurus a *dinosaur*
waterlily frog spawns on waterlilies
water moccasin venomous American
 snake

14

boa constrictor a large constrictor
cobra da capello an *asp*
earless monitor a lizard
egg-eating snake incredible swallowing
 capacity
emerald tree boa a constrictor
fire salamander a type of newt
flowerpot snake small blind snake
four-lined snake European snake

golden tree-frog arboreal frog
gopher tortoise desert-dwelling tortoise
labyrinthodont extinct amphibian
leathery turtle thick-skinned turtle
mole salamander unusual Mexican
  amphibian
red spotted newt *'eft'* stage on land
roofed tortoise African tortoise
saw-scaled viper the deadliest viper
snapping turtle aggressive turtle
spider tortoise partly articulated
  armour

swamp crocodile length to 13ft.

15

alligator lizard snake-like lizard
common milk snake harmless snake
giant salamander largest living
  amphibian
golden tree snake a flying snake
hawksbill turtle the source of
  'tortoiseshell'
rhinoceros viper a puff adder

FLORA

adv any plant of the division of
afm any plant of the family of
ags any plant of the genus of
ak. akin to
ex in former times was used as a
ff fruit, fruit of
fl. flower, flowers
fm family, family of
gs genus, genus of
Gs The genus of
m marine
papilio. papilionaceous
pl. plant, plants
scf source of
sp. a species of
tf a type of
tfs a type of all the following
trop. tropical
vf variety of
vp various kinds of plants/trees
vr various
wd the wood of ------- (tree)
notes (1) Many hyphenated words are optional forms.
  (2) Headwords in ***bold italics*** are botanical terms or non-specific words.
  (3) Headwords in CAPITALS are flowers or plants which, as a gift, have a traditional
    meaning.
  (4) Crossword addicts: In clues 'flower' often means 'river'!

2

bo *bo tree*
ti a small liliaceous tree

3

ala (1) *ff* membranous outgrowth
ala (2) pea *fm* side petal

ala (3) milkworts' side sepal
ala (4) a leafy expansion
ash tree of olive *fm*
asp *aspen*
ava *sp.* pepper
awn beard of barley (etc.)
bay the laurel tree (etc.)
bel *bael*
ben horse-radish seed
BOX* 'loyalty and courage'
box evergreen tree/shrub
bud rudimentary shoot
bun a dry stalk
bur *burr*
bur club-moss (Scotland)
cep *tf* edible mushroom
cos a long-leaved lettuce
dal the pigeon-pea
elm any tree of *Ulmus*
ers the bitter vetch
fig tree/fruit
fir various conifers
fog grass after haymaking
fog moss (Scotland)
haw *ff* hawthorn
hay dry cut grass (etc.)
hep *hip*
hip *ff* (dog) rose
hop *pl.* of mulberry *fm*
imp a shoot or graft (obs.)
ita miriti palm
ivy an evergreen climber
jak *jack*
kat shrub, spindle-tree *fm*
kex a dry (hollow) stalk
kex any tall umbellifer
koa Hawaiian acacia
lis (1) fleur-de-lys
lis (2) a plural of (1)
may may-blossom
meu baldmoney or spignel
nep catmint
nim margosa, *sp.* Melia
nip *nep*
nur *knur*
nut (1) hard dry indehiscent *ff*
nut (2) seed in hard shell
oak *gs* trees, beech *fm*
oat *gs* grasses
oca *tf* wood-sorrel

ore seaweed
pan *pl.*/seed (*peas, pease, peason*)
pia tropical *pl. scf* arrowroot
pip fruit seed/fruitlet
pit (to remove) fruit-stone
Poa* large *gs* grasses
pod fruit, shell, legume
rue *vr* shrubby plants
rye a grass *ak.* wheat
sal a large Indian tree
sap vital juice: sapwood
soy a *papilio. pl.*/bean
tea tree/leaves *ak.* Camellia
tef a cereal grass
til sesame
tod a bush (usually ivy)
udo *sp.* Aralia
ule *tf* rubber tree
uva grape: grape-like berry
wud wood (Scotland)
yam (1) *sp.* Dioscorea/tuber
yam (2) *vf* potato (Scotland)
yam (3) sweet-potato (USA)
yew any tree of Taxus
zea styles/stigmas of maize

4

Acer *Gs* maple
alae plural of *ala*
alfa *halfa*
alga a seaweed: *m* thallus
Aloe* *gs* liliaceous trees/shrubs
anil indigo *pl., scf* dye
arar the sandarac tree
Arum* *Gs* cuckoo-pint, *wakerobin*
atap the nipa palm
axil angle between leaf/stem
axis main stem/root
bael the Bengal quince
bark rind of trunk/branch
bast inner bark: phloem
bean *vr* leguminous *pl.*/seed
bear barley
beet *pl.* of goosefoot *fm*
bell one of the *bells*
benj *bhang*
bent *gs* slender grass
bent (1) any stiff wiry grass

FLORA

bent (2)   old dried grass stalks
bere *bear*
bhel *bael*
bigg *bear*
bine (1)   slender stem of climber
bine (2)   a flexible shoot
birk *birch*
bito a tree with oily fruit
Bixa *gs trop.* American *pl.*
bulb a subterranean bud
bunt fungus causing stink-brand
burr prickly seed-case
bush large shrub/small tree
chat small, poor quality potato
chay *pl.* of madder *fm*
chou cabbage
cive *chive*
coca Peruvian shrub *ak.* flax
coco coconut-palm
cola *gs* W. African trees
cole various cabbage
coma head of a tree
cone flower/fruit of *vp*
conk a tree disease
cork outer bark of cork-tree
corm short bulbous stem
corn kernel: small hard seed
crab wild, bitter apple/tree
culm a grass or sedge stem
cyme a young shoot
dali tree *ak.* nutmeg
date *ff* date-palm
deal soft wood
dhak an Indian Butea
dhal *dal*
dika wild-mango tree
dill annual *ak.* parsnip
dita tree with a tonic bark
dock weed, nettle-sting antidote
doob dog's-tooth grass
dura *durra*
ebon *ebony*
eddo tuber of *vr* plants
**FERN* 'trust and devotion'
fern a cryptogram
flag iris: reed-grass (Bible)
flax Linum
funk touchwood
gall abnormal growth on *pl.*
gean European wild cherry

**Geum* *gs* rose *fm*
gnar *knar*
gold corn-marigold
guar *tf* legume
haft a winged leaf-stalk
halm *haulm*
hemp *pl.* of mulberry *fm*
herb (1)   *pl.* without woody stem
herb (2)   a medicinal plant
herb (3)   aromatic cooking *pl.*
hule *ule*
husk dry-fruit/seed case
**Ilex* *Gs* holly
ilex holm-oak
irid *afm* iris
iris *fm* plants *ak.* lily
jack tree/fruit (breadfruit *gs*)
kail *kale*
kale cabbage
kali prickly saltwort: glasswort
kans grass *ak.* sugar-cane
kava *sp.* pepper
kelp *vr* brown seaweed
khat *ket*
kilp *kelp*
kina *quina*
knag a knot in wood
knar a knot on a tree
knop a bud
knot (1)   buried base of branch
knot (2)   joint in (grass) stem
knur knob/knot of wood
kola *cola*
lana genipap wood
leaf transpiration organ of *pl.*
lily (1)   *sp.* Lilium
lily (2)   fleur-de-lys
lima Lima bean
lime (1)   *tf* lemon tree/fruit
lime (2)   the linden tree
lind *lime* (2)
line *lime* (2)
ling heather
lobe division of a leaf
loco *vr* leguminous *pl.*
lote lotus
mace a spice from nutmeg
mate *sp.* holly
**MINT* 'passion consumes me'
mint *ags* Mentha

moly *sp.* wild onion
more root: stump
MOSS* 'constant friendship'
moss (1) any of the Musci
moss (2) *vr* Musci-like *pl.*
moss moss-rose
mowa *mahwa*
Musa *Gs* banana
nabk Christ's thorn
nard spikenard: matweed
neem *nim*
neep turnip (Scotland)
Nipa a brackish-water palm
node point where leaf attaches
nurr *knur*
okra *sp.* Hibiscus
Olea *Gs* olive, Oleaceae *fm*
ombu a S. American tree
palm a (branchless) tree *fm*
pawn *pan*
pear tree/fruit of Pyrus
peas new plural of *pea*
peel rind of fruit
pepo melon/cucumber *tf* fruit
pili nut of *vr* trees
pina pineapple (obs.)
pine (1) *ags* Pinus
pine (2) trees similar to (1)
pine (3) pineapple *pl.*/fruit
pink *ags* Dianthus: *vr* others
pipi a Brazilian *Caesalpina*
pith *pl.* soft tissue
plum tree/fruit (rose *fm*)
poke *vr sp.* Phytolacca
pome an apple-like fruit
poon an Indian tree *scf* oil
pulp soft part of plant
ragi a millet
rami rhea or China grass
rams original singular of *ramson*
Rapa *vr* beet *scf* sugar
rape *pl. ak.* turnip
rasp raspberry
rata a N. Zealand tree
reed tall stiff water grass
rhea *rami*
Rhus* *gs* of cashew-nut *fm*
rice valuable food grass
rice twig(s), small branch(es)
rind bark or peel

root (subterranean) base part
Rosa *Gs* rose, Rosaceae *fm*
ROSE* 'your beauty enchants'
rose shrub/flower of Rosa
rusa an Indian grass
rush *ags* Juncus
rust fungus and *pl.* disease
Ruta *Gs* rue
SAGE* 'my deepest respect'
sage a garden labiate *pl.*
sale *sallow*
seal *sallow*
seed plant embryo
sego a liliaceous *pl.*
seta stalk of moss capsule
shaw visible garden vegetables
shea tree/nut
Sida* *Gs* Queensland hemp
Sium *Gs* water-parsnip
sloe blackthorn bush/fruit
soja *soy*
sola hat-plant or spongewood
soma *pl.* worshipped by Indians
soya *soy*
spud a potato
star *vr* grass/sedge/rush
stem (1) *pl.* leaf-bearing axis
stem (2) a stalk
stem (3) deprive of (1)/(2)
sunn Indian *pl., scf* fibre
sybo cibol: a young onion
tang coarse seaweed
tare (1) various vetch
tare (2) darnel? (Bible)
taro *pl.* of arum *fm*
teak an Eastern timber tree
teel *til*
teff *tef*
tell linden or lime tree
Thea *Gs* tea
toon Indian tree *ak.* mahogany
tree large *pl.* with single trunk
tule large American bulrush
tuna prickly-pear *pl./ff*
tutu a N. Zealand shrub
twig small shoot/branch
ugli grapefruit/tangerine cross
Ulex* *Gs* gorse
upas (1) a fabulous toxic tree
upas (2) toxic tree, mulberry *fm*

FLORA

vine   a woody climber
ware   seaweed
weed   any useless plant
weld   dyer's-rocket
whin   gorse, furze
woad   *gs* of crucifers
wort   any herb/vegetable
yang   *vr* timber trees
Yuca*   *Yucca*
yuca   cassava
zest   orange/lemon peel

5

abele   the white poplar tree
Abies*   *Gs* true firs
Abrus   crab's-eye (*gs* bean)
acorn   fruit of the oak
Agave*   *gs* amaryllids (aloe-like)
agila   eaglewood
ajwan   *ajowan*
alder   *ags* Alnus (*ak.* birch)
Algae*   *fm m* thallophytes
algae   plural of *alga*
algum   (Bible) *wd* red sandalwood?
anana   *ananas*
anise   an umbellifer
Anona   *Gs* custard-apple (etc.)
apple   tree/fruit of Pyrus
apple   pine/custard/oak, etc.
Areca*   *Gs* betel-nut palm
argan   a Moroccan timber-tree
arnut   earth-nut
aspen   the trembling poplar
aspic   *tf* lavender
assai   a S. American palm
ASTER*   'Are you deceiving me?'
aster   Michaelmas daisy
attap   *atap*
Avena   *Gs* oat, grass *fm*
avens   *ags* Geum
babul   *bablah*
bacca   a berry
balsa   corkwood
basil   an aromatic labiate *pl.*
bells   *Campanula*
berry   a simple fruit
berry   coffee bean: cereal grain
betel   leaf of betel-pepper

bhang   leaves/shoots of hemp
birch   a hardy forest tree
blite   various goosefoots
bloom   (to) blossom or flower
borse   *vr* wattle-trees
bract   leaf with *fl.* in axil
brake   a fern: bracken
brank   buckwheat
briar   *brier* (1) (2)
brier (1)   prickly shrub: wild rose
brier (2)   Algerian *white heath*
broom   *tf* shrub
buaze   an African shrub
buchu   S. African medicinal *pl.*
bucku   *buchu*
bugle   *gs* labiate *pl.*
bunya   *sp.* monkey-puzzle
burry   plant with a burr
bussu   *tf* palm
Butea   *gs papilio.* trees
bwazi   *buaze*
cacao   tree *scf* cocoa, chocolate
cacti   a plural of *cactus*
calyx   flower's outer covering
camas   small *pl. ak.* lily *fm*
Canna*   *Gs* Indian shot
Carex*   *gs* sedges, Cyperaceae *fm*
carob   algarroba/locust-tree
carvy   caraway (seed)
cedar   large evergreen conifer
Chara*   *gs* freshwater plants
chard   edible (artichoke) stalks
chaya   *chay*
chich   chick-pea
chile   *chilli*
chili   *chilli*
china   *quina*
chive   an onion-like herb
choux   plural of chou
chufa   sedge with edible tubers
cibol   *vf* onion
clary   a sage
clote   burdock (etc.)
clove   a division of a bulb
clove   clove-tree flower-bud
cocci   plural of coccus
colza   *cole-seed*
copra   dried coconut kernel
couch   *gs* grass *ak.* wheat
cress   various crucifers

cumin an umbellifer
cuple cup-shaped *ff*-envelope
cycad *pl.* resembling fern/palm
dagga Indian hemp
daisy a composite
dholl *dal*
drupe fleshy *ff* with stone
dulse edible red seaweed
durra *tf* grass *ak.* sugar-cane
dwale deadly nightshade
ebony various trees
elder small tree, honeysuckle *fm*
ergot a grass disease
Erica* *Gs* heath
exine *extine*
Fagus *Gs* beech
flora particular *pl.* list
folia plural of *folium*
frond palm or fern leaf
fruit fructification from ovary
fungi a plural of *fungus*
furze whin or gorse
ganja female heads of hemp
gemma a plant bud
Glaux fleshy seaside *pl.*
GORSE* 'thoughts of you'
gorse a *papilio. pl.*
gourd (1) large hard-rinded fruit
gourd (2) any *pl.* with a *gourd*
gowan daisy: oxeye daisy
grain (1) a small hard seed
grain (2) plate of wood
grama an American grass
grape *ff* grapevine
grass common herbage
guaco *vr* medicinal *pl.*
guava small Amer. tree/fruit
gumbo okra or its pods
gutta a latex from trees
halfa esparto (N. Africa)
haulm straw
haver the wild oat
hazel tree of birch *fm*
heath a *fm* of shrubs
henna small oriental shrub
HOLLY* 'be cautious'
holly an evergreen shrub
hypha a fungus thread
icker an ear of corn
istle valuable *pl.* fibre

ixtle *istle*
Jaffa orange from Jaffa, Israel
jalap a purgative root
jambu a rose-apple tree (etc.)
jarul Indian bloodwood
karri an Australian gum tree
kauri a N. Zealand conifer
Khaya* *gs* trees, *ak.* mahogany
knosp unopened flower bud
knurr *knur*
kokra tree of spurge *fm*
kokum an E. Indian tree
kudzu *pl.* with edible tubers
latex 'milk' of rubber tree (etc.)
laver *vr* edible seaweeds
Lemna *Gs* duckweed
lemon tree/citrus fruit
liana any climbing plant
liane *liana*
lilac tree of olive *fm*
loofa *luffa*
lotos *lotus*
lotus (1) various water-lilies
lotus (2) mythical tree (jujube?)
luffa *gs* of gourd *fm*
LUPIN* 'I need consolation'
lupin *fl.* on long spikes *pl.*
mahua *mahwa*
mahwa *tf* butter-tree
maize a staple cereal
Malva* *gs* in Malvaceae
mango (1) tree/fruit cashew-nut *fm*
mango (2) pickled green musk-melon
manna (1) sugary extract *vr* trees
manna (2) float-grass seeds
manna (3) honey-dew
manna (4) edible parts *tf* lichen
maple *ags* Acer
maqui an evergreen shrub
mazer maple
Melia *Gs* nim tree
melic *tf* grass
melon *vr* plants/gourds
merry a *gean*
morel *vr* edible fungi
mould *vr* small fungi
mowra *mahwa*
mulga an Australian acacia
Musci mosses (Bryophyta)
mvule a huge mulberry *fm* tree

FLORA

myall *vr* Australian acacia
myrrh sweet cicely
naras *narras*
navew (1) rape or coleseed
navew (2) a wild Swedish turnip
nelis (1) a winter pear (nelies)
nelis (2) a plural of *nelis*
ngaio a N. Zealand tree
nival growing among snow
nopal *tf* cactus
ocrea a stem sheath
olive tree/oily fruit
ombus plural of *ombu*
onion edible bulb, lily *fm*
orach *gs* of goosefoot *fm*
orpin a stonecrop
Oryza *gs* grasses incl. rice
oshac the ammoniac plant
oxeye a wild chrysanthemum
oxlip *sp.* Primula
paddy rice
padma the sacred lotus
palas *dhak*
palay small tree, dogbane *fm*
Panax* *gs ak.* Aralia
PANSY* 'frequent thoughts of you'
pansy *vr sp.* of violet
papaw (1) tree/fruit (USA)
papaw (2) *papaya* (1)
peach tree/fruit
pease original word for *pea*
pecan hickory tree/nut
PEONY* 'please forgive'
peony *vp* buttercup *fm*
petal a corolla leaf
Phlox* *gs* of garden *pl.*
Picea *Gs* spruce
pilei plural of *pileus*
pinna leaflet
pinon tree/edible pine-seed
Pinus *gs* N. temperate conifers
pipal bo tree
pipul *pipal*
Piper* *Gs* pepper
plane any of Platanus
plant (1) any of vegetable kingdom
plant (2) to set for growth
plant (3) (1) ready for (2)
plant (4) (1) having been (2)
plant (5) sapling: cutting: offshoot

plump a cluster (of trees)
poppy (1) *ags* Papaver
poppy (2) horned poppy (Glaucium)
poppy (3) blue poppy (Meconopsis)
praty potato
prune a dried plum
pulse leguminous seeds as food
Pyrus *Gs* apple/pear (rose *fm*)
quick a couch-grass
quill reed, hollow stalk (obs.)
quina chichona bark
raggy *ragi*
ramee *rami*
ramie *rami*
ratan *rattan*
regma dehiscent splitting *ff*
resin *vr* substances from sap
Rheum* *Gs* rhubarb
Ribes *Gs* red/blackcurrant
rivet bearded wheat
roble various (oak) trees
roosa *rusa*
rowan rose *fm* tree/fruit
Rubia *Gs* madder
Rubus *Gs* bramble, rose *fm*
Rucus *gs* evergreen shrubs
Rumex *Gs* dock and sorrel
runch charlock: wild radish
Sabal *gs* palms incl. Chamaerops
salal an American shrub
salep dried Orchis tubers
Salix* *Gs* willow
sally sallee: sallow
sapan *sappan*
sarsa *sarsaparilla*
sarza *sarsaparilla*
sauch *sallow*
saugh *sallow*
savin *sp.* juniper
scale a reduced leaf (-base)
scrog (1) stunted tree/bush
scrog (2) a broken branch
scrog crab-apple tree/fruit
scrub stunted tree(s)
sedge *ags* Carex
senna *vr* Cassia shrubs
sepal member of a *calyx*
shaya *chay*
shoot stem, leaf parts of *pl.*
shrub a low woody plant

sisal *tf* grass
sorgo *vr* durra
spart esparto
spike *fl.* on a long axis
spike (1) an ear of corn
spike (2) *tf* lavender
spine thorn (modified leaf/branch)
sprig small shoot/twig
sprue inferior asparagus
stalk stem of a plant
starr *star*
Stipa* *Gs* feather-grass
stole *stolon*
stone a hard fruit-kernel
strae straw (Scotland)
straw dried stalks of corn (etc.)
sumac any tree/shrub of Rhus
syboe *sybo*
sybow *sybo*
Taxus *Gs* yew
thorn spine
thorn hawthorn
thyme *ags* Thymus
Tilia *Gs* lime or linden
timbo a S. American climber
trunk stem of a tree
Tsuga *Gs* hemlock spruce
tuart *sp.* Eucalyptus
tuber **(1)** stem swelling (i.e. potato)
tuber **(2)** root swelling (i.e. dahlia)
Tuber* *Gs* truffle (*tf* fungus)
TULIP* 'your beauty dazzles'
tulip *ags* Tulipa
Typha *Gs* reedmace
Ulmus *Gs* elm (*ak.* nettles)
umbel *tf* flat-topped inflorescence
urali *wourali*
urari *wourali*
Usnea* *gs* lichens, tree-moss
varec kelp, wrack
vetch *vr sp.* Vicia esp. tare
Vicia a *papilio. gs*
Viola* *Gs* violet and pansy
Vitis *gs* climbers inc. vine
viver rootlet
volva sheath for *vr* fruit
vraic fuel/manure seaweed
wahoo (1) the burning bush
wahoo (2) a Californian buckthorn
wahoo (3) winged elm: rock elm

wheat *vr* cereal grasses
wicky *quicken* (2)
witch wych-elm: rowan (etc.)
withy any willow
wrack seaweed
xenia double fertilisation
xylem woody tissue
Xyris *gs* sedge-like *pl.*
yacca two different evergreens
yapon *yaupon*
yeast minute fungi
yerba a herb
Yucca* *gs* liliaceous *pl.*
yucca *yuca*
yulan a Chinese magnolia
yupon *yaupon*
Zamia* *gs* palm-like trees
zante (1) wood of smoke-tree
zante (2) satinwood

6

Acacia* *gs* wattle *ak.* Mimosa
acajou cashew tree: *tf* mahogany
acanth acanthus
achene dry indehiscent fruit
Acorus *gs* sweet-flag (arum *fm*)
adnate attached to another organ
agamic asexual: parthenogenic
agaric a fungus (*tf* mushroom)
Aizoon *gs ak.* goosefoots
ajowan *pl.* of caraway *gs*
alerce *wd* sandarich: *tf* arbor vitae
Alisma* *Gs* water-plantain
almond *ff* almond-tree
alsike *tf* clover
Amomun* *gs* ginger *fm*
ananas pineapple: pinguin
anbury a turnip disease
angico a mimosaceous tree
anlage first rudiment of an organ
annual *pl.* with one year's life
anther pollen part of stamen
antiar the upas-tree
Arabis *Gs* rockcress
Aralia* *gs* ivy family
arbute *sp.* Arbutus
archil a lichen, *scf* dye
arolla *tfs* stone-pine, cedar

FLORA

Arnica* *gs* composites
ash-key winged *ff* ash
Aucuba* *Gs* Japan laurel
AZALEA* 'vain regrets, passing fancy'
Azalea* *gs ak.* Rhododendron
bablah *sp.* Acacia
balsam *sp.* Impatiens
bamboo gigantic tropical grass
banana tree-like *pl.*/fruit
banian *banyan*
banyan an Indian fig-tree
baobab (1) monkey-bread tree
baobab (2) cream of tartar tree
barley a hardy-grass
batata the sweet-potato
bennet herb-bennet
bennet a dry grass stalk
betony *vr* labiate plants
Betula *Gs* birch
biffin *vf* apple
bilian an ant-proof tree
bondue the nicker seed
bonsai (Japanese) dwarf tree
borage prickly *pl.* with nutlets
bo tree (1) Buddha's holy tree
bo tree (2) pipal (temple garden *pl.*)
brazil *wd* sappan
briony *bryony*
bryony (1) *white bryony*, English *pl.*
bryony (2) *black bryony*
bulbil bud as potential *pl.*
burnet *great burnet*/*salad burnet*
byssus a fine yellowish flax
cacoon seed, mimosa *fm* climber
cactus *afm* Cactaceae
camash *camas*
camass *camas*
Carapa *gs* trees, mahogany *fm*
Carica *Gs* papaw *ak.* passion-flowers
carpel modified leaf gymnaeceum
carrot *pl.*/root, an umbellifer
cashaw *tf* US pumpkin: mesquite
cashew a spreading *trop.* tree
Cassia* *gs* shrubs, *scf* senna
cassia tree *scf* cinnamon
catkin spike of unisexual *fl.*
catnep *catnip*
catnip catmint
caulis stem of a plant
celery an umbellifer

cembra Swiss stone-pine
cerris the Turkey oak
cherry tree/fruit
chibol *cibol*
chilli pod of Capsicum
chinks *chincherinchee*
cicely *vr, ak.* chervil
Cicuta* *gs* toxic umbellifers
cirrus a tendril
Cistus* *Gs* rock-rose
citron tree/citrus fruit
CLOVER* 'Any hope for me?'
clover *gs papilio. pl.*
Cnicus *gs* thistles
coccus segment of dry fruit
codlin *codling*
cohune *trop.* American palm
conker *ff* horse-chestnut
coonty *coontie*
cornel small tree: alpine herb
corozo (1) a short-stemmed palm
corozo (2) cohune palm
cortex bark or outer skin
corymb flattish-topped raceme
Cosmos* *gs* composites *ak.* dahlia
cotton plant and fibres
cow-pea a leguminous *pl.*
crocus a bulbous iridaceous *pl.*
Croton* *gs trop. pl.* spurge *fm*
cummin *cumin*
cuscus (1) grain of African millet
cuscus (2) root of an Indian grass
DAHLIA* 'Your promises mean nothing'
Dahlia* *gs* Mexican composites
damson a small purple plum
Daphne* *gs* of shrubs
darnel (1) *sp.* rye-grass
darnel (2) the Biblical tares?
Datura* *Gs* thorn-apple, potato *fm*
deodar a Himalayan cedar
Derris* *gs pl., scf* insecticide
diarch having two xylem strands
dodder leafless *pl. ak.* convolvulus
dog-hep *dog-hip*
dog-hip hip of dog-rose
durian a lofty fruit-tree
eddoes plural of *eddo*
endive salad *pl., gs* chicory
eryngo sea-holly

extine   outer skin of spore
farina   pollen
fat-hen   *vr* (goosefoot) *pl.*
fennel   an umbellifer
fescue   *gs* grasses *ak.* brome-grass
fimble   male hemp
fiorin   *vf* creeping bent-grass
floral   of flora/flowers
floret (1)   a small flower
floret (2)   (1) in inflorescence
florid   flowery
folium   a leaf
frijol   kidney-bean
frutex   a shrub
fungus   a sans-chlorophyll
   thallophyte
Funkia*   *gs ak.* day lilies
fustet   Venetian sumach
fustic   *wd sp. trop.* tree
fustoc   *fustic*
garget   poke
garjan   *gurjun*
garlic   a bulbous liliaceous *pl.*
gilcup   buttercup
ginger   root of *sp.* Zingiber
gingko   *gingko*
ginkgo   maidenhair – tree
gollan   *vr* yellow flowers
gomuti   *sp.* palm, *scf* black fibre
gomuto *gomuti*
gru-gru   *vr* American *pl.*
gurjun   a dipterocarp
Hedera   *Gs* ivy, Aralia *fm*
hen-bit   ivy-leaved speedwell
hyphae   plural of *hypha*
Hypnun*   *gs* mosses
hyssop (1)   an aromatic labiate
ʰyssop (2)   an unknown Biblical *pl.*
ilexes   *ilices*
ilices   a plural of *ilex*
intine   pollen inner *film*
irides   a plural of *iris*
irises   *irides*
Isatis   *Gs* woad, Cruciferae *fm*
jarool   *jarul*
jarrah   an Australian tree
jujube   shrub/fruit, blackthorn *fm*
Juncus*   *gs* grass-like marsh *pl.*
jupati   *sp.* Raphia
kamala   tree, spurge *fm*

karaka   N. Zealand tree/fruit
karite   shea-tree
kermes   *kermes oak* (also an insect)
kernel   seed within hard shell
kie-kie   shrub, screw-pine *fm*
kiss-me   *vr* incl. wild pansy
kittul   jaggery palm
knawel   a cornfield weed
kowhai   a shrub: glory-pea
kumara   sweet potato
lablab   a tropical bean
lalang   *tf* coarse grass
LAUREL*   'love triumphant'
laurel (1)   sweet bay tree (classical)
laurel (2)   any *sp.* Laurus
laurel (3)   cherry-laurel
laurel (4)   any Rhododendron
Laurus   *Gs* laurel
lebbek   *trop.* timber tree
legume   a pod of one carpel
lentil   a *papilio. pl.*/seed
lichen   fungus/alga symbiosis
lignum   wood
lignum   *vr* Australian shrubs
Lilium   *gs* in Liliaceae *fm*
linden   *lime* (2)
lisses   *lis* (2)
litchi   *lychee*
locust   locust-bean/-tree
longan   tree/fruit *ak.* lychee
loofah   *luffa*
lovage   *vr* umbellifers
lucern   *lucerne*
lunary   moonwort fern: honesty
lupine   *lupin*
Luzula   *gs* hairy-leaved *pl.*
lychee   Chinese tree/fruit
macoya   palm tree/nut
madder   *pl., scf* red dye
mallee   dwarf Eucalyptus
mallow   *ags* Malva
mammee   W. Indian tree/fruit
mangel   mangel-wurzel
manioc   *sp.* Manihot
manuka   tree of myrtle *fm*
marram   a dune grass
marrum   *marram*
mastic   tree *scf* a gum resin
matico   a Peruvian pepper shrub

FLORA

[1]**mealie (f)** an ear of maize
medick a clover-like grass
medlar small tree/fruit *ak.* apple
Mentha *gs* aromatic labiates
mildew a fungus
millet various grain
mimosa *gs* sensitive plants
miriti various palms
murphy a potato
MYRTLE* 'I, too, care for you'
myrtle an evergreen shrub
nardoo an Australian Marsilea
narras shrub/melon-like fruit
neb-neb bablah pods
nelies singular/plural of *nelis*
nerine an amaryllid *gs*
nettle *ags* Urtica
nickar *nicker*
nicker seed of Caesalpina (etc.)
nucule nutlet
nutlet (1) one seed *ff* portion
nutlet (2) stone of a drupe
nutmeg kernel of a *sp. trop.* tree
obeche large W. African tree
oidium vine-mildew conidial stage
oilnut butter/buffalo-nut (etc.)
orache *orach*
orange tree/citrus fruit
ORCHID* 'I give you all'
orchid any *pl./fl.* Orchideae
Orchis* *gs* (British) orchids
orpine *orpin*
Oxalis* *gs ak.* geranium *fm*
ourali *wourali*
ourari *wourali*
padauk a Burmese tree
padouk *padauk*
paeony *peony*
papaya (1) S. Amer. tree/fruit
papaya (2) *papaw* (1)

pawpaw *papaw* (1) and (2)
peacod pea-pod
peanut *sp.* Arachis
pea-pod pod of pea
peason plural of *pease*
peecul pipul
pepper (1) *ags* Piper
pepper (2) entire berry = black pepper
pepper (3) skinned berry = white pepper
pepper (4) Capsicum *gs* = Cayenne/red
[2]**pig-nut** earthnut (*St Anthony's nut*)
pileus cap of a fungus
pineal pine-cone shaped
pippin *vr vf* apple
pistil ovary of a flower
platan plane
pomelo grapefruit
poplar (1) *gs* trees, willow *fm*
poplar (2) tulip-tree (USA)
PRIVET 'I am wary'
privet shrub of olive *fm*
Protea* *gs* S. African shrubs
Pteris *gs* ferns
ptyxis leaf folding in bud
Pyrola *Gs* wintergreen *ak.* heath
quince (1) tree/fruit *ak.* Pyrus
quince (2) bael-fruit (etc.)
quinoa *sp.* edible goosefoot
quitch couch-grass
raceme *tf* inflorescence
radish a crucifer
raffia Raphia palm/leaf bast
raggee *ragi*
raisin a dried grape
ramsom see *rams, ramsoms*
Raphia* *gs* palms *scf* raffia
rattan a climbing palm
red-bud Judas-tree
red rot an oak disease
rennet *vr sp.* apple
retama *vr* desert switch-plants
Riccia *gs* liverworts
ricker young tree trunk
rocket (1) a salad crucifer
rocket (2) dame's violet (etc.)

[1] Games players note: *mealie* may be acceptable for play as its currency of use is given in *Chambers* as 'esp. in South Africa' implying usage elsewhere. This is confirmed by the entry for *maize* which mentions *mealies*. It is accepted by the *Official Scrabble Players' Dictionary* as valid but other authorities (e.g. *Oxford Illustrated*) confine currency to South Africa.

[2] Games players note: to discover *pignut* (without hyphen) in *Chambers* see *St Anthony's nut*.

rocket (3) winter-cress (etc.)
rocket (4) monkshood (etc.)
rocket (5) larkspur, weld (etc.)
rubber rubber plant/tree
runner ground-running rooting stem
runner kidney-bean *gs* climber
sallal *salal*
sallee *vr* Acacia: *sp.* Eucalyptus
sallow *vr* willow
Salvia* *Gs* sage
samara a winged dry fruit
sandal sandalwood
santal *sandal*
sapele a mahogany-like tree
sappan *sp.* Caesalpina
savine *savin*
savory a labiate herb
saxual grotesque tree, goosefoot *fm*
Scilla* *gs* lily *fm*
senega an American milkwort
sesame *pl. scf* gingili oil
shalot *shallot*
she-oak a casuarina tree
sissoo a *papilio.* tree
Smilax* (climbing) *pl. gs,* lily *fm*
sobole a creeping underground stem
sorgho *sorgo*
sorrel *vr sp.* Rumex
sprout a Brussels sprout
sprout (1) a new growth
sprout (2) young shoot: side bud
sprout (3) to shoot
spruce spruce-fir
spurge *ags* Euphorbia
spurry *spurrey*
squash plant/gourd
squill *vr* incl. sea-onion
stamen pollen organ (male)
stolon a shoot from *pl.* base
struma a cushion-like swelling
sumach *sumac*
[3]**sun-dew** an insectivorous bog *pl.*
sunder *sundari*
sundra *sundari*
sundri *sundari*
syboes a plural of *sybo*
sybows *syboes*

[3] Games players note: to discover *sundew*
(without hyphen) in *Chambers* see *Drosera.*

tamanu a lofty gamboge tree
tangle coarse (edible) seaweed
tewart tuart
Thymus* *gs* low half-shrubby *pl.*
timber growing/cut wood
titoki a N. Zealand tree
tomato *pl./*fruit *ak.* potato
tooart *tuart*
troely *troolie*
Tulipa* *gs* bulbous liliaceous *pl.*
tupelo an American gum-tree
turino an underground bud
turnip *pl./*edible root
tutsan *sp.* St John's wort
twitch *quitch*
Urtica* *Gs* nettles *ak.* elms
varech *varec*
VIOLET* 'modest charm'
violet *ags* Viola: *vr* others
Viscum* *gs* parasitic *pl.*
waboom (f) *wagenboom*
wampee an edible *ff ak.* orange
wattle rods, branches, etc.
wattle *vr* acacias
wicker a small pliable twig
wicken *quicken* (2)
willow *ags* Salix
yarrow two scented plants
yaupon evergreen *ak.* holly

7

abaxial away from the axis
abjoint to cut off
absinth wormwood
acantha a thorn, prickle
aconite wolfsbane, monkshood
acrogen a fern or moss
acerose needle-pointed
ailanto the tree of heaven
alecost costmary
alfalfa a valuable forage *pl.*
alizari levantine madder
alkanet *vp scf* a red dye
allheal valerian
allseed weed *ak.* flax
Alyssum* *gs* crucifers
Amanita* *gs* toadstools
amarant (1) fabled unfading *fl.*

FLORA

amarant (2) *ags* Amarantus
ambatch a pith-tree
ANEMONE* 'a parting'
Anemone* *gs* crowfoot *fm*
aniseed seed of anise
annulus any ring-shaped structure
apricot tree/fruit *ak.* plum
Arachis* Brazilian *gs* of pea *fm*
Arbutus* *Gs* strawberry-tree
babassu a Brazilian palm
Baldwin American *vf* apple
bebeeru Guyanese *greenheart* tree
BEGONIA* 'inconstancy in affection'
Begonia* *gs* tropical *pl.*
bilimbi tree of wood-sorrel *fm*
bistort *pl.* of dock *fm*
blawort harebell
blossom (to) bloom or flower
blue gum *sp.* Eucalyptus
bogbean buckbean
bog-moss *ags* Sphagnum
box-tree *box*
boxwood *box*
bracken a fern
bramble blackberry bush *ak.* raspberry
brinjal (*ff*) egg-plant
bubinga *sp.* W. African tree
bugloss *vr* borage *fm pl.*
bulbous of/pertaining to bulbil
bullace shrub *ak.* sloe
bulrush (1) reed-mace or cat's-tail
bulrush (2) *clubrush*, sedge *fm*
burdock composite: any Xanthium
bur-reed reedlike water *pl.*
Bursera *gs trop.* Amer. trees
burweed *vr* burry *pl.*
cabbage (1) a common vegetable
cabbage (2) edible bud of palms
Calamus* *gs* palms
calamus sweet-flag
Calluna *Gs* heather
campion various plants
cam-wood W. African tree, *scf* dye
Canella *gs* small aromatic trees
caraway an umbellifer
cardoon *ak.* true artichoke
carline any Carline thistle
cascara a Californian buckthorn
cassava (*manioc*) *scf* tapioca

catmint mint-like labiate *pl.*
cat's-ear *vr* British composites
catawba an American grape
Cedrela *gs* trees *ak.* mahogany
champac *champak*
champak Indian tree *ak.* magnolia
chervil an umbellifer
climber a climbing plant
clivers goose-grass
clotber burdock
codling an elongated apple
collard cole-wort
conifer a cone-bearing tree
coontie an American cycad
coquito a Chilean palm
corn-cob axis of a maize ear
corolla floral envelope whorl
Corylus *Gs* hazel
costard large *tf* apple
cowbane water hemlock
cowslip *sp.* primrose
cow-tree tree of mulberry *fm*
cow-weed cow-chervil
creeper any creeping plant
cudweed a woolly composite
Curcuma* *gs* ginger *fm*
cypress a conifer
dagwood *dogwood*
day-lily lily with diurnal *fl.*
Dionaea Venus's fly-trap
dittany an aromatic rutaceous *pl.*
dogbane of Apocynum
dog-rose *sp.* wild rose
dogwood *vr* small trees
Drosera* *Gs sundew* (Droseraceae)
dum-palm *doum-palm*
duramen heartwood
dye-wood any dye-yielding *wd*
egg-pium yellowish egg-shaped plum
Ephedra* *gs* leafless desert *pl.*
epicarp outermost skin of fruit
epithem water-exuding leaf cells
esparto strong (Spanish) grass
felwort a gentian
figwort *vr* incl. *pilewort*
filbert nut of cultivated hazel
Filices the (true) ferns
flybane *vr* insecticidal *pl.*
foliage (1) leaves collectively
foliage (2) a mass of leaves

foliole leaflet of compound leaf
foliose leafy, leaf-like
fox-tail *gs* grasses
frijole *frijol*
frogbit *ak.* water-soldier
FUCHSIA* 'not wanted'
fuchsia *sp.* evening-primrose *fm*
Fumaria *gs* of *fm ak.* poppy
galanga *galingale* (1) (2)
geebung Australian tree/fruit
genipap W. Indian tree/fruit
Genista* *gs* shrubby *pl.*
gentian *vr* herbs
gherkin a small cucumber
giltcup buttercup
gingili *sp.* sesame
ginseng *sp.* Panax/Aralia
Goa bean a *papilio. pl.*/bean
goat-fig the wild fig
Godetia* *gs ak.* evening-primrose
golland *gollan*
gowland *gollan*
gum tree a gum-yielding tree
Gunnera* a gigantic-leaved herb *gs*
hadrome xylem
hag-weed broom
hanepot (f) *haanepot*
haricot kidney-bean
harmala 'African rue'
hawkbit *pl. ak.* dandelion
hayseed grass seed
heather ling, a low shrub
hemlock (1) a toxic umbellifer
hemlock (2) a N. American tree
henbane toxic *pl.,* nightshade *fm*
herbage herbs collectively
herblet a small herb
hickory *gs ak.* walnut
hog-plum tree/fruit, cashew *fm*
hogweed cow-parsnip (etc.)
holm-oak the evergreen oak
honesty a crucifer
hop-tree an American shrub
hop-vine hop
horn-nut water-chestnut
Ipomoea* *gs pl.,* Convolvulus *fm*
ivy-bush bush/branch of ivy
jasmine *gs* oleaceous shrubs
Jew's-ear an ear-like fungus
jinjili *gingili*

JONQUIL* 'love drives me mad'
jonquil *vr sp.* narcissus
Juglans *Gs* walnut
juniper evergreen shrub-conifer
kingcup buttercup
kumquat *tf* orange
labiate of *Labiatae*
Lactuca *Gs* lettuce
Lantana* *gs* shrubs, vervain *fm*
leaflet a little leaf
leafbud bud of leaf
leechee *lychee*
lentisk the mastic tree
lettuce a composite
linseed lint or flax seed
LOBELIA* 'loving thoughts'
Lobelia* *gs* blue-flowered *pl.*
lucerne purple medick, alfalfa
lumbang candle-nut tree (etc.)
lycopod club moss (etc.)
madrona *madrono*
madrono an evergreen arbute
malmsey *vf* grape
mangoes plural of *mango*
mangold mangel-wurzel
mandioc manioc (Manihot *gs*)
Manihot *gs pl.* spurge *fm*
manjack W. Indian tree/fruit
margosa tree *scf* nim oil
marybud the marigold bud
mastich mastic or lentisk
matweed a small moorland grass
mawseed poppy seed
maycoya palm tree/nut
may-duke *vf* sour cherry
mayweed (1) stinking camomile
mayweed (2) corn feverfew (etc.)
melitot a clover-like *gs*
milfoil yarrow (etc.)
Mimulus* *gs* of figwort *fm*
monarch having one xylem strand
moriche the miriti palm
mudwort a small mud-growing *pl.*
mugwort a British wormwood
mullein a tall stiff woolly *pl.*
mustard seeds of *vr* Brassica
naartje *nartjie*
nartjie *vf* small orange
nut-pine *vp* incl. stone-pine
nut-tree *vp* especially hazel

FLORA

oak-fern *tf* fern
oak-gall gall on oak
oakling a young oak
oak-lump the lichen lungwort
oak-mast acorns collectively
oarweed *oreweed*
oil-palm any palm *scf* palm-oil
oil-seed any seed *scf* oil
Opuntia* *Gs* prickly-pear, cactus *fm*
oreweed seaweed
palmiet aloe-like riverside *pl.*
palmyra (1) *sp.* palm, *scf* toddy
palmyra (2) palm timber
Papaver *gs* poppy incl. opium poppy
paprika Hungarian red pepper
papyrus a tall *pl.*, sedge *fm*
pareira a tropical climber
parsley an umbelliferous herb
parsnep *parsnip*
parsnip an umbellifer
paxiuba a Brazilian palm
pedicle a little stalk
penguin *pinguin*
perique a Louisiana tobacco
petiole a leaf stalk
PETUNIA* 'anger' or 'why angry?'
Petunia* *gs pl. ak.* tobacco
pigweed goosefoot, amaranth (etc.)
pilcorn the naked oat
pimento tree/wood/dried fruit
pinguin W. Indian *pl.*/fruit
pitcher a fly-trapping leaf
platane *plane*
pollard tree with crown removed
pompelo grapefruit
pompion pumpkin
PRIMULA* 'joy of youth'
Primula* *Gs* primrose
puccoon bloodroot: *vr* gromwell
pumpkin plant/gourd
pupunha peach-palm/fruit
putamen a fruit-stone
quamash *camas*
quassia a S. American tree
Quercus *Gs* oak, beech *fm*
quetsch *vf* plum
quicken (1) *quick*
quicken (2) rowan
ragwort *vr* composites
ramsoms *sp.* wild garlic (plural)

red-root *gs* of buckthorn *fm*
redwood *sp.* Sequoia
regmata plural of *regma*
rhatany *pl.*/astringent root
Rhellia *gs* of acanthus *fm*
rhizome basic underground stem
rhodora *sp.* Rhododendron
rhubarb *sp.* Rheum, dock *fm*
ribwort ribwort plantain
Robinia* locust or false acacia
rose-bay (1) oleander: rhododendron
rose-bay (2) fireweed
rose-bud bud of rose
rose-hip fruit of rose
rosella an E. Indian hibiscus
rozella *rosella*
ruderal growing in waste places
rye-corn rye
saffron *sp.* of crocus
saguaro the giant cactus
saksaul *saxaul*
salfern gromwell
saligot water-chestnut
Salsola *Gs* saltwort, goosefoot *fm*
sampire *samphire*
sanders (red) sandalwood
sanicle *vr* umbellifers
sapling a young tree
sapwood *alburnum*
sarment a long weak twig
saw-wort *vr* composites
Scandix *gs* umbellifers
Scirpus *gs* of sedge *fm*
sea-bean cacoon
sea-kale a fleshy crucifer
sea-moss carrageen
sea-pink thrift
sea-reed marram grass
sea-tang tangle
seaweed any marine alga
Sequoia* *gs* gigantic conifers
seringa (1) a Brazilian rubber-tree
seringa (2) *syringa*
service a rowan-like tree
shallot garlic flavoured *sp.* onion
shea-nut nut *scf* shea-butter
skirret *tf* water-parsnip
Solanum* *Gs* potato, nightshade
Solpuga *gs* toxic *pl.*
Sorghum* *gs* grass *ak.* sugar-cane

sorosis *ff* formed by *fl.* cluster
sour-sop tree/fruit
sourock sorrel
soy bean bean of soy
spignel baldmoney
spinach *sp.* of goosefoot *fm*
spinage *spinach*
Spiraea* *Gs* meadow-sweet
spurrey *ags* Spergula
staddle (1) small tree left unfelled
staddle (2) stump left for coppice
stamina a plural of *stamen*
stubble straw
sultana small seedless raisin
sundari an E. Indian tree
SYRINGA* 'safeguard our friendship'
Syringa* *Gs* lilac
syringa mock-orange
talipat *talipot*
talipot a Ceylon fan-palm
Tamarix *gs* of xerophytic *pl.*
tangelo TANGErine/POMELO hybrid
tarweed *vr* composites
taughin tree *scf* poison
TEA-ROSE 'Our love breeds good'
tea-rose tea-smelling rose
thallus *pl.* of irregular natural form
thistle a prickly composite
timothy cat's-tail grass
tobacco *ags* Nicotiana
treetop top of a tree
trefoil (1) leaf of 3 leaflets
trefoil (2) a trefoilate plant
troelie *troolie*
troolie bussu palm/leaf
truffle any fungus of Tuber
valonia acorns of valonia oak
vanilla a climbing orchid
Verbena* *gs ak* labiates
vervain a wild *verbena*
wallaba a Brazilian tree
waratah *vr* Australian shrubs
wax-palm two different palms
wax-tree any tree *scf* wax
whangee *vr* grasses *ak.* bamboo
witchen mountain ash: wych elm
witloof *tf* chicory
woorali *wourali*
woorara *wourali*
wourali *pl. scf* curare (poison)

wych-elm a common wild elm
Xylopia *gs* trees, custard-apple *fm*
zedoary *vr sp.* Curcuma
Zizania *gs* tall aquatic grasses
Zostera *Gs* grasswrack

8

absinthe wormwood
abstrict to set (spores) free
Abutilon* *gs* mallow
Acanthus* *gs ak.* figwort *fm*
ACANTHUS* 'undying devotion'
achenial of/pertaining to *achene*
adhesion concrescent of unlike parts
Adiantum *Gs* maidenhair ferns
Aesculus *Gs* horse-chestnut
agrimony *gs* small yellow rose
aguacate the avocado pear
alburnum *sapwood*, soft outer layer
allogamy cross-fertilization
allspice pimento
amaracus marjoram
amaranth *amarant* (1) (2)
amelcorn emmer
anthesis (1) opening of flower-bud
anthesis (2) flower's lifetime
ANGELICA* 'inspiration and joy'
Angelica* *gs* umbellifers
Apocynum *gs ak.* periwinkle
apricock (former name) apricot
Arenaria *Gs* sandwort *ak.* chickweed
ash-plant an ash sapling
asphodel (1) mythical *pl.* of the dead
asphodel (2) *pl.* of lily *fm*
Aspidium* *Gs* shield-fern
Aubretia* *gs* crucifers
autocarp self-fertilised fruit
autogamy self-fertilisation
barberry a thorny shrub
bayberry *ff* bay/candle-berry
beam tree whitebeam
bearbine a bindweed
bedeguar rose-branch soft gall
bedstraw *vr* plants
beef-wood *wd vr* trees
beetroot root of the beet
Berberis* *Gs* barberry *ak.* buttercup
bergamot (1) *tf* citron or orange

FLORA

bergamot (2) a fine pear
betel-nut the areca nut
biennial *pl.* with two years' life
Bignonia *gs* of tropical *pl.*
bilberry whortle/blaeberry shrub
bindweed convolvulus
blackboy Australian grass-tree
blimbing *bilimbi*
blowball dandelion head in seed
bluebell (1) wood-hyacinth
bluebell (2) harebell (Scotland)
blueweed viper's bugloss
borecole kale
bountree *bourtree*
bourtree elder
Brassica* *Gs* turnip and cabbage
breadnut *ak.* breadfruit (*trop. Amer.*)
broccoli hardy *vf* cauliflower
buckbean marsh *pl.*, gentian *fm*
bull-hoof a W. Indian passion flower
buplever hare's-ear
cactuses *cacti*
calabash *ff* calabash tree: gourd
calamint *pl. ak.* mint and thyme
CAMELLIA* 'undying love'
Camellia* *gs* evergreen shrubs
camomile *vr pl. ak.* chrysanthemum
camphire henna
canaigre a Texan dock
Cannabis* *Gs* hemp
Capsicum* *gs* shrubs, potato *fm*
carl-hemp female hemp (see *fimble*)
carraway *caraway*
caruncle small fleshy outgrowth
Caryocar *Gs* butternut
Castanea *Gs* chestnut
cat's-tail (1) catkin on a willow (etc.)
cat's-tail (2) Timothy grass
cat's-tail (3) reed-mace or bulrush
celeriac *vf celery*
centuary *vr* plants
Centurea *gs* composites incl.
  knapweed
charlock wild mustard
chay-root chay, *scf* red dye
chestnut tree/edible nut
chichory a blue-flowered composite
chick-pea *sp.* pea (*pl.* edible seed)
chorisis multiplication by branching
choy-root *chay-root*

Cinchona *gs* (Peruvian bark) trees
cinnamon tree and bark
cleavers goose-grass
Clematis* *gs* Virgin Bower, etc.
clotebur burdock
club-moss of Pteridophyta
[4]**club-rush** *ags* Scirpus (*bulrush (2)*)
Cocculus *gs* tropical climbers
cocoplum tree/fruit
coco-wood kokra-wood (trade name)
cole-seed seed of rape
cole-wort (heartless) cole
conferva *gs* freshwater algae
conidial of spore production
coolabah *vr* Aust. eucalypti
coquilla piassava palm/nut
cork-tree *tf* oak
costmary S. European composite
cowberry red whortleberry
cow-grass (1) perennial red clover
cow-grass (2) wild chervil
cow-plant *pl.* with a milky juice
cow-wheat yellow-flowered *pl.*
crab-nuts *ff* Carapa
crab's-eye jequirity, a *tf* bean
crab-wood *wd* Carapa
cream-nut the Brazil nut
crowfeet plural same *sp.* crowfoot
crowfoot buttercup (see *crowfoots*)
crucifer of the *Cruciferae*
cucumber gourd-like creeper
cyclamen *gs* S. European *pl.*
DAFFODIL* 'mistrust your love'
daffodil yellow-*fl.* narcissus
Danewort *wallwort* (1)
date-palm *sp.* palm
death-cap a very toxic toadstool
death-cup *death-cap*
deer-hair small *sp.* club-rush
[5]**dew-berry** *tf* bramble
Dianthus* *Gs* carnations, pinks
dioecius sexes on separate *pl.*
dividivi Carib. *pl.*, curved pods
dog's bane *dogbane*

---

[4] Games players note: to discover *clubrush* (without hyphen) in *Chambers* see *bulrush*.

[5] Games players note: *dew-berry* is the form in which this word appears in *Chambers* even though other authorities prefer *dewberry*.

dogberry *ff* wild cornel/dogwood
dog-daisy daisy: oxeye daisy
dog-grass couch-grass (etc.)
dog-wheat *dog-grass*
doum-palm tree/fruit
duckweed *vr* water plants
earthnut an edible tuber
earth-pea peanut
eelgrass *m pl. ak.* pondweed
eelwrack eelgrass/*grasswrack*
egg-apple *egg-fruit*
egg-fruit *ff* egg-plant
egg-plant E. Indian annual
eglatere eglantine
epiphyte non-parasitic *pl.* on *pl.*
escarole *tf* endive
eucalypt a eucalyptus tree
Euonymus* *Gs* spindle tree
fen-berry cranberry
feverfew a composite
filament stalk of a stamen
fireweed rose-bay willow-herb
flagelot *vf* kidney bean
flax-lily a N. Zealand *pl.*
flix-weed *sp.* hedge-mustard
floscule floret
floweret a small flower
fluellin *vr* speedwells
follicle single carpel fruit
foxberry *bearberry*: cowberry
foxglove (1) *ags* Digitalis
foxglove (2) fairy foxglove (Erinus *gs*)
Fraximus *Gs* ash
frutices plural of *frutex*
fumitory *ags* Fumaria
funguses *fungi*
fuss-ball *fuzz-ball*
fuzz-ball puffball
galangal *galingale* (1) (2)
GARDENIA* 'secret passion for you'
Gardenia* *gs pl.,* madder *fm*
Geranium* *gs* incl. cranesbill
gingelly *gingili*
⁶gladiole gladiolus

gladioli a plural of *gladiolus*
glory-pea a *papilio. gs*
goat's-rue a *papilio. pl.*
goatweed *goutweed*
goosegog gooseberry
goutweed an umbellifer
goutwort *goutweed*
greening *vf* apple
gromwell *vr* plants
groo-groo *gru-gru*
gulfweed a large seaweed
haanepot (f) a kind of grape
hagberry bird-cherry: hackberry
hag-taper mullein
hairbell harebell
hardfern the northern fern
harebell Scottish bluebell
hare's-ear an umbellifer
hat-plant *sola*, used for topees
hawkweed a composite
hawthorn small tree, rose *fm*
hazelnut *ff* hazel
heartpea *heartseed*
hedgehog prickly plant or fruit
hempbush an Aust. fibre *pl.*
hemp-palm a palmetto
hemp-seed seed of hemp
henequen a Mexican agave
Hesperis *Gs* dame's violet
Hibiscus* *gs* tropical *pl.*
holly-oak holm-oak
honeypot *haanepot*
hornbeam beech-like tree
hornwort a rootless water *pl.*
Huon-pine a Tasmanian conifer
hyacinth *gs* bulbous *pl.*, lily *fm*
iceplant *pl.* with glistening leaves
ironwood hard timber (-trees)
itchweed *hellebore* (2)
ivory-nut *ff* ivory-palm
jack-pine *vr* N. Amer. trees
jack-tree jack or jak
jambolan *jambu*
japonica (1) Japanese quince
japonica (2) camellia (etc.)
Java plum jambolana
kail-runt a cabbage stem
kalumpit a Philippine tree/fruit
kinakina quina
kingwood a Brazilian tree

---

⁶ Games players note: whilst *gladiola* is a
form current in the UK and found in the
Official Scrabble Players' Dictionary it is
ignored by such authorities as *Chambers*
and the *Complete Oxford*.

FLORA

knapweed spineless thistle-like *pl.*
kohlrabi *tf* cabbage
Labiatae *fm* lipped flowers
LABURNUM* 'despair of your coldness'
laburnum small toxic *papilio.* tree
lace bark lofty W. Indian tree
lady-fern a pretty British fern
LARKSPUR* 'my feelings are obvious'
larkspur *ags* Delphinium
LAVENDER* 'steadfast devotion'
lavender a labiate *pl.*
Lecanora* *gs* lichens
lent-lily daffodil
licorice liquorice
Lima* bean *ak.* French bean
lima-wood *tf* brazil-wood
lime-tree linden tree
lime-wood *wd lime* (2)
lintseed linseed
livelong luchee: orpine
loblolly *vr* American pines
loco-weed *loco*
long moss rootless *pl. ak.* pineapple
lungwort a borage; a lichen
macahuba *macoya*
mad-apple (1) *ff* egg-plant
mad-apple (2) *apple of Sodom* (2)
mad-apple (3) *tf* gall on eastern oak
Magnolia* *gs* beautifully leaved trees
mahogany *trop.* tree/timber
male-fern a woodland fern
malvasia malmsey
malvesie malvasia
mandarin *vf* small orange
mandioca manioc
mandrake (1) toxic *pl.*, potato *fm*
mandrake (2) white bryony (etc.)
mangrove *vr* swamp trees
manna-ash tree, *scf* manna (1)
many-root of Ruellia
MARIGOLD* 'all is not well'
marigold a composite
MARJORAM* 'comfort and sympathy'
marjoram an aromatic labiate *pl.*
Marsilea *gs* aquatic ferns
martagon Turk's cap lily
matfelon the greater knapweed
matgrass matweed
May-apple tree/*ff* Podophyllum
may-bloom may-blossom

mesquite a leguminous tree
milk-tree tree (i.e. cow-tree) *scf* 'milk'
milk-weed *sp.* Asclepias
milkwood *vr* trees *scf* latex
milkwort *ags* Polygale
moonseed *pl.* with lunate seeds
moonwort *vr* ferns: honesty
mulberry tree/edible fruit
murphies plural of *murphy*
mushroom any (edible) fungus
musk-pear *vf* pear
musk-plum *vf* plum
Myosotis* *gs* of borage *fm*
naked oat *sp.* oat
napiform turnip-shaped
narcissi a plural of Narcissus
nenuphar *vr* water-lilies
nisberry *naseberry*
noisette China/moss rose hybrid
nut-grass *vr* sedges
oak-apple gall on oak leaf
oat-grass a fodder grass
Oleaceae *fm* incl. ash, privet, jasmine
oleander an evergreen shrub
oleaster the true wild olive
ovenwood brushwood
palmetto palm of Sabal *gs*
paspalum *gs* pasture grasses
patience *sp.* dock
peaberry a small coffee seed
pearmain *vr* apple
peasecod pea-pod
pea-straw pease-straw
peduncle stalk of solitary *fl.*
perianth calyx and corolla
pericarp the wall of a fruit
phyllode petiole with leaf function
phyllome any (homologue of) leaf
piassaba *piassava*
piassava palm *scf* piassava-fibre
[7]**pile-wort** the lesser celandine
  (*figwort*)
pinaster cluster pine
pine-cone cone of pine
pinkroot *vp gs ak.* gentians
pipe-tree (1) (white) mock-orange
pipe-tree (2) (blue) lilac

---

[7] Games players note: to discover *pilewort*
(without hyphen) in *Chambers* see *figwort*.

pipewort rare rush-like *pl.*
pisiform pea-shaped
pith-tree *sp. papilio.* tree
plantule a plant embryo
plantain (1) *gs* roadside plants
plantain (2) *pl.*/fruit (coarse banana)
Platanus *Gs* bark-shedding trees
Plumbago* *gs* ornamental *pl*
pokeweed *poke*
polyarch having many xylem strands
Polygala* *Gs* milkwort
polypody *sp.* fern
pond-lily a water-lily
pondweed *vr* plants
primrose *vr* Primula
prophyll a bracteole
prunello a little prune
puffball *sp.* gasteromycete fungus
purslane a pot/salad herb
pyriform pear-shaped
quandong small tree/edible drupe
rain-tree S. Amer. tree, mimosa *fm*
rambutan tree/hairy edible fruit
red cedar *vr* cedars: juniper
RED* POPPY* 'Rest and tranquillity'
reed-mace *cat's-tail* (3)
rib-grass ribwort plantain
Roccella *gs* lichens incl. *scf* litmus
rock-rose *vr* plants
rockweed *bladderwrack* (etc.)
rose-bush shrub of rose
ROSEMARY* 'you alone I love'
rosemary a labiate shrub
rose-root a stonecrop
rose-tree a standard rose
rosewood wood of *vr* trees
rutabaga the Swedish turnip
Rutaceae *fm* incl. Ruta, orange
rye-grass a fodder grass
sack-tree *upas* (2)
sago-palm palm *scf* sago
sainfoin a legume fodder *pl.*
salt-bush *vr* Australian shrubs
salt-wort *vr* goosefoots (*Salsola*):
   glasswort
Salvinia *gs* water-ferns
samphire an umbellifer
sandwort *ags* Arenaria
sapucaia Brazilian tree/nut
sargasso a gulfweed

sarrasin a buckwheat
sarrazin *sarrasin*
Scabiosa a *gs* of teasel *fm*
scabious of Scabiosa: *vr* others
scallion shallot: leek
scallion onion with defective bulb
seaberry *ags* Halorhagis
sea-blite a salt-marsh *pl.*
sea-grape (1) any Ephedra (fruit)
sea-grape (2) glasswort: gulfweed
sea-grass any seaside grass
sea-heath a wiry heath-like *pl.*
sea-holly thistle-like umbellifer
sea-onion a liliaceous *pl.*
sea-wrack coarse seaweeds
sebesten tree/plum-like fruit
seedling a young plant
sengreen the house leek
shadbush *sp. ak.* rose *fm*
shaddock tree/citrus fruit
shamrock lesser yellow trefoil
shea-tree tree (nuts *scf* shea-butter)
Silphium* *gs* Amer. composites
sloebush blackthorn bush
sloetree *sloebush*
smallage wild celery
snowball guelder-rose
SNOWDROP* 'promise of happy future'
snowdrop early spring flower
soap-bark a S. American tree
soap-root *vr* plants
soapwort a tall herb, pink *fm*
soja bean soya bean
sow-bread cyclamen
soya bean bean of soy
Spergula *gs ak.* chickweed
Sphagnum *gs* peat or bog moss
spikelet a small crowded spike
Spinifex* (1) *gs* Australian grasses
Spinifex* (2) porcupine grass
Stapelia* *Gs* carrion-flower
starwort *vr* plants
subshrub an undershrub
sugar-gum *sp.* Eucalyptus
sun-drops *sp.* evening-primrose
sunn-hemp *sunn*
swamp oak Casuarina
sweet-bay laurel: *tf* magnolia
sweetpea a *papilio. pl.*
sweet-sop an Amer. evergreen

FLORA

sycamine   mulberry-tree (Bible)
sycamore (1)   *tf* fig-tree
sycamore (2)   great maple: plane
sycomore   *sycamore* (1)
syconium   a multiple fruit
tacahout   a tamarisk gall
tamarack   American/black larch
tamarind   large tree/pod
tamarisk   *ags* Tamarix
tarragon   an aromatic Artemisia
teil tree   lime: terebinth (Bible)
toadflax   *vr pl. ak.* snapdragon
toadrush   a low rush
tree-fern   a tree-like fern
tree-lily   a xerophytic *pl.*
tree-moss   Usnea
Tremella   a gelatinous fungus
trichome   a plant hair
Trillium*   *gs* of lily *fm*
tuckahoe (1)   edible underground
   fungus
tuckahoe (2)   *vr* edible foodstock
tung-tree   tree *scf* tung-oil
Turk's cap   *sp.* Lilium
turnsole   *pl.* with 'sun facing' *fl.*
upas-tree   *upas* (1) (2)
valerian   all-heal *ak.* teasel
vallonia   *valonia*
Veronica*   *Gs* speedwell
Victoria*(1)   *gs* water-lilies
Victoria*(2)   a large red plum
wall-moss   a yellow lichen
wall-wort (1)   a dwarf elder
wall-wort (2)   pellitory: wall-pepper
wartweed   *tf* spurge
wartwort   *fm* lichens: *wartweed*
wild oats   *sp.* oat
wild rice   Zizania
WILD* ROSE*   'constancy'
windfall   *ff* blown off tree
Wistaria*   *gs papilio. pl.*
witch-elm   wych elm
withwind   bindweed, *vr* climbers
woodbind   *woodbine* (1) (2)
woodbine (1)   honeysuckle
woodbine (2)   *vr tf* ivy
woodruff   *gs* rubiaceous *pl.*
wood-rush   *ags* Luzula
wormwood   *pl. ex* vermifuge
xenogamy   cross-fertilization

xylocarp   a hard, woody fruit
Zingiber*   *gs* tropical herbs
Zizyphus   *Gs* jujube-trees

9

Aaron's rod   mullein, golden rod (etc.)
abcission (1)   shedding of a part
abcission (2)   liberation of fungal spore
Adansonia   *Gs* baobab
adderwort   bistort or snakeweed
ailanthus   ailanto
albespine   *albespyne*
albespyne   hawthorn
algarroba   carob: mesquite
Amarantus   *Gs* love-lies-bleeding
amaryllid   *afm* Amaryllidaceae
Amaryllis*   *Gs* belladonna lily
Anacharis*   *gs* water plants
Andromeda*   *gs* heath shrubs
Anthurium*   *gs trop.* American *pl.*
apetalous   without petals
aphyllous   without foliage
apple-tree   tree *ak.* pear, rose *fm*
Aquilegia*   *Gs* columbine
Araucaria*   *Gs* monkey-puzzle
arracacha   umbellifer with edible
   tubers
Artemesia*   *gs* composites incl.
   wormwood
artichoke   *pl.* with edible receptacles
asclepiad   *ags* Asclepias
Asclepias*   *gs fm ak.* periwinkle
Asparagus*   *gs* of Liliaceae
Asplenium   *gs* of ferns
aubergine   *ff* egg-plant
baldmoney (1)   spignel, a subalpine *pl.*
baldmoney (2)   *vr* gentian
balsam fir   an American fir
baneberry   *pl.* with toxic fruit
bean caper   *gs* steppe/desert shrubs
[8]bear-berry   *vr* plants *(foxberry)*
bear's-foot   black hellebore
berg-cedar   a rare *tf* cedar
bilimbing   bilimbi
birthwort   *pl., ex* midwife use

[8] Games players note: to discover *bearberry*
(without hyphen) in *Chambers* see *foxberry*.

blaeberry whortleberry/bilberry
bloodroot *pl*. of poppy *fm*
bloodwood *vr* trees
blueberry *vr* fruit
bluegrass *tf* grass
BLUE* PHLOX* 'you enchant me'
blush-rose pink *vf* rose
bodhi tree bo tree
bog-myrtle *tf* bog-plant
bolletrie bully tree
bracterole leaf on flower axis
Brazil* nut seed of Bertholletia
breadroot prairie-turnip: yam
breadtree *vr* trees
brooklime *tf* speedwell
brookweed water pimpernel
broomrape *gs* parasitic on broom
brushwood broken branches, etc.
Bryophyta mosses and liverworts
bryophyte any *sp*. Bryophyta
buckthorn shrub *scf* sap-green paint
buckwheat a Polygonum
bulletrie bully tree
bully tree *vr* W. Indian trees
butterbur *butterdock*
BUTTERCUP* 'spitefulness, mockery'
buttercup crowfoot
butternut white walnut tree/nut
Cactaceae *fm* fleshy xerophytes
Calendula* *Gs* marigold
CAMPANULA 'Pride mars your charm'
Campanula *gs* bellflowers incl.
   harebell
candle-nut *ff* Pacific spurge
candytuft a crucifer
caprifole honeysuckle
carambola tree, wood-sorrel *fm*
Carmadine *gs* cress
carnation *vf* clove pink
carrageen an edible seaweed
cashew-nut *ff* cashew
Casuarina *Gs* she-oak or beef-wood
celandine swallow-wort
chickling chick-pea
chickweed *sp*. stitchwort
China* jute *sp*. Abutil
China* rose *vr* garden roses
chincapin *chinkapin*
chinkapin Amer. dwarf-chestnut
circinate rolled inwards

clove-pink *vf* pink
Coccoloba *Gs* grapetree
cockscomb *vr* plants
cocksfoot *gs* grass
cocoa-wood kokra-wood
cocus-wood kokra-wood (trade name)
Colchicum* *gs* medicinal plants
colocynth *tf* cucumber
COLUMBINE* 'passionate love'
columbine *ags* Aquilegia
coltsfoot a composite
Combretum* *gs* of *fm ak*. myrtle
composite *afm* Compositae
coral-root (1) *sp*. Carmadine
coral-root (2) *gs* orchid
coral-tree *gs trop*. trees
coral-wort *coral-root* (1) (2)
Corchorus *Gs* jute
coriander *pl*., seeds used as spice
corn-salad lamb's lettuce
Cotyledon* *gs* S. African *pl*.
cotyledon a seed-leaf
courbaril W. Indian locust tree
cranberry shrub/red acid berry
Crataegus *Gs* hawthorn
cremocarp *ff* an umbellifer
crosswort a bedstraw
crow-berry small creeping shrub
crowfoots plural *vr sp*. crowfoot
cryptogam of Cryptogamia
curry-leaf an Indian tree
dae-nettle *day-nettle*
DANDELION* 'Jealousy tortures me'
dandelion yellow *fl*. composite
day-nettle dead-nettle: hemp-nettle
deciduous all leaves shed together
deerberry huckleberry (etc.)
Dicksonia *gs* tree-ferns (etc.)
Digitalis *gs* foxglove, figwort *fm*
dittander pepperwort
dog-violet scentless wild violet
doorn-boom a S. African acacia
duck's-foot lady's-mantle
duck's-meat duckweed
dulcamara bittersweet
Dutch* rush scouring rush
dyer's-weed *vr* dye-yielding *pl*.
dyer's-weld dyer's yellowweed
eaglewood *gs* trees, daphne *fm*
earth-star fungus *ak*. puffballs

FLORA

eglantine sweet-brier
epilobium a willow-herb
eschallot shallot
eucalypti a plural of *eucalypt*
Eumycetes the higher fungi
Euphorbia* *gs* Angiospermae
evergreen *pl.* in leaf all year
fabaceous bean-like
fenugreek *pl. ak.* meliot
flagellum a long runner
flame-leaf Poinciana
fly orchis *tf* orchid
footstalk stalk of a leaf
Forsythia* *gs* flowering shrubs
friar's cap wolf's-bane
galengale *galingale (1) (2)*
galingale (1) *sp.* sedge: its rootstock
galingale (2) rootstock *vr pl.* ginger *fm*
gama-grass *sp.* tall grass
gelsemium Carolina jasmine
germander *tf* labiate herb
gladiolus *gs pl.* iris *fm*
glasswort *vr pl.*, *scf* soda
GOLDENROD* 'please be kind'
goldenrod a composite
goosefoot *vr pl.* beet *fm*
grapeseed seed of the vine
grapetree tree/fruit, dock *fm*
grapevine *vr sp.* Vitis
grass-tree Aust. *pl.*, lily *fm*
greenweed *vr* shrubby plants
ground-ash a sapling of ash
ground-ivy a British creeper
[9]**ground-nut (1)** peanut or monkey-nut
[9]**ground-nut (2)** earthnut
groundsel a common composite
gynaeceum flower's female organs
gypsywort a labiate plant
hackberry Amer. tree *ak.* elm
hair-grass *sp.* grass
Haloragis *Gs* seaberry
Hamamelis *Gs* Amer. witch-hazel
hardgrass cocksfoot, etc.
heartseed balloon-vine
heartwood inner wood of tree

[9] Games players note: *ground-nut* is the
form in which this word appears in
Chambers even though other authorities
prefer *groundnut*.

hellebore (1) *vr pl.* buttercup *fm*
hellebore (2) *vr pl.* lily *fm*
herb-grace rue
herb-Paris *pl.* of lily *fm*
herb-Peter* cowslip
herd grass timothy
hindberry raspberry
holly-fern a spiny-leaved fern
HOLLYHOCK* 'admiration of beauty'
hollyhock Holy Land *pl.*, mallow *fm*
honey-blob sweet yellow gooseberry
horse bean *vr* broad bean (etc.)
horsemint (1) any wild mint
horsemint (2) sweet horsemint
horsetail any scouring rush
house-leek *pl.* of stonecrop *fm*
HYDRANGEA* 'Too cool for me'
Hydrangea* *gs* shrubby *pl. ak.*
  saxifrage
Hypericum *Gs* St John's wort
Impatiens* touch-bursting pod *gs*
Indian fig banyan tree
involucre a ring of bracts
Irish moss carrageen
ivorypalm *sp.* palm
ivory-tree palay
jacaranda a S. American tree
jack-fruit *ff* jacktree or jack
jambolana *jambu*
jequity *ff* Indian liquorice *(Abrus)*
Jew's thorn Christ's thorn
jewel-weed *ags* Impatiens
Job's* tears involucres of a *tf* grass
John*-apple (apple-John) *vf* apple
Judas-tree flowers before leafing
Juneberry *ff* shadbush
kauri-pine *kauri*
kermes oak tree where *kermes* breed
king-apple *vf* apple
knee-holly butcher's broom
Kniphofia *gs pl.* lily *fm*
knotgrass a common weed
kurrajong *vr* Australian trees
lady-smock *lady's-smock*
lignaloes aloes-wood
Liliaceae *fm* in Angiospermae
liquorice a *papilio. pl.*
loco-plant *loco*
love-apple tomato
lyme-grass a coarse grass

macaw-palm *macoya*
macaw-tree *macoya*
Malpighia *Gs* Barbados cherry
Malvaceae hollyhock *fm ak.* lime
malvoisie malmsey
mandarine *mandarin*
mandiocca *manioc*
mangostan *mangosteen*
manzanita Californian bearberry
maple leaf emblem of Canada
mare's-tail (1) a tall marsh *pl.*
mare's-tail (2) horsetail
marihuana hemp
marshwort marsh *pl. ak.* celery
matchwood wood suitable for matches
mayflower hawthorn (etc.)
meadow-rue *gs* buttercup *fm*
mead-sweet meadow-sweet
melocoton large *vf* peach
milk-vetch a fodder *pl.*
MISTLETOE* 'nothing shall separate'
mistletoe a hemiparasitic *pl.*
mocker-nut *tf* hickory-nut
moneywort a loosestrife
monkey-nut peanut or ground-nut
monkey-pot shell of sapucaia nut
monkshood wolfsbane
mouse-tail small *pl.*, buttercup *fm*
musk-melon common melon
myrobalan (1) *ff vr sp.* Terminalia
myrobalan (2) *vf* plum
naked lady meadow saffron
NARCISSUS* 'selfishness will part us'
Narcissus* *Gs* daffodil, Amaryllis *fm*
naseberry tree/plum
navelwort *pennywort*
neesberry *naseberry*
Nicotiana* *Gs* tobacco, *ak.* Solanum
nonpareil *vf* apple
nux vomica tree/seed *scf* strychnine
oleaceous of Oleaceae
Orchideae *fm* (tropical) flowers
parrot-jaw parrot-beak
patchouli a labiate shrub
patchouly *patchouli*
pellitory *vp* incl. feverfew, yarrow
[10]**penny-wort** *vr* plants

[10] Games players note: to discover *pennywort* (without hyphen) in *Chambers* see *navelwort*.

perennial lasting over 2 years
petty whin *papilio.* shrub, pea *fm*
Phytolaca *Gs* pokeweed
physic-nut tree/nut, spurge *fm*
pigeon-pea *dal*, a pealike *pl.*
PIMPERNEL* 'victory'
pimpernel *pl.* of primrose *fm*
pineapple *pl.*/pineal fruit
pitchpine *vr* American pines
pitch-tree tree *scf* pitch
pixy-stool toadstool/mushroom
plantling a little plant
Poinciana* *gs* Caesalpina *fm*
poison-ivy *tf* sumac
poison-nut nux vomica
poison-oak *tf* sumac
pokeberry poke
Polygonum* *Gs* knotgrass (dock *fm*)
pre-vernal flowering before spring
quebracho *vr* hardwood trees
quickbeam *quicken* (2)
raspberry plant/fruit
red pepper *pepper* (4)
redstreak *vf* apple
remontant (1) re-blooming same season
remontant (2) plant (i.e. rose) doing (1)
rhapontic rhubarb
rhizocarp (1) a heterosporus fern
rhizocarp (2) a perennial herb
rhizocarp (3) *pl.* fruiting underground
riverweed Podostermon
rock-brake parsley-fern
rockcress Arabis, a crucifer
rootstock (short, erect, thick) rhizome
rosaceous rose-like: of rose *fm*
rose-apple tree/fruit (clove *gs*)
rose-elder the guelder-rose
rowan-tree mountain-ash
royal fern a British fern
royal palm *sp.* cabbage-palm *gs*
rusa grass rusa, *scf* rusa oil
rutaceous of the Rutaceae
Saccharum *Gs* sugar-cane (grass *fm*)
safflower a thistle-like composite
sage-apple edible gall on *sp.* sage
sagebrush Artemisia
saintfoin sainfoin
sand-grass any dune grass

FLORA

sapodilla a large evergreen tree
saskatoon shad-bush/fruit
sassafras tree of laurel *fm*
satinwood *vr* (Indian) trees
Saxifraga *gs ak.* rose *fm*
SAXIFRAGE* 'your indifference wounds'
saxifrage *ags* Saxifraga: *vr* others
Scotch* elm wych elm
Scotch* fir *Scots pine*
Scots* pine only UK native pine
sea-bottle *bladderwrack*
sea-girdle tangle
sea-lentil gulfweed
sea-rocket a fleshy crucifer
sea-tangle tangle
sloethorn blackthorn bush
smart-weed *water-pepper*
snakeroot bistort: milkwort (etc.)
snakeweed bistort
snakewood letter-wood
snow-berry shrub, honeysuckle *fm*
snowflake a snowdrop-like *pl.*
snowfleck *snowflake*
snowflick *snowflake*
soapberry tree/soapy fruit
sour-gourd cream-of-tartar tree
spear-wood *sp.* Acacia: *sp.* Eucalyptus
spearwort lance-shaped leaf *gs*
speedwell *ags* Veronica
spikenard *pl. scf* an aromatic oil
spike-rush a spiked sedge
spruce fir any conifer of Picea
staff-tree shrub *ak.* spindle-tree
Staphylea *Gs* bladder-nut shrubs
star-grass *star*
Stellaria *Gs* chickweed, pink *fm*
stinkhorn a stinking gasteromycete
stinkwood *vr* ill-smelling wood
stonecrop *ags* wall-pepper
stone-pine *tf* Mediterranean nut-pine
stonewort *vr* plants
sugar-bean Lima bean
sugar-beet *vr* beet esp. Rapa
sugar-cane woody grass *scf* sugar
sugar-palm *vr* palms
sugar-pine an American pine
SUNFLOWER* 'thoughts only of you'
sunflower a composite
sun-spurge *sp.* spurge
sweet-corn *vf* maize

sweet-flag an aromatic pond *pl.*
sweet-gale bog-myrtle
sweetwood *vr* trees
sweet-wort wort
sword-bean *pl.*/edible pods
tacamahac the balsam poplar
tangerine mandarin orange
Taraxacum* *Gs* dandelion
terebinth the turpentine tree
thorntree hawthorn (etc.)
TIGER-LILY 'richness and abundance'
tiger-lily *tf* lily
tiger-wood *vr* timber
toad-grass toadrush
toadstool a mushroom-like fungus
toddy palm any palm *scf* toddy
tonga-bean *tonka-bean*
tonka-bean *tf* scented seed
touchwood decayed timber
tree-onion *vf* onion
tubercule small tuber
tulip-root an oat disease
tulip-tree tree of magnolia *fm*
tulip-wood *wd* tulip-tree
Turkey*oak *sp.* oak
umbellate having umbels
vetchling *ags* sweet-pea
wagenboom (f) a S. African tree
wakerobin (1) cuckoo-pint *(Arum)*
wakerobin (2) the spotted orchis
wakerobin (3) *ags* Trillium
wall-cress *ags* Arabis
water-fern *vr* fern-like *pl.*
water-leaf *vr* plants
waterlily *vr* plants
water rice Zizania
water-vine *vr* plants
water-weed *vr* incl. Anacharis
wax-flower *vr* plants
wax-myrtle *candleberry* tree
whitebeam two different trees
whitewood *vr* trees/timber
wild-grape (1) a wild grape-vine
wild-grape (2) Coccoloba
wild olive oleaster
withywind *withwind*
wolfsbane an aconite
wolf's-claw *wolf's-foot*
wolf's-foot a club-moss
xerophyte *pl.* of arid areas

yerba mate *yerba*
zebra-wood a Guinea tree

10

acanaceous prickly
accrescent enlarged and persistent
adder's-wort *adderwort*
afrormosia tree *ak.* teak
alexanders *pl.* used as celery
alliaceous garlic-like
almond-tree tree *ak.* peach
Amaranthus *Amarantus*
ampelopsis Virginia creeper
Anacardium* *Gs* cashew-nut
angiosperm *adv* Angiospermae
arbor vitae *gs* conifer *ak.* cypress
asarabacca hazelwort
Aspidistra* *gs* of asparagus group
Astralagus* *Gs* milk-vetch
badderlock an edible seaweed
barrenwort a herb, barberry *fm*
beard-grass *tf* bearded grass
beaver-tree *sp.* magnolia
beaver-wood *beaver-tree*
BELLADONNA* 'bad luck'
belladonna deadly nightshade
[11]**bell-flower** *ags* Campanula
bird-cherry small wild tree/fruit
bishopweed goutweed
bitter-king shrub, quassia *fm*
bitter-root *pl.*, purslane *fm*
bitterwood *vr* trees
blackberry *ff* bramble
blackheart a dark *tf* cherry
BLACK* POPPY* 'neglect and
  forgetfulness'
BLACKTHORN* 'love isn't smooth'
blackthorn a sloe-bearing thorn
bladder-nut *ags* Staphylea
bluebottle the blue cornflower
bottle-tree an Australian tree
brazil-wood *brazil* NOT *Bertholletia*
breadfruit *ff* S. Sea Islands' tree
brome-grass an oat-like grass

[11] Games players note: *bell-flower* is the
  form in which this word appears in
  Chambers even though other authorities
  prefer *bellflower*.

brown algae brown seaweeds
brown jolly brinjal
bullet-tree *bully tree*
bunya-bunya *bunya*
burnet rose *sp.* wild rose
bur-thistle spear-thistle
busy Lizzie *sp.* Impatiens
butterdock *pl. ak.* coltsfoot
butter-tree *vr* trees *scf* buttery
  substance
butterwort *vr* bog plants
button-bush shrub *ak.* madder
button-wood (1) tree of myrobalan *fm*
button-wood (2) plane-tree (USA)
Caesalpina *Gs* brazil-wood, dividivi
calamander *Gs* ebony
candelilla a Mexican spurge
candle-wood *vr* Mexican/Carib trees
carragheen *carrageen*
Chamaerops only European palm
champignon mushroom/edible fungus
cherry-bean cow-bean
cherry-plum cherry-flavoured plum
China* grass rami
chinquapin *chinkapin*
Chionodoxa* *Gs* glory of the snow
cinque-foil (1) *sp.* Potentilla
cinque-foil (2) 5 leaf clover
citronella a Ceylon grass
clementine *tf* orange
cloudberry *pl.*/edible fruit *ak.* bramble
coffee-bean seed of coffee-tree
coffee-tree *ak.* madder
Compositae *fm* bell-flowers
CORNFLOWER* 'I love your innocence'
cornflower a composite weed
cotton-weed cudweed
cotton-wood *vr* American poplar
couch-grass *couch*
cow-chervil wild chervil
cow-parsley *cow-chervil*
cow-parsnip hogweed
cranesbill any wild *sp.* Geranium
Cruciferae cross-shaped *fl. fm*
cuckoo-pint *sp.* Arum
Dane's blood *wallwort* (1)
dead-finish an Australian shrub
dead-nettle stingless nettle-like *pl.*
Delphinium* *Gs* larkspurs, stavesacre
dog-parsley fool's parsley

FLORA

dog's-fennel mayweed
dog's-tongue hound's-tongue
dragonhead a labiate garden-*pl.*
dragon-root a medicinal *pl.*
dragon-tree a great Canaries tree
dyer's-broom *dyer's-greenweed*
elderberry *ff* elder
Eucalyptus* *gs* trees, myrtle *fm*
filmy ferns *fm* thin-leaved ferns
flamboyant *trop.* tree *sp.* Poinciana
fleur-de-lis *fleur-de-lys*
fleur-de-lys iris
Flindersia* *gs* Australian trees
florescent bursting into flowers
Fontinalis* *gs* aquatic mosses
frangipani red jasmine (etc.)
Fraxinella dittany
French* bean kidney-bean
French* plum prune (dried plum)
friar's cowl wake-robin
fringe tree shrub of olive *fm*
fritillary *gs* lily *fm*
gelder-rose *guelder-rose*
goat-sallow the great sallow
goat's-beard a composite
goat's-thorn an Astralagus shrub
goat-willow *goat-sallow*
golden-seal a medicinal *pl.*
goldilocks *sp.* buttercup
gooseberry *ff* gooseberry-bush
goose-grass cleavers: silverweed
grapefruit *vf* shaddock
grapestone pip of the grape
grasswrack eelgrass *(eelwrack)*
greenheart tree, laurel *fm (bebeeru)*
gum juniper sandarach
gymnosperm *pl.* with open ovary
Gypsophila* perennial *ak.* pinks
hawksbeard hawkweed-like *pl.*
heart of oak oak duramen
heliotrope a *turnsole*, borage *fm*
hemp-nettle coarse labiate weed
herbaceous (1) of/pertaining to herbs
herbaceous (2) like ordinary foliage
herb-bennet avens
herb-Robert stinking cranesbill
herd's grass timothy
hobble-bush wayfaring-tree
hop-trefoil a yellow clover
horse-gowan oxeye daisy

Idaean vine cowberry
Indian corn maize
Indian hemp *sp.* Cannabis
Indian pink pinkroot
Indian pipe an American *fl.*
Indian poke white hellebore
Indian rice Zizania
Indian shot a *trop. pl.*
insane root hemlock? (Plutarch)
Jew's-mallow *tf* jute
Jew's-myrtle butcher's broom
jimson-weed thorn-apple
kaffir-boom coral-tree
kaffir corn Sorghum
kidney-bean *sp.* Phaseolus
lady's-smock a meadow crucifer
laurustine a winter-flowering shrub
leguminous possessing legumes
letter-wood a S. American tree
liliaceous of Liliaceae
locust-bean carob-bean
locust-tree carob or false acacia
loganberry a supposed hybrid
maidenhair (1) fine footstalked *sp.* fern
maidenhair (2) maidenhair spleenwort
maiden pink a wild *sp.* pink
maidenweed mayweed
male orchis early purple orchis
manchineel *trop.* tree, spurge *fm*
mangosteen tree/fruit
manna-grass *scf manna* (2)
MARGUERITE* 'Is there hope?'
marguerite oxeye daisy
marshlocks *sp.* cinquefoil
MAUVE* LILAC* 'still same feelings?'
may-blossom hawthorn flower
melocotoon *melocoton*
melicotton *melocoton*
MIGNONETTE* 'modesty, quiet
  affection'
mignonette a fragrant Reseda
missel-tree tree/edible berries
mock-orange (1) shrub, saxifrage *fm*
mock-orange (2) *tf* cherry-laurel (USA)
mock-privet shrub *ak.* privet
monkey-rope a liana
moon-flower oxeye daisy
motherwort a labiate *pl.*
musk-mallow *sp.* mallow
NASTURTIUM* 'you inspire me'

Nasturtium* *Gs* water-cress
nasturtium Indian cress
nettle-tree (1) tree, elm *fm*
nettle-tree (2) stinging-leafed tree
nightshade *vr* (toxic) *pl.*
nuciferous nut-bearing
oak-leather *tf* fungus
orange-lily *tf* lily
oxeye daisy *oxeye*
pagoda tree *vr* trees
palm-kernel kernel of oil-palm
Parana pine a Brazilian tree
parkleaves tutsan
parrot-beak a *papilio. pl.*
parrot-bill *parrot-beak*
Passiflora* *gs* climbers
pennyroyal *sp.* mint
peppercorn dried pepper-berry
peppermint *sp.* mint
pepperwort dittander (etc.)
periscaria *sp.* knotgrass
PERIWINKLE* 'happy past memories'
periwinkle an evergreen creeper
pileorhiza a root-cap
pine-kernel edible kernel *vr* pine
pine-needle a pine leaf
Podostemon *gs thallus*-like (!) *pl.*
poinsettia a spurge
polycarpic fruiting many times
pompelmous grapefruit
Potentilla *gs* rose *fm*
prickly ash toothache tree
pumpel-nose grapefruit
quaking ash aspen
quick-grass *quick*
quinsy-wort squinancy-wort
receptacle (1) end of axis (floral *pl.*)
receptacle (2) 'sex' section (non-floral)
redcurrant shrub/fruit
RED* JASMINE* 'love leads us astray'
red jasmine shrub *ak.* periwinkle
red-sanders *tf* sandalwood tree
red seaweed *tf* seaweed
rest-harrow a tough-rooted *pl.*
Rheinberry *Rhineberry*
Rhineberry buckthorn/berry
rock-plant *pl.* adapted to rock life
rose-laurel rose-bay
rose-mallow hollyhock: hibiscus
rowan-berry *ff* mountain ash

rubber tree any *pl. scf* rubber
rubiaceous of madder *fm*
salal-berry edible *ff* salal
sand-cherry *sp.* dwarf cherry
sandalwood red/white sandalwood
sappan-wood *sappan*, brazil-wood
Sarracenia* *gs* insectivorous *pl.*
scorzonera dandelion-like *pl.*
Scotch* **kale** *vf* kale
Scotch* **rose** the burnet rose
sea-burdock clotber (Xanthium)
sea-lettuce *tf* seaweed
sea-whistle *tf* seaweed
setterwort stinking hellebore
shield-fern Aspidium
silverweed *sp.* Potentilla
snapdragon Antirrhinum
sow-thistle *gs* thistle-like *pl.*
spear-grass spear-like grass
spike-grass *vr* grasses with spikes
spleenwort *ags* Asplenium
spongewood sola
springwood secondary wood
springwort a magical root
  (mandrake?)
starr-grass *star*
stavesacre a tall larkspur
stitchwort *gs ex* stitch remedy
stork's-bill (1) *gs* geranium *fm*
stork's-bill (2) Pelargonium
strawberry *pl.*/fruit
strophiole a caruncle
Sudan grass a fodder grass
sugar-apple sweet-sop
sugar-grass sweet sorghum
sugar-maple a N. Amer. maple
sugar-wrack *tf* tangle
sweet-briar *sweet-brier*
sweet-brier fragrant wild rose
sword-grass *vr* sword-like grass
tallow-tree *vr* trees *scf* tallow
Terminalia *gs ak.* Combretum
thale-cress a crucifer wall-*pl.*
thalliform of/pertaining to *thallus*
thorn-apple (1) toxic *pl. ak.* potato
thorn-apple (2) haw
throatwort (1) bellflower *ex* medicinal
throatwort (2) giant bellflower
touch-me-not balsam
towel-gourd luffa

FLORA

tragacanth shrub *scf* gum
tree-mallow Lavatera
tree-tomato shrub/fruit
tree of life arbor vitae
tropaeolum *gs* climbers
[12]*tumble-weed* windblowable *tf pl.*
umbellifer *afm* Umbelliferae
valonia oak a Levantine oak
Venus's comb an umbellifer
wallflower *vr* crucifers
wall-pepper *Gs* stonecrop
wall rocket wall-mustard
water-bloom large masses of algae
water-cress a perennial cress
water-lemon *sp.* passion flower
water-melon *pl.* of cucumber *fm*
water-plant aquatic *pl.*
water thyme Canadian pondweed
weeping-ash *vf* European ash
Welsh* onion cibol
white heath *brier, scf* briar (pipe)
white-heart cherry *ak.* gean
WHITE* LILAC* 'love is dawning'
WHITE* PHLOX* 'I love you'
WHITE* POPPY* 'my affections are dead'
whitethorn hawthorn
wild-cherry gean (etc.)
wild-indigo a tumble-weed
willow-herb *sp.* evening-primrose *fm*
willow-weed *vr* plants
wind-flower (wood-) anemone
witch-alder *gs* shrubs *ak.* wych elm
witch-hazel wych elm: hornbeam (etc.)
wolf's-peach tomato
wooden pear an Australian tree
wood-sorrel *ags* Oxalis
xerophytic able to stand drought
yellow-root golden-seal
[13]**yellow-weed** ragwort: goldenrod
yellow-wood trees *scf* pale wood
yellow-wort annual, gentian *fm*
ylang-ylang a Malayan tree
youngberry black/*dewberry* cross

[12] Games players note: *tumble-weed* is the
form in which this word appears in
Chambers even though other authorities
prefer *tumbleweed*.
[13] Games players note: to discover
yellowweed (without hyphen) in
Chambers see *Dyer's-yellowweed*.

11

Aaron's beard (1) *sp.* saxifrage
Aaron's beard (2) *tfs* toadflax, wort, etc.
Amboina pine tree *scf* resin
Amelanchier *Gs* shadbush rose
Antirrhinum* *gs ak.* figwort
balloon-vine *trop.* Amer. climber
bastard teak dhak
bear's-breech acanthus
betel-pepper *sp.* Piper
bitter-apple colocynth
bitter-cress *sp.* Cardamine
bittersweet woody nightshade
bitter vetch *vr* plants
black bryony climber, yam *fm*
black walnut *sp.* N. Amer. walnut
bladdermint *ags* Staphylea
bladderwort *sp.* floating plants
blood orange *tf* orange
blue thistle blueweed
bottle-gourd a climbing annual
boysenberry bramble hybrid
bramble-bush *bramble*
bur-marigold a composite
burning bush volatile seed *pl.*
burning bush (1) dittany
burning bush (2) spindle-tree (etc.)
cabbage-palm palm with *cabbage* (2)
cabbage-rose cabbage-like rose *fl.*
cabbage-tree cabbage-palm
Calabar-bean witchdoctor's seed
camel's thorn desert *pl.*, camel food
[14]**candle-berry** wax-myrtle, bayberry
caper-spurge *tf* spurge
caraway-seed *ff* caraway/carraway
cashew-apple stalk of cashew
cauliflower *vf cabbage* (1)
cherry-stone endocarp of cherry
clover-grass clover
cluster-pine pine with clustered cones
coconut-palm curving-stem palm
CONVOLVULUS* 'suspect you flirt'
Convolvulus* *Gs* bindweed
cotton-grass *gs* sedges
Cryptogamia flowerless plants
Cupuliferae *fm* cupuliferous trees

[14] Games players note: to discover
candleberry (without hyphen) in
Chambers see *wax-myrtle*.

dame's violet fragrant crucifer
dipterocarp *vr* (Indian) trees
discomycete *vr* fungi
dog's-mercury *tf* spurge
dragon's-head *dragonhead*
Droseraceae *fm* insectivorous *pl.*
dwarfed tree bonsai
dyer's-rocket *dyer's yellowweed*
ELDERFLOWER* 'Hope of further
   favours'
elderflower *fl.* of *elder*
elkhorn fern *gs* ferns
epiphyllous growing upon a leaf
false acacia Robinia
feather-palm *vr* palms
flamboyante *flamboyant*
fleurs-de-lis ⎫ plural forms of
fleurs-de-lys ⎭ fleur-de-lys
florescence (1) a bursting into *fl.*
florescence (2) time of flowering
FORGET-ME-NOT 'reminder of love'
forget-me-not *ags* Myosotis
fothergills witch alder
French* berry *vr* buckthorn berry
frugiferous fruit-bearing
gelder's-rose *guelder-rose*
giant fennel an umbellifer
gillyflower clove-smelling *fl.*
gladioluses *gladioli*
globe-flower of buttercup *fm*
gobe-mouches (f) an insectivorous *pl.*
goldenberry Cape gooseberry
goose-flower *sp.* Aristolochia
great burnet a meadow *pl.*
guelder-rose tree of honeysuckle *fm*
hedge-hyssop *pl.* of figwort *fm*
herb-of-grace rue
herb Trinity* pansy
HONEYSUCKLE* 'always together'
honeysuckle (1) a climbing shrub
honeysuckle (2) clover (etc.)
horned poppy *tf* poppy
horseradish *pl. ak.* scurvy-grass
huckleberry shrub/fruit
Iceland moss a lichen
indehiscent not opening when mature
Indian berry *ff sp.* Cocculus
Indian bread a Virginian fungus
Indian cress a Peruvian climber
india-rubber juice of *vr pl.*

jaggery palm tree *scf* sugar
Jaffa orange *Jaffa*
Jamaica plum hog-plum
Japan* laurel shrub *ak.* dogwood
jimpson-weed *jimson-weed*
kaffir bread pith of cycad
kidney-vetch *vr papilio. pl.*
kiss-me-quick wild pansy (etc.)
Labrador tea shrub, heather *fm*
lacquer-tree *sp.* Rhus
lady's-finger *vr pl.* incl. kidney-vetch
lady's-mantle *gs* rosaceous *pl.*
laurustinus *laurustine*
leopard-wood letter-wood
loblolly-bay tree, tea *fm*
loosestrife *vr pl.* primrose *fm*
London pride nancy-pretty
love-in-a-mist fennel: passion-flower
lucken-gowan globe flower
Madonna lily a white lily
mammee apple *mammee*
mammoth tree Sequoia
manna-lichen *scf manna* (4)
marshmallow *m pl. ak.* hollyhock
meadow-grass *ags* Poa
[15]meadow-sweet queen of the meadows
melakatcone *melocoton*
milk-thistle lady's thistle
millet-grass tall *sp.* grass
Molucca bean nicker nut, bonduc
monkey-bread baobab tree/fruit
monkey-grass coarse grass fibre
mountain ash rowan tree
mountain-tea an Amer. evergreen
mulberry-fig the true sycamore
musk-thistle *tf* thistle
mustard-tree *tf* shrub
nancy-pretty a saxifrage
narcissuses *narcissi*
needle-furze the petty whin
night-flower night-opening *fl.*
OLIVE* BRANCH* 'reconciliation'
orange-grass *tf* St John's wort
oyster-plant two seaside *pl.*
palm-cabbage bud of cabbage-palm
pampas-grass a reed-like grass

[15] Games players note: *meadow-sweet* is the
   form in which this word appears in
   Chambers even though other authorities
   prefer *meadowsweet*.

FLORA

pampelmoose grapefruit
pampelmouse grapefruit
Paraguay tea mate
PARMA VIOLET* 'Will you accept me?'
Parma violet Neapolitan violet
parsley fern *sp.* fern
parsley-pert *parsley-piert*
Pelargonium* *gs* geranium *fm*
[16]**pepper-grass** cress: pillwort
Pimpernella *gs* umbellifers
Podophyllum *gs* barberry *fm*
poison-sumac *tf* sumac
pomegranate tree/fruit
pompelmoose grapefruit
pompelmouse grapefruit
pussy-willow *vr sp.* willow
quandoug-nut edible kernel
queez-maddam a French pear
quicken-tree *quicken* (2)
quinsy-berry blackcurrant
quitch-grass *quitch*
RED* GERANIUM* 'no use for you'
red-hot poker Kniphofia, Tritonia
rescue-grass *tf* brome-grass
rhodium-wood Canary Is. convolvulus
Roman* **sorrel** *sp.* Rumex
rose-campion *sp.* campion
rubber plant *sp* mulberry
St* **John's*** **wort** *ags* Hypericum
Saintpaulia *gs* African plants
salad burnet common burnet
sallal-berry *salal-berry*
sallow-thorn sea-buckthorn
sanderswood (red) sandalwood
sapucaia-nut monkey-pot seed
scuppernong a N. Carolina grape
scurvy-grass a crucifer
sea-colewort sea kale: wild cabbage
sea-furbelow a brown seaweed
sea-lavender *vr* salt-marsh *pl.*
sea-milkwort Glaux
sea-purslane (1) *tf* sandwort
sea-purslane (2) *vr* orach
sesame-grass zama grass
Sitka spruce *tf* spruce

snail-flower *fl.* pollinated by snail
spatterdock (f) yellow water-lily
spindle-tree shrub *scf* spindle-wood
spring-wheat spring-sown wheat
swallow-wort an asclepiad
[17]**sweet-Cicely*** an umbellifer
sweet-potato batata, convolvulus *fm*
sweet sultan *sp.* Centaurea
sweet-willow *vr* trees
swine's-cress wasteland crucifer
switch-plant shoots-ape-leaves *pl.*
sycamore fig *sycamore* (1)
Thallophyta all the thalliform *fms*
thallophyte a thallus
tiger-flower a Mexican *pl.*
tonquin-bean *tonka-bean*
trumpet-tree a S. American tree
trumpet-wood *trumpet-tree*
tussac-grass tussock-grass
twitch-grass *twitch*
viper's grass black salsify
wall-mustard a crucifer
[18]**water-pepper** *sp.* Polygonum
water-violet *sp.* Hottonia
weeping-tree pendant-branch tree
white bryony gourd *fm* climber
white walnut butternut
whitlow-wort *vr* plants
wintergreen *vr* plants
witches' meat tremella
wood-anemone *vr* anemone
Xanthoxylum *gs* S. Amer. trees
Xeranthemum* *gs pl. ak.* thistle

12

achlamydeous without perianth
Adam's flannel mullein
adder's tongue *gs* fern
agamogenesis reproduction without sex
American poke white hellebore

---

[16] Games players note: *pepper-grass* is the
form in which this word appears in
Chambers even though other authorities
prefer *peppergrass*.

[17] Crossword note: to compare *sweet-Cicely*
and *sweet cicely* in *Chambers* also see
cicely.

[18] Games players note: *water-pepper* is the
form in which this word appears in
Chambers even though other authorities
prefer *waterpepper*.

Angiospermae closed-ovary division
apple of Sodom (1) 'turned to ashes'
apple of Sodom (2) a toxic fruit
Aristolochia *Gs* birdwort
autumn-crocus meadow-saffron
balsam poplar an Amer. poplar
benjamin tree (1) Styrax
benjamin tree (2) Amer. spice-bush
benjamin tree (3) *tf* fig-tree
Bertholletia *Gs* Brazil nut
blackcurrant *ff* shrub *ak.* gooseberry
black salsify scorzonera
[19]**bladder-wrack** a brown seaweed
  (*rockweed*)
BLUE* HYACINTH* 'suspect deceit'
bramble-berry blackberry
calabash tree has melon-like *ff*
Canadian rice Zizania
carraway seed *ff* carraway/caraway
Carolina pink pinkroot
cherry-laurel *sp.* cherry
Chinese aster *sp.* aster
chiquichiqui a piassava palm
Christ's thorn (1) *sp.* buckthorn
Christ's thorn (2) jujube tree
citrus fruits citrons, oranges, limes, etc.
cuckoo flower Lady's-smock: ragged
  robin
cucumber-tree (1) bilimbi/tulip trees
cucumber-tree (2) magnolia
cupuliferous bearing cuples
custard-apple *ff* W. Indian tree
Dead Sea apple *apple of Sodom* (1) (2)
Dead Sea fruit *apple of Sodom* (1) (2)
Enteromorpha *gs* green seaweeds
everlastings *sp.* Xeranthemum
feather-grass *tf* grass
floriculture culture of *fl./pl.*
flower delice ⎫ plural forms of
flower deluce ⎬ fleur-de-lys, also
flower de-luce ⎭   see *fleurs-de-lys*
fool's parsley a toxic umbellifer
French* sorrel *Roman sorrel*
frog's lettuce *tf* pondweed
globe-thistle a composite
ground-cherry (1) *vr* dwarf cherries

ground-cherry (2) husk tomato
ground-cherry (3) Cape gooseberry
hedge-mustard tall stiff crucifer
hedge-parsley an umbellifer
Hemerocallis day-lily
hemp-agrimony a composite
Hercules club Xanthoxylum
hound's-tongue *sp.* borage *fm*
Indian millet durra
Indian turnip *pl.*/starchy tuber
Jacob's-ladder ladder-like leaved *pl.*
Jamaica cedar bastard Barbados cedar
Jamaica ebony cocus-wood
kidney-potato *vf* potato
lady's-cushion mossy saxifrage
lady's-fingers *lady's-finger*
lady's-slipper *gs* orchid
lady's-thistle milk thistle
lamb's lettuce *gs pl.*, valerian *fm*
leopard's-bane a composite
loblolly-pine *loblolly*
loblolly-tree leathery-leaved tree
mangel-wurzel *vf* beet
massaranduba Brazilian milk-tree
massaranduba *massaranduba*
monkey-flower *sp.* Mimulus
monkey-puzzle *vr* prickly-leaved trees
monk's rhubarb patience-dock
orchard-grass *sp.* cocksfoot
parsley-piert dwarf *sp.* lady's-mantle
passion-fruit any edible *ff* Passiflora
patience-dock used like spinach
pease-blossom blossom of pea
pickerel-weed a pondweed
PINK* GERANIUM* 'you act foolishly'
[20]**pitcher-plant** *tf* insectivorous *pl.*
pleurisy-root an Amer. asclepiad
poison-sumach *tf* sumac
Pteridophyta ferns, lycopods,
  horsetails
RED* CARNATION* 'worldliness will
  separate'
reindeer moss a lichen
Rhododendron* *gs* trees/shrubs
roebuck-berry stone-bramble
rose of Sharon *sp.* hibiscus

---

[19] Games players note: to discover
  bladderwrack (without hyphen) in
  Chambers see either *rockweed* or
  sea-bottle.

[20] Games players note: *pitcher-plant* is the
  form in which this word appears in
  Chambers even though other authorities
  prefer *pitcherplant.*

FLORA

St* John's* bread carob bean
St* Peter's* wort *vr* plants
sandarch tree a Moroccan tree
sarsaparilla *ags* Smilax
sassafras nut the pitchurim bean
sea-buckthorn a willow-like shrub
seaside-grape grape-tree/fruit
service-berry (1) pear-shaped *ff* service
service-berry (2) shadbush/fruit
sheep's sorrel *sp*. Rumex
Shirley poppy *vf* common poppy
skunk-cabbage stinking *pl*., arum *fm*
snowdrop-tree *vr* incl. fringe tree
snow-in-summer *tf* chickweed
Solomon's-seal *gs* lily *fm*
Spanish broom a broom-like shrub
Spanish grass esparto
Spanish onion large mild *tf* onion
[21]sparrow-grass asparagus |
spear-thistle two *sp*. thistle
staghorn moss club moss
swamp cypress a deciduous conifer
SWEET* WILLIAM 'you are perfect'
sweet-william *sp*. pink
timothy-grass a fodder grass
tree of heaven ailanto
tussock-grass a Falkland Is. grass
Umbelliferae carrot/hemlock *fm*
Victoria* plum *Victoria* (2)
virgin's-bower *sp*. Clematis
wandering Jew *vr* creepers
Washingtonia* *gs* fan palms
water-flowers *water-bloom*
water-hemlock *sp* water-dropwort
water-milfoil finely divided leaf *pl*.
water-parsnip *ags* Sium
water-soldier a common aquatic *pl*.
weeping-birch *vf* white birch
WHITE* JASMINE* 'the sweetness of love'
whitlow-grass *vr* plants
whortleberry bilberry
wood-hyacinth English bluebell
yellow sultan *sp*. Centaurea
Yorkshire fog a tall grass
Zantedeschia *gs* calla lily

[21] Games players note: *sparrow-grass* is the form in which this word appears in *Chambers* even though other authorities prefer *sparrowgrass*.

13

African violet *sp*. Saintpaulia
Barbados cedar a Cedrela
Barbados pride W. Indian shrub
black saltwort Glaux
brown seaweeds a division of Algae
bullock's heart custard-apple
butcher's broom shrub, lily *fm*
butterfly-weed pleurisy-root
caliature-wood red sanders
camphor laurel *sp*. cinnamon-tree
carrion-flower *pl*. with stinking *fl*.
chinkerinchee *chincherinchee*
Christmas rose flowers in winter
Christmas tree any (fir) tree
Chrysanthemum* *gs* composites
cotton thistle emblem of Scotland
cranberry-tree guelder-rose (USA)
creeping Jenny* moneywort
creosote-plant an American bush
dead-men's bells foxglove
dog's-tail grass a common grass
elephant grass *tf* reed-mace
elephant's-ears begonia
elephant's-foot *pl*. of yam *fm*
eucalyptusses *eucalypti*
false calabash bottle-gourd
garlic mustard a tall crucifer
gasteromycete of the Gasteromycetes
good-King-Henry a goosefoot
grape hyacinth *ak*. hyacinth
honeydew melon *tf* melon
horse chestnut tree/fruit
horse mushroom a large coarse fungus
inflorescence aggregate of *ff* on axis
Indian tobacco an Amer. lobelia
Jamaica pepper allspice
Jamestown-weed *jimson-weed*
Jerusalem sage S. European perennial
kangaroo-apple plant/fruit
kangaroo-thorn a prickly acacia
Lady's bedstraw *gs* Galium
mangold-wurzel *mangel-wurzel*
marmalade plum *ff* marmalade tree
marmalade tree *trop*. Amer. tree
marsh-marigold kingcup
marsh-samphire a glasswort
meadow saffron *sp*. Colchicum
noli-me-tangere *sp*. balsam

orange-blossom worn by brides
Papilionaceae butterflylike-corolla *fm*
partridge-wood (1) a S. American tree
partridge-wood (2) tree with *sp.* fungus
[22]**passion-flower** *ags* Passiflora
pelican-flower goose-flower
pineapple-wood rayless mayweed
PINK* CARNATION* 'you are welcome'
prairie-turnip breadroot
quadrifoliate four-leaved
Quaker-buttons nux vomica seeds
Queensland-nut tree/edible nut
red sandalwood two different trees
roe-blackberry roebuck-berry
rose-bay laurel *rose-bay*
rose of Jericho a crucifer
St* Anthony's nut earthnut/*pignut*
sapodilla plum *ff* sapodilla
scorpion grass forget-me-not
Scotch* thistle cotton thistle
shepherd's club mullein
squinancy-wort *sp.* woodruff
swine's-succory small *pl. ak.* chicory
toothache-tree Xanthoxylum
traveller's joy virgin's-bower
trumpet-flower *vr* plants
Venus's fly-trap an insectivorous *pl.*
water-chestnut *vr pl.*/edible seed
water-dropwort *gs* umbellifers
water-plantain *pl.* of Alisma *gs*
water-starwort *ags* Callitriche
wayfaring-tree shrub *ak.* guelder-rose
weeping-willow a Chinese willow
WHITE* HYACINTH* 'I wish you well'
winter aconite *sp. gs ak.* buttercup
YELLOW* JASMINE* 'passionately in
   love'

14

alder-buckthorn *sp.* buckthorn
Amaryllidaceae narcissus, snowdrop
   fm
bastard saffron safflower

[22] Games players note: ignored by the
   Complete Oxford, given as two words in
   the *Oxford Illustrated*, hyphenated in
   Chambers, it appears as one word in *Funk
   and Wagnalls*.

belladonna lily S. African pink *fl.*
cabbage lettuce *tf* lettuce
calabash nutmeg *ff* tropical tree
cannonball-tree a S. American tree
Canterbury* bell bell-flower/throatwort
Cape* gooseberry strawberry-tomato
Carline thistle *gs ak.* true thistles
chickling vetch chick-pea
chincherinchee *sp.* star-of-Bethlehem
dog's-tooth grass a dune grass
dogtooth violet *vr* plants
dyer's-greenweed shrub *scf* dye
false hellebore itchweed, Indian poke
Gasteromycetes an order of fungi
gold-of-pleasure a crucifer
gooseberry-bush shrub, saxifrage *fm*
Jack*-by-the-hedge garlic mustard
lavender cotton *sp.* Santolina
love-in-idleness pansy
maidenhair-tree a Japanese holy tree
papilionaceous of *Papilionaceae*
partridge-berry *pl.*/fruit, madder *fm*
provincial-rose cabbage rose
Rogation* flower milkwort
St* Dabeoc's heath a rare heath
St* Ignatius's nut *ak.* nux vomica
Scotch* bluebell harebell
sea-gilliflower thrift
sensitive plant irritable when touched
Spanish needles weed: hooked fruits
strawberry-tree small tree, heath *fm*
sweet horsemint dittany
traveller's-tree tree of banana *fm*
treacle-mustard a crucifer
water-pimpernel crucifer-like *pl.*
white hellebore *hellebore (2)*
WHITE* CARNATION* 'your purity
   inspires'
witches' thimble foxglove (etc.)
wood-nightshade bittersweet
worcester-berry *sp.* gooseberry

15

Brussels sprouts *vf* cabbage
butterfly-flower butterfly pollinated
butterfly-orchis *vr* orchids
Christmas cactus red *ff* cactus
Christmas flower Christmas rose

FLORA

DOUBLE* CARNATION* 'let me think'
dyer's-yellowweed *pl.*, *scf* dye
evening-primrose a N. American *pl.*
glass-cloth plant ramie
golden saxifrage *sp.* saxifrage
hens-and-chickens *vr pl.* incl. daisy
horseradish tree two different trees
Hottentot's bread elephant's-foot
Indian liquorice tree *scf* crab's-eye
Jack*-in-the-pulpit *pl.* like cuckoo-pint
king of the forest oak
LILY OF THE VALLEY* 'hope of
  reconciliation'
lily of the valley Convallaria *gs*,
  Liliaceae *fm*
marsh-cinquefoil marshlocks

meadow saxifrage *sp.* saxifrage
Michaelmas daisy a wild aster
mountain bramble cloudberry
mountain tobacco *sp.* Arnica
PURPLE* CARNATION* 'no feeling for
  you'
Spanish chestnut the true chestnut
star-of-Bethlehem *pl.* of lily *fm*
strawberry-shrub Calycanthus
Tasmanian myrtle an evergreen beech
Virginia creeper climber *ak.* vine
wall-gillyflower wallflower
wandering sailor *wandering Jew*
white sandalwood a parasitic tree
winter hellebore winter aconite
woody nightshade *sp.* Solanum

PERSONAL NAMES

BOYS

dim. diminutive of
pet pet form of
v variant form of

2

Al *dim.* mainly Albert
Cy *pet* Cyrus
Eb *dim.* Ebenezer
Ed *pet* various Ed---
Es* *pet* Esmond
Ez *pet* Ezra
Hi* *pet* Hiram
Hu *v* Hew
Jo* *v* Joe
Lu *dim.* various Lu---
Mo* *pet* Moses
Si* *pet* Silas: *dim.* Simon

3

Abe *dim.* Abraham
Aby* *pet* Abraham
Art* *dim.* Arthur
Asa 'God healeth'
Ben* *dim.* Benjamin
Bob* *dim.* Robert
Cal *dim.* Calvin
Car* *dim.* Carmichael
Col* *pet* Colin
Dai 'to shine'
Dan* *dim.* Daniel
Day* Anglicized Dai
Don* *dim.* Donald
Dhu 'he of swarthy countenance'
Eli 'high'
Ern *pet* Ernest
Geo.* *dim.* George
Gif* *pet* Gifford

Gil *pet* Gilbert/Gilchrist
Gip* *pet* Gilbert
Gus* *pet* Augustus
Guy* 'leader'
Hal *dim.* Henry
Ham* *pet* Hamilton
Hew* 'mind'
Ian *v* John
Ike *pet* Isaac
Ira 'watchful'
Ivo *v* Yves
Jan *v* John
Jay* the bird of that name
Jed *dim.* Jedediah
Jem *dim.* James
Jim *dim.* James
Job* 'persecuted'
Joe* *dim.* Joseph
Ken* *pet* Kenneth
Kit* *pet* Christopher
Lee* 'a meadow'
Len *pet* Leonard
Leo 'a lion'
Les* *pet* Leslie
Lew* *dim.* Lewis
Lin* *dim.* Lionel
Lou *dim.* Louis
Mal *pet* Malcolm
Mat* *dim.* Matthew
Max *pet* Maxwell
Mel* *pet* Melvin
Nap* *pet* Napoleon
Nat *dim.* Nathan/Nathaniel
Ned* *dim.* Edward
Nev *pet* Neville
Pat* *dim.* Patrick

BOYS

Pip* *dim.* Philip
Rab *dim.* Robert
Ran* *pet* Randolph
Ray* *dim.* Raymond
Reg *dim.* Reginald
Rex 'king'
Rip* origin obscure
Rob* *dim.* Robert
Rod* *dim.* Roderick/Rodney
Rog *pet* Roger
Ron *dim.* Ronald
Roy 'king'
Sam *dim.* Samuel
Sax* origin obscure
Sid *dim.* Sidney
Sim* *dim.* Simon
Sol* *dim.* Solomon
Tad *dim.* Thaddeus
Tam* *v* Tom
Ted* *dim.* Edward
Tim *dim.* Timothy
Tod* *v* Tad
Tom* *dim.* Thomas
Val *dim.* Valentine
Van* from surname
Vic *pet* Victor
Vin *pet* Vincent
Viv *pet* Vivian
Wat* *dim.* Walter

4

Abel 'vanity'
Abie *pet* Abraham
Adah 'an ornament'
Adam 'man'
Alan origin obscure
Alec *dim.* Alexander
Alex *dim.* Alexander
Algy *pet* Algernon
Alun *v* Alan
Amos 'borne'
Andy *pet* Andrew
Bart *dim.* Bartholomew
Bede* 'prayer'
Benj.* *pet* Benjamin
Bert *dim.* Albert
Bill* *dim.* William
Bing* pet name

Boyd 'yellow'
Bram *dim.* Abraham
Bran* 'raven'
Brod* *dim.* Broderick
Burl* possibly 'high'
Cain* 'a murderer'
Carl* *v* Karl
Cary from surname
Chad* *dim.* Ceadda
Chay* possibly 'me'
Chip* origin obscure
Clay* possibly 'man'
Clem* *pet* Clement
Clif *dim.* Clifton
Cole* 'dove'
Conn* possibly 'knowledge seeker'
Dale* possibly 'valley'
Dane* 'valley'
Dave *dim.* David
Davy *dim.* David
Dean* 'valley'
Dick* *dim.* Diccon
Doug *pet* Douglas
Drew* 'sturdy'
Duff* 'dark man'
Duke* *pet* Marmaduke
Earl* 'warrior'
Eddy* *dim.* various Ed---
Eoan* *v* Eoin
Eoin *v* Iain
Eric* 'ever king'
Erne* *v* Ern
Esau 'hairy'
Evan *v* John: *v* Ewan
Ewan 'young warrior'
Ewen 'young warrior'
Ezra 'help'
Fess* 'a band'
Fred *pet* Frederick
Fulk 'folk'
Gary *v* Gareth
Gene* *dim.* Eugene
Gert *dim.* Gertrut
Glen* possibly 'valley'
Hank* *dim.* Henry
Herb* *pet* Herbert
Hoel *v* Hywel
Hugh 'thought'
Hugo *v* Hugh
Iain *v* John

Ifor *v* Ivor
Ikey *pet* Isaac
Iolo possibly *v* Julius
Issy *pet* Isador
Ivan *v* John
Ivor 'Ing protector'
Jack* *v* John
Jago *v* Jacob
Jake* *pet* Jacob
Jean* *v* John
Jeff* *dim.* Jeffrey
Jess* *v* Jesse
Jock* *pet v* John
Joel 'Jahweh is God'
Joey* *dim.* Joseph
John* 'God is gracious'
Josh* *dim.* Joshua
Jude *v* Judah
Jule *dim.* Julius
Karl 'a man'
Kean 'vast'
Leon *v* Leo
Levi 'joined'
Liam *v* William
Lief* 'beloved'
Llew *dim.* Llewellyn
Lorn* *dim.* Loarn
Ludo* *dim.* Ludovic
Luke* 'he of Lucania'
Marc* *dim.* Marcus
Mark* possibly *v* Marc
Matt* *dim.* Matthew
Mick* *dim.* Michael
Mike* *dim.* Michael
Milo* *v* Michael
Mort* *dim.* Mortimer
Neal* *v* Niul
Neil *v* Niul
Nial *v* Niul
Niel *v* Niul
Niul 'a champion'
Nick* *dim.* Nicholas
Noah 'rest'
Noel 'birth'
Noll* *pet* Oliver
Norm* *pet* Norman
Obie *dim.* Obadiah
Otto* 'rich'
Owen possibly 'youthful warrior'
Paul* 'small'

Phil *dim.* Philip
Plum* *pet* Pelham
Pugh* 'son of *Hu*'
Ralf *v* Ralph
Rene 'born again'
Rhys 'warrior'
Rice* *v* Rhys
Rich* *pet* Richard
Rick* *pet* Eric
Rock* origin obscure
Rolf *dim.* Rodolph
Roly *v* Roland
Rory* 'ruddy'
Ross from the surname
Rube *pet* Reuben
Rupe *pet* Rupert
Russ *pet* Russell
Saul* 'asked for'
Sean* *v* John
Seth 'appointed'
Shan* *v* John
Stan *pet* Stanley
Stew* *pet* Stewart
Theo *dim.* Theo---
Toby* *v* Tobias
Tony* *pet* Anthony
Vere possibly from surname de Vere
Walt *pet* Walter
Wilf *pet* Wilfred
Will* *pet* William
Yang* 'positive force'
Yves *v* John
Zack *dim.* Zachariah
Zeke *pet* Ezekiel

5

Aaron possibly 'light'
Abner 'father of light'
Adolf *v* Adolphus
Alaric 'all-ruler'
Alban 'of Alba'
Aldis male *v* Alda
Aldus male *v* Alda
Alick *dim.* Alexander
Allan *v* Alan
Allen *v* Alan
Alwyn *v* Aylwin
Amias origin obscure

BOYS

Amyot 'loved by God'
Angus origin obscure
Ansty *dim.* Anastasius
Artie *dim.* Arthur
Barny *dim.* Barnaby/Barnard
Barry 'good spearman'
Basil* 'a king'
Basty *dim.* Sebastian
Benjy *dim.* Benjamin
Benny *dim.* Benjamin
Bevis 'bull'
Billy* *dim.* William
Blase* *v* Blaise
Blaze* *v* Blaise
Bobby* *dim.* Robert
Boris 'fight'
Brand* 'a flame'
Brian 'strong'
Brien *v* Brian
Bruce from the surname
Bruno 'brown'
Brush* *dim.* Ambrose
Bryan *v* Brian
Bunny* origin obscure
Caleb 'a dog'
Carlo *v* Charles
Carol* *v* Charles
Cecil 'blind'
Chris *dim.* Christopher
Claud *v* Claudius
Cliff* *dim.* Clifford
Clive 'cliff'
Colan 'a dove'
Colin* *v* Colan
Conal 'high courage'
Conan 'wise'
Cosmo *v* Cosimo
Craig* 'crag'
Cyril 'lordly'
Cyrus 'the sun'
Dafod *v* David
Darby *v* Diarmid
D'Arcy 'he of Arcy'
Daryl 'darling'
David 'to love'
Davie *dim.* David
Denis *v* Dionysos (god of wine)
Derek *v* Derrick
Digby from surname
Dolly* *pet* Adolphus

Dowal *v* Dugald
Dylan 'ocean'
Eamon *v* Edmund
Eddie *pet* various Ed---
Edgar 'prosperous spear'
Edwin 'rich friend'
Elias 'God the Lord'
Elihu 'God is Yahweh'
Eliot *v* Elias
Ellis *v* Elias
Elmer *v* Aylmer
Emery* *v* Emmery
Emile 'industrious'
Emlyn 'work serpent'
Emrys *v* Ambrose
Enoch 'dedication'
Ermin a Teutonic demi-god
Ernie *pet* Ernest
Errol 'wanderer'
Ethel* 'noble'
Ewart *v* Everard
Felix 'happy'
Frank* *v* Francis
Fritz *v* Frederick
Fulke 'one of the folk'
Garry *v* Garth
Garth* *v* Gareth
Gavin possibly 'Hawk of May'
Gawan *v* Gavin
Geoff *pet* Geoffrey
Gerry *pet* Gerald
Giles possibly 'religious servant'
Greig *v* Gregory
Guido *v* Guy
Gyles *v* Giles
Hanno *v* Hannibal
Harry* *pet* Henry
Harty male *v* Harriet
Henri *v* Henry
Henry* 'ruler of an enclosure'
Hiram 'most noble'
Homer* 'pledge'
Horst* 'gardener'
Hosea 'salvation'
Hywel 'lordly'
Idris origin obscure
Isaac 'laughter'
Jabez 'height'
Jacob 'a supplanter'
James* 'a heel'

Jamie *dim.* James
Jemmy* *dim.* James
Jerry* *dim.* Jeremiah
Jesse 'the lord is'
Jimmy* *dim.* James
Jonah 'a dove'
Jonas *v* Jonah
Joyce 'Goth'
Judah *v* Judas
Judas* 'praised'
Karol *v* Charles
Keith 'the wind'
Kenny *dim.* Kenneth
Kevin *v* Kenneth
Lance* *v* Lancelot
Larry *dim.* Lawrence
Leigh 'a meadow'
Lenny *pet* Leonard
Lewis* *v* Llewellyn/Louis
Lloyd 'grey'
Lorne 'love-lorn'
Louis* 'famous war'
Lucas *v* Luke
Madoc 'strong and handsome'
Manus* *v* Magnus
Marco *v* Mark
Maris male *v* Mary
Maxim* *v* Maximilian
Meara 'merry'
Melva 'chief'
Micky* *dim.* Michael
Miles* *v* Michael
Monty *dim.* Montagu
Morty *dim.* Mortimer
Moses possibly 'law-giver'
Mungo* 'beloved'
Myles *v* Miles
Natty* *dim.* Nathan/Nathaniel
Neddy* *pet* various Ed---
Neill *v* Niul
Niall *v* Niul
Nicky* *dim.* Nicholas
Nicol* *dim.* Nicholas
Nigel 'black'
Ollie *dim.* Oliver
Orson 'a bear's cub'
Oscar *v* Osgar
Osgar 'divine spear'
Osric 'divine power'
Paddy* *dim.* Patrick

Perce *pet* Perceval
Percy 'pierce-hedge'
Perry* *dim.* Peregrine
Peter* 'rock'
Piers* *v* Peter
Ralph 'wolf counsel'
Reece *v* Rhys
Robin* *dim.* Robert
Roddy *dim.* Roderic/Rodney
Rodger 'fame spear'
Rolfe *dim.* Rodolph
Rollo *dim.* Rodolph
Rolph *dim.* Rodolph
Rorie *v* Rory
Rufus 'red-haired'
Sandy* *dim.* Alexander
Savvy* *pet* Xavier
Shane *v* John
Silas *dim.* Silvanus
Simon 'the snub-nose'
Solly *dim.* Solomon
Taffy* *dim.* David
Teddy* *pet* Edward/Theodore
Terry* *dim.* Terence
Tibal *dim.* Theobald
Titus possibly 'I honour'
Tolly *pet* Bartholomew
Tommy* *pet* Tom
Tudor *v* Theodore
Ulric *v* Wulfric
Vince *dim.* Vincent
Vinny *dim.* Vincent
Waldo 'power'
Wally* *pet* Walter
Willy* *dim.* William
Yvain *v* John
Zacky *dim.* various Zach---

6

Adolph *v* Adolphus
Adrian 'of the Adriatic'
Albert* *dim.* Aethelbearht
Aldous male *v* Alda
Alfred 'elf in council'
Andrew *dim.* Andreas
Anselm 'divine helmet'
Antony *dim.* Antonius
Arnold *dim.* Arnwald

BOYS

Arthur completely unknown origin
Aubrey 'elf ruler'
August* *dim.* Augustus
Austen *dim.* Augustin
Austin *dim.* Augustin
Aylmer possibly 'nobly famous'
Barney* *dim.* Barnaby/Barnard
Bartie *dim.* Bartholomew
Bartle *dim.* Bartlemy
Bennet* *pet* Benedict
Bernie *pet* Bernard
Blaise possibly 'splay-footed'
Bobbie *dim.* Robert
Cadell 'strength in war'
Caesar* 'hairy'
Calvin 'bald'
Caspar 'horseman'
Casper 'horseman'
Cedric *v* Cerdic
Cerdic 'chieftain'
Cicero* 'vetch'
Claude *dim.* Claudius
Colman 'dove'
Connal 'high courage'
Connel *v* Connal
Connor *v* Connaire
Conrad 'shrewd in advice'
Cormac 'charioteer'
Cosimo 'order'
Curtis possibly 'courteous'
Damian 'one who tames'
Damien *v* Damian
Dandie *v* Andrew
Darius 'wealthy'
Darrel 'darling'
Delius 'of Delos'
Dennis *dim.* Dionysos (Greek god)
Densil origin obscure
Denzil origin obscure
Dermot *dim.* Diarmaid
Dhugal 'black'
Diccon (obsolete) *dim.* Richard
Dickey* *dim.* Richard
Donald 'world-ruler'
Dougal *v* Dhugal
Dudley from surname
Dugald 'dark stranger'
Duggie *dim.* Douglas/Dugald
Duncan 'brown warrior'
Eachan 'a horse'

Edmond 'happy protection'
Edmund 'happy protection'
Edward 'rich guardian'
Egbert 'edge-bright'
Egmont 'sword protection'
Elijah 'Jahweh is God'
Elisha 'God is salvation'
Elliot *dim.* Ellis
Ernest *v* Ernust
Ernust 'earnestness'
Esmond 'divine protection'
Eugene 'well born'
Evelyn possibly 'pleasant'
Fabian 'bean grower'
Ferdie *dim.* Ferdinand
Fergus 'excellent choice'
Fingal 'fair stranger'
Franco 'a free lord'
Freddy *pet* Frederick
Garnet* 'little warren'
Gareth *dim.* Garrath
Garret* *dim.* Garrath
Gaston 'a Gascon'
Gawain *v* Gavin
George 'earth worker'
Georgy *dim.* George
Gerald *dim.* Gerwald
Gerard 'spear hard'
Gervas *v* Gervase
Gibbon* *v* Gilbert
Gideon 'a destroyer'
Godwin 'God-friend'
Gordon 'three-cornered hill'
Graham 'grey hamlet'
Gwilym *v* William
Hamish *v* James
Harald 'army-wielder'
Harold 'army-wielder'
Harvey 'warrior-war'
Hector* 'defender'
Hedley from surname
Heirom 'most noble'
Herbie *pet* Herbert
Hilary 'cheerful'
Hobart *v* Hubert
Horace 'punctual'
Howard 'sword guardian'
Howell *v* Hywel
Hubert 'mind bright'
Humfry possibly 'giant peace'

Ingram 'Ing's raven'
Irving from surname
Isidor 'gift of Isis'
Israel 'contenting with the Lord'
Jarvis *v* Gervas
Jasper* 'master of the treasure'
Jemmie *dim.* James
Jenkin *v* John
Jeremy *v* Jeremiah
Jermyn 'a German'
Jerome 'holy name'
Jerram *v* Jerome
Jimmie *pet* James
Johnny* *dim.* John
Jordan 'descender'
Joseph* 'he shall add'
Joshua 'Jahweh is salvation'
Julian *v* Julius
Julius 'first growth of beard'
Justin 'just'
Kenelm 'bold helmet'
Kieren 'black'
Kieron *v* Kieren
Lalage 'prattler'
Launce* *dim.* Launcelot
Laurie *dim.* Laurence
Lemuel 'devoted to God'
Lennox 'chieftain'
Leslie from surname
Lester from surname
Lionel* 'little lion'
Lothar 'famous warrior'
Lucian *v* Lucius
Lucius 'born at daylight'
Luther *v* Lothair
Magnus 'great'
Marcus Mars, god of war
Marius 'of Mars'
Markus *v* Marcus
Martin* 'of Mars'
Melvin *v* Melva
Mervyn 'famous friend'
Mickie* *dim.* Michael
Morgan 'a sea dweller'
Morris* *v* Maurice
Murray* 'a seaman'
Nathan 'a gift'
Nelson* from Lord Nelson
Nichol *dim.* Nicholas
Norman* 'a Northman'

Nowell *v* Noel
Oengus 'unique choice'
Oliver* 'the olive'
Osbert 'divinely bright'
Osmond *v* Osmund
Osmund 'divinely bright'
Oswald 'divine power'
Pelham* from surname
Philip 'fond of horses'
Pierce* *v* Peter
Pompey* 'of Pompeii'
Rabbie *pet* Robert
Ranald *v* Ronald
Randle *dim.* Randolf
Reggie *dim.* Reginald
Reuben 'behold, a son'
Robert 'bright fame'
Rodney from Lord Rodney
Rodolf 'wolf fame'
Roland 'land fame'
Ronald *v* Reginald
Rudolf *v* Rodolf
Rupert 'bright fame'
Samson 'child of the sun god'
Samuel 'heard of God'
Seamus *v* James
Seumas *v* James
Sholto 'sower'
Sidney possibly St Denis
Simeon 'obedient'
Sydney *v* Sidney
Talbot* 'faggot cutter'
Talmai 'abounding in furrows'
Thomas 'twin'
Tobias 'God is good'
Tolley *pet* Bartholomew
Trefor from ancient surname
Trevor *v* Trefor
Ulrick 'wolf rule'
Vernon 'flourishing'
Victor* 'victorious'
Virgil 'flourishing'
Vivian 'alive'
Walter folk ruler'
Warren* 'protecting friend'
Wilmer 'willing fame'
Wilmot 'resolute mood'
Wilson Will's son
Xavier 'splendid'

BOYS

7

Abraham 'father of a multitude'
Alaster *v* Alexander
Alfonso *v* Alphonso
Alister *v* Alexander
Almeric 'work ruler'
Ambrose 'immortal'
Andreas 'a man'
Aneurin* 'truly golden'
Anthony 'inestimable'
Aonghus *v* Oengus
Aonguas *v* Oengus
Arnwald 'eagle strong'
Baldwin 'bold friend'
Barnaby 'son of exhortation'
Barnard *v* Bernard
Barnett *v* Bernard
Bartlet *dim.* Bartholomew
Bartley *dim.* Bartholomew
Bartram 'bright raven'
Bernard 'courage of a bear'
Bertram 'bright raven'
Cadogan pertaining to 'war'
Caradoc origin obscure
Carolus *v* Charles
Charles 'a man'
Charley* *pet* Charles
Charlie* *pet* Charles
Chauncy from surname
Christy* *dim.* Christopher
Clarrie *dim.* Clarence
Clemens 'the merciful'
Clement* *v* Clemens
Colbert 'cool brightness'
Colborn 'black bear'
Cormick *v* Cormac
Cradock *v* Caradoc
Crispin* 'curly haired'
Cuthbert 'famous bright'
Cyprian 'of Cyprus'
Darrell 'darling'
Deiniol *v* Daniel
Derrick *pet* Theodoric
Desmond 'of South Munster'
Diarmid 'a freeman'
Diggory possibly 'lost'
Douglas 'dark stream'
Dunstan 'hill stone'
Eachaid 'a horse'

Eadward 'rich guardian'
Elliott *dim.* Elias
Emanuel *v* Immanuel
Ephraim 'doubly fruitful'
Erasmus 'I love'
Ethered 'counsel'
Eustace 'rich harvest'
Everard 'brave as a boar'
Everett 'brave as a boar'
Ezekiel 'God will strengthen'
Francis *v* Franco
Frankie *pet* Francis
Freddie *pet* Frederick
Fredric 'peaceful ruler'
Fulbert 'exceedingly bright'
Gabriel 'man of God'
Garrath 'firm spear'
Garrett *v* Garth
Gawaine *v* Gavin
Geordie* *v* George
Georgie *dim.* George
Gervase 'spear eagerness'
Gerwald 'spear wielder'
Gifford origin obscure
Gilbert* 'bright pledge'
Gillies* 'servant of Jesus'
Godfrey 'God's peace'
Goronwy origin obscure
Gregory* 'watchman'
Griffin* *v* Rufus
Haldane 'half-Dane'
Harding *v* Hardwin
Hardwin 'firm friend'
Hartley 'stony meadow'
Herbert 'bright army'
Hesketh from surname
Horatio *v* Horace
Humbert 'bright giant'
Humfrey 'giant peace'
Ishmael 'God harkens'
Isidore 'gift of Isis'
Jacobus* *v* James
Jacques *v* James
Jeffery *v* Geoffrey
Jeffrey *v* Geoffrey
Joachim 'appointed of the Lord'
Joannes* *v* John
Jocelin 'merry'
Jocelyn *v* Jocelin
Johnnie* *dim.* John

Kenneth 'handsome'
Lachlan 'warlike'
Lambert* 'land pride'
Lazarus 'whom God assists'
Leander 'lion-man'
Leonard 'lion-strong'
Leopold 'people bold'
Lincoln surname, President Lincoln
Lothair v Lothar
Lowther v Lothar
Macaire 'blessed'
Macbeth 'son of life'
Madison surname, President Madison
Malachi 'God's messenger'
Malcolm 'servant of Columb'
Marcius v Marcus
Matthew 'gift of the Lord'
Maurice 'a moor'
Maxwell* v Maximilian
Menzies v Clarence
Meyrick 'work ruler'
Michael 'like to God'
Montagu 'peaked will'
Morrice* v Maurice
Morvryn 'sea king'
Murdoch 'sea warrior'
Murtagh 'sea warrior'
Murtoch 'sea warrior'
Myrddin possibly 'sea hill'
Neville 'new city'
Nicolas 'victory of the people'
Norbert 'Niord's brightness'
Obadiah 'servant of the Lord'
Orlando 'fame of the land'
Padriac v Patrick
Patrick* 'patrician'
Percival 'pierce value'
Phineas possibly 'whitehouse'
Prosper* 'fortunate'
Quentin v Quintus
Quintin v Quintus
Quintus 'the fifth child'
Randolf 'house wolf'
Raphael 'God's healing'
Raymond 'wise protection'
Redmond 'counsel-protection'
Reynold 'power and might'
Richard 'stern ruler'
Ritchie dim. Richard
Roderic 'famous ruler'

Rodolph 'wolf fame'
Rowland v Roland
Rudolph v Rodolph
Russell 'red head'
Sanders* v Alexander
Solomon 'peaceable'
Stanley from surname
Stephen 'crown'
Tancred 'grateful speech'
Tantony* from St Anthony
Terence 'tender'
Thorold 'Thor's rule'
Tiernan 'kingly'
Timothy* 'honouring God'
Vincent 'conquering'
Wilfred 'resolute peace'
Wulfric 'wolf rule'
Wilfrid v Wilfred
William 'helmet of resolution'
Winston from surname
Zachary v Zachariah

8

Adolphus 'noble wolf'
Adrianus 'of the Adriatic'
Alaricus 'ruler of all'
Alastair v Alexander
Algernon 'whiskered'
Alistair v Alexander
Alisteir v Alexander
Almerick v Almeric
Aloysius v Louis
Alphonso origin obscure
Antonius 'inestimable'
Augustin dim. Augustus
Augustus 'majestic'
Barnabas 'son of exhortation'
Bartlemy dim. Bartholomew
Barthram 'bright raven'
Benedict 'blessed'
Benjamin* 'son of the right hand'
Bertrand v Bertram
Biddulph 'commanding wolf'
Boniface* 'well-doer'
Chauncey from surname
Clarence* 'renowned'
Claudius 'lame'
Connaire 'high will'

BOYS

Constant* 'constant'
Cuthbert 'famous splendour'
Diarmaid 'a freeman'
Donoghue 'brown chieftain'
Ebenezer* 'stone of help'
Emmanuel *v* Immanuel
Ethelred 'counsel'
Franklin* 'freeholder'
Frederic 'peaceful ruler'
Geoffrey 'God's peace'
Geoffroy *v* Geoffrey
Gervaise 'spear eagerness'
Griffith *v* Rufus
Gruffydd *v* Rufus
Gustavus 'divine staff'
Hamilton from surname
Hannibal 'grace of Baal'
Heinrich 'ruler of enclosure'
Hercules 'lordly fame'
Humphrey *v* Humphrey
Ignatius 'fiery'
Immanuel 'God with us'
Innocent* 'harmless'
Jedidiah 'God is my friend'
Jeremiah 'appointed by Jahweh'
Johannes* *v* John
Jonathan 'the Lord's gift'
Justinus 'just'
Lancelot possibly 'boy servant'
Laurence 'laurel tree'
Lawrence *v* Laurence
Lothario *v* Lothair
Ludovick *v* Lewis
Matthias *v* Matthew
Meredith 'sea protector'
Montague 'peaked hill'
Mortimer 'sea warrior'
Napoleon* 'belonging to new city'
Nicholas 'victory of the people'
Octavius eighth child
Perceval 'pierce value'
Percival 'pierce value'
Randolph 'house wolf'
Reginald 'judgement power'
Roderick 'famous ruler'
Saunders *v* Alexander
Sebastos 'venerated'
Septimus 'seventh child'
Thaddeus possibly 'praise'
Theobald 'folk-bold'

Theodore 'God's gift'
Theodric 'people's ruler'
Tristram possibly 'a herald'
Valerius 'strong'
Xenophon 'strange voice'

9

Alexander 'defender of men'
Archibald 'truly bold'
Balthasar origin obscure
Cadwallon 'war lord'
Christian 'follower of Christ'
Cornelius 'regal'
Demetrius 'of Demeter'
Ferdinand 'venturous life'
Frederick 'peaceful ruler'
Gilchrist 'servant of Christ'
Gillespie 'servant of Bishop'
Gwalchmai *v* Gavin
Kentigern 'head chief'
Launcelot original form of Lancelot
Llewellyn 'lion-like'
Lodowick *v* Lewis
Marcellus *dim.* Marcus
Marmaduke possibly 'sea leader'
Nathaniel 'gift of God'
Peregrine* 'a wanderer'
Sebastian 'venerated'
Silvester 'of the forest'
Stanislas disputed origin
Sylvester *v* Silvester
Theodoric 'people's ruler'
Valentine* 'strong'
Zachariah 'God has remembered'

10

Anastasius 'he who awakes'
Athanasius 'immortal'
Belshazzar origin obscure
Carmichael 'friend of Michael'
Crispianus 'curly haired'
Gwenwynwyn 'thrice-white'
Hildebrand 'battle-sword'
Hortensius 'a gardener'
Maximilian 'greatest'
Stanislaus 'martial glory'

Theophilus 'beloved of God'	**Cadwallader** 'battle arranger'
	Christianus 'follower of Christ'
11	**Christopher** 'bearer of Christ'
	Constantine 'constant'
Bartholomew 'son of Talmai'	**Sacheverell** from surname

GIRLS

dim. diminutive of
fem. feminine of
pet pet form of
v variant form of

2

Ag *dim.* Agnes
Di *dim.* Dinah/Diana
Em* *pet* Emily
Jo* *pet* Josephine/Joanna
Lu *dim.* various Lu---
Mo* *pet* various M---
Si* *pet* Simone
Vi *dim.* Viola/Violet
Zo* *pet* Zoë

3

Ada possibly 'happy'
Amy 'a woman beloved'
Ann* *v* Anna
Ava* *v* Avis
Bab *dim.* Barbara
Bar* *dim.* Barbara
Bea *dim.* Beatrice
Bet* *dim.* Elizabeth
Cal *dim.* Calliope
Cec *dim.* Cecilia
Cis *dim.* Cicely/Cicily
Clo *dim.* Chloe
Cyn *pet* Cynthia
Dan* *pet* Danielle
Deb* *dim.* Deborah
Dee* *dim.* Delia
Dot* *dim.* Dorothy/Dorothea
Eda *dim.* Edith

Ena possibly 'praise'
Eth *pet* Ethel
Eva 'life'
Eve* 'life'
Fay* *v* Faith
Flo *pet* Florence
Gay* 'lively and merry'
Gus* *pet* Augustina
Het* *dim.* Hetty
Ida *dim.* Idonia
Ira 'watchful'
Ivy* the plant of that name
Jan *pet* Janet
Jay* *pet* various J---
Jen *dim.* Jane: *pet* Jennifer
Joe* *pet* Josephine/Joanna
Joy* 'joy'
Kay* *dim.* various K---
Kit* *dim.* Kitty
Les* *pet* Lesley
Lil *dim.* Lil---
Lin* *dim.* Lindsay
Liz *dim.* Elizabeth
Lou *dim.* Louisa
Lyn *v* Lynn
Mae* *v* May
Mag* *dim.* Margaret
May* *dim.* Mary
Meg *dim.* Margaret
Mel* *dim.* Melanie
Nan* *pet* Ann
Pat* *dim.* Patricia
Peg* *pet* Margaret

GIRLS

Pet* *dim.* Petula
Pru *dim.* Prudence
Ray* *v* Raye
Ria* *pet* Maria
Rue* *pet* Ruth
Sal* *pet* Sally
Sam *pet* Samantha
Sim* *pet* Simone
Sis* *dim.* Cicely/Cicily
Sue* *pet* Susan/Susannah
Tab* *pet* Tabitha
Ted* *pet* Theodora
Tib *pet* Isabel
Una 'one'
Val *pet* Valerie
Van* *pet* Vanessa
Vic *pet* Victoria
Vin *pet* Lavinia
Viv *pet* Vivienne
Win* *dim.* Winifred
Wyn *v* Win
Yin* 'negative force'
Zoë 'life'

4

Abbe* *v* Abbey
Addy *pet* various A---
Alda 'old'
Alex *dim.* various Alex---
Alix *dim.* Alicia
Ally* *dim.* Alice
Alma* 'maiden'
Alys *v* Alice
Anna* 'grace'
Anne *v* Anna
Atty possibly 'high'
Auda 'rich'
Avis 'bird'
Avvy *pet* various Av---
Babs *pet* Barbara
Bell* *pet* Isabel/Isabella
Bess *dim.* Elizabeth
Beth *dim.* Elizabeth
Cara 'friend'
Cass *pet* Cassandra
Cleo *dim.* Cleopatra
Cora 'maiden'

Daff* *dim.* Daphne
Dale* 'valley dweller'
Daly *dim.* Elaine
Dawn* *v* Aurora
Dixy* *v* Dixie
Dodo* *pet* Dorothy
Doll* *pet* Dorothea
Dora *v* Dorothea
Edda *pet* Edwina
Edie *pet* Edith
Edna *v* Edina
Ella *v* Ellen
Elma 'love'
Elsa *v* Else
Else* 'noble maiden'
Elza *v* Elsa
Emma* *v* Imma
Enid 'spotless purity'
Esme 'to esteem'
Etta *v* Henrietta
Etty *dim.* Esther
Fran *pet* Frances
Gaby* *pet* Gabriella
Gail *dim.* Abigail
Gale* *v* Gail
Gene* *dim.* Eugenia
Gert *dim.* Gertrude
Gill* *dim.* Gillian
Gwen *dim.* Gwendolen
Hebe* 'youth'
Hero* 'a lady'
Hild 'battle'
Hope* 'hope'
Imma *v* Irma
Ines *v* Agnes
Inez *v* Ines
Iris* 'rainbow'
Irma 'maid of high degree'
Issy *pet* Isadora
Izzy *pet* Isadora
Jane* *fem.* John
Jean* *v* Jane/Joan
Jess* *dim.* Jasmine
Jill* *v* Gillian
Joan *v* Jane/Johanna
Judy* *dim.* Judith
Jule *pet* various Ju---
June the month
Kali* Hindu goddess
Kate *dim.* various Kat---

Kath *dim.* various Kath---
Katy *dim.* Kathleen
Lana* *fem.* Lancelot
Leah 'wearied'
Lena *dim.* various ---len---
Leot *v* Loise
Lida 'people's love'
Lila *v* Leila
Lily* origin obscure
Lina *v* various ---lin---
Lisa *v* Elizabeth
Lise *v* Louise
Liza *v* Elizabeth
Lois 'better'
Lola *pet* Dolores
Lora *pet* Leonara
Lucy *fem.* Lucius
Lulu* *dim.* Louise
Lynn possibly 'a lake'
Mall* *dim.* Matilda
Mara* *dim.* various Mar---
Mari *v* Mary
Mary *dim.* Miriam
Matt* *dim.* Matilda
Maud* *v* Matilda
Meta *v* Margaret
Mima *dim.* Jemima
Mina* *pet* Wilhelmina
Mira *dim.* Miranda
Moke* *v* Molly
Moll* *v* Molly
Mona* 'noble'
Myra *v* Mira
Nell *dim.* various --el--: *fem.* Neal
Nina *pet* Anna
Nita 'bright'
Nona 'ninth child'
Nora *dim.* various ---nora
Olga *v* Helga
Poll* *v* Mary
Prue *dim.* Prudence
Rene *dim.* Irene
Rina *dim.* Katherine
Rita *v* Margaret
Rona *fem.* Ronald
Rosa *v* Rose
Rose* flower of that name
Ross *pet* Rosalind
Ruby* the jewel
Ruth* possibly 'beauty'

Sara 'a princess'
Suse *pet* Suzanne
Suze *pet* Suzanne
Tara* royal Irish connection
Tess *dim.* Theresa
Theo *dim.* Theo---
Tina *dim.* various ---tin---
Trix *dim.* Beatrix
Ursy *dim.* Ursula
Vera 'true'
Vida *fem.* David
Zona* 'girdle'
Zora 'dawn'

5

Abbey* *dim.* Abigail
Addie *pet* Audrey
Adela 'noble'
Aggie *dim.* Agnes/Agatha
Agnes 'pure'
Ailie *dim.* Alison
Ailsa *v* Elsa
Alice 'truth'
Aline *dim.* Adeline
Allie *dim.* Alice
Amber* jewel name
Amice* *v* Amy
Angie *dim.* Angela
Anita *dim.* Anna
Annie *pet* Ann
Annis *v* Agnes
Annot *dim.* Agnes
Annys *v* Agnes
Anona Ann + Oona
April *v* Averil
Audry *v* Audrey
Avice 'war refuge'
Avril *v* Averil
Babie *dim.* Barbara
Becky *pet* Rebecca
Bella *dim.* various ---bella
Belle* *v* Bella
Beryl* jewel name
Bessy *dim.* Elizabeth
Betsy *dim.* Elizabeth
Betta *dim.* Elizabeth
Bette *dim.* Elizabeth
Betty* *dim.* Elizabeth

GIRLS

Biddy* *dim.* Bridget
Bride* *dim.* Bridget
Bunny* origin obscure
Bunty* possibly 'short and stout'
Carol* *v* Charlotte
Carry* *v* Charlotte
Celia 'heavenly'
Chloe 'green and tender shoot'
Chris *dim.* Christina
Cissy* *pet* Cicely
Clair *v* Clara
Clara 'clear'
Clare *v* Clara
Coral* a 'jewel' name
Daisy* 'day's eye' flower
Debby* *dim.* Deborah
Delia surname of Artemis
Della 'noble'
Detta *dim.* Benedetta
Diana Roman goddess
Dinah 'judged'
Dolly* *dim.* Dorothea
Dotty* *dim.* Dorothy
Doris 'a Doric girl'
Dreda possibly *dim.* Etheldreda
Edina *fem.* Edwin
Edith 'prosperous war'
Effie *dim.* Euphemia
Elise *v* Eliza
Eliza *v* Elizabeth
Ellen *v* Helen
Elsie *v* Elizabeth
Emily *fem.* Emile
Emmie *dim.* Emma
Emott possibly 'universal'
Eppie *dim.* Euphemia
Erica* *fem.* Eric
Essie *dim.* Esther
Ethyl* *dim.* various Ethyl---
Ettie *dim.* Esther
Faith* 'faith'
Fanny* *pet* Frances
Fiona 'white'
Fleur 'flower'
Flora* 'flower'
Freda *pet* Winifred
Frida *v* Frieda
Gabby* *pet* Gabrielle
Gatty *dim.* Gertrude
Gemma* 'precious stone'

Glory* *pet* Gloria
Grace* 'grace'
Greta *v* Margaret
Gussy *dim.* Augusta
Hatty *v* Harriet
Hazel* 'hazel'
Helen 'the light'
Helga 'holiness'
Hetty *dim.* Esther
Hilda 'battle'
Holly* 'holly'/'holy'
Honor 'honour'
Hulda 'muffled'
Irene 'peace'
Isold *v* Ysolt
Janet *v* Jane
Jenny* *pet* Jennifer: *dim.* Johanna/Jane
Jerry* *fem.* adoption Jerry
Jinny *dim.* Jane
Josie *dim.* Josephine
Joyce 'Goth'
Julia *fem.* Julius
Julie *v* Julia
Karen *v* Katherine/Karin
Karin 'pure'
Karol *v* Carol
Kathy *dim.* Kathleen
Katie *dim.* Katherine
Keren *dim.* Kerenhappuch
Kitty* *dim.* Katherine
Laura* 'laurel tree'
Leila 'darkness'
Letty *dim.* Letitia
Libby *dim.* Elizabeth
Liddy *dim.* Lydia
Lilly *dim.* Lilian
Linda *dim.* various ---linda
Lindy *pet* Linda
Lizze *pet* Elizabeth
Lizzy *pet* Elizabeth
Lolly* *pet* Laura
Lorna *v* Lorne
Lorne 'love-lorn'
Lotty *pet* Charlotte
Lucia *dim. fem.* Lucius
Lucie *v* Lucy
Lydia 'a woman of Lydia'
Mabel *dim.* Amabel
Madge* *v* Margaret
Magda *dim.* Magdalene

Mamie *dim.* Margaret
Mandy *dim.* Amanda
Marge* *pet* Marjorie
Maria* *v* Miriam
Marie *v* Maria
Marta *v* Martha
Marty *pet* Martina
Matty *pet* Matilda
Maude *v* Matilda
Maura *v* Moira
Mavis* 'song thrush'
Meggy *dim.* Margaret
Mercy* 'mercy'
Merle* 'blackbird'
Milly *dim.* Emily/Millicent
Minna *v* Minnie
Moggy* *v* Molly
Moira 'soft'
Molly* *dim.* Mary
Morna 'affection'
Moyna *v* Mona
Nancy* *v* Anne/Agnes
Nelly* *dim.* Helen
Nessa *dim.* Agnes
Nesta *dim.* Agnes
Netta *v* Nita
Nicky *pet* various Nic---
Nicol* *fem.* Nicholas
Norah *dim.* various ---ora
Norma* 'a pattern'
Odila 'the fatherhead'
Odile *v* Odila
Olive* *v* Olivia
Oriel* 'window'
Paddy* *dim.* Patricia
Pansy* the flower
Patsy* *dim.* Patricia
Paula *fem.* Paul
Pearl* 'pearl'
Peggy* *v* Margaret
Penny* *dim.* Penelope
Phebe *pet* Phoebe
Polly* *pet* Mary
Poppy* the flower
Rayda *dim.* Raymonda
Rhoda 'roses'
Rhode 'rose-bush'
Rosie *dim.* various Ros---
Sadie *pet* Sarah
Sally* *v* Sarah

Sarah 'princess'
Sibyl* 'a prophetess'
Sonia 'wise one'
Sophy 'wisdom'
Stacy *dim.* Anastasia
Susan *dim.* Susanna
Susie *dim.* Susan
Sybil *v* Sibyl
Tabby* *pet* Tabitha
Tammy* *pet* Thomasina
Tania *dim.* Natalia
Tansy* origin obscure
Tanya *dim.* Natalia
Terry* *dim.* Teresa
Tessa *dim.* Teresa
Tilda *dim.* Matilda
Tilly *pet* Tilda
Tracy *v* Teresa
Trixy *pet* Beatrix
Truda *pet* Gertrude
Trude *pet* Gertrude
Unity* 'unity'
Ursie *dim.* Ursula
Vassy *dim.* Vashti
Vesta* goddess of the hearth
Vinny *pet* Lavinia
Viola* 'violet'
Wanda 'stem, stock'
Wenda 'wanderer'
Wendy invented by J. M. Barrie
Willa 'resolute'
Winnie 'white'
Winny *pet* Una
Ysolt possibly a Celtic goddess

6

Agatha 'good'
Aileen *v* Helen
Alexia* *v* Alicia
Alexis *dim.* Alexandra
Alicia 'truth'
Alison *dim.* Alice
Almira 'of Almeria'
Althea 'healthy'
Amabel 'lovable'
Amecia *v* Amy
Amelia* *v* Emily
Amicia *v* Amy

GIRLS

Andrea *fem.* Andrew
Angela *dim.* Angelica
Anthea 'lady of flowers'
Astrid 'divine strength'
Audrey *dim.* Etheldreda
Aurora* 'dawn'
Averil 'wild-boar battle maid'
Averyl *v* Averil
Awdrey *v* Audrey
Beatie *dim.* Beatrice
Bertha* 'the bright one'
Bessie *dim.* Elizabeth
Bethia 'servant of Yahweh'
Blanch* 'white'
Bobbie *pet* Roberta
Brenda *fem.* Brand
Bridie* *dim.* Bridget
Brigid *dim.* Brighid
Brigit *dim.* Brighid
Carmel 'vineyard'
Carola *fem.* Carolus
Carole *v* Carol
Carrie *dim.* Carola
Cecily *v* Cecilia
Chatty* *pet* Charlotte
Cherry* *dim.* Charity
Cicely* *v* Cecily
Cicily *v* Cecily
Cissie *pet* various Ci/Ce---
Connie *dim.* Constance
Corrie* *dim.* Cornelia
Daphne* 'bay-tree'
Denise *fem.* Denis
Derdre *v* Deirdre
Dorcas 'gazelle'
Dulcia 'sweet'
Dulcie 'sweet'
Edwina *fem.* Edwin
Eileen *v* Helen
Elaine *v* Helen
Elinor *v* Eleanor
Eloisa *fem.* Louis
Eloise *fem.* Louis
Elspie *dim.* Elizabeth
Elvina 'friendly'
Elvira 'elf counsel'
Emilia *fem.* Emile
Esther 'star'
Eunice 'wife'
Evadne 'well-tamed'

Evelyn 'pleasant'
Flower* 'flower'
Frieda 'peace'
Garnet* the jewel
Georgy *pet* Georgina
Gladys *v* Claudia
Gloria* 'fame'
Graina *v* Graine
Graine* 'love'
Grizel *dim.* Griseldis
Gwenda *dim.* Gwendolen
Gwenny *dim.* Gwendolen
Gwynne 'white'
Haidee possibly 'modest'
Hannah *v* Anne
Hester *v* Esther
Hilary 'cheerful'
Honora *v* Honor
Ianthe 'violet flower'
Imogen 'daughter'
Ingrid 'Ing's ride'
Isabel* *v* Elizabeth
Iseult *v* Ysolt
Isobel *v* Elizabeth
Isolda *v* Ysolt
Isolde *v* Ysolt
Jeanie *dim.* Jean
Jemima* 'dove'
Jessie* *pet* Jessica
Joanna *v* Johanna
Judith 'a Jewess'
Juliet *v* Julia
Kathie *dim.* various Kath---
Keziah 'cassia'
Kirsty *v* Christine
Leilah 'darkness'
Leonie *fem.* Leo
Lesley *v* Leslie
Leslie from surname
Lilian 'lily'
Lilias *v* Lilian
Lilith 'serpent'
Lottie *pet* Charlotte
Louisa *fem.* Louis
Louise *fem.* Louis
Maddie *dim.* Madeline
Maggie *pet* Margaret
Maidie *dim.* Margaret
Maisie *dim.* Margaret
Marcia *fem.* Marcus

314

Marian *v* Marion
Marina* *v* Mary
Marion *v* Marie
Martha 'lady'
Martie *d.* Martha
Mattie *pet* Matilda
Maudie *pet* Maud
Meggie *dim.* Margaret
Melody* 'melody'
Mercia 'of border-lands'
Meriel *v* Muriel
Millie *dim.* Emily
Minnie* 'love'
Miriam 'bitterness'
Monica 'unique'
Muriel 'sea bright'
Myrtle* 'bilberry'
Nadine 'hope'
Nellie* *dim.* Helen, etc.
Nessie *dim.* Agnes
Nichol *fem.* Nicholas
Noreen *dim.* Nora
Odette *dim.* Odile
Olivia *v* Olive
Oonagh *v* Una
Oriole* possibly *v* Oriel
Pamela 'all honey'
Paulie *pet* Pauline
Phoebe 'radiant'
Porcia 'pig'
Portia *v* Porcia
Prissy* *pet* Priscilla
Rachel 'a ewe'
Regina* 'queen'
Robina *fem.* Robin
Rosina *v* Rose
Rowena *v* Rhonwen
Sabina 'a Sabine'
Salome 'peace'
Sancha *v* Sanchia
Sandra *dim.* Alexandra
Selima *fem.* Solomon
Selina 'heaven'
Serena 'calm'
Sheila *v* Sheelah
Silvia *v* Sylvia
Sissie *pet* various Ci---
Sisley *v* Cicely
Sophia* 'wisdom'
Sorcha 'bright'

Stacey *dim.* Anastasia
Stella 'star'
Sylvia* 'wood-dweller'
Teresa 'reaper'
Tessie *dim.* Teresa
Tirzah *v* Thirzah
Tricia *pet* Beatrice
Ultrica *fem.* Ulric
Ursula 'little bear'
Vanora 'white wave'
Vashti 'star'
Venise from Venus
Violet* 'violet'
Vivien 'alive'
Yseult *v* Yseulte
Yvette *fem.* Yves
Yvonne *fem.* Yves

7

Abigail* 'father's joy'
Adelina *v* Adela
Adeline *v* Adela
Adriana *fem.* Adrian
Ailleen *v* Helen
Alberga 'noble'
Alberta *fem.* Albert
Alfreda *fem.* Alfred
Annabel *v* Amabel
Annette *v* Anne
Anstace *v* Anastasia
Anstice *v* Anastasia
Antonia *fem.* Anthony
Augusta *fem.* Augustus
Aurelia* 'golden'
Barbara 'stranger'
Beatrix 'blessed'
Bethiah 'servant of Yahweh'
Bettrys *v* Beatrice
Blanche 'white'
Bridget *dim.* Brighid
Bridgit *dim.* Brighid
Brighid 'strength'
Bronwen 'white-breasted'
Camilla 'temple maiden'
Candida 'white'
Carmela 'vineyard'
Cecilia 'blind'
Cecilie *v* Cecilia

GIRLS

Celeste* 'heavenly'
Charity* 'love'
Charlot *fem.* Charles
Clarice 'renowned'
Clarrie *dim.* Clara
Claudia 'lame'
Clemmie *dim.* Clemency
Clodagh from an Irish river
Colette *v* Nichol
Coralie *v* Cora/Coral
Corinna *v* Cora
Crystal* jewel name
Cynthia moon goddess (Artemis)
Deborah 'a bee'
Deirdre *v* Derdriu
Delicia 'delight'
Derdriu 'The Raging One'
Dolores 'grief'
Dorinda *v* various Dor---
Eadgifa 'giver of bliss'
Eadgifu 'rich gift'
Eadgyth 'prosperous war'
Eadwine 'rich friend'
Eiluned possibly *v* Helen
Eleanor *v* Helen
Elspeth *v* Elizabeth
Erminia *fem.* Ermin
Estelle *dim.* Esther
Eugenia *fem.* Eugene
Eveleen 'pleasant'
Evelina *v* Eveline
Eveline *fem.* Evelyn
Felicia *v* Felicity
Fenella 'white shoulders'
Finella 'white shoulders'
Florrie *dim.* Flora/Florence
Flossie *dim.* Flora/Florence
Frances *fem.* Francis
Frankie *pet* Frances
Freddie *pet* Frederica
Genevra *v* Guinevere
Georgie *pet* Georgina
Gertrud *dim.* Gertrut
Gertrut 'beloved spear'
Gillian *v* Julia
Grainne 'love'
Grisell *v* Grizel
Grissel *v* Grizel
Grissil *v* Grizel
Grizzie *pet* Grizel

Gwennie *pet* Gwen
Gwladys *v* Claudia
Gwyneth 'blessed'
Harriet 'home rule'
Harriot *v* Harriet
Heather* from the flower
Helena 'light'
Heloisa *fem.* Louis
Hilaria *v* Hilary
Honoria *v* Honor
Horatia *fem.* Horatio
Imogine *v* Imogen
Isadore 'equal gift'
Jasmine* flower
Jemimah 'handsome as the day'
Jessica 'God is looking'
Jocelyn 'jocular'
Johanna *fem.* John
Jonquil* flower
Josepha *fem.* Joseph
Katrine *dim.* Katharine
Kirstin *v* Christian
Lavinia 'of Lavinium'
Leonora *v* Eleanora
Letitia 'gladness'
Letizia *v* Letitia
Lettice *v* Letitia
Lillian possibly 'lily'
Lindsay 'of gentle speech'
Lindsey *v* Lindsay
Lucilla *dim.* Lucia
Lucille *dim.* Lucia
Malachi 'God's messenger'
Malvina 'friendly'
Margery *v* Margaret
Mariana *v* Maria
Marilyn *v* Mary
Matilda 'might of battle'
Maureen *v* Mary
Maurine *v* Maureen
Melanie 'dark complexioned'
Melinda possibly 'of the ash tree'
Melissa 'honey'
Mildred 'mild power'
Mildrid *v* Mildred
Mirabel 'wonderful'
Miranda 'worthy of admiration'
Morgana *fem.* Morgan
Myfanwy 'child of the water'
Natalia 'birth'

Natalie v Natalia
Octavia eighth child
Ophelia 'assistance'
Patricia fem. Patrick
Pauline fem. Paul
Peggoty dim. Margaret
Petrina fem. Peter
Phyllis 'a green leaf'
Queenie possibly from queen
Rebecca 'a snare'
Rebekah v Rebecca
Rhonwen 'white skirt'
Roberta fem. Robert
Robinia fem. Robin
Rosabel 'pretty rose'
Rosalia* 'rose-like'
Rosalie 'rose-like'
Rosanna Rosa + Anna
Rosella* Rosa + Ella
Rosetta pet Rose
Sabrina River Severn
Sanchia 'saintly'
Sheelah v Celia
Shirley from surname
Sighile v Cecilia
Susanna 'graceful white lily'
Suzanne v Susanna
Tafline fem. v David
Theresa v Teresa
Thirzah 'pleasantness'
Valerie fem. Valerius
Vanessa* Van + Esther
Venetia 'blessed'
Yolande possibly v Viola
Yseulte possibly a Celtic goddess

8

Adelaide 'nobility'
Adrienne fem. Adrian
Amabella v Amy
Angelica* 'a messenger'
Angelina dim. Angela
Arianwen 'silver'
Averilla 'wild-boar battle-maid'
Beatrice dim. Beatrix
Brunhild 'brown battle-maid'
Calliope* 'beautiful voice'
Carolina v Carol

Caroline v Carol
Cathleen v Katharine
Charissa 'love'
Charmian 'joy'
Charmion v Charmian
Chrissie pet Christina
Christie* pet Christina
Claribel dim. Clara
Clarinda dim. Clara
Clarissa v Clarice
Claudine v Claudia
Clemence v Clemency
Clemency* 'mercy'
Clotilda 'famous battlefield'
Clotilde 'famous battlefield'
Cordelia 'daughter of the sea'
Cornelia 'regal'
Danielle fem. Daniel
Dorothea 'a gift of God'
Eleanora v Helen
Eleanore v Helen
Euphemia 'fair speech'
Felicity* 'happiness'
Florence* 'flourishing'
Georgina fem. George
Gertrude v Gertrud
Griselda v Griseldis
Guenever v Guinevere
Hermione 'daughter of Hermes'
Iolanthe possibly v Yolande
Isabella* v Isobel
Jacobina fem. Jacob
Jamesina fem. James
Jennifer v Guinevere or Winifred
Julienne* v Julia
Juliette v Julia
Kathleen v Katharine
Madeline v Magdalen
Magdalen* 'of Magdala'
Marcella* fem. Marcus
Margaret 'a pearl'
Marianne Mary + Anne
Marigold* v Margaret
Mathilde v Matilda
Mercedes 'Mary of the mercies'
Milicent 'work-strong'
Myrtilla dim. Myrtle
Patience* 'patience'
Patricia fem. Patrick
Penelope 'a weaver'

GIRLS

Perpetua 'everlasting'
Philippa *fem.* Phillip
Phyllida *v* Phyllis
Primrose* 'first bloom'
Prudence* 'prudent'
Raymonda *fem.* Raymond
Raymonde *fem.* Raymond
Rosalind 'fair as a rose'
Rosaline *v* Rosalind
Rosamond *v* Rosamunda
Rosamund *v* Rosamunda
Rosemary* Rose + Mary
Samantha *fem.* Samuel
Sapphira 'lapis lazuli'
Sheelagh *v* Celia
Susannah 'graceful white lily'
Theodora *fem.* Theodore
Tryphena 'dainty'
Veronica* 'true image'
Victoria* 'victory'
Virginia 'of spring'
Walburga 'powerful protectress'
Winifred 'white wave'
Winifrid *v* Winifred

9

Albertina *fem.* Albert
Albertine *fem.* Albert
Alexandra *fem.* Alexander
Anastasia 'she who awakes'
Annabella Anna + Bella
Arthurine *fem.* Arthur
Augustina *v* Augusta
Bathsheba 'daughter of the oath'
Brunhilda 'brown battle-maid'
Cassandra 'helper of men'
Catharina *v* Katharina
Catharine *v* Katharine
Charlotte* *fem.* Charles
Christian original *fem.* of Christina
Christina 'follower of Christ'
Christine *v* Christina
Cleopatra 'fame of one's father'
Columbine* 'dove-like'
Constance 'firm of purpose'
Dominique 'Sabbath born'
Elizabeth 'consecrated to God'
Emanuelle *fem.* Emanuel

Ernestine *fem.* Ernest
Esmeralda 'an emerald'
Francesca *v* Frances
Frederica *fem.* Frederic
Gabriella *fem.* Gabriel
Gabrielle *fem.* Gabriel
Genevieve 'white'-(poss.)'browed'
Georgiana *fem.* George
Georgette* *fem.* George
Geraldine *fem.* Gerald
Griseldis 'grey battle-maid'
Guendolen *v* Gwendolen
Guenevere *v* Guinevere
Guinevere 'white'-(poss.)'wave'
Gwendolen 'white'-(poss.)'browed'
Gwendolin *v* Gwendolen
Gwenfrewi *v* Winifred
Henrietta *fem.* Henry
Hepzibah 'my delight is in her'
Hildegard 'battle-maid'
Hortensia 'a gardener'
Jessamine* *v* Jasmine
Josephine *fem.* Joseph
Katharina *v* Katharine
Katharine 'pure'
Magdalene* 'of Magdala'
Maribelle 'lovely Mary'
Melisande *v* Millicent
Millicent 'work-strong'
Mirabella *v* Mirabel
Nicolette *fem.* Nicholas
Priscilla 'ancient'
Rosabella 'pretty rose'
Rosalinda 'fair as a rose'
Rosamunda 'horse-protection'
Stephanie *fem.* Stephen
Thomasina *fem.* Thomas
Thomasine *fem.* Thomas
Tryphaena 'dainty'
Victorine* *v* Victoria

10

Brunehilda 'brown battle-maid'
Caintigern 'fair lady'
Christabel *v* Christian
Christiana* *v* Christian
Clementina *v* Clementine
Clementine* 'merciful'

Constantia 'constancy'
Ermintrude 'maid of the nation'
Ethelburga 'noble protectress'
Etheldreda 'noble might'
Gwendoline *v* Gwendolen
Gwenhwyfar *v* Guinevere
Hildegarde 'battle-maid'
Jacqueline *fem.* Jacques
Margaretta *v* Margaret
Marguerite* *v* Margaret
Petronella* *fem.* Peter
Petronilla *fem.* Peter

Thomassina *fem.* Thomas
Thomassine *fem.* Thomas
Wilhelmina *fem.* William

11

Alexandrina *fem.* Alexander

12

Kerenhappuch 'horn of eyelash-paint'

RELIGION AND MYTHOLOGY

BIBLICAL CHARACTERS

OLD TESTAMENT

2

Er brother of *Onan*
Og huge, king of Bashan

3

Asa king of Judah
Dan son of *Jacob*/*Bilhah*
Eli high priest
Eve first woman
Gad (1) son of *Zilpah* (2) *David's* seer
Gog of land of Magog
Ham son of *Noah*
Hur aided *Moses*
Ira 2 served *David*
Job 'patience'
Lot escaped from Sodom

4

Adah (1) wife of *Lamech* (2) wife of
  Esau
Adam first man
Agag king of the Amalekites
Agur a writer, Proverbs
Ahab king of Israel
Ahaz king of Judah
Amon son of *Manasseh*
Amos foreign missionary
Boaz g/grandfather of *David*
Cain first son of *Adam*/*Eve*
Doeg *Saul's* cattle man

Eber gave name to Hebrews
Ehud assassinated *Eglon*
Elah king of Israel
Esau twin brother *Jacob*
Ezra leading Persian Jew
Hiel rebuilt Jericho
Iddo 8, incl. a seer
Jael wife of Heber, killed *Sisera*
Jair judge from Gilead
Jehu (1) anti-Baal king (2) prophet
Joab son of *Zeruiah*, general
Joel prophet
Leah sister of *Rachel*, wife of *Jacob*
Levi son of *Leah*/*Jacob*
Moab incestuous son of *Lot*
Noah patriarch
Oded prophet, Israel
Omri king of Israel
Onan refused *Tamar* lawful sex
Oreb a Midianite leader
Ruth widow of *Mahlon*, wife of *Boaz*
Saul first king of Israel/Judah
Seth 3rd son of *Adam*/*Eve*
Shem son of *Noah*, ancestor of *Eber*
Tola judge

5

Aaron elder brother of *Moses*
Abihu son of *Aaron*
Abner general, *Saul's* cousin
Abram *Abraham*
Achan criminal
Amasa nephew of *David*

Asaph musician to *David*
Asher 8th son of *Jacob*
Bakak king of Moab
Barak judge
Caleb survived wilderness
Cyrus great warrior king of Persia
David great king of Israel/Judah
Dinah daughter of *Jacob*/*Leah*
Eglon fat king of Moab
Eldad assistant to *Moses*
Enoch a devout man
Gomer wife of *Hosea*
Hagar *Sarah's* personal maid
Haggi prophet
Haman attempted Jewish massacre
Hiram (1) king (2) craftsman
Hobab marriage relative of *Moses*
Hosea prophet
Ibzan minor judge, Bethlehem
Isaac son of *Abraham*/*Sarah*
Ittai one of *David's* generals
Jabal began cattle breeding
Jabin king of Hazor
Jacob renamed *Israel*
Javan son of *Japheth*
Jesse father of *David*
Joash (1) father of *Gideon* (2/3) kings
Jonah prophet
Joram son of *Ahab*/*Jezebel* (*Jehoram* (1))
Jubal musical instruments inventor
Judah sold *Joseph* as slave
Korah rebel vs *Moses*/*Aaron*
Laban provided wives *Isaac*/*Jacob*
Lahmi brother of *Goliath*
Magog son of *Japheth*
Merab daughter of *Saul*
Mesha king of Moab
Micah (1) thief (2) *Micaiah* (3) prophet
Moses patriarch and prophet
Nabal rich sheep farmer
Nadad (1) son of *Aaron* (2) king
Nahum prophet
Naomi *Ruth's* mother-in-law
Ornan *Araunah*
Pekah assassinated *Pekahiah*
Peleg son of *Eber*
Perez twin son of *Judah*/*Tamar*
Rahab reformed prostitute
Reuel father-in-law of *Moses*

Rezin last king of Damascus
Sarah wife of *Abraham*, mother of *Isaac*
Sihon powerful Amorite king
Tamar (1) wife of *Er* (2) daughter of *David*
Tibni opposed *Omri*
Tidal king of Goyim (nations)
Uriah (1) husband of *Bathsheba* (2) prophet
Uzzah king of Judah
Zadok high priest
Zimri assassinated *Elah*

6

Abijah 9 different people
Abriam a Reubenite
Achish king of Gath
Ahijah 6 incl. a prophet
Ahikam consulted *Huldah*
Arioch (1) king (2) guard captain
Asahel nephew of *David*
Baalis king of Ammon
Baasha usurper (Israel)
Baalam a psychic
Baruch secretary to *Jeremiah*
Bilhah *Rachel's* personal maid
Daniel prophet
Darius various kings of Persia
Dathan brother of *Abiram*
Elijah prophet
Elisah *Elijah's* successor
Esther chief wife of *Ahasuerus*
Gehazi servant of *Elisha*
Gideon defeated the Midianites
Hanani brother of *Nehemiah*
Hannah mother of *Samuel*
Hazael became king of Syria
Hophni immoral priest, son of *Eli*
Hoshea last king of Israel
Huldah prophetess
Hushai spy for *David*
Isaiah great prophet
Israel *(Jacob)* patriarch
Jethro father-in-law of *Moses*
Jocheb mother of *Moses*/*Aaron*
Joseph son of *Jacob*, assisted *Pharaoh*
Joshua (1) took Jericho (2) priest

Josiah king of Israel
Jotham (1) son of Gideon (2) king
Lamech (1) son of Methushael (2) son of *Methuselah*
Mahlon son of *Naomi*, husband of *Ruth*
Michal daughter of *Saul*, wife of *David*
Miriam sister of *Moses/Aaron*
Naaman Syrian general
Naboth vineyard owner
Nahash king of Ammon
Nathan prophet
Nimrod the mighty hunter
Orpath Moabite, son of *Ruth*
Rachel wife of *Jacob*
Rechab reformed prostitute
Reuben son of *Jacob/Leah*
Rizpah *Saul's* concubine
Samson exceptionally strong man
Samuel judge, prophet
Sargon king of Assyria
Shemer owned hill (Samaria)
Shimei 20 incl. curser of *David*
Simeon son of *Jacob/Leah*
Sisera defeated by *Barak*
Vashti chief wife of *Xerxes*
Xerxes *(Ahasuerus)* king of Persia
Zillah wife of *Lamech*, mother of *Tubal-cain*
Zopher friend of *Job*

7

Abigail (1) sister of *David* (2) wife of *David*
Abishag aged *David's* young nurse
Abishai nephew of *David*
Abraham the great Patriarch
Absalom 3rd son of *David*
Ahaziah (1) son of *Ahab* (2) son of *Jehoram*
Ahimaaz 3 incl. a spy
Amaziah king of Judah
Araunah owner of Temple site
Asenath wife of *Joseph*
Azariah 28 different people
Benaiah officer to *David/Solomon*
Deborah prophetess
Delilah tricked *Samson*

Eleazar high priest, son of *Aaron*
Elhanan killed *Goliath's* brother
Eliakim siege negotiator
Eliezer (1) son of *Moses* (2) steward
Eliphaz friend of Job
Elkanah father of *Samuel*
Ephraim son of *Joseph/Asenath*
Eshbaal *(Ishbosheth)* son of *Saul*
Ezekiel prophet
Goliath Philistine giant
Hanamel cousin of *Jeremiah*
Hilkiah found lost book of Law
Ichabod son of *Phineas*
Ishmael son of *Abraham/Hagar*
Japheth son of *Noah*
Jehoram (1) king of Israel (2) king of Judah
Jezebel wife of *Ahab*, worshipped Baal
Johanan various people
Keturah concubine wife of *Abraham*
Malachi prophet
Micaiah foretold death of *Ahab*
Obidiah several incl. prophet
Othniel first judge of Israel
Pashhur (1) priest (2) attacked *Jeremiah*
Pharaoh various Egyptian kings
Phineas (1) high priest (2) son of *Eli*
Rebekah wife of *Isaac*, mother of *Jacob*
Shallum 15 incl. 2 kings
Shamgar killed 600 Philistines
Shaphan assisted *Josiah*
Shechem raped *Dinah*
Solomon last king of Israel/Judah
Zeruiah mother of *Abishai, Asmael, Joab*

8

Abed-nego friend of *Daniel*
Abiathar high priest
Abinadad citizen
Adonijah 4th son of *David*
Amraphel king of Shinar
Athaliah evil, only ruling queen
Ben-Hadad 3 kings of Damascus
Benjamin son of *Jacob/Rachel*

Eliashib high priest
Gedaliah governor of Judea
Hananiah false prophet
Hesekiah king of Judah
Issachar son of *Jacob*/*Leah*
Jeduthun leading musician
Jehoahaz (1) king of Judah (2) king of Israel
Jehoiada high priest, saved *Joash*
Jephthah had 'Shibboleth' password
Jeremiah prophet
Jeroboam succeeded *Solomon*, Israel only
Jonathan various incl. son of *Saul*
Lot's wife became pillar of salt
Manasseh (1) son of *Joseph* (2) son of *Hezekiah*
Meremoth priest, son of *Uriah* (2)
Mordecai influential Persian Jew
Naphtali son of *Jacob*/*Bilhah*
Nehemiah governor of Jerusalem
Pekahiah king of Israel
Potiphar husband of seductress
Rehoboam succeeded *Solomon*, Judah only
Shadrach friend of *Daniel*
Shemaiah (1) prophet (2) captive
Zedekiah last king of Judah
Zipporah wife of *Moses*

9

Abimelech 3 different people
Ahasuerus *Xerxes*
Ahimelech priest at Nob
Ahithopel wise man, advisor
Barzillai old friend of *David*
Bathsheba wife of *David*, mother of *Solomon*
Elimelech husband of *Naomi*

Jehosheba daughter of *Athaliah*, saved *Joash*
Sanballat opponent of *Nehemiah*
Tubal-cain first used iron/copper
Zachariah 30 incl. king, prophet
Zacharias *Zachariah*

10

Adonibezek king of Bezek
Artaxerxes king of Persia
Belshazzar king of Babylon
Ebed-melech aided *Jeremiah*
Esar-haddon son of king of Assyria
Ishbi-benob a Philistine giant
Ishbosheth *(Eshbaal)* ruled north
Methuselah lived 969 years

11

Adrammelech murdered *Sennacherib*
Jehoshaphat king of Judah
Melchizedek king-priest, Salem
Nebuzaradan Babylonian general
Sennacherib king of Assyria
Shalmaneser king of Assyria

12

Evil-merodach (Amel-Marduk) king of Babylon
Jehoshabeath *(Jehosheba)* wife of *Jehoiada*
Queen of Sheba visited *Solomon*

14/15

Nebuchadnezzar king of Babylon
The witch of Endor consulted by *Saul*

NEW TESTAMENT

4

Anna   prophetically gifted
John   (1) apostle (2) the Baptist
Jude   brother of *James*
Luke   apostle, evangelist, doctor
Mark   evangelist
Mary   see list 13
Paul   *(Saul)* apostle, tentmaker
Saul   *(Paul)* Pharisee, Roman Jew

5

Annas   High priest
Chloe   a Corinthian lady
Chuza   *Herod*'s steward
Demas   fellow worker, *Paul*
Felix   procurator of Judea
Herod   see lists 9/12/13/15/16
James   see SAINTS (p. 354)
Judas   (1) Iscariot (2) *Jude*, etc.
Linus   in prison with *Paul*
Lydia   *Paul's* first convert
Peter   prince of the Apostles
Rufus   son of *Simon of Cyrene*
Simon   (1) *Peter* (2) leper: see 10/13
Titus   gentile disciple

6

Agabus   Christian prophet
Andrew   apostle, brother of *Peter*
Apphia   poss. wife of *Philomen*
Aquila   Christian Jew
Aretas   father-in-law *Antipas*
Caesar   Augustus: Tiberius: Nero, etc.
Cephas   *Peter*
Dorcas   *(Tabitha)* woman disciple
Eunice   mother of *Timothy*
Festus   succeeded *Felix*
Jairus   daughter restored to life
Joanna   wife of *Chuza*

Joseph   (1) husband of *Mary* (2) of Arimathea
Julius   Roman officer
Manaen   disciple
Martha   fed Jesus and disciples
Philip   (1) apostle (2) evangelist (3) *Herod*
Pilate   *Pontius Pilate*
Pudens   associated with *Paul*
Salome   (1) disciple (2) daughter *Herodias*
Simeon   recognized infant Christ
Thomas   apostle

7

Agrippa   brother of *Herodias*: see 12
Ananias   (1) high priest (2/3) disciples
Antipas   son of *Herod the Great*: see 12
Apollos   Alexandrian Jew
Bernice   daughter of *Herod Agrippa*
Claudia   British wife of *Pudens*
Clement   fellow worker of *Paul*
Cleopas   disciple
Gabriel   archangel
Lazarus   (1) raised from dead (2) leper
Malchus   *Peter* cut ear off
Matthew   apostle, evangelist
Nicholas   disciple
Publius   entertained *Paul/Luke*
Stephen   martyr
Tabitha   restored to life
The Magi   followed star
Theudas   revolutionary
Timothy   leading disciple
Zebedee   father of *James/John*

8

Alphacus   father of *Matthew*: of *James*
Barabbas   received Passover amnesty
Bar-Jesus   practitioner of magic
Barnabus   disciple

Caiaphas high priest
Drusilla daughter of *Herod Agrippa*
Epaphras citizen of Colossae
Eutychus restored to life
Gamaliel tutor of *Paul*
Herodias married two uncles
Lysanias tetrach of Abilene
Nicholaus disciple
Onesimus slave, convert
Philemon Christian, slave owner
Tiberius Caesar (AD 14–37)
Tyrannus schoolteacher

9

Alexander various people
Archelaus (son of *Herod*) inherited ⅓
Archippus poss. son of *Philomen*
Boanerges nickname *James/John*
Cornelius Roman convert
Demitrius silversmith, Ephesus
Elisabeth mother of John the Baptist
Nathanael disciple
Nicodemus fair-minded Pharisee
Quirinius governor of Syria
Stephanas early convert
Tertullus lawyer
Zacchaeus convert

10

Andronicus 'kinsman' of *Paul*
Bartimaeus cured blind beggar
Simon Magus magician, gnostic

11

Aristarchus companion of *Paul*
Bartholomew an apostle
Onesiphorus dead, prayers for

12

Epaphroditus *Paul's* prison visitor
Herod Agrippa (I and II) followed
   Philip
Herod Antipas (son of *Herod*)
   inherited ⅓

13

Herod the Great king of the Jews
Judas Iscariot ex-apostle, betrayer
Mary of Bethany sister of *Martha*
Mary Magdalene reformed sinner
Simon of Cyrene helped carry Cross
The Virgin Mary mother of Jesus
Pontius Pilate sent Jesus to *Antipas*

14/15/16/17

Claudius Lysias garrison commander
The Three Wise Men *The Magi*
Herod the Tetrarch *Herod Antipas*
Mary, wife of Clopas stood at Cross
Philip the Tetrarch (son of *Herod*)
   inherited ⅓

BIBLICAL PLACES

COUNTRIES, STATES, LANDS, TERRITORIES, PROVINCES, REGIONS AND DISTRICTS

2

Uz

3

Dan
Gad
Ham
Kue
Lud
Nod
Put
Tob

4

Amaw
Arah
Cush
Edom
Elam
Hazo
Maon
Moab
Seba
Seir
Tema
Uzal

5

Ammon
Argob
Asher
Choba
Dedan

Dumah
Egypt
Gebal
Goiim
Golan
Judah
Ludim
Magog
Massa
Media
Mesha
Minni
Negeb
Ophir
Paran
Pekod
Ragae
Sabta
Sheba
Teman
Timna
Tubal
Uphaz
Zobah

6

Abarim
Ararat
Beulah
Canaan
Cushan
Geshur
Gilead
Goshen
Hauran
Israel
Jeruel
Kittim

Maacah
Mearah
Padden
Sabtah
Sharon
Shinar

7

Abilene
Arbatta
Arbella
Ascalon
Assyria
Babylon
Bashan
Chaldea
Cilicia
Elishah
Ellasar
El-Paran
Elymais
Ephraim
Galilee
Havilah
Ituraea
Lebanon
Lehabim
Maacath
Meshech
Nabatea
Parvaim
Pathros
Sabteca
Samaria
Shaalim
Sheleph
Zebulun

8	Merathaim	Anti-Lebanon
	Pamphylia	Hazarmaveth
Arzareth	Philistia	Trachonitis
Ashkenaz	Phoenicia	
Benjamin	Shalishah	
Beth-Eden	Shephelah	12
Bithynia		
Issachar		Aram-Naharaim
Jeshimon	10	Land of Mizpah
Manasseh		Land of Moriah
Naphtali	Aram-Maacah	
Philippi	Cappadocia	
Rathamin	Coelesyria	15/16/17
	Gennesaret	
	Land of Zuph	Wilderness of Sin
9	Padden-Aram	Wilderness of Zin
		Wilderness of Moab
Aphairema		Wilderness of Shur
Aram-Zobah	11	Wilderness of Ziph
Beth-Rehob		Wilderness of Judah
Land of Nod	Akrabattene	Wilderness of Tekoa

CITIES
(including City or Temple Gates in CAPITALS)

2	Cuth	Accad
	Gath	Admah
On	Gaza	Adora
Ur	Geba	Alema
	Hena	Almon
	Kain	Aphek
3	Moab	Ariel
	Myra	Arpad
Ain	Nain	Arvad
Dor	Sela	Babel
Pai	Side	Betah
Pau	Tyre	Bezer
Zer	Zela	Calah
	Zion	Calno
	Ziph	Debir
4	Zoan	Derbe
	Zoar	Dibon
Acco		Dimon
Anem		Ebron
Aner	5	Edrei
Arad		Eglon
Bela	Abdon	Ekron

BIBLICAL PLACES   COUNTRIES, STATES, ETC.

Erech	Jattir	Jarmuth
Geder	Kadesh	Jericho
Gerar	Kartah	Jezreel
Gezer	Kartan	Jokmeam
Haran	Kedesh	Jokneam
Hazor	Keilah	Kerioth
Iwah	Lesham	Kibzaim
Jahaz	Librah	Kishion
Jebus	Lystra	Lachish
Joppa	Mailus	Medeba
Laish	Mashal	Megiddo
Lasea	Medeba	Memphis
Madon	Mizpah	Nahalal
Perga	Myndos	Nahalol
Rages	Paphos	NEW GATE
Rehob	Pithon	Nineveh
Resen	Rabbah	OLD GATE
Salem	Ramoth	Rogelim
Sidon	Raphon	Salamis
Sodom	Rezeph	Samaria
Tamor	Rhodes	Sheehem
Tekoa	Riblah	Shimron
Troas	Shiloh	SUR GATE
Zemer	Smyrna	Taanach
	Tadmor	Tibhath
	Tarsus	Zeboiim
6	Thebes	Zephath
	Thebez	Zeredah
Adamah	Tirzah	
Aradus	Zeboim	
Ashdod	Ziddim	8
Asshur		
Bethel		Abel-Maim
Bileam	7	Achshaph
Bozrah		Anathoth
Calneh	Adoraim	Askcalon
Cnidus	Adullam	Ashkalon
Cuthah	Aijalon	Ashkelon
Cyrene	Alemeth	Berothai
Dimnah	Antioch	Beth-Meon
Dothan	Ascalon	Beth-Shan
Gadara	Beth-Zur	Caesarea
Gazara	Corinth	Chorazin
Gerasa	Eltekeh	Colossae
Gibeah	Ephesus	Damascus
Gibeon	Eshtaol	Dibon-Gad
Hamath	Hadrach	Dinhabah
Hammon	Hamonah	DUNG GATE
Hebron	Helkath	EAST GATE
Hepher	Heshbon	Ecbatana

COUNTRIES, STATES, ETC.   BIBLICAL PLACES

En-Gannim	SHEEP GATE	EPHRAIM GATE
Eshtemoa	Tahpanhes	Kir-Hareseth
Eshtemoh	UPPER GATE	Kiriath-Arba
FISH GATE	WATER GATE	MUNSTER GATE
Gomorrah	Zarephath	
Horonaim		
Kir-Heres		12
Laodicea	10	
Lasharon		City of the Sun
Mahanaim	BATH-RABBIM	FOUNTAIN GATE
Makkedah	Be-Eshterah	Hazazon-Tamar
Mephaath	Beth-Maacah	Philadelphia
Mitylene	Carchemish	POTSHERD GATE
Pergamum	Chinnereth	Ramoth-Gilead
Phaselis	Chinneroth	Thessalonica
Pirathon	City of Moab	Timnath-Serah
Shaalbim	City of Salt	
Thyatira	CORNER GATE	
	Hammoth-Dor	13
	Heliopolis	
9	Kiriathaim	BEAUTIFUL GATE
	Persepolis	Elon-Beth-Hanan
Ashtaroth	Rehoboth-Ir	Kiriath-Sannah
Beersheba	Sepharvaim	Kiriath-Sepher
Beth-Hanan	VALLEY GATE	
Bethlehem		
Beth-Shean		14/15
Capernaum	11	
Chephirah		Abel-Beth-Maacah
En-Mishpat	Beth-Shemesh	Ramoth in Gilead
HORSE GATE	City of David	GATE OF THE GUARDS
Jerusalem	City of Palms	Ur of the Chaldees

TOWNS AND VILLAGES, ETC.

(Stopping places of the Wilderness-wandering in CAPITAL LETTERS)

2	4	Cana
		ELIM
Ar	Abel	IYIM
	Amad	Jaar
	Amam	Nebo
3	Anab	Soco
	Anim	
Ain	Arab	5
Cun	BEER	Ahlab
Lod	Beon	ALUSH

BIBLICAL PLACES

TOWNS AND VILLAGES, ETC.

Aphik	Shunem	NAHALIEL
Aroer	Tephon	Nazareth
Ashan	Ziklag	REPHIDIM
Avvim		Shaaraim
ETHAM		Sharuhen
Jabez		Tel-Meiah
Jazer	**7**	Tiberias
LABAN		Tripolis
Lydda	Aphekah	Zemaraim
Maked	Beeroth	
MARAH	Bethany	
OBOTH	DOPHKAH	
Ocina	En-Hazor	**9**
PUNON	Ephraim	
Ramah	HARADAH	Anaharath
Shema	Iconium	Beth-Anoth
Socoh	Jabneel	Beth-Phage
TERAH	MITHKAH	HASHMONAH
Ummah	MOSERAH	Ir-Shemesh
Yiron	Rabbith	IYE-ABARIM
Zenan	Rakkath	JOTBATHAH
Zorah	RITHMAH	MAKHELOTH
	Salecah	Tel-Harsha
	Shilhim	
6	Succoth (1)	
	SUCCOTH (2)	**10**
Achzib	TABERAH	
Ashnah	Tappuah	Antipatris
Athach	Tappush	Bamoth-Baal
Azekah	Taralah	BENE-JAAKAN
Azotus		Ezion-Geber
BAMOTH		KEHELATHAH
Beroea		PI-HAHIROTH
Canneh	**8**	Shahazumah
Dessau		
Emmaus	Adithaim	
Ephron	Arubboth	**11**
Hushah	Baal-Meon	
Ibleam	Beer-Elim	Allammelech
Irpeel	Ge-Harash	Kiriath-Arim
Jabesh	GUDGODAH	Kiriath-Baal
Jabneh	HARIROTH	RIMMON-PEREZ
Juttah	HAZEROTH	
LIBNAH	Irnahash	
Marisa	Jogbehah	**12**
MASSAH	Kedemoth	
Ophrah	MATTANAH	Ataroth-Addar
Rakkon	Mareshah	Beth-Baal-Meon
RISSAH	MOSEROTH	

UNDESIGNATED PLACES	BIBLICAL PLACES	
Beth-le-Aphrah	13	15
HOR-HAGGIDGAD		
Jabesh-Gilead	**Beth-Haccherem**	ALMON-DIBLATHAIM
Shimron-Meron	**Chephar-Ammoni**	**Ramah of the Negeb**
Zereth-Shahar	**Gibeath-Elohim**	**Ramathaim-Zophim**
	Kiriath-Jearim	

UNDESIGNATED PLACES

2

Ai

3

Ain
Dok
Gob
Iim
Kir
Luz
Nob
Ono
Sur

4

Adam
Aija
Baal
Eden
Etam
Hara
Kola
Kona
Lehi
Shur
Zair

5

Adasa
Addan
Adida
Bezek

Elasa
Elath
Ether
Gedor
Gidom
Gimzo
Gozan
Hadid
Helam
Immer
Kamon
Mamre
Moreh
Rumah
Sores
Syene
Tabor
Zabad

6

Arumah
Bochim
Charax
Cherub
Chesil
Chezib
Daphne
Elkosh
En-Gedi
Gallim
Gilgal
Helbah
Jotbah
Madmen
Migdol
Mizpeh
Naioth

Peniel
Penuel
Pethor
Siloam
Tishbe
Tophel
Tophet

7

Caphtor
Dizahab
En-Rogel
Magdala
Shittim

8

Baal-Peor
Beth-Peor
Bethulia
Eben-Ezer
El-Bethel
Golgotha
Manahath
Michmash
Nadabath
Tarshish

9

Beth-Horon
Bethsaida
Machpelah
Pas-Dammim
Zaanannim

10

Armageddon
Baal-Zephon
Gethsemane
Ramath-Lehi

11

Baal-Perazim
Ephes-Dammim
Hamath-Zobah

12

Capharsalama

Garden of Eden
Kadesh-Barnea
Timnath-Heres

13

Baal-Shalishah

GEOGRAPHICAL

Fld field, vineyard, threshing floor or other site
Ht hill or ascent
Mt mount or mountain
Pl pool, spring or well
R river, brook or stream
Val. valley

3

Gur *(Ht)*

4

Atad *(Fld)*
Peor *(Mt)*

5

Abana *(R)*
Abron *(R)*
Achor *(Val.)*
Ahava *(R)*
Amana *(R:Mt)*
Ammah *(Ht)*
Ardat *(Fld)*
Arnon *(R)*
Bozez (crag)
Gareb *(Ht)*
Gihon *(R:Pl)*
Habor *(R)*
Harod *(Pl)*
Mizar *(Ht)*
Nacon *(F)*
Ophel *(Ht)*
Seneh (crag)

6

Asphar *(Pl)*
Chebar *(R)*
Chidon *(Fld)*
Olivet *(Mt)*
Pisgah *(Mt)*
Pishon *(R)*
Red Sea
Rimmon (rock)
Shibah *(Pl)*
Theras *(R)*
Tigris *(R)*

7

Araunah *(Fld)*
Calvary *(Ht)*
Cherith *(R)*
Salt Sea

8

Akeldama *(Fld)*
Bethesda *(Pl)*
Great Sea
Hachilah *(Ht)*
Hamon-Gog *(Val.)*

Me-Jarkon *(Pl)*
Mount Hor
Rehoboth *(Pl)*
Rock Oreb

9

Baal-Hamon *(Fld)*
Beth-Zatha *(Pl)*
Euphrates *(R)*
Mount Ebal
Mount Nebo
Mount Seir
River Nile

10

Brook Besor
Brook Kanah
Coelesyria *(Val.)*
Eastern Sea
Jacob's Well
Mount Halak
Mount Horeb
Mount Senir
Mount Sinai
Mount Tabor
Oak of Tabor

Sea of Reeds
Sea of Sodom
Western Sea

11

Abel-mizraim *(Fld)*
Ascent of Ziz
Brook Kidron
Diviners' Oak
Hill of Moreh
Jehoshaphat *(Val.)*
Mount Carmel
Mount Ephron
Mount Gilboa
Mount Gilead
Mount Hermon
Mount Jearim
Mount Sirion
Plain of Dura
River Jabbok
River Jordan
River Kishon
Sea of Arabah

12

Beer-Lahai-Roi *(Pl)*
Brook of Egypt
Brook of Zered
Brook Mochmur
Fuller's Field
Ladder of Tyre *(Mt)*
Mount Gerizim
Mount Perazim
Mount Shepher
Plains of Moab
Pool of Shelah

Pool of Siloam
Potter's Field
Ridge of Judea
River of Egypt
Rock of Escape
Sea of Galilee
Stone of Bohan
Valley of Aven
Valley of Baca
Valley of Elah
Valley of Salt

13

Ascent of Heres
Brook of Arabah
Brooks of Gaash
Field of Zophim
Mount of Olives
Sea of Tiberias
Serpent's Stone
Vale of Succoth
Valley of Salem
Valley of Zered
Waters of Merom

14

Ascent of Luhith
Cistern of Sirah
Forest of Hereth
Meribath-Kadesh *(Pl)*
Oak of the Pillar
Plain of Megiddo
Sea of the Arabah
Valley of Eshcol
Valley of Hinnom
Valley of Mizpeh

Valley of Shaveh
Valley of Siddim
Waters of Nimrin
Wildgoats' Rocks

15

Ascent of Adummin
Forest of Ephraim
Mountain of Gaash
Plains of Jericho
River Eleutherus
Sea of Chinnereth
Sea of Chinneroth
Valley of Aijalon
Valley of Beracah
Valley of Jezreel
Valley of Lebanon
Valley of Rephaim
Valley of Shittim
Valley toward Gad
Waters of Megiddo
Waters of Shiloah

16

Ascent of Akrabbim
Lake of Gennesaret
Plain of Esdraelon
Valley of Iphtah-El
Waters of Nephtoah

17

Brook of the Willows
Mount of Corruption
Valley of Craftsmen

ANCIENT GODS

gs goddess

EGYPTIAN

2

Ra the sun

3

Bes fun and war
Geb earth
Keb *Geb*
Min virility
Mut Nile, wife of *Amen (gs)*
Net war *(gs)*
Nut life after death
Seb *Geb*
Set twin, murdered *Osiris*
Shu supporter of heaven
Tum *Atum*

4

Amen Thebes
Amsu *Min*
Apis sacred bull
Aten *Aton*
Aton sun as disk
Atum setting sun
Bast cat *gs*, sexual passion
Hapi breasted-male, Nile
Isis wife-sister of *Osiris (gs)*
Khem fertility
Maat wisdom *(gs)*
Menu *Min*
Munt hawk-headed deity
Ptah the giver of life

5

Ammon *Amen*
Horus the rising sun

Khnum ram-headed deity
Khons son of *Amen-Ra*
Neith *Net (gs)*
Sebek crocodile deity
Thoth ibis-headed, wisdom

6

Amen-Ra Glorious Thebes
Anubis weighed the soul
Hathor cow-headed deity
Khepra *Kheperi*
Khopri *Kheperi*
Kknemu *Khnum*
Mekhet vulture deity
Osiris greatest of the gods
Qetesh love *(gs)*
Sekhet lioness, mother of *Nefertem*
Tefnet 2-headed wife of *Shu (gs)*

7

Kheperi *Ra* as rising sun
Imhotep medicine, son of *Ptah*
Sekhmet wife of *Ptah (gs)*
Serapis Ptolemy I's monotheistic god

8

Herakhti falcon-headed *Horus*
Nefertem son of *Ptah*
Nekhebet Upper Nile *(gs)*
Nephthys wife of *Set (gs)*

11/12

Heru-pa-Khret *Horus* the child
Ra-Atum-Khepra the sun

EUPHRATES – TIGRIS

A Assyrian
B Babylonian
C Carthaginian
also Canaanite, Hittite, Moabite, Persian, Phoenician, Phrygian, Sumerian, etc.

2

Ea (*B*) waters

3

Aja (*B*) wife of *Shamash (gs)*
Anu (*B*) chief god
Bel (*B*) father of gods
Sin (*B*) moon

4

Adad (*A*) storm, thunder
Apsu (*B*) primeval male
Baal Canaanite/Phoenician chief god
Nana Phoenician, mother *Attis (gs)*
Nebo (*B*) wisdom, writing

5

Andtu wife of *Anu (gs)*
Ashur *Assur*
Assur (*A*) chief god
Attis Phoenician: emasculation
Belit (*B*) wife of *Bel (gs)*
Dagon Philistines: fish
Diana Ephesus: *Astarte (gs)*
Enlil (*B*) earth, *Bel*
Igigi (*B*) visible stars, gods
Khefa Hittite: *Khepit (gs)*
Ninib (*A B*) battle
Nusku (*A B*, etc.) fire
Tanit (*C*) *Astarte (gs)*

6

Allatu (*B*) the dead *(gs)*
Arbela (*A*) war *(gs)*
Baalim various Semitic, sun
Cybele chief Phrygian *gs*
Eshmun (*C*) trinal with *Moloch*
Iolaus (*C*) local god
Ishtar (*B*) *Astarte (gs)*
Khepit Hittite: sun *(gs)*
Lilith (*A*) evil *(gs)*
Mazdah Persian: great creator
Mithra Persian: fire
Molech (*C*, etc.) *Moloch*
Moloch (*C*, etc.) *Baal*
Nergal (*A*) the chase
Ningal (*B*) wife of *Sin (gs)*
Ramman (*B*) *Adad*
Tammuz (*B*) vegetation, Spring
Teshub Hittite: *Adad*
Tiamat (*B*) primeval female *(gs)*

7

Anahita Persian: fertility *(gs)*
Anaitis *Anahita (gs)*
Astarte Canaanite, etc. sex *(gs)*
Cabeiri Asia Minor divinities
Chemosh Moabite, national god
Damkina (*B*) wife *Ea*, mistress gods
Derketo (*A*) fish aspect of *Atargatis (gs)*
Marduck (*B*) city of Babylon
Melkart (*C*) local: Tyre, *Baal*
Mithras *Mithra*
Mylitta (*B*) sacred prostitution *(gs)*
Shamash (*B*) sun

8

Anunnaki (B) hidden stars, gods
Merodach (B) *Marduck*, son of *Ea*
Sabazios Phoenician, harvest

9

Ashtaroth Phoenician, *Astarte (gs)*
Ashtoreth *Ashtaroth (gs)*
Atargatis (A) water *(gs)*

Baal-Ammon (C) *Baal*
Beelzebub Canaanite, *Baal*
Gilgamesh (B) mythical deified king

10/12

Baal-Hammon Phoenician colonies
   Baal
'golden calf' (Biblical) Hittite deity
Tammuz-Adonis (C) local god

GREEK, ROMAN, CRETAN

Rm Roman
T Titan (Greek)

2

Ge earth *(gs)*

3

Dis (Rm) *Hades*
Eos dawn *(gs)*
Pan flocks, herds
Pax (Rm) *Irene (gs)*

4

Ares war
Eros love
Gaea *Ge*
Hebe youth *(gs)*
Hera sister, wife *Zeus (gs)*
Jove (Rm) *Jupiter*
Juga (Rm) *Juno* as marriage guardian
Juno (Rm) *Hera (gs)*
Kore *Persephone*
Maia ancient Italian *gs*, Spring
Mars (Rm) *Ares*
Nike *Athena (gs)*
Rhea earth *(gs)*
Zeus supreme Olympian

5

Atlas (T) supported world
Ceres (Rm) *Demeter (gs)*
Chaos primeval god
Cupid (Rm) *Eros*
Diana (Rm) *Artemis (gs)*
Dione a wife of *Zeus (gs)*
Fates Clotho, Lachesis, Atropos
Flora (Rm) flowers *(gs)*
Hades netherworld
Hymen marriage
Irene peace *(gs)*
Janus (Rm) openings
Minos a judge of dead
Orcus punished perjurers
Pluto *Hades*
Titan giant, early deity
Tyche chance *(gs)*
Venus (Rm) *Aphrodite (gs)*
Vesta (Rm) *Hestia (gs)*

6

Aeacus a judge of dead
Apollo sun
Athena wisdom *(gs)*
Athene *Athena*

GREEK, ROMAN, CRETAN

Aurora *Eos (gs)*
Cronus (T) father of *Zeus*
Erebus hell
Hecate a trinal (earth) *gs*
Helios (T) son of *Hyperion*
Hermes luck, wealth
Hestia the hearth
Lucina (Rm) *Eilithyia*
Matuta (Rm) matrons *(gs)*
Moneta (Rm) *(Juno)* finances *(gs)*
Phoebe (T) supplanted by *Artemis*
Plutos wealth
Pomona (Rm) fruit *(gs)*
Rumina (Rm) breast-feeding mothers
    (gs)
Saturn (Rm) *Cronus*
Selene moon *(gs)*
Tethys wife of *Oceanus (gs)*
Uranus (early) chief god
Vulcan (Rm) *Hephaestus*

7

Artemis hunting, chastity *(gs)*
Bacchus *Dionysus*
Bellona (Rm) war *(gs)*
Bona Dea (Rm) women's rites *(gs)*
Demeter corn, agriculture *(gs)*
Fortuna (Rm) *Tyche (gs)*
Hygieia health *(gs)*
Iacchos of Eleusinian mysteries
Jupiter (Rm) *Zeus*
Mercury (Rm) *Hermes*
Minerva (Rm) *Athena (gs)*
Neptune (Rm) *Poseidon*
Oceanus (T) sea
Phoebus *Apollo* as man
Priapus procreation
Pronuba (Rm) a *Juno* manifestation
    (gs)
Proteus son of *Oceanus*
Sospita (Rm) *(Juno)* women's peril *(gs)*

8

Dionysus wine
Dispater (Rm) *Dis*
Hyperion (T) sun
Juventas (Rm) *Hebe (gs)*
Libitina (Rm) *Persephone (gs)*
Morpheus dreams
Olympian displaced *Titan* as deity
Portunus (Rm) harbours, gates
Poseidon sea
Quirinus (Rm) trinal with *Mars, Jupiter*

9

Aphrodite love *(gs)*
Asclepius medicine
Eilithyia childbirth *(gs)*
Vortumnus (Rm) orchards, fruit

10

Hephaestus fire
Juno Lucina (Rm) *Eilithyia (gs)*
Persephone wife of *Hades (gs)*
Proserpina Persephone *(gs)*

11

Aesculapius *Asclepius*

12

Pallas-Athene *Athena (gs)*

13

Phoebus-Apollo *Apollo*

SCANDINAVIAN, TEUTONIC, CELTIC, GAELIC

(Cel.) Celtic
(Ga.) Gael
(Teu.) Teutonic

2

Ve son of *Bor*

3

Bor father of *Odin*
Eir hearing *(gs)*
Hel death *(gs)*
Hod night
Lir (Ga.) sea
Lug (Cel.) luck, wealth
Sif wife of *Thor (gs)*
Tiu *Tyr*
Tiw *Tyr*
Tyr bravest of *aesir*
Urd *Norn* time past
Vor punished faithless lovers *(gs)*

4

Bure father of *Bor*
Danu (Cel.) mother of the gods *(gs)*
Frey fertility
Hela *Hel (gs)*
Idun wife of *Bragi (gs)*
Liyr (Cel.) *Llyr*
Llyr (Cel.) sea
Lofn reunion of lovers
Loki evil personified
Lopt *Loki*
Norn any of the *Norns*
Odin chief god
Saga history and narration *(gs)*
Surt fire
Thor thunder
Vali of the *aesir*
Vile son of *Bor*

Ymer first *jotun*

5

aesir the greater gods
Bragi eloquence
Dagda (Cel.) (possibly) earth
Donar (Teu.) *Thor*
Freya love and night *(gs)*
Freyr *Frey*
Frigg *Frigga*
Gerda frozen earth *(gs)*
Hodur *Hod*
Hulde (Teu.) marriage *(gs)*
Iduna *Idun*
jotun primeval giant, evil
Nanna wife of *Balder (gs)*
Niord of the *Vanir*
Norns the 3 fates of time
Sigyn wife of *Balder*
Skuld *Norn* time future
Uller of the *aesir*
Vanir the atmosphere gods
Vidar forests
Woden (Teu.) *Odin*
Wotan (Teu.) *Odin*

6

Balder wisest of *aesir*
Baldur *Balder*
Bertha (Teu.) *Berchta*
Bestla *Jotun*, mother of *Odin (gs)*
Freyja *Freya*
Frigga wife of *Odin (gs)*
Gerdhr *Gerda*
Hermod of the *aesir*
Hertha (Teu.) *Nerthus (gs)*

Skadhi wife of *Niord (gs)*
Snotra sagacity *(gs)*
Surtur *Surt*

9

Manannain (*Cel.*) three-legged (Isle of Man)
Valkyries divine battle maids

7

Berchta (*Teu.*) spinners *(gs)*
Camulos (*Cel.*) war
Forsete of the *aesir*
Grannos (*Cel.*) sun
Hemidal of the *aesir*
Nerthus (*Teu.*) earth *(gs)*
Njordhr *Niord*

10

Fenriswolf monster son of *Loki*

12

Dea Brigantia (*Cel.*) wisdom *(gs)*
Jormungander *Midgard-Serpent*

8

Keridwen (*Cel.*) nature *(gs)*
Verdande *Norn* time present

14

Midgard-Serpent son of *Loki*

MYTHOLOGICAL CHARACTERS
(including part-human)

Bry. Brythonic Celtic
Gk Greek
Ir. Irish
Teu. Teutonic
X magically transformed
Names in CAPITALS see GODS.

2

al (f) Armenian demon
Io *Gk* heroine: Maori god
ka Egyptian *wraith*
ob Hebrew familiar

hex witch/bewitching
Ing Teutonic hero
Ith death avenged by *Bile*
Kay Kt of the Round Table
lar Roman house-spirit

3

aes *Ir.* fairies
Ask Norse Adam
elf perverse fairy
hag witch: she-devil

4

Aine *Ir.* fairy
Airi powerful Indian ghost
Bile (*Ir.* myth) King of Spain
Bran *Bry.* sea-giant
Brut Trojan, founded Britain

MYTHOLOGICAL CHARACTERS

deva Hindu god or spirit
Dido deserted by *Aeneas*
Echo *oread* desired by PAN
Egil tended THOR's goats
Gy(g)es *Gk* giants
Hero *Gk* priestess
jinn Muslim *sprite*(s)
juju Ibo fetish-*spirit*
Leda amour of ZEUS (swan)
Ogma Ogam alphabet inventor
ogre cannibalistic giant
para Finnish *sprite*
peri Persian fairy
pixy *pixie*
puck malicious *goblin*
Rahu Hindu, eclipse demon
Thok LOKI as *hag*
trow Orkney/Shet. *troll*

5

afrit Arabic evil demon
Argus giant: dog: craftsman
Balor *Ir.* giant-king
Boann mother of *Angus Og*
bogle English *hobgoblin*
Circe *Gk* sorceress
Conla *Ir.* warrior-hero
djinn *jinn*
dryad *Gk* tree *nymph*
dwarf underground being
Dylan *Bry.* sea-hero
Faust medieval magician
fetch living spirit-double
ghoul demonic corpse-eater
gnome deformed *dwarf*
golem Hebrew robot
Helle *Gk* villainess
houri heavenly perpetual-virgin
  (Islam)
Iambe *Gk* slave-maiden
Isolt beloved of *Tristan*
Ixion fathered the *centaurs*
Jason *Gk* hero
Kappa Jap. malicious *spirit*
Kesil Semitic giant
larva Roman evil *spirit*
manes Roman ghosts

Medea *Gk* priestess-witch
Midas king of Phrygia
Muses nymphs of the arts
nymph beautiful female semi-divine
oread *Gk* mountain *nymph*
Paris prince of Troy
pixie small *sprite*
Regin Norse dwarf/smith
satyr *Gk* man-goat
Siren *Gk* sea-nymph
Thrym Norse frost-giant
troll Norse supernatural
zombi soulless body

6

Aarvak Norse hero
Adapta human son of EA
Adonis *Gk* hero
Aeneas Trojan hero
Aeolus king of Aeolia
Afreet *afrit*
Alviss Norse *dwarf*
Amadan *Ir. stroke lad*
Arthur British hero-king
Befind Celtic fairy
Cadmus *Gk* hero
Charon *Gk* ferryman of dead
Codrus last Athenian king
Cormac *Ir.* hero-king
Dvalin dwarf-inventor of runes
Europa amour of ZEUS (Bull)
Fafnir *Teu.* dwarf-prince
Fatima Arabian heroine
Furies the *Erinyes*
goblin household *sprite*
Icarus flew too near sun
kobold German *bogle*
Lycaon Arcadian king *X* wolf
maenad ecstatic, frenzied female
Merlin poet, wizard, prophet
nereid *Gk* sea-nymph
Oenone nymph-wife of Paris
ogress female *ogre*
spirit disembodied essence
sprite *spirit*-manifest
wraith living double
zombie *zombi*

7

Actaeon *Gk* hunter *X* stag
Admetus *Gk* king
Ali Baba Arabian hero
Angus Og the Irish *Adonis*
Arachne *Gk* weaver *X* spider
banshee *Ir*. female fairy
berserk frenzied Norse warrior
brownie British *goblin*
centaur *Gk* man-horse
Cheiron wisest *centaur*
Clootie (Scots) devil
Croesus last king of Lydia
Cyclops one-eyed giant
Dactyls fabulous *Gk* smiths
Echidna *Gk* woman-serpent
Erinyes divine female avengers
Firbolg pre-Celtic Irish
Galatea *nereid*: Pygmalion's statue
Grainne *Ir*. heroine
gremlin 20th C. air-*sprite*
harpies *Gk* hags
Hesione Trojan princess
Hjordis Norse heroine
Jocasta wife/mother *Oedipus*
Laocoon Trojan priest
Leander illicit lover of *Hero*
Lorelei 19th C. Rhine-nymph
mermaid woman-fish
Mordred *Arthur*'s traitor
Oedipus tragic hero-king
Omphale Lydian queen
Orestes avenging *Gk* prince
Orpheus tragic musician-hero
Pandora the all-endowed woman
Perseus *Gk* hero
Phineus *Gk* soothsayer-king
sandman nursery-sleep figure
Sigmund Norse hero
Tristan Celtic hero
Ulysses *Odysseus*
vampire living corpse

8

Achilles *Gk* hero
Asmodeus Semitic evil spirit
Baba Yaga Russian *ogress*

[1]barghest dog-like goblin
Callisto Arcadian *nymph*
Cercopes *(Gk)* ape-like pigmies
Daedalus great *Gk* craftsman
Dardanus ancestor of Trojans
Gigantes *Gk* earth-giants
Grimhild *Teu*./Norse sorceress
Hercules great *Gk* hero
Hiawatha Iroquois prophet
Iphicles Hercules twin ½ brother
John Bull England personified
Lancelot Kt of the Round Table
Minotaur man-bull
Morpheus son of Hypnos
Odysseus *Gk* hero-king
Pentheus king of Thebes
Polyidus *Gk* soothsayer
Sisyphus crafty *Gk* king
Tantalus tormented king
Uncle Sam USA personified
werewolf man *X* wolf

9

Androcles exploits with lion
Andromeda *Gk* beauty in peril
Bluebeard European villain
Cassandra Trojan prophetess
Davy Jones sailors' sea-spirit
Finnbeara *Ir*. king of fairies
Friar Rush medieval mischief-maker
Friar Tuck Sherwood outlaw
Gilgamesh Babylonian hero
hamadryad *Gk* oak-tree *nymph*
Hippolyta Amazon queen
hobgoblin mischievous fairy
Iphigenia *Gk* heroine
Jack a Kent outwitted devil
Lohengrin Teutonic swan-knight
Narcissus vain youth *X* flower
Pecos Bill cowboy hero
Robin Hood outlaw-hero
Siegfried Teutonic hero
stroke lad dangerous fairy-fool

[1] Various alternative spelling forms: *bargest,*
bargaist and (Derbyshire) *bar-ghost.*

MYTHOLOGICAL CHARACTERS

10

changeling human/fairy offspring
Cinderella folklore heroine
Hag of Beare Gaelic *hag*
Hippolytus *Gk* hero
Lady Godiva wife of Earl Leofric
leprechaun roguish elf *(Ir.)*
leprechawn *leprechaun*
Maid Marian amour of *Robin Hood*
Paul Bunyan USA super-lumberjack
Peeping Tom observed *Lady Godiva*
Tannhauser German hero

11

Blunderbore giant killed by Jack
Gog and Magog pre-*Brut* giants
Morgan le Fay fairy-priestess
Mother Goose nursery folklore figure
Prester John magical king
William Tell Swiss hero

12

Allison Gross Scottish witch

little people goblins, elves, etc.
Rip Van Winkle slept 20 years

13

Fionn MacCumal great *Ir.* hero
Lord of Misrule Christmastide reveller

14

Abbot of Misrule *Lord of Misrule*
Fergus mac Roich Ulster hero
Hermaphroditus *Gk* man-woman
Herne the Hunter Windsor ghost
Old Man of the Sea evil *jinn*

15

Abbot of Unreason *Lord of Misrule*
Hansel and Gretel lost children
Robin Goodfellow *puck*
Rumpelstiltskin *dwarf*
Washer of the Ford death omen

MYTHOLOGICAL ANIMALS, ARTIFACTS, PLACES, ETC.

3

Ahi Vedic cosmic dragon

4

Argo Jason's ship
Gram Odin's magic sword

5

Hades underworld of dead
Hydra many-headed monster

kelpy Scottish horse-sprite
Khara Iranian giant ass
Ladon apple-guarding dragon
Lethe river of *Hades*
Munin Odin's raven
orgia winter-worship ritual

6

Aeolia a floating island
amulet lucky mascot
Asgard Norse heaven
Avalon Arthur's isle of apples

Camlan   Arthur's fatal battlefield
kelpie   *kelpy*
kraken   Norwegian sea-monster
Python   female dragon

7

Acheron   river of woe
Beltane   Celtic May Day
Bifrost   Norse rainbow-bridge
Camelot   seat of Arthur's court
Elysium   land of the blessed
griffin   monster
Pegasus   divine winged horse
Reynard   crafty fox-hero
unicorn   single-horned 'horse'

8

Acephali   land of headless
ambrosia   food of the gods
Atlantis   long-vanished island
Cerberus   dog-like Hades guardian:
   Hercules' 12th task
Derby Ram   colossal beast
familiar   animal-attendant of witch
Labyrinth   complex Cretan prison
Ragnarok   end of the world
Sleipnir   Odin's horse
Valhalla   part of *Asgard*

9

Charybdis   whirlpool monster
dream time   Aborigine golden age
fairy food   dangerous to humans
fairy ring   dark circle in grass
fairy tale   traditional folklore
fairy wind   sudden gust of wind
fire-drake   fire-breathing dragon
hag-ridden   suffered a Succubus
Typhoseus   Greek monster
Yggdrasil   the world tree

10

Book of Life   enlists the good

Brer Rabbit   trickster
Cretan Bull   Hercules' 7th task
fetch-light   nocturnal supernatural light
Hellespont   where Helle fell in sea
Hippocreue   sacred fountain
Nemean Lion   Hercules' 1st task
Open Sesame   magic phrase

11

Abracadabra   magic word
Book of Death   enlists the evil
Chanticleer   proper name for cock
corpse light   *fetch-light*
fetch-candle   *fetch-light*
Geryon's oxen   Hercules' 10th task
Hippocampus   sea monster
Pandora's box   source of ill
Puss in Boots   enchanted prince

12

Golden Fleece   taken by Jason
jack-a-lantern   *fetch-light*
Kilkenny cats   fought till death
Lernean Hydra   Hercules' 2nd task
will-o-the-wisp   *fetch-light*

13

Augean stables   Hercules' 5th task
Ceryneian Hind   Hercules' 3rd task
Delphic Oracle   Apollo's shrine
friar's lantern   *fetch-light*
glass mountain   land of the dead
king of the cats   huge Irish troglodyte

14/15/16/21

Flying Dutchman   phantom ship
Erymanthian Boar   Hercules' 4th task
Gotterdammerung   *Ragnarok*
Hippolyta's girdle   Hercules' 9th task
horses of Diomedes   Hercules' 8th task
Stymphalian birds   Hercules' 6th task
apples of the Hesperides   Hercules' 11th
   task

RELIGIONS, RELIGIOUS AND ECCLESIASTICAL TERMS

Also see TIME (p. 223).

Bud. Buddhist
CE Church of England
Chr. Christian
eChr. early Christian
Heb. Hebrew
Mhm Mohammedan
Prot. Protestant
RC Roman Catholic
Zor. Zoroastrianism

3

alb long, white vestment
ark chest or coffer
ave hail
Dom monastic title
fra (f) brother or friar
Jew follower of Hebrew faith
lay non-clerical
nun woman of religious order
pax the kiss of peace
pew fixed bench in church
pie a book of Church rules
pix *pyx*
pye *pie*
pyx a vessel for the *host*
see diocese: office of bishop
sin a moral offence
sir priest's title (obs.)
use local form of *rite*

4

abba Syriac or Coptic bishop
abbe courtesy title for priest, etc.
acta ecclesiastical court proceedings
alma soul, essence
ambo raised platform or pulpit
apse semicircular recess in church
bead a prayer (obs.): see *beads*

bull serious papal edict
cell solitary religious apartment
cope vestment worn over *alb*
Copt N.E. African Christian
cowl monk: monk's hood
cure French parish priest
dean cathedral dignitary
fane a temple
fast special abstinence from food
font vessel for baptismal water
form medieval theological term
gild *guild*
guru spiritual teacher
hadj Islam pilgrimage to Mecca
hajj *hadj*
halo saint's aura, aureole
Hell* abode of evil dead
Holi a Hindu spring festival
holy morally perfect
host consecrated wafer of the eucharist
icon religious image (Greek, Russian, etc.)
idol an object of worship
ikon *icon*
imam an officer of a mosque
Jain adherent of Jainism
joss a Chinese idol
jube rood-loft, screen in church
kirk church, in any sense
lama Tibetan Buddhist priest
mass celebration of Eucharist

monk man of religious order
naos temple, temple inner cell
nave main part of a church
neum *neume*
obit mass for dead person
Pace* *Pasch*
pall a chalice cover
pica *pie*
pome hand-warming ball of hot water
pope bishop of Rome: Greek priest
rite ceremonial form or observance
rood a cross or crucifix
rota *RC* supreme ecclesiastical tribunal
sect a body of followers
sext office of sixth hour
Sufi a pantheistic Islam mystic
Veda any of four holy books (Hindu)
Zion Jerusalem: Christian Church:
  heaven

5

abbey (convent and) church
abbot male head of abbey
agape *eChr.* love-feast: God's love
aisle side division of nave: passage
altar the Eucharist table
ambry *aumbry*
amice linen neck-cloth
Arian early heretic: Unitarian
awmry *aumbry*
banns proclamation of intended
  wedding
beads the rosary: *Bud.* similar device
benet an exorcist *(RC)*
brief a papal edict
canon rule, law: clerical dignitary
cella *naos*
cerge a large wax-candle
chela a novice in Buddhism
choir eastern part of church
clerk a member of the *clergy*
cotta short surplice
creed summary of belief
crook pastoral staff
curia court of the papal *see*
deify to exalt to rank of god
deism belief in unrevealed God
deist adherent of *deism*

deity a god or goddess
dirge funeral song or hymn
dogma authoritative doctrine
dulia inferior veneration of saints
elder Presbyterian Church officer
ephod a surplice
fakir a religious mendicant (esp. *Mhm*)
farse vernacular explanation of Latin
  epistle
friar a *Chr.* mendicant
guild association for religious purpose
habit official garment(s)
hadji one who has performed a *hadj*
hajji *hadji*
hejra *hegira*
herse (obs.) *hearse*
hijra *hegira*
Hindu believer in a form of
  Brahmanism
imaum *imam*
index *RC* official list of forbidden
  books
Islam the Mohammedan religion
Jaina *Jain*
Jesse Christ's genealogical tree:
  candlestick
Kaaba holy building at Mecca *(Mhm)*
karma *Bud.* theory of consequences
Koran the *Mhm* scriptures
laity non-clerical people
lauds post-matins prayers
laura group of recluses' cells
laver ritual washing vessel
lavra *laura*
Logos the Word of God incarnate
manse an ecclesiastical residence
matin a canonical church hour
mitre bishop's high head-dress
morse a cope fastening
myrrh a bitter aromatic transparent
  gum
neume successive one-syllable notes
  (chanting)
Nones a church *office*
pagan non-*Chr.*/Jew/*Mhm*
panim (obs.) *paynim*
papal of the pope or papacy
Parsi *Parsee*
Pasch the Passover
paten communion plate: chalice-cover

RELIGIONS AND RELIGIOUS TERMS

pieta picture of the Virgin with dead Christ
piety devoutness, etc.
pious dutiful: having piety
prime the *office* for 6 a.m.
prior abbot's deputy: head of priory
prone a service (obs.): part of church (obs.)
psalm devotional song or hymn
purim Feast of Lots (Hebrew)
qibla *Mhm* prayer-facing point
rabbi Jewish doctor of the law
rebus pictorial pun
relic personal memorial of saint
sadhu Hindu holy man
serge *cerge*
Shiah a *Mhm* sect: member of
stole scarf-like vestment
stoop *stoup*
stoup a holy-water vessel
summa a summary of theology, etc.
Sunna *Mhm* traditional teaching
sutra Sanskrit aphoristic rule book
synod an ecclesiastical council
terce *office* of the third hour
tithe a levy for the Church
Torah the Mosaic law: book of law
tract a pamphlet or leaflet
trope a phrase added to the mass
vicar parson *(CE)*: bishop's deputy *(RC)*
vigil celebrated eve of holy day

6

abbacy the office of abbot
abbess female head of abbey
adytum sacred part of temple: chancel
almery *aumbry*
ashram Indian hermitage
aumbry a recess for church vessels
awmrie *aumbry*
banner one who curses
beadle a church petty official
beguin *beghard*
bethel nonconformist chapel: ship
bishop a spiritual lord
cantor leader of church singers
censer a pan for burning incense
chrism consecrated or holy oil

cierge *cerge*
clergy the clerks in holy orders
cleric one of the *clergy*
corban a sacrifice fulfilling vow
Culdee an early Scottish monk
curate a minor *cleric*
cursal of/pertaining to *cursus*
cursus a daily prayer
datary an officer of papal court
deacon minor official (clerical, lay)
decani *decanal*
dharma the law (Sanskrit)
donary sacred donation
dossal cloth hanging rear of altar
dossel *dossal*
dosser chancel tapestry or hanging
Dunker a German-American baptist
exequy funeral procession/rites
Exodus* second book of Old Testament
flamen ancient Roman priest
friary convent of friars
Gemara second part of *Talmud*
gloria halo
gospel the teaching of Christ
gradin a ledge behind altar
hallow to make holy
Hebrew Jew (faith, race, language)
hearse a frame for 15 candles
hegira flight of Mohammed from Mecca
hejira *hegira*
heresy heterodoxy
hermit a solitary religious ascetic
housel the eucharist
hymnal a hymn-book
hyssop holy-water sprinkler
Jesuit member of Society of Jesus
Jewess female Jew
Judaic Jewish
keblah *kiblah*
kiblah facing-point in prayer *(Mhm)*
latria *dulia*
lavabo ritual washing of fingers
lector a minor *cleric*
legate *papal* ambassador
Levite* ancient Jewish inferior priest
litany a prayer of supplication
living a benefice
mantra a Vedic hymn

Mishna first part of *Talmud*
mollah *mullah*
moolah *mullah*
Mormon member of an American sect
Mosaic* pertaining to Moses
Moslem a Mohammedan
mosque *Mhm* place of worship
mullah *Mhm* teacher (law, theology)
Muslim *Moslem*
mystic seeker/attainer of mystical experience
novice pre final vows religious inmate
nuncio papal ambassador to monarch
oblate one dedicated to religious life
office act of worship
Ophite* gnostic *ophiolaier*
orison a prayer
pagoda an Eastern temple
painim (obs.) *paynim*
palmer pilgrim
Parsee Indian *Zor.* believer
parson incumbent of a parish
pastor a clergyman
paynim (obs.) heathen
priest official conductor of religious rites
primus a Scottish bishop
proper service/psalm, etc. for particular day
pulpit raised preaching structure
Purana various sacred Sanskrit books
Quaker one of a puritanical sect
rector a parish priest
rochet a surplice-like vestment
rosary a string of prayer beads
rubric liturgical direction
saddhu *sadhu*
santon Eastern dervish or saint
Shaker* member of (various) sect
shaman magic doctor-priest (Asia)
Shiite member of *Shiah* sect
Shinto Japanese nature and hero cult
shrine place hallowed by association
shrive hear and absolve confession
Talmud *Heb.* code of civil and canon law
Tantra Hindu instructional writings
temple a place of worship
tunker *Dunker*
votary a devoted worshipper

verger one having care of church
vestry vestment room
virger verger at St Paul's
votive observed in fulfilment of vow
Wahabi one of a *Mhm* sect

7

Aaronic pontifical
Abaddon Hell
acolyte one in minor orders
acolyth *acolyte*
Adamite N. African 2nd C. sect member
alms-fee Peter's pence
alms-man man who lives by alms
ampulla a vessel for holy oil
angelus bell: devotional exercise
ashrama *ashram*
Baptist* believer in cognizant baptism
beghard un-vowed monastic
beguine female *beghard*
biretta square cap worn by clergy
Brahman one of the Hindu priestly caste
Brahmin *Brahman*
caloyer a Greek monk
cassock long robe or outer coat
chalice a communion cup
chancel eastern part of a church
chaplet a string of prayer beads
chapter an assembly of canons
chrisom a baptismal robe for child
Cluniac monk or nun (Benedictine)
collect a short prayer
complin *compline*
confirm admit to full communion
convent monastery or nunnery
convert to change: one changed
crosier abbot or bishop's *crook*
crozier *crosier*
dataria *datary*
deanery dean's house/office/parishes
decanal pertaining to a dean
diocese extent of bishop's jurisdiction
diptyeh writing-tablet: register, etc.
douleia *dulia*
Elohist writer(s) of Elohistic parts of Bible

RELIGIONS AND RELIGIOUS TERMS

epistle letter from an apostle
Essenes ancient Jewish ascetics
evangel gospel, doctrine
fasting religious abstinence
frontal an altar hanging
Gehenna Hell
Genesis* first book of the Bible
gentile any non-Jew
Gnostic* an early heretic
gradine *gradin*
gradual part of the *mass*
gremial Bishop's ordination cloth
heathen polytheist, atheist
heretic upholder of *heresy*
hexapia an edition of the Bible
hosanna exclamation of praise to God
hymnary hymn-book
impiety want of veneration
incense fragrant-fume material
incubus sleep sex-devil (male)
infidel non-believer
in petto (f) secret choice (of cardinal)
introit *mass* anthem
Jainism an Indian religion
Judaism the Hebrew religion
Lamaism Tibetan Buddhism
Lateran of the Pope's cathedral
lectern church reading desk
lection lesson read in church
liturgy regular ritual of a church
Lollard a follower of Wycliffe
low mass sans music and incense
maniple a eucharist vestment
minaret a mosque tower
minster an abbey/priory church
muezzin *Mhm* official who calls to
  prayer
narthex vestibule between porch and
  nave
nirvana *Bud.* aspired state
Numbers* 4th book of Old Testament
nunnery a house for nuns
Oratory* a *RC* church
ordinal a service book
orphrey vestment embroidery
Parsism *Parseeism*
penance sacrament of confession
Peshito a Syriac translation of Bible
piscina basin in old churches
pontiff pope: bishop: high priest

prebend a share of cathedral revenue
primate archbishop
prophet a spokesman of deity
Psalter* the Book of Psalms
Puritan* extreme protestant
rectory province/residence of rector
requiem mass for dead: music
reredos screen behind altar
retable shelf behind altar
retreat period of meditation
sacring consecration
sedilia seats for officiating clergy
shaster holy writing
shastra *shaster*
soutane *cassock*
tonsure mode of cutting monk's hair
unfrock depose from priesthood
vespers an evening service
Vulgate* a Latin version of the
  Scriptures
Wee* Free* nickname for a Scots *Prot.*
  sect

8

advowson right of patronage
affusion baptismal pouring on
anchoret *anchorite*
Anglican of the Church of England
antiphon alternate chanting or singing
antipope a rival pope
apostasy revolt from obedience,
  defection
apostate one who has apostatized
Arianism an early heresy
asperges short introductory to *mass*
basilica *RC* church with honorific
  privileges
beadroll iist of the dead
beadsman one endowed to pray
bedesman *beadsman*
benefice a church living
breviary book containing daily services
Buddhism religion founded by Buddha
Buddhist follower of *Buddhism*
cantoris north side of choir
Capuchin* a Franciscan friar
canonise enrol in list of saints
cardinal a prince of the church

catacomb   subterranean burial-place
Catholic*   Roman C.: Anglo C.: Old C.: etc.
cenobite   *coenobite*
chasuble   a sleeveless vestment
ciborium   a chalice-like vessel
compline   last service of day
conclave   the body of cardinals
corporal   cloth covering Eucharist
crucifer   cross-bearer in procession
crucifix   figure of Christ crucified
dalmatic   a loose-fitting vestment
demoniac   one possessed: of demons
diocesan   of diocese: bishop: cleric
Docetism   a 2nd C. heresy
donatism   early African sect
Donatist   believer in *donatism*
doxology   a hymn or liturgical formula
ebionism   early Judaico-Christian sect
Ebionist   believer in *ebionism*
ethereal   heavenly, airy, spirit-like
etherial   *ethereal*
evensong   evening prayer
exegesis   (Biblical) interpretation
exorcise   cast out devil(s)
exorcism   the act of exorcising
exorcist   one who exorcises
exorcize   *exorcise*
feretory   a shrine for relics
footpace   *predella*
God's acre   burial ground
hierarch   ruler in holy things
hieratic   priestly
high mass   mass with full ceremonial
holy coat   seamless coat of Jesus
holy rood   Christ's cross
holy writ   the Scriptures
Huguenot   a French Protestant
hymn-book   book of hymns
idolater   worshipper of idols
idolatry   worship of idol(s)
lichgate   roofed churchyard gate
Lutheran   of Luther: his doctrines/followers
lychgate   *lichgate*
mass-book   *RC* missal
menology   calendar of saints
Miserere*   a psalm
modalism   a Trinity doctrine
modalist   believer in *modalism*

Mohammed   founder of Mohammedanism
Moravian   of the Moravians (*Prot.* sect)
navicula   incense boat
Nethinim   old Jewish temple servants
Novatian   of the *antipope* Novatian(us)
oblation   act of offering: sacrifice
ordinary   judge: death-cell chaplain
Orthodox*   Eastern Church
paganism   heathenism
Pantheon   all the gods: temple
pardoner   licensed seller of indulgences
Parsiism   *Parseeism*
Pharisee   strict observer of the law (*Heb.*)
pontifex   ancient Roman priest
predella   the altar platform
Proverbs*   an Old Testament book
Psalmist*   David
quietism   a doctrine of tranquillity
quietist   follower of *quietism*
recollect   a Franciscan friar
sacristy   *vestry*
Sadducee   aristocratic traditionalist (*Heb.*)
sequence   a pre-gospel hymn
succubus   female *incubus*
suffrage   a prayer for the dead
superior   head of an order
surplice   a white linen vestment
swastika (1)   (clockwise) male, good (Hindu)
swastika (2)   (anti-clockwise) female, bad (NAZI)
tenebrae   matins, lauds in Holy Week
thurible   *censer*
thurifer   carries the *thurible*
transept   part at right angles to *nave*
Trimurti   Hindu trinity (Brahma, Vishnu, Siva)
triptych   three tablets, hinged together
unaneled   without extreme unction
viaticum   Eucharist at danger of death
vicarage   residence of a vicar
vicaress   deputy abbess: vicar's wife
zoolatry   animal worship

9

ablutions   ceremonial washing

RELIGIONS AND RELIGIOUS TERMS

anchorage a recluse's cell
anchorite a recluse
apocrypha hidden or secret
apostolic proceeding from the apostles
arch-druid chief druid
arch-enemy Satan
Athenaeum a temple of Athene
ave Maria* the Hail Mary prayer
baptistry where baptism occurs
beatitude Heavenly happiness: Orthodox title
bishopric office/jurisdiction of bishop
bismillah in the name of Allah
black mass devil worship
Black* Pope* head of Jesuits
blasphemy contempt of God
Calvinism predestination protestantism
Carmelite* friar/nun of Mount Carmel
catechism question/answer instructions
cathedral principal church of diocese
Celestine monk of Pope Celestine
cere-cloth winding sheet
Christian a believer in Christ's divinity
coenobite monk in solitary community
confessor priest: persecuted believer
Cordelier a Franciscan friar
dalai lama head of Tibetan *(Bud.)* hierarchy
deaconess various serving women
Dominican friar/monk of St Dominic
episcopal governed by bishops
epistoler epistle reader in service
Eucharist Holy Communion
Eutychian follower/doctrine of Eutyches
evangelic of the Gospels
gospeller protestant preacher
Gregorian of Pope St Gregory
hierarchy the angels: church government
hierogram a sacred symbol
holy grass strewn on floor at festivals
holy water blessed water
incumbent one holding benefice
interdict papal prohibition
joss-house a temple
joss-stick a stick of incense
Lazarists *RC* missionary society
Leviticus an Old Testament book

Low* Church* *CE* evangelical wing
Maronites Lebanese Christians
martyrdom death of a martyr
Methodism akin to *Low Church*
Methodist* follower of *Methodism*
moderator a Presbyterian president
monachism monasticism
monastery a house for monks
Mussulman Moslem (plural Musselmans)
Mussulmen facetious plural of *Musselman*
Nestorian of the heresy of Nestorius
offertory verses sung during collection
ostensory monstrance
pantheism identification of God with universe
Parseeism Indian *Zor.* belief
patriarch Biblical leader: pontiff
plainsong unmeasured music
prayer-rug a Moslem's small carpet
precentor leader of choir
presbyter an elder: senior priest
priestess female priest
proselyte a convert
prothesis Greek Eucharist table, etc.
pyrolatry fire-worship
reliquary a receptacle for relics
rural dean has charge of certain parishes
sabbatism observance of the Sabbath
Sabainism akin to Islam
sacrament very special religious rite
sacrilege profanation of anything holy
sacristan one having care of movables
sanctuary chancel: refuge: immunity, etc.
sepulchre tomb: recess, etc.
Shamanism* N. Asian magic religion
solemnise to celebrate with rites
solemnize *solemnise*
succentor subcantor: bass soloist
suffragan a coadjutor-bishop
synagogue Jewish place of worship
teleology a doctrine of purposes
theomachy opposition to divine will
theomancy divination by oracles
theomania religious madness
theotokos mother of God
theurgist agent of divine action

Vaishnava a worshipper of Vishnu
venerable worthy of reverence
Waldenses followers of Waldo

10

Albigenses French 13th C. heretics
altar-cloth the covering of the altar
altarpiece a work of art
altar-rails dividing rails
altar-stone stone as altar
Anabaptist* German Baptist sect
Antichrist great opponent of Christ
Apocalypse* last book of New
  Testament
apotheoses plural of *apotheosis*
apotheosis a deification
archbishop metropolitan with own
  diocese
archdeacon the 'bishop's eye'
arch-priest various senior priests
assumption taking up bodily into
  heaven
Athanasian relating to Athanasius
baptistery *baptistry*
Bernadine *Cistercian*
black friar a *Dominican*
Brahmanism worship of Brahma
Brahminism *Brahmanism*
Carthusian monk/nun of St Bruno
catechumen one being taught
  Christianity
Chronicles* two Old Testament books
churchyard burial-ground
Cistercian monk of Citeaux, France
confession sacrament: body of belief
  (etc.)
conformist follower of Established
  Church
consecrate *hallow*
consistory ecclesiastical court
dragonnade Louis XIV's *Prot.*
  persecution
ecumenical general, universal
episcopacy church government:
  bishops (etc.)
episcopate bishopric: office of bishop
  (etc.)
evangelism Protestantism

evangelist author of Gospel: preacher
  (etc.)
Free* Church* a Scots Presbyterian
  sect
Gnosticism an early heresy
gospel side north side of church
hallelujah praise be the name of God
heliolater a sun-worshipper
heliolatry sun-worship
Heptateuch first 7 Old Testament
  books
hierocracy priestly government
High* Church* the episcopal wing of
  CE
high priest a chief priest
Holy* Office* the Inquisition
holy orders sacrament of priesthood
Holy* Willie* a religious hypocrite
hyperdulia veneration of the Virgin
  Mary
iconoclasm act of breaking images
iconoclast image-breaker
iconolater image-worshipper
iconolatry image worship
iconomachy opposition to *iconolatry*
idolatress female *idolater*
indulgence remission of punishment
  for sin
invocation prayer: spirit-raising
Juggernaut* an incarnation of Vishnu
Lady* Chapel* dedicated to Virgin
  Mary
lay brother unprofessed monastic
  worker
lectionary a book of church lessons
Magnificat the song of the Virgin
monotheism belief in one god
monotheist believer in monotheism
monstrance vessel for consecrated host
occurrence two feasts on the same day
omnipotent all powerful
ophiolater a snake-worshipper
ophiolatry snake-worship
Pentateuch first 5 books of Old
  Testament
prayer-bead a rosary bead
prayer-book a book of prayers
prebendary a canon with *prebend*
preceptory community of Knights
  Templar

RELIGIONS AND RELIGIOUS TERMS

presbytery court: district: priest's house (etc.)
priesthood office of priest
priest-king king with priestly functions
priestling a contemptible priest
prophetess female *prophet*
Protestant* member of Reformed Church
Puritanism* extreme Protestantism
rock-temple temple hewn from rock
rood-screen an ornamental partition
sacerdotal priestly
sacrosanct inviolable
sanctified made holy
schismatic one who assists breach
Septuagint the Greek Old Testament
tabernacle temple: human body: receptacle (etc.)
Tridentine of the Council of Trent
unannealed *unaneled*
unbaptised without baptism
white friar a Carmelite
worshipper one who worships
Zend-Avesta ancient, sacred Parsi writings

11

archdiocese an archbishop's diocese
Benedictine monk/nun of St Benedict
benediction blessing
bibliolatry superstitious reverence for book
Christendom Christian lands: Christians
convocation provincial synod of clergy
devil-dodger ranting preacher
ecclesiarch a ruler of a church
epistle side south side of church
Erastianism control of church by state
eschatology doctrine of final things
Geneva* Bible* English, published Geneva 1560
genuflexion bending the knee in respect
Hagiographa books of Old Testament
Inquisition* tribunal of heresy, unbelief, etc.
intercessor bishop acting for vacant see

Karmathians *Mhm* pantheistic/socialistic sect
miracle play medieval religious drama
Nicene Creed* creed of first Nicene Council
parishioner a member of a parish
oecumenical *ecumenical*
passing-bell rung for prayers for dead
Passionists *RC* missionaries, etc.
Passion-play drama of the Crucifixion
paternoster the Lord's Prayer: *bead*
patron saint for examples see SAINTS (p. 353).
pontificate office/dignity of pope
pontificies plural of *pontifex*
prayer-wheel *Bud.* drum of prayers
protomartyr a first martyr of cause
sacring bell rung for solemn parts of mass
Scientology an Australian cult
uncanonical not canonical

12

Annunciation* angelic announcement to Our Lady
chapel of ease subordinate to parish church
chapter-house a monastic assembly building
church-parade military assembly for church
church-warden a parish officer
confessional cubicle for confession
devil-worship Satanism
dispensation permission to neglect a rule, etc.
Ecclesiastes an Old Testament book
ecclesiastic of church
episcopalian of bishops: Anglican
frankincense a type of incense
hot gospeller a revivalist preacher
interdiction a papal ban
metropolitan archbishop: of mother church
nunc dimittis (f) the song of Simeon
red-letter day saint's feast day
sanctus bell *sacring bell*
spiritualism a doctrine: spiritism

Sunday school religious instruction
vicar-general various clerical/lay
officers

13

Anglo-Catholic *High Church*

beatification first step to canonisation
burnt-offering a sacrifice by fire
Eastern* Church* Greek Orthodox
Nonconformist* *Prot.* apart from CE
Roman* Catholic* Catholic
Salvation* Army* *Prot.* missionary
workers
Way of the Cross Stations of the Cross

SAINTS, EASTERN AND WESTERN TRADITION

Also see POPES (p. 117).

fdr founder of religious order
pat. patron(ess)
x invoked against
SJ Society of Jesus (Jesuits)

2

Ia *pat.* St Ives, Cornwall

3

Abo Arab perfumer, martyred 786
Ann Mary's mother (tradition)
Bee Irish refugee, 7th C.
Foi *Faith*
Foy *Faith*
Ivo *pat.* St Ives, Huntingdon
Odo French abbot 879–942 (see 10)

4

Afra ex-prostitute, martyred c.304
Bavo penitent, died c.653
Bede monk, scholar, 673–735 (see 16)
Chad English bishop, died 672
Cnut King of Denmark, died 1086
Dewi *David*, abbot-bishop 6th C.
Elmo *Erasmus, pat.* sailors
Enda *fdr* first Irish monastery
Eric king, *pat.* Sweden

Fare sister of *Faro*, died c.660
Faro bishop of Meaux, died c.672
Gall Irish monk, died c.640
John (see 14/15/16)
Jude apostle, *x* desperation
Lucy died c.304, *x* eye disease
Luke evangelist, Greek
Mark evangelist
Maro *pat.* Lebanese Maronites
Mary The Blessed Virgin (see 12/13)
Neot King Alfred association
Nino slave-girl, died c.340
Olaf King of Norway 995–1030
Paul apostle of the Gentiles (see 13)
Pius popes, Pius v, Pius x
Roch *Rock*
Rock 14th C. *x* physical diseases
Sava c.1175–1235, *pat.* Serbs
Yves 'an honest lawyer', 1303–47

5

Agnes Roman child, martyred c.304
Aidan missionary: bishop
Alban Romano-Briton, martyred c.209
Asaph Welsh bishop, 6th C.

SAINTS

Boris *Boris and Gleb*
Bride *Brigid*
Bruno *fdr* 'Charterhouse': archbishop
Budoc Celtic bishop 6th C.
Clare *fdr* 'Poor Clares' (see 13)
Cloud Frankish prince, c.520–60
David *Dewi, pat.* Wales
Denis *Denys, pat.* France (see 16)
Denys *Denis*, bishop martyred c.258
Edith of Wilton: Polesworth: Tamworth
Edwin Paulinus of York, died 644
Faith possibly French martyr
Felix 67 Western saints (see 14)
Giles hermit, *pat.* cripples, indigent
Helen empress, mother of Constantine
James (see 12/15)
Leger Frankish bishop, c.616–79
Linus succeeded *Peter* as pope
Menus Egyptian, martyred c.303
Moses Ethiopian ex-bandit, died 405
Mungo Celtic nickname *Kentigern*
Osyth East Saxon queen, 7th C.
Peter leader of Apostles (12)
Sabas *fdr* extant monastery, 439–532
Simon apostle, 'the Zealot'
Vitus *x* epilepsy, chorea, etc.

6

Adrian martyr: bishop
Agatha martyr, *pat.* bell-founders
Alexis 'the man of God', 5th C.
Andrew apostle, *pat.* Scotland (see 13)
Anselm historic English archbishop, c.1033–1109
Anskar Scandinavian missionary, 801–65
Antony hermit, c.251–356 (see 12/13/16)
Blaise bishop, *x* throat infections
Brigid Swedish *fdr*, c.1303–73
Cecily martyr, *pat.* musicians
Edmund martyr, English king, 841–69
Edward (the Confessor) c.1004–66 (see 15)
Fiacre Irish hermit, *pat.* gardeners
George martyr, *pat.* England
Godric died 1170, English lyric poet

Hubert *pat.* hunters and trappers
Jerome c.342–420, great scholar
Joseph husband of *Virgin Mary*
Marina woman-monk *'Pelagia'*
Mesrop died 439, devised Armenian alphabet
Monica mother of *Augustine of Hippo*
Philip apostle
Teresa *fdr*, mystic 1515–82 (see 15)
Thomas (see 10/13/14)
Wandru *pat.* Mons (Belgium)

7

Alberic (Aubrey) abbot, *fdr*, died 1108
Aldhelm bishop, Wessex, died 709
Ambrose great Latin scholar, c.334–97
Barbara *x* lightning, *pat.* gunners, miners
Bathild queen, ex-slave, English, died 680
Bernard 'the Honey-sweet Teacher'
Brendan (the Voyager) abbot, 486–578
Bridget Swedish, *fdr*, c.1303–73
Casimir Polish prince, 1458–84
Cecilia *Cecily*, early Roman martyr
Clement succeeded *Linus* as pope
Columba abbot: nun: maiden
Crispin *pat.* shoemakers, leatherworkers
Dominic 1170–1221, *fdr* Order of Preachers
Donatus Irish bishop in Italy, died c.876
Dunstan compiled (UK) coronation rite (973)
Erasmus martyred 303, *Elmo*, 'St Elmo's fire'
Francis (see 13/14/15)
Gabriel Archangel
Gilbert 1085–1189, *fdr* only English order
Gothard Bavarian bishop, c.960–1038
Gregory (the Wonderworker) died 270 (see 14/15)
Leonard hermit, *pat.* prisoners
Malachy Irish bishop, 1094–1148
Marinus hermit, 4th c., *San Marino*
Matthew apostle, evangelist

Michael Archangel
Pancras Roman boy, martyred c.304
Patrick c.385–c.461, *pat.* Ireland
Pelagia 'Pelagia the Penitent' legends
Raphael Archangel
Sergius Russian abbot, c.1314–92
Stephen first Christian martyr
Swithin bishop, died Winchester 862
Swithun *Swithin*, '40 days' rain'
Timothy converted by *Paul*
Zachary father of *John the Baptist*

8

Adelaide empress, c.931–999
Aloysius Lombard student *(SJ)* 1568–91
Attracta Irish nun, c.5th C.
Barnabas styled apostle, Cypriot Jew
Benedict patriarch of monks, died
  c.547 (see 16)
Boniface missionary: bishop
Camillus 1550–1614, *pat.* nurses, sick
Cure d'Ars *pat.* parish clergy (see 11)
Cuthbert English bishop, c.634–687
Euphemia martyred at Chalcedon,
  c.307
Gelasius pope, poss. African, died 496
Hallvard martyred 1043, *pat.* Oslo
Ladislas heroic Hungarian king,
  1040–95
Lawrence famous Roman martyr, died
  258
Margaret various incl. Scottish queen
Matthias apostle, replaced Iscariot
Nicholas *pat.* children, Russia, virgins
Notburga c.1265–1313, *pat.* hired
  hands
Polycarp bishop, martyred Smyrna,
  c.155
Seraphim Russian mystic, 1759–1833
Veronica wiped Christ's suffering face
Vladimir Russian prince, c.955–1015
Walburga feast day 'Walpurgisnacht'
Werburgh Mercian princess, died
  c.700

9

Alexander early Roman martyr (see
  15)

Anastasia martyred in Yugoslavia 304
Apollonia martyred 249, *x* toothache
Augustine (of Canterbury) died c.605
  (see 16)
Callistus (the First) pope, martyred
  c.222
Dubricius 'Dubric' of Arthurian legend
Elizabeth biblical: princess: queen, etc.
Ethelbert king of East Angles, died 794
  (see 15)
Expeditus *x* pressing emergency
Hildegard 'the Sibyl of the Rhine'
Januarius blood still liquefies,
  martyred 305
Joan of Arc historic maid, c.1412–31
Katherine (of Alexandria) 'wheel' (see
  16)
Kentigern Scots bishop, died c.612
Marcarius (the Elder) stigmatic
  c.300–90
Pantalcon martyr, *pat.* medical men
San Marino republic named after
  Marinus
Sebastian famous early martyr
Valentine birds pair 14th February
  (trad.)
Wenceslas prince, *pat.* Czechoslovakia

10

Athanasius great Greek scholar
  c.296–373
Barba'shmin Persian bishop, martyred
  341
Bernadette visionary, Lourdes,
  1844–79
Crispinian martyred with *Crispin*,
  same *pat.*
Frideswide *pat.* Oxford, city/university
Oda the Good *Odo*
Santa Claus *Nicholas* of Asia Minor
Thomas More (Sir) historic chancellor,
  1485–1535
Virgin Mary mother of Christ

11

Bartholomew apostle
Bonaventure bishop, theologian,
  1221–74

Christopher martyr, *pat.* wayfarers
John Vianney 1786–1859, *Cure d'Ars*
Leo the Great historic pope, died 461
Wilgefortis *x* troublesome husbands

12

Anthony Daniel *SJ* martyred by Red
 Indians 1648
Boris and Gleb Russian princes,
 murdered 1015
Gemma Galgani laywoman, stigmatic,
 1878–1903
James the Less apostle, died c.62
Mary Magdalen first witness of
 Resurrection
Peter Nolasco died 1256, *pat.* midwives

13

Andrew of Crete preacher, poet,
 c.660–740
Antony of Padua preacher, 1195–1231
Basil the Great great Greek scholar,
 died 379
Clare of Assisi friend of *Francis* (see 5)
Francis Borgia *(SJ)* of the infamous
 Borgias
Francis Xavier *pat.* RC missionaries
Gerard Majella bilocation facility,
 1726–55
Gildas the Wise Scots historian,
 c.500–70
Hugh of Lincoln anti-semitic legend
John the Divine apostle, died c.100
Louis of France king, crusader 1214–70
Paul the Hermit first Christian hermit
The Three Marys evangelized
 Provence (legend)
Thomas a' Becket historic archbishop,
 1118–70
Thomas Aquinas theologian c.1225–74
Vincent de Paul missionary *fdr*,
 c.1580–1660

14

Albert the Great 1206–80 'the
 Universal Teacher'

Doubting Thomas the apostle
Felix of Dunwich Felixstowe named
 after
Frances Cabrini 1850–1917, *pat.* all
 emigrants
Francis de Sales bishop, writer,
 1567–1622
Gregory of Sinai mystic, c.1290–1346
John Chrysostom great Greek scholar,
 died 407
John of the Cross mystic, poet,
 1542–91
John the Baptist herald of Christ, died
 c.29
Magnus of Orkney died c.1094, son of
 ruler

15

Alexander Nevsky Russian prince,
 1219–63
Angela of Brescia *fdr* Ursulines, died
 1540
Canute the Fourth *Cnut*
Charles Borromeo cardinal, 1538–84
David of Scotland king, died 1153
Edward the Martyr English king,
 c.962–78
Ethelbert of Kent king, c.560–616
Four Crowned Ones early martyrs,
 stonemasons
**Germanus of
 Paris** Saint-Germain-des-Pres
Gregory the Great historic pope,
 c.540–604
James of the March missionary, died
 1476
James the Greater apostle, died 44
John of Rochester John Fisher,
 1469–1535
Teresa of Lisieux nun, 1873–97
The Forty Martyrs Romans: British

16

Antony of the Caves Russian abbot,
 983–1073
Augustine of Hippo great Latin
 scholar, died 430

Benedict the Black ex-slave, 1526–89
Cyril of Jerusalem bishop, scholar, c.315–86
Daniel the Stylite succeeded Simeon (below)
Dionysius of Paris *Denis, Denys*
Genesius the Actor early Roman martyr
Hilary of Poitiers 'Hilary term' named after
Ignatius of Loyola *fdr SJ*, 1491–1556

John the Almsgiver *pat.* Knights of Malta
Katherine Laboure 'miraculous medal', 1806–76
Katherine of Siena stigmatic, c.1347–80
Nicholas the Great pope, died 867
Simeon the Stylite 36 years atop pillar
The Holy Innocents murdered by Herod
The Venerable Bede only Englishman in 'Paradiso'

SCIENCE AND TECHNOLOGY

ABBREVIATIONS

For scientific bodies and qualifications see ABBREVIATIONS (p. 379).
For scientific units of measure see MEASUREMENT (ABBREVIATIONS) (p. 210).
note The asterisk * indicates that the abbreviation is also a word, usually with a totally different meaning, and valid for most word games.

1

A   argon
B   boron
C   carbon
D   deuterium
E   einsteinium (also Es)
E   energy
F   flourine
F   force
H   hydrogen
I   iodine
I   electric current
K   (kalium) potassium
m   mass
N   nitrogen
O   oxygen
P   phosphorus
P   power
S   sulphur
T   tritium
U   uranium
V   vanadium
W   (wolframium) tungsten
Y   yttrium

2

AC (**ac**)   alternating current
Ac   actinium
Ag   (argentum) silver

Al   aluminium
AM*   amplitude modulation
Am*   americium
aq.   (aqua) water
Ar   argon
As*   arsenic
AT*   alternative technology
At*   astatine
Au   (aurum) gold
AV   audio-visual
az.   azimuth
Ba   barium
Be*   beryllium
Bi   bismuth
Bk   berkelium
Br   bromine
Ca   calcium
Cd   cadmium
Ce   cerium
Cf   californium
c.g.   centre of gravity
Cl   chlorine
Cm   Curium
CN   an irritant 'gas'
Co   cobalt
Cr   chromium
CS   an irritant 'gas'
Cs   caesium
Cu   (cuprum) copper
DC (**dc**)   direct current
DP   data processing
DS   disseminated sclerosis

DT data transmission
DT (dt) delirium tremens
Dy dysprosium
EP electroplated
Er* erbium
Es* einsteinium (also E)
Eu europium
Fe (ferrum) iron
Fm fermium
Fr francium
Ga gallium
Gd gadolinium
Ge germanium
Gl glucinum (now beryllium)
Ha* hahnium
HE* high explosive
He* helium
Hf hafnium
Hg (hydragyrum) mercury
Ho* holmium
HT high tension
IC integrated circuit
ID* infectious diseases
In* indium
Ir iridium
Kr krypton
La* lanthanum
Lr lawrencium
LT low tension
Lu lutetium
Lw now Lr
Md mendelevium
Mg magnesium
Mn manganese
Mo* molybdenum
MS multiple sclerosis
Mv now Md
Na* (natrium) sodium
Nb niobium
Nd neodymium
Ne neon
Ni nickel
No* nobelium
Np neptunium
op.* operation
Os osmium
OT occupational therapy
Pa* protactinium
Pb (plumbini) lead
Pd palladium

PK psychokinesis
Pm promethium
Po* polonium
Pr praseodymium
Pt platinum
Pu plutonium
Ra radium
Rb rubidium
Re* rhenium
Rf rutherfordium
Rh rhodium: rhesus
RT radiotele (phone/phony)
Ru ruthenium
Sb (stibium) antimony
Sc scandium
Se selenium
sg specific gravity
Si silicon
Sm samarium
Sn (stannum) tin
sp. species
Sr strontium
Ta* tantalum
TB tuberculosis
Tb terbium
Tc technetium
Th thorium
Ti* titanium
Tl thallium
Tm thulium
TT tuberculin tested
Xe xenon
Yb ytterbium
Zn zinc
Zr zirconium

3

ADP automatic data processing
AGR advanced gas-cooled reactor
agr. agriculture
alg. algebra
alt.* altitude
ans. answer
APT* advanced passenger train
arg. same as Ag
art.* article: artificial: artillery
ASM air-to-surface missile

ABBREVIATIONS

ATC automatic train control
atm. atmosphere
ATS anti-tetanus-serum
aut. automatic
bcg a strain of tubercule bacillus
BOD* biochemical oxygen demand
bot.* botany
CLR computer language recorder
CLT computer language translator
CNS central nervous system
COL* computer-oriented language
COM computer output microfilm
CRO cathode-ray oscillograph
CRT cathode-ray tube
cva cerebrovascular accident
cwr continuous welded rail
DDT dichlorodiphenyltrichloroethane
dil. dilute
DNA deoxyribonucleic acids
dyn dynamo: dynamometer
ECG electrocardio (gram/graph)
ECT electroconvulsive therapy
EDT electronic data processing
EEG electroencephalo(gram/graph)
ENT Ear, Nose and Throat
ent. entomology
ESP extra-sensory perception
ety. etymol(ogy/ogical)
FET field-effect transistor
GPI general paralysis of the insane
hor. horology
ich. ichthyology
LED* light emitting diode
LNG liquefied natural gas
LPG liquefied petroleum gas
LSD lysergic acid diethylamide
mag.* magnetic
med. medical: medicine
met.* metaphysics: meteorology
min. mineralogy
mmf magnetomotive force
neg. negative
PVC polyvinyl chloride
QSO quasi-stellar object (quasar)
RNA ribonucleic acids
sol.* solution
TCP trichlorophenylmethyliodosalicyl
TNT trinitrotoluene
TVP texturized vegetable protein
vac.* vacuum

4

ammo ammunition
anal.* analysis
anat. anatomy
arch.* archaic: architecture
astr. astronomy
at.* no.* atomic number
auto.* automatic
biol. biology
comp.* compound
conc. concentrate(-ed/-ion)
dent.* -al/-ist/-istry
elec. electric(ity)
EPNS electroplated nickel silver
etym. same as *ety.*
geog. geography
geol. geology
hort. horticult(-ure/-ural)
icon.* iconography
math.* same as *maths*
mech. mechanical
meth. same as *meths.*
MOS(T)* metal oxide silicon
(transistors)
phar. *pharm.*
Phil. -ology/-ological/-osophy/
-osophical
phon.* phonetics
phot.* photography
phys. -iology/-ics/-ician
PTFE polytetrafluoroethylene
trig.* trigonometry

5

agric. agriculture
ALGOL (**Algol**) algolrithmic language
arith. arithmetic(-al)
COBOL an English computer language
contr. contract(-ed/-ion)
D and C dilatation and curettage
(med.)
DATEC data and telecommunications
elect.* same as *elec.*
entom same as *ent.*
ichth same as *ich.*
LASER* radiation amplified light
MASER* radiation amplified microwave

maths* mathematics
metal* metallurgy
meths.* methylated spirits
pharm. -acy/-aceutical/-acopoeia

6

arccos inverse cosine
archit. architecture
arcsin inverse sine
arctan inverse tangent
astrol. astrology
astron. astronomy
at.* numb.* same as *at. no.*

con.* sec.* conic section
cosmog. cosmography
hortic. horticulture
metaph. metaphysics
meteor.* meteorology
metall. metallurgy
Nat. Sci. Natural Science(s)
phonet. phonetics

7

archeol. archeology
nat. hist.* natural history

CHEMICAL ELEMENTS
(of known isotopic weight)

note The chemical symbol followed by the atomic number is given within the brackets. The higher the atomic number the higher the atomic weight. Except where the spelling is very similar the previous or alternative name is given in CAPITALS.

R/A artf mtl radioactive, artificially made metallic element

3

tin (Sn/50) malleable metal

4

gold (Au/79) precious metal
iron (Fe/26) metal
lead (Pb/82) soft metal
neon (Ne/10) gas
zinc (Zn/30) metal

5

argon (Ar/18) gas
boron (B/5) amorphous powder
radon (Rn/86) radioactive gas
xenon (Xe/54) heavy gas

6

barium (Ba/56) malleable metal
carbon (C/6) graphite, diamond
cerium (Ce/58) metal
cobalt (Co/27) hard metal
copper (Cu/29) metal
curium (Cm/96) *R/A artf mtl*
erbium (Er/68) rare metal
helium (He/2) light inert gas
indium (In/49) rare soft metal
iodine (I/53) chemical
nickel (Ni/28) malleable metal
osmium (Os/76) metal, heaviest
  substance
oxygen (O/8) gas
radium (Ra/88) radioactive metal
silver (Ag/47) precious metal
sodium (Na/11) soft metal

CHEMICAL ELEMENTS

7

arsenic (As/33) chemical
bismuth (Bi/83) brittle metal
bromine (Br/35) chemical
cadmium (Cd/48) metal
caesium (Cs55) soft metal
calcium (Ca/20) metal
fermium (Fm/100) *R/A artf mtl*
gallium (Ga/31) soft metal
hafnium (Hf/72) metal, CELTIUM
holmium (Ho/67) rare-earth metal
iridium (Ir/77) hard brittle metal
krypton (Kr/36) inert gas
lithium (Li/3) lightest metal
mercury (Hg/80) liquid metal,
    QUICKSILVER
niobium (Nb/41) metal, COLUMBIUM
rhenium (Re/75) rare metal
rhodium (Rh/45) hard metal
silicon (Si/14) amorphous powder,
    SILICIUM
sulphur (S/16) mineral, BRIMSTONE
terbium (Tb/65) rare metal
thorium (Th/90) radioactive metal
thulium (Tm/69) rare-earth metal
uranium (U/92) radioactive metal
yttrium (Y/39) rare-earth metal

8

actinium (Ac/89) radioactive metal
americum (Am/95) *R/A artf mtl*
antimony (Sb/51) crystalline metal
astatine (At/85) *R/A artf mtl*
chlorine (Cl/17) gas
chromium (Cr/24) metal
europium (Eu/63) rare-earth metal
fluorine (F/9) gas
francium (Fr/87) radioactive chemical,
    VIRGINIUM
hydrogen (H/1) gas
lutetium (Lu/71) rare-earth metal
nitrogen (N/7) gas
platinum (Pt/78) noble metal
polonium (Po/84) radioactive metal
rubidium (Rb/37) soft metal
samarium (Sm/62) rare-earth metal
scandium (Sc/20) rare metal

selenium (Se/34) chemical
tantalum (Ta/73) rare, hard metal
thallium (Tl/81) soft metal
titanium (Ti/21) metal
tungsten (W/74) rare metal
vanadium (V/23) hard metal

9

aluminium (Al/13) light metal
berkelium (Bk/97) *R/A artf metal*
beryllium (Be/4) very light metal
germanium (Ge/32) brittle metal
lanthanum (La/57) rare-earth metal
magnesium (Mg/12) combustible metal
manganese (Mn/25) hard brittle metal
neodymium (Nd/60) metal
neptunium (Np/93) *R/A artf mtl*
palladium (Pd/46) rare metal
plutonium (Pu/94) *R/A artf mtl*
potassium (K/19) metal
ruthenium (Ru/44) rare hard metal
strontium (Sr/38) metal
tellurium (Te/52) rare crystalline
    element
ytterbium (Yb/70) rare-earth metal
zirconium (Zr/40) metal

10

dysprosium (Dy/66) rare-earth metal
gadolinium (Gd/64) rare-earth metal
molybdenum (Mo/42) brittle metal
phosphorus (P/15) waxy substance
promethium (Pm/61) rare-earth metal
technetium (Tc/43) *R/A artf mtl*

11

californium (Cf/98) *R/A artf mtl*
einsteinium (E/99) *R/A artf mtl*

12

praesodymium (Pr/59) rare-earth
    metal
protactinium (Pa/91) radioactive metal

MEDICINE
(Ailments, Anatomy, etc.)

2

ee eye
op operation
os (f) a bone

3

ail indisposition: indisposed
ana equal quantities
een eyes
fit (1) convulsion, paroxysm
fit (2) in good condition
flu influenza
ill sick, diseased
ova plural of *ovum*
pox eruptive disease: plural of *pock*
pus suppurative fluid
sty inflamed tumour on eyelid
tic muscular convulsive motion
wen sebaceous cyst

4

ache continued pain
acne sebaceous follicle inflammation
ague shivering fit
bile a liver secretion
bleb a transparent blister
boba *yaws*
boil an inflamed swelling
buba *yaws*
bubo a glandular swelling
burn heat injury
clot soft concentrated mass
cold *coryza*
corn small hard growth
cure care: remedy
cyst a bladder
damp lowness of spirits
derm the true skin

diet remedial feeding plan
disc *disk*
disk layer of fibrocartilage
dope *drug* (2): to drug
dose a medicinal portion
drug (1) any medicinal substance
drug (2) stupefying substance
gena side of face
gene a DNA unit
germ (1) rudimentary living form
germ (2) micro-organism (malign)
gore blood: clotted blood
gout a swelling disease
heal to cure effectively
iris coloured part of eye
lame disabled: to disable
limb arm or leg
limp flaccid: drag a leg
lint dressing for wound
lobe a bodily division
loof palm of hand
lung respiratory organ
mole small skin elevation
otic of the ear
ovum egg
pain bodily suffering
pang painful emotion
pock small skin eruption
pill little ball of medicine
rale sound from diseased lung
rash skin eruption
rete network (nerves, blood-vessels)
scab crust over a sore
scar mark or blemish
sick ill: diseased: vomit(ing)
sore ulcer:boil: painful spot, etc.
stye *sty*
swab (1) cleaning material
swab (2) morbid specimen
Tolu* a balsam
ulna a forearm bone
vein blood vessel to heart

MEDICINE

ward (1)   hospital multi-bed room
ward (2)   the patients of *ward* (1)
wart   hard excrescence on skin
weal   mark of lash
womb   organ of development
X-ray   photograph by *X-rays*
yaws   contagious tropical disease

5

agony   extreme suffering
algid   cold, chill
aloes   a bitter purgative drug
ancon   elbow
angst   anxiety
aorta   great blood artery
ataxy   *ataxia*
aural   of the ear
botch   boil, pimple, etc.
chill   shivering cold
chyle   a bodily fluid
cilia   plural of *cilium*
colic   an abdominal disease
colon   the large intestine
cough   symptom of an ailment
cramp   involuntary muscular
   contraction
croup   inflammation of larynx
derma   *derm*
ether   stupefying agent
faint   swoon
femur   thigh bone
fever   heat-manifesting disease
gland   secreting structure
lance   a surgeon's lancet
leech   blood-sucking worm
lepra   *leprosy*
loins   lower part of back
lymph (1)   a bodily fluid
lymph (2)   a vaccine
mania   a mental illness
mucus   a slimy discharge
mumps   swelling of parotid gland
nerve   impulse-conveying cord
ovary   female genital gland
palsy   paralysis
plice   *plice Polonica*
polio   *poliomyelitis*
probe   a medical instrument

pulmo   *lung*
pulse   heart-beat
reins   the kidneys
rheum   a mucous discharge
rigor   chillness, skin contraction
salve   ointment: remedy
sarsa   *sarsaparilla*
sarza   *sarsaparilla*
scurf   flakes of dead skin
senna   a purgative
serum   a watery liquid
sinus   a nasal cavity
sling   support for injury
spasm   violent *cramp*, etc.
sprue   a tropical disease
stone   a diseased state
stupe   medicated tow
swoon   a fainting fit
tabes   wasting away
tibia   shinbone
tones   bodily conditions
tonic (1)   of *tones*
tonic (2)   re-invigorating
tonus   tonic spasm
torse   *torso*
torso   trunk
toxic   poisonous
toxin   *ptomaine*
truss   a surgical appliance
tumor   *tumour*
ulcer   an open sore
ulnae   plural of *ulna*
unfit   not *fit* (2)
uvula   part of palate
varix   an abnormal vein
virus   a pathogenic agent
wound   to injure: injury
X-rays   body-penetrating rays

6

ailing   unwell
anetic   soothing
angina   *quinsy*: *croup*
apepsy   a digestion weakness
artery   blood vessel from heart
asthma   chronic breathing disorder
ataxia   lack of co-ordination
axilla   the armpit

biceps a two-headed muscle
bruise discoloration from injury
buboes plural of *bubo*
bunion lump on big toe joint
cancer malignant growth
caries decay, esp. tooth
cauter *cautery*
chorea a nervous disease
cilium eyelash
coryza nasal catarrh
dengue an acute tropical fever
dermis *derm*
dorsal of the back
dosage proper size of dose
dropsy an excess of fluid
eczema a skin disease
elixir panacea, nostrum, etc.
emetic vomit-causing medicine
fibula a lower-leg bone
flexor a muscle
foment apply warm lotion to
goitre Derbyshire neck
gripes intestinal pain
grippe influenza
growth a morbid formation
herpes various skin diseases
infirm feeble, sickly, weak, frail
iritis inflammation of iris
larynx upper part of windpipe
lesion injury, wound
looves plural of *loof*
lotion a medicinal liquid
lumbar of/near the loins
maimed crippled
megrim *vertigo*: *migraine*
morbid sickly: unwholesome
myopia shortness of sight
neural of/relating to nerves
opiate sleep-inducing *drug* (2)
pelvis a bony cavity
pepsin a medical preparation
phenol a powerful disinfectant
physic (a) medicine
pimple a small swelling
plague a deadly epidemic
pleura lung membrane
poison any malignant influence
potion draught, dose
pyemia *pyaemia*
quinsy suppurative tonsillitis

ranula a tongue cyst
remedy cure, redress
retina sensitive layer of eye
scurvy a gum disease
sepsis putrefaction
spleen blood-modifying organ
splent *splint*
splint a medical contrivance
sprain muscle/ligament injury
stroma part of blood-corpuscle
stupor torpor, lethargy, stupefaction
tablet medicinal confection
tendon fibrous tissue
tetany painful muscular cramps
thorax chest
thrush a throat infection
torpid numb, lethargic, sluggish
torpor numbness, inactivity, dullness
trepan to remove piece of skull from
troche round *tablet*
tumour swelling, turgidity
typhus a dangerous fever
uterus womb
vermis part of brain

7

abdomen the belly
abscess cavity of pus
aconite poison
adenoid glandlike: glandular
adipose fatty
ailment pain: indisposition, etc.
allergy abnormal sensitivity
amnesia loss of memory
anaemia lack of red corpuscles
anatomy science of the body
anodyne pain-relieving medicine
antacid (1) internal counteracting
  agent
antacid (2) a medicine
anthrax (1) carbuncle: malignant boil
anthrax (2) woolsorter's disease
antigen an antibody stimulant
apepsia *apepsy*
aspirin acetyl-salicylic acid
atrophy wasting away: degeneration
autopsy post-mortem examination
bandage wound cloth dressing

MEDICINE

bedridd *bedridden*
bilious of bile disorder
blister a skin bladder
bromide a sedative
bubonic accompanied by *buboes*
cardiac (1) of the heart
cardiac (2) of the upper end of stomach
cardiac (3) a heart stimulant
cascara a tonic *aperient*
catarrh chronic cold
cautery burning with hot iron (etc.)
cholera a deadly disease
cranium the skull
cupping extraction of blood
disease ailment: cause of pain
dresser a medical student
earache pain in the ear
empyema a collection of pus
endemic locally-present disease
enteric of the intestines
febrile of/like *fever*: feverish
fistula (1) artificially-made opening
fistula (2) narrow pipe-like ulcer
forceps a pincer-like instrument
gastric of the stomach
glottis entrance to windpipe
gumboil abscess on the gum
hepatic of/pertaining to the liver
hormone an internal secretion
humerus the funny bone
invalid sick/disabled person
leprosy a chronic disease
linctus a syrup-like medicine
lockjaw *tetanus*
lozenge a small sweetmeat
lumbago lumbar rheumatism
lunatic an insane person
malaria a fever
measles an infectious fever
morphew a skin eruption
morphia *morphine*
myalgia pain in the muscle
nostrum (1) secret/patent medicine
nostrum (2) quack/favourite remedy
occiput back of the head
otalgia earache
panacea a universal medicine
patella the knee-cap
pharynx upper part of gullet
pink-eye acute conjunctivitis

polypus a type of tumour
pustule pimple with pus
pyaemia infection of the blood
pyretic of cure/nature of fever
pyrexia fever
quinine used against fever
rickets child's bone disease
roseola rose-coloured rash: *rubella*
rubella a mild form of measles
scabies the itch
scalpel small operating knife
sciatic of/in hip region
seasick sickness from wave action
sick-bay ship's sickroom
sternum the breast-bone
styptic checking bleeding
sunburn solar skin-damage
surgeon (1) one who operates
surgeon (2) military doctor
surgery (1) art of *surgeon* (1)
surgery (2) Dr's consulting room
syncope a fainting fit
syringe an injection instrument
tetanus jaw muscle disease
therapy curative treatment
trachea wind pipe
triceps an arm muscle
tympana plural of *tympanum*
tympany any swelling
typhoid (1) like typhus
typhoid (2) typhoid fever
vaccine immunity preparation
vertigo giddiness, dizziness
whitlow *paronychia*
wryneck a cervical vertebrae disease

8

acidosis excessive acid in blood
adenoids nasal glandular enlargement
aneurysm dilation of an artery
antibody a defensive substance
antidote an anti-poison agent
aperient laxative
apoplexy sudden loss of sensation
appendix a blind sac
asphyxia suspended animation
backache a pain in the back
bacteria agents of disease, etc.

beriberi an Eastern disease
botulism sausage poisoning
cataract a condition of the eye
compress a pressure pad
cystitis bladder inflammation
dandriff *dandruff*
dandruff scaly scurf on scalp
debility weakness, languor
delirium state of being *delirious*
delivery act of birth
demented insane
dementia a form of insanity
diabetes a disease
dyslexia word blindness
epidemic a widespread outbreak
epilepsy chronic functional disease
feverish slightly fevered
first-aid pre-doctor treatment
fumigate disinfection by fumes
ganglion (1) a tumour
ganglion (2) a nerve-centre
gangrene death of part of body
gingival pertaining to the gums
glaucoma an eye disease
hay fever a nasal irritation
heatspot a skin blotch
hospital a treatment centre
hysteria a psychoneurosis
impetigo a skin disease
insanity want of sanity
iodoform an antiseptic
jaundice excess of bile
laudanum tincture of opium
laxative a purgative medicine
lethargy *torpor*
ligament bonding tissue
ligature a bandage
liniment a thin ointment
mal de mer seasickness
medicine (1) the curative science
medicine (2) any curative substance
migraine intense head pain
morphine a *drug* (2)
narcosis *narcotic*-induced torpor
narcotic a *drug* (2), gas, etc.
neuritis inflammation of a nerve
neurotic (1) affected by *neuritis*
neurotic (2) obsessive: hypersensitive
ointment medicinal grease
paranoia a mental disorder

paranoid resembling *paranoia*
paroxysm a sudden acute fit
phthisis a wasting disease
pleurisy inflammation of the *pleura*
plumbism poisoning by absorbed lead
poultice a soft application
ptomaine various animo-compounds
pyogenic pus-forming
Red Cross international nursing
  organization
remedial (in)tending to remedy
rest-cure treatment by resting
ringworm a skin disease
sanitary conducive to health
schizoid exhibiting *schizophrenia*
sciatica neuritis of *sciatic* nerve
sedative *drug* (2): calming, composing
shingles an eruptive disease
sickness illness
sickroom place of confinement
smallpox a contagious *febrile* disease
specific a medicine, remedy
surgical pertaining to surgery
tapeworm segmented parasitic worm
tincture alcoholic solution of a drug
tympanum the middle ear
varicose of/pertaining to *varix*
vertebra a joint of the backbone

9

adrenalin a *hormone*
allopathy orthodox medical practice
analgesic an anodyne
antitoxin *toxin* neutralizer
antiviral acting against a *virus*
arthritis (1) inflammation of a joint
arthritis (2) gout
asthmatic of *asthma*
bedridden confined to bed (ill/senile)
Caesarian of *delivery* by operation
carbuncle an inflamed ulcer
cartilage gristle (often, later, bone)
castor-oil a medicinal oil
catalepsy state of insensibility
cauterise burning with hot iron
cauterize *cauterise*
chilblain a painful red swelling
cirrhosis wasting of organ-tissue

MEDICINE

cold-cream   a cooling *ointment*
contagion   contact-transmitted disease
contusion   (act/state of) bruise(ing)
delirious   insane
diaphragm   the midriff
diathermy   electrical internal heating
dietetics   dietary rules
dietitian   an authority on diet
disinfect   to free from infection
disinfest   to free from pests
dysentery   an infection
dyspepsia   indigestion
emollient   a softening application
epileptic   one suffering *epilepsy*
epidermis   protective outer skin
frostbite   injury from exposure to cold
gastritis   inflammation of stomach
gathering   a suppurating swelling
germicide   a germ-killing agent
hartshorn   an ammonia solution
heartburn   internal burning feeling
hepatitis   *hepatic* infection
infirmary   a hospital
influenza   an epidemic virus disease
inoculate   protective infection
lead colic   *lead poisoning*
leucaemia   *leuchaemia*
leukaemia   *leuchaemia*
Listerism   antiseptic treatment
monomania   an obsessive madness
nephritis   inflammation of kidneys
neuralgia   pain in the nerve(s)
nyctalops   one suffering *nyctalopia*
osteopath   practitioner of *osteopathy*
paralysis   loss of power of action
paranoiac   resembling *paranoia*
pertussis   an infectious disease
phlebitis   inflammation of a vein
physician   one skilled in *physic*
pleuritis   *pleurisy*
pneumonia   inflammation of the lung
psychosis   a serious mental disorder
psychotic   of/one suffering, *psychosis*
pulmonary   of the lungs
pyorrhoea   pus in tooth socket
rheumatic   one suffering rheumatism
Rock fever   undulant fever
sclerosis   morbid hardening
silicosis   a respiratory disease
sinusitis   inflammation of a *sinus*

soporific   a sleep-bringing agent
sterilise   to destroy
sterilize   *sterilise*
stone-dead   dead as a stone
stone-deaf   deaf as a stone
stretcher   frame for carrying the sick
sudorific   causing sweat
sunstroke   a nervous disease
toothache   pain in a tooth
umbilicus   the navel
vaccinate   to administer a *vaccine*
vertebrae   plural of *vertebra*
water-cure   treatment by water

10

amputation   cutting off (a limb)
antibiotic   micro-organism destroyer
antisepsis   destruction of bacteria
antiseptic   agent for *antisepsis*
apoplectic   of/pertaining to, *apoplexy*
blood count   measurement of
   corpuscles
blood donor   one who gives blood
blood-group   type of blood
blood-wagon   ambulance (slang)
bloody flux   dysentery
bronchitis   a respiratory disorder
chicken-pox   a contagious *febrile*
   disease
concussion   state of being shaken
convalesce   to regain health
convulsion   involuntary muscular
   contraction
dandy-fever   *dengue*
diphtheria   an infectious throat disease
dipsomania   a morbid craving for
   alcohol
dispensary   place for medicine
   dispensing
dissection   act/art of cutting: anatomy
Epsom salts   a purgative medicine
erysipelas   an inflammatory disease
fibrositis   inflammation of fibrous tissue
gingivitis   *gingival* inflammation
homeopathy   *homoeopathy*
hydropathy   disease treatment by water
hypodermic (1)   pertaining to
   hypodermis

hypodermic (2) a hypodermic injection
hypodermic (3) drug used in (2)
hypodermic (4) syringe used for (2)
hypodermis tissue under *epidermis*
incubation fostering bacteria
indisposed slightly disordered in health
infectious apt to spread/infect
insanitary not *sanitary*
interferon a natural bodily protein
laryngitis inflammation of the larynx
leuchaemia a blood disease
medicament (external) medical
  substance
meningitis brain membrane
  inflammation
metabolism food conversion process
nettlerash rash like nettle-sting effect
nyctalopia *night-blindness*
osteopathy healing by manipulation
oxygen tent enveloping breathing aid
palliative that which lessens pain
paronychia inflammation near
  fingernail
penicillin anti-bacteria substances
psychiatry study of mental disorder
pyretology study of fevers
quarantine (1) (40 days) compulsory
  isolation
quarantine (2) place where (1) is spent
recuperate to recover
rheumatism various painful diseases
sanitarium sham Latin for *sanitorium*
sanitorium chronic diseases hospital
scarlatina (mild) scarlet fever
shellshock wartime mental disturbance
spinal cord the main neural axis
stone-blind completely blind
tourniquet artery-compressing
  appliance
tracheitis inflammation of the *trachea*

11

acupuncture science of skin puncture
amniobutene a pain-relieving drug
anaesthetic of/agent for, insensibility
astigmatism a defect in an eye
barbiturate a kind of sedative drug
cod-liver oil a medicinal oil

consumption pulmonary tuberculosis
consumptive wasting away
corn plaster remedial plaster for corns
embrocation act of moistening: lotion
fingerstall protective cover for finger
haemophilia tendency to bleed
  excessively
haemorrhage a discharge of blood
homoeopathy a system of treatment
hydrophobia (1) horror of water
hydrophobia (2) inability to swallow
  water
hydrophobia (3) rabies: (2) symptom of
  (3)
hypothermia subnormal body
  temperature
inoculation see *inoculate*, act of
ipecacuanha a valuable emetic
jungle fever a severe malarial fever
nursing home a private hospital
peritonitis an abdominal inflammation
psittacosis parrots' disease
radiography X-ray photography
restorative a medicine
sal volatile *smelling-salts*
spina bifida a spinal condition
stethoscope instrument for *auscultation*
stomach-ache pain in the belly
stomach-pump a medical instrument
thalidomide a drug (withdrawn 1961)
therapeutic curative
tonsillitis tonsil inflammation
tracheotomy cutting into the *trachea*
trench-fever lice-transmitted disease
vaccination administering a *vaccine*
yellow-fever an acute tropical disease

12

appendicitis appendix inflammation
auscultation heart/lung examination
chemotherapy chemical treatment
court-plaster silk sticking plaster
disinfectant infection destroyer
Dover's powder a *sudorific* compound
enteric fever *typhoid fever*
fever therapy cure by fever inducement
friar's balsam a *tincture*
gastric fever a bilious fever

MEDICINE

growing pains   *neural* pains in young
heart disease   any morbid heart
  condition
hooping-cough   *whooping-cough*
hysterectomy   removal of *uterus*
hysteromania   hysterical mania
inflammation   heat of body part
neurasthenia   nervous debility
prescription   a medical recipe/direction
prophylactic   (of) disease prevention
psychiatrist   mental illness specialist
radiotherapy   X-ray (etc.) treatment
recuperation   recovery
sarsaparilla   a medicinal preparation
scarlet fever   an infectious fever
spinal column   the *vertebrae*, backbone
thyroid gland   a gland in the neck
tuberculosis   *phthisis* of the lung
typhoid fever   an infectious disease
zinc ointment   a medicinal grease

13

adipose tissue   stores fat
bubonic plague   an epidemic disease
elephantiasis   a tropical disease
German measles   *rubella, roseola*
hydrocephalus   *dropsy* of the brain
lead poisoning   *plumbism*
materia medica   (science of) medical
  material
medicine-chest   chest for medicines
mononucleosis   a blood disorder
osteomyelitis   bone (marrow)
  inflammation
painter's colic   *lead poisoning*
pharmacopoeia (1)   drug list/book

pharmacopoeia (2)   a collection of drugs
plica Polonica   an infested hair
  condition
poliomyelitis   spinal cord inflammation
pyretotherapy   induced heat treatment
St Vitus's dance   *chorea*
schizophrenia   an introversion
  psychosis
smelling-salts   a stimulant in faintness
tranquilliser   a sedative drug
varicose veins   distorted veins
whooping-cough   *pertussis*

14

Achilles' tendon   calf to heel-bone
  tendon
angina pectoris   a heart disease
blood-poisoning   *pyaemia*, etc.
Bright's disease   various kidney
  diseases
conjunctivitis   an eye inflammation
floating kidney   abnormally mobile
  kidney
Gregory's powder   a laxative
hallucinogenic   causing delusions
housemaid's knee   a knee sac
  inflammation
medicine-bottle   bottle for medicine
mustard-plaster   plaster of mustard
  flour
night-blindness   sightless in dim light
patent medicine   a proprietary medicine
plastic surgery   shaping, formative
  surgery
psychoanalysis   mental investigation
psychoneurosis   a mental disease

STRANGERS

A section concerned with less familiar descriptions of people (including historical, dialect and slang descriptions).
For racial and similar designations, use LANGUAGES (p. 189).
For nationalities add suitable suffixes to countries.
For musicians add suffixes to instruments in MUSIC (p. 38).

2

bo man (USA)
ex one who once was
jo beloved one (Scotland)
oe *oy*
oo we (Scotland)
oy grandchild (Scotland)
pi a sanctimonious person
un one, him

3

aga a Turkish commander
auf oaf (an elf's child)
Ban* Hungarian military governor
bey a Turkish governor
bor neighbour
bot irritating pest (Australia)
bub boy (USA)
cad an Oxford townsman
chi *chai*
cit townsman (contemptuous term)
coz cousin
Dan* master (martial art: poetry)
deb débutante
dey a dairy maid
dux leader: head schoolboy/girl
erk aircraftman
faw a gypsy
gin Australian aboriginal woman
gob sailor in US navy
gyp Cambridge/Durham college servant
hob rustic: lout
joe *jo*
lez lesbian

lud lord
mor *mawr*
nib important person
Nip* Japanese
oye *oy*
rag worthless beggarly person
ras an Abyssinian prince
rom a gypsy man
rye gentleman (gypsy word)
sib (twin) brother/sister; kins(wo)man
Ted* Teddy boy
tit girl, young woman
tod a sly person
wog a (coloured) foreigner
wop Italian (or similar)

4

Adam a gaoler
agha *aga*
amir a Muslim princely title
ayah Indian/S. African (nurse)maid
babu Indian clerk: Mr (etc.)
bint girl, woman
cadi a Muslim judge
chai feminine of *chal*
chal fellow: person
chit child: girl
dalt a foster child
dell a young girl
doge chief magistrate Venice/Genoa
doxy woman of loose character
emir Muslim chieftain
esne Old English domestic slave
eten a giant
feme a woman (legal term)
foud Orkney/Shetland magistrate

frow a Dutchwoman
gaby a simpleton
gink a fellow
goop fool: fatuous person
gump a foolish person
hobo tramp: vagrant workman
jarl noble, chief, earl
Jehu a (furious) driver
Judy* frump, odd-looking woman
kaid a N. African chief
kami Japanese lord/deified hero
mawr (great, awkward) girl
minx a pert young girl
mort a (loose) woman
naik lord, governor: corporal
pais potential jurors
pard partner (USA)
peon labourer: soldier: policeman:
  messenger
Pict ancient N. Briton
qadi *cadi*
quiz odd-looking person: hoaxer
rana a Rajput prince
rani feminine of raja/rajah
ryot an Indian peasant
Saba an ancient Yemenese people
said *sayyid*
snab *snob*
snob (apprentice) shoemaker
Sorb* *Wend*
swad country lout: soldier
tiro beginner, novice
tyro *tiro*
vert convert: pervert
weft waif, castaway (obs.)
Wend* old Germanic Slav
Whig* a Liberal forebear
yegg (f) safe-breaker, burglar (USA)

5

amban a Chinese official
ameer *amir*
amman *amtman*
ardri a head king
baboo *babu*
begum Muslim princess/lady
betty a male housewife
billy brother: comrade

boyar old Russian aristocrat
brock a dirty stinking fellow
bucko swaggerer, domineering bully
bunia *bunnia*
butty chum, (coal-mine) partner
calif caliph/khalif (Muslim leader)
ceorl pre-1066 freeman
chuff boor, oaf, surly type
churl rustic (labourer): *chuff*
coarb head of Irish family sept
coffle a (slave) gang
dault *dalt*
darzi a tailor
dewan Indian state prime minister
  (etc.)
dhobi Indian washerman
Dives* rich and luxurious person
diwan *dewan*
dutch a wife
ettin *eten*
ghazi various Muslim titles
gilpy a boisterous girl
helot (Spartan) serf
issei Japanese immigrant (USA)
jager a (German) huntsman (etc.)
janty *jonty*
jawan Indian common soldier
jonty naval master-at-arms
jurat magistrate (etc.)
kulak rich peasant: exploiter
looby a clumsy, clownish fellow
lubra (f) Australian aboriginal woman
matlo matelot, sailor
milor milord, a rich Englishman
mpret ex Albanian ruler's title
mudir a local governor
mufti civilian: Muslim law exponent
mujik *muzhik*
myall wild Australian aboriginal
nawab various Eastern titles
nazir various Indian officials
nizam Indian prince: Turkish soldier
ollav ancient Irish doctor/master
omrah a Muslim lord
ozeki a champion sumo wrestler
pawaw *powwow*
putti plural of *putto*
putto young (winged) boy (art)
quean (saucy) girl: fallen woman
qui-hi Englishman in India

ranee *rani*
rayah non-Muslim Turk
sambo *zambo*
sayid *sayyid*
sepoy soldier: policeman
sewer table service superintendent
Sheba *Saba*
spahi French Algerian cavalryman
squaw Red Indian woman/wife
sumph a soft sheepish fellow
sutor a cobbler
syren siren, fascinating woman
thane Old English nobleman
theow Old English slave
thete Greek freeman/serf
tiros *tyrones*
titty sister (Scotland)
vrouw woman, goodwife, housewife
zambo Red Indian and negro offspring

6

amtman a European magistrate
apache a lawless (French) ruffian
archon ancient Athenian magistrate
ascian dweller in torrid zone
atabeg (Turkish) ruler, high official
atabek *atabeg*
ataman Cossack general/headman
banian Hindu trader/broker/financier
banyan *banian*
bashaw haughty man: pasha
bodger a travelling pedlar
brehon ancient Irish judge
brunet masculine of brunette
buckra white man (Negro word)
bunnia a Hindu merchant
bunter rag-picker: low woman
bursch a German student
carder one who combs wool
chough *chuff*
circar *sircar*
cotwal *kotwal*
cuffin a man
cummer gossip: woman: girl
dacoit Indian/Burmese robber
daimio Japanese noble
dakoit *dacoit*
drazel a slut

durgan a dwarf
dyvour a bankrupt
ephebe ancient Greek young citizen
ephebi plural of *ephebe*
evzone a Greek infantryman
fautor favourer: patron: abettor
fizgig a giddy girl
foozle a tedious fellow
fossor a grave digger
gossip baptism sponsor: natal friend[1]
grieve farm overseer: sheriff
halver one who halves
hetman Polish officer: Cossack general
induna S. African tribal councillor
jaunty *jonty*
kanaka S. Sea Is. labourer
kotwal Indian chief
   constable/magistrate
lascar Oriental sailor/camp-follower
lurdan dull heavy sluggish fellow
lurden *lurdan*
manred (obs.) a body of vassals
marque a privateer
marrow mate, companion
moujik *muzhik*
mousme *mousmee*
mucker fanatical reformer: hypocrite
muzhik a Russian peasant
oecist founder of a colony
ollamh *ollav*
pakeha a white man
pariah a social outcast
parser a type of grammarian
parter one who parts
Pathan an Afghan
pedder a pedlar
peeler plunderer: policeman
pennal German university freshman
pether a pedlar
pezant peasant (old spelling)
powwow Red Indian conjuror
pandit pundit, learned man
qui-hye *qui-hi*
raiyat *ryot*
relict a widow
ritter a knight
Sabine an ancient Italian person
sachem (1) Red Indian chief

---

[1] see *kenno*, FOOD (p. 173).

sachem (2) a Tammany leader
sannup squaw's husband: brave
savant a learned man
sayyid descendant of Fatima (Muslim)
sbirro Italian police officer
schout a (Dutch) municipal officer
scouse a Liverpudlian
serang a *lascar* boatswain
sherif *sayyid*: prince: magistrate
shiksa non-Jewish woman
sircar Indian clerk/factotum
sirdar military head: C. in C.
sirkar *sircar*
socman *socager*
soutar *souter*
souter cobbler, shoemaker
sowter *souter*
sutler a military camp hawker
syndic ancient Greek judge (etc.)
tanist Celtic chief's heir-elect
taupie *tawpie*
tawpie clumsy, headless girl
tindal *lascar* petty officer
tiroes *tyrones*
tonsor a barber
tyroes *tyrones*
vidame a minor French noble
wahine a Maori woman
wanter one who wants
warman warrior
yagger a pedlar
zendik practitioner of magic

7

abactor cattle thief
abigail a lady's maid
ardrigh *ardri*
atamans plural of *ataman*
cacique W. Indian chief: political boss
caitiff a mean despicable fellow
capitan chief Turkish admiral
chapman itinerant dealer: pedlar
charlie a night-watchman
charley *charlie*
custrel knight's attendant: knave
dilling darling: youngest child
dobhash an interpreter

dvornik Russian concierge
ephebos *ephebe*
ephebus *ephebe*
fedayee an Arab commando
hetmans plural of *hetman*
hidalgo Spanish nobleman: gentleman
jackman type of medieval soldier
janizar *janizary*
Jenkins Society reporter: toady
jauntie *jonty*
ladrone a robber
lordkin would-be/little lord
lurdane *lurdan*
montero a huntsman
mormaor a high steward
mousmee Japanese waitress/girl
mugwump (self) important person
mulatta female *mulatto*
mulatto negro-European offspring
mynheer a Dutchman
navarch ancient Greek admiral
papoose Red Indian child
Partlet* a woman (hen's proper name)
patroon captain: coxswain: land-holder
pindari a mercenary freebooter
praetor ancient Roman magistrate
quashee West Indies negro
quashie *quashee*
rooinek Englishman (Afrikaans nickname)
samurai (member) Japanese military caste
shereef *sherif*
shikari *shikaree*
sibling (1) (half) brother/sister
sibling (2) (distant) kins(wo)man
sibship sibs: blood/clan relationship
socager service tenant
staretz a Russian holy man
Stentor* a loud-voiced person
suffete ancient Carthage official
sultana wife/mistress of sultan
Switzer a Swiss (mercenary)
Szekler a Transylvanian Magyar
tranter hawker: carrier
tsigane *tzigany*
Turkess a female Turk
tyrones a plural of *tiro*
tzigany a Hungarian gypsy

vaquero (Spanish American) herdsman
venerer gamekeeper: hunter
victrix a feminine of victor
webster (obs.) a weaver
whittaw a saddler
yeggman (f) *yegg*
younker a young person
zabtieh *zaptieh*
zaptiah *zaptieh*
zaptieh Turkish policeman

8

Abram man *Abraham man*
ambivert non-introvert/extravert
Benjamin* youngest/favourite son
bimbashi Turkish/Egyptian officer
bostangi Turkish palace guard
burgrave town/castle ruler/governor
caboceer W. African headman
calender a dervish
chasseur hunter: French soldier: (etc.)
chee-chee Eurasian (person and speech)
croupier a vice president
dragoman Eastern guide/interpreter
fedayeen plural of *fedayee*
feme sole legally unmarried woman
fletcher one who makes arrows
janizary former Turkish footguard
kaimakam Turkish Lt. Col./Lt. Governor
Mameluke slave: Egyptian sultan
mouchard a police spy
novercal of/pertaining to stepmother
octaroon *octoroon*
octoroon one who is ⅛th negro
omadhaun a fool
parcener a co-heir
peter-man fisherman
peterman safe blower
pindaree *pindari*
pirrauru aboriginal supplementary spouse
proditor a traitor
quadroon mulatto and white offspring
runagate vagabond: renegade: fugitive
sagamore Red Indian chief

shikaree a hunter
slyboots a sly cunning person
squarson a clergyman squire
starosta (1) Russian village headman
starosta (2) Polish life-estate noble
stradiot a Venetian light horseman
strelitz old Muscovite guard
streltzi plural of *strelitz*
tacksman Scottish lessee
tanaiste Eire's deputy prime minister
tipstaff a sheriff's officer
truchman an interpreter
Xantippe a scold, shrew

9

ami de cour court/untrustworthy friend
amplosome short stocky human type
archimage chief magician/enchanter
Aristarch a severe critic
Autolycus thief: plagiarist
backfisch young girl, flapper
beglerbeg a former Turkish governor
bourgeois (of) (middle class) citizen
brinjarry Indian travelling grain dealer
catchpoll constable, petty judicial officer
chaprassi orderly: messenger
concierge warden: janitor: porter(ess)
dragomans plural of *dragoman*
Jack* Ketch* a public hangman
Jack* Nasty* sneak: sloven
landgrave a German count
moonraker a Wiltshire man
multipara mother of more than one
palsgrave a count palatine
paraclete advocate, legal helper, intercessor
paranymph groomsman, bridesmaid: helper
petticoat of women: a woman
philander a male flirt: lover
philomath a lover of learning
pillicock a boy
primipara mother (to be) of one
promachos champion, defender
quintroon *octoroon* and white offspring
sallee-man Moorish pirate

Sephardim Spanish/Portuguese Jews
Simon Pure* the real person/thing
spadassin swordsman: bravo
tabellion Roman official scrivener
taoiseach Eire's prime minister
termagant (woman) brawler, bully
tipstaves a plural of *tipstaff*
Tom* and Tib anybody
waldgrave a German noble

10

Abraham man a sturdy beggar
Ashkenazim Polish and German Jews
austringer a keeper of goshawks
condisciple fellow disciple/student
corregidor a Spanish chief magistrate
feme covert married woman
khidmutgar table servant
khitmutgar *khidmutgar*
peelgarlic *pilgarlick*
pilgarlick a poor wretch: oneself
propraetor a Roman provincial governor
scaramouch bragging cowardly buffoon
strelitzes *streltzi*
tramontane (1) dweller beyond the mountains
tramontane (2) foreigner: barbarian

troglodyte a cave dweller

11

apparatchik a Soviet bureaucrat
John* o'dreams a dreamy impractical person
landsknecht 16th C. mercenary
pettifogger paltry cavilling lawyer
philanderer one fond of men/husband
philogynist one who loves women
rouping wife woman at/running an auction
Scotch* cuddy *Scotch draper*
waldgravine wife of a *waldgrave*
witenagemot Anglo-Saxon supreme council

12

bluestocking (pedantic) learned woman
cousin-german a first cousin
every man Jack* one and all
Jack*-in-office arrogant petty official
kakistocracy govt by the worst
Peep*-o-day Boys* old Ulster protestant society
scattermouch any Latin/Levantine
Scotch* draper itinerant credit dealer

376

APPENDICES

APPENDIX 1

ABBREVIATIONS

For units of measure (including scientific) see MEASUREMENT (ABBREVIATIONS) (p. 210).
For scientific terms see SCIENCE AND TECHNOLOGY (ABBREVIATIONS) (p. 358).
For geographical names and terms see GEOGRAPHY (ABBREVIATIONS) (p. 49).
For musical terms see MUSIC (ABBREVIATIONS) (p. 38).

note
(1) 'of' or 'and' replaced by a comma (,) in many instances.
(2) ● denotes a descriptive explanation.
(3) The asterisk* indicates that the prefix is also a word, usually with a totally different meaning, and valid for most word games.
(4) The letter R, where undefined, stands for Royal.
(5) The use of full stops is optional and these are included where modern convention usually retains them.

ASSOCIATIONS, COMPANIES, CIVIL OR MILITARY UNITS, TRADE UNIONS

1

C   Conservative
H   Hospital
L   Liberal
U   Unionist

2

AA   Automobile Association
AC   Alpine Club
AG   (Aktiengesellschaft) German *Co.*
AP   Associated Press
BA   British Association (Science)
BB   Boys' Brigade
BE*   Board of Education
BL   British Legion/Library
bn   battalion
BP   British Petroleum/Pharmacopoeia
BR   British Rail

BS   British Shipbuilders
CA   Chartered Accountant
CC   County Council: Cricket Club
CD   Civil Defence
Co.   Company
CP   Communist Party
DE   Department of Employment
FA*   Football Association
FC   Football Club
FO   now *FCO*
GM   General Motors
GS   Geological Society
HK   House of Keys (Isle of Man)
HQ   headquarters
IA   Institute of Actuaries
IB   Institute of Bankers
ID*   Intelligence Department
IL   Institute of Linguists
KC   Kennel Club
LA*   Library Association
LP   Labour Party

MG   Morris Garage
PA*   Press/Publishers Association
PS   Pharmaceutical Society
RA   Royal Academy
RB   Rifle Brigade
RE*   Royal Engineers
RI   Royal Inst., Painters, Water
Colours
RM   Royal Marines
RN   Royal Navy
RP   Royal Soc., Portrait Painters
RR   Rolls Royce
RS   Royal Society
RU   Rugby Union
SE   Society of Engineers
TA*   now *T and AVT*
UU   Ulster Unionist
VW   (Volkswagen) People's car
WD   War Department

3

AAA   Amateur Athletic Association
ABA*   Amateur Boxing Association
ABC   American Broadcasting Corp.
AEA   Atomic Energy Authority (UK)
AEB   Associated Examining Board
AEC   Atomic Energy Commission (USA)
AEI   Associated Electrical Industries
AEU   Amalgamated Engineering Union
AFA   Amateur Football Association
AID*   Agency, International
Development
AMA   Assistant Masters Association
AMC   American Motors Corporation
AOF   Ancient Order of Foresters
ARC*   Agricultural Research Council
ASA   Amateur Swimming Association
ASC   American Soc., Cinematographers
ASE   Amalgamated Soc., Engineers
Ass.*   Association: Associated
ATC   Air Training Corps
ATS   now *WRAC*
ATV   Associated Television
AUT   Assoc., University Teachers
BAA*   British Airports Authority
BAC   British Aircraft Corp.
BAT*   British–American Tobacco Co.
bat.*   battalion: battery

BBC   British Broadcasting Corp.
BCS   British Computer Soc.
BDA   British Dental Association
Bde   Brigade
BDH   British Drug Houses
●BDI   Federation of German Industry
BEF   British Expeditionary Force
BHS   British Home Stores
BIM   British Inst. of Management
BIR   British Inst. of Radiology
BIS*   Bank, International Settlements
BMA   British Medical Association
BMW   Bavarian Motor Works
BOA*   British Optical Assoc.
BOC   British Oxygen Company
BRS   British Road Services
BSA   Birmingham Small Arms
BSC   British Steel/Sugar Corp.
BSI (1)   British Standards Institute
BSI (2)   Building Societies Inst.
CAA   Civil Aviation Authority (UK)
CAB*   Civil Aeronautics Board (USA)
CAT*   College of Advanced Technology
CBC   Columbia Broadcasting Corp.
CBI   Confederation, British Industry
CBM   California Business Machines
CBS   Columbia Broadcasting System
CCF   Combined Cadet Force
CCS   Corp., Certified Secretaries
CEF   Canadian Expeditionary Force
CEI   Council of Engineering Institutions
CIA   Central Intelligence Agency
Cia   (Compagnia) Italian *Co.*
CID   Criminal Investigation Dept.
Cie   (Compagnie) French *Co.*
CII   Chartered Insurance Institute
CIS   Chartered Inst., Secretaries
CIT*   Chartered Inst., Transport
CML   Colonial Mutual Life
CNR   Canadian National Railway
COI   Central Office of Information
CPR   Canadian Pacific Railway
CSP   Chartered Soc., Physiotherapists
CTC   Cyclists Touring Club
CWS   Co-operative Wholesale Society
●daf   a Dutch motor company
DCL   Distillers Company Limited
DEA   Dept. of Economic Affairs
DEP   Dept., Employment and
Productivity

ASSOCIATIONS, COMPANIES, ETC. **ABBREVIATIONS**

DEP. (dep.) Department (also *dpt.*, *dept.*)
DES Dept., Education and Science
DOE* Dept. of the Environment
dpt department (also *dep., dept.*)
DTI Dept. of Trade and Industry
EBU European Broadcasting Union
ECU* English Church Union
EDC European Defence Community
EDS English Dialect Society
EMI Electric and Musical Industries
ETU Electrical Trades Union
FBI Federal Bureau of Investigation
FCO Foreign and Commonwealth Office
●FIQ International Tenpin Association
FOE* Friends of Earth/Europe
GEC General Electric Company
GKN Guest, Keen and Nettlefold
GPO General Post Office
●GUM* Russian State Store
GUS* Great Universal Stores
HAC Honourable Artillery Company
HLI Highland Light Infantry (*RHF*)
HMC His/Her Majesty's Customs
HMI His/Her Majesty's Inspector(ate)
HMS His/Her Majesty's Ship/Service
HMV His Master's Voice (Comp.)
IAM Inst. of Advanced Motorists
IBA Independent Broadcasting Authority
IBM International Business Machines
ICE* Institution of Civil Engineers
ICI Imperial Chemical Industries
ICL International Computers Ltd.
IEE Institution, Electrical Engineers
IFC International Finance Corporation
ILP Independent Labour Party
IMM Institution, Mining and Metallurgy
Inc. Incorporated
IOB Institute of Building
IPA Inst. of Practitioners in Advertising
IPC International Publishing Corp.
IQS Inst. of Quantity Surveyors
ITA* now *IBA*
ITT Int. Telephone, Telegraph Corp.
JAL Japan Airlines
●KLM Royal Dutch Airlines

Lab.* Labour
LGU Ladies Golf Union
Lib.* Liberal
LOB* Location of Offices Bureau
LTA Lawn Tennis Association
Ltd. Limited Liability (see *Co. Ltd.*)
MCC Marylebone Cricket Club
MIT Massachusetts Inst. of Technology
MOD* Ministry of Defence
MOT Ministry of Transport
MSC Manpower Services Commission
Nat. National
NBC Nat. Broadcasting Comp. (USA)
NCB National Coal Board
NCR Nat. Cash Register Comp.
NEB* Nat. Enterprise Board
NFS National Fire Service
NFU National Farmers' Union
NGA Nat. Graphical Assoc.
NRA Nat. Rifle Assoc.
NUJ Nat. Union, Journalists
NUM Nat. Union, Mineworkers
NUR* Nat. Union, Railwaymen
NUS Nat. Union, Seamen/Students
NUT* Nat. Union, Teachers
OTC Officer Training Corps
PGA Professional Golfers Assoc.
PIA* Pakistan International Airlines
PLP Parliamentary Labour Party
PRO* Public Record Office
Pru. Prudential Assurance Comp.
PWD Public Works Department
RAC Royal Automobile Club
RAD* Royal Academy of Dance
RAF Royal Air Force
RAM* Royal Academy of Music
RAN* Royal Australian Navy
RAS* Royal Astronomical Soc.
RCA Radio Corp. of America
RCM Royal College of Music
RCN Royal Canadian Navy
RCO Royal College, Organists
RCP Royal College, Physicians/Preceptors
RCS (1) Royal College, Surgeons
RCS (2) Royal Corps of Signals
RCT Royal Corps of Transport
RDS Royal Dublin Society
RFC now *RAF*

ABBREVIATIONS   ASSOCIATIONS, COMPANIES, ETC.

RGG Royal Grenadier Guards
RGS Royal Geographical Soc.
RHA Royal Horse Artillery
RHF Royal Highland Fusiliers
RHG Royal Highland Guards
RHS R. (Humane/Horticultural/Hist.)
Soc.
RIA* Royal Irish Academy
RIC Royal Inst. of Chemistry
RMP *CRMP*
RMS Royal Microscopic Soc.
RNR Royal Naval Reserve
ROC* Royal Observer Corps
ROI Royal Inst., Oil Painters
RPS Royal Photographic Soc.
RSA R. (Soc. Antiquaries/Arts): Scot.
Acad.
RSE Royal Society, Edinburgh
●**RTE** Irish Television
RTZ Rio Tinto Zinc Corp. Ltd.
RYA Royal Yachting Assoc.
RYS Royal Yacht Squadron
RZS Royal Zoological Society
SAA S. African Airways
SAS Special Air Service
SDP Social Democratic Party
SED Scottish Education Dept.
SFA Scottish Football Assoc.
SGF Scottish Grocers Federation
SMC Scots. Mountaineering Club
SNP Scottish National Party
Soc.* society
SPR Soc., Psychical Research
SRU Scottish Rugby Union
TPI Town Planning Institute
TUC Trades Union Congress
TWA* Trans World Airlines
UDR Ulster Defence Regiment
UDT United Dominions Trust
USN United States Navy
USS United States Ship/Steamer
UUU United Ulster Unionists
VCD Volunteer Defence Corps
WBA World Boxing Assoc.
WLA Women's Land Army (obs.
1950)
WNP Welsh Nationalist Party
WRI Women's Rural Inst.
WVS now *WRVS*
YHA Youth Hostels Assoc.

4

ABTA Assoc., British Travel Agents
ACAS Advisory Concilation, Arbit.
Serv.
ACCA Assoc. Certified, Corporate
Accts.
ACGB Arts Council, Great Britain
AERE Atomic Energy Research Estab.
APEX* Assoc. Professional Executive
(etc.) Staff
AWRE Atomic Weapons Research
Estab.
BAOR British Army of the Rhine
●**BASF** a German chemical company
batt.* battalion: battery
BBBC British Boxing Board, Control
BBFC British Board, Film Censors
BCAL British Caledonian (Airways)
BEAB Br. Electric. Approvals Board
BICC Br. Insulated Callender's Cables
BLMC Br. Leyland Motor Corp.
BNEC Br. Nat. Export Council
BNFL Br. Nuclear Fuels Ltd.
BNOC Br. National Oil Corp.
BOCM Br. Oil and Cake Mills
BRCS Br. Red Cross Society
BSAC Br. Sub Aqua Club
BUPA Br. United Provident Assoc.
●**CARE*** a USA relief organization
CEGB Cent. Elect. Generating Board
●**CERN** European Nuclear Research
CG(L)I City and Guilds, (Lond.) Inst.
C of E Church of England
C of I Church of Ireland
C of S Church of Scotland
Corp. Corporation
CRMP Corps, Royal Military Police
Dept. (dept.) Department
DHSS Dept., Health, Social Services
ECG(D) Export Credits Guarantee
(Dept.)
EFTA European Free Trade Assoc.
EKCO E. K. Cole (electrical goods)
●**El*Al** Israeli airline
ESRO Euro Space Research Org.
ESSO Standard Oil
●**FIAT*** Italian motor comp., Turin
●**FIFA** Federation, Int. Football
Assocs.

GmbH German *Co. Ltd.*
HMAS H.M. Australian Ship
HMCS H.M. Canadian Ship
HMSO H.M. Stationery Office
IATA International Air Transp. Assoc.
●**IBRD** World Bank
ICWA Inst., Cost, Works Accountants
Inst. (inst.) Institute
ISCh Inc. Soc. of Chiropodists
MAFF Min., Agric. Fisheries, Food
mech. mechanical
mfrs manufacturers
NASA Nat. Aeronautics, Space Admin.
NFWI Nat. Federation, Women's Insts.
NUBE Nat. Union, Bank Employees
NUPE Nat. Union, Public Employees
OCTU Off. Cadet Training Unit
OHMS* On Her(His) Majesty's Service
PDSA People's Disp., Sick Animals
RAAF Royal Australian Air Force
RADA Royal Acad., Dramatic Art
RADC Royal Army Defence Corps
RAEC Royal Army Educ. Corps
RAeS Royal Aeronautical Society
RAMC Royal Army Medical Corps
RAOB R. Antediluvian Ord., Buffaloes
RAOC Royal Army Ordnance Corps
RAPC Royal Army Pay Corps
RAVC R. Army Veterinary Corps
RCAF Royal Canadian Air Force
RCVS R. College, Vet. Surgeons
REME R. Electrical, Mech. Engineers
RIAM R. Irish Academy, Music
RIBA R. Inst., British Architects
RICS R. Inst., Chartered Surveyors
RNAS R. Naval Air Service
RNVR R. Naval Volunteer Reserve
RNZN Royal New Zealand Navy
RSGS R. Scots. Geographical Soc.
RSSA R. Scots. Soc. of Arts
RZSE R. Zoological Soc., Edin.
SMMT Soc., Motor Mfrs., Traders
●**SNCF** French National Railways
STUC Scottish *TUC*
TGWU Transp., Gen. Workers' Union
UEFA Union, Euro. Football Assocs.
USAF United States Air Force
WAAC now *WRAC*
WAAF now *WRAF*
WFTU World Fed., Trade Unions

WRAC Women's Royal Army Corps
WRAF Women's Royal Air Force
WRNS Women's Royal Naval Serv.
WRVS Women's Royal Voluntary Serv.
YMCA Young Men's Christian Ass.
YWCA Young Women's Christian Ass.

5

Alcan Aluminium Comp., Canada
●**ASLEF** Loco. Engineers, Firemen
(Union)
Assoc. Association (also Ass.)
ASTMS Ass. Sci. Tech. Managerial Stfs.
BALPA Brit. Airline Pilots Assoc.
Bart's St Bartholomew's Hosp.
BEAMA Brit. Elec. Allied Mfrs. Assoc.
Buffs* see *RAOB*
C and A Clements & August (Comp.)
C and G City and Guilds (Lond. Inst.)
CENTO* Central Treaty Organization
COHSE Confed., Health Serv.
Employees
Co. Ltd. Limited Liability Company
I Mun E Institute Municipal Eng.
InstP Institute of Physics
LAMDA Lond. Acad., Dramatic Art
NALGO Nat., Assoc. Loc. Govt. Off.
●**NUGMW** General, Municipal Workers
(Union)
Pan* Am* Pan American Airways
P and O Peninsular and Oriental
R and A Royal and Ancient (Golf)
RMetS Royal Meteorological Soc.
RNZAF Royal New Zealand Air Force
●**SLADE*** Litho. Artists, Designers, etc.
(Union)
●**SOGAT** Graphical, Allied Trades
(Union)
UKAEA U.K. Atomic Energy Auth.
●**USDAW** Shop, Distributive Workers
(Union)

6

ARAMCO Arabian–American Oil Co.
●**BLESMA** Limbless ex-Servicemen's
Ass.

IChemE Institution, Chem. Engineers
IMechE Institution, Mech. Engineers
Incorp. incorporated (also *Inc.*)

Lonrho London Rhodesian (Comp.)
RHistS Royal Historical Soc.
●**SABENA** Belgian National Airline

DECORATIONS, DEGREES, QUALIFICATIONS (usually suffixes)

note: Space does not permit a complete list. However, it is possible to supplement by a combination of the first and second sections of this chapter. Most of the professional organizations mentioned use some or all of the following designations: Associate (**A**), Fellow (**F**), Member (**M**), Associate Fellow (**AF**), Associate Member (**AM**), President (**P**), past President (**PP**). Example: FCII = Fellow of the Chartered Insurance Institute.

1

A Associate: Academician
B Bachelor
F Fellow
M Member
P President

2

AB Bachelor of Arts
AF Associate Fellow
AM* Associate Member: Master of Arts
BA Bachelor of Arts
BD Bachelor of Divinity
BE* Bachelor of Engineering
BL Bachelor of Law/Letters
BM Bachelor of Medicine
BS Bachelor of Science/Surgery
CA Chartered Accountant (Scotland)
CB Companion, Order of the Bath
CD Canadian Forces Decoration
CE Civil Engineer
CH Companion of Honour
CM Master of Surgery
DA* Diploma of Art
DD Doctor of Divinity
DF Defender of the Faith
FD   Defender of the Faith
GC George Cross
GM George Medal
JP Justice of the Peace

KB Knight Bachelor/of the Bath
KC King's Counsel
KG Knight, Order of the Garter
KM Knight of Malta
KT Knight of the Thistle
Kt Knight
MA* Master of Arts
MB Bachelor of Medicine
MC Military Cross
MD Doctor of Medicine
ME* Mining/Mechanical Engineer
MM Military Medal
MO* Medical Officer
MP Member of Parliament
MS Master of Surgery
NP Notary Public
OM Order of Merit
OP* (of) Order of Preachers
PC Privy Councillor
PP Past President
QC Queen's Counsel
RA Royal Academician
SJ (of) Society of Jesus
SL Solicitor/Sergeant at Law
TD Territorial Decoration
VC Victoria Cross
VD Volunteer (Officers) Decoration
VS Veterinary Surgeon

3

AFC Air Force Cross
AFM Air Force Medal

DECORATIONS, DEGREES, ETC.   **ABBREVIATIONS**

ARA   Associate, Royal Academy
BAI   Bachelor of Engineering
Bar.* Barrister
BCh   Bachelor of Surgery
BCL   Bachelor of Civil Law
BDS   Bachelor of Dental Surgery
BEd* Bachelor of Education
BEM   British Empire Medal
BSc   Bachelor of Science
CBE   Companion, Order, British
   Empire
ChB   Bachelor of Surgery
CMG   Companion, Order, St Michael,
   St George
CPA   Chartered Patent Agent
CVO   Commander, Royal Victorian
   Order
DBE   Dame Commander, Order, British
   Empire
DCL   Doctor of Civil Law
DDS   Doctor of Dental Surgery
DEd   Doctor of Education
DFC   Distinguished Flying Cross
DFM   Distinguished Flying Medal
DIC   Diploma, Imperial College
DIH   Diploma, Industrial Health
Dip.* Diploma
DPH   Diploma, Public Health
DPh   Doctor of Philosophy
DPM   Diploma, Psychological Medicine
DSC   Distinguished Service Cross
DSc   Doctor of Science
DSM   Distinguished Service Medal
DSO   Distinguished Service Order
DTh   Doctor of Theology
EdB   Bachelor of Education
FAS* Fellow, Society of Arts
FBA   Fellow, British Academy
FCA   Fellow, Institute, Chartered
   Accountants
FJI   Fellow, Institute of Journalists
FRS   Fellow, Royal Society
GBE   (Knight/Dame) Grand Cross,
   Order, Brit. Emp.
GCB   (Knight) Grand Cross, Bath
GCH   (Knight) Grand Cross, Hanover
HNC   Higher National Certificate
HND   Higher National Diploma
HSS   Fellow, Historical Society
ISO   Imperial Service Order

JCD   Doctor of Civil Law
JUD* Doctor of Canon and Civil Law
KBE   Knight, Order, British Empire
KCB   Knight Commander, of the Bath
KLH   Knight, Legion of Honour
LCh   Licentiate in Surgery
LHD   Doctor of Letters
LLB   Bachelor of Laws
LLM   Master of Laws
LSA   Licentiate, Society of
   Apothecaries
LTh   Licentiate in Theology
MBE   Member, Order, British Empire
MCh   Master of Surgery
MDS   Master of Dental Surgery
MJI   Member, Institute of Journalists
MPS   Member,
   Pharmaceutical/Philological Soc.
MSc   Master of Science
MTh   Master of Theology
MVO   Member, Royal Victorian Order
OBE   Officer, Order, British Empire
OSA   (of) Order of St Augustine
OSB   (of) Order of St Benedict
OSF   (of) Order of St Francis
PhB   Bachelor of Philosophy
PhD   Doctor of Philosophy
RSS   Fellow of the Royal Society
SAS   Fellow, Society of Antiquaries
ScB   Bachelor of Science
ScD   Doctor of Science
SCM   State Certified Midwife
SEN* State Enrolled Nurse
SRN   State Registered Nurse
SRS   Fellow of the Royal Society
STP   Professor of Theology
ThD   Doctor of Theology
UJD   Doctor of Civil and Canon Law

4

BAgr   Bachelor of Agriculture
BCom   Bachelor of Commerce
BEng   Bachelor of Engineering
B ès L   Bachelor of Letters (Fr)
B ès S   Bachelor of Sciences (Fr)
BLit   Bachelor of Literature/Letters
BMus   Bachelor of Music

CDSO Companion, Distinguished Service Order

CEng Chartered Engineer

DCVO Dame Commander, Royal Victorian Order

DEng Doctor of Engineering

DIng* Doctor of Engineering

DLit Doctor of Literature

DMus Doctor of Music

DOMS Diploma, Ophthalmic Medicine, Surgery

FRCP Fellow, Royal College of Physicians

FRPS Fellow, Royal Photographic Society

GCMG (Knight) Grand Cross, SS Michael, George

GCVO (Knight/Dame) Grand Cross, R. Vic. Ord.

KCMG Kt Commander, St Michael, St George

KCVO Kt Comdr. Royal Victorian Order

KGCB Knight, Grand Cross, Bath

LitD Doctor of Letters

LLCM Licentiate, London College of Music

LRAM Licentiate, Royal Academy of Music

LRCP Licentiate, Royal College of Physicians

LRCS Licentiate, Royal College of Surgeons

MRCP Member, Royal College of Physicians

MusB Bachelor of Music

MusD Doctor of Music

MusM Master of Music

OStJ Officer, Order, St John of Jerusalem

SRCh State Registered Chiropodist

5

BComm Bachelor of Commerce

BLitt Bachelor of Literature

BPhil Bachelor of Philosophy

CLitt Companion of Literature

Dip.* Ed. Diploma in Education

DLitt Doctor of Literature

DPhil Doctor of Philosophy

LChir Licentiate in Surgery

LittD Doctor of Letters

MLitt Master of Letters/Literature

6

BAgric Bachelor of Agriculture

BPharm Bachelor of Pharmacy

DesRCA Designer, Royal College of Art

Fid.*Def. Defender of the Faith

Kt Bach.* Knight Bachelor

LRCP (Ed.) *LRCP* Edinburgh

LRCS (Ed.) *LRCS* Edinburgh

MusBac Bachelor of Music

MusDoc Doctor of Music

7

Dip.*Tech. Diploma in Technology

Vet.*Surg. Veterinary Surgeon

8

FRCP (Edin.) *FRCP* Edinburgh

FRCP (Irel.) *FRCP* Ireland

FRCP (Lond.) *FRCP* London

LRCP (Irel.) *LRCP* Ireland

LRCP (Lond.) *LRCP* London

LRCS (Irel.) *LRCS* Ireland

LRCS (Lond.) *LRCS* London

10

FRCPS (Glasg.) *FRCP* and Surgeons, Glasgow

MILITARY RANKS, TITLES, OFFICES, FORMS OF ADDRESS (usually Prefixes)

1

A/ Acting (poss. prefix to most Ranks)
B Baron
J Judge: Justice
M Monsieur (French)
P President: Prince
R King: Queen (suffix)
S Saint

2

AB able-bodied seaman
AC aircraftman
AF Admiral of the Fleet
AG Adjutant/Attorney-General
AS* Assistant Secretary
BM Brigade Major
Bn Baron
Bp Bishop
Br. Brother
Bt Baronet (suffix)
CA County Alderman
Ch. Chief
CJ Chief Justice
CO Commanding Officer
DA* District Attorney
DL Deputy Lieutenant
Dr Doctor (see Sect. 2): Drummer: Driver
Ed. Editor
FO Field/Flying Officer
Fr. Father: Friar
HE* His Excellency/Eminence
HG His/Her Grace
HH His/Her Highness: His Holiness
HM His/Her Majesty
Hr Herr (German)
JC Justice Clerk
JP see Section 2
Ld Lord
LJ Lord Justice
LP Lord Provost
Lp Lordship

Lt. Lieutenant
MC Master of Ceremonies
MD Managing Director
ME* Most Excellent
MM (Their) Majesties: Messieurs (Fr.)
Mr Mister: Master
OC Officer Commanding
OS ordinary seaman
PC Police Constable
PM Prime Minister: Provost-Marshal
PO* Petty/Pilot Officer
PP Parish Priest: past President
Pr. Priest: Prince
QM Quartermaster
Qu. Queen
RA Rear Admiral
RH Royal Highness
RR Right Reverend
SC Special Constable
SG Solicitor General
SM Sergeant-Major: Sa Majesté (Fr.)
SO* Staff/Signal Officer
St* Saint
TO* Transport Officer
US* Under-secretary
ux. (uxor) wife
VC Vice-Chancellor/Consul
VG Vicar-General
VP Vice-President
WO* Warrant Officer
Wp Worshipful

3

Abb.* Abbess: Abbot
Abp Archbishop
ACW aircraftwoman
ADC aide-de-camp
Adm. Admiral
Ald. Alderman
AOC Air Officer Commanding
AVM Air Vice Marshal
Bro. Brother
Cdr Commander

CGS   Chief of the General Staff
Ch.J.   Chief Justice
Cll   Councillor
Col.*   Colonel
Com.   Commander: Commodore: Commissioner
Cor.*   Coroner
Cpl   Corporal
CPO   Chief Petty Officer
CSM   Company Sergeant-Major
DAG*   Deputy Adjutant-General
Dep.   Deputy
Dir.   Director
DOC   District Officer Commanding
DPP   Director of Public Prosecutions
Emp.   Emperor: Empress
Esq.   Esquire (suffix)
FOC   father of the chapel
Gen.*   General
GOC   General Officer Commanding
Gov.*   Governor
HBM   His/Her Britannic Majesty
HCF   Honorary Chaplain, Forces
HCM   His/Her Catholic Majesty
HEH   His/Her Exalted Highness
HIH   His/Her Imperial Highness
Hon.   (The) Honourable
HRH   His/Her Royal Highness
HSH   His/Her Serene Highness
Imp.*   (Imperator) Emperor (suffix)
Jud.*   Judges
LAC*   Leading Aircraftman
LCJ   Lord Chief-Justice
Ldp   Lordship
Maj.   Major
Mdm   Madam
MFH   Master of Foxhounds
Mgr   Monseigneur: Monsignor
Mme   Madame (French)
Mrs   Mistress
NCO   non-commissioned officer
OCF   Officiating Chaplain, Forces
PMG   Post/Pay/master General
Pmr   Paymaster
PMO   Principal Medical Officer
PPS   Parliamentary Private Secretary
PRO*   Public Relations Officer
Pte   Private (military rank)
QMG   Quartermaster-General
QMS   Quartermaster-Sergeant

Rev.*   Reverend
RSM   Regimental Sergeant-Major
SAC*   Senior aircraftman
Sec.*   Secretary
Sen.*   Senator
Sir*   prefix of Knight or Baronet
SMO   Senior Medical Officer
SSD   Most Holy Lord (the Pope)
Ste   Sainte (Fr. fem. of Saint)
TRH   Their Royal Highnesses
Ven.   Venerable
Vic.   Vicar
Vis.   Viscount
WPC   Woman Police Constable

4

Adjt.   Adjutant
Asst.   Assistant
Bart   Baronet (suffix)
Brig.*   Brigadier
Capt.   Captain
Card.*   Cardinal
Chap.*   Chaplain
CIGS*   Chief, Imperial General Staff
C-in-C   Commander-in-Chief
comm.   commander
Corp.   Corporal
CQMS   Company Quartermaster-Sergeant
DAAG   Dep. Asst. Adjt-General
Esqr.   Esquire (suffix)
Genl   General
Judg.   Judges
LACW   Leading aircraftwoman
L/Cpl   Lance Corporal
Marq.   Marquis
Mlle   Mademoiselle (French)
Mmes   Mesdames (French)
Preb.   Prebendary
Pres.   President
Prin.   Principal
Prof.*   Professor
Prov.   Provost
Rect.   Rector
SACW   Senior aircraftwoman
Secy   Secretary
Serg.   Sergeant
Serj.   Serjeant

MILITARY RANKS, TITLES, ETC.   **ABBREVIATIONS**

Supt Superintendent
Surg. Surgeon
Visc. Viscount
W/Cdr Wing Commander

5

Archd. Archdeacon: Archduke
Chamb. Chamberlain
Chanc. Chancellor
Comdr Commander
Comdt Commandant
Flt Lt. Flight Lieutenant
Hon.CF Honorary Chaplain, Forces
Lieut Lieutenant
Lt. Col.* Lieutenant-Colonel
Lt. Com. Lieutenant-Commander

Lt. Gen.* Lieutenant-General
Lt. Gov. Lieutenant-Governor
Mdlle Mademoiselle (French)
Mlles Mademoiselles (French)
Rt Hon. Right Honourable
Rt Rev.* Right Reverend
Sergt Sergeant
Serjt Serjeant

6

AOC in C Air Officer
   Commanding-in-Chief
Maj. Gen.* Major General
Man.* Dir. Managing Director
Messrs Messieurs (Fr.): plu. of Mr
Monsig. Monsignor

APPENDIX 2

PREFIXES

note The asterisk* indicates that the prefix is also a word, usually with a totally different meaning, and valid for most word games.

1

a- an, on, in
a' all
y- with, together

2

ab- centimetre-gram-second-electromagnetic-unit
be-* forms verb from noun, adjective
bi- twice, double
co- with, together
de- down from, away: reversal
di- two, twice, double
em-* }
en-* } em before b, m or p
otherwise en to form verbs
sense of in, into, upon:cause to be
ex-* former but surviving
im- }
in-* } form verbs/nouns/adjs.
with sense of in, into:
ir- } intensive: negative
on-* same as *un-*
oo-* egg
re-* again
sy- together, with
un-* not, reversal, reversal (emphasis)
up-* sustain, raise
ur-* primitive, original

3

aut- self, same, self-caused, *auto-*
azo- nitrogen

bio-* living organisms
con-* with
dia- through, across
dis- in two: not: removal: intensive
dys- ill, bad, abnormal
eco- environment
eka- provisional name (science)
ent- inside
Eur- European
exo- outside
for-* forms verbs away, off, etc. (obs.)
geo-* earth
gri- grey (obs.)
hem-* blood
hex-* six
hol- whole
iso- equal
lip-* fat
mal-* bad, badly
meg- big: (in units) a million
mes-* middle
met-* among
mid-* middle part
mis-* wrong, ill
mon- single
myc- fungus
myo- muscle
neo- new, young, revived
oct- eight
oen- wine
oin- wine
ovi- egg, ovum
pan-* all
ped-* child, boy
pod-* foot
pre- in front (of): beforehand: surpassing

pro-* before: earlier: in favour of etc.
sex-* six
sub-* under: subordinate: almost: etc.
sur-* over
syl- together, with
sym- together, with
syn- together, with
tel-* far, distant
ter- thrice
tra- *trans-*
tri- three
twi- two, double
twy- two, double
uni-* one
uro- urine
vas-* vessel, tube, duct (+ liquid)
xen- strange, foreign, guest
xer- dry
zoo-* animal
zyg- yoke, union

4

acet- vinegar
acro- tip, point, summit
aden- gland
aero- air
agro- soil
allo- other
andr- man, male
ante-* before
anti-* against, rivalling
aqua- water
arch-* first, chief
atto- one million, million, millionth
auto-* *aut-*, automobile, automatic
cryo- frost, ice
cycl- cycle, ring, circle, cyclic
cyto- cell
deca- ten
deci- one tenth
demi- half
dino- huge, terrible
dipl- double
ecto- outside
endo- inside
ento- inside
equi- equal
erio- wool fibre

Euro- European
fore-* before
gamo- writing
giga- ten to the ninth power
gymn- naked (esp. biological)
gyno- woman, female
haem-* blood
hagi- holy
hect- 100 times
heli- helicopter
hemi- half
hemo- blood
hexa- six
hist-* tissue, sail
holo- whole
homo-* same
hydr- of, like, by means of, water
hypo-* under, defective
Indo- Indian
kilo-* 1000 × attached unit
levo- on or to the left
leuc- white
leuk- white
lipo- fat
lith-* stone: calculus
mega- big: (in units) a million
meso- middle
meta- among
metr- of the uterus
micr- see *micro-*
midi-* middle size, length
mini-* small
miso- hater of
mixo- mixed
mono-* single
mult- much, many
myco- fungus
nano- one thousand millionth
naso- of the nose
near-* almost
neur- nerve cell, fibre, tissue, system, etc.
octa- eight
octo- eight
oeno- wine
oino- wine
olig- little, few
omni- all
ophi- snake
opto- sight, eye

PREFIXES

oste- bone
over-* above, beyond, down, upper, etc.
paed- child, boy
paid-* child, boy
pale-* old, very distant past
pant-* all
para-* faulty, abnormal: parachute
pedo- child, boy
pent-* five
peri-* around
phag- feeding, eating
phen- showing, visible; benzene
phil- loving, lover
phon-* sound, voice
phot-* light
pico- *micromicro-*
pleo- more
plio- more
podo- foot
poly-* many
post-* after
prae- *pre-*
prot- *proto-*
pter- feather, wing
pyro-* fire, heat, fever
rect- right, straight
rere- rear
rheo- current, flow
rhin- nose
rhiz- root
rhod- rose, rose-coloured
sapr- rotten, decayed
scia- shadow
scio- shadow
self-* acting upon the agent
semi-* half
sept-* seven
sero- serum
sexi- six
Sino- Chinese
sino- sinus
skia- shadow
skio- shadow
sono- sonic
step-* affinity by another marriage
tach-* speed, speedy
taut-* the same
tele- far, distant, television
tera- ten to the twelfth power

tetr- four
theo- god
thio- sulphur
tran- *trans-*
vaso- vessel, tube, duct (+ liquid)
vice-* in place of
vivi- alive, living
xeno- strange, foreign, guest
xero- dry
xiph- sword
zygo- yoke, union
zymo- a ferment, disease-germ

5

aceto- vinegar
adren- adrenal (-glands), adrenalin
ailur- cat
andro- man, male
anemo- wind
Anglo- English
aniso- unequal
antho- flower
astro- star
bathy- deep
bibli- book
brady- slow
centi- 1/100th of unit named
copro- dung
crypt-* hidden
cyclo-* cycle, ring, circle, cyclic
deino- huge, terrible
diazo- 2 nitrogen atoms + hydrocarbon radical
diplo- double
eigen- proper, own
enter-* intestines: also *inter-*
extra-* outside
femto- thousand million millionth
gymno- naked (esp. biological)
haemo- blood
haplo- single
hecto- 100 times
helio- sun
hemet- blood
hepta- seven
heter- other, different
histo- tissue, sail
homeo- like, similar

hydro-* of, like, by – water
hygro- wet, moist
hyper-* over, excessive
hypso- height
impar- unequal
inter-* between, among, midst of, etc.
intra- within
intro-* within, into
Italo- Italian
laevo- on, to – the left
lepid-* scale
leuco- white
leuko- white
litho-* stone: calculus
macro- long, great
medio- middle
micro-* abnormally small: microscopy: magnifying: reducing: a millionth part, etc.
milli- a thousandth part
multi- much, many
myria- 10,000: v. large number
necro- dead, dead body
nepho- cloud
nephr- kidney
neuro- nerve cell, fibre, tissue, system, etc.
nitro- nitrogen
odont- tooth
oligo- little, few
ophio- snake
organ-* organ
ortho- straight, upright, right, genuine, etc.
osteo- bone
pachy- thick
paedo- child, boy
paido- child, boy
palae- old, very distant past
paleo- old, very distant past
panto-* all
penta- five
phaen- *pheno-*
phaeo- dusky
phago- feeding, eating
pheno- showing, visible: benzene
philo- loving, lover
phono- sound, voice
photo-* light
phyco- seaweed

physi- nature
phyto- plant (botanical)
piezo- pressure
pleio- more
pluri- several
pneum- lung
proto- first, primitive, ancestral, etc.
pseud-* sham, false, spurious, temporary, etc.
psych- soul, spirit, mind, mental, etc.
ptero- feather, wing
pubio- grown up, downy
pycno- dense, close
pykno- dense, close
quadr- four
quint-* fifth
radio-* rays, radiation, radium, radius, radio, etc.
recti- right, straight
recto-* rectum
retro-* backwards, behind
rhino-* nose
rhizo- root
rhodo- rose, rose-coloured
sacro- sacrum (a bone)
sapro- rotten, decayed
sarco- flesh
schiz- cleave, cloven
scoto- dark
septi- seven
siala- saliva
sialo- saliva
socio- social
spino- spine
spiro- coil, spire
stann- tin
stato- standing
stear- suet, fat
steat- suet, fat
stego- covered, roofed, hidden, watertight
steno- contracted
super-* above, beyond, in addition/excess
supra- above
tache- speed, speedy
tachy- speed, speedy
tauto- the same
tetra-* four
theri- beast, mammal

PREFIXES

thero- beast, mammal
trans- across, beyond, through
trich- hair
troph- nutrition
ultra-* beyond
  place/position/limit/ordinary, etc.
under-* below, beneath, subordinate,
  etc.
vibra- vibration
vibro- vibration
visco- viscous
visuo- sight
vitro- glass
xanth- yellow
xipho- sword

6

adreno- *adren-*
ailour- cat
ailuro- cat
ampeli- vine, vine-like
ampelo- vine, vine-like
blasto- sprout, bud, germ
brachy- short
cardio- heart, upper stomach
centri- centre
centro- centre
cephal- head
crypto-* hidden
dodeca- twelve
entero- intestine
erythr- red
Franco- French
gastro- belly
gyneco- woman, female
haemat- blood
hemato- blood
hetero- other, different
histio- tissue, sail
homoeo- like, similar
homoio- like, similar
hyster- womb
ichthy- fish
impari- unequal
lepido- scale
megalo- big: (in units) a million
nephro- kidney
odonto- tooth

opisth- behind
organo- organ
palaeo- old, very distant past
phaeno- *pheno-*
physio-* nature
pneumo- lung
preter- beyond
pseudo-* sham, false, spurious,
  temporary, etc.
psycho-* *psych-* psychological
quadri- four
quadru- four
quinqu- five
rhynch- snout
sangui- blood
schizo- cleave, cloven
septem- seven
sesqui- ratio 1½ to 1: 1 to nth of 1
speleo- cave, cave dwelling
stereo-* solid, hard, 3 dimensional
subter- under
thauma- wonder, miracle
therio- beast, mammal
tricho- hair
tropho- nutrition
xantho- yellow

7

ailouro- cat
anthrop- man, human
counter-* against
dibromo- 2 atoms of bromide
dichlor- 2 atoms of chlorine
dinitro- 2 nitro-groups
dolicho- long
electro- electric
erythro- red
gastero- belly
gynaeco- woman, female
haemato- blood
Hispano- Spanish
hystero- womb
ichthyo- fish
opistho- behind
pneumon- lung
praeter- beyond
quinque- five
rhyncho- snout

spaeleo- cave, cave dwelling
spectro- spectrum
stegano- *stego-*
strepto- bent, flexible, twisted
thaumat- wonder, miracle

8

anthropo- man, human
dichloro- 2 atoms of chlorine
ophthalm- eye
pneumono- lung
trichlor- 3 atoms of chlorine

trinitro- 3 nitro-groups

9

micromicr- million of millionth part
ophthalmo- eye
trichloro- 3 atoms of chlorine

10

micromicro- million of millionth part
ultramicro- smaller than *micro-*

APPENDIX 3

SUFFIXES

note The asterisk* indicates that the suffix is also a word, usually with a totally different meaning, and valid for play in most word games.

2

-er* agent designating person, thing
-ia used in scientific naming
-or* agent, non-personal agent

3

-ana* belonging to, typical of
-asm abstract condition/system
-ise verbs from nouns/adjectives
-ish* somewhat
-ism* abstract condition/system
-ite names people/fossils/minerals etc.
-ize verbs from nouns/adjectives
-kin* diminutive
-let* diminutive
-oma tumour
-sis action, process: caused by

4

-able* capable of being
-acea zoological orders, classes
-fest party, gathering
-form* a form, form of
-gram* written/drawn record
-head* state, nature
-hood* state, nature
-iana belong to, typical of
-ible capable of being
-itis disease
-less* free from: wanting
-ling* diminutive
-logy science, theory, discourse, etc.
-phil lover of, loving

-phor carrier
-self* reflective, emphatic
-some* full of
-tomy surgical incision
-tron* agent, instrument
-type* same type, resembling
-ward* motion towards

5

-aceae plant families
-icism abstract condition/system
-ology* *-logy*
-otomy *-tomy*
-phaga eaters
-phage eater, destroyer
-phagy eating of a specified nature
-phile lover of, loving
-phily lover of, loving
-phore carrier
-ptera wings, wing-like parts
-shire* county
-stomy (surgical) opening

6

-ostomy *-stomy*
-phagus feeding, particular way/thing
-philia love of
-philus (zoological) lover of (food)

7

-phagous feeding on
-philous loving

APPENDIX 4

WORDS FOR WORD GAMES

2-LETTER WORDS

The following 2-letter interjections and exclamations are valid for most word games played in the UK.

ah, aw, bo, eh, er, fy, ha, hi, ho, io, oh, oi, ou, ow, sh, st, ta, um, ur, yo together with the dialect verb (to loathe or to excite loathing in) **ug**.

The remaining 2-letter words which may be permissible and are not given elsewhere in this book are:

ad, am, an, as, at, ax, be, by, el, es, go, he, if, in, is, it, ma, my, na, no, ob, od, of, on, or, to, up, us, we, and **ye**.

Note Us and **we** are non-plural words in royal usage and, as such, are valid for those word-games which specifically bar plurals. Ye, whilst an archaic word, means 'the' as well as 'you' in both the singular and plural senses. Only **ky**, listed in FAUNA-ANIMALS, cannot be considered for those games which bar plurals. Dixit players will need to exercise caution as such standard words as **an** are not listed in their reference dictionary.

6-LETTER WORDS

To supplement the 6-letter words discovered in the main body of this dictionary the following words are valid for Sylabex:

barted from barter, to trade by exchange
bating from bate, to abate, lessen, diminish or blunt
curred from curr, to make a purring sound
looten from loot, the Scottish verb to let
tented from tent, to canopy or camp in a tent
wanned from wan, to make pale or sickly
warred from war, to make war upon